The Cavalry of the Army
of the Cumberland

ALSO BY DENNIS W. BELCHER
AND FROM MCFARLAND

*General David S. Stanley, USA:
A Civil War Biography* (2014)

*The 11th Missouri Volunteer Infantry in the Civil War:
A History and Roster* (2011)

*The 10th Kentucky Volunteer Infantry in the Civil War:
A History and Roster* (2009)

EDITED BY DENNIS W. BELCHER
AND FROM MCFARLAND

*"This Terrible Struggle for Life":
The Civil War Letters of a Union Regimental Surgeon
by Thomas S. Hawley, M.D.* (2012)

The Cavalry of the Army of the Cumberland

Dennis W. Belcher

Foreword by David A. Powell

McFarland & Company, Inc., Publishers
Jefferson, North Carolina

LIBRARY OF CONGRESS CATALOGUING-IN-PUBLICATION DATA

Names: Belcher, Dennis W., 1950– author.
Title: The cavalry of the Army of the Cumberland /
Dennis W. Belcher ; foreword by David A. Powell.
Description: Jefferson, North Carolina : McFarland & Company, Inc.,
Publishers, 2016. | Includes bibliographical references and index.
Identifiers: LCCN 2016012528 | ISBN 9780786494804
(softcover : acid free paper) ∞
Subjects: LCSH: United States. Army of the Cumberland. Cavalry Corps. |
United States—History—Civil War, 1861–1865—Cavalry operations. |
United States—History—Civil War, 1861–1865—Campaigns.
Classification: LCC E470.5 .B45 2016 | DDC 973.7/3—dc23
LC record available at http://lccn.loc.gov/2016012528

BRITISH LIBRARY CATALOGUING DATA ARE AVAILABLE

ISBN (print) 978-0-7864-9480-4
ISBN (ebook) 978-1-4766-2396-2

© 2016 Dennis W. Belcher. All rights reserved

*No part of this book may be reproduced or transmitted in any form
or by any means, electronic or mechanical, including photocopying
or recording, or by any information storage and retrieval system,
without permission in writing from the publisher.*

Front cover: chromolithograph of Sheridan's final
charge at Winchester (Library of Congress)

Printed in the United States of America

*McFarland & Company, Inc., Publishers
Box 611, Jefferson, North Carolina 28640
www.mcfarlandpub.com*

To the deacon, for all her support,
love, kindness and friendship

Table of Contents

Acknowledgments	ix
Foreword by David A. Powell	1
Preface	5

Part I: Major General David S. Stanley, Chief of Cavalry

1. The Union Cavalry of the Army of the Cumberland	9
2. The Battle of Stones River	33
3. Middle Tennessee, January–June 1863	57
4. The Tullahoma Campaign, June 23–July 5, 1863	87
5. The Advance on Chattanooga	103

Part II: Brigadier General Robert B. Mitchell, Acting Chief of Cavalry

6. The Battle of Chickamauga	143
7. The Union Cavalry Guards the Tennessee River; Wheeler's Raid	164

Part III: Brigadier General Washington Lafayette Elliott, Chief of Cavalry

8. The Knoxville Campaign and Campaigning in East Tennessee: A New Beginning	177
9. Preparation for the Atlanta Campaign: Two Divisions Divided	191
10. Rocky Face Ridge to the Chattahoochee River, May–July 9, 1864	211
11. Chattahoochee River to Atlanta, July 10–August 7, 1864	243
12. Atlanta to Lovejoy's Station, August 8–October 26, 1864	265

Epilogue	286
Appendix A: Biographical Notes	293
Appendix B: Organization of the Cavalry of the Army of the Cumberland	299
Chapter Notes	305
Bibliography	328
Index	335

Acknowledgments

One of the advantages of writing about the cavalry of the Army of the Cumberland is the depth of material available to support this history. The sources for this book are drawn from a wide variety of collections, so let me begin by thanking the many people who have contributed to making it a reality.

I am always grateful to Molly Kodner, associate archivist, Missouri History Museum and Research Library, for her efforts to find materials for this book. Molly is ever helpful, regardless of the number of times I call upon her for assistance. I also want to thank Brent Abercrombie, manuscripts librarian at the Indiana State Library, and Justin Davis, librarian, for their help in locating primary sources and other materials about the Union cavalry. Lacey Herington, collections assistant, Reference Services, Indiana Historical Society, was particularly helpful with material from Indiana used in this book. Becki Plunkett, special collections archivist, State Historical Society of Iowa, provided much needed assistance with the Iowa sources. Emma Hawker, assistant archivist at the Bentley Historical Library, was very helpful with Michigan material used in the book. Lori B. Bessler, reference librarian, at the Wisconsin Historical Society, was a lifesaver in obtaining the essential material from Wisconsin. Eric Willey, Jennifer Cole, and Heather Stone of the Filson Historical Society really went beyond all expectations in their diligence in providing material about the Kentucky cavalry. I am also grateful to Kyle Hovious, Hodges Library, University of Tennessee, for his assistance with primary source material from Tennessee. Darla Brock, archivist, Tennessee State Library and Archives, was so very helpful as I researched the sources regarding Tennessee and the Union cavalry. She repeatedly went out of her way to assist in this project. Samantha Ashby, reference archivist at Bowling Green State University, was of enormous assistance with materials located at that institution. M'Lissa Kesterman, Reference Services, Cincinnati History Library and Archives, was very helpful in providing material regarding the 4th Ohio Cavalry. Barry Brown, reference specialist at the Switzerland County Public Library, was extremely helpful in providing biographical information about the Indiana Cavalry. Jennie Russell, archivist at Michigan State University, provided important material regarding the 2nd and 4th Michigan cavalries. Kate Collins, of the David M. Rubenstein Rare Book and Manuscript Library at Duke University, provided important material used in this book. Finally, to the archivists at the United States Military Heritage and Education Center, I want to express my great appreciation for their efforts in preserving and providing materials used in this book. In particular, Marlea D. Leljedal was very helpful with material from the USAHEC.

I want to specifically thank Edward Singer for his much needed assistance with materials located in the National Archives. Sara Borden and Dana Dorman of the Historical Society of Pennsylvania provided significant information about the Pennsylvania regiments described. I also want to especially express my appreciation to Tutti Jackson, Ohio Historical Society, who provided much of the valuable and hard-to-find material regarding the Ohio regiments. Deborah Wood, Wilson's Creek National Park, continues to be an invaluable resource for those studying the Civil War and is always helpful and willing to assist those researching this time period.

In addition, I am truly fortunate to have an expert group of reviewers for this work. The efforts of Greg Biggs, Dr. Michael Bradley, Charlie Crawford, and David A. Powell were most gratefully received and helpful in the completion of this project. I am very thankful for the comments, time and efforts of these individuals. I also want to express my deep appreciation to David Powell for writing the foreword. Powell is the expert on cavalry and infantry operations at the Battle of Chickamauga, and his book, *Failure in the Saddle*, is the recognized definitive work on the Confederate cavalry during this battle. I am honored to have his opening comments for this present work.

This is my fourth collaboration with George Skoch, mapmaker extraordinaire. I cannot say enough good things about his maps. Maps are an invaluable component to any Civil War history, and I am always thankful to have the benefit of his skill, experience, knowledge and dedication.

Then I saw an angel standing in the sun, and with a loud voice he called to all the birds that fly in mid-heaven, "Come, gather for the great supper of God, to eat the flesh of kings, the flesh of captains, the flesh of the mighty, the flesh of horses and their riders—flesh of all, both free and slave, both small and great." Then I saw the beast and the kings of the earth with their armies gathered to make war against the rider on the horse and against his army.

Revelation 19:17–20

Foreword
by David A. Powell

Twenty-five years ago the study of the American Civil War's mounted forces and their role in our great conflict was limited to a few classic volumes. Most of those focused on Confederates, with an even tighter focus on J.E.B. Stuart and his fellow cavaliers in Virginia. This is largely a legacy of the Civil War's centennial era, which also seemed heavily focused on Virginia. While other theaters were not entirely ignored, the preponderance of publishing was weighted toward the epic four-year struggle between Robert E. Lee's vaunted Army of Northern Virginia and the Union Army of the Potomac.

Things have changed. We have seen a flowering of attention on Civil War mounted forces, their use, their battles, and the men in their ranks. Still, some things have not really changed. The publishing focus is still weighted toward the Eastern Theater, especially towards that "cockpit of the war," Virginia. To be sure, the federal cavalry in the East has finally received its due, garnering a full measure of credit for its role in bringing the Army of Northern Virginia to bay.

There is good news for students of the war in the West, however. A similar flowering is now underway in the overall literature of the Western Theater. In the past few years, a spate of campaign and battle studies have examined the fighting in Tennessee, Mississippi, and Georgia. Biographies of important Western Theater generals both blue and gray are appearing with increasing frequency. Even regimental histories and personal narratives are making their way into print. I welcome this trend and hope it swells into a veritable flood.

Most of these combat narratives, however, have so far been individual battle monographs, focused on the intense action and bloodletting of specific engagements such as Shiloh, Peachtree Creek, Chickamauga, and Atlanta. While such works are always welcome and often bring fresh new information and interpretation to their topics, by their nature tactical battle narratives don't tell a complete story. The operational level of military history (the history of a whole campaign, or what the 19th century called Grand Tactics) has much to teach the interested student, especially with regard to mounted operations.

The role of Civil War cavalry is complicated. It has been widely acknowledged—perhaps too widely—that by the 1860s the mounted arm had been eclipsed by both the rise of the rifled musket and new artillery technology, which rendered mounted battlefield charges obsolete. By the 1860s, massed heavy cavalry squadrons—sabers and cuirasses flashing in the sun—charging home against crumbling infantry formations were a thing of the past. Despite the hopes of a few overly romantic European tacticians, by the mid–19th century even European conflicts were foreshadowing the demise of those heavy-cavalry, boot-to-boot charges.

As a result, Civil War cavalry fights tended to be on the periphery of the war's big battles, seemingly indecisive sideshows waged while the infantry and artillery bore the brunt of the bloodiest actions. Given the propensity of Civil War literature to focus on massive in-depth tactical studies of those selfsame "big battles," perhaps it is not surprising that it took so long for historians to turn their attention to the primary role of 19th-century cavalry.

Even in the Napoleonic era, which in the modern era is arguably the peak of cavalry's role on the battlefield proper, mounted-force missions were far more diverse than riding down formed infantry. The essence of operational warfare in the age of the musket, rifled or smoothbore, was maneuver. Armies had grown large enough to become unwieldy unless they were divided into subunits—corps, most familiarly—and marched separately, uniting only for that climactic struggle at some unfortunate crossroads village or market town.

"March divided, fight united" is a doctrine that offers both risks and opportunities for commanding generals. If Force A can concentrate more quickly than Force B, then Force A will bring a tactical advantage in numbers to the battlefield, even if Force B has the greater overall numbers. Accomplish this feat enough times, and you will have defeated your opponent in detail, which is the best measure of martial skill, a fact as true in 1861–1865 as it was in 1760, 1805, or 1815.

While easy enough to theorize about, in practice victories rooted in grand maneuvers are much harder to achieve. Information is the currency of mobile warfare. A commander needs to know the terrain between him and his opponent, the location of the enemy forces, and, of course, have a firm grasp of his own dispositions—sometimes easier said than done. Ideally, he must deny his opponent access to similar intelligence. To accomplish all this, generals turn to their cavalry.

The space between two armies becomes contested ground, with each side's cavalry seeking dominance in that space. This, then, was the real war for the average cavalryman: hours in the saddle interspersed with sudden, short, and intense combats. A fight for a crossroads or a captured dispatch often proved more important than a massed, boot-to-boot charge against formed infantry. In between campaigns, cavalry still had no chance to rest. Chasing partisans or raiders, escorting foraging parties, even rounding up deserters and renegades, were all part of a trooper's existence.

By mid–1863, the Confederacy deployed an impressively large mounted force in the Western Theater. At one point that spring, the Rebel horsemen numbered nearly 30,000, a staggering figure that included both conventional cavalry and various partisan units like those led by Nathan Bedford Forrest and John Hunt Morgan. That investment paid off when, in the second half of 1862, a series of successful cavalry raids helped stymie Union forces that had seemed nearly unstoppable earlier that year. With too much terrain to defend and too few regular troops to defend it with, in 1863 Confederate commanders conceived of the idea of using those same mounted forces as a sort of mobile reserve operating between Mississippi and Tennessee, where Union armies prepared for new offensives.

In contrast, the Federals were slower to augment their own mounted arm or to properly organize the cavalry they did have on hand. As a result, the cavalry of the Union Army of the Cumberland found itself at a numerical—and sometimes a qualitative—disadvantage for nearly all of the first year of its existence.

This imbalance of forces is mirrored by a similar imbalance in historical attention. Works on Western cavalry focus almost exclusively on the Southern mounted arm, and of those, the dominant topic, by far, centers on one man: Nathan Bedford Forrest. The list of titles examining Forrest is longer than that of all other western cavalry works combined, both Union and Confederate. While Forrest is a fascinating character, he is certainly not the only important figure to be found out West. In fact, for much of the war Forrest was merely a minor player, commanding small forces and operating in arenas that lacked first-string strategic importance. Conversely, the Confederacy's most significant western cavalry commander, Joseph Wheeler, has been the subject of only a couple of monographs.

And what of their opponents, the Federals? There we have a paucity indeed—which is unfortunate. Though the Army of the Cumberland never had a formally designated cavalry corps, it did field such a force in all but name. Only division-sized at the battle of Stones River, by the spring of 1863 this force had grown to two divisions numbering between 8,000 and 10,000 men. Thereafter it met and often mastered its primary opponent, Wheeler's cavalry of the Confederate Army of Tennessee. By war's end Union cavalry columns would range at will across much of the South, unstoppable strike forces that could go anywhere they chose.

The story of that rise to dominance has heretofore garnered too little attention in Civil War history, but fortunately Dennis Belcher has now given us a new and fresh look at the Army of the Cumberland's mounted arm. Dennis traces the development of the army's cavalry through its three most important commanders and its first two years of life, documenting the command's growth from an under-equipped and outnumbered handful to the principal cavalry force in William T. Sherman's army group during the campaign for Atlanta.

The cavalry's story really begins in the fall of 1862 when a new army commander, William S. Rosecrans, brings with him another new man to lead the cavalry, David S. Stanley. Within a few months, Stanley is leading that same cavalry into battle at Stones River, where it was made clear that despite valiant efforts on the part of the blue-clad troopers the Union cavalry was at a severe disadvantage.

As a result, Rosecrans and Stanley were determined to build the army's cavalry arm into a force capable of dominating the enemy. They spent the winter and spring of 1863 doing exactly that. When Rosecrans launched his next campaign at the end of June, the triumph of Tullahoma was the result. The Union cavalry established itself as a force to be reckoned with.

The author next takes us through the complex operations of the Chickamauga Campaign, a far-flung enterprise across some of the most difficult terrain of the war where the Union cavalry again faced daunting challenges, including a change of commanders midway through the operation. The battles for Chattanooga followed, and then in 1864 came the Atlanta Campaign, undertaken with yet a third man in charge.

Dennis Belcher concludes his narrative there, with the fall of Atlanta and the dispersal of the Army of the Cumberland to various other duties. Along the way, however, he has both shined a light on the critical incubation of the Army of the Cumberland's cavalry corps and documented this force at the peak of its operational capability. It is a worthy story.

David Powell earned a BA from the Virginia Military Institute in 1983. His published works include: *The Maps of Chickamauga* (2009); *Failure in the Saddle* (2010); *The Chickamauga Campaign*, volumes 1 (2014) and volume 2 (2015); and essays in Steven Woodworth's *The Chickamauga Campaign* (2010) and Evan Jones and Wiley Sword's *Gateway to the Confederacy* (2014).

Preface

Louis Douglass Watkins, James P. Brownlow, Archibald Campbell, Joseph Dorr, Eli Long, William W. Lowe, Robert Byington Mitchell, Eli Murray, Washington Elliott. These are not names many people except those immersed in Civil War military history would readily recognize. Robert Minty, Edward McCook, Judson Kilpatrick and David Stanley are perhaps more familiar historical figures. All these men, and others, were members of the largest cavalry force in the central theater of the Civil War, and yet they remain unknown to many people. The Union cavalry of the Army of the Cumberland served the United States during one of the most bitter and challenging times in its history.

The Union cavalry of the Army of the Cumberland fought in some of the largest conflicts of the war, participated in raids, and faced the more commonly recognized Confederate cavalrymen—Nathan Forrest, John Hunt Morgan and Joseph Wheeler. After fighting for parity during its first few months, the Union cavalry gained its place on the battlefield with its Confederate opponents. The cavalry of the Army of the Cumberland (November 1862–October 1864) fought most of its actions in central and eastern Tennessee, northern Alabama, and Georgia and had active service during the Battle of Stones River, the Tullahoma Campaign, the Battle of Chickamauga, the Knoxville and East Tennessee Campaign, and the Atlanta Campaign. It was finally reorganized into the cavalry of the Military Department of Mississippi and the regiments continued to the end of the war under that designation. The troopers were drawn from a variety of states: Pennsylvania, Michigan, Ohio, Indiana, Kentucky, Tennessee, Wisconsin, and Iowa. The history of this cavalry unit is presented in this book.

I want to acknowledge the work that has previously been completed on this topic, in particular Edwin Bearss's work on the cavalry at the Battle of Stones River, Michael Bradley's research on the Tullahoma Campaign, David Powell's analysis of the Confederate cavalry at Chickamauga, and David Evans' very complete research on the cavalry raids during the Atlanta Campaign. In addition, there has been an impressive amount of research and analysis on the Tullahoma, Chickamauga and Atlanta campaigns completed by the U.S. Army Command and General Staff College. These materials were very important in the completion of this work. Probably the areas which needed the most additional investigation were the period after the Battle of Stones River, the Battle of Chickamauga, and the actions of the cavalry in East Tennessee after the Battle of Chickamauga until the beginning of the Atlanta Campaign.

As with all research, not all the accounts can be declared factual. Hyperbole and rationalization are common in many Civil War accounts and no doubt will be found in this work despite all efforts to make the account factual. It is also important to note that there is no attempt to slight the Southern forces in the war. If anything, in regard to the cavalry, the

Southern opponents of the Union cavalry often had the upper hand. In addition, the Southern cavalry suffered through the same hardships and performed with the same gallantry as their Union counterparts. However, this is a history of the Union cavalry and by its nature has a Union perspective.

Most of the information presented is designed not to be overly technical. The use of cavalry terms are intended to be general. Note that "saber" and "sabre" are used interchangeably in this work, both terms used to describe the curved cavalry sword used in the Civil War.

In addition, a few points need to be clarified. This work is directed at the Union cavalry of the Army of the Cumberland (1862–1864). It does not include cavalry regiments outside of this group, although some discussion of other regiments has been included. For example, the 15th Pennsylvania Cavalry is included within this work only in regard to the months of December 1862 through February 1863. After that time, the 15th Pennsylvania Cavalry was detached and served under the command of the army commander and was not under the command of the chief of cavalry of the Army of the Cumberland. In addition, only the mounted infantry attached to cavalry is included. For example, the 39th Indiana Mounted Infantry was part of the cavalry for a short time in the spring of 1863 and then transferred back to the command of the infantry. However, the 39th Indiana Mounted Infantry was reorganized and included in the cavalry corps as the 8th Indiana Cavalry in 1864. This rule also applied to Wilder's mounted infantry brigade and its amazing story. However, Wilder's brigade was included in the cavalry corps after the Battle of Chickamauga and Colonel Abram Miller generally commanded the brigade at this time due to Wilder's ill health. Wilder's Brigade is included in the manuscript at the point it was assigned to the cavalry division.

It is also important to note that the cavalry of the Army of the Cumberland was never designated as a cavalry corps, even though it operated as a corps in reality. The cavalry was officially identified as divisions. A cavalry corps was formally organized when James H. Wilson reorganized the cavalry in the West in the fall of 1864.

The cavalry of the Army of the Cumberland was commanded by three chiefs of cavalry: David Stanley, Robert B. Mitchell, and Washington L. Elliott. The book is divided into three sections to reflect the influence of the chief of cavalry. In the end, this might be somewhat unfair, as will be seen. Only David Stanley could be called an important chief of cavalry for the Army of the Cumberland. Mitchell, as it turns out, was a reluctant and temporary chief of cavalry and Elliott had almost no influence on the command of the cavalry of the Army of the Cumberland.

The objective of this book is to compile and analyze the actions, successes, failures and sacrifices of this cavalry "corps," which has been neglected for far too long. A more dedicated, effective, and hardworking command would be difficult to find. This is a story of a small group of troopers who fought for parity with their Southern foes and finally achieved it. Stanley's cavalry moved from a handful of regiments to two full divisions; under Elliott's command two additional divisions were added. This was a formidable fighting force in the Civil War.

As this work developed, a second objective emerged, particularly relating to the actions of the cavalry during the Chickamauga and Atlanta campaigns. Many existing sources refer to the poor actions of the Union cavalry during these campaigns. Certainly the cavalry actions during these campaigns could have produced better results, but the fault does not necessarily lie with the cavalry. Contrary to conclusions that the Union cavalry failed Sherman during the Atlanta Campaign, it actually performed extraordinary service in 1863 and 1864. These troopers literally rode their horses to death in many instances. The historical evidence shows excellent cavalry commanders who would be referred to as the "best cavalry officers I ever saw" by Major General James H. Wilson when he assumed command of the cavalry in the West in October 1864. The allegations of poor service came from poor and impractical mission objectives rather than the inability of the cavalry to accomplish its duty. One in three cavalrymen would be lost in the Atlanta Campaign and many regiments were dismounted because they no longer had serviceable horses.

It is also important to note the correct description of the campaign from May through September 1864. This would ultimately be titled the Atlanta Campaign, but when the campaign began Sherman's objective was not Atlanta but the destruction of Johnston's Confederate army. As the campaign developed, Johnston chose to withdraw to the defenses of Atlanta. Once Hood, who had superseded Johnston, had evaded Sherman's advance, the term "Atlanta Campaign" was adopted and is commonly used today, perhaps, erroneously.

This is a story of victories and defeats, of humor and profound sadness, of life and death, as this great country struggled to define itself. The cavalry of the Army of the Cumberland played an integral part in this struggle and has a proud history worthy of being remembered.

PART I: MAJOR GENERAL DAVID S. STANLEY,
CHIEF OF CAVALRY

1. The Union Cavalry of the Army of the Cumberland

The cavalry had been sadly neglected. It was weak, undisciplined....
—Major General David S. Stanley

Brigadier General David S. Stanley was greeted with the neighing of horses and the smell of manure as he rode into the headquarters of the Union cavalry of the newly formed Army of the Cumberland on November 23, 1862. Stanley had traveled by riverboat from Memphis to Louisville after receiving orders directing him to Nashville as the new chief of cavalry serving under the command of Major General William Starke Rosecrans. Before journeying to Nashville, Stanley met his wife and spent some time with her. Once on the way to Nashville, he rode the last forty miles on horseback because Confederate raiders had caused so much destruction to the rails that trains could not travel.

David Stanley was a tall man with broad shoulders and a narrow waist. His dark brown hair and voluminous beard, along with a steely stare, made him an impressive general. It was his calmness that caused one to sense danger in this general in blue. When he arrived in Nashville there were stories circulating about him, including ferocity in battle; he had hewn an enemy soldier almost in half at Corinth. The calm and gentlemanly appearance of Stanley hid another side of this West Point graduate.[1]

The Army of the Cumberland was less than two months old when Stanley arrived. In fact, the army was the reorganization of the Army of the Ohio, which had been commanded by Major General Don Carlos Buell. Buell was relieved of command after the Battle of Perryville, and Rosecrans was ordered to command the Department of the Cumberland on October 24, 1862. The initial orders included direction to first drive the enemy out of Kentucky and Middle Tennessee and second to secure East Tennessee. In securing East Tennessee, the Union commanders hoped to separate the rail connections with Virginia, Georgia and other southern states.[2] Rosecrans relieved Buell of command on October 30. Rosecrans, ever the gentleman, wrote to Buell as follows:

> I know the bearer of unwelcome news has a "losing office," but feel assured you are too high a gentleman and too true a soldier to permit this to produce any feelings of personal unkindness between us. I, like yourself, am neither an intriguer nor newspaper soldier. I go where I am ordered; but propriety will permit me to say that I have often felt indignant at the petty attacks on you by a portion of the press during the past summer, and that you had my high respect for ability as a soldier, for your firm adherence to truth and justice in the government and discipline of your command. I beg you, by our common profession and the love we bear our suffering country, to give me all the aid you can for the performance of duties of which no one better than yourself knows the difficulties.[3]

Rosecrans assumed command of the Army of the Cumberland after commanding the Army of the Mississippi, which had just gone through an extensive campaign in Missouri, Tennessee and Mississippi. Rosecrans commanded the Army of the Mississippi in two Union victories during the Battle of Iuka and the Battle of Corinth in September and October 1862. Although Rosecrans was successful in both battles, he had disappointed his commanding officer, Ulysses Grant, in each engagement.

Brigadier General David S. Stanley, first chief of cavalry for the Army of the Cumberland (photograph taken between 1860 and 1870, Library of Congress).

Rosecrans announced upon taking command of the troops who had served under Buell that the organization would be designated the Fourteenth Army Corps. Rosecrans began to organize his new department and knew exactly what he wanted to do about the weak cavalry component, which consisted of only eight cavalry regiments. On the same day he assumed command, he wrote to Major General Henry Halleck:

> I find we have here eight regiments of cavalry. Would be able to do wonders under an able chief. Brigadier-General Stanley, besides being an able and indefatigable soldier, is a thorough cavalry officer. He can do more good to the service by commanding a cavalry than an infantry division. I beg you for that reason to send him to me. You know the expense of cavalry, and what the rebel cavalry has done. Stanley will double our forces without expense.

Halleck agreed.[4]

Rosecrans made a good decision when he asked for Stanley. He was a West Point graduate of the class of 1852, finishing ninth in his class, and he had nine years of service on the frontiers, first in the dragoons and then in the U.S. Cavalry. He had experience in the "Bloody Kansas" fight as the state sought to determine if it would be a free state or a slave state; and since the beginning of the war, he had fought in the Wilson's Creek Campaign, commanded infantry divisions during the Siege of New Madrid and Island Number 10, the siege of Corinth, the Battle of Iuka and the Battle of Corinth. The last three engagements were under the direct command of Rosecrans, who liked the way Stanley commanded his soldiers.

Although Stanley had commanded infantry since the beginning of the war, the Union high command had trained their eyes on him to command cavalry for a long time. In January 1862 George McClellan, chief of the Union army, wrote to Henry Halleck, "Can you spare Stanley to Buell as chief of cavalry, or shall I look elsewhere to get him one? He has not asked for him, but I know him to be a first-rate officer."[5]

Although Rosecrans requested Stanley to command his cavalry, there were still a few unpleasantries which needed to be navigated. The biggest obstacle was Ulysses Grant, Stanley's commanding officer, and Grant seemed to be in no hurry to give Stanley up. Although Rosecrans' need for him was immediate, it would be three weeks before Stanley would arrive. Six days after his last message Rosecrans wrote to Halleck: "I have considerable cavalry in much confusion for want of a head. I am greatly in need of General Stanley, and request that you order him to join me at once. General Grant is pushing him south."[6] Stanley still did not arrive at the Army of the Cumberland and on November 9 Rosecrans wrote again to Halleck: "Our great wants are arms and a chief for the cavalry. Nothing yet from Stanley." On the same day, he also appealed to Edwin Stanton, the secretary of war: "General Halleck has ordered Stanley for a chief. He has not reported. No promise of arms. What can you do for us?" Grant finally issued orders for Stanley's transfer on November 11.[7]

Rosecrans Reorganizes His Army

While Rosecrans waited for Stanley's arrival, he reorganized his infantry into three wings—Thomas L. Crittenden commanding the Left Wing, Alexander McCook commanding the Right Wing, and George Thomas commanding the Center Wing. Crittenden exemplified the Civil War. The Kentucky native and his father supported the Union cause, while his brother offered his talents to the Confederacy. Crittenden served in the Mexican War as lieutenant colonel of the 3rd Kentucky Infantry. Also, he had commanded the II Corps of the old Army of the Ohio. Alexander McCook was an old classmate of David Stanley and both men graduated from West Point in 1852. McCook, part of the famous "Fighting McCooks," commanded the I Corps in the Army of the Ohio. Finally, George Thomas served as second-in-command to Don Carlos Buell in his army, and Thomas was not at all happy with Rosecrans' choice to command the Department of the Cumberland.

Thomas wrote to Halleck on the date Rosecrans assumed command about his unhappiness at serving under a commander of lower rank. Thomas soon found Rosecrans' promotion to the rank of major general was antedated so that Rosecrans' rank superseded Thomas's. Thomas complained that Halleck had requested he assume command of the Department of Tennessee and also of Buell's troops just the month before and now he was ordered to report to Rosecrans. He explained he had done good and loyal service for the Union and he had turned down the command so as not to impede the Union effort just as Buell was preparing to follow Bragg into Tennessee. He wrote, "Feeling convinced that great injustice would be done him if not permitted to carry out his plans I requested that he might be retained in command. The order relieving him was suspended, but today I am officially informed that he is relieved by General Rosecrans, my junior. Although I do not claim for myself any superior ability, yet feeling conscious that no just cause exists for overslaughing me by placing me under my junior, I feel deeply mortified and aggrieved at the action taken in this matter." Thomas concluded by saying an officer of superior rank would need to command the Department of the Cumberland if Thomas was expected to stay. Halleck replied that Rosecrans' date of promotion actually superseded Thomas's and Rosecrans' appointment resulted because Thomas refused to assume command over Buell the prior month. Thomas, thus being informed he was not serving under a junior officer, accepted command of the Center Wing.[8]

When Rosecrans assumed command of what was soon to be designated the Army of the Cumberland, General Braxton Bragg was in the process of concentrating his troops at Murfreesboro. Bragg positioned Polk's and Hardee's corps around Murfreesboro and utilized his cavalry to watch Rosecrans' movement and disrupt his communications whenever possible. By early December the Department of the Cumberland was simply designated as the Army of the Cumberland, a title it would carry to the end of the war. Rosecrans initially established his headquarters at Bowling Green, Kentucky, and Brigadier General James Negley commanded Union troops in occupied Nashville. Soon the Confederate cavalry threatened Nashville and Rosecrans sent McCook's infantry corps to relieve the city. This gave Rosecrans the excuse he needed not to follow Halleck's direction to carry a campaign into eastern Tennessee.

William S. Rosecrans, David Stanley's commanding officer, wrote, "I am greatly in need of General Stanley" (Wilson's Creek National Battlefield).

McCook arrived at Nashville on November 17 and secured the city. Rosecrans followed soon afterwards and established his new headquarters there.

The Cavalry of the Army of the Cumberland

The cavalry Stanley found when he arrived was weak and under the command of Colonel John Kennett. The Union cavalry was totally outmanned by its Confederate counterpart. The cavalry under the organization of the Army of the Ohio was dispersed throughout the army under command of specific infantry corps commanders. Colonel Edward McCook had commanded a brigade of cavalry in Thomas L. Crittenden's II Corps made up of three regiments: 2nd Indiana Cavalry, 1st Kentucky Cavalry, 7th Pennsylvania Cavalry, and Battery M of the 4th U.S. Light Artillery. In addition, Captain Ebenezer Gay commanded a three-regiment brigade of cavalry as part of Charles Gilbert's III Corps: 9th Kentucky Cavalry, 2nd Michigan Cavalry, 9th Pennsylvania Cavalry and a section of the 2nd Minnesota Light Artillery. Colonel Lewis Zahm also commanded a cavalry brigade of the 5th Kentucky, 3rd Ohio, and 4th Ohio cavalries. The 2nd Kentucky Cavalry and the 1st Ohio Cavalry served as escorts for the various commanders of the infantry corps, and the 4th U.S. Cavalry and the "Anderson Troop" served as escorts for the commanding general. When the cavalry moved from Kentucky to Tennessee, Gay's brigade remained in Kentucky.

John Kennett had the most precarious position in the new cavalry organization. Prior to Stanley's arrival he had commanded the entire cavalry division of the Army of the Cumberland. With Stanley's arrival, Kennett had a more undefined role, especially in light of Stanley's decision to take direct command of the Reserve Cavalry Brigade. Kennett failed to impress Rosecrans, and, in fact, caused the commanding general much trouble. While Rosecrans was trying to deal with the organization of the entire army, he seemed to be bombarded with daily messages from his wing commanders about the failure of the cavalry to communicate and to check the enemy's actions. In Kennett's defense, he was more accustomed to the command style of Buell, and the efficient Rosecrans was very different. Probably the biggest problem for Kennett was simply being out-soldiered by the enemy, whose cavalry numbers more than doubled his own.

The Left Wing commander, Major General Thomas Crittenden, was asked on November 6, "Do you hear anything of Colonel Kennett or his cavalry force?" This message reverberated in headquarters until Stanley arrived: Where was the cavalry? In fact, Kennett was earnestly doing his duty. The cavalry tried to rid the countryside of guerrillas and enemy cavalry, and the necessity of communicating with Rosecrans didn't seem to Kennett a priority at that moment.[9]

Again on November 6, Rosecrans received a disturbing communication from one of his subordinates, J.B. Anderson, about the dominance of the Confederate cavalry in Tennessee: "The whole country from Richland to Gallatin has been occupied by bands of mounted men, who will cut off working parties and destroy their work unless a sufficient force is placed on the line." The message continued by saying that unless a large enough force of Union cavalry was present to intimidate the Confederate raiders, much of the necessary work on the railroad would not be completed.[10]

The seriousness of the threat of Southern cavalry was also communicated to Rosecrans from Major General Alexander McCook, commanding his Right Wing, on November 6. McCook observed that John Hunt Morgan's cavalry had attacked Edgefield, Tennessee, the previous day but was repulsed. While the Union infantry was dealing with this, a simultaneous attack was made at Nashville by Nathan Bedford Forrest's cavalry. McCook noted this movement was also repulsed. It seemed all the Union army could do was to act defensively. McCook wrote that Morgan was next seen six miles north of Nashville heading for Gallatin. McCook dispatched some of his cavalry to observe Morgan's movements and promised to relay the information to Thomas Crittenden.[11]

The Confederate cavalry seemed to be everywhere. Rosecrans' frustration was evident when he responded to McCook through his acting chief of staff, Arthur Ducat: "We have nothing from Colonel Kennett as to where he is: did he go toward Scottsville, as ordered? He has not communicated with General Crittenden, and the general does not know whether he has cavalry on his front or not. One regiment was ordered to go on General Crittenden's front. When Colonel Kennett marched it was never reported to him."[12]

On November 7, Rosecrans wrote a chastisement of Kennett's silence in a communication to Crittenden. Rosecrans identified the intent of the Confederate cavalry as preventing the use of the railroad to Nashville, and he told Crittenden to order Kennett to strongly defend Hartsville from the enemy's cavalry. He also told Crittenden to use some of the cavalry assigned to his corps to serve as a screen near Lebanon: "At this distance you must be the best judge of the position of the rebel cavalry.... Order Colonel Kennett to keep up communication."[13] The distance was too great and Rosecrans had more to do than give Kennett detailed orders for each action. Ducat wrote to Kennett, "The general commanding expects that you will exercise your own judgment in many respects, governed by the several movements ordered. You will, on receipt of this, communicate rapidly with General Crittenden, and cooperate with him.... The general wishes me to state that he does not consider your dispatches satisfactory, and would like them oftener; that communication with his headquarters must at all times be kept up, wherever they are."[14]

Colonel Lewis Zahm, commanding the Second Brigade, soon grasped and accepted the need to increase communication, and on November 7 he reported to Rosecrans the location of McCook's corps and information of Morgan's 3,000 cavalry at Gallatin. Zahm had only 600 troopers and could not engage Morgan. In addition, he was unaware of the exact location of the wings of the army and had sent troopers to try to find Crittenden's corps to open communications with him. Rosecrans reinforced the importance of intelligence from Zahm and encouraged him to keep the messages going: "Inform him [Crittenden] of all you know, and keep up communications with him. If you have to communicate, will Colonel Kennett act on the principle that the cavalry are the eyes of the army? Take orders for co-operation from General Crittenden. Always keep up your communication with headquarters." While Zahm acted on Rosecrans' wishes that his cavalry work in conjunction with the entire army, it was disturbing that Zahm had to be urged to influence Kennett to serve the army through his role as a commander of cavalry.[15]

Rosecrans had had enough of the cavalry's operating without communication. He had gotten one of his cavalry brigades on board and he issued General Orders No. 7 announcing Captain Elmer Otis, 4th U.S. Cavalry, as chief of the courier lines. Otis organized an effective courier service utilizing troopers who had horses but no weapons. One way or another, he needed to get information from his "eyes of the Army" and between his three corps.

Crittenden used his infantry to attempt to capture Morgan, and on November 8 Colonel Charles Harker's infantry brigade and Zahm's cavalry reached the location where Morgan had been observed only to find him gone. They did manage to capture eighteen men, some horses, and equipment. Crittenden wrote, "The want of cavalry greatly embarrasses my operations. Colonel Kennett has not yet reported, so I have none to send to General Smith, as you have ordered. Without a cavalry force at Hartsville, I fear a single regiment would not be safe here, and I have no means of opening communication with General McCook." He lamented the lack of cavalry to support his actions and the continued lack of communication from Kennett.[16]

Rosecrans' commander of his Center Wing, General Thomas, arrived in Gallatin, Tennessee, on November 12 offering experience and stability to his newly forming army. Thomas's first questions went to the heart of the struggle Rosecrans was facing: "Arrived here today.... Where is Crittenden and the cavalry?" Almost immediately, the weakness of the cavalry was evident. Thomas needed to know how to position his troops and he needed to know where the Union cavalry was placed. On November 12, Kennett and 2,000 Union cavalry were in Hartsville, Tennessee, and Thomas was informed Kennett was "requested to keep up communications."[17]

The next day, Brigadier General James Negley reported Nathan B. Forrest's cavalry threw aside the pickets of the 4th Ohio Cavalry. Again on November 14, Rosecrans wrote to Thomas: "Have you any news from Kennett today? He was anxious on yesterday. Satisfied there was no cause. Find out how much of a train it will take to haul his spoils from Hartsville, and send for them. Direct your infantry at Hartsville to collect the stores discovered by Colonel Kennett." Thomas responded disparagingly regarding his interactions with Kennett:

A dispatch from Colonel Kennett, just received, states that one of his scouts had just returned from Lebanon, and tells him that Morgan and Forrest are at Lebanon with 4,200 men and eight pieces of artillery. Colonel Kennett thinks it will be an unequal fight, and, therefore, would return to Hartsville. He thinks a combined movement should be agreed upon to move from this place and Lebanon on the rebels. Confess I do not understand him, and his dispatch has something of the appearance of a stampede.[18]

Within three days of Thomas's arrival in Gallatin, he summarized the cavalry situation of the Army of the Cumberland Rosecrans had desperately tried to remedy. Thomas wrote to Rosecrans on November 15: "When will Stanley arrive? It is a great pity he is not now in command of the cavalry." On November 18, Arthur Ducat slapped Colonel Kennett verbally with an unpleasant and thinly veiled message about the way the cavalry was being handled: "Dispatch received. Had information some time before of the affair at Gallatin. It is to be regretted that our cavalry has proved too slow for Morgan. It is hoped that you will execute your orders promptly."[19]

On a positive note, Halleck came through on his promise to furnish new and effective cavalry arms to the Army of the Cumberland on November 17. Although the type of cavalry arms was not specified in his message, the new and technically superior Colt revolving rifles were also being sent to Rosecrans. Edwin Stanton promised 1,600 of the revolving rifles moved by passenger train to Louisville for use by Rosecrans. During the intervening weeks the constant struggle of communication with Kennett on one hand and the hit and run tactics of Morgan, Forrest, and Wheeler on the other was enough to distract Rosecrans. By the middle of November, Kennett's communications were somewhat improving.[20]

At long last, on November 24, Rosecrans issued General Orders No. 22, which announced David Stanley's arrival. When Stanley made his appearance he saw an army in desperate need of a chief of cavalry because communication, organization, and reliability of the cavalry were poor. Almost immediately upon his arrival, all messages about communication and coordination with the cavalry ceased.[21]

With him Stanley brought an intimate friend who would serve with him throughout the remainder of the war, Major William Henry Sinclair. Sinclair was born near Akron, Ohio, and enlisted in the 7th Michigan Infantry. Soon thereafter, he was promoted to the rank of lieutenant in Dee's 3rd Michigan Artillery. The two men became acquainted during the Siege of Island Number 10, and when Stanley moved to Nashville in the fall of 1862 Sinclair came along as his adjutant general and remained in that role until the end of the war. During the Battle of Corinth, Sinclair had been sent with a message for Stanley. Just as Sinclair arrived, Stanley's aide was killed and Stanley turned to Sinclair and appointed him to his staff on the spot. Stanley had no more efficient, loyal subordinate and better friend than Sinclair.[22]

Upon his arrival, Stanley organized the cavalry regiments into a single division:

CAVALRY[23]
Brigadier General David S. Stanley

CAVALRY DIVISION
Colonel John Kennett

First Brigade
Colonel Edward McCook, Colonel Robert H.G. Minty
2nd Indiana, Company M, Captain Joseph A.S. Mitchell
3rd Kentucky, Colonel Eli H. Murray

4th Michigan, Lieutenant Colonel William H. Dickinson
7th Pennsylvania, Major John E. Wynkoop

Second Brigade
Colonel Lewis Zahm
1st Ohio, Colonel Minor Millikin
3rd Ohio, Lieutenant Colonel Douglas A. Murray
4th Ohio, Major John L. Pugh

Artillery
1st Ohio, Battery D (section), Lieutenant Nathaniel M. Newell

Unattached
4th U.S. Cavalry, Captain Elmer Otis

What was thought to be one of the more pleasant bits of news which awaited Stanley was the anticipated arrival of the Anderson (15th) Pennsylvania Cavalry. The Anderson Troop was an independent cavalry command formed in Pennsylvania and it served primarily as escort for the commanding generals of the army. The Anderson Troop expanded to a full regiment in 1862 and officially comprised the 15th Pennsylvania Cavalry. The 15th Pennsylvania would serve in the cavalry reserve brigade for the Army of the Cumberland but did not reach the army until December 24.

Stanley summarized his assessment of the cavalry upon his arrival at the Army of the Cumberland: "The cavalry had been sadly neglected. It was weak, undisciplined and scattered about a regiment to a division of infantry. To break up this foolish disposal of cavalry and to form brigades and eventually divisions, was my first and most difficult work. Generals commanding divisions, declared they would not give up their cavalry regiments, but I insisted that they do so and General Rosecrans sustained me."[24] Despite some resistance to Stanley's reorganization, Brigadier General John Beatty was impressed with him upon Stanley's arrival and recorded the following in his diary: "Major-General Stanley, the cavalryman, is of good size, gentlemanly in bearing, light complexion, brown hair."[25]

Both Stanley and Rosecrans wanted time for their new troops to drill, equip and train in preparation for the upcoming campaign, but by December 4 Henry Halleck informed Rosecrans the president was becoming impatient with the Army of the Cumberland's stay in the area around Nashville. In return, Rosecrans had several issues of his own and felt these needed to be rectified before he could march, including obtaining a supply of shoes, arms, and tents. In regard to the cavalry, he lamented the lack of horses and he felt he had about half the number the cavalrymen needed. When Stanley arrived he had 3,038 troopers present for duty and a total number of cavalrymen of 4,534. The 15th Pennsylvania (Anderson) Cavalry, which was en route, as well as two regiments of Tennessee cavalry increased the number by 2,883 men. The new total of cavalry was 7,400 and even with the new arms received from Washington there were still 1,300 troopers without arms. Another 1,200 horses were also needed.

Cavalry Division

The cavalry division was commanded by Colonel John Kennett, born in St. Petersburg, Russia, in 1809. He attended Harvard College and returned to Russia after his education.

Later he returned to Cincinnati, where he became a United States citizen. Prior to the war, Kennett co-owned a large tobacco company in Cincinnati. He assisted in the organization of the 4th Ohio Cavalry and served as the first colonel of the regiment. During the Battle of Perryville, Kennett commanded the cavalry division, of which he was given command on September 5.[26]

The First Brigade

Twenty-nine-year-old Colonel Edward McCook commanded the First Brigade of Cavalry under Buell and continued in that capacity under Rosecrans. Before the war McCook was a lawyer and served in the Kansas Territory legislature. He enlisted without military experience and had risen in rank through his performance in the field. In September 1862 his brigade successfully captured the 3rd Georgia Cavalry near New Haven, Kentucky. In October McCook led the brigade in the Battle of Perryville. His health began to fail and he was granted a leave of absence in mid–December; the command of the First Brigade fell to Colonel Robert Minty, 4th Michigan Cavalry. The First Brigade was made up of four regiments: 2nd Indiana, 3rd Kentucky, 4th Michigan, and 7th Pennsylvania.[27]

The 2nd Indiana Cavalry was the first complete cavalry regiment organized in Indiana, in Indianapolis in September 1861, and John A. Bridgeland was the first colonel of the regiment. Troopers enlisting in the 2nd Indiana were promised "good quarters, a handsome uniform and first rate horse." In addition, those in the regiment were offered a salary of $14–$24 per month. In November 1862, the 2nd Indiana was a battle-hardened regiment with service extending to the Battle of Pea Ridge and it had experience sparring with Confederate cavalry in Kentucky and Tennessee. At full strength it contained 1,200 men. On December 7, 1862, John Hunt Morgan's Confederate cavalrymen captured most of those in a raid at Hartsville, Tennessee. Only Company M, commanded by Captain Joseph Mitchell, avoided this fate and was available for service in Stanley's cavalry division. Mitchell, a 26-year-old attorney from Goshen, Indiana, was a native of Pennsylvania and had no prior military experience.[28]

The 3rd Kentucky Cavalry's commanding officer was nineteen-year-old Colonel Eli H. Murray. Murray, born into a prosperous family in Breckinridge County, Kentucky, was commissioned major when the regiment was mustered into service and received a battlefield promotion when Brigadier General James Jackson was killed during the Battle of Perryville. Murray, though very young, was described as "always cool, self-possessed ... and equal to every emergency." The regiment commanded by Murray was organized in September and October 1861 with the troopers drawn from central

Robert Minty, Stanley's trusted cavalry commander, commanded his First Brigade (*Minty and the Cavalry*, 1886).

Kentucky. The 3rd Kentucky had active service beginning in the fall of 1861 and was involved in a skirmish with Forrest's cavalry at Sacramento, Kentucky, the second day of battle at Shiloh, the siege of Corinth, the Battle of Perryville and actions in northern Alabama, Tennessee and Kentucky. The regiment also participated in the capture of the 3rd Georgia Cavalry regiment near New Haven.[29]

The 4th Michigan Cavalry was mustered into service on July 29, 1862, and Colonel Robert Minty commanded the regiment. Minty had been serving as lieutenant colonel of the 3rd Michigan Cavalry. Born in County Mayo, Ireland, on December 4, 1831, the son of an English soldier serving in Ireland, Minty did not consider himself an Irishman. Following in his father's footsteps, he enlisted as an ensign in the British Army and served five years in the West Indies, Honduras, and the west coast of Africa. His service in the Union army began when he was commissioned major of the 2nd Michigan Cavalry in 1861. Stanley had great respect for Minty and enjoyed his style of horsemanship, both officers realizing the need to wield the saber when fighting in close quarters with enemy cavalry. Minty's brigade would ultimately be nicknamed the "Sabre Brigade" because of his insistence on the use of this weapon.[30]

The 4th Michigan had traveled to Louisville, Kentucky, and clashed with Forrest's cavalry near Stanford and escorted the infantry to Nashville. While the 4th Michigan was a green regiment with over 1,200 men and officers on the rolls, the influence of Minty instilled confidence and steadiness to the troopers.

The 7th Pennsylvania Cavalry was an experienced regiment mustered into service during the fall of 1861; George Wynkoop was appointed as its first colonel. The regiment contained men from various counties in eastern Pennsylvania. Wynkoop, a cavalry officer for more than twenty years, provided the much needed experience necessary to command the regiment. He had served in a three-month regiment prior to the organization of the 7th Pennsylvania Cavalry. Wynkoop's subordinate officer was Lieutenant Colonel William B. Sipes, a newspaper editor from Philadelphia. Sipes temporarily assumed command of the regiment as it became part of the Army of the Cumberland. Sipes would permanently assume command of the regiment in April 1863 when Wynkoop resigned due to disability.[31]

The regiment had previously been assigned to duty under Buell primarily in central Tennessee. The duty included heavy skirmishing with Forrest's and Morgan's Confederate cavalry, including a particularly bloody affair near Gallatin, Tennessee, where the 7th Penn-

Colonel Eli Murray was nineteen years old and "equal to every emergency" (MOLLUS-MASS Civil War Collection, United States Army Heritage and Education Center, Military History Institute, Carlisle, Pennsylvania).

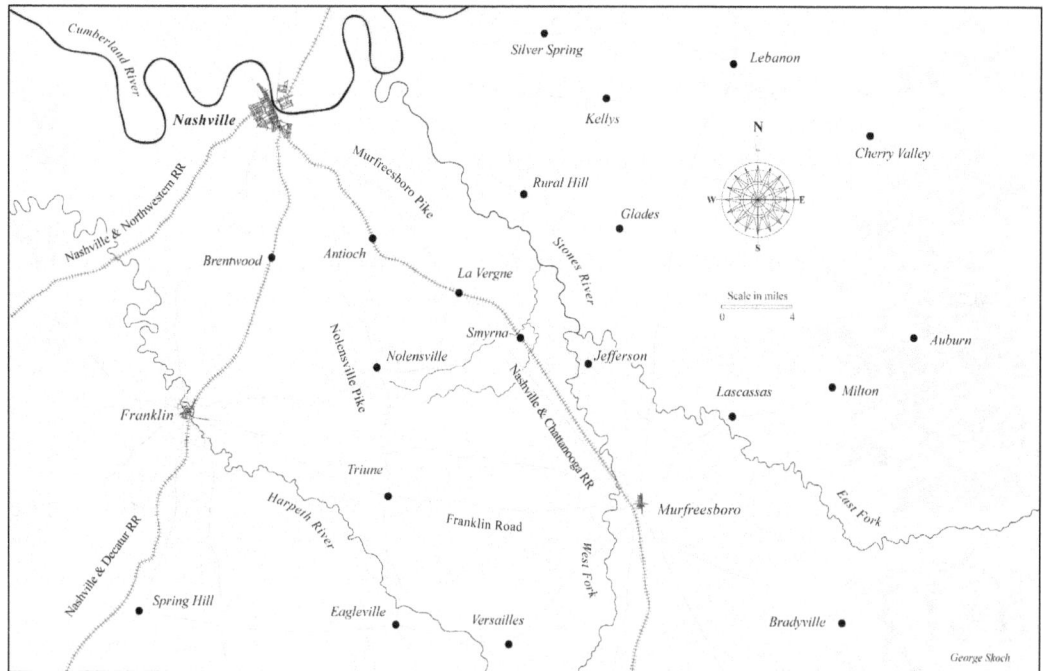

Central Tennessee, December 1862

sylvania lost 140 men killed or wounded. In addition, Major John E. Wynkoop, whose brother, Battalion Adjutant Nicholas Wynkoop was killed in action at Gallatin, Tennessee, on August 21, 1862, led the First Battalion during the Battle of Perryville where the regiment recorded seven casualties.

The Second Brigade

Colonel Lewis Zahm commanded the Second Brigade. Born in Bavaria on August 7, 1820, Zahm eventually came to America with his two sisters and travelled to Ohio, where his brother lived. When the Civil War began he was urged to raise a regiment of cavalry, which he did after some deliberation. He became the first colonel of the 3rd Ohio Cavalry, which was mustered into service in September 1861. The Second Brigade was made up of three regiments of cavalry and a section of artillery: the 1st Ohio, 3rd Ohio, and 4th Ohio cavalries, and the 1st Ohio Artillery Battery D (Newell's section).

The 1st Ohio Cavalry, with the majority of troopers being drawn from central Ohio, was one of the most experienced of Stanley's regiments. This regiment saw action in the siege of Corinth and in engagements in northern Mississippi and Alabama and participated in the Battle of Perryville. The first colonel of the regiment was O.P. Ransom, but he resigned in February 1862. Colonel Ransom, a regular army officer, was a strict disciplinarian. He had been disparaged by men of the regiment who referred to him as a tyrant, but soon the training and discipline he instilled were recognized and appreciated. After Ransom's resignation, Colonel Minor Millikin assumed command. Millikin was from a prosperous family from southern

Ohio and had attended Hanover College and Miami College. He also attended Harvard and was an attorney, newspaper editor and farmer before the war.[32]

Millikin was an outspoken and energetic officer, and he had chafed under the command of Ransom not because of his discipline but due to his excesses. Millikin was commissioned as major when the 1st Ohio was organized as a three-year regiment. When he served as major, he wrote to his commanding officer: "Your habits, Colonel Ransom, your intemperate excesses, are of such a character as to entirely negative negate my faith in and respect for your other good qualities." Millikin, obviously referring to Ransom's drinking, declared he would prefer charges against his colonel if the problem continued. When Ransom resigned, Millikin was promoted to the command of the regiment. Dissatisfaction resulted in the regiment because the thirty-year-old Millikin passed some older and more experienced officers. Nevertheless, he retained command of the regiment and was in the saddle when Stanley arrived.[33]

Colonel Lewis Zahm, born in Bavaria, first colonel of the 3rd Ohio Cavalry, commanded the Second Cavalry Brigade (MOLLUS-MASS Civil War Collection, United States Army Heritage and Education Center, Military History Institute, Carlisle, Pennsylvania).

The 3rd Ohio Cavalry recruited troopers from northern Ohio and was also an experienced regiment. The 3rd Ohio arrived at Shiloh on the second day of the battle, participated in the siege of Corinth, served in northern Alabama, sparred with Confederate cavalry in Tennessee and Kentucky, and fought in the Perryville Campaign. When fully mustered, 1,200 men made up the regiment who "wanted to get at it, get it done, and get home again." The first colonel of the regiment was Colonel Lewis Zahm, who had been given brigade command in the fall of 1862. Next, Lieutenant Colonel Douglas A. Murray commanded the regiment. Murray, a Scotsman, was experienced and had been promoted from the 2nd U.S. Cavalry. Murray's experience in the regular cavalry made him the ideal choice for training of the regiment, and he began training the volunteers in the skills needed to fight in the war. Sergeant Thomas Crofts recalled Murray's "very peculiar brogue, rolling his rs in a wonderful fashion."[34]

The 4th Ohio Cavalry was recruited from various locations across the state, primarily Cincinnati but also Hamilton, Dayton, Lebanon, South Charleston, Ironton, Lima and St. Mary's. The 4th was also an experienced regiment, having been mustered into service in the fall of 1861. Like other cavalry regiments in the brigade, it had seen action in various engagements in Kentucky, Tennessee and Alabama. Colonel John Kennett was instrumental in its organization, and when Kennett was promoted to command the cavalry division Lieutenant Colonel Henry W. Burdsall assumed command of the regiment. Burdsall resigned the day before Stanley arrived in Nashville and Major John L. Pugh, a 29-year-old Madison, Indiana, native, commanded the regiment through the upcoming months.[35]

The artillery assigned to the cavalry division was the 1st Ohio, Battery D (section), commanded by Lieutenant Nathaniel M. Newell. The battery was captured in Munfordville, Kentucky, on September 17, 1862, but Newell's section escaped that fate because it was attached to Brigadier General James S. Jackson's Tenth Division. Newell's section was at the Battle of Shiloh, in the siege of Corinth, northern Alabama, Tennessee and the Battle of Perryville.[36]

Battery D was mustered into three year's service in October 1861 under the command of Colonel James Barnett. Newell's section contained two 3-inch rifled cannon which were noted for exceptional accuracy. It was proudly claimed the cannon could hit the end of a flour barrel at any distance less than a mile.[37]

The final cavalry regiment attached to headquarters was the 4th U.S. Cavalry, commanded by Captain Elmer Otis. The thirty-two-year-old Otis, an 1853 West Point graduate, was a professional soldier and commanded an expert regiment of cavalry. Prior to the war he had experience on the frontier similar to Stanley's. Otis was promoted to the rank of captain in May 1861 and had commanded the 4th U.S. Cavalry thus far in the war. The professional regiment had seen extensive service in Missouri, Fort Donelson, New Madrid, Shiloh, and Perryville.[38]

Chief of Cavalry: David S. Stanley

Brigadier General David Sloan Stanley brought years of cavalry experience to the Army of the Cumberland. He graduated 9th in his class at the United States Military Academy in 1852. Raised in modest circumstances in Cedar Valley, Ohio, he was sent in his early teens to live with Dr. Leander Firestone. Stanley was training to be a physician when he was offered an opportunity to attend West Point. He accepted and was educated with many of the men who were to play important roles in the Civil War. Thomas Casey graduated first in the class of 1852, which included such individuals as Henry Slocum, George Hartstuft, Alexander McCook, George Crook, and Hezekiah H. Garber of Illinois, who graduated last in the class of 43.[39]

On his way to West Point, Stanley met a man who was destined to become a lifelong friend. As Stanley traveled to Cleveland on his initial trip to West Point he rode with a lovely young woman and a "little dapper, rather dandified young man." By coincidence, the young man was Philip Sheridan, "small and red faced, long black wavy hair, bright eyes, very animated and neatly dressed in a brown broadcloth sack suit." Stanley recorded that, once Sheridan reached West Point, his suit was replaced with a brown linen jacket and his locks were removed, revealing a rather "insignificant"-looking person. To Stanley, this new appearance meant nothing because Sheridan was a "good fellow and he and I remained friends until his death." Phil Sheridan also remembered his first encounter with David Stanley and recalled that their friendship grew while they were on the steamship crossing Lake Erie. Sheridan recalled, "I found out that he had no 'Monroe shoes,' so I deemed myself just that much ahead of my companion, although my shoes might not conform exactly to regulations in Eastern style and finish."[40]

After graduation Stanley attended cavalry training at Carlisle Barracks in Pennsylvania and then accompanied Lieutenant A.W. Whipple's Topographical Engineers expedition consisting of about 20 men. The engineers surveyed a route from Fort Smith, Arkansas, to San Diego, California. The expedition began on July 24, 1853, and reached San Bernardino on March 14, 1854. Stanley then spent years in various locations on the western frontier dealing with issues between settlers and Native Americans. While on the frontier Stanley met and served with a myriad of men who would lead troops in the Civil War. Ironically, future Confederate cavalry legend J.E.B. Stuart saved Stanley's life in a skirmish with Indians in Kansas. In 1857, Stanley's command went in search of a group of marauding Cheyenne Indians near Solomon Fork, Kansas. While pursuing the Indians, the quarry dispersed and as luck would have it, Lieutenant Stanley and Lieutenant Stuart rode stirrup to stirrup after one of the Indians. The chase took four miles and the horses were winded when the Indian stopped and fired at Stuart. Stanley recorded, "I turned my horse and rode in on the Indian, firing one shot, but as I fired near my horse's ear, it scared him, and immediately jumping off my horse, tried to get a good aim at the Indian, but to my horror, my pistol stood firmly cocked and refused to fire. The Indian saw my fix in a flash and ran towards me, presenting his pistol." Stanley dropped his pistol drew his saber and waited for the shot, but Stuart rode ahead and swung his saber at the Indian. Stuart hit his target, but at the same time the Indian's pistol went off, wounding Stuart in the chest.[41]

When the war began Stanley turned down a commission in the Confederate army and later led troops during the Wilson's Creek Campaign, the Siege of New Madrid and Island Number 10, the Siege of Corinth, the Battle of Iuka, and the Battle of Corinth. He was commissioned a brigadier general in September 1861 and had successfully led infantry divisions thus far in the war.

It was during the advance on Corinth in May 1862 that Stanley first served under wing commander William S. Rosecrans. Rosecrans grew to value Stanley's professional attitude toward the war and, despite the fact Rosecrans privately censured Stanley's late arrival at the Battle of Iuka, the two men were mutually supportive of each other. The relationship between them revealed a common spiritual nature. While Rosecrans was well known for his verbal tirades, he never blasphemed. Rosecrans was a devout Roman Catholic and his brother was a priest in the church and later would become a bishop. Stanley, on the other hand, was raised in the Presbyterian church and was also noted for his spiritual nature.

A significant event occurred during the summer of 1862 that explained much in regard to the relationship of David Stanley and his immediate commander, William Rosecrans. Stanley was baptized into the Roman Catholic church in Mississippi in 1862 and Rosecrans was his godfather. Rosecrans wrote his wife about the baptism: "I had also the great joy to be God father to Genl. David S. Stanley who was baptized this morning at seven o'clock this morning previous to the Holy Sacrifice which was offered by the Rev. Father Tracy of Tuscumbia or rather of Huntsville in whose mission the region lies and who has come here to administer the sacraments to those he finds willing...." Before Stanley entered the United States Military Academy, he was a Presbyterian, but the war caused him to search the core of his personal convictions. John Ireland, chaplain of the 5th Minnesota Infantry, and after the war Archbishop of St. Paul, Minnesota, recalled that Stanley's public conversion occurred during Mass held in a public square in Iuka with a very large congregation. Before this group Stanley publicly read his profession of faith and was conditionally baptized. Word of the event swept through the army. Ireland stated, "Not many weeks later I met General Stanley, and he told me that he was most happy in realizing that he had obeyed the calling of his conscience; and that by so doing he was nearer to his God, and ready to meet Him, if death came to him in the performance of his duty on the battle field." Afterward, it was common to see Stanley kneeling on the ground with the common soldiers with his prayer book in his hand. Ireland noted, "Catholics and non–Catholics expressed their respect for him on account of his open profession."[42]

Rosecrans most certainly was influential in this decision of Stanley's conversion to Catholicism, but a remarkable Roman Catholic priest coincidentally entered Stanley's life and changed him forever. The priest was Father Jeremiah F. Trecy, a native of Ireland, who was noted for ministering to troops of both sides during the Civil War. Trecy's involvement in the Union army began after the Battle of Shiloh when he asked to tend to the religious needs of the Southern wounded and prisoners. Permission was granted and soon the good father was providing spiritual care for both sides.[43] Trecy moved from place to place providing much needed spiritual support and was often accused of being a spy.[44]

Stanley and the Cavalry

When Stanley arrived at the Army of the Cumberland, a correspondent of the *Cincinnati Commercial Newspaper*, William D. Bickham, described him as a "man of sanguine nervous temperament, of vehement and fiery spirit, with blazing blue eyes and a lithe figure somewhat above medium stature." Stanley faced many challenges in improving the weak Union cavalry to meet his formidable adversaries. When he arrived at the Army of the Cumberland, he assessed the poor organization of the cavalry and gained Rosecrans' support to improve his new command. Stanley declared, "I soon had three pretty substantial brigades formed and commanded by good officers. We made several sudden marches upon the enemy's outposts, where they were collecting provisions and running mills and we ran the enemy away."[45]

If imitation is the sincerest form of flattery, then the Confederate cavalry had to be pleased with Stanley's decision to reorganize the cavalry of the Army of the Cumberland. The Confederates began organizing their cavalry in brigades early in 1862. Stanley's reorganization of the cavalry was unique in the West. Stanley served under Rosecrans in Mississippi and that cavalry was organized just as it had been under Buell in the Army of the Ohio. The decision to form a cavalry division was met with almost universal approval by the cavalrymen under Stanley's command. They felt they had provided hard service for the infantry corps or division commanders and had accomplished very little. Small groups of cavalry had faced large Confederate forces and the Union troopers had no significant offensive role. The situation immediately changed with Stanley's arrival, as he and Rosecrans began to develop a plan to build parity with the enemy's horsemen. The Federals needed to be able to mount a force large enough to meet the enemy on equal terms and this could not be accomplished under the old Union organization.

Next, Stanley realized he had some very experienced cavalry regiments mixed with newer regiments, and his entire command had really never participated in a battle as a significant cavalry presence. The Army of the Ohio had really participated in only two battles, Shiloh and Perryville, and in both of them the cavalry played a minor offensive role. As the Army of the Cumberland faced Forrest, Wheeler and Morgan, the Union cavalry needed to learn to fight. Stanley assumed command of cavalry, which had been utilized according to the policy applied to the Eastern Theatre. At the beginning of the war, the high command of the Union army felt that, due to the geographic obstacles, cavalry could not be efficiently used, therefore little emphasis was placed on this arm of the service. In addition, it was commonly accepted that a cavalryman could be fully trained only after two years. Most believed the war would be over in a short period and discounted any efforts for a long-term expansion of the cavalry. This neglect was obvious when Stanley assumed command.[46]

Training was important to newly forming cavalry. Stanley wrote, "Our cavalry had been poorly instructed and depended upon their carbines instead of the saber. I insisted on the latter. I sent grindstones and had the sabers sharpened, each squadron being provided with the means for this work. This soon gave confidence to our men, and the opportunity was only lacking to show their superiority over the enemy." This quote by Stanley has generated numerous comments from historians, some positive, most not. Stanley believed the new volunteers needed as much training as possible. Granted, the cavalry tactics were rapidly changing with the effectiveness of firearms becoming more important. This was still a time of transition for cavalry tactics and Stanley never minimized the importance of firearms for his troopers. He felt the cavalry needed to be trained to be fully capable of utilizing not only pistols, muskets, rifles and carbines, but the saber also. The cavalry in 1862 still charged and in close-quarters combat the saber proved to be an effective weapon of the day. The cavalry under Stanley, and fully supported by his experienced brigade commander, Robert Minty, would need to use the saber. Discounting some views of Stanley's over reliance on the saber, Rosecrans and Stanley armed as many troopers as possible with breech-loading, revolving and repeating rifles, the new technology in weaponry at the time.[47]

Next, the Union cavalry needed more men, desperately, and also better firearms and good horses. Remarkably, the Union cavalry in Tennessee had many troopers without horses and weapons this late in the war. Stanley convinced Rosecrans of the need and Rosecrans began sending messages urging Washington to send more men, weapons and horses.

Not only was Rosecrans happy to have Stanley, with his skills, in charge of the cavalry, so too were many in the Union cavalry. W.L. Curry, 1st Ohio Cavalry, wrote:

> General D.S. Stanley, a cavalry officer of long, active service in the regular army, had just been assigned to duty as Chief of the Cavalry, Army of the Cumberland, and as he was very active and aggressive, a long felt want in that arm of the service seemed to have been supplied. He was always on the alert for duty required of his command, and he did not propose to settle down and wait for the enemy to come to him, but went after the enemy, and usually found him, as Forrest, Wheeler and Morgan were tireless riders and were making raids on the railroads almost daily.[48]

The need to neutralize the Confederate cavalry was emphasized on December 7 when the Union command became aware Morgan was again on the move. In a message full of foreboding, Rosecrans asked George Thomas, "Where is Dumont's division now lying?" This message referred to Brigadier General Ebenezer Dumont, who commanded the 12th Division. One of Dumont's brigades, commanded by Colonel Absalom B. Moore, held the town of Hartsville, Tennessee. John Hunt Morgan's cavalry attacked Moore's brigade on December

7 and virtually the entire brigade surrendered by 9:00 a.m. to a force half its size. The Union prisoners totaled about 1,800 men, including most of the 2nd Indiana Cavalry. The bold raid by Confederate cavalry yielded significant results.[49]

Confederate Adversaries

In Middle Tennessee David Stanley's cavalry faced three legendary Confederate cavalry officers—Nathan Bedford Forrest, John Hunt Morgan and Joseph Wheeler. These Confederate commanders literally rode circles around the Union army in Middle Tennessee in November and December 1862.

John Hunt Morgan, "Thunderbolt of the Confederacy," was born in Huntsville, Alabama, and was the grandson of John Wesley Hunt, an early founder of Lexington, Kentucky. Morgan attended Transylvania College for two years but was suspended in 1844 for dueling. He enlisted as a private in the U.S. Cavalry during the Mexican War.

Typical Union cavalryman with saber, carbine and Colt revolver (Library of Congress).

Stanley's adversaries in central Tennessee: (left) John Hunt Morgan (Library of Congress) and Nathan B. Forrest (Library of Congress).

Afterwards, he became a hemp manufacturer and took over his grandfather's mercantile business in Kentucky. In 1857, Morgan raised an independent infantry company known as the "Lexington Rifles" and in September 1861, he took his militiamen to the Confederacy. Initially, he was promoted as colonel of the 2nd Kentucky Cavalry and promoted to the rank of brigadier general on December 11, 1862. At the first, Morgan gained notoriety by leading a raid deep behind Buell's lines in Kentucky in July 1862.[50]

A native of Tennessee, Nathan Bedford Forrest, "Wizard of the Saddle," proved to be one of the most talented Confederate cavalry officers in the war. Forrest made a living in the Mississippi Delta before the war and when the war began he enlisted and raised a regiment at his own expense. He gained national attention when he refused to surrender his cavalry at Fort Donelson and led his men through Union lines rather than surrender. He had participated in the Battle of Shiloh and had caused havoc to the Union army in Tennessee and Mississippi since then.[51]

Joseph Wheeler, a native of Georgia and graduate of the United States Military Academy in 1859, was the third Confederate cavalry commander in Middle Tennessee. In September 1861 he was commissioned colonel of the 19th Alabama Infantry and led the regiment during the Battle of Shiloh. In July 1862, he was given command of a cavalry brigade in Bragg's Army of Mississippi. Wheeler commanded a cavalry brigade during the Battle of Perryville and had been rewarded with a promotion to the rank of brigadier general at the end of October. He had been constantly harassing the Union army in Tennessee since his return to that state. While Stanley's cavalry would face all three of these commanders, perhaps Joseph Wheeler was his most immediate threat.[52]

On November 20, Bragg renamed his Army of Mississippi the Army of Tennessee and appointed 25-year-old Joseph Wheeler as his chief of cavalry in October 1862. Certainly this decision did not improve relations between Bragg and Forrest or Morgan; but Bragg did allow Forrest and Morgan to maintain independent commands while Wheeler was attached to Bragg's army. Wheeler was loyal to Bragg and the two worked well together. For a time, Morgan, Forrest and Wheeler effectively worked to impede Rosecrans' army in Middle Tennessee.

The Union Reserve Brigade

By December, Stanley and Rosecrans had successfully added three new regiments of cavalry—the 15th Pennsylvania Cavalry, 1st Middle Tennessee (5th Tennessee) Cavalry, and 2nd East (2nd) Tennessee Cavalry. A battalion of the 3rd Indiana was also loosely assigned to this brigade. At the beginning of the war, Tennessee regiments carried designations from the part of the state where they were organized, e.g., East Tennessee, Middle Tennessee, West Tennessee. Eventually these geographic designations were dropped, but

Another of Stanley's adversaries in central Tennessee: Joseph Wheeler (Wilson's Creek National Battlefield; WICR 31412).

at this point in the war they were still used. The 2nd East Tennessee Cavalry would be renamed the 2nd Tennessee Cavalry and the 1st Middle Tennessee Cavalry would be renamed the 5th Tennessee Cavalry.

While the 15th Pennsylvania Cavalry would not arrive until Christmas, the three new regiments of cavalry, although very inexperienced, did add important numbers of men to fill the ranks of the Union cavalry. Stanley and Rosecrans concluded they should add additional cavalry regiments. By December 25, the Army of the Cumberland would have ten regiments of cavalry plus the 4th U.S. Cavalry, which was attached to army headquarters, and Stanley formed three brigades. The First Brigade was initially commanded by Edward McCook and by mid–December the highly regarded Robert Minty had assumed command of the brigade in McCook's absence. The capable Lewis Zahm commanded the Second Brigade and David Stanley assumed direct command of the greenest of the troops in the Reserve Brigade.

RESERVE CAVALRY
3rd Indiana (four companies), Major Robert Klein
15th Pennsylvania, Major Adolph G. Rosengarten, Major Frank B. Ward
1st Middle (5th) Tennessee, Colonel William B. Stokes
2nd East (2nd) Tennessee, Colonel Daniel M. Ray

The 3rd Indiana Cavalry's unique organization resulted in four companies (G–K), the West Battalion being assigned to the Army of the Cumberland while six companies served in the Army of the Potomac. The companies assigned to the Army of the Cumberland were organized after the first six companies had been sent to fight in the East. These four companies performed escort, courier and provost duties until they were formed into an independent cavalry battalion commanded by Major Robert Klein, who had served as captain of Company K. The battalion also saw action during the Perryville Campaign while protecting the army's supply train and served during the advance of Buell's army. A twenty-six-year-old German-born ex–Prussian soldier, Klein was a resident of Switzerland County, Indiana, before the war.[53]

The 2nd Tennessee Cavalry was organized in eastern Tennessee and began service in September 1862. The regiment had little combat experience by November 1862. It participated in the Union retreat from Cumberland Gap to Greensburg, Kentucky, and then served about a month in the Kanawha Valley before being moved to Nashville. Colonel Daniel M. Ray commanded the regiment. The 29-year-old Ray was a North Carolina native and the son of a farmer. He resided in Tennessee and taught school for three years prior to the war. Ray served in the 3rd Tennessee Infantry before the 2nd Tennessee Cavalry was organized.[54]

The 5th Tennessee Cavalry had been mustered into service as the 1st Middle Tennessee Cavalry on July 15, 1862, under the command of Colonel William B. Stokes. The 48-year-old Stokes was a farmer and had served in the house and senate in the Tennessee General Assembly prior to the war. Previously, Stokes had served for a short time as a major in the Tennessee volunteer infantry. The 5th Tennessee Cavalry had been assigned to the Union garrison at Nashville until Stanley added the regiment to the Reserve Brigade. The regiment generally performed reconnaissance but had little combat experience except in skirmishes at Nashville and Kinderhook.[55]

The highly anticipated 15th Pennsylvania Cavalry was requested for service in the Army of the Cumberland and permission had been granted for the regiment to be transported to Nashville. This cavalry regiment was originally organized as an independent cavalry company (or troop) attached for army headquarters duty by Brigadier General Robert Anderson. The troop was recruited in the fall of 1861 and organized at Carlisle Barracks, Pennsylvania, under command of Captain William J. Palmer. The troop moved to Louisville in December 1861 and moved with Buell's army during the Battle of Shiloh. The troop performed its assigned duty, primarily as dispatch carriers and scouts, with high recommendations from the commanding general.[56]

In July 1862 permission was given to raise three more companies, but the order was changed to raise an entire regiment. The name was changed from the Anderson Troop to the Anderson Cavalry and subsequently changed to the 15th Pennsylvania Cavalry, with 1,200 troopers, when the regiment was assigned duty with the Army of the Cumberland. Twenty-seven-year-old William J. Palmer, a native of Delaware, was the commanding officer of the regiment. He served as secretary and treasurer of the Westmoreland Coal Company before he took the post as secretary to John Edgar Thompson, president of the Pennsylvania Coal Company. Unfortunately, he was captured the day after the Battle of Antietam and remained a prisoner of war until January 1863. The newly expanded regiment was assigned combat duty instead of courier duty and it had just lost its commander. This combination of factors would make the 15th Pennsylvania's inclusion into the cavalry corps a difficult one.[57]

Cavalry Action, December 1862

The capture of Colonel Absalom B. Moore's brigade at Hartsville on December 7 was an embarrassment to all involved. This involved 1,855 Union troops, including much of the 2nd Indiana Cavalry (357 troopers) and 44 cavalrymen of the 11th Kentucky Cavalry. Afterward, Stanley decided to take the offensive whenever possible and practical as he tried to prevent the Confederate cavalry from doing more damage. He needed to instill a fighting spirit in his command.[58]

On December 11, Stanley took the offensive as he rode with Colonel Edward McCook's First Cavalry Brigade (3rd Kentucky, 4th Michigan, and 7th Pennsylvania), along with the 5th Tennessee Cavalry, with the objective of opening the roads from Franklin toward Murfreesboro. After traveling a few miles south of Brentwood, the Union troopers clashed with Confederate pickets and then encountered a full regiment of Colonel Baxter Smith's 4th Tennessee Cavalry (CSA) of Brigadier General John Wharton's brigade. Stanley drove Smith's cavalry about two miles and decided to continue on his way toward Murfreesboro but soon found Smith's regiment dismounted and prepared to make a stand. As Stanley advanced upon the 4th Tennessee, they again retreated. Stanley bivouacked for the night, and pickets exchanged gunfire through the night.[59]

The next morning McCook's brigade rode for Franklin and encountered enemy pickets about one and a half miles east of the town. The Federal cavalry drove them toward the town and found a concentration of Wharton's cavalry along the bank of the Harpeth River. After the running fight on the previous day, Wharton placed 400 troopers at Franklin to meet the Union threat. The Confederate cavalry was promised infantry reinforcements but these did not reach Wharton's position in time for the fight. McCook ordered the 4th Michigan and the 7th Pennsylvania to dismount and move forward. A stiff fight resulted but the Confederates gave way under the pressure of McCook's brigade. Wharton lamented the fact Smith's force at Franklin was outnumbered 5 to 1, and he was forced to withdraw until Brigadier General Patrick Cleburne's infantry could be moved forward to defend the town. Stanley claimed four enemies killed, nine more wounded, and eleven prisoners; one Union trooper was mortally wounded and four horses were killed. Wharton recorded he had three men killed and six wounded. Stanley initially planned to burn the grain mill the enemy defended but decided it could result in a fire in the town. Instead, his troopers destroyed the mill equipment and confiscated four wagons of flour and ten horses. He also destroyed a wagon full of brandy and whiskey intended for the Confederate army. Stanley gave the credit for most of the fighting to the 7th Pennsylvania Cavalry.[60]

While this engagement was no match for Morgan's success over Absalom Moore's brigade, it was a first step in gaining the offensive. "It was a handsome little affair (the first time the troopers had ever used their new revolving rifles)," noted historian Larry Daniel. Significant was the use of new technologically superior weapons, new troops (5th Tennessee Cavalry) and an experienced, professional commander. These three factors would continue to be important as the Union cavalry struggled to gain equality on the field with the Confederate cavalry.[61]

For the next few weeks Stanley continued training his cavalry and ensuring it was supplied with horses and arms. His cavalry scouted, guarded supply trains, screened for the infantry and struck where it could find an advantage against the Confederates. Stanley also waited patiently for the arrival of the 15th Pennsylvania Cavalry, which had been due weeks earlier.

Four important events occurred in mid to late December: Nathan Forrest withdrew his cavalry from Middle Tennessee to harass Ulysses Grant's communications in western Tennessee; John Hunt Morgan moved into Kentucky to repeat his successful summer expedition; Earl Van Dorn attacked and destroyed Grant's supply base in Holly Springs, Mississippi; and pressure from Washington convinced Rosecrans it was time move against Bragg at Murfreesboro.

Morgan's movements were detected by the Army of the Cumberland on December 19, 1862. He was observed with 4,000 troopers near Lebanon, Tennessee. David Stanley was ordered by Colonel Julius P. Garesche, Rosecrans' chief of staff, to distribute his cavalry along the north side of the Cumberland River and to probe Morgan near Lebanon to discern his strength and intentions. Garesche, an 1841 West Point graduate, was well liked and efficient and had twenty-one years' experience in the regular army. The close of 1862 was going to be busy for Stanley and his cavalry, but the real challenge lay in store for the Union forces in Kentucky as Morgan began his "Christmas Raid." While the Army of the Cumberland occupied Middle Tennessee the Confederates saw an opportunity to create havoc to communications, supplies and morale by raiding into Kentucky using their cavalry, which could strike fast and disappear before Union troops could react. The Confederates intended to destroy communication and supply lines and to isolate or draw Union forces from Tennessee to defend Kentucky

By Christmas 1862, Morgan and his 3,900 troopers reached Glasgow, Kentucky, and began their grim task of disrupting Union transportation and communications. General George Thomas ordered Colonel John Harlan to load his infantry brigade onto the rail cars of the L&N Railroad at Gallatin, Tennessee, and travel north to assist in preventing Morgan's cavalry from continuing their activities and particularly preventing them from reaching Louisville.[62]

The Union army, still short of cavalry, relied on infantry to try to capture Morgan. Despite the failure of the infantry to "bag" Morgan's raiders, Union units soon converged on him. The Union objective now was to prevent Morgan's return to Tennessee. Morgan had troubles of his own; the weather was turning cold and unfavorable. On the evening of December 30, he stayed at Bardstown and the next day moved east to Springfield, Kentucky. As the Union army converged on him, Morgan was able to elude capture and move back to the safety of Tennessee after a very successful raid. While Morgan was in Kentucky, Nathan Bedford Forrest's cavalry had left Middle Tennessee over a week earlier to harass Ulysses Grant's supply line from western Tennessee to northern Mississippi.

Four cavalry brigades remained in Middle Tennessee: Brigadier General Joseph Wheeler, Brigadier General John Wharton, Brigadier General John Pegram and Brigadier General Abraham Buford, all under the command of Wheeler. While Morgan moved throughout Kentucky and Forrest in western Tennessee, Wheeler's Confederate cavalry continued their usual tactics of frustrating the Union troops. Despite the reduction in numbers of Confederate cavalry, Wheeler's troopers were still formidable.

The 15th Pennsylvania Cavalry

On December 24, 1862, the 15th Pennsylvania Cavalry arrived in Nashville for service in the Army of the Cumberland, specifically requested by William Rosecrans. But soon there was great dissatisfaction within the regiment, and the troopers expressed their dissatisfaction by refusing to perform their duty. This highly anticipated regiment arrived in Nashville under a veil of controversy and the events over the next week resulted in one of the largest mutinies in the Union army during the Civil War.

Although there are several accounts of the mutiny, the official version was recorded by Assistant Adjutant General Major N.H. Davis, who investigated the mutiny. The Anderson Troop was organized in the fall of 1861, commanded by Captain William J. Palmer, to serve as an escort for Brigadier General Robert Anderson. When General Don Carlos Buell assumed command of the Army of the Ohio, he retained the Anderson Troop. This cavalry troop was made up of intelligent men of high character, and the company had proven itself highly efficient at its duties. When permission was granted to raise three additional companies, the response from the enlistment process resulted in greater than 1,000 men volunteering for service. All of the men wishing to enlist and meeting the standards set by Captain Palmer were allowed to do so, although there was some question of whether Palmer had the authority to organize a full cavalry regiment.[63]

Based on the terms of enlistment, the officers were appointed rather than elected by men of the regiment. Most of the officers were drawn from the old Anderson Troop and the full complement of officers was not yet appointed, as Lee's army moved northward culminating in the Battle of Antietam. On the day after the battle, Captain Palmer was captured by the Confederates and made a prisoner of war. The regiment returned to Carlisle, Pennsylvania, to complete its organization and training while negotiations were made to return Palmer to the regiment. In the meantime, Rosecrans requested this new regiment of cavalry, the 15th Pennsylvania Cavalry, and permission was granted to send it to the Army of the Cumberland. The regiment arrived in Louisville on November 9, 1862, and awaited transportation to

Nashville. It was while the regiment remained in Louisville that the dissatisfaction began. While the Pennsylvanians languished, awaiting transportation south, the regiment drilled and trained, but, Major Davis noted, "The preparations were retarded, discipline lax, and camp or garrison duties more or less neglected from insufficiency of company officers."[64]

With William Palmer in a Confederate prison, the selection of officers was imperative. First Lieutenant William Spencer was commissioned lieutenant colonel on October 1, 1862. Additionally, two very capable majors were appointed—Adolph G. Rosengarten and Frank B. Ward. Additional officers were by appointment but only eleven other officers were commissioned for the twelve-company regiment.

When the regiment arrived in Nashville, there were seven regimental officers and twelve officers for the companies and only two-thirds of the noncommissioned officers were appointed. The regiment had a list of grievances when it arrived in Nashville and the next day, during its first assignment of guarding a supply train, the Confederates attacked. The attack was successfully repulsed but one trooper of the 15th Pennsylvania was killed. Major Davis reported the evening after the first duty in Nashville that the men of the regiment had concluded their officers were "inexperienced and incompetent." However, Davis determined the officers of the 15th Pennsylvania compared favorably to officers of others volunteer regiments. As a result, the men decided they would not do further duty and demanded to be disbanded or discharged. The decision to refuse to perform the assigned duty was made during meetings of members of the regiment without consulting superior officers.[65]

Quartermaster George Fobes of the 15th Pennsylvania wrote that the troubles that arose within the regiment resulted from Palmer's tight control of it. Palmer wanted to "organize, equip, and discipline a regiment" alone. Certainly when Palmer was captured the regiment was not organized and was "left almost alone." Fobes noted jealousy resulted between the new enlistees and members of the old Anderson Troop. The latter felt, based on their experience, they would receive all the commissions over the new enlistees. Fobes wrote, "Witnessing the rivalry, suffering from the consequent delays and neglect, was it unreasonable that the men began at length to feel that they had been enlisted not for the good of the service, but for the purpose of the furnishing commissions to a body of men who looked upon them as their aristocratic right." Great distrust developed between the old Anderson Troop and the new 15th Pennsylvania Cavalry.[66]

Fobes explained that the dissatisfaction continued in Louisville, as Company A of the old Anderson Troop was given privileges not offered to the new enlistees. The lieutenant colonel of the new regiment was also constantly at odds with the two majors, who in Fobes' opinion diligently tried to get the regiment prepared for their new assignment. Fobes noted that much of the problem resulted from the poor command abilities of Lieutenant Colonel Spencer. When on one occasion the 15th Pennsylvania was ordered to ride on an expedition, Fobes, serving as quartermaster, tried for a day to obtain ammunition for the regiment. Spencer signed the requisition only after Fobes threatened to report the matter to General Stanley. But others of the regiment were kinder to Spencer, who was very ill during this time and had to be transported by ambulance.[67]

The day after the regiment's first duty, the troopers stacked their arms and refused to do further duty. The dissatisfaction of the regiment included the understanding that the new enlistees were to form a single battalion for the purpose of being a bodyguard for Buell. The troopers also complained they had not been properly mustered, the regiment did not have sufficient officers, they were not properly armed, they were assigned duty unsuitable for them, and they had, in fact, been deceived into enlisting in the regular Union cavalry service. Also, the members of the regiment stated their dissatisfaction was discussed in Louisville, but they were promised their issues would be addressed once they reached the Army of the Cumberland.[68]

Davis determined there was no deception to entice men to enlist and the men were told "their duties would be the same as those of the old troop, viz., scouting, secret expeditions, escorts, guards, service of a daring and dashing character, and that they would probably be kept at or about the headquarters of the commanding general, and under his orders." He also found authority was granted to raise the regiment and that all the men were properly mustered into service with the exception of about twenty of them. In addition, the men of the regiment were found to have adequate officers and proper arms, equipment and mounts. However, the real rankle came when it was determined the regiment would "discharge duties of the regular cavalry."[69]

The dissatisfaction within the regiment escalated, according to Davis, with the movement from Louisville to Nashville when "squads of the men visited disloyal families, and reported to them their grievances, and exhibited a disposition to refuse or avoid doing a soldier's duty." When instructed by the officers to stop these practices certain individuals replied "they dared any general to interfere with their rights; that they had money and influence, which would secure them their rights, discharge."[70]

These events within the 15th Pennsylvania Cavalry all occurred on the eve of the beginning of the Stones River Campaign, and when David Stanley ordered the men to duty only 200–300 agreed to service, while another 600 remained in Nashville under arrest. Only about a half of a battalion of this regiment would participate in the upcoming battle.

David Stanley faced many challenges within the Union cavalry on the eve of the Battle of Stones River.

2. The Battle of Stones River

Let's charge them boys! Let's charge them!
—Major General David S. Stanley

Stanley and Rosecrans immediately brought a sense of professionalism and discipline to the Army of the Cumberland. Stanley wanted control of the cavalry in his hands and not in those of the infantry commanders and Rosecrans supported this decision. Next, Stanley wanted his men properly trained, which would take months. Surprisingly, perhaps the greatest need for the Union cavalry in Nashville was being properly supplied with horses and weapons. Before Stanley's arrival Rosecrans wrote to the War Department asking for improved arms. On November 18, Edwin Stanton replied that 1,600 revolving rifles were being sent to Rosecrans for use by the cavalry, and by early December the arms were slowly being received by it. Upon his arrival, Stanley's cavalry reported only 3,038 troopers present for duty but slightly less than 2,000 carbines and 2,500 pistols.[1]

Stanton made good his promise of providing improved arms, such as the five-shot Colt revolving rifle. The Colts were shipped from the Army of the Potomac, which had recently obtained newer arms. Not everyone was pleased, however. Sergeant Otis G. Gerould, 7th Pennsylvania Cavalry, noted in his diary on December 8 that the 4th Michigan had just received the rifles: "Good gun, but too long and heavy for cav[alry]." On the next day, he wrote pleasantly, "Receiving and issuing more carbines."[2]

Secretary of war Edwin Stanton began supplying Rosecrans with the equipment he had requested and replied, "[B]ut something is expected of you." Rosecrans, however, was not ready to march. Piqued, he replied that he was doing all that was necessary to begin his advance but he faced a dangerous adversary and he had the task of protecting an insecure communications and supply line. He lamented,

> Many of our soldiers are to this day barefoot, without blankets, without tents, without good arms, and cavalry without horses. Our true objective now is the enemy's force.... If the Government which ordered me here confides in my judgment, it may rely on my continuing to do what I have been trying to—that is, my whole duty. If my superiors have lost confidence in me, they had better at once put some one in my place and let the future test the propriety of the change.... To threats of removal or the like I must be permitted to say that I am insensible."[3]

Slightly over a month into his new command, General David Stanley was soon to lead his cavalry in the Battle of Stones River. His organization on December 26 included two active brigades and a reserve brigade. The highly regarded Colonel Robert Minty commanded the First Brigade and the capable Colonel Lewis Zahm commanded the Second Brigade.

Union cavalry lieutenant, mounted with saber (Library of Congress).

Stanley had direct command of the Reserve Brigade, which included the green and untested regiments. John Kennett still had nominal command of the entire cavalry division, but his role diminished when Stanley assumed command.

THE STONES RIVER CAMPAIGN: CAVALRY[4]
Brigadier General David S. Stanley

CAVALRY DIVISION
Colonel John Kennett

First Brigade
Colonel Robert H.G. Minty
2nd Indiana, Company M, Captain J.A.S. Mitchell
3rd Kentucky, Colonel Eli H. Murray
4th Michigan, Lieutenant Colonel William H. Dickinson
7th Pennsylvania, Major John E. Wynkoop

Second Brigade
Colonel Lewis Zahm
1st Ohio, Colonel Minor Millikin/Major James Laughlin
3rd Ohio, Lieutenant Colonel Douglas A. Murray
4th Ohio, Major John L. Pugh

Artillery
1st Ohio, Battery D (section), Lieutenant Nathaniel M. Newell

Reserve Cavalry
3rd Indiana, Battalion, Major Robert Klein
15th Pennsylvania, Major Adolph G. Rosengarten/Major Frank B. Ward
1st Middle (5th) Tennessee, Colonel William B. Stokes
2nd Tennessee, Colonel Daniel M. Ray

Unattached
4th U.S. Cavalry, Captain Elmer Otis

It would soon become clear that thirty days were just not enough time to overcome the neglect of the cavalry that continued from the Army of the Ohio; however, Stanley had good material to work with to transform into an effective cavalry division. If anyone could lead this cavalry force successfully, it was Stanley. The importance of having the right person in command of even a marginal force was immeasurable. Stanley clearly identified concerns about his cavalry—the mutinous 15th Pennsylvania Cavalry, green regiments and cavalry commanders who were yet to be tested.

In other areas of the war, the Union campaigns in Virginia and Mississippi were bogged down. The Battle of Fredericksburg had just concluded in a decisive Confederate victory; Holly Springs had just fallen to Earl Van Dorn; and Sherman was struggling in Mississippi. The Union army needed good news. Halleck pushed Rosecrans to begin a campaign against Bragg, and Rosecrans finally decided it was time to move. Much of the Confederate cavalry which had been so troublesome to the Union forces in middle Tennessee were gone—Morgan raiding Kentucky and Forrest in western Tennessee. The Union command also believed the Confederates would be complacent, having settled into winter quarters. On December 26, Rosecrans' army of 43,000 seized the opportunity to attack Bragg's army of 37,000.

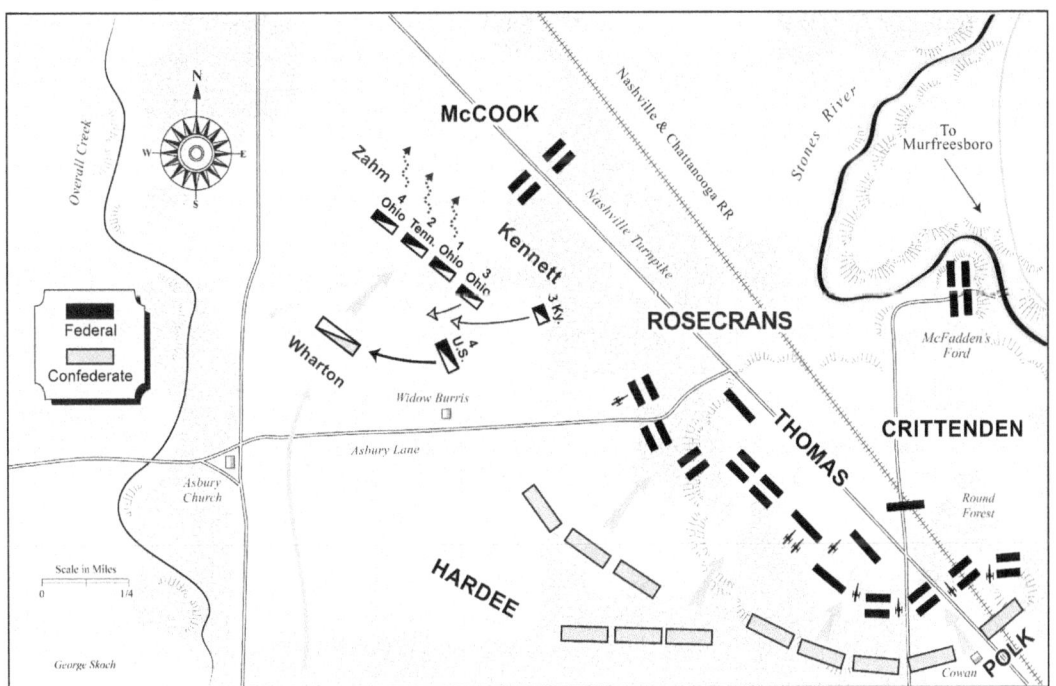

Cavalry Actions at the Battle of Stones River (December 31, Morning)

The Advance of Murfreesboro

Thirty miles south of Nashville lay Bragg's Army of Tennessee, which had the unenviable task of guarding a fifty-mile front. But it was late December, and Bragg felt confident Rosecrans would not venture out of the friendly confines of his strong defenses in Nashville to mount a winter advance on Murfreesboro. Rosecrans was to prove him wrong.

Rosecrans' plan called for Alexander McCook, with three divisions, to move toward Triune along the Nolensville Pike. General Thomas's divisions of Negley and Rousseau were to advance along McCook's right by the Franklin and Wilson pikes to Nolensville. Crittenden's divisions commanded by Wood, Palmer and Van Cleve were to advance along the Murfreesboro Pike to La Vergne. McCook planned to attack Hardee at Triune with the support of Thomas. If there was enemy resistance from the east, Crittenden was to join in the attack.

Stanley organized his cavalry to meet the requirements of the advancing infantry. He received a message from Rosecrans' chief of staff and started moving 1,300 of his men on December 24 and allowed the remainder to complete foraging their horses. On December 26, Stanley divided the cavalry into three columns, putting Minty's First Brigade on the Union left along the Murfreesboro Pike to screen Crittenden's corps. Zahm's Second Brigade was ordered to move on the right flank, riding to Franklin to remove any threat of the enemy's cavalry swinging to the rear of McCook's corps. Stanley's Reserve Brigade of cavalry, under his personal command, planned to ride in advance of McCook's corps along the Nolensville Pike. Colonel John Kennett, commanding the cavalry division, advanced with Minty's brigade on the left flank.[5]

Rosecrans' plan for his cavalry established a pattern he would use during the next two campaigns. Rosecrans and Stanley decided the left column of the Union cavalry, Minty's brigade, would coordinate its actions very closely with the infantry and would push the enemy resistance out of the way of the advance. Minty's primary role was to screen the Union advance while protecting the flanks as he served as the "eyes and ears" of the army. The right flank of the Union cavalry, Zahm's brigade, would provide greater mobility and would serve in a more, although limited, offensive role. Stanley felt he needed direct supervision over his newer regiments located in the center, at the same time offering his support and leadership should either of his cavalry wings run into trouble.

December 26

As the Union advance began, the soldiers of both armies were reminded it was winter as a cold rain began to fall. In addition, the ever-present Confederate cavalry faced the Union horsemen. Joseph Wheeler's brigade occupied the Nashville Turnpike stretching to the east and joining with Brigadier General John Pegram's brigade. Pegram, a West Point graduate and ex-regular army officer, had command of a four-regiment brigade in the upcoming battle—the 1st Georgia, 1st Louisiana, and 1st and 2nd Tennessee cavalries. Pegram, a Virginian, had commanded infantry and served as an engineer prior to appointment as cavalry brigade commander. He had been captured in Virginia and exchanged. Although his performance was inconsistent, he was still a highly regarded officer for the Confederacy, commanding cavalry for the first time in the Civil War. To the west of Wheeler lay John Wharton's brigade, which extended to Franklin. John A. Wharton was Wheeler's most able brigade commander. The 34-year-old Wharton, a native Tennessean, was an attorney residing in Texas prior to the war. He was severely wounded during the Battle of Shiloh and was again wounded in the summer of 1862. Wharton commanded a brigade made up of men drawn from several states. Abraham "Abe" Buford's brigade was posted eighteen miles southwest of Murfreesboro at Rover. Buford, a giant of a man at 320 pounds, was a native of Kentucky and a graduate of West Point, class of 1841. The 42-year-old Buford served in the regular army service until 1854 when he returned to Kentucky. He opposed secession but finally offered his services to the Confederacy and was appointed brigadier general in November 1862. The Confederate cavalry had three primary objectives: to screen the Confederate positions, resist the

Top left: Colonel John Wharton was one of Wheeler's most effective officers (Alabama Department of Archives and History, Montgomery). *Bottom:* Abraham Buford, a native Kentuckian and West Point graduate, commanded one of Wheeler's brigades (Alabama Department of Archives and History, Montgomery). *Top right:* John Pegram, a highly regarded officer for the Confederacy, commanded a brigade of Wheeler's cavalry (Library of Congress).

advance of Rosecrans' army, and when possible, offensively strike the Union positions. The Southern cavalry had shown, and continued to show, the ability to attack the Union communications and supply lines, almost at will, much to the frustration of Stanley and Rosecrans.[6]

The plan on December 26 called for Stanley's Reserve Brigade to screen the advance of the center of the Army of the Cumberland. However, by the time Stanley arrived at McCook's headquarters the infantry had already marched and had possession of the roads leading southward, making it impossible for the cavalry to lead the advance. The pike was "full of wagons, troops, and artillery," noted John McLain, 4th Michigan Cavalry. As the Union infantry advanced, John Wharton's cavalry prepared to meet the advance at Nolensville with dismounted troopers and artillery. Once the infantry deployed in battle line, Wharton had accomplished his intent, slowing the Union advance, so he mounted and rode south to defend Knob Gap. The Union artillery and infantry followed, pushing him further southward toward Triune.[7]

Meanwhile, Colonel Lewis Zahm's 950 troopers rode eastward in search of General George Thomas along the Wilson Creek Pike. Upon determining Thomas's location was unreachable due to the congestion along the roads, Zahm proceeded to Franklin as ordered. He ran into John Wharton's Confederate pickets about a half-mile from Franklin. After heavy skirmishing along the Big Harpeth River Zahm engaged the enemy skirmishers and then flanked the Confederate cavalrymen. The Confederates—4th Tennessee and Davis's Tennessee Battalion—retreated followed by Zahm's troopers close behind, and the chase continued for two miles. Zahm's brigade surprised the Tennessee cavalry, which became disorganized and the Union troopers never gave them a chance to prepare a proper defense. As a result, the Confederate troopers scattered in several directions while trying to stop then slow the Union pursuit, but to no avail. Among the prisoners captured was a lieutenant of General Braxton Bragg's escort. During the day's ride, Zahm also discovered a large number of infantry nine miles from Franklin and another infantry concentration near Triune. He returned to the main Union line, but was still unable to find Thomas. Zahm made his report of General Lovell Rousseau and the two decided the Second Cavalry Brigade would best serve by scouting the front and right until further orders were received. Zahm wrote,

> I shall therefore send some 500 men toward Petersburg and Triune to reconnoiter; shall likewise send a smaller force over toward Franklin, to ascertain whether the enemy has come back again or not.... My command behaved nobly, both officers and men. The Third [Ohio] Cavalry had the advance, and did the principal part of the fighting; there was no flinch to them.[8]

On the left flank of the Union advance, Minty's First Brigade began its advance toward Murfreesboro moving along the Murfreesboro Pike. Minty ran into Confederate skirmishers as the march began on December 26 and the 3rd Kentucky Cavalry covered the left flank, the 7th Pennsylvania the right and the 4th Michigan moved along the road in the center. Minty recorded, "Ten miles from Nashville I met the enemy's pickets, who, as they fell back before us, were continually re-enforced, until, arriving at La Vergne, they disputed our progress with a force of 2,500 cavalry and mounted infantry, supported by four pieces of artillery, under the command of General Wheeler." As the skirmish intensified, Minty moved his cavalry to protect a knoll where Newell's section of 1st Ohio Artillery was unlimbered to return the barrage. He ordered two companies of the 4th Michigan to dismount behind a fence and provide cover for the artillerymen. General John Palmer's Second Division added its guns to the artillery duel for an hour and a half exchange. Lieutenant Nathaniel M. Newell's artillery fired sixty rounds after he wheeled his artillery to the right of the pike and opened fire. The Union infantry pushed ahead but darkness put an end to the fighting.[9]

Being convinced the Union advance was serious, Bragg decided to concentrate his army near Murfreesboro. Wheeler rode to headquarters after the day's skirmishing to attend a meeting to decide what action should be taken. Bragg asked Wheeler how long he could delay the Union advance and various answers were recorded—ranging from two to four days. Wheeler began over the next few days a "fight-withdraw-fight" method of slowing the Union advance while Bragg hastily brought in his army. As Wheeler developed his strategies, Stanley's Reserve Brigade moved into position and, freed from the congestion with the infantry, the cavalry would precede the infantry the next day.[10]

December 27

After the rain stopped on December 27, a dense fog blanketed the area around Murfreesboro. Because of the problems with visibility, Alexander McCook chose not to advance until the fog lifted about 1:00 p.m. Due to his proximity to Stanley, Lewis Zahm coordinated his column with Stanley's reserve cavalry brigade. After having discovered two large concentrations of Confederates on the previous day, Zahm set out to determine the identity and the concentration of the enemy he was facing. He sent the 1st Ohio Cavalry and most of the 4th Ohio Cavalry to reconnoiter the situation at Triune. These regiments scouted to within two miles of Triune when they encountered enemy pickets and the Confederate artillery began to shell them.

Wharton's cavalry, supported by Brigadier General S.A.M. Wood's infantry brigade, waited for the Union troops, hoping to surprise their advance. But Stanley, coordinating his advance with Alexander McCook, called upon the infantry of Richard Johnson's division to assist with the Confederate defenders. While Johnson's infantry advanced to face Wood's defenders, the weather again turned for the worse as it started to sleet. The poor conditions convinced Johnson to withhold his attack, but the 3rd Indiana and the 15th Pennsylvania cavalries, riding from the west, continued forward. Earlier in the day, Stanley had stopped to talk to Major Robert Klein, 3rd Indiana Cavalry, and remarked the 3rd Indiana "knew how to take these rebels." Certainly, the remark served as an inspiration for the upcoming fight. The 15th Pennsylvania Cavalry and the 3rd Indiana approached Triune and soon encountered a large force of Confederates in line of battle. Major Robert Klein recorded the following:

> Here we were ordered by General Stanley, with one company of the Fifteenth Pennsylvania Cavalry, to attack the enemy on the right side of the pike. They were posted behind a stone wall, heads only visible, one or more regiments strong. We advanced across the open fields, and were pouring in a steady fire at easy range, when two pieces of artillery on our left, about 500 yards, and two in front, opened on us, obliging us to retire to the cover of the woods from where we advanced. This movement was done promptly, but in good order.

Stanley complimented Major Adolph Rosengarten and Major Frank Ward of the 15th Pennsylvania Cavalry for their leadership during the fighting. Both majors performed admirably with the 15th Pennsylvania despite the regiment's other problems. Stanley said, "Tell the Anderson Cavalry I am extremely pleased with their behavior today."[11]

Meanwhile, the 3rd Ohio went back to Franklin only to find the rebels had returned in

Major Robert Klein (officer in center of photograph) commanded the 3rd Indiana Cavalry at the Battle of Stones River (Library of Congress).

force and were prepared to meet them. The Ohioans skirmished about two hours but could not drive the Confederates away. The next day Zahm moved his brigade, along with the infantry, to Triune.

On the left flank of the Army of the Cumberland, ninety troopers of the 4th Michigan Cavalry, commanded by Captain James Mix, preceded Crittenden's advance toward Stewart's Creek. Three miles north of Stewart's Creek, Mix encountered enemy cavalry and the chase began with Confederates giving way. Mix chased the enemy past the bridge over Stewart's Creek, securing an easy march over the creek for Crittenden. The 4th Michigan Cavalry battalion rode past the bridge chasing what began as the rear guard. Once the retreating rear guard caught up with and unnerved the main column of the 51st Alabama Cavalry, the entire 51st raced to the rear. Crittenden's infantry hastily seized the bridge before it could be burned and made an easy crossing.[12]

December 28 and 29

The next day was relatively uneventful for the Army of the Cumberland. The various cavalry regiments continued screening and pushing the Confederate resistance to the front;

but on the other side of the line Wheeler and Bragg successfully pulled the Confederate army together. As Rosecrans continued his advance, Bragg prepared a defensive line near Murfreesboro and waited.

On December 29, Rosecrans' three wings steadily marched toward Murfreesboro. Zahm's brigade moved from Triune east along the Franklin Road while Stanley's Reserve brigade, four miles north, moved parallel, eastward along the Bole Jack Road. Minty's brigade moved southward along the Nashville Turnpike. Coincidentally all three of Stanley's columns became engaged in skirmishing almost simultaneously.

Zahm's three cavalry regiments—1st Ohio on the left, 3rd Ohio in the center and 4th Ohio on the right—advanced about a mile apart. After marching for five miles, Zahm met enemy pickets and drove them to the rear. Zahm recorded,

> [W]e came upon the enemy's cavalry [Wharton's brigade], engaged them for three hours, some time the right wing, then the left, then the center, receiving several charges, which were repulsed, driving the enemy some 2 miles, when the brigade concentrated, repelling a heavy charge from the enemy, driving him back under his guns, which were only a short distance from us. We then retired some 2 miles and went into camp.

By the end of December 29, Zahm and McCook were within four miles of Murfreesboro.[13]

Meanwhile, Stanley's column moved along the Bole Jack Road, and another clash of cavalry occurred at Wilkinson's Crossroads. The Union cavalry pushed the defenders beyond Overall Creek and within a half-mile of the Confederate line manned by the 10th and 19th South Carolina infantry regiments. During the fighting, the 15th Pennsylvania Cavalry under the command of majors Rosengarten and Ward were determined to show the value of their cavalry. The Pennsylvania cavalry led the attack and pushed the enemy pickets six miles in a running fight. Finally, the Union troopers rode into an ambush and received a full volley from the South Carolina infantry. The two majors became casualties. Rosengarten was killed during the exchange and Ward was mortally wounded. Another five troopers were killed and six additional troopers were wounded. Stanley observed the 15th Pennsylvania had shown great courage in the charge but he remarked in discouragement, "With the loss of these two most gallant officers the spirit of the Anderson Troop, which gave such fine promise, seems to have died out, and I have not been able to get any duty out of them since." Meanwhile, along the left wing, Minty recorded skirmishing all day as his brigade pushed forward.[14]

On the evening of December 29, there was little surprise in store for Bragg. He clearly knew Rosecrans' intention. John Pegram's two regiment cavalry brigade pulled back to Murfreesboro and Abraham Buford's 3rd, 5th and 6th Kentucky cavalries, reinforced with artillery, established a defensive position at Rover should Rosecrans attempt a flanking movement.

December 30

December 30 was to prove to be a long day for the Union cavalry. They worked to protect the flanks of Rosecrans' army, and light skirmishing occurred throughout the day. Early in the morning of December 30, Zahm personally commanded the 1st Ohio, 3rd Ohio and 2nd Tennessee and moved forward, quickly encountering more enemy pickets. The 4th Ohio Cavalry was sent on reconnaissance southward and met another strong enemy force, Hardee's infantry. Soon, heavy concentrations of cavalry and artillery advanced to meet Zahm's probes, on which he made no further progress.

On the left flank of the army, parts of the 7th Pennsylvania and the 3rd Kentucky (U.S.) cavalries performed duty in the rear of Crittenden's Left Wing, pushing the stragglers to their regiments. While Rosecrans' attention had been focused on Bragg's concentrating army to his front, General Wheeler decided it might be opportune to utilize his superior number of cavalry to attack the Union rear. Bragg and Wheeler decided to distract Rosecrans by creating problems with his communications while a full infantry attack was planned for the morning of December 31 on the Union right flank. Wheeler's raid on the Union rear accomplished all Bragg and Wheeler had hoped. Wheeler attacked wagon trains at Jefferson, La Vergne, Rock Springs and Nolensville and claimed "500 wagons, 600 prisoners and many mules."[15]

In response to the Confederate raid, Minty accompanied the 4th Michigan Cavalry and a battalion of the 7th Pennsylvania Cavalry rearward along the Nashville Pike to prevent further ravages by Wheeler's cavalry, which had just caused havoc on a Union supply train. When Minty arrived he found about one hundred Confederate raiders in what he described as Union uniforms. He sent this group scampering away, but Wheeler's main force had long since moved westward in his raid around the rear of Rosecrans' army.[16]

As McCook's corps advanced on Murfreesboro, David Stanley brought information which could have changed the battle. At 2:00 p.m. on December 30 Stanley sent a local citizen who had knowledge of the Confederate concentration of forces to McCook, who subsequently sent the citizen to Rosecrans. The civilian stated,

> I was up to the enemy's line of battle twice yesterday and once this morning, to get some stock, taken from me. The enemy's troops are posted in the following manner: The right of Cheatham's division rests on the Wilkinson pike; Withers is on Cheatham's left, with his left resting on the Franklin road; Hardee's corps is entirely beyond that road, and his left extending toward the Salem pike.

McCook recorded,

> This made me anxious for my right. All my division commanders were immediately informed of this fact, and two brigades of the reserve division, commanded, respectively, by Generals Willich and Kirk, two of the best and most experienced brigadiers in the army, were ordered to the right of my line, to protect the right flank and guard against surprise there.

At 6:00 p.m. Rosecrans sent an order to McCook to work in conjunction with Stanley to try to deceive the enemy. McCook and Stanley made very large campfires, some outside the camp, to make the enemy think there were more soldiers on the Union right.[17] Ever diligent, Stanley wanted to determine the veracity of the citizen's description of the Confederate position. "[I] rode, with only an escort, beyond our extreme right and so I reported to McCook and Rosecrans. One division of two brigades, sent this evening to support Johnson's right would have averted disaster. McCook seemed utterly indifferent," noted Stanley.[18]

While the Union army settled in for the night, the report that General Joseph Wheeler had caused havoc in the Union supply train by moving along the rear of the Union army resulted in action on the part of Rosecrans. Even though Robert Minty had been dispatched earlier in the day to protect the Union rear, Rosecrans wanted more action from his cavalry to prevent further attacks.[19] When Stanley returned to his bed after meeting with McCook, an orderly roused him with a message from Colonel Garesche, Rosecrans' chief of staff, about the attack of Confederate cavalry on the supply trains in the Union rear. Rosecrans ordered Stanley to see to the protection of the trains.

At 11:00 p.m. on December 30, Stanley left for La Vergne with the 5th Tennessee and the 15th Pennsylvania cavalries and met Minty with the 4th Michigan and one battalion of the 7th Pennsylvania Cavalry near La Vergne early the next morning. Stanley rode toward the supply train, arriving at Stewart's Creek at 5:00 a.m. He found three infantry regiments, safe and sound. Father O'Higgins, chaplain of the 10th Ohio Infantry, was also present and they were in the company of a pot of tea and some Irish whiskey. Stanley visited with the colonel and the chaplain until his scouts returned reporting the trains were safe. No Confederate cavalry was found lurking in the countryside, but at 9:30 a.m. Stanley received a note from Colonel Garesche: "The enemy have attacked McCook's corps in great force, and the Corps is falling back in a good deal of disorder. Fasten to the right and do your best to restore order."[20] The Battle of Stones River had begun.

The Union Cavalry at the Battle of Stones River, December 31

Colonel Lewis Zahm had his brigade up and moving early on December 31 and had the misfortune of being on the right flank of the Army of the Cumberland. He bivouacked his brigade about a mile and a half from the concentration of Hardee's infantry along the right of McCook's wing. By 6:00 a.m. he had sent two squadrons on reconnaissance and soon heard heavy firing and cannonading to his left and front. "The roar of the cannon and the rattle of the musket were terrific," noted Sergeant Thomas Crofts, 3rd Ohio Cavalry. Zahm observed what was left of General Richard Johnson's 2nd Division of McCook's wing in full retreat being chased by Lieutenant General William Hardee's Confederate infantry. Zahm saw the Confederate infantry in close pursuit of McCook's soldiers and observed Wharton's cavalry moving to his right. Bragg's infantry had crushed the Union right, which was flowing to the rear.[21]

Wharton's Confederate cavalry, divided into three commands, moved in concert with the Confederate infantry as the Union right was propelled rearward. Meanwhile, Joseph Wheeler's cavalry moved back toward Murfreesboro, after riding in a complete circle around Rosecrans rear, when he heard the noise of the battle. In addition, Abraham Buford's cavalry brigade was also ordered forward to exploit the Southern successes. John Pegram's brigade remained on the Confederate right flank during the battle, providing reconnaissance and protection along the flank.

The genius of Wheeler's foray in the Union rear now yielded its fruit. The Confederate cavalry concentrated along the collapsing Union right flank, contending with only Lewis Zahm's four regiments of Union cavalry. Although a considerable amount of Union cavalry was still available to Kennett for use during the battle, only Zahm's regiments operated as a brigade. Certainly the order sending Stanley with a large portion of cavalry to the rear was lamented by those along the Union right flank. Nevertheless, Lewis Zahm had several options: attempt to rally the retreating troops, engage the enemy, or keep the Confederate cavalry from gaining the Union rear. Zahm recorded his situation: "[T]he enemy pressing hard on me; kept him at bay with my skirmishers. I retired in this wise for a mile, when I formed a line of battle with the First and Third [Ohio Cavalry], when the enemy charged on them with their cavalry, but were repulsed by my men. About this time the enemy began to throw shells into my lines pretty lively." The first barrage of Captain Benjamin F. White's artillery mortally wounded Major David A.B. Moore, 1st Ohio, setting the stage for a difficult day for Zahm's cavalry. Facing superior numbers and being shelled, Zahm fell back and formed a new screen only to be charged by the Confederate cavalry. Zahm repulsed the Southern attack and again the Confederate artillery found his position. The Union cavalry again retreated and found support among some of Brigadier General Augustus Willich's First Brigade of Johnson's division. The Confederate cavalry again charged Zahm's troopers only to be repulsed, but Zahm was giving way throughout the morning, being attacked by Wharton's cavalry and artillery. In addition, the Confederate infantry's success left Zahm in a position of holding the enemy's cavalry but being nearly cut off by the advance of the Southern infantry. Zahm noted that no matter what successes he made in repulsing the cavalry charges there were more than enough replacements on their heels.[22]

Zahm faced Confederate infantry and cavalry pressing hard on the Union right flank and he set up a screen with the 1st Ohio and the 3rd Ohio, supported by the 4th Ohio, covering the extended right flank of the army while sparring with Brigadier General John Wharton's cavalry brigade consisting of a mixture of Tennessee, Alabama, Georgia, Texas and Confederate regular army troopers. White's Battery of Tennessee artillery followed the advance and shelled the Union cavalry at every opportunity. While Zahm was withdrawing with too many things to handle, Stanley was unaware of the situation. He was still in the rear of the army with orders to protect the army's supply train. Upon being informed of the Confederate attack, Stanley rode, as ordered, back to the main Union line, but he would not arrive until the morning's combat was over. He was delayed as he encountered McCook's soldiers running from the battlefield. As he rode in the direction of Murfreesboro he had to leave some of his troopers to protect the supply trains, which were sent to the rear. He also detached some of his cavalry to collect stragglers and send them forward.[23]

A Union cavalry counterattack successfully stymied Colonel John Cox's 1st Confederate Cavalry and part of the 8th Texas Cavalry, which had captured some guns of the 1st Ohio Light Artillery and men of Colonel William Gibson's First Brigade. Gibson had assumed command of the brigade because August Willich had been captured during the early morning attack. Zahm's charge "threw the greyclads in momentary confusion. Taking advantage of the situation [Brigadier General Richard] Johnson and most of his men made good their escape," noted historian Edwin Bearss.[24]

Zahm's cavalry regiments were performing remarkably well and they slowly gave way while being heavily pressed, repulsing three charges from Wharton. By 9:00 a.m. they were pushed back to Overall Creek and by 11:00 a.m. they were pushed further north, losing contact with the creek. As Zahm withdrew his cavalry from the collapsing right flank, an officer approached with a message. Zahm noted, "When we arrived on the open ground, General McCook's aide told me the whole of General McCook's ammunition train was close by, on a dirt road running by that point, and that I must try to save it." The withdrawal was over for Zahm and his cavalry, and he had found the place to stand and fight.[25]

Zahm took up position near McCook's supply train and had withdrawn as far as he could go. He formed his line, the 3rd Ohio, 1st Ohio, 2nd Tennessee, and 4th Ohio (east to left), and waited for Wharton's move. Zahm noted the following:

> The enemy made his appearance in a position occupying two-thirds of a circle. They prepared to charge upon us; likewise commenced throwing shells, at which the Second East Tennessee broke and ran like sheep. Likewise, the Fourth [Ohio], after receiving several shells, which killed some of their men and

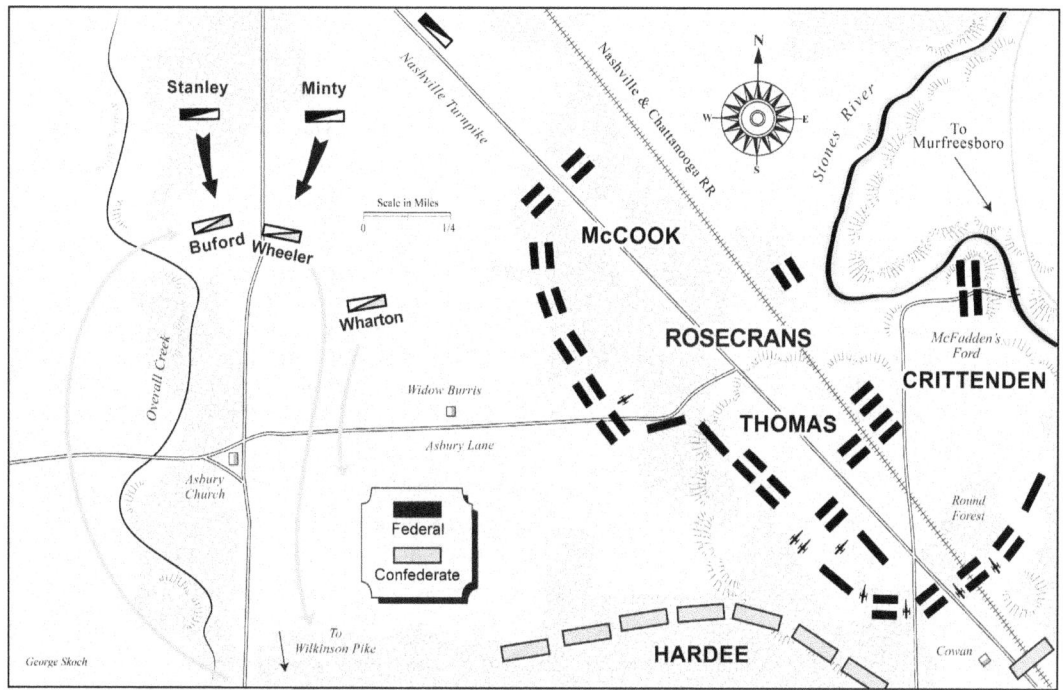

Stanley's Counterattack at the Battle of Stones River (December 31, Afternoon)

horses, retired from their line, as it became untenable. The First had been ordered to proceed farther on into another lot, to form and to receive a charge from another line of the enemy's cavalry. The Third moved to the left, in the vicinity of a white house. About the time the First was formed, the enemy charged upon the Fourth, which, being on the retreat, owing to the shells coming pretty freely, moved off at a pretty lively gait. The Third moved farther to the left, and, somewhat sheltered by the house and barns, the First charged upon the enemy; did not succeed in driving them back.[26]

Captain Valentine Cupp of the 1st Ohio Cavalry recalled the charge into the Confederate cavalry, which resulted in Colonel Minor Millikin's death, the serious wounding of his adjutant, Lieutenant William Scott, and the death of Lieutenant Timothy Condit. Millikin was described as "a rare character, intense, impatient and dramatic." Cupp noted Millikin reasoned that to permit Wharton's cavalry to proceed any further into the Union flank "would have been ruinous." The 1st Ohio's charge fulfilled Colonel Minor Millikin's stated desire to lead his regiment in a full-blown saber charge. Millikin, a highly regarded cavalry officer who had led a brigade of cavalry after the Perryville Campaign, had been frustrated leading the Union cavalry and he lamented that in no instance were the resources at his disposal sufficient to meet his Southern cavalry adversaries. Millikin's brigade was disbanded after the campaign, but now at Murfreesboro:

> His officers and soldiers were falling around him rapidly, Major Moore had been mortally wounded early in the day by a shell while the regiment was maneuvering for position, and Adjutant W.H. Scott had been severely wounded in attempting to capture a rebel flag, and Lieutenant Sam Fordyce, of Company B, was also wounded.... He must act at once, or his regiment would be stampeded and driven from the field, as they were being pushed and crushed ... [and] then Colonel Millikin ... gave the command "Charge!" which was repeated to right and left along the line.... Commending their souls to God, they charged home.

The 1st Ohio's charge cut through the Confederate cavalry and in the process Millikin was shot in the neck and died. As the Confederate cavalry closed around the 1st Ohio, the regiment lost thirty-one killed and wounded in this charge, including five officers.[27]

After the unsuccessful charge of the 1st Ohio, the regiment was forced to retire and was attacked again by its pursuers. Next, the Confederate cavalry took possession of a wagon train. Zahm had clashed with Wharton throughout the morning and finally his troopers facing Wharton's cavalry, fled except for the 3rd Ohio Cavalry. Louis Zahm wrote,

> At this juncture the First and Fourth retired pretty fast, the enemy in close pursuit after them, the Second East Tennessee having the lead of them all. Matters looked pretty blue now; the ammunition train was supposed to be gone up, when the Third charged upon the enemy, driving him back, capturing several prisoners, and recapturing a good many of our men, and saved the train. I was with the three regiments that skedaddled, and among the last to leave the field. Tried hard to rally them, but the panic was so great that I could not do it. I could not get the command together again until I arrived at the north side of the creek.[28]

Despite the fact Zahm's brigade were finally overwhelmed by the Confederate cavalry, two timely counterattacks by Elmer A. Otis and John Kennett allowed the rest of the Union cavalry regain the wagon train and hold its position on the right. Otis's regiment participated in two notable actions during the battle. The attack resulted in sending an unidentified unit of Confederate cavalry to the rear. The second attack occurred after the 1st Ohio Cavalry unsuccessfully charged the 2nd Tennessee and McCown's Escort Company, which freed several of the 1st Ohio, which had been captured. A member of the 4th U.S. recorded, "On we came, yelling like so many savages, and scattering them like chaff." Next, Otis prepared to take on White's artillery that had caused so much damage to Zahm throughout the morning, but Otis was ordered to duty near the ammunition train before he could make the attack. He wrote, "The train on the pike ... was in possession of the enemy, with a large number of stragglers, who were being disarmed at the time. These stragglers did nothing at all to protect the wagons, scarcely firing a shot....[T]he Fourth U.S. Cavalry charged at this time an entire brigade of cavalry, and routed them to such an extent that they disappeared from the field at that point entirely."[29]

Despite Union setbacks, it was along the Union supply trains that cavalry began to have success. Wharton had pushed too far. Major Robert Klein was an experienced and calm commander of 3rd Indiana Cavalry during the battle on December 31. Klein recorded his command had been posted to the right and rear of Richard Johnson's Second Division. As the Union right collapsed, Klein lamented,

> [T]he efficiency of my battalion was destroyed in being divided by one of our own cavalry regiments running through our ranks and scattering the men. This movement, had it been in the opposite direction, would have been a most gallant charge, and, doubtless, from its determination, an efficient one. We kept falling back, forming and charging at intervals, until forced across to the Murfreesborough pike, where one of my companies was first to form to drive the enemy from our train.[30]

Of Zahm's cavalry, the 3rd Ohio Cavalry held its ground. Major J.W. Paramore, 3rd Ohio Cavalry, commanded his battalion after retreating as far as the ammunition train after the collapse of the Union right. The 32-year-old James Wallace Paramore, commanding the 3rd Ohio (born in Mansfield, Ohio), had been a lawyer before the war. He now faced the challenge of his life and later noted,

> We had been forced back as far as General McCook's ammunition train, and were drawn up in front of it for its protection, the furious charge of the enemy's cavalry, preceded by a shower of shells, caused a pretty

general stampede of our cavalry, led off by the Second Tennessee on our right, and followed by the Fourth and First Ohio, and the First Battalion of the Third Ohio Cavalry. At that juncture an aide of General McCook came up to me, and informed me that "that was their entire ammunition train, and must be held at all hazards."

Paramore ordered his regiment to hold their position although it was receiving a "galling fire," but his troopers suffered the attack without budging. As the enemy moved away from the 3rd Ohio and 3rd Indiana, the Union cavalry was able to charge the retreating cavalry. The charge effectively dispatched the Confederate cavalry, killing an unrecorded number and claiming 10–12 prisoners.[31]

Next, the 3rd Ohio and the 3rd Indiana cavalries encountered a group of Confederate cavalry near the Union hospital intending to capture a supply train. Paramore ordered his troopers to attack although Klein estimated he faced twice his numbers. The battle was severe and several men were lost on both sides. A squadron of Paramore's cavalry engaged another group of Southern cavalry farther along the pike in an effective counterattack led by Colonel John Kennett. Paramore proudly wrote in his after action report, "Then be it spoken to their praise that the Second and Third Battalions of the Third Ohio Cavalry did not run nor break their lines during that day's severe fighting."[32]

Kennett's Counterattack

After dispatching Zahm's troopers to the rear, Wharton's cavalry captured a large wagon train consisting of several hundred wagons. In addition, Wharton claimed prisoners, caissons and cannons and quickly began moving the booty toward the Confederate lines. Wharton's further advance on the Union right flank was stopped as Federal infantry emerged from the woods near the Nashville Pike.

John Kennett's service to the Army of the Cumberland had been inconsistent; however, on this occasion he showed his value by doing the right thing at the right time and without question helped save the Union supply train. During the battle on December 31, Rosecrans ordered Kennett, in Stanley's absence, to attempt to rally the collapsed right wing and organize the cavalry into an effective screen. Rosecrans had to realize the error of sending his chief of cavalry and best cavalry brigade commander to the rear to deal with raids on his supply train. Kennett was up to the task and performed exemplary service on this day. As he rode with Colonel Eli Murray's 3rd Kentucky Cavalry, they observed the Union wagon train being moved by the Confederate cavalry. Colonel Paramore, observing the arrival of Kennett on the field, dispatched two companies to aid in the attack. Kennett noted, "We found a complete stampede—infantry, cavalry, and artillery rushing to the rear, and the rebel cavalry charging upon our retiring forces on the Murfreesborough pike."[33]

Kennett ordered the Union cavalry to attack, which surprised the Confederate cavalry in possession of the wagon train:

> Colonel [Eli] Murray, with great intrepidity, engaged the enemy toward the skirts of the woods, and drove them in three charges. His men behaved like old veterans. Between his command and the field the space was filled with rushing rebel cavalry, charging upon our retreating cavalry and infantry, holding many of our soldiers as prisoners. I rallied the Third Ohio, some two companies, which was falling back, and formed it in the rear of a fence, where volley after volley had the effect of driving back the rebels upon the run,

they [the Third Ohio] charging upon them effectually, thereby relieving the pike of their presence, saving the train, one piece of artillery, and rescuing from their grasp many of our men taken as prisoners.

Murray, 3rd Kentucky Cavalry (U.S.), noted,

We came upon the enemy in all directions. Here were engagements hand-to-hand, but dashing onward my men were doing in earnest the work before them. The open field gave us the place for charging. The enemy were marching about 250 of our men to their rear as prisoners. These we recaptured ... saved the baggage and ammunition of a great part of our army; recaptured a portion of the Fifth Wisconsin Battery and a section of, I think, the First Ohio Battery, and, at least calculation, 800 of our men.

Kennett was in the middle of the battle and was nearly killed by Confederate troopers. Corporals Farrish and Jacquith, Kennett's orderlies, shot two Southern troopers converging on Kennett and captured a third who had a pistol leveled in Kennett's face. Kennett's counterattack successfully reclaimed the supply train and stopped the Confederate cavalry's advance along the Union right flank.[34] So aggressive were Otis's and Kennett's charges "the Rebels decided that the attacking force must be the regulars reinforced by Zahm's brigade." Wharton moved away from the Union line and the Union cavalry moved back to defend the Union flank.[35]

Meanwhile, on the Union left flank Major John Wynkoop commanded the remainder of the 7th Pennsylvania near Murfreesboro while Minty was with Stanley at Stewart's Creek. During the morning Wynkoop's command screened the left flank of the army and served as couriers. The 7th Pennsylvania performed a yeoman's task of rallying the retreating troops. Once the Union right collapsed, Wynkoop pulled his troopers together and began the duty of stopping the panic-stricken solders running to the rear; but he was unable to stop the stampede of men running away. In exasperation, he asked for orders from Rosecrans, who directed him to proceed to the rear to try his best to pull the troops together into fighting units. The 7th Pennsylvania rallied the troops until about 2:00 p.m., when the regiment was ordered back to the front by Kennett.[36]

Stanley's Reserve and First Cavalry Brigades

After a ten-mile ride, David Stanley's reserve cavalry and portions of Minty's First Brigade were the last to arrive to assist Zahm and Kennett's troops. David Stanley and Minty rode hard to the collapsing wing of the army with the 1st Middle (5th) Tennessee and a portion of the 15th Pennsylvania Cavalry. With Minty's First Brigade in tow (4th Michigan and Jennings Battalion, 7th Pennsylvania), the combined cavalry moved to the right along Overall Creek to support McCook's damaged flank. Minty left 130 men of the 4th Michigan to provide cover for Battery D, 1st Ohio Battery, and as they hastened to Overall Creek, his cavalry came under friendly fire.

As Stanley reached the right wing of the army he met many stragglers, "first a few dozen, then a hundred and finally not less than five thousand." He left a troop of cavalry to rally the troops and return them to their lines. He later learned that his troopers returned over two thousand soldiers back to the line. Stanley consulted with Rosecrans and then he joined Minty's fresh cavalry before assessing the situation in the field. Stanley was faced with a difficult situation but he was itching for a fight when he realized Zahm's cavalry had been scattered.[37]

Once at Overall Creek, the 4th Michigan dismounted and formed a line of skirmishers and drove some Confederate cavalry from a wooded area to their front near Asbury Church. The 4th Michigan was supported by a portion of the dismounted 1st Middle (5th) Tennessee. To the right and rear of the 4th Michigan, Captain Jennings' battalion of the 7th Pennsylvania and two companies of the 3rd Kentucky Cavalry joined in the preparation for battle. The 15th Pennsylvania Cavalry was immediately behind the 4th Michigan. The entire Union cavalry defense comprised 950 men and they soon saw the approaching troopers of General Wheeler's cavalry, which had moved onto the battlefield after its circuitous ride around Rosecrans' army. Stanley and Minty rode among the cavalry encouraging them to maintain the line.[38]

When Minty and Stanley arrived, Wharton's brigade was "fought out," but Wheeler's and Buford's brigades were still present and effective on the field. Minty, who commanded the new contingent of Union cavalry while Stanley and his staff visited Rosecrans, described it as follows:

> The enemy advanced rapidly with 2,500 cavalry, mounted and dismounted, with three pieces of artillery, all under the command of General Wheeler. They drove back the Fourth Michigan to the line of the First [Middle] Tennessee skirmishers, and then attacked the Seventh Pennsylvania with great fury, but met with determined resistance. I went forward to the dismounted skirmishers and endeavored to move them to the right, to strengthen the Seventh Pennsylvania, but the moment the right of the line showed itself from behind the fence where they were posted, the whole of the enemy's fire was directed on it, turning it completely around.

The unreliable 15th Pennsylvania Cavalry continued to be so, rapidly riding to the rear. This left the 7th Pennsylvania Cavalry dismounted and without any support and in a very vulnerable position. The Union cavalry fell back and re-formed, unseen and outside the range of the Southern artillery.[39]

The Union cavalry was not to be pushed aside so easily and Stanley met with Minty on the field. Together, Minty and Stanley led a coordinated charge that would end the day. At four o'clock, Minty noted Wheeler's cavalry, in force, moved to the right collecting more Union infantry as prisoners. Shadowing the Rebel cavalry, Minty moved at a distance of about six hundred yards. Stanley noted,

> My first impression was that these covered infantry, but I learned soon that they were only dismounted cavalry. We successfully held them at bay for one-half an hour with the Fourth Michigan and Seventh Pennsylvania, dismounted, when, being outflanked, I ordered our line to mount and fall back to the open field. The enemy followed here, and being re-enforced by detachments of the Anderson and Third Kentucky Cavalry, and the First [Middle] Tennessee, we charged the enemy and put him to rout.[40]

Minty recorded the remainder of the action: "The rebel cavalry had followed us up sharply into the open ground, and now menaced us with three strong lines, two directly in front of my position and one opposite our left flank, with its right thrown well forward, and a strong body of skirmishers in the woods to our right, and threatening that flank."[41] Simultaneously, David Stanley led his own charge. The adjutant of the 15th Pennsylvania observed of Stanley, "General Stanley was everywhere, and in a moment he saw the best that could be done was to order a charge. Let's charge them boys! Let's charge them!"[42]

David Stanley gave the order to charge. Stanley and Minty split the leadership of the cavalry in the attack. Stanley rode at the head of the two companies of the 4th Michigan Cavalry and what group he could rally of the 15th Pennsylvania Cavalry. The attack was successful and the Confederate troopers hustled away. While Stanley was leading his troopers, Minty charged with his regiments of cavalry, which made two charges. Minty's command captured one stand of colors and he noted, "The enemy was again broken and driven from the field."[43]

At this point in the day, Stanley was fearless and decided to put the fighting spirit into his horsemen despite the odds. He knew he had to inspire whatever part of the 15th Pennsylvania Cavalry who would fight. As he divided the assignment of the cavalry, he said to Minty, pointing at Wheeler's cavalry, "You look after those fellows in the front and I will take care of this force." Stanley was preparing to lead the 4th Michigan. He stopped and considered, and Minty recalled Stanley told the men of the 4th Michigan, "'Wait here and I will bring you assistance." He rode over to the men of the troublesome 15th Pennsylvania. He told the men to prepare to charge the Confederates. Minty recounted,

> I then witnessed one of the most heroic scenes of the war. Stanley, standing in his stirrups, his soldierly figure erect, his saber raised straight above his head, in a voice distinctly heard above the noise of battle exclaimed, "The man who does not follow me is a _____ coward!" and wheeling his horse dashed back to the two companies of the 4th Michigan. The 15th followed and the 4th, and with a raging cheer this little band of heroes, led by the gallant Stanley, charged home into the center of Wharton's Brigade and drove it from the field.

When the charge was over, Sergeant Eugene Bronson, 4th Michigan, rode across the area where Stanley, Minty and Zahm had fought during the day and observed, "The number of horses that was killed almost covered the ground."[44]

At the end of a difficult day, the Union cavalry had stabilized the extended right flank of the army. Rosecrans and Stanley's policy of rearming the cavalry contributed to its efficiency during the battle. The Confederate cavalry had many troopers armed only with shotguns, but most were armed with better weapons at the end of the day. The 4th Michigan, 5th Tennessee, and 7th Pennsylvania cavalries held the Union line and the remainder of the Union cavalry settled in for the night north of Asbury Church. While Wheeler had gotten some booty from the Union supply train, it was minimal. General John Wharton recorded, "Owing to this and to my being detained to defend the battery, we were able only to bring off a portion of the wagons, 5 or 6 pieces of artillery, about 400 prisoners, 327 beef cattle, and a goodly number of mules cut from the wagons." Wheeler had been concerned that Stanley and Minty's actions were an attempt to turn the Confederate left flank, but he soon concluded the Union cavalry was making no further efforts to drive forward. Confident there was no further risk to the flank, Wheeler retired his cavalry for the day, exhausted after the entire expedition around Rosecrans' army and the day's battle.[45]

After that day's battle Rosecrans met with his commanders on the evening of December 31. He asked this question: "Shall we fight it out here, or withdraw to an advantageous position covering our depots at Nashville?" Crittenden declined to offer an opinion but agreed to obey any orders of Rosecrans, and Thomas gave a similar answer. It was McCook who said, "I therefore advise that we retire on Nashville and await reinforcements." The officers looked toward Stanley, who said, "I agree with what Gen'l. McCook has recommended." Rosecrans thanked the officers for their opinions and for two hours he and Stanley inspected the ground he held. At 1:00 a.m. Stanley asked him, "'General, what are you going to do?' He immediately answered, 'By God's help, I am going to beat the enemy right here.' No more was said and we immediately went to bed."[46]

Rosecrans returned to headquarters and told the commanding generals, "Well, gentlemen, we shall not retreat, but fight it out here and to the front. Go at once to your posts and hold your commands ready to receive any attack from the enemy." He had concluded he would establish a defensive position and not resume his advance until the arrival of ammunition and supplies from Nashville.[47]

Cavalry Actions: January 1–January 5

While the Union and Confederate cavalries had clashed, it was the infantry regiments that suffered the carnage of the hard-fought battle on December 31. On January 1, the two opposing armies stared across the fields and streams at each other; but the Confederate cavalry was not idle. Bragg had hoped Rosecrans would withdraw after the previous day's battle, but the Union line remained unchanged. So he ordered Wheeler to make a reconnaissance of the enemy's position and to stop any flow of supplies or trains by attacking Rosecrans' communications. This meant another long day for the Union cavalry, Zahm's Second Brigade.[48]

Wheeler took three brigades of cavalry north to the rear of Rosecrans' army and was rewarded with a wagon train along the Nashville Pike, which was defended by the 2nd Tennessee Cavalry and the 22nd Indiana Infantry. Wheeler and Buford rode together to attack the train and Wharton's brigade was sent north to cut off the retreat. Seeing the large number of enemy cavalry, the 2nd Tennessee rode away, the teamsters panicked, and ninety-five of the infantrymen surrendered to Buford. With the 2nd Tennessee Cavalry riding for their lives, and after he burned 30 wagons, Wheeler sought more booty.

For the remainder of Lewis Zahm's Second Cavalry Brigade, January 1 began early after the difficult time his troopers had experienced the previous day, but his horses were fresher than the other Union regiments. Zahm's brigade was saddled and moving at 3:00 a.m. to escort ambulance and ammunition wagons to Nashville and then escort badly needed supplies to replenish those destroyed or captured on the previous day. After burning the first wagon train, Wheeler rode toward Zahm's column, which approached La Vergne. Along the way, Wheeler dispatched Wharton's brigade to deal with Colonel William P. Innes's 1st Michigan Engineers and Mechanics at La Vergne, who obstinately defended their position and successfully repulsed all of Wharton's efforts. Meanwhile, Zahm, with only the 3rd Ohio Cavalry, 4th Ohio Cavalry, and 15th Pennsylvania Cavalry (Anderson), faced Wheeler and Buford's brigades. Zahm discovered he was being attacked when he found the 2nd Tennessee Cavalry riding hard toward him and toward the rear. He threw a company of cavalry across the road to stem the retreat and proceeded to stop the Confederate attack, only to see the 2nd Tennessee again race to the rear "like sheep." While the 2nd Tennessee showed no willingness to fight, the 15th Pennsylvania Cavalry showed even less. When the Confederates attacked, the 15th Pennsylvania ran off in every direction to avoid the fight. Zahm's remaining cavalry repulsed the Confederate attacks twice at the rear of the train at the cost of only 2 or 3 wagons and he was able to save some cannons that were almost captured. While Wheeler was attacking the rear, Zahm was held in check and the baggage train proceeded northward until the Union cavalry was a half-mile from the rear wagon. He noted, "The Anderson Troop, I am sorry to say, were of very little benefit to me, as the majority of them ran as soon as we were attacked."[49]

It was the retreat of the two regiments that stampeded some of the supply wagons, resulting in the breakdowns. Despite the poor performance of the 2nd Tennessee and 15th Pennsylvania

(Anderson) Cavalry, Zahm coordinated his remaining regiments with the 4th Michigan Cavalry, 4th U.S. Cavalry and infantry and finally drove the raiders away.

Lieutenant Colonel Joe Burke, 10th Ohio Infantry, in charge of protecting the Stewart's Creek bridge, made a point in his report to mention Lieutenant James Gilbert, 2nd Tennessee Cavalry, as a member of the cavalry who was connected with "the disgraceful panic." But Burke also noted Lieutenant Rendelbrook, 4th U.S. Cavalry, and the noncommissioned officers and men of his command, and also Lieutenant Thomas Maple, 15th Pennsylvania Cavalry, for their exemplary service during this engagement. General John Wharton claimed possession of about 100 wagons, 150 prisoners, 300 mules, and 1 piece of artillery during his successful raid.[50]

While Zahm was escorting supply trains, Minty's First Cavalry Brigade stayed at the front with the Army of the Cumberland and was involved in skirmishing with enemy cavalry pickets. Minty maintained this duty on January 1, 2, and 3. Stanley's Reserve Brigade also remained with the army on January 1 and had little to report except some skirmishing.[51]

Wheeler's cavalry returned to the friendly confines of the Confederate line after dark. The following morning they were given an opportunity to rest and resupply, but Bragg needed to know if Rosecrans planned to stay and fight or retreat to Nashville. So John Wharton and Pegram's brigades were ordered to the right flank of the Army of Tennessee to support the Confederate right flank. Wheeler and Buford's brigades were ordered again to strike the Union rear and at the same time definitely determine Rosecrans' movements. On January 2, Bragg ordered John C. Breckinridge to lead an attack on Rosecrans' defenses. Breckinridge's attack was initially successful; however, as the Confederates advanced, fifty-seven Union guns decimated the attack, resulting in the loss of more than 1,800 Confederate soldiers killed or wounded.

On January 2, Zahm found time to gather his troopers and forage the horses after two days of activity. Stanley's Reserve Brigade maintained its position and scouted the flanks of the army. On the next day, somewhat rested and replenished, Zahm was again guarding hospital and ammunition trains supplying Rosecrans' army and again found himself fighting the Confederate cavalry. Much to his relief, he had the 1st Ohio, 4th Ohio and 3rd Tennessee cavalry regiments to perform this duty with much better results. The cavalry formed the escort around a hospital supply and ammunition train, and with two and half regiments of infantry, the train began to move south at 11:00 a.m. After marching for eight miles, Wheeler's cavalry attacked and was repulsed; they attempted a second attack later. Fourteen hours later the train arrived safely and Zahm's cavalry had killed 15 Confederate troopers, wounded an unknown number and captured twelve prisoners. This was a much better day for Zahm.[52]

On January 4, Zahm scouted toward Murfreesboro and found Bragg had withdrawn. After receiving reports from Wheeler's reconnaissance that Rosecrans was not withdrawing but was, in fact, moving in what was thought to be reinforcements, Bragg withdrew southward from Murfreesboro. Rosecrans marched into Murfreesboro, claiming the victory on January 5.

On January 5, Stanley's cavalry pursed Bragg's army. Minty advanced through Murfreesboro and down the Manchester Pike southward and within a mile encountered Confederate pickets. David Stanley took command of the advance and drove ahead, riding with the 4th U.S. Cavalry. As the advance continued, the Union cavalry crossed a creek another mile forward and came under attack from Confederate artillery. The advance, which included the 1st

Tennessee, 3rd Kentucky, 7th Pennsylvania, 4th Michigan, 4th U.S. and 2nd Tennessee cavalries, pushed onward. Six miles south of Murfreesboro, a stiff skirmish resulted, with most of the fighting being successfully done by the 4th U.S., 5th Tennessee and 7th Pennsylvania. Afterward, the Union cavalry withdrew and camped just south of Murfreesboro.[53]

Summary of the Cavalry's Role

After the Battle of Stones River, the Union cavalry suffered 357 casualties and lost 77 horses. In addition to the total losses, Colonel Minor Millikin, Major David Moore, and 2nd Lieutenant Timothy Condit, all of the 1st Ohio Cavalry, were killed. Major Frank B. Ward and Major A.O. Rosengarten, 15th Pennsylvania, were killed just prior to the battle. Although they were not listed in Stanley's official report, the cavalry would soon receive resignations from Colonel John Kennett (February 1863) due to ill health and Colonel Lewis Zahm (January 1863), who had been wounded during the battle. In addition, Captain Wortham, 1st Middle (5th) Tennessee Cavalry; Captain Eli Long, 4th U.S. Cavalry; Lieutenant William H. Scott, 1st Ohio; and Lieutenant Thomas V. Mitchell, 4th Michigan Cavalry, were all wounded during the battle.[54]

Perhaps one of the most interesting casualties during the Battle of Stones River was that of Private Frank Martin, 2nd Tennessee Cavalry. The 18-year-old had enlisted about six months prior to the battle and while being examined for a shoulder wound was found to be a woman. Martin was, of course, discharged, but she later enlisted, again hiding her gender, in the 8th Michigan Infantry.[55]

Report of Casualties in Cavalry Command, Fourteenth Army Corps, from the Advance from Nashville on the 26th December, Including the Battle of Stones River[56]

Command	Killed Officers	Killed Men	Wounded Officers	Wounded Men	Missing Officers	Missing Men	Total
First Brigade, Colonel Robert H.G. Minty							
2d Indiana, Company M	0	1	0	0	1	13	15
3d Kentucky	0	1	1	7	0	1	16
4th Michigan	0	1	1	6	0	12	26
7th Pennsylvania	0	2	0	9	0	50	61
Total First Brigade	0	5	2	22	1	76	106
Second Brigade, Colonel Lewis Zahm							
1st Ohio	3	2	1	10	1	14	31
3d Ohio	0	6	0	15	0	13	34
4th Ohio	0	7	0	18	0	31	56
Total Second Brigade	3	15	1	43	1	58	121
Artillery							
1st Ohio Light, Battery D	0	1	0	0	0	0	1
Total Cavalry	3	21	3	65	2	134	228
Reserve Cavalry							
3rd Indiana (West Battalion)	0	0	0	0	0	0	0
15th Pennsylvania	1	8	1	8	0	53	71

Command	Killed		Wounded		Missing		Total
	Officers	Men	Officers	Men	Officers	Men	
Reserve Cavalry							
1st Middle (5th) Tennessee	0	0	1	5	1	8	15
2d Tennessee	1	2	0	10	0	5	18
Total Reserve Cavalry	2	10	2	23	1	66	104
Unattached							
4th United States	0	3	1	9	0	12	25
Total Cavalry	5	34	6	97	3	212	357

Certainly accounts vary regarding the number of men present for duty, but Rosecrans recorded that 3,200 Union cavalry troopers participated in the battle. The refusal of most of the 15th Pennsylvania Cavalry to participate in the battle accounts for some of the reduction in accounting for Union troopers.

The battle was over and for the Union cavalry of the Army of the Cumberland it marked a new beginning. Stanley really had eight regiments he could count on during the battle: Minty's First Brigade, Zahm's Second Brigade and the 4th U.S. Regulars, although this regiment was not attached to the Union cavalry division. The 15th Pennsylvania and the 2nd Tennessee regiments were just too green for reliable service at Murfreesboro. Stanley had only a month to work with his cavalry. Reginald Stuart, in his analysis of the Union cavalry at Stones River, noted that despite the early retreats during the battle the cavalry demonstrated increased aggressiveness and energy under "Stanley's guiding hand in combination with Rosecrans' lavish attention," which together produced positive results.[57]

Certain changes in command were necessary after the actions at Stones River. Major Frank Mix, 4th Michigan Cavalry, did not shy away from his thoughts about the commander of that regiment after Minty assumed command of the brigade. Mix wrote to his brother:

> That d___ coward of a Dickenson has spoiled all I done for the Regt. and more too. It is like this. Minty is in command of the Brigade and Dickenson was left in command of the Regt. Two of our Majors have gone home and the other one on standby staff, so I was sent in one direction with six companies and Dickenson another.... On the other hand, Dickenson was attacked and was scared to death. Showed the white feather and his ass too. Lost our wagons, came near losing his men. And I will not attempt to tell you all, only has brought a pile of disgrace on himself and the Regt and he had some of the best officers under him we have in the Regt. And if he does not leave the Regt. you will soon see your humble servant and a number of others at home in quick time. I never will march a rod under his command if I am cashiered for it.[58]

Major Frank Mix commanded a battalion of 4th Michigan Cavalry (*Minty and the Cavalry*, 1886).

In addition, a change in command occurred in the 4th Ohio, which was commanded by Major John Pugh; but Pugh was not to command the regiment for long. On November 20, the officers of the regiment signed a petition demanding Pugh "resign immediately and unconditionally." The demand was based on charges of cowardice and disobeying orders. Oliver P. Robie, who would be promoted to the rank of lieutenant colonel in February 1863, replaced Pugh. Robie was born in Cumberland County, Maine, and had moved to Cincinnati by 1860, when his occupation was a salesman. He began the war in a three-month regiment, H.W. Burdsall's Independent Cavalry Company, and then enlisted in the 4th Ohio Cavalry. The 29-year-old Robie began his service in the 4th Ohio Cavalry as captain of Company A. He was captured at Lexington, Kentucky, in October 1862 by John Hunt Morgan's raiders and exchanged.[59]

There were moments of absolute embarrassment for the Union cavalry at Stones River, but there were also moments of ultimate heroism and glory. It was a start, and having David Stanley in the saddle leading this command had been invaluable. Others noted the efforts of the cavalry, too. Alexander McCook wrote of the actions of Stanley and the cavalry after the battle was over: "To Brig. Gen. D.S. Stanley, chief of cavalry, my thanks are particularly due. He commanded my advance from Nolensville and directed the cavalry on my right flank. A report of the valuable services of our cavalry will be furnished by General Stanley. I commend him to my superiors and my country." Rosecrans also lauded the role of the cavalry: "Brig. Gen. D.S. Stanley, already distinguished in four successful battles ... at this time in command of our ten regiments of cavalry, fought the enemy's forty regiments of cavalry, and held them at bay, or beat them wherever he could meet them. He ought to be made a major-general for his service, and also for the good of the service."[60]

Stanley mentioned in his report those individuals who in his opinion deserved recognition for their actions during the battle:

Major Robert Klein	3rd Indiana Cavalry	For Action on December 27
Major Frank Ward	Anderson Cavalry	Great Bravery
Major Adolph Rosengarten	Anderson Cavalry	Great Bravery
Colonel Robert Minty	4th Michigan Cavalry	Command in Several Actions
Captain Eli Otis	4th U.S. Cavalry	Important and Distinguished Service
Colonel Eli Murray	3rd Kentucky Cavalry	Important and Distinguished Service
Major John Wynkoop	7th Pennsylvania Cavalry	A Model to Faithful Soldiers
Colonel Lewis Zahm	Second Brigade	Personal Example
Colonel John Kennett	Divisional Command	Rendered Good Service[61]

It is also important to note that Private John Tweedale and Private John Bourke, both of the 15th Pennsylvania Cavalry, would be awarded the Medal of Honor for gallantry in action during the Battle of Stones River in 1887. Of the Battle of Stones River, Stanley wrote, "The battle of Stones River was no great victory but retreating to some extent demoralized, the rebel army, and coming about the time of Burnside's miserable failures in the east, our victory helped to sustain the courage of the country."[62]

Stanley and Rosecrans learned much in regard to the Union cavalry at the Battle of Stones River and Rosecrans had accurately identified his needs in a communication to Henry Halleck on November 2: "We must have cavalry and cavalry arms, and a capable division commander." The first lesson learned was that Stanley needed some parity in arms, experience, and numbers to the Confederate cavalry he faced. His and Rosecrans' numbers included two untried Tennessee regiments along with the wholly unreliable 15th Pennsylvania Regiment. In addition, Stanley had only one company of the 2nd Indiana Cavalry and a demi-regiment of the 3rd Indiana at his disposal.[63]

The addition of David Stanley as chief of cavalry was an excellent choice. He immediately added collegiality, experience and confidence to the cavalry. When he was present, the Union cavalry performed well, even in the presence of overwhelming odds. The counterattack on Wheeler's cavalry by Stanley and Minty on the afternoon of December 31 was an example of an experienced cavalryman stalemating a superior force by rallying troopers while capitalizing on weaknesses of his adversaries. A correspondent of the *Cincinnati Commercial Newspaper*, William D. Bickham, described David Stanley after the Battle of Stones River:

> He is an active, enterprising soldier, familiar alike with the abstract science, and the practical art of war.... It was his good fortune to be loved by all whom he commanded. The soldiers had faith in his zeal and skill, and his fiery courage inspired them with confident enthusia[s]m. They compared him not inaptly with Murat, and airily applied to him the soubriquet of "gay old Stanley"—singing merrily at festive board or cheerful bivouac fire "Here's to gay old Stanley [/] Pass him round, Pass him round."[64]

Finally, the reorganization of the cavalry of the Army of the Cumberland was of great importance in the Battle of Stones River and subsequently for the Union cavalry. Only by concentrating the cavalry, although still outnumbered, could Stanley have made the progress he did. It is not difficult to imagine the havoc Wheeler's cavalry could have created had the Union cavalry regiments been dispersed throughout the various infantry corps working directly under the command of divisional or even brigade commanders. Stanley receives credit for this improved organization despite complaints of the infantry commanders, and Rosecrans saw the wisdom of this change. This organization was the first step in gaining parity with Wheeler, Forrest, and Morgan, who, until this point, had literally ridden circles around the Union army.[65]

3. Middle Tennessee, January–June 1863

"… the game is worth the candle," we will slap away at them.
—Major General David S. Stanley

David Stanley's assessment of the Battle of Stones River was this: "[T]otally indecisive … this victory counted more for its moral effect upon the soldiers of each side than for any material or physical advantage." Clearly, Rosecrans did not gain a decisive victory, but in the end his army claimed Murfreesboro and Bragg retreated southward about thirty miles and began preparing defenses along the Highland Rim south of the Duck River. The removal of Bragg southward resulted in immediate accolades for Rosecrans from Washington. This much needed "victory" offered balm to Washington in light of the defeat at Fredericksburg, the stalemate along the Mississippi River and the recent raid by Major General Earl Van Dorn on the Union supply depot at Holly Springs, Mississippi. At least for now, the Army of the Cumberland was the darling of the Union Army.[1]

Almost immediately, pressure mounted for Rosecrans to continue with his offensive. Secretary of war Edwin Stanton wrote on January 7, "[T]his opens Eastern Tennessee; and if General Rosecrans takes possession of it, 200,000 rebel troops cannot drive him out." Rosecrans had no intention to resuming the offensive; instead he felt he was on the defensive anticipating Bragg was about to receive an influx of reinforcements. In addition, Rosecrans needed supplies. His army had rations to last only until January 15. He had no plans of moving away from his base of supplies, particularly as he was perilously low on provisions and because Wheeler's cavalry had shown an ability to cut Rosecrans' supply line.[2]

After withdrawing from Murfreesboro, Bragg established his headquarters at Tullahoma, while Polk's Corps settled in at Shelbyville and Hardee moved into winter quarters near Tullahoma. While the Union and Confederate infantry remained relatively stationary, the cavalry of both armies worked hard during the first six months of 1863. Bragg established a defensive line of cavalry across a 75-mile front stretching from Spring Hill to the west to McMinnville in the east.[3]

Reorganization of the Cavalry of the Army of the Cumberland

Taking advantage of his success, Rosecrans again asked for additional troops, and this proved to be advantageous for David Stanley's fledgling cavalry division. On January 5 Rosecrans requested the 1st Tennessee Cavalry and the door opened on January 7, when Edwin Stanton wrote to Rosecrans: "There is nothing you can ask within my power to grant to yourself or your heroic command that will not be cheerfully given." Then began, over the next six months, a process of increasing the number of cavalry regiments assigned to the Army of the Cumberland. While the army remained in the area around Murfreesboro, Stanley's cavalry arm increased by 13 regiments, with all but two of the regiments being ready for service by April 1863.[4]

Immediately upon the Union's taking possession of Murfreesboro, the work of Stanley's cavalry began again as he faced the strong Confederate cavalry just south of the town protecting the retreating infantry along the Shelbyville and Manchester pikes. Faced with the same old problem of a strong Confederate cavalry, Stanley and Rosecrans sought numerical and technological solutions to the problem. On January 14, Rosecrans explained to secretary of war Stanton that the Confederates outnumbered his cavalry by four to one and plagued his communications and supply lines. One solution planned by Rosecrans was to mount an infantry brigade to supplement the traditional cavalry. He wanted to be able to move quickly like cavalry but bring to bear the new technology of repeating rifles, which would increase the firepower of the mounted infantry as a way to tame the Confederate cavalry. Rosecrans wrote, "I must have horses and saddles to mount some infantry, and have asked authority to buy the horses and saddles for 5,000." Thus began months-long exchanges of messages between Rosecrans and Washington in which Rosecrans demanded repeating rifles, more cavalry regiments, authority to mount infantry, and more horses to do so. Initially, Washington tried to meet Rosecrans' needs, largely based on the success at Stones River while other Union armies were stalemated; but the constant demands by Rosecrans soon became tiresome. His numerous requests would finally be met with a reply from Washington that enough was enough.[5]

In the first six months of 1863 the Union cavalry's organization was fluid as regiments entered the developing cavalry divisions. Only the 3rd Kentucky Cavalry left the cavalry division of the Army of the Cumberland and returned to Kentucky. Initially, Robert Minty and Edward McCook were permanent brigade commanders and other officers were given temporary brigade command as needed. The cavalry was reorganized in April and May to include four brigades and two divisions.

By June, Stanley's cavalry increased to twenty-two regiments with three sections of artillery. On January 20, fifty-five hundred troopers reported for duty, but when all the new regiments of cavalry were present more than 10,000 troopers made up the cavalry division. This was a far cry from the slightly greater than 3,200 reported by Rosecrans at the Battle of Stones River. Despite the increase in the Union cavalry, Stanley struggled to gain numerical equality against the impressive Confederate cavalry operating in Middle Tennessee.

Relative Strength of Union and Confederate Cavalries 1863[6]

Date	Present for Duty—Union	Present for Duty—Confederate
January 31	4,549	8,707
February 28	5,040	9,101
April 30	4,961	15,125
May 20	–	15,096
May 31	4,961	–
June 10	–	13,868
June 30	10,560	–

The final reward awaiting the cavalry was a promotion to the rank of major general for David Stanley. Rosecrans' report of the Battle of Stone's River stated Stanley proved himself worthy of the rank. In addition to Rosecrans' recommendation, a group of citizens from Ohio and the officers of his command petitioned Abraham Lincoln to promote Stanley to the rank of major general. In the petition Stanley's prior actions were cited: "On behalf of the soldiers of his command, we ask it! In the name of justice and for the country's good we ask his promotion." The officers ended their request by penning, "Under Stanley, always forward, efficient and brave."[7]

Joseph Wheeler, chief of cavalry for Bragg's army, was promoted on January 22 to the rank of major general, the youngest man of this rank in the Confederate army. Wheeler had been rewarded for his service during the Battle of Stones River and his subsequent action at Harpeth Shoals, where he captured four large transports on the Cumberland River.

Union Cavalry Actions: January–April

While new regiments continuously poured into the Army of the Cumberland, many arrived untrained, poorly horsed or poorly equipped. On February 2, Rosecrans, still prodding Stanton and Halleck for more matériel, lamented, "We have now 1,000 cavalrymen without horses, and 2,000 without arms. We don't want revolvers so much as light revolving rifles." Meanwhile, the cavalry commanders trained their troopers, and the officers attempted to develop a fighting spirit in this new Union cavalry.[8]

Many of Stanley's men preferred his style of command because he did not believe in

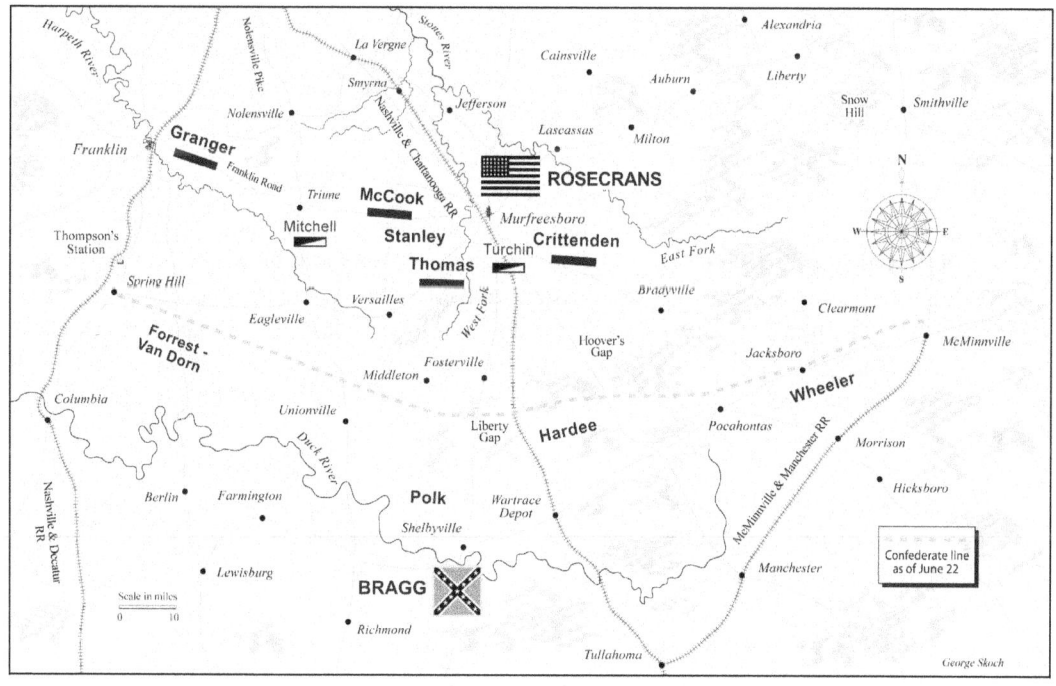

Middle Tennessee (January–June 1863)

drilling veteran cavalry just for the purpose of drilling. Nor did he feel military reviews were routinely necessary for his cavalry, which was a marked contrast from the previous cavalry commander. Captain Joseph Vale, 7th Pennsylvania Cavalry, noted, "The change from the constant irksome drills and reviews of the preceding year to the rest and recuperation of camp life now permitted was highly appreciated by the soldiers, and endeared their commander to them, as one who cared for their comfort rather than for display."[9]

Training was important for the volunteer cavalry and the common belief within the army was that it took as much as two years to fully train a cavalryman. The common method of training followed the guidelines of the *Poinsett Tactics*, authorized by secretary of war J.R. Poinsett in 1841. These tactics were printed in three volumes and included a wide variety of skills including formations, training of horses, conducting a cavalry charge, methods of riding and a manual of arms. The complexities of handling horse, arms (carbines, pistols, sabers) and the various formations required many hours of practice and instruction. Early in the war, the use of cavalry was more traditional horsemanship, but as the war continued the extensive use of dismounted cavalry in battle was common. To be properly trained, the cavalry trooper needed to be proficient with close-quarters combat on horseback and marksmanship in line of battle while dismounted. New regiments drilled as much as six hours per day when not on reconnaissance or guard duty.[10]

The winter was difficult for many in the Union cavalry, particularly those whose baggage had been destroyed during one of the many Confederate raids on the supply trains. The 2nd Tennessee Cavalry was one such regiment and Lieutenant John Andes recorded, "It had turned very cold, and the men having got their clothing wet, their clothes were frozen stiff, and the men were frozen almost to death.... It was not unusual to find men dead in their tents in the morning." The 1st Ohio Cavalry also had unpleasant experiences during January. Sergeant Major C.M. Riggs noted on January 14, "During the night the waters of the creek had flooded the valley where a part of our boys were camped. In the morning many of the tents were swimming in the angry waters, the occupants having escaped, although many of them barely saving their lives, by wading or swimming to higher ground." Major Will McTeer, 3rd Tennessee Cavalry, also lamented the condition of the camp, complaining that the mud was knee-deep and the ground was so full of water the men slept on cornstalks in an effort to stay dry. More unpleasant was the smell of rotting flesh that came from the Stones River battlefield. McTeer exclaimed, "The whole atmosphere was foul."[11] L.K. Dunn, trooper of the 3rd Kentucky Cavalry, described some of the hardships in January: "I slept in a tent last night for the first time since Thursday.... Our Reg. was ordered on a scout last Friday night, was a week without anything of the shelter kind and was out in all that snow and you may know that we suffered to some extent ... but a soldier is hard to freeze. We are used to exposure in all shapes."[12]

But officers were officers, and soldiers were soldiers. On February 24, the commanders of the Army of the Cumberland had a large dinner and speeches were made during the event. Sergeant Daniel Prickitt, 3rd Ohio Cavalry, humorously recorded in his diary that various generals made speeches, but noted, "If the Generals & Officers crush the rebellion, what will the privates do?"[13]

Although the two armies remained relatively stationary during the winter of 1863, skirmishes were commonplace. The next major action for the Army of the Cumberland would not begin until June 23 with the Tullahoma Campaign, but the Union cavalry was constantly in action from January until that time. Nine expeditions, nine reconnaissance actions, and fifty skirmishes occurred in the first six month of 1863.[14]

The command situation within Stokes' 5th Tennessee Cavalry deteriorated from January through March, although the battalions commanded by Lieutenant Colonel Robert Galbraith and Major John Murphy provided notable service. However, in January the regiment elected a major and one of the candidates was Captain Eli Fleming, Company F. Fleming lost the election and he felt he lost because he had been charged with being absent without leave by Colonel William B. Stokes. During a heated exchange between the two, Fleming shot Stokes in the leg. Fleming was court-martialed and the sentence was reduced, with Fleming returning to service due to Rosecrans' intervention. Later, Stokes faced a court-martial for his harshness and tyranny toward the regiment, but he was acquitted.[15]

Despite these irritating drawbacks, things were starting to fall into place for the Union cavalry with more experience and better leadership, but more training was needed. On January 22, Captain Elmer Otis commanded a reconnaissance to Liberty, Tennessee, bagging a dozen Confederate soldiers and "five or six noted secessionists." The 1st Tennessee Cavalry assisted in the capture of the prisoners and transferred them to the 2nd Tennessee Cavalry, riding in the rear of the column, which promptly allowed seven of the prisoners to escape much to the disgust of professional soldier Otis.[16]

Obviously, more training was needed. So training became part of the daily activities of the cavalry regiments and the troopers learned the many bugle calls. Each regiment had a chief bugler and then one man from each of the twelve companies had duty as a company bugler. "The tr-r-r-r-rat, tr-rat-tat, tr-rat-atat-tat of the drums was sweet music compared with the horrid sound from all the blare of bugles as they took up the cavalry calls, as follows: reveille, roll-call, stable-call, sick call, drill-call, officers'-call, retreat and taps or lights out," noted a trooper of the 1st Tennessee Cavalry.[17]

15th Pennsylvania Cavalry

William Rosecrans offered another chance for the mutinous and inconsistent regiment from Pennsylvania on January 20 when he sent the men of the 15th Pennsylvania Cavalry an opportunity to return to service. "Rev. Dr. McCauley and Mr. Kerr, of Philadelphia, have called to see me in behalf of those members of the Fifteenth Pennsylvania," noted Rosecrans. An appeal from citizens of Pennsylvania helped him to decide what to do with this regiment that had caused Stanley and him so much trouble. Rosecrans realized it was not good politics to punish the many sons of well-connected citizens of a state as important as Pennsylvania. It was better to forgive and move forward. He decided to use this regiment as a headquarters escort and for the courier service for the Army of the Cumberland, the service which they had desired. Rosecrans also promised a proper organization of the regiment, including the electing of officers, not appointing them. In return, the professional and reliable 4th U.S. Cavalry was assigned to Stanley's cavalry division. The 4th U.S. Cavalry was commanded by Captain James McIntyre, a native of Tennessee. McIntyre was a classmate of David Stanley at West Point and (appointed from Texas) graduated in 1853. McIntyre, a thoroughly professional cavalryman, served in the army before the war and saw action during the Antietam Campaign before moving to the Western Theatre.[18]

All but about 200 men agreed to the terms outlined by Rosecrans. On February 8, Colonel William J. Palmer, the commander of the 15th Pennsylvania who had been captured and subsequently exchanged, was ordered to Murfreesboro to assume command of the regiment. When Colonel Palmer arrived he noted he found the condition of the regiment "was just about as bad as it was possible to be." Rosecrans selected fifteen members of the 15th Pennsylvania to be tried for mutiny as an example to the rest of the army, but he finally decided to put the entire matter behind him by discharging the remainder of the regiment who refused to perform their duty. Those court-martialed had their sentences suspended and were discharged also. This was a turning point for those left in the regiment, which was reorganized and served through the end of the war.[19]

The refusal of the 15th Pennsylvania Cavalry to perform its duty in December was also twisted into propaganda, as it was speculated the cause of the mutiny was that the regiment disagreed with the Emancipation Proclamation. The situation, implied Southern sympathizers, was a result of Union troops' disagreement with Lincoln's decision to free slaves and they refused to perform their duties. Although untrue, the reputation of the regiment was ruined until it was reorganized. In a letter written by Sergeant George Garrett, 4th Missouri Cavalry, he wanted to be sure the folks at home knew his service was not to be confused with those who mutinied at Stones River.[20]

Franklin Expedition

Meanwhile, the Union cavalry was on the move. Colonel Robert Minty, in a joint expedition with Brigadier General Jefferson C. Davis's infantry division, made a sweep to the west of Murfreesboro from January 31 through February 13 to reconnoiter and to maintain the respective defensive lines. Minty commanded six regiments of cavalry (7th Pennsylvania, 4th Michigan, 3rd Kentucky, 4th U.S., 2nd Tennessee and 3rd Tennessee) on the expedition, consisting of 1,300 troopers, and surprised the 51st Alabama and 8th Confederate cavalries at Middleton and captured eight officers and 84 troopers. Minty proudly noted he collected another 49 wounded at Rover, all suffering from saber wounds. However, the expedition was a miserable experience whether the soldier wore blue or gray. It was described as "a succession of rain, snow, and sleet, alternated with the most intense cold; the roads knee deep with mud and slush."[21]

Minty's cavalry riding through the Tennessee countryside had a devastating effect on the local citizens. Tennessee resident Mary Pearre wrote, "A Federal force is at Franklin. Cavalry are scouting all over the country, stealing money, clothes, foraging, pressing horses and capturing 'Secesh' soldiers. I am fearful Robert will be taken prisoner. Not a dog barks but what I think, 'The Yankees are coming.' Oh! when will it end?"[22]

Wilder's Mounted Infantry

Colonel John T. Wilder's brigade became the first mounted infantry Rosecrans would use against the Confederate army. Wilder's brigade (17th Indiana Infantry, 72nd Indiana Infantry, 98th Illinois Infantry, 123rd Illinois Infantry) was the 2,000-man Second Brigade

Company D, 2nd Tennessee Cavalry was organized in eastern Tennessee and commanded by Colonel Daniel Ray (courtesy Tennessee State Library and Archives).

of General J.J. Reynolds' division. Wilder was a frustrated commander. He had been captured by Brigadier General James R. Chalmers during the Perryville Campaign in September 1862 and had been unable to contain his disappointment since that time. He wanted a way to fight the Confederate cavalry and he had argued his case with Rosecrans. Once mounted, Wilder's brigade proved a valuable resource that complemented the traditional cavalry.[23]

On February 16, 1863, Rosecrans authorized Wilder to mount his brigade, and Wilder began to train the brigade in this new type of warfare. Not only were the upcoming days ones of change for the infantry but the traditional Union cavalry also needed to change to work in a coordinated manner with the mounted infantry. While Rosecrans saw the value of mounted infantry, General in Chief Henry Halleck did not. While allowing Rosecrans to shape his army as he saw fit, Halleck cautioned him on March 21: "It is believed that you weaken your force by mounting too many. Mounted infantry are neither good infantry nor good cavalry."[24]

Dover and Fort Donelson

While Minty was on the expedition west of Murfreesboro, Joseph Wheeler and Nathan Bedford Forrest made an unsuccessful cavalry raid at Fort Donelson at Dover, Tennessee. Colonel Abner Harding, commanding the Union defenses, held his position during the seven-hour Confederate attack. The 5th Iowa Cavalry, soon to become part of Stanley's cavalry, detected the enemy's advance and sounded the alarm. The repulse led Forrest to declare he would never serve under Wheeler.[25]

The failure of the Confederate attack, and Forrest's position in regard to Wheeler, resulted in Bragg dividing his cavalry command between Wheeler and Earl Van Dorn. Forrest would serve as second-in-command under Van Dorn and, as promised, would not serve under Wheeler's command. Van Dorn would command the cavalry on Bragg's left flank while Wheeler worked on the right flank.

Bradyville

Skirmishing continued weekly as the cavalry of both armies sparred in the countryside. On February 22, along the Manchester Pike near Murfreesboro, a picket of the 1st Middle [5th] Tennessee Cavalry scampered to the rear after an enemy attack, but the 4th Michigan Cavalry stabilized the Union line. The Union cavalry had a better day on March 1 in a skirmish at Bradyville, Tennessee. Stanley rode with a large group of cavalry including the 5th Tennessee, 3rd Ohio, 4th Ohio and 4th U.S. cavalries, while Minty's command covered the rear. The column escorted 400 wagons on a foraging expedition about 10 miles southeast of Murfreesboro, near Bradyville. The 5th Tennessee led the advance and clashed with two Confederate regiments, the 2nd Kentucky (CSA) and the 14th Alabama Battalion. The 5th Tennessee engaged the enemy cavalry initially until they were pushed back and then the 3rd and 4th Ohio cavalries arrived on both flanks, compelling the Confederates to withdraw. News reporters heralded the action at Bradyville as the "most brilliant affair since the battle of Stones River."[26]

Thompson's Station

Shortly afterwards, on March 4, a different fate awaited another Union foraging and reconnaissance expedition near Thompson's Station just outside Franklin, Tennessee. About 600 Union cavalry, commanded by Colonel Thomas Jordan from the 9th Pennsylvania, 4th Kentucky and 2nd Michigan cavalries, escorted Colonel John Coburn's brigade of infantry (19th Michigan, 22nd Wisconsin, 33rd and 85th Indiana) south toward Spring Hill where Major General Earl Van Dorn was reported to be massing a large concentration of troops. The Union column, 2,800 men strong, pushed the enemy cavalry pickets but ran into determined resistance about five miles south of Franklin at Thompson's Station. Van Dorn would officially become part of Bragg's Army of Tennessee on March 16 and his arrival added significant numbers of cavalry, about 8,000 men, to the Southern army. Van Dorn also assumed command of Nathan Forrest's Confederate cavalry. Both Wheeler and Van Dorn would formally have control of the two cavalry corps of the Army of Tennessee.[27]

Thomas Jordan, a graduate of Dickinson College, was an attorney in Harrisburg, Pennsylvania, before the war. When the war began, he was an aide to Major General William Keim and served in the East early in the war. When the 9th Pennsylvania Cavalry was organized, Jordan was commissioned major and subsequently gained command of the regiment. He was captured at Tompkinsville, Kentucky, when his battalion was surprised by Confederate cavalry during John Hunt Morgan's Kentucky raid in July 1862. He remained a prisoner until he was exchanged in December 1862.[28]

Major Leonidas S. Scranton, commanding the 2nd Michigan Cavalry, reported the relative position and strength of the enemy Coburn faced. Scranton also reported what he thought were the indications of a trap being set for the advancing Union column but Coburn thought "the major unnecessarily alarmed." Scranton, who would serve throughout the war with the 2nd Michigan Cavalry, was forty years old and a native of Covington, New York. He was a surveyor before the war and had been elected to the office of Register of Deeds in Kent County, Michigan.[29]

Colonel Thomas Jefferson Jordan, Dickinson College graduate and attorney, commanded the 9th Pennsylvania Cavalry (MOLLUS-MASS Civil War Collection, United States Army Heritage and Education Center, Military History Institute, Carlisle, Pennsylvania).

The skirmishing resulted in a stalemate on March 4. On March 5 Coburn awoke to what he thought to be an absence of the enemy. Colonel Thomas Jordan, commanding the Union cavalry, was convinced the Confederate force facing Coburn was large. Jordan urged Coburn to obtain reinforcements before advancing but, he wrote, "failed to convince him." Soon Confederate troops were discovered in front of the Union column but fell back, drawing Coburn's soldiers closer to a strong Confederate position. As Coburn advanced to silence Confederate artillery he found he had walked into a trap and Confederates who had concealed themselves behind a stone wall rose and unleashed volleys into the unsuspecting Union lines. Under the fire of the concentrated Southern attack the Union troops battled but began to withdraw. Coburn determined he would have to fall back toward Franklin if Jordan could hold the road open for him. Captain Marshall Thatcher, 2nd Michigan, explained the Union artillery was useless because it had been placed between two hills by Coburn and there was no way to fire on the enemy. The Confederate attack pushed Coburn away from his escape route and he was becoming encircled. Colonel Jordan noted the enemy artillery "literally rained upon them," forcing the troopers to the rear and also noted he issued orders to withdraw some of the artillery about to be captured by the charging Confederate lines. After the five-hour battle, Coburn surrendered when he was encircled, resulting in a loss of 48 killed, 247 wounded, and 1,446 captured.[30]

The reports of the action at Thompson's Station by Coburn and Jordan are very different. Coburn placed much of the blame for his defeat on the Union cavalry, which rode from the field of battle. Most scholars support Jordan's action, as he successfully prevented the cavalry and artillery from being captured while he tried to maintain an escape route for the infantry. Coburn had been alerted to the situation on the previous day by Jordan and did not use his cavalry on the second day to ascertain the position of the enemy he faced. But certainly when Jordan withdrew with the artillery Coburn lost about 1,000 men and with them any hope of reaching the escape route. Rosecrans summarized the defeat as a want of caution in Coburn's advance and indecision on the part of Brigadier General Charles Gilbert, Coburn's superior officer, about reinforcing him. A court of inquiry demonstrated that Coburn never asked for reinforcements from Gilbert. However, much finger pointing resulted after this engagement. Colonel Emerson Opdycke, 125th Ohio Infantry, wrote to his wife on March 26 from Franklin and claimed the disaster at Thompson's Station was Coburn's fault "owing to his rashness," despite Coburn's attempt to shift the blame to the cavalry.[31]

Small Cavalry Expeditions from Murfreesboro

On March 4, while Colonel Jordan was involved in the action at Thompson's Station, Minty led detachments of all three Union cavalry brigades with orders to drive the Confederate cavalry out of Rover, Tennessee, at which Minty was successful. Minty's cavalry totaling 863 troopers drove about 600 Southern troopers to within five miles of Shelbyville, bagging 51 prisoners along the way. "The 7th Penn was ahead with their sabres. They won't stand the sabres," noted Lieutenant Albert Potter, expressing pride in what would be named Minty's Saber Brigade.[32]

On March 9 Minty's command ventured to Thompson's Station and sparred with Colonel Frank Armstrong's Southern troopers along the way before pushing them aside. A soldier of the 121st Ohio Infantry observed Minty's troopers passing: "Artillery, wagons, cavalry & troops, to battle trod." Minty initially pushed Armstrong's troopers before him but realized he faced a larger Confederate force immediately to his rear. He broke off the pursuit, not because he faced stiffer resistance but because he was waiting on a second column of cavalry commanded by Brigadier General Green Clay Smith, former colonel of the 4th Kentucky Cavalry, who was serving as brigade commander. Joseph Vale incredulously observed that Smith had halted his column and moved into battle line "fourteen miles away from the enemy, anticipating an attack!" Minty's problems with Smith were not over. On March 11 Minty's First Brigade advanced upon another Confederate force, sending it quickly to the rear. Minty sought approval from Smith to start a vigorous pursuit only to be denied by Smith, who felt he might suffer the same fate Coburn had at Thompson's Station.[33]

The skirmishing continued. Colonel Thomas Jordan led another expedition with the 9th Pennsylvania, 7th Kentucky, 4th Kentucky and 2nd Michigan cavalries to Spring Hill on March 19 and pushed a large group of Southern cavalry before them. The next day Minty's brigade provided reconnaissance for Colonel Albert Hall's infantry brigade, which resulted in an intense skirmish that repulsed John Hunt Morgan's cavalry at Vaught's Hill.

While the Union cavalry was having some successes, their adversaries were having successes of their own. On March 25 Nathan Bedford Forrest's Southern cavalry attacked and captured Lieutenant Colonel Edward Bloodgood's 400-man command, which defended a station of the Nashville & Decatur Railroad at Brentwood. Bloodgood found the enemy had encircled his stockade and cut his communications and reluctantly surrendered. The 9th Pennsylvania, 6th Kentucky, 4th Kentucky and 2nd Michigan cavalries commanded by Brigadier General Green Clay Smith pursued Forrest's cavalry in possession of the booty captured at Brentwood. The Union cavalry fought to a standstill after recapturing most of the wagons taken at Brentwood. As the Confederate cavalry counterattacked, they had to abandon the wagons. William Thomas, 9th Pennsylvania, recorded, "We recaptured 5 of our teams back, but had to leave them in the hands of the Rebs again."[34]

Another minor skirmish occurred on March 27 when a small detachment of the 3rd Ohio Cavalry was sent to aid William B. Hazen's 41st Ohio Infantry. The 3rd Ohio, rushing ahead of Hazen's regiment, faced a much larger force of two regiments of Confederate cavalry and were soon surrounded but were able to cut their way through the encirclement with a loss of eleven men. The 3rd Ohio had its hands full, even after cutting its way out, fighting a determined running rearguard action. The significance of this event linked three men even after the war. Hazen's report of the action to Brigadier General James A. Garfield, Rosecrans' chief of staff, thanked Garfield for sending the cavalry ahead. However, David Stanley complained of the misuse of the cavalry when the infantry should have handled the situation. Moreover, Stanley questioned the useless loss of good men and retorted that the cavalry should be handled with more discretion in the future. For various reasons, Stanley, Hazen and Garfield were destined to become bitter enemies and the feud would last for years after the war.[35]

In addition to the fights with their Southern foes, many of the regiments of Union cavalry suffered health problems associated with living outdoors during the winter months. This was particularly true for some of the Tennessee regiments that suffered exceptionally high losses. For example, the 1st Tennessee cavalry lost 75 men to disease during the first six months of 1863. The 3rd Tennessee lost 48 men for the same reason and the 4th Tennessee fared similarly during the first six months. The 7th Pennsylvania also suffered through a bout of "fever." The constant exposure, poor diet (resulting in scurvy), and fatigue took its toll on the cavalry. Disease was not the only health problem. Horses and mules were large animals capable of causing problems of their own. Captain Elisha Culver, 3rd Ohio Cavalry, was "severely if not fatally kicked on the right side of his face and head," noted Daniel Prickitt. Serving in the cavalry was a dangerous occupation in Tennessee in 1863. Many of the dedicated troopers continued to ride even though they were sick, sometimes to the point of falling from the saddle.[36]

Despite the give and take with the Confederate adversaries, the camaraderie within the Union cavalry increased. The troopers of the 3rd Tennessee and 7th Pennsylvania delighted in mutual verbal exchanges and the unique accent of each regiment. The brigade officer of the day made fun of the 3rd Tennessee by commanding the troops using this language: "Now, all you critter-back fellows of the Third Tensee regiment, fall in heah—*lively now—foh toa strings*; and march ouet *endwise*—like youh sauh th' Penselvana fellows do yesterday—d___m youa, git." It took a short time for the 3rd Tennessee troopers to become "veteranized" but not before they joked that the 7th Pennsylvania would "steal their whole camp," after they had involuntarily traded their old bridles for the new ones issued to the 3rd Tennessee. Another story recorded by Major Will McTeer recounted a near disaster as the 3rd Tennessee Cavalry crossed a rain-swollen river only to have four troopers unhorsed and swept away in the torrent. McTeer noted the rescue of the men by a single member of the 4th Indiana Cavalry who "leaped into the river, with all his accoutrements and swimming to the drowning men, rescued everyone."[37]

New Regiments Arrive

New regiments slowly filled the ranks of the cavalry in the first months of 1863. The veteran 2nd Kentucky was one of the first regiments to arrive at David Stanley's cavalry in

January. The 2nd Kentucky Cavalry regiment was organized in the fall and winter of 1861 and had various assignments, including service at the Battle of Shiloh, the Union campaign in northern Alabama and Middle Tennessee, and the Battle of Perryville. The 2nd Kentucky was assigned to the Army of the Cumberland in November 1862, but it was attached to the infantry corps and was not part of the cavalry division during the Battle of Stones River. It was assigned duty to the cavalry in Tennessee in January 1863 under the command of Lieutenant Colonel Thomas P. Nicholas, the son of noted Kentucky judge Samuel Smith Nicholas.[38]

Dates of Arrival of Cavalry Regiments, January–April[39]

Regiment	Arrival at Murfreesboro
4th Indiana Cavalry	January 1863
39th Indiana Mounted Infantry	April 1863 (previously assigned to 20th Army Corps)
2nd Kentucky Cavalry	January 1863 (unattached since November 1862)
4th Kentucky Cavalry	February 1863
5th Kentucky Cavalry	February 1863
6th Kentucky Cavalry	February 1863
7th Kentucky Cavalry	March 1863
2nd Michigan Cavalry	March 1863
10th Ohio Cavalry	March 1863
9th Pennsylvania Cavalry	February 1863
1st Tennessee Cavalry	January 1863

Next the 4th, 5th, 6th and 7th Kentucky Cavalry regiments arrived for duty. The 4th Kentucky Cavalry was mustered into service in December 1861, with most of the troopers from Louisville and the surrounding counties. General Green Clay Smith assumed command of the regiment in May 1862 and continued in that capacity as the regiment moved to Tennessee in February 1863. Smith, born in Richmond, Kentucky, was 30 years old and served in the 1st Kentucky Infantry in the Mexican War. He graduated from Transylvania University in 1850 and practiced law in Richmond and Covington prior to the war. He remained active in Kentucky politics while serving in the cavalry; he was a member of the state legislature and later in the year was elected to a seat in Congress. When Smith served as brigade commander, the command of the regiment initially fell to Colonel Jesse Bayles, who resigned. Subsequently Colonel Robert Wickliffe Cooper assumed command of the regiment. Cooper, 31 years old and a native of Lexington, Kentucky, was a lieutenant in the 20th Kentucky Infantry before being promoted to lieutenant colonel and then colonel of the 4th Kentucky Cavalry. He had been taken prisoner and paroled after the Battle of Richmond, Kentucky, in August 1862.[40]

The 943-man 5th Kentucky Cavalry regiment was mustered into service on March 31, 1862, under command of Colonel David R. Haggard, but Lieutenant Colonel William T. Hoblitzell commanded the regiment when it became part of the cavalry arm of the Army of the Cumberland. Hoblitzell had served on Alexander McCook's staff and also as an aide to William Sherman. He was a native of Maryland born in 1834 and was an engineer involved in railroad construction before the war.

The 6th Kentucky Cavalry was organized in the summer of 1862 and was mustered into service in October 1862. Colonel Louis Watkins was promoted to colonel of the regiment on February 1, 1863, when it arrived for duty. The highly regarded 29 year-old was a native of Florida and a member of the National Rifles, a District of Columbia volunteer regiment, until he found the men disloyal to the Union. At that point he resigned and joined the 2nd U.S. Cavalry. He was later transferred to the 5th U.S. Cavalry and participated in the Peninsular Campaign, where he was severely wounded in the Battle of Gaines Mill. Next he was ordered to report to General Gordon Granger commanding the army in Kentucky and participated in Carter's Expedition to eastern Tennessee. He was given command of the 6th Kentucky Cavalry on February 1, 1863, based on his excellent performance in the war.[41]

Finally, the 7th Kentucky Cavalry was mustered into service on August 16, 1862, in Paris, Kentucky, initially under command of Leonidas Metcalfe. Colonel John K. Faulkner commanded the regiment when it arrived for service in March 1863. Faulkner was a native of Garrard County, Kentucky, attended Centre College in Danville and was a farmer before the war. The 27year-old Faulkner was rebuilding his regiment after the resignation of the previous colonel, Metcalfe, and had made great strides in instilling confidence in his troops. He was described as a "gallant officer" who rebuilt the 7th Kentucky Cavalry.[42]

Colonel Louis Watkins, severely wounded in the Battle of Gaines Mill, commanded the 6th Kentucky Cavalry (Library of Congress).

These four regiments would often be brigaded together during the winter and spring of 1863. For the 4th, 5th, and 6th Kentucky cavalries, their experience until this time was primarily guard and reconnaissance duty. These regiments also had experience as cavalry in Kentucky in various units prior to the organization of the Kentucky cavalry regiments such as Mundy's Battalion. They were all involved to some extent in the pursuit of Bragg in the fall of 1862. When they arrived at the Army of the Cumberland they were not veterans; nor were they green troops but they had yet to be tried in battle. Only the 7th Kentucky Cavalry had the dubious distinction of being involved in a major engagement, at Big Hill, Kentucky. During the Battle of Richmond, 4,000 Union soldiers were captured and the 7th Kentucky Cavalry regiment was "shattered," resulting in 5 men killed, 25 wounded, and 238 captured. After this event, Colonel Leonidas Metcalfe resigned, although he was cited for bravery during the battle, and Faulkner assumed command of the regiment.[43]

Also joining Stanley's cavalry was the 4th Indiana Cavalry, a regiment of 1,223 troopers organized in August 1862 in Indianapolis. They had a little experience skirmishing with Confederate cavalry but were involved in tracking John Hunt Morgan during his Christmas Raid. The regiment arrived in Murfreesboro in January under the command of John A. Platter. Company C of this regiment served as escort for Major General A.J. Smith, Sixteenth Army Corps, in Mississippi and Tennessee while the rest of the regiment was in Middle Tennessee.

Platter, 31 years old, was an Indiana native and a plasterer before the war. He started the war as a captain in the 16th Indiana Infantry, a one-year regiment. He had been severely wounded in September 1862 by a gunshot wound to the head during a skirmish in Kenucky.[44]

Perhaps the 2nd Michigan Cavalry was the most prominent regiment to arrive in 1863. The 2nd Michigan was a veteran regiment, organized and mustered into service in Detroit in October 1861. It produced very notable commanders: Colonel Robert Minty, Colonel Archibald Campbell, General Gordon Granger (its first colonel) and General Phil Sheridan. Its service included action at New Madrid and Island Number 10, the Siege of Corinth, the pursuit of Bragg's army in Kentucky and the Battle of Perryville. The 2nd Michigan arrived in March ready for service with the Army of the Cumberland. When Archibald Campbell was given command of the First Cavalry Brigade, Major John Godley assumed command of the 2nd when it arrived for service. Godley, who lived in Flint, Michigan, before the war, was the first captain of Company A, which consisted of men drawn from the Saginaw Valley.

The 10th Ohio Cavalry was a green regiment. Organized in Cleveland in October 1862, its first assignment was as part of Stanley's cavalry in Middle Tennessee. The 10th Ohio arrived in Tennessee in early March and rode on its first expedition in April to Snow Hill. Colonel Charles C. Smith commanded the regiment. He was commissioned colonel of the 10th Ohio after serving as captain in the 2nd Ohio Cavalry, where he was reported to be one of the "best officers" of the regiment. He was born in Lawrence County, Ohio, in 1828 and later moved to Painesville, where he was an engineer before the war.[45]

The 9th Pennsylvania Cavalry, also known as Lochiel Cavalry, was organized in the fall of 1861. The officers of the regiment were Colonel Edward C. Williams, Lieutenant Colonel Thomas C. James and Major Thomas Jefferson Jordan. The regiment served in Kentucky beginning in May 1862, sparring with Confederate cavalry and guerrillas, and it participated in actions around Perryville in October 1862 and the East Tennessee raid in December and early January 1863. Its nickname, Lochiel Cavalry, was in honor of a Scottish clan. By January 1863 Thomas J. Jordan commanded the regiment after the resignation of Colonel Williams and Lieutenant Colonel Thomas James's unexpected death on January 1, 1863. The 41-year-old, Jordan had attended Dickinson College and was an attorney in Harrisburg, Pennsylvania, before the war. He had served as an aide to Major General William Keim before joining the 9th Pennsylvania Cavalry. Captured along with three companies of cavalry near Tompkinsville, Kentucky, in July 1862, he had been exchanged in December 1862.[46]

The 1st Tennessee Cavalry was organized from the 4th Tennessee Infantry mustered into service in March 1862. The regiment was made up of men from East Tennessee, primarily Bradley, Knox, Union, Grainger, Jefferson, Greene, Hawkins and Hancock counties. The 4th Tennessee was involved in actions in eastern Tennessee and Kentucky and was part of Stevenson's retreat from Cumberland Gap. In November 1862 the regiment (1,260 troopers) was mounted and designated the 1st Tennessee Cavalry. It was commanded by Colonel Robert Johnson, son of Andrew Johnson, military governor of Tennessee. The cavalry regiment's first duty was to pursue John Hunt Morgan during his Christmas Raid into Kentucky in December 1862 taking up position along the Salt River at Shepherdsville, Kentucky. After Morgan's return to Tennessee, the 1st Tennessee moved to Nashville in mid–January and began its service with the Army of the Cumberland.[47]

At the end of May, Lieutenant Colonel James P. Brownlow was promoted to the rank of colonel of the 1st Tennessee Cavalry when Robert Johnson resigned due to ill health. While

Johnson commanded, allegations of excessive alcohol use were rumored. He was finally thrown out of the army for alcoholism and died of a laudanum overdose in 1869. In fact, Rosecrans had tried to intervene to stop Johnson's drinking, which "had become a subject of remark everywhere." Brownlow had been effectively commanding the regiment even before this promotion due to Johnson's incapacity. "Col Brownlow takes charge of the regt today he is by far the best officer and the most competant to command us," noted Julius Thomas of the 1st Tennessee Cavalry in June 1863. The 6-foot 6-inch Brownlow—the son of "Parson" William G. Brownlow, a preacher, newspaperman, and future governor and U.S. senator from Tennessee—was 21 years old when he assumed command of the regiment. He also had a brother in the Union army, Colonel John Bell Brownlow of the 9th Tennessee Cavalry.[48]

Colonel James Brownlow commanded the 1st Tennessee Cavalry (MOLLUS-MASS Civil War Collection, United States Army Heritage and Education Center, Military History Institute, Carlisle, Pennsylvania).

April 1863: Cavalry Action

At the beginning of April, the organization of Stanley's cavalry was set, although some of the principals had yet to arrive. As the weather improved, the action between the two stagnant armies intensified. The cavalry under Stanley improved daily and this arm of the Army of the Cumberland, which had served primarily in a defensive role, changed dramatically. As the confidence of the Union cavalry improved with training, leadership, equipment and arms, so the offensive posture grew. W.L. Curry, 1st Ohio, wrote of the change in attitude among the Union cavalry as successes mounted against their Southern adversaries. He noted the skills of the troopers improved to the point "horsemen in the regiment ... could pick up a hat or saber from the ground without dismounting."[49]

Cavalry Reorganization: Division Commanders

The final component in completing the organization of the cavalry was the assignment of permanent division and brigade commanders. Stanley, while pleased with the selection of brigade commanders, had the divisional commanders appointed by Rosecrans' headquarters and not by Stanley. Stanley was greatly displeased, and rightly so, with the selection of Brigadier General Robert Mitchell and Brigadier General John Turchin to command the two cavalry divisions. When he was informed of the men selected to command his two divisions, he was very angry at the outcome. Perhaps at the rank of major general the politics of the army became more intense and perhaps this was the source of Stanley's intense dislike of James Garfield. Whatever the case, as a result of the reorganization of the cavalry Stanley was shackled with two divisional commanders who were totally unsuitable to him. Turchin, a native Russian, was born Ivan Turchaninoff in 1822. He had been involved in the "Rape of

Athens" the previous year and had been court-martialed for actions taken in Athens, Alabama. Immediately after the conclusion of the court-martial Lincoln promoted him to the rank of brigadier general, although the court recommended he be dismissed from the service. The presiding officer of the court-martial was Brigadier General James A. Garfield. So disgusted was his commanding officer, Major General Don Carlos Buell, by the actions being taken on Turchin's behalf, that he wrote, "I…now find it necessary to relieve him from it in consequence of his utter failure to enforce discipline and render it efficient." Nevertheless, on April 17 Turchin was given command in Stanley's cavalry. Stanley's other divisional commander was Brigadier General Robert B. Mitchell, a man Stanley had known since the beginning of the war and had served with during the Wilson's Creek campaign. Mitchell, a native Ohioan, was living in Linn County, Kansas, at the beginning of the war. He was wounded while leading the 2nd Kansas Infantry at the Battle of Wilson's Creek and had most recently commanded the garrison at Nashville. Stanley rightly appraised Mitchell as a political appointee.[50]

These appointments, and obvious battles fought by Stanley to resist them, jaded Stanley's outlook. He resented Garfield's meddling in the selection of divisional officers and this alienated Stanley. He believed, correctly, that it weakened the cavalry. It is important to note he laid the blame of the selection of the division cavalry officers at the feet of Garfield, but this blame was assigned many years after the war. It was Rosecrans who made the final decision on the appointment of Turchin and Mitchell, and there is little evidence to demonstrate the full extent of Garfield's involvement in making the decisions. Stanley and Rosecrans had struggled from November through April to

Left: John Turchin commanded the Second Cavalry Division (MOLLUS-MASS Civil War Collection, United States Army Heritage and Education Center, Military History Institute, Carlisle, Pennsylvania). *Right:* Robert Mitchell commanded the First Cavalry Division (Wilson's Creek National Battlefield).

develop a skilled cavalry that could meet the enemy. Both Lewis Zahm and John Kennett resigned from the cavalry after the Battle of Stones River and had been replaced with improved commanders. Stanley had excellent officers capable of commanding divisions—Eli Long, Robert Minty, and Edward McCook—but he felt shackled with Turchin and Mitchell after making so much progress. Certainly for the remainder of 1863 David Stanley was less pleased with his time in the army than at any other time in the war.[51]

Despite Stanley's opinions of his division commanders, they had supporters within the army. Captain James Love, 8th Kansas Infantry, serving under Mitchell, wrote, "Genl Mitchell has been removed and Genl Wood is in command. Genl Mitchell is home on sick leave and is assigned to the command of a Cavalry Brigade—he is a dashing Cavalry officer if his health & wounds will allow. Our Cavalry at present is doing good service all over Dixie."[52]

Cavalry Reorganization: Brigade Commanders

Under Mitchell's command was Archibald Campbell and Edward McCook. Campbell, who began the war serving as a captain in the 2nd Michigan Cavalry and had demonstrated an exceptional ability to lead cavalry, commanded the First Brigade in the First Division. Campbell, a 34-year-old native Scotsman, was promoted to the rank of lieutenant colonel after his actions at Booneville, Mississippi, in July 1862; he was promoted to the rank of colonel during the Perryville Campaign. Captain Marshall Thatcher, 2nd Michigan, opined that Campbell "was from private life and advanced rapidly—too rapidly, perhaps, for his own good—had much to learn." The 2nd Michigan had distinguished service under the command of Campbell and, prior to his appointment, Phil Sheridan and Gordon Granger. Soon Campbell gained the respect of all who served under his command.[53]

Edward McCook, returning from a leave of absence, was again in command of a brigade of cavalry. Under Turchin's command was Robert Minty, whose performance at the Battle of Stones River secured permanent brigade command. Along with Minty, Eli Long, who was most recently an officer in the 4th U.S. Cavalry, was given command of Turchin's Second Brigade. Long was wounded in the shoulder during the Battle of Stones River. A Kentucky native, he graduated from the Kentucky Military Institute in 1855 and served along with David

Colonel Archibald Campbell, a 34-year-old native Scotsman, commanded Mitchell's First Brigade (courtesy Archives of Michigan).

Stanley in the 1st U.S. Cavalry before the war. Long was serving as escort for Buell's headquarters when the Army of the Cumberland was formed. After being wounded at the Battle of Stones River, he was appointed colonel of the 4th Ohio Volunteer Cavalry upon the resignation of John Pugh due to health reasons, in February 1863. The pipe-smoking colonel was noted for placing his favorite pipe in his teeth prior to action with the enemy. When he took over the 4th Ohio, he found a demoralized regiment with officers waiting to resign, but he made an immediate positive impact on the regiment. Captain Thomas Osborn, 4th Ohio Cavalry, noted that with the appointment of Long the regiment was stabilized and brought back to its full fighting potential. In March, Long's leadership resulted in his promotion to brigade command.[54]

Despite Stanley's unhappiness with his divisional commanders, he was pleased with the four brigade commanders who had direct command of the actions of the troopers in the field. The Union cavalry in 1863 was better prepared than the group of regiments available for duty during the Battle of Stones River.

Colonel Eli Long, a regular army cavalry officer, commanded Turchin's Second Brigade (MOLLUS-MASS Civil War Collection, United States Army Heritage and Education Center, Military History Institute, Carlisle, Pennsylvania).

When Turchin was given division command Robert Minty, initially placed in Mitchell's division, was assigned command of the First Brigade in Turchin's Second Division. Minty's experience and coolness under pressure was seen as a way of strengthening Turchin's command. This reorganization did not take place until April and May, even though the assignments were officially dated March. In the months of February through April, the various Union cavalry command designations were fluid and official reports vary on command assignment in the official records. Some of the records are postdated, with the actual changes occurring earlier or later than the official orders. For example, Thomas Jordan and G. Clay Smith both commanded brigades of cavalry at various times but this was never formally recorded in command.

Snow Hill

On April 2, General Stanley rode along with Minty, who was commanding about 1,000 troopers of the 7th Pennsylvania, 4th Michigan, 5th Tennessee and 10th Ohio cavalries along with Newell's section of Ohio artillery in a reconnaissance from Murfreesboro to Liberty. Skirmishing began with the cavalry of physician Richard M. Gano's Confederate First Brigade of Morgan's cavalry division as the column advanced toward Auburn, Tennessee. The expedition continued the next day and Minty found the enemy in a strong defensive position near Liberty. Minty's cavalry gained the enemy's flank and forced a retreat towards Snow Hill. Again, Gano's cavalry attempted to make a stand and opened on the Federal cavalry with four cannons, but Minty assigned the 4th Michigan the task to again gain the enemy's flank and sent his remaining cavalry charging forward. The Confederate cavalry again retreated to fixed defenses at Snow Hill. Stanley next ordered infantry support but the enemy retreated from Snow Hill before reinforcements arrived.[55]

Snow Hill, an important engagement, demonstrated the ability of the Union cavalry to dominate the eastern flank of both armies. In this significant action, the Union cavalry forced the retreat of Morgan's cavalry, which would be a contributing factor in the decision to remove Morgan from his position defending the eastern flank of Bragg's army.

Engagement at Franklin

On April 10, Earl Van Dorn advanced on Franklin, which made a tense and exciting morning for the Union cavalry. Van Dorn intended to march to Franklin and capture the town to relieve pressure on Bragg at Tullahoma. On April 10, Stanley took a large cavalry force of 1,600 troopers in conjunction with Major General Gordon Granger's infantry to repulse Van Dorn's forces, reportedly at a strength of 10,000–18,000 men, located near Franklin. In fact, Van Dorn advanced with about 6,000 men. Granger requested Stanley's assistance after receiving intelligence of Van Dorn's advance.[56]

This affair at Franklin, a rare case of overaggressiveness on Stanley's part, almost cost the cavalry dearly but achieved an important objective. Stanley's force included the First Brigade—4th Michigan, 7th Pennsylvania, 2 companies of the 1st Middle Tennessee, 2nd East Tennessee, 4th U.S., and Newell's artillery and his Second Brigade with 3 companies of the 3rd Indiana, and two Ohio regiments (3rd and 4th) commanded by Lieutenant Colonel Oliver Robie. Stanley camped about four miles east of Franklin on the evening of the April 9 and reached Franklin at 10:00 a.m. on April 10. Granger estimated Van Dorn's force "consisted of about 9,000 cavalry and mounted infantry and two regiments of infantry proper." Though outnumbered, David Stanley felt confident in the ability of his cavalry to meet Van Dorn. He sent a message to Rosecrans on the morning of April 10: "At 7 o'clock this morning Van Dorn was still at Spring Hill. Steedman thinks he has 18,000 men. Granger put it at 12,000. I think this latter probably about right. With one of our old divisions we could whip them out of their boots. I do not know whether it would be judicious to attack with this green force, but if you think 'the game is worth the candle,' we will slap away at them."[57]

Van Dorn marched on Franklin and met the 40th Ohio Infantry, which held its ground in the town. Stanley watched the advance and ordered a counterattack into Van Dorn's flank. He crossed his Second Brigade at Hughes Mill and the Lewisburg Pike. Once across the Harpeth River, the road forked about a mile from the pike leading to Franklin, which carried Van Dorn's column. Lieutenant Colonel Oliver Robie commanded the Second Brigade, supported by Colonel Daniel Ray's 2nd Tennessee Cavalry and Lieutenant Colonel Robert Klein's 3rd Indiana Cavalry battalion, which rode along the road that forked to the right. The 4th U.S. Cavalry rode alone on the left fork.[58]

As Stanley's cavalry advanced on the Confederate cavalry, an ex-slave was taken to him and the slave reported he had just escaped from the enemy. Stanley had ordered his cavalry to swing around Van Dorn's flank and, much to his consternation, he was told Van Dorn was moving between Stanley's troopers and Franklin with 4,000 men. To prevent his cavalry from being trapped, Stanley rushed the 4th Kentucky Cavalry (U.S.) with two cannons to Ewing's

Ford on the Big Harpeth River, but by the time the regiment reached the ford Van Dorn was already crossing. Stanley's cavalry needed the ford to avoid being encircled by Van Dorn's troopers. Fortunately, the 4th Kentucky (U.S.) was able to capture the crossing. The Union cavalry being outnumbered, they hastily moved to the ford to escape capture. In the meantime, the 4th U.S. Cavalry had captured a battery of enemy artillery, Freeman's Tennessee Battery, but the Confederate advance prevented the Union cavalry from escaping with the guns. The 4th U.S. Cavalry cut the spokes on the wheels and tried to spike the guns then hastily headed back to the ford. The Union cavalry fought off three attacks before they reached it. Fortunately, darkness prevented any further action. Although this had been a close affair for Stanley, he was able to extract his troopers. Rumors abounded about David Stanley on April 11 after the battle. Lieutenant Lewis Hanback, a member of the 27th Illinois Infantry, wrote a letter to his family about the action at Franklin: "They [Confederates] also attacked Franklin, Tenn. with a large force. But were repulsed with severe loss though I learn this evening that Gen. Stanley who commanded our cavalry, a brave and skillful officer was captured." The rumors were false, but the letter reflects the feeling of the soldiers for Stanley.[59]

Captain Potter of the 4th Michigan Cavalry wrote of the engagement at Franklin on April 14: "We were over near Franklin. Van Dorn is hovering around to see what he may devour. He made a dash into Franklin on Friday. But got rather severely handled. We killed about one hundred, officers and all, while our loss was but a trifle compared to theirs." Granger reported Van Dorn was advancing on his infantry at Franklin, and Stanley's flanking action, while dangerous for the cavalry, had caused Van Dorn to divert his attack from Franklin. Although Stanley was pushed back across the river, the Confederates moved back toward Spring Hill. Granger wrote, "Since Van Dorn's repulse, he facetiously calls his attack an armed reconnaissance in force."[60]

An unfortunate situation developed as a result of the capture of Freeman's Tennessee (CSA) artillery. Captain Samuel Freeman commanded the artillery that was captured and he was killed by Sergeant Major H.A. Strickland of the 4th U.S. Cavalry. Accusations circulated that Strickland had murdered Freeman, but members of the Union cavalry vehemently denied this. Instead, they claimed, Freeman was killed in self-defense. Regardless of which version was true, members of the Union cavalry believed that Forrest pledged never to take a member of the 4th U.S. Cavalry prisoner, and rumors circulated that Forrest would hang Strickland if he ever caught him.[61]

Expedition to McMinnville and Conflict with Washington

On April 17, Stanley was ordered to Louisville along with 1,200 of his cavalrymen who were without horses. The purpose of the trip was to at last secure mounts for his cavalry. Yet, on April 24 Rosecrans wired secretary of war Edwin Stanton that Stanley was still in Louisville and horses were not to be found. While Stanley was in Louisville, neither of the new division commanders, Turchin and Mitchell, were yet present with the cavalry. Robert Minty assumed command of the cavalry and cooperated in an expedition to McMinnville, about 40 miles southeast of Murfreesboro, with 1,700 troops of three cavalry brigades, from April 20 to 30. Under the command of Major General Joseph J. Reynolds the expedition included the various commands of mounted infantry, infantry and cavalry totaling about 7,000 men.[62]

The combination of Wilder's Mounted Infantry and Minty's cavalry surprised the Confederate cavalry at McMinnville and scattered them as the Union horsemen charged through the town. Before returning to Murfreesboro the expedition succeeded in capturing Confederate stores and destroying bridges and railroads used by Confederates. Major Will A. McTeer, 3rd Tennessee Cavalry, described the cavalry charge through the town and said a boy came running out and mounted a box at the end of the street and proudly unfurled "the stars and stripes and joyously waved it to cheer us on…. This was something we had not met anywhere in Middle Tennessee, so that it raised the spirits of tired and worn soldiers until they were ready to do and to dare anything." At McMinnville, the cavalry captured Major Dick McCann, a notorious guerrilla, and various accounts of his capture were recorded; but unfortunately for the Union cavalry, McCann escaped and returned to the Confederate lines.[63]

Not everyone in McMinnville welcomed Minty's cavalry. Lucy Virginia French, an ardent secessionist, exclaimed, "How I did hate them! That imp of the devil, McKenzie, after he had been up stairs and searched for provisions—met Mollie in the hall and said to her in the hatefullest, taunting way, 'is that all ye got? if it is I pity ye!' Oh how I did want to kill him—the reptile!—They did not behave as badly in town as they did here." French made extensive notations of the Union raid and search for McCann. French had reasons to be angry with the Union cavalry, which did extensive damage during the expedition. John McLain, 4th Michigan Cavalry, described it: "We burnt the depot and railroad buildings and mill, burnt 1 train, 2 passenger cars, 8 flat cars, 2 engines and their load, captured the mail and burnt 2 bridges." McLain noted McCann escaped due to drunkenness on the part of the Union guards.[64]

During this expedition Colonel Eli Long clashed with two of the officers of the 2nd Kentucky (U.S.) Cavalry on April 21. Captain Owen Star told Long he didn't think the expedition could be carried out by his regiment. Colonel Long replied, "I gave him to understand that he was at perfect liberty to do as he chose." But Long advised him to keep up with the rest of the cavalry, which was determined to carry out its assignment. Captain John D. Wickliffe, originally assigned to command the 2nd Kentucky, became ill and had turned command over to Star. To make matters worse, the ill Wickliffe fell from his horse and spilled a batch of letters on the ground. This being noticed by the provost marshal, it was found they were letters written to Confederate soldiers. Long later spoke to Wickliffe, who explained that the letters, written by citizens of his hometown, were to be taken to the Confederate lines under a flag of truce. Kentucky, being a border state, had soldiers fighting on both sides. Wickliffe was returned to duty. The local newspapers in Kentucky reported the "illness" as drunkenness, but Wickliffe strongly denied the allegation.[65]

New Regiments, Streight's Expedition, Rosecrans Battles Washington

As the expansion of regiments in the Army of the Cumberland developed in the spring of 1863 the issue of mounted infantry took an unfortunate turn when Colonel Abel D. Streight led a newly formed mounted infantry brigade too far to the rear of Bragg's army. Streight and infantry under the command of Colonel Grenville Dodge marched together and then separated with the hope General Nathan B. Forrest would follow Streight's mounted infantry. This was exactly what happened and, in May, Streight, isolated and exhausted, surrendered his entire force of 1,446 men and officers. Stanley felt this was another example of poor judgment by Garfield and through him Rosecrans. Stanley was always a proponent of well-trained and disciplined soldiers in all actions. In Stanley's criticism of the Streight affair, he clearly places the blame not on the mounted infantry but on the unwise decision by Garfield and Rosecrans, which resulted in the loss of such good soldiers. Stanley also severely criticized Streight for advocating such an attempt to ride through Confederate territory.

Giving punch to his cavalry divisions, Stanley added the 39th Indiana Mounted Infantry to his regiments in April. The experienced regiment was mustered in August 1861 and saw service during the Battle of Shiloh, the Siege of Corinth, and the pursuit of Bragg's army in October 1862. The regiment was posted on the Union right flank during the Battle of Stones River and suffered about 380 causalities during the battle. It was mounted in April and joined the cavalry corps. The 39th Indiana was commanded by Colonel Thomas Jefferson Harrison, a 40-year-old Kentucky native who had lived in Indiana since he was a boy. He attended Wabash College and practiced law after he graduated, served as state legislator prior to the war and served in a three-month regiment, the 6th Indiana Infantry, at the beginning of the war in western Virginia.[66]

By April 20 Washington had quite enough of Rosecrans' constant appeals for a plethora of items needed and the increasingly frustrated general-in-chief, Halleck, responded that Rosecrans made more requests than any other general in the army: "For example, you have telegraphed at least a dozen, and, perhaps, twenty times in the last few months that you require more cavalry. The Government is fully aware of your wants, and has been doing all in its power to supply them. It certainly was not necessary to remind it every day and every hour of its duty." Rosecrans had remained stationary in Middle Tennessee for four months while building his army and he sent many telegrams demanding immediate action. The War Department finally came to the end of its tether and soon the demands would be on Rosecrans to make a move against Bragg. But in regard to the cavalry, Rosecrans was justified in his demands for more regiments. At the end of April, Rosecrans had slightly fewer than 5,000 troopers.[67]

The relationship between Rosecrans and Washington took a decided downturn in April. Not only did Halleck take Rosecrans to task regarding the constant requests for matériel, on April 28 he again chastised Rosecrans for wishing to seize horses and mules from loyal citizens: "I do not precisely understand why you so often urge me to give you authority to violate the law. If you wish to violate the law, you certainly should not throw upon me the responsibility of your illegal acts." The exultant tone of the communications between the two in January had turned clearly antagonistic by April. Even the quartermaster general, M.C. Meigs, who had endeavored diligently to fulfill all of Rosecrans' needs, joined in the exchanges with Rosecrans' suggesting the misuse of horses and mules. Meigs noted he had sent 14,063 horses and 11,842 mules since November: "Is efficiency gained by service which breaks down horses, tasking them beyond their strength? Three cavalry regiments have been broken down by long return marches, without necessity marching 50 miles a day returning to camp." In a series of unpleasant exchanges, Rosecrans and Meigs argued about the use of animals and the actual number of serviceable animals on hand. Again, whoever was correct is less important than the tenor of the communications between the Army of the Cumberland and Washington. There was no doubt the warm relationship between Washington and Rosecrans had come to an end.[68]

Stanley probably agreed with Meigs. He noted that Rosecrans was "given to sending cavalry upon aimless raids, invariably resulting in using up their cavalry without accomplishing anything." Certainly Stanley's cavalry worked hard during the first months of 1863.[69]

May 1863 Cavalry Action

The month of May began with increased activity on both sides. Colonel Archibald Campbell's First Cavalry Brigade skirmished with the enemy near Thompson's Station, bagging 24 prisoners and killing 2. On May 5, Lieutenant Colonel James Brownlow's 1st Tennessee Cavalry surprised the 4th Tennessee Cavalry (CSA) near Caney Fork. Brownlow succeeded in capturing Colonel Baxter Smith, commander of the 4th Tennessee, along with a lieutenant and two privates. The Confederates counterattacked the Union cavalry in an attempt to free Smith but Brownlow succeeded in returning with his prize. Despite the constant skirmishes, the morale of the Union cavalry was high even in the area where Van Dorn and Forrest had been successful. Colonel Thomas Jordan, 9th Pennsylvania Cavalry, wrote his wife on May 5 that Van Dorn was close to his regiment but he didn't except further trouble from the Confederate cavalry. He told her his regiment was in a good position and that he hoped Van Dorn would attack. He exclaimed, "I wish he would try it, and give us a chance of walloping him soundly."[70]

David Stanley's unhappiness about his Second Division commander could not be expressed more clearly than his report demonstrated after the expedition to Middleton, Tennessee, which occurred from May 1 through May 22. Stanley discovered "a force of the cavalry of the enemy was lying about carelessly at Middleton. I started on the evening of the 21st, with a portion of General Turchin's division and Colonel Thomas Harrison's 39th Indiana Infantry (Mounted) regiment, to attack them. I was furnished by General Sheridan with the best guide I have ever yet followed." Stanley approached the Confederate camp during the evening and remained about three miles away, intending to attack at dawn. On the morning of May 22, he rode along with Lieutenant O'Connell of the 4th U.S. Cavalry, the advance element of his cavalry. He ordered the remainder of the cavalry to follow his advance. General Turchin commanded the remainder of the cavalry and Colonel Harrison's regiment of mounted infantry followed. After riding for about a mile and a half, Stanley looked to his rear:

> [T]o my surprise and indignation, [I] saw no one following. At the same instant I heard shots in front. I sent one orderly after another, and finally rode as fast as my jaded horse could carry me back, and found the entire column at a walk and turned upon a by-road at direct right angle to the road we were going on. By tours, by companies, and by squadrons I turned them back, and soon arrived in the enemy's camp, to find that Lieutenant O'Connell, to whom the word gallant applies, not as a compliment, but in its true old English signification, had, with his intrepid squadron, whipped the enemy out of his three camps. The rebels, with the exception of a few men in the Eighth Confederate Regiment and some Georgians, escaped to the cedar thicket—literally *sans culottes*. An attempt at a stand was made by the fugitives 1 mile from Fosterville, but they fled upon the approach of our support.[71]

Although this was a successful attack by the 4th U.S. Cavalry, the Confederate cavalry escaped and Stanley settled for "800 stand of arms, all the camp equipage and saddles, blankets, and clothing in all the camps, some wagons, and, perhaps, captured about 300 horses."

However, from the reports of some of Stanley's regiments, the 4th Ohio Cavalry, 3rd Ohio Cavalry, 3rd Indiana Cavalry, and 7th Pennsylvania Cavalry all contained notations suggesting the embarrassment of not being in position to support the 4th U.S. Cavalry. The wrath of Stanley fell on Turchin in Stanley's sharp report to James A. Garfield as chief of staff.[72]

Stanley described Turchin in his memoirs as "a fat short-legged Russian, who could not ride a horse." The apologetic reports submitted by Stanley's regimental commanders carried the same message. In Stanley's report, he wrote the following:

> My staff officers came and told me that General Turchin, was not supporting me and indeed had not followed me. I was in the presence of two thousand rebels with only one hundred men. Turchin, after receiving the order to gallop, had deliberately commanded trot, and although the road we were on was broad and plain, he deliberately led his column into a wood road at right angles to the main road and leading away from the sound of the battle. The fight for our small force was becoming perilous, when relief came in the shape of a charge over the fields by Colonel Eli Long's and Colonel H.G. Minty's Brigades. The valiant and brilliant soldiers heard our firing and without waiting for orders, threw down fences and charged across the fields to our rescue.[73]

After this incident, Stanley reported directly to General Rosecrans and marched into his headquarters. He declared Rosecrans could choose between Stanley and Turchin. Rosecrans chose to keep Stanley. Turchin would be formally relieved of duty in the cavalry in July 1863. William H. Sinclair, assistant adjutant general, informed Stanley by messenger of Turchin's exit in July from the cavalry: "Turchin relieved of duty this morning. Good!" Once Stanley had an opportunity to reflect on Turchin's lack of support at Middleton, Tennessee, he concluded Turchin simply could not ride. Stanley described his riding style as of one who is sitting in a rocking chair; he concluded that the fact Turchin did not gallop or charge was because he was afraid he would fall off the horse. More disturbing was Stanley's description of Turchin's leadership style, which called to mind the actions in Athens, Alabama: "A perfectly cold blooded foreigner—he did not care a fig what became of me or of the few men who followed me. He did not care to be jostled in a rush of cavalry for anybody's sake.... Garfield who was everlastingly looking out for votes, had imposed Turchin on the cavalry without any inquiry as to his fitness."[74] Turchin's wife chronicled her feelings about her husband's time in the cavalry: "My husband—despite his learning (which they cannot deny, ignorant as they are), despite his distinguished manners and his noble bearing does not count for much with them."[75]

The unhappiness of Stanley with the way the cavalry was handled was evident in his writings after the Battle of Stones River. In his reflections later in his life on the organization of the cavalry, he included disappointment in Garfield and also Rosecrans. Garfield agreed to serve as Rosecrans' chief of staff in February after the death of Julius P. Garesche during the Battle of Stones River. After Garfield's appointment the relationship between Stanley and Rosecrans cooled somewhat. Stanley would write,

> Garfield disgraced himself eventually on Rosecrans' staff and the latter did himself great discredit by listening to such humbugs.... Neither Rosecrans, Sherman or Grant ever understood the true uses of cavalry. All these commanders were given to sending cavalry upon aimless raids, invariably resulting in using up their cavalry without accomplishing anything. Generals Thomas and Sheridan had more correct views of cavalry and used it to protect their flanks, to keep themselves in order of battle, and then ... threw the whole cavalry upon the enemy's flank at the critical time of the battle and crushed the opposing force. This is true application of cavalry.[76]

While the Union cavalry had troubles, violence erupted in the Confederate cavalry. On May 7 Earl Van Dorn, who had been commanding Bragg's cavalry on the left flank and causing so much trouble near Franklin, was shot and killed by an outraged husband, Dr. James Bodie Peters. Van Dorn was reported to be having an affair with Peters' wife. While Van Dorn sat at his desk at his headquarters, Dr. Peters shot him and killed him. Nathan Bedford Forrest assumed command of the cavalry previously commanded by Van Dorn.

As Stanley's cavalry faced its Confederate adversaries in May, he found John Hunt Morgan's cavalry gone. Morgan had been ordered along the Cumberland River in Kentucky. Stanley had effectively gained enough successes during April along Morgan's line of defense that Morgan's reputation declined to such an extent Wheeler dispatched him to a place he could rest and regain his confidence. John Wharton's cavalry brigade took over the position previously held in Wheeler's line. Morgan's cavalry regained its strength and in July of 1863 participated in another raid into Kentucky and Indiana in July 1863.[77] In addition, the pressure from Washington began to intensify by urging Rosecrans to move against Bragg. On May 18, Halleck advised Rosecrans the best way to neutralize an apparent Confederate concentration of force was to move against Bragg in Tennessee. Rosecrans replied, "If I had 6,000 cavalry, in addition to the mounting of the 2,000 now waiting horses, I would attack Bragg within three days. As it is, all my corps commanders and chief of cavalry are opposed to an advance, which, they think, hazards more than the probable gains." Halleck simply replied to Rosecrans that there were no more cavalry regiments available for him.[78]

The Union cavalry obtained another 800 horses from Kentucky during May. Major Peter Mathews, 4th Ohio Cavalry, was in charge of the animals as they were unloaded from the boats on the Ohio River. Mathews communicated to David Stanley that the horses were ready for service but told him not to send any Kentuckians, who were more interested in visiting, or sick officers, who were not interested in work. Mathews had two sick officers from the 7th Pennsylvania Cavalry "who have not done an hour's work since they came here." It took seventy-five to one hundred men to escort a shipment of horses by train to Tennessee.[79]

Finally, May ended with President Lincoln gently trying to persuade Rosecrans into moving against Bragg. On May 28 the president wrote, "I would not push you to any rashness, but I am very anxious that you do your utmost, short of rashness, to keep Bragg from getting on to help Johnston against Grant."[80]

June 1863 Cavalry Action—New Regiments Arrive

June began with Washington's continued pressure on Rosecrans to move against Bragg. On June 3 Henry Halleck telegrammed Rosecrans: "If you cannot hurt the enemy now, he will soon hurt you." This message followed a veiled threat from Halleck the day before: "If you can do nothing yourself, a portion of your troops must be sent to Grant's relief." Washington watched as Grant besieged Vicksburg. Because the siege was lasting so long there was the threat that Confederate General Joseph Johnston could concentrate a force great enough to punch a hole in Grant's lines, allowing Pemberton's army to escape. Halleck needed Rosecrans to advance and hold Bragg's troops in place; but Rosecrans had finally gotten the message and realized it was time to move.[81]

David Stanley watched the quarrel between Halleck and Rosecrans as a trusted member of Rosecrans' army. He observed as Rosecrans' constant appeals for more supplies finally fall upon deaf ears in Washington and saw that Rosecrans refused to move until spring crops were mature and could be used by the advancing army as it foraged for supplies. Stanley wrote, "Rosy was powerful then, but his head was marked and it only awaited the slightest excuse to bring his dooms day."[82]

While Rosecrans delayed, James A. Garfield committed the indiscretion of writing his dissatisfaction with the inaction of the army to secretary of the treasury, Salmon Chase: "I cannot conceal from you the fact that I have been greatly tried and dissatisfied with the slow progress that we have made in this department since the battle of Stone River.... Thus far the General [Rosecrans] had been singularly disinclined to grasp the situation with a strong hand and make the advantage his own." That slip on the part of Garfield would haunt both Rosecrans in the upcoming months and Garfield in the future.[83]

As Stanley prepared his troopers for active campaigning, the men were trained to travel "light." The large Sibley tents, which comfortably housed a dozen or more soldiers, were replaced with "dog" tents, which accommodated only two men. W.R. Carter, 1st Tennessee Cavalry, noted, "This new-fangled tent was very appropriately named by the boys, and was little better than no tent." In addition, the cavalryman's "haversack contains his rations, while from his belt or saddle clatters a small coffeepot or pail, and in less than a half-hour after a halt the veteran knows how to prepare a wholesome meal of bacon, coffee and crackers, familiarly known as "hard-tack.""[84]

Dates of Arrival of Cavalry Regiments (May–June)

Regiment	Arrival at Murfreesboro
5th Iowa Cavalry	June 1863
1st Wisconsin Cavalry	June 1863
Chicago Board of Trade Battery, Illinois Light Artillery (Stokes)	June 1863

Stanley received two final cavalry regiments and one battery of artillery in June. The Chicago Board of Trade Artillery was organized and mustered into service as a response to a call from President Lincoln for 3,000 recruits. The battery was mustered into service on August 1, 1862, under the command Captain James H. Stokes and boasted six James rifled six-pounder field artillery guns; however, it exchanged four six-pound guns for four smooth-bored ones. The battery first met the enemy in October in Lawrenceburg, Kentucky, and gained the attention of the Army of the Cumberland with outstanding service during the Battle of Stones River on December 31. The battery was ordered to service with the cavalry effective May 16, 1863, as horse artillery but retained its guns. The Chicago Board of Trade became the only battery of horse artillery for the cavalry in contrast to light artillery of the other batteries. A six-pound gun was captured from the enemy and used to replace a disabled one. After the battle, Rosecrans made this a seven-gun battery in recognition of its performance during the battle.[85]

Born in 1814, Captain James H. Stokes was mustered in as captain of the battery. He graduated seventeenth in his class at West Point in 1835. He was a Marylander by birth and served in the U.S. Army until 1843 in the artillery and as a quartermaster. He was involved in manufacturing and railroading prior to the war.[86]

The 5th Iowa Cavalry regiment, originally organized companies A–D as the "Curtis Horse" by the order of Major General John C. Fremont in Omaha, Nebraska; Company E in Dubuque; Company F in Missouri (Fremont's Hussars); Company H organized at Benton Barracks, Missouri; Companies G, I, K as 1st, 2nd and 3rd Independent Companies; Minnesota Cavalry at Fort Snelling, Minnesota; Company L as Naughton's Irish Dragoons at Jefferson City, Missouri; and finally Company "M" as Osage Rifles at St. Louis. All the companies were organized from September through the end of December 1861. The various components of the regiment were consolidated as the 5th Iowa Cavalry in June 1862, which was assigned to the Army of the Cumberland in June 1863 and arrived on June 11, 1863. The regiment had various duties during the war, including participating in the Siege of Corinth, but it spent most of its time around Fort Henry, Fort Heiman, and Fort Donelson in late 1862 and into 1863. The 5th Iowa Cavalry was reportedly nicknamed "Lowe's Hell Hounds" by the troopers of Forrest's cavalry.[87]

The 5th Iowa was commanded by Colonel William Warren Lowe, who was born in 1841 in Greencastle, Indiana. Lowe was a West Point graduate, class of 1853. He served in the 2nd U.S. Cavalry prior to the war and spent a great deal of time in Texas after leaving the United States Military Academy. He served in the defense of Washington, D.C., in 1861 and participated in the First Battle of Bull Run. Lieutenant Colonel Mathewson T. Patrick—born in Pennsylvania about 1832 and a resident of Omaha, Nebraska, prior to the war—commanded the regiment in June 1863 due to Lowe's temporary absence.[88]

The 1st Wisconsin Cavalry was organized during the fall and winter of 1861 and was mustered into service in March 1862 with the original strength of 1,124 men. The regiment had extensive duty in Missouri and Arkansas skirmishing with various Confederate regiments. Part of the 2nd Battalion was attacked at L'Anguille Ferry, Arkansas, while loaded down with wagons and freed slaves; various accounts of the engagement exist. Reportedly many of the ex-slaves were "shot down in cold blood," reinforcing for this regiment the brutality of the war. In the spring of 1863 the request for the 1st Wisconsin Cavalry was made by Rosecrans and the regiment arrived in Middle Tennessee in mid–June.[89]

In June 1863, the 1st Wisconsin was commanded by Colonel Oscar La Grange. Born in Fulton, New York, in April 1837, La Grange's family moved to Ripon, Wisconsin, when he was a child. Later an ardent abolitionist, he traveled to Kansas while still in his teens to assist in the anti-slavery efforts in that state. He attended Ripon College and the University of Wisconsin. La Grange continued his strong anti-slavery actions and helped an abolitionist editor escape from a Milwaukee jail in 1860. He evaded arrest and in April 1861 aided in the organization of the "Ripon Rifles," company D of the 4th Wisconsin Infantry. Four months later he was elected major in the 1st Wisconsin Cavalry, and in June 1862

Colonel William W. Lowe, a regular army cavalry officer before the war, commanded the 5th Iowa Cavalry (**MOLLUS-MASS Civil War Collection, United States Army Heritage and Education Center, Military History Institute, Carlisle, Pennsylvania**).

he was promoted to the rank of lieutenant colonel. In February, he was commissioned colonel of the regiment. The fiery La Grange "enjoyed nothing more than a headlong cavalry charge, when he was in the front rank." Another observer said, "He looked like a berserker, and was full of daring. His fixed rule was to let no man get deeper into the battle than himself."[90]

By June 15, Stanley had an impressive group of cavalry regiments:

Colonel Oscar La Grange, commander of the 1st Wisconsin Cavalry, "enjoyed nothing more than a headlong cavalry charge" (MOLLUS-MASS Civil War Collection, United States Army Heritage and Education Center, Military History Institute, Carlisle, Pennsylvania).

CAVALRY
Major General David S. Stanley

FIRST CAVALRY DIVISION
Brigadier General Robert B. Mitchell

First Brigade	*Second Brigade*
Colonel Archibald P. Campbell	**Colonel Edward M. McCook**
4th Kentucky, Col. Wickliffe Cooper	2nd Indiana, Lt. Col. Robert R. Stewart
6th Kentucky, Col. Louis D. Watkins	4th Indiana, Lt. Col. John A. Platter
7th Kentucky, Col. John K. Faulkner	5th Kentucky, Lt. Col. William T. Hoblitzell
2nd Michigan, Maj. John C. Godley	2nd Tennessee, Col. Daniel M. Ray
9th Pennsylvania, Col. Thomas J. Jordan	1st Wisconsin, Col. Oscar H. La Grange
1st Tennessee, Lt. Col. James P. Brownlow	

SECOND CAVALRY DIVISION
Brigadier General John B. Turchin

First Brigade	*Second Brigade*
Colonel Robert H.G. Minty	**Colonel Eli Long**
3rd Indiana [West Batt], Lt. Col. Robert Klein	2nd Kentucky, Col. Thomas P. Nicholas
5th Iowa, Lt. Col. Matthewson T. Patrick	1st Ohio, Col. Beroth B. Eggleston
4th Michigan, Maj. Frank W. Mix	3rd Ohio, Lt. Col. Charles B. Seidel
7th Pennsylvania, Lt. Col. William B. Sipes	4th Ohio, Lt. Col. Oliver P. Robie
5th Tennessee, Col. William B. Stokes	10th Ohio, Col. Charles C. Smith
4th United States, Capt. James B. McIntyre	Stokes's (Illinois) battery, Capt. James H. Stokes
1st Ohio Artillery, Battery D (one section), Lieut. Nathaniel M. Newell	

Unattached
39th Indiana Infantry (mounted), Col. Thomas J. Harrison

Concluding Cavalry Actions in June

Turchin would continue to command the Second Cavalry Division into July and the trouble with him continued on June 3. Minty's First Brigade came under attack by a "brigade of rebel cavalry and mounted infantry, with seven pieces of artillery," along the Manchester Pike and the Wartrace Road just south of Murfreesboro. Minty's brigade was soon in the saddle riding southward along the Manchester Pike and Wartrace Road to insure no further enemy probes occurred and to support to the 7th Pennsylvania and 4th Michigan cavalries, which were skirmishing with the enemy. Minty rode to find Turchin, who was watching a review of Negley's division. Minty reported the situation and Turchin ordered him to take three regiments along the Manchester Pike to meet the enemy. Minty, in what could only be described as an attempt to teach Turchin how to command cavalry, "suggested" an alternative command: "…my representing to him that Major Mix was engaged on the Wartrace road with a superior force, and that by going out on that road I could support him, and also take the attacking force on the Manchester road in flank and rear." Minty rode forward with the approved plan and brought Newell's 1st Ohio Artillery and repulsed the advance with only minor casualties.[91]

Meanwhile, outside Franklin the enemy continued probing the Union lines attempting to capitalize on any mistakes. On June 4, three brigades and two regiments of Forrest's cavalry advanced on Franklin planning to surround the town occupied by Gordon Granger's troops. The Union cavalry rode to meet the threat. Amid the "clatter of hoofs, sabers, and spurs" Colonel Archibald Campbell's First Cavalry Brigade of Mitchell's division sparred with Frank Armstrong's cavalry, repulsing the advance in a brisk skirmish that resulted in a serious wound to Colonel John K. Faulkner, 7th Kentucky, and Colonel Wickliffe Cooper, 4th Kentucky, when he suffered a severe fall from his horse. Private Tom Dixon, 2nd Michigan, and his company were ambushed from the flank and the troopers dismounted with their revolving rifles. Their horses were lost in the subsequent volleys and a Confederate yelled, "Cut down the cowardly S____ b____!" when the 2nd Michigan's volley knocked him off his horse. Dixon remarked after capturing the officer who was wounded, "Learn to keep a civil tongue in your head, will you!"[92] Colonel Thomas Jordan, 9th Pennsylvania Cavalry, wrote to his wife: "I did not fire a shot, but charged the enemy with the sabre…. Col. Faulkner 7th Ky was so badly wounded that I fear he will die although he was not so exposed as I was."[93]

A few days later, in one of the most brazen incidents of the war, Colonel Louis Watkins, 6th Kentucky Cavalry, discovered two spies attempting to determine the strength and position of the Union troops at Franklin. On the afternoon of June 6 Colonel Orton and Major Dunlap arrived at the Union headquarters at Franklin with orders from the secretary of war to make a "critical inspection" of the troops in Tennessee. After the inspection by the two officers, the commander of the garrison hosted the two at lunch. After lunch, Colonel Louis Watkins and his orderly sergeant observed the men, and Watkins recognized Orton as a Confederate officer. The two officers were returned to the garrison headquarters and Watkins pulled the sword from Orton's scabbard. Written on the sword was "C.S.A." and both men were arrested. Colonel Thomas Jordan was the president of the "military commission" that tried the men and found them guilty. The two were hanged the next day as spies. Jordan wrote his wife that he pitied the men but declared "death is the lot of the spy."[94]

The daily skirmishing continued. Because of the increased Confederate cavalry activity around Franklin, Gordon Granger requested Robert Mitchell's First Cavalry Division. On June 11, the enemy again probed Granger's defenses, but Edward McCook's and Archibald Campbell's cavalry brigades were on hand to drive the enemy back across the Harpeth River. The skirmishing was brisk and resulted in 28 casualties for the Union cavalry, while Mitchell reported 23 enemies killed and an unknown number of wounded.[95]

Summary of January 6–June 22, 1863

The cavalry actions during the first six months of 1863 resulted in varying degrees of success for each army. Historian Michael Bradley summarized the results of the engagements of Wheeler on the east and Forrest and Van Dorn on the west of the Confederate defensive line. Rosecrans was far more successful in these encounters with Wheeler and Morgan and in turn was roughly handled by Van Dorn and Forrest on the west.

Results of Cavalry Actions on the Eastern and Western Flanks[96]

Western Flank	Eastern Flank
March 3, Thompson's Station: Confederate Victory	March 1, Bradyville: Union Victory
March 24, Brentwood: Confederate Victory	March 19–20, Liberty: Union Victory
April 10, Franklin: Confederates Achieved Goals	April 3, Snow Hill: Union Victory
April 29–May 3, Streight's Raid: Confederate Victory	April 19, McMinnville: Union Victory

For six months the Federal and Confederate cavalries probed each other's line and W.L. Curry, 1st Ohio Cavalry, described the stalemate as the two sides "glaring at each other like two gladiators, watching for any advantage he may take over his antagonist from some weak place in his lines." But the stalemate was coming to an end. Historian Bradley concluded the successes in the cavalry action on the eastern flank decided the Union advance during the Tullahoma campaign: "Although the terrain was more challenging in the east, the success of Union cavalry probes revealed that the Confederate defenses were vulnerable in that sector and the potential rewards were much greater." The six months in the saddle had allowed Stanley to amass twenty-two regiments and had determined the route of the advance on the Confederate positions at Tullahoma.[97]

4. The Tullahoma Campaign, June 23–July 5, 1863

> ... *reflecting in full splendor the bright sabers and arms, and kissing the flags, banners, and streamers, as a harbinger of victory.*—Captain Joseph Vale

Over the six-month period following the Battle of Stones River both William Rosecrans and Braxton Bragg rebuilt their armies. By June the Union army needed a victory. Lee was marching aggressively through Maryland and Pennsylvania, and Grant was still bogged down with the siege at Vicksburg. It was incumbent on Rosecrans to put his army in motion.

The six months of rebuilding the Army of the Cumberland yielded good results for Rosecrans and David Stanley. The army had swelled in size and Stanley now commanded two strong divisions of cavalry boasting twenty-two regiments and a mounted infantry regiment, which were well supplied with the most advanced weapons. Stanley's cavalry now had the ability to protect Rosecrans' supply line while providing offensive duty.

The Union army faced Bragg's Army of Tennessee along an impressive geographic obstacle, the Highland Rim Plateau. Bragg extended his army from Shelbyville on the left flank to Beech Grove near Hoover's Gap on the right. The left flank of his cavalry extended to Columbia and McMinnville on the right flank. The center of Bragg's army was Tullahoma, which lay between two rivers, the Duck, which flowed from Manchester through Shelbyville and was north of Tullahoma, and the Elk, south of Tullahoma meandering in a southwest direction about midway toward Winchester. The Highland Rim contained gaps the main roads used as passages toward Tullahoma. The eastern road, the Murfreesboro-Manchester Road, passed through Hoover's Gap, a three-mile long valley. Liberty Pike passed through Liberty Gap, two miles west of Hoover's Gap, along a southward path to Wartrace. Finally, the Murfreesboro-Shelbyville Turnpike traveled through Guy's Gap just west of Liberty Gap. Rosecrans needed to develop a plan to move through these three gaps, where a determined defense by Confederate troops threatened to stall his entire advance.

Bragg had no intention of moving against Rosecrans but he was faced with the question regarding Rosecrans' advance against him. Bragg's defensive positions should have been fully developed during the preceding months. Unknown to Rosecrans, the discord within Bragg's army resulted in a "squandered" opportunity to complete the defenses in Tennessee. Bragg's illness, the animosity among the commanding general and his subordinates, and the constant struggle for supplies all contributed to the Confederates being in a less strong position than Rosecrans had supposed.[1] On June 8, Rosecrans sent a message to his seventeen corps and division commanders that contained five questions regarding the officers' perceived impressions about the size of Bragg's army and the advisability of attacking the Army of Tennessee.[2]

Various explanations have been given for these questions, including Rosecrans' need to reassess the position of his army and to gain support from his commanders in his verbal battle with Halleck. Turchin, Mitchell and Stanley responded on behalf of the cavalry. Turchin replied that he felt Bragg was weakened but that an advance southward without first capturing East Tennessee was very risky. Comparing Tennessee to Switzerland, he urged Rosecrans to capture East Tennessee before advancing on Bragg. Mitchell, on the other hand, lamented his own personal illness and felt he was not current with the affairs in Middle Tennessee. He stated he did not feel Bragg was weakened and urged caution. Mitchell gave little hope in the ability of the Army of the Potomac to defeat Lee in the East and noted that a loss by Grant would put the Union at terrible peril. Mitchell noted, "I would most earnestly advise against any unnecessary risks being taken here."[3] David Stanley wrote to Rosecrans:

> I believe the enemy is so reduced by detachments sent to reinforce Johnston, that we may hope to defeat him, provided we can meet his force fairly upon the field.... I believe an advance upon the enemy at this time would prevent their sending any more detachments from their force.... I have reasoned that an advance would bring on a decisive battle. Battles must be fought for political or military reasons. Had Hooker succeeded upon the Rappahannock, there would have been no political reason for now fighting a battle. Should Grant succeed at Vicksburg there will be no reason of such nature for a battle. Should Grant fail, the necessity would in my humble view be imperative.... I think our people have now comprehended that a battle is a very grave thing.

In the end, it is unlikely Rosecrans received any information that surprised him. Finally, he concluded that Grant had the situation in Vicksburg in hand, which freed Rosecrans to move against Bragg. He began his march against Bragg beginning on June 23, 1863.[4]

Various figures have been offered for the total forces of the two armies facing each other during the Tullahoma Campaign, but Rosecrans fielded about 50,000 men including 6,806 cavalry and 3,065 artillerymen. In addition, Rosecrans had over 12,000 men held in reserve. Bragg, on the other hand, had 46,000 men, with 13,962 cavalry and 2,254 artillerymen. Facing Stanley's cavalry was Forrest, Wharton, Wheeler and Brigadier General William Thomas Martin. Martin was a new face in Wheeler's cavalry. He was a Kentucky native whose family had moved to Natchez, Mississippi. Martin graduated from Centre College in Kentucky and was admitted to the bar in Mississippi. Having performed well under J.E.B. Stuart's command in Virginia, he was rewarded with a transfer west and division command in May 1863 in Wheeler's command.

Opening Moves

Bragg's army was entrenched at Shelbyville and Tullahoma. Rosecrans knew the cost that would be associated with attacking well-constructed defenses and he had to find a way around them. Leonidas Polk's corps was located near Shelbyville and William Hardee was near Wartrace. The Confederates also had the advantage of holding the highland passes along the three primary roads—Shelbyville Pike, Liberty Pike and Manchester Road—leading to Tullahoma. Rosecrans estimated Polk commanded about 18,000 men, Hardee had 12,000 and the Confederate cavalry was thought to have about 8,000 troopers. Rosecrans planned to push Bragg southward, then quickly capture the bridges at Estill Springs or Pelham, trapping

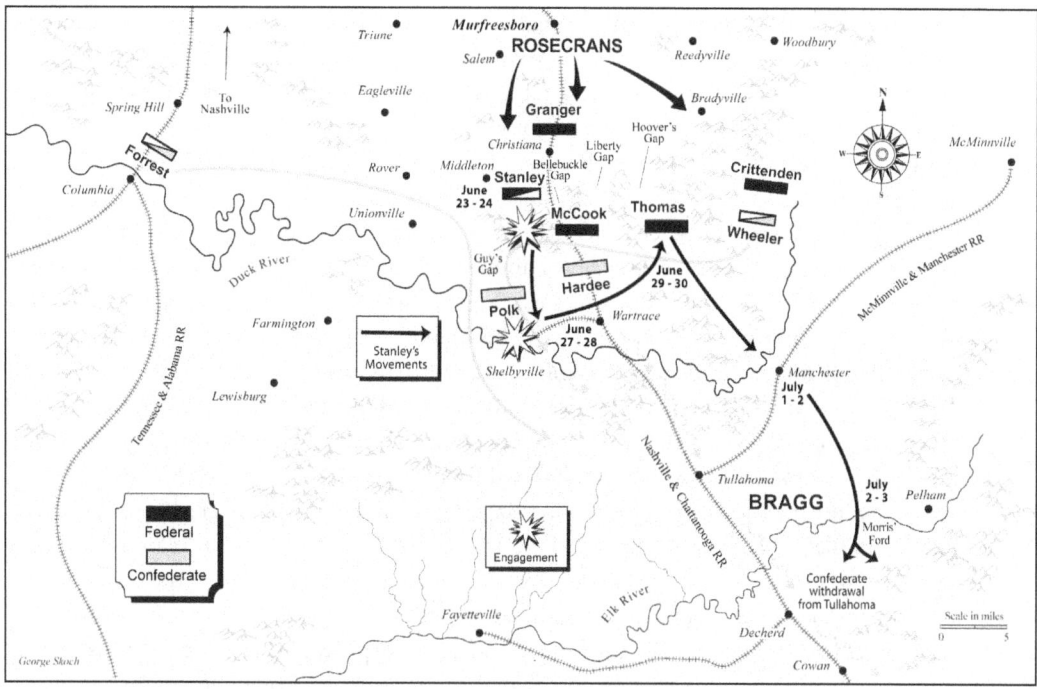

Cavalry Advance, Tullahoma Campaign (June 23–July 5, 1863)

Bragg before he could cross the Elk River. Rosecrans planned to feint west and then attack the Confederate east flank, which the cavalry operations over the past months suggested was more vulnerable. Rosecrans wanted to develop his full strength near Manchester and in a wheeling movement turn Bragg's right flank, placing him in the position of facing the Union infantry away from his entrenchments.[5]

Rosecrans' plan called for Thomas's Fourteenth Corps to move along the Manchester Pike and seize and hold Hoover's Gap. Rosecrans ordered Thomas and McCook to advance, each corps within supporting distance of the other. Meanwhile, Crittenden's Twenty-first Corps was to advance and concentrate at Bradyville, forming the left flank of the Army of the Cumberland. Eli Long's Second Brigade of cavalry under the command of General Turchin was ordered to operate in conjunction with Crittenden. David Stanley and the remainder of the cavalry were ordered toward Versailles, west of the Shelbyville Road. They were then to move southward to unite with Mitchell's cavalry division, which had been placed under Gordon Granger's command.

Major General Gordon Granger, commander of the Reserve Corps during the Tullahoma Campaign (Library of Congress).

On the eve of the beginning of the Tullahoma Campaign, the 5th Iowa Cavalry prepared for the expedition. Each man collected three days' rations and one hundred rounds of ammunition. The regiment lit up the night in a sublime, silent scene: "At night the boys lit up the camp with pieces of candles and even climbed the trees and put them there. Everybody seemed to desire to have his light the highest. It was a very beautiful sight. The lights in the trees seemed at a distance to be very bright stars. There was not a breath of air stirring."[6]

Meanwhile, Rosecrans called a meeting of his corps commanders to explain their orders. Because it was imperative to deceive Bragg about the direction of his attack, Rosecrans was secretive about his plans even to his highest ranking officers. He kept his plans so closely guarded that he sent only one day's orders to his commanders. McCook's Twentieth Corps was to begin its march on the Shelbyville Road and then advance on Wartrace along the Wartrace Road. One of McCook's divisions was to cover Granger's left flank. Next Granger was to march along the Middleton Road, covering the movement of the Thomas's Fourteenth Corps. Crittenden was to move forward toward Bradyville.[7]

As the campaign began, Rosecrans sent Major General Gordon Granger's Reserve Corps and David Stanley's cavalry to Triune in a feint to confuse Bragg as to his true plan. He hoped Bragg would send troops to an area Rosecrans did not plan to attack. Initially, the cavalry was to seek and push back the Confederate cavalry at Eagleville, Rover, Middleton and Unionville. Interestingly, Granger commanded the Reserve Infantry Corps and Mitchell's cavalry division. He also had overall supervisory command of all the cavalry except Long's brigade, which was working with Crittenden's corps. On June 23, Granger ordered Robert Mitchell's First Cavalry Division along the Eagleville and Salem roads, pushing the enemy's cavalry and pickets in front of them. The 9th Pennsylvania Cavalry led the Union advance and battled the 2nd and 4th Georgia and the 7th and 51st Alabama Cavalry which fell back only to fight from hill to hill in the first resistance of the campaign. Due to the stiff resistance by the Confederate cavalry, the 2nd Michigan Cavalry relieved the 9th Pennsylvania after the first two miles. Granger marched Brannan's division to Salem and Palmer's division and a brigade of cavalry to Readyville. Mitchell had sharp fights as he pushed from Eagleville and Rover.

As the 2nd Michigan led the column, it ran into stiff resistance and the advance stopped. The regiment dismounted and moved forward only to find themselves in a bad situation. As the Union troopers faced the enemy in their front, a regiment of Confederate cavalry appeared on the flank and prepared to charge. Just when things looked bleak, the 1st Tennessee Cavalry (U.S.) charged forward, to the relief of Sergeant Henry Mortimer Hempstead, 2nd Michigan Cavalry:

> And just at this moment we heard artillery open back in our rear where our horses were left, and again we started on a run but found only a few able to get up a decent appearance of running. We had not long to remain in suspense before the firing that followed up the first peal of artillery ceased and the well known cheer of the 1st Tenn. was born down upon us, and we knew all was safe. It afterwards appeared that the enemy had come out of the woods on our right and rear with a Regt of Cavalry and one gun and attempted to charge upon and capture our horses; but fortunately the 1st Tennessee had been held back in the rear of the horses ... coming on the ground in the nick of time given them a volley and then made a counter-charge and sent them flying.

Outside of Unionville, the Union cavalry ran into Confederate infantry battled by the 4th Kentucky (U.S.), 1st Tennessee (U.S.), 1st Wisconsin, and Battery D of the 1st Ohio Artillery in a brisk skirmish. Mitchell accomplished his task and fell back to Eagleville that night. His return to Eagleville filled the Confederate cavalry with confidence. A member of the 3rd

Georgia Cavalry wrote, "This day was a brilliant and glorious day for the 3rd Ga. Cav. We whipped them in every attempt to drive us."[8] Stanley recalled,

> [O]ne of the ridiculous things that sometimes happen to lighten up the death roll, occurred [during the skirmish on June 23]. The Confederates made a charge on our line of skirmishers, but recoiled when they met a brisk fire. One trooper continued to charge straight down our lines. As he passed across the line of skirmishers of the 1st Tennessee cavalry [Union] every man took a shot at the bold horse soldier. He dashed into our lines with his gray clothes full of bullet holes but with a whole skin, when it was discovered that a bullet had cut both his reins, and it was the horse that did the charging, the trooper being an unwilling participant.[9]

The next day Mitchell moved on to Middleton and again faced stiff resistance in the town. Stanley, becoming aware of the resistance, rode with Minty's Brigade and Stoke's Chicago Board of Trade Battery to join Mitchell. By the time the reinforcements arrived, Mitchell had moved the enemy from the town and the cavalry returned to Christiana. In an engagement with Confederate cavalry during the day Colonel James Brownlow, 1st Tennessee Cavalry, found himself in an awful situation similar to the example described by Stanley. His horse was wounded in the fight and his bridle was cut. The horse, wild with pain, ran directly for the Confederate lines. Brownlow was soon to become a prisoner unless he could find a solution. He found he had only one choice. He pulled his revolver and shot the horse in the back of the head.[10]

After riding to Mitchell, Stanley recorded, "That day the rain set in, which has continued to this present date, and which, converting the whole surface of the country into a quagmire, has rendered this one of the most arduous, laborious, and distressing campaigns upon man and beast I have ever witnessed." Also on June 25 the 5th Iowa and 4th Michigan cavalries skirmished with Confederate cavalry near Guy's Gap. The following day the Union cavalry on the western flank rested the horses and rationed its men. Colonel Thomas Jordan, 9th Pennsylvania Cavalry, wrote to his wife of the terrible conditions of the campaign: "The weather has been awful. It has rained steady for four days & we have not a tent to cover us. Wet to the skin all the time, we lie down in the water & sleep comfortable."[11]

Meanwhile, on the Union left flank on June 25, Crittenden's drive toward Manchester, unopposed by the Confederates, was grinding to a halt; the wet and muddy conditions all but stopped his advance. Eli Long's Second Brigade of cavalry pushed ahead to prevent any resistance to the march. Crittenden hoped Long would make progress by swinging around Bragg's flank. Long secured his objective, Lumley's Stand, and held his position until June 27.

The actions of Stanley's cavalry and Granger's reserve infantry corps accomplished all that was hoped and had confused Wheeler to "such an extent that for days he sent army headquarters erroneous, conflicting, and incomplete reports of enemy movements and intentions." In fact, one day before Rosecrans began his advance Wheeler moved Wharton's troopers toward Shelbyville from the exact objective of the Union advance, leaving the critical Highland Rim gaps weakly defended as Rosecrans' main thrusts moved forward. Crittenden's Twenty-first Corps swung to the east on the Bradyville Road and met almost no resistance as they marched toward Manchester. Alexander McCook's Twentieth Corps marched through Liberty Gap, and Thomas's Fourteenth Corps marched through Hoover's Gap and Matt's Hollow. Much of the success at Hoover's Gap was attributable to John T. Wilder's mounted infantry brigade, which performed admirably in the advance.[12]

Rosecrans' plan to deceive Bragg had worked. Two Confederate divisions were placed at Shelbyville to defend against the phantom attack that never came. Instead, Thomas, McCook and Crittenden had successfully moved through the treacherous gaps marching toward Manchester. Realizing Rosecrans' success, the Confederate infantry began its retreat to Tullahoma on the morning of June 27.[13]

Cavalry Battle at Shelbyville

Guy's Gap remained uncaptured and behind this gap was the concentration of Wheeler's cavalry, which had been moved from the right flank. To Wheeler's credit, he was determined to hold back the Union advance with just his cavalry as Polk and Hardee marched toward Tullahoma. Stanley's cavalry took to the saddle on June 27 in what was destined to be a long but productive day. Stanley, commanding 5,000 cavalrymen, set out in search of their enemy. Captain Joseph Vale, 7th Pennsylvania Cavalry, recalled, "Here was presented a scene of great military pageantry, as rare as it was inspiring. The sun, for a few hours after rising, shone out clear and bright, reflecting in full splendor the bright sabers and arms, and kissing the flags, banners, and streamers, as a harbinger of victory." At 9:00 a.m. Stanley advanced on Guy's Gap under Rosecrans' orders to "dislodge the enemy" at that location. Stanley, commanding Mitchell's division and Minty's brigade, approached Guy's Gap. Next he sought Granger's permission to make a direct attack on the defenders and Granger "acquiesced in this, and, pushing forward, our forces deployed." Vale noted that Mitchell's First Division had an unaccountable delay in advancing on Guy's Gap and Minty was "raging like a chained lion" at the

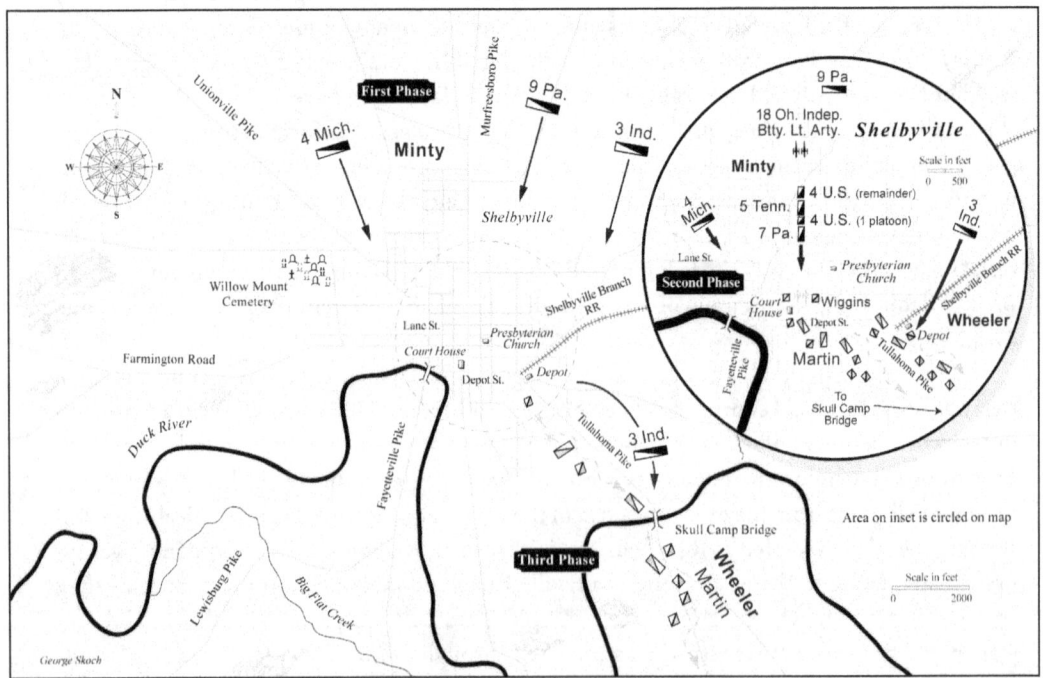

Cavalry Battle at Shelbyville (June 27, 1863)

lack of progress. Stanley sent a rider to Minty asking him to move his brigade ahead and attack the gap, exclaiming that the brigade in the lead was "so d___d slow, he couldn't do anything with it." The slowness of the lead brigade was attributed to Mitchell's illness and delays in sending orders to the regimental commanders.[14]

Stanley placed his best brigade commander, Robert Minty, with the 4th U.S. and the 5th Tennessee cavalries in front of the gap, while the 7th Pennsylvania, 4th Michigan, and 3rd Indiana cavalries were positioned to flank Confederate defenders. Minty promptly led the attack by swinging the 4th U.S. Cavalry to the right, and the 5th Tennessee Cavalry charged home in column of fours. Historian Michael Bradley noted, "Observing that not much defensive fire was coming out of the place Lieutenant Colonel Galbraith sent forward some men from his 1st Middle [5th] Tennessee Cavalry (U.S.), cleared the barricade off the road, and then charged the earthworks mounted. The few Confederates holding the place immediately scattered and for about two miles there was a horse race." Stanley also gave credit to the two columns of infantry from Granger's reserve corps that were deployed and moved to attack the defenders. The enemy abandoned the position and fled toward Shelbyville.[15]

While the fighting at Guy's Gap was relatively light, there was one incident that perhaps set the tone for the rest of the day. The 7th Pennsylvania Cavalry captured some of the Confederate defenders who could not escape. Private Felix Herb captured two men who had surrendered, only to be surprised as one of the men pulled a pistol and shot Herb in the head. Sergeant James Wilson rode down on the two and killed both of the men and exclaimed to the adjutant, "The devils shot Felix Herb after they surrendered." The day's work had just begun and Wilson would have further satisfaction.[16]

As the Union cavalry pursued the Confederates toward the critical engagement at Shelbyville, no one knew that the results there would mark the change in the balance of power in the Civil War. Minty's troopers rode toward Shelbyville, where William "Will" Martin's cavalrymen, about 900 strong, defended the town in entrenchments. Stanley ordered Minty to attack with his entire brigade of 2,522 men. Minty ran into the first defensive line about four miles north of Shelbyville when he came under artillery fire. The 3rd Indiana Cavalry moved to the left and the 4th U.S. and 7th Pennsylvania held the center. The 4th Michigan swung to the right and dismounted, but they were too far from the defenses. The 4th Michigan remounted, rode through the abates, and struck the defenders in the flank. Martin had too few troopers to man the defenses and retreated again toward Shelbyville.[17]

Minty moved the 7th Pennsylvania Cavalry to the lead to replace the 4th U.S. Cavalry, whose horses were fatigued. Wheeler and Martin, outnumbered and closely pursued, set up another defensive line near the courthouse square in Shelbyville centered around Wiggins' Arkansas Battery. Minty brought artillery of his own and as he approached Shelbyville he paused to organize his command and unlimbered Aleshire's 18th Ohio Battery. Then he decided to attack Shelbyville with the 7th Pennsylvania, 1st Middle (5th) Tennessee and 4th U.S. Cavalry by column of fours with their sabers drawn.[18]

Historian Michael Bradley noted, "This should have been a recipe for disaster—a cavalry column charging a battery of artillery supported by a full body of cavalry." Luck favored the bold as other factors played an important part in the battle. The weather caused much of the Confederate ammunition to become wet. Rather than ride to meet Minty's charge, the Confederate horsemen were ordered to receive the charge at a "standstill." Further, Martin's troopers were told to fire one shot and then retreat across the Skull Camp Bridge over the Duck River, which was swollen from the incessant rain.[19]

On charged Minty. While Stanley and Minty's insistence on training the cavalry in the use of the saber has been discounted by many, the battle at Shelbyville showed the value of this weapon. This saber charge was made by troopers of the same column that had just "demonstrated comparable skill as dismounted skirmishers." As one of the defenders later wrote, "On either side of the highway ... in columns of fours, they advanced at a steady gallop.... The Union troopers, with sabers high in the air, made no sound whatever, beyond the rumbling tattoo which their horses' hoofs played upon the ground.... No more gallant work was ever done by any troops than was done this day by the Seventh Pennsylvania."[20]

Minty was charging directly into the mouths of the cannons but as he charged, Wiggins' artillery boomed and emptied "precisely two saddles—the gunners appeared to have failed to depress the muzzles." There are no second chances in war and Minty charged forwarded. Major Charles Davis would be awarded the Medal of Honor for his actions during the charge of the Union cavalry. The citation would recognize that Davis "led one of the most desperate and successful charges of the war." The 7th Pennsylvania Cavalry was selected to lead the attack and Davis, who was in command of the troops on the right of the column, volunteered to lead the charge, which was conducted by column of fours because the pike was very narrow. This was a perilous attack for the Union cavalry, and "Major Davis rode well in front of the leading sabres, the beau ideal of a trooper."[21]

Lieutenant Colonel William B. Sipes, the ex-newspaper editor from Pennsylvania, commanded the 7th Pennsylvania Cavalry, which charged the Confederate defenders concentrated at the courthouse square at Shelbyville. He led the 7th Pennsylvania at the walk and maintained that pace until the Confederate cannon fired and he ordered the charge. Sipes wrote,

First Lieutenant Amos Rhoads, 7th Pennsylvania Cavalry, was killed during the conflict at Shelbyville (courtesy Ronald Coddington).

Never did men move more gallantly and daringly into the face of the most imminent danger than did this little force. The street up which it moved was perfectly straight, gradually ascending to the court-house, where the enemy had four guns planted so as to command it completely, and these supported by a brigade of cavalry. To look upon these preparations, it seemed that utter destruction was inevitable to all those who dared advance, and yet, with sabers drawn, and with shouts of defiance, the men rushed onward, never faltering for an instant, and, to all appearance, utterly destitute of any apprehension of danger.

According to Sipes, the Confederate artillery sent three rounds, the last being canister as the Union cavalry closed on its target.[22]

The Confederate cavalrymen unleashed a volley and broke for the bridge. One piece of artillery was captured near a railroad depot, followed by a second taken in a sharp fight and a third captured at the Skull Camp Bridge. The pursuit did not stop at the river and the Union cavalry chased their prey for another two miles before breaking off the pursuit. Although the Union cavalry pushed back the Confederate cavalry, troopers fell on both sides. Trooper Henry Snyder rode next to Frances Reed as the 7th Pennsylvania charged ahead. Snyder wrote to Reed's wife that Reed was riding next to him and then was gone. He never saw how Reed died. After the fighting, Snyder found his body and his face was covered with blood.[23]

In the meantime, Colonel Archibald Campbell's brigade swung around to cut off the retreat at the bridge over the Duck River. Hand-to-hand fighting took place as the 3rd Indiana Cavalry slammed into the remaining Confederate defenders as some of the Confederates rode into the river to escape capture with the 3rd Indiana on their heels. So fierce was the fighting, some of the 3rd Indiana used carbines to club their enemy. Once the 7th Pennsylvania, followed by the 4th U.S., charged the cannon, the 4th Michigan Cavalry commanded by Major Frank Mix succeeded in riding from the flank into the escaping Confederate cavalry, turning it to the left and causing it to ride into a heavily fenced garden, which resulted in the capture of about 250 men.[24]

According to Major Mix, the troopers of the 4th Michigan set to the deadly work. Corporal Hofmaster, of Company L of the 4th Michigan,

charged into town, and selected a position where the enemy would have to pass him, and, with drawn saber, hewed away at them until he was disabled, receiving a wound in the left arm, also one in the right hand, nearly severing the grip of his saber, and cutting some of his fingers nearly off. A ball also hit his hat, cutting it entirely open on the top. Private Mason Brown, of Company I, having found a carbine, tried to fire it at the enemy, but, missing fire, he immediately changed ends with it and did good service among the rebels with whom he was in close contact.[25]

The defenders had been totally defeated and lost three artillery pieces; 591 men were taken prisoner and an estimated 200 troopers had chosen to take their chances in the swollen Duck River rather than be captured. Stanley observed, "[T]he annals of this war will not probably show a more gallant charge…. [T]wo of their generals—Wheeler and Martin—escaped by swimming the river."[26]

There are various accounts of this engagement, but one complicating factor might have been Wheeler's belief that Forrest's cavalry was rushing to his aid. Wheeler was informed Forrest was coming with two full brigades of cavalry and he was on the north side of the Duck River. Wheeler had planned to burn the bridge and prevent Stanley's cavalry from crossing the river, but he knew this would trap Forrest and his Southern cavalry. However, Michael Bradley pointed out this was unlikely, because once Wheeler had been pushed to the courthouse square he was in no position to offer any aid to Forrest on the north side of the river. It is more likely Wheeler was attempting a delaying action to get his trains across the river. Regardless of circumstance, Wheeler was in a very uncomfortable position as the Union cavalry swung to the left and came charging directly into his flank. Wheeler had had enough to deal with as Minty charged his front. This flanking movement proved to be too much. Any Confederates not across the bridge were trapped. "After a four-day downpour, Duck River was a roaring torrent, with its crest fifteen feet below the level of the streets of Shelbyville and with a nearly vertical drop from the riverbank to the water below. Wheeler, 'saber in hand, shouted to his men that they must cut their way through and swim the river, ordered the charge, and, with General Martin, led in the desperate venture,'" observed Stephen Starr, author of *The Union Cavalry in the Civil War*. Bradley also noted the belief that Wheeler jumped off the Skull Camp Bridge with saber in hand into the torrents of the river has probably been overstated. There is no doubt Wheeler and Martin swam the river, but the 3rd Indiana followed those retreating into the same river, losing only one man, without the hyperbole of a dramatic leap into the water.[27]

The Union cavalry's ability to defeat Wheeler at Shelbyville revealed the results of increased numbers of troopers, mounts and efficient weapons. The engagement at Shelbyville also demonstrated the benefits of being properly trained, as the Union cavalry had just implemented two successful saber charges. The Union cavalry had finally come into its own.[28]

David Stanley wanted to extend the efforts of a good day's work, because at midnight he learned the formidable Nathan Bedford Forrest's cavalry had struggled through the mud and crossed the Duck River downstream as he retreated toward Tullahoma. The day belonged to Stanley and his cavalry. The aggressive Stanley was satisfied with what he had gained, but with his blood up he decided to go after Forrest. Unfortunately, Rosecrans had shackled Stanley to Granger. Stanley pleaded with Granger for permission to pursue Forrest, but he recorded that Granger "was of the opinion that the command was too much wearied to move in the night. As the matter turned out, I think it was very unfortunate that this attack was not made, as I think we could have completely routed this part of Forrest's force." Stanley had to have been particularly frustrated when he received a message from Lieutenant Colonel C. Goddard, assistant adjutant general, which encouraged to him to take the battle to Wheeler and Forrest: "Pitch in and use them up," only to find out he had been ordered not to pursue Forrest by his new commanding officer, Granger.[29]

The engagement at Shelbyville carried great significance in terms of the strategic situation in future campaigns in the central theater of the Civil War. This engagement is generally recognized as a point where the dominance of Confederate cavalry over Union cavalry in Tennessee ended. David Stanley wrote, "The Confederate cavalry never recovered from the demoralizing effect which it experienced that day of being ridden down by the Union cavalry." Rosecrans and Stanley had worked diligently to bolster the Union cavalry in terms of men, horses, training and firepower. They could now stand on their own, on equal terms, against the Confederate cavalry. Stanley gave credit for the success of the engagement at Shelbyville to the confidence and training of his cavalry.[30]

Advance on Tullahoma

The infantry advance had also moved smoothly. McCook seized Liberty Gap. General Joseph Reynolds' division, including Wilder's Mounted Infantry, claimed the critical Hoover's

Gap. The infantry struggled through the same mud as the cavalry and the rain continued for the remainder of the Tullahoma campaign. On June 26, Bragg had retreated to Fairfield and Wilder's Brigade captured Matt's Hollow, another very important position. By June 27, Rosecrans' army had crossed the Duck River and Rosecrans ordered Wilder's Brigade to destroy the bridge over the Elk River, therefore preventing Bragg's escape. Squire Elbert, 4th Michigan Cavalry, described the terrible condition of the roads due to the incessant rains: "And Oh! What roads! They were worse than any I have ever traveled over before. We halted Saturday night [June 27] ... and I slept in my wet clothing soundly."[31]

On June 28, Stanley resupplied and rested the horses, but on June 29 he sought the Southern cavalry and was unsuccessful in locating the Confederate horsemen. He sent Mitchell with the First Brigade to Beech Grove while he moved the remainder of the cavalry to Fairfield, and Turchin remained on duty on the army's left flank. Rosecrans advanced his infantry and ordered Stanley to join the army at Manchester.

The next day, after remaining in tents all day, many of Eli Long's Second Brigade were ordered to saddle at 7:00 p.m. The orderly passed among the tents, exclaiming, "Strike the tents and be ready to march in half an hour!" W.L. Curry, 1st Ohio Cavalry, noted in his diary, "We feel more inclined to strike the orderly." The troopers packed up their gear, which was waterlogged from the rain, and saddled their horses in the dark.[32]

Colonel Eli Long was still establishing his command of the Second Brigade of Turchin's division. Colonel James Paramore, 3rd Ohio Cavalry, chafed under the style of command of the ex-regular officer, and the friction exploded into confrontation on June 29 in an argument over a captured horse. When the 3rd Ohio Cavalry returned from a foraging expedition, Long ordered the forage to be given to the 4th Ohio Cavalry. Even though the 3rd Ohio had received eighteen sacks of forage from the 1st Ohio Cavalry the day before, Paramore was not in a sharing mood. Paramore "told [Long] what he thought" of him, and then Long placed him under arrest. Paramore simply told Long he did not recognize his authority to do that and returned to his tent. The next morning Long sent an order to claim a horse that had been captured by the 3rd Ohio Cavalry and Paramore ordered his men not to release the horse to Long. Long marched to Paramore's headquarters, accompanied by the provost guard, to seize the horse. Paramore ordered out three companies of troopers and, under orders of a lieutenant, told Long if he made one further step they would shoot him. Long returned to his headquarters, but the incident was not over. He reported the incident to Turchin and then to Rosecrans, who arrested both Paramore and Lieutenant Brown, who had been ordered to resist the seizure of the horse. Paramore was discharged from the service, and command of the regiment fell to Major Charles Seidel. Brown was returned to duty. Long continued to offer good service to the cavalry as brigade commander. Charles B. Seidel, the new commander of the regiment, was a native of Germany. He was born in Berlin in 1835 and later immigrated to the United States. A carriage maker before the war, he had military service in Germany, enlisted as a U.S. private in 1861 and fought at the first Battle of Bull Run. He next joined the cavalry and quickly advanced in rank due to his leadership abilities.[33]

Now, Rosecrans needed to complete his plan to maneuver Bragg away from his fixed defenses at Tullahoma. To accomplish this, he planned to swing Thomas and Crittenden to the south, cut the railroad and turn the Confederates, forcing them into a less strong line of defenses. Rosecrans ordered Stanley's cavalry to work in concert by capturing bridges over the Elk River, thus preventing Bragg from retreating.

Wilder, who was dispatched to destroy the Elk River Bridge, was unsuccessful; but his expedition, along with the line of Federal march, revealed Rosecrans' intent. On June 30, Bragg realized he could not hold Tullahoma, and by July 1 Bragg successfully retreated from Tullahoma. On the same day, Robert Minty's brigade rode back to Walker's Mill (between Beech Grove and Manchester) and Stanley's cavalry found Bragg had evacuated Tullahoma. Then the cavalry led the pursuit of the retreating army toward Pelham with the hope of cutting off the retreat at Elk River and trapping Bragg's army. The 2nd Kentucky (U.S.) Cavalry, accompanied by the 39th Indiana Mounted infantry, pushed forward on July 2 into Tullahoma; they clashed with Forrest's pickets about three miles from town and sent them to the rear. Lieutenant Colonel Elijah Watts, commanding the Kentucky cavalry battalion, rode ahead into Tullahoma. As he entered, a large number of Confederate cavalry rode out the other side, giving up the town. Elijah S. Watts, the son of a tailor, was born December 16, 1836, in Bardstown, Kentucky. In 1861, he joined a local Home Guards company, the Wickliffe Blues. After the first battle of the war, he enlisted and was elected captain of Company A in 2nd Kentucky Cavalry. He was promoted to major in February 1862 and to lieutenant colonel in January 1863.[34]

Rosecrans did not want to lose contact with Bragg's retreating army and on July 2 he ordered his infantry corps to aggressively follow the retreating Confederates. "Additional instructions to George Thomas indicated Rosecrans expected Stanley to work for Thomas. Thomas and Stanley were then to cooperate to destroy the Confederate cavalry and trains," noted military historian Richard Brewer. More practically, Rosecrans needed Stanley to capture the bridges to insure he could pursue Bragg even if he could not trap him. Under Stanley's orders, Turchin started for Hillsboro and Mitchell's division rode for Manchester.

The next day, it was confirmed the route of retreat was not through Pelham but Estill Springs. Upon this discovery, Stanley ordered Turchin to ride to Decherd but Turchin's advance was blocked at Morris's Ford by a Confederate rear guard. Turchin, riding with Long's brigade made up of mostly Ohio cavalry, crossed the ford and attempted to protect the crossing, but enemy artillery forced the Ohioans to retreat to the north side of the river. On the opposite side of the river were the 51st Alabama Cavalry and the 25th and 26th Tennessee infantries backed by Darden's Mississippi Battery. Mitchell's cavalry was dispatched to assist in the crossing. Stanley recorded, "General Turchin, having arrived in advance of my column, immediate measures were taken to force the passage. General Mitchell was directed to cross the upper and General Turchin the lower ford. This was effected with little opposition—a fortunate circumstance, as the current was swift, and almost swam a horse." Long got his brigade across the river first and fought a determined rearguard action by Confederate cavalry as he advanced toward Decherd. Once Long was across the ford, Turchin and Mitchell pressed their pursuit until nightfall and Stanley's cavalry claimed a Confederate colonel killed and a second mortally wounded, in addition to another twenty soldiers killed. John Allan Wyeth, 4th Alabama Cavalry, recalled that Wheeler had set a trap for Long's brigade, which led the pursuit, but Long discovered and avoided the ambush.[35]

The reports by Turchin and Stanley fairly drip with the animosity between the two men. Stanley stated a simple crossing of the Elk River was unable to be accomplished by Turchin. He also made almost no reference to Turchin in his overall report, except this incident. Turchin lamented the fact that his cavalry brigade "was scattered by battalions, under command of majors and lieutenant-colonels, on the front of the two army corps, the regimental commanders and the brigade commanders remaining in camp with twelve companies of different regiments, and at the head of all was the division commander himself." In regard to his failure to cross the Elk River, he felt he faced an entrenched enemy with superior numbers of men supported by cavalry and artillery. He also wrote he decided to guard a second ford to prevent the enemy from threatening the army's flank. Clearly, Stanley had not forgiven Turchin for leaving him to die in the face of the enemy earlier in the summer.[36]

Turchin's reputation continued to suffer under the pen of T.F. Dornblaser, 7th Pennsylvania Cavalry, who noted Turchin decided to take a nap before attempting to push the Confederates from the ford at Elk River. "Here we halted for a few hours. Turchin took a nap in the shade of a tree. While he was napping the writer saw the enemy on the south side of the river, placing a battery in position. The orderly felt it his duty to wake the general, and before a 'mad Dutchman' was done growling at the unnecessary interruption, the aforesaid battery opened fire, and dropped the shells in such close quarters as to cause the general and his staff to 'get up and dust.'" Turchin's self-importance was also recorded by a member of the 3rd Ohio Cavalry, who recorded that Turchin's coffee pot was stolen on June 27, and the brigade waited as a member of the staff was dispatched to try to find the culprit and the pot.[37]

By the end of the day on July 2, the Army of the Cumberland had successfully claimed several points to cross the Elk River, despite Bragg's attempts to destroy bridges and guard the fords. However, the high water and Confederate resistance at the fords accomplished what Bragg desperately needed—time to withdraw his army.

On July 4, the 5th and 6th Kentucky cavalries moved in search of Bragg with hopes of gaining his rear. After the 5th Kentucky rode a mile toward University Place, it was ambushed by the 3rd and 4th Georgia cavalries, who wounded six of the Kentucky cavalrymen. The 5th Kentucky fell back to the main column and the 6th Kentucky Cavalry charged forward, engaging the enemy. The two sides battled for three-quarters of an hour until the Confederates were forced back, fighting "obstinately for every foot of ground." The Union cavalry moved to within a half-mile of University Place and fell back after capturing fifteen prisoners and some band equipment. Sergeant Robert Burr, 2nd Kentucky Cavalry, recorded the perilous nature of the pursuit of Bragg's Army: "The Rebs was lying in ambush and ... they opened fire on our men. It was a narrow road and it was impossible for us to get to them. It is not known how many we killed of them. They had fallen trees a crost the road and we could not get up with our a[m]bulance and when they came back a carring theire dead thrown a crost theire horses you can imagine how I felt."[38]

Cavalry Corps, Tullahhoma Campaign Casualties[39]

Command	Killed Officers	Killed Men	Wounded Officers	Wounded Men	Captured/Missing Officers	Captured/Missing Men	Total
FIRST DIVISION, Brigadier General Robert B. Mitchell							
First Brigade, Colonel Archibald P. Campbell							
4th Kentucky	0	0	0	2	0	0	2
6th Kentucky	1	1	1	4	0	0	7
2nd Michigan	0	0	0	2	0	3	5
9th Pennsylvania	1	1	0	2	0	0	4
1st Tennessee	0	2	0	1	0	1	4
Total First Brigade	2	4	1	11	0	4	22

Command	Killed		Wounded		Captured/Missing		
	Officers	Men	Officers	Men	Officers	Men	Total
Second Brigade, Colonel Edward M. McCook							
4th Indiana	0	0	0	2	0	0	2
5th Kentucky	0	0	0	6	0	1	7
2nd Tennessee	0	0	0	1	0	0	1
1st Wisconsin	0	0	0	2	0	0	2
Total Second Brigade	0	0	0	11	0	1	12
Total First Division	2	4	1	22	0	5	34
SECOND DIVISION, Brigadier General John B. Turchin							
Staff	0	0	1	0	0	0	1
First Brigade, Colonel Robert H.G. Minty							
3rd Indiana	0	1	1	2	0	0	4
4th Michigan	0	0	1	7	0	2	10
7th Pennsylvania	1	4	1	10	0	0	16
5th Tennessee	0	0	1	1	0	1	3
4th United States	0	0	1	1	0	0	2
Total First Brigade	1	5	6	21	0	3	36
Second Brigade, Colonel Eli Long							
2nd Kentucky	1	0	0	2	0	2	5
1st Ohio	0	2	0	1	0	0	3
3rd Ohio	0	0	0	6	0	0	6
4th Ohio	0	0	1	4	0	0	5
Total Second Brigade	1	2	1	13	0	2	19
Total Second Division	2	7	7	34	0	5	55
Total Cavalry Corps	4	11	8	56	0	10	89

Officers killed: Lieutenant William G. Jenkins, 2nd Kentucky Cavalry; Lieutenant Amos B. Rhoads, 7th Pennsylvania Cavalry; Captain Gilbert Waters, 9th Pennsylvania Cavalry

One of the most unfortunate things about the Tullahoma Campaign is the absence of official records by the Confederate cavalry. This was not one of Wheeler's best campaigns, but the lack of records from Wheeler and his subordinates resulted in a less than complete story. On the Union side, Rosecrans was well pleased with the action of his cavalry and he wrote in his after action report, "It affords me pleasure to return my thanks to Major-General Granger and Major General Stanley, commanding the cavalry, for their operations on our right, resulting in the capture of Shelbyville." Opinions vary on the success of the Tullahoma Campaign. Some hold this campaign as a model of maneuver to achieve success with the least amount of loss while others point out that Bragg's army slipped southward to fight again. Stanley agreed with the latter opinion but quickly pointed to weather as the primary reason for Bragg's escape.[40]

The Union cavalry performed well during the Tullahoma Campaign and David Stanley aggressively drove his horsemen to victory. One additional accomplishment would have claimed a major victory: the capture of the bridges over the Elk River. Historian Michael Bradley wrote of the possibility of the Union cavalry's trapping Bragg's infantry along the Elk River: "[T]he idea that the blue cavalry would have trapped the Army of the Tennessee asks too much of the Union cavalry. Rosecrans' mounted arm had improved vastly during the first six months of 1863 but his troopers did not have the firepower or the élan to hold a river line against Reb infantry and artillery. Wilder's Brigade of mounted infantry could have held a bridge, but Stanley's cavalry could not have held the line of the Elk."[41] In addition, Rosecrans intended to turn Bragg's army and force it to fight at a disadvantage and not to capture it. Therefore he delayed dispatching Stanley's cavalry and Crittenden's corps to swing to the rear of the enemy, and Bragg, realizing the precarious situation, was allowed to withdraw from Tullahoma aided by a sea of mud.[42]

For an unexplained reason, Rosecrans placed Mitchell's cavalry, and really much of the bulk of the Union cavalry, under the command of Gordon Granger early in the campaign. Historian Stephen Starr, wrote, "Rosecrans may have become disenchanted with Stanley's performance as an adequately aggressive cavalry commander ... or he may have decided that it would be convenient to have the commander of the infantry corps with which the cavalry was to work, control the operations of all three arms." Initial orders show only Mitchell's cavalry under Granger's command. Turchin worked with Crittenden, while Stanley commanded the remainder of the cavalry—Minty's cavalry brigade. Perhaps illuminating the mistake of assigning command to Granger, the greatest successes occurred with the cavalry under Stanley's immediate command. Messages from Garfield on June 26 were directed to Stanley and the wording appeared to show Stanley and Granger as relative equals: "The above order to feel the enemy at Guy's Gap will not be carried out if there are reasons why Generals Stanley and Granger regard the expedition as fruitless or too hazardous; in that case, General Stanley will come forward at once."

Once Bragg began his retreat, Stanley was again placed in a position to "work for Thomas" in the pursuit. This strongly suggests Rosecrans intended to put the cavalry at the disposal of his infantry corps commanders as situations changed in the campaign to achieve the desired result. Despite everything he had learned during the past eight months, he reverted to the old organization, which Stanley had resisted when he assumed command of the cavalry. Perhaps Rosecrans wanted to improve communications and offer mobility should it be immediately needed, but it took command away from the chief of cavalry. This mistake on the part of Rosecrans caused little problem during the Tullahoma Campaign, but restricting the command abilities of the chief of cavalry would prove to be problematic during the upcoming Chickamauga Campaign, and then later in the Atlanta Campaign.[43]

It is important to remember that Stanley was under Granger's command early in the campaign, and it was Stanley's initiative that resulted in the capture of Guy's Gap, a critical strategic position. Stanley stated he urged Granger to allow his cavalry to make a direct attack on the position and Granger "acquiesced." A second situation resulted after the success at Shelbyville when Stanley wanted to battle Forrest but Granger's reluctance kept him from further actions. These reports clearly showed Stanley shackled when he aggressively wanted to move forward. If Rosecrans had been disenchanted with Stanley, his performance during the Tullahoma campaign allayed any concerns. Stanley's philosophy was to face his opponents with "hindward feather and with forward toe."[44]

Historically, the success of Stanley's cavalry in the Tullahoma Campaign is overshadowed by the success of Colonel John T. Wilder's mounted infantry. There can be no doubt Wilder's brigade was a very successful experiment that contributed directly to Rosecrans' victory at Tullahoma. David Stanley is often referred to as a sarcastic fellow and he was certainly an officer who believed in the traditional cavalry methods; but as a regular cavalry officer he was comfortable with the role dragoons. Although Colonel Abel Streight's expedition earlier in the year resulted in his entire command being captured, Wilder was a different commander. When he realized he was being stalked by Forrest, he wisely abandoned the attempt to destroy the bridge over the Elk River and turned his attention to the destruction of railroads. He returned before he was forced into a dangerous position. Wilder returned to enjoy the successes of the campaign.[45]

Clearly the Tullahoma Campaign was a great success for Stanley, who was described by historian Robert Delassandro: "The Cavalry Corps commander, Major General David S. Stanley, was not the stereotypical cavalryman. Stanley was an apt leader described as 'bold and dashing, his action tempered and guided by skill and prudence, which make him a successful commander.' Stanley was universally liked by his subordinates." Despite Stanley's later assessment of Garfield, there is evidence Garfield also liked Stanley and had sent a photograph of Stanley in a letter to his family on June 21, 1863, saying, "A photograph of my friend General Stanley, our chief of cavalry. He is an able and gallant officer."[46]

In conclusion, much of the success of Tullahoma was attributable to the actions of the Union cavalry, and much of this resulted from seemingly endless days of riding from January through June. Because the Union cavalry worked so hard, Rosecrans was given proper intelligence of Bragg's army and its strengths and weaknesses. Stanley's cavalry played an important part in deceiving Bragg regarding Rosecrans' intentions in wheeling from the left to cut Bragg's retreat. Along the way, Minty, in particular, played a key role in increasing the parity of Union cavalry with its Southern counterparts.[47]

5. The Advance on Chattanooga

So far your command has been a mere picket guard for our advance.
—Major General William S. Rosecrans

Wheeler and Forrest's cavalries provided effective rearguard action for the Army of Tennessee after it evacuated Tullahoma. By July 7, Braxton Bragg had moved his army across the Tennessee River; but this was an unremarkable feat because Rosecrans did not mount a vigorous pursuit. For the Union cavalry, the ten-day campaign through continuous rainfall and subsequent mud had taken a toll on the horses and men. After Stanley had time to fully appraise the condition of the cavalry, he summarized from his headquarters in Winchester: "The incessant rain and consequent condition of the roads rendered the operations of the cavalry difficult and exceedingly trying to men and horses. The impossibility of bringing up forage in wagons, and the absence of feed in the 'Barrens' of the Cumberland Mountains, the constant rain depriving our poor beasts of their rest, has reduced the cavalry considerably. They now require some little rest and refitting."[1]

Great strides had been made in the Union cavalry and at last Stanley's cavalry exceeded the combined strength of that of Wheeler and Forrest after the Tullahoma Campaign. Morgan's cavalry, still detached from Bragg's army, was on a raid in the north.

Comparison of Union and Confederate Cavalry Commands, July 1863[2]

Confederate Command	Total (Present and Absent)	Union Command	Total (Present and Absent)
Wheeler's Cavalry	5,547	Mitchell's Division[a]	5,696
Forrest's Cavalry	3,807	Crook's Division	5,187
Total	9,354	Total	10,883

[a]Includes Corps Command and Staff

Rosecrans settled his army around Middle Tennessee as Bragg marched for Chattanooga. The railroad was a critical source of communication and supply for his army and he set his infantry and engineers the task of making it operational. He desperately needed the rails as he contemplated his next advance on Bragg's army. Bragg's retreat and the low morale of his army would prove to be helpful for the Army of the Cumberland. Fortunately, when Bragg retreated he did not destroy the Cumberland Mountain tunnel, an important link in keeping the supplies moving south through the Cumberland Mountains. Phil Sheridan also provided excellent news to Rosecrans on July 7 when he reported that Bragg did not burn all the railroad bridges leading to the Tennessee River, but left several intact.[3]

Washington Pushes Rosecrans to Move

Almost immediately after the end of the Tullahoma Campaign, the ill will between Washington and Rosecrans began again. Rosecrans proudly wired Halleck about his victory at Tullahoma. Rosecrans felt he had just performed a remarkable piece of generalship by pushing Bragg out of middle Tennessee at a cost of less than 700 casualties, but Washington wanted more results. Secretary of War Stanton replied, on July 7, "You and your noble army now have the chance to give the finishing blow to the rebellion. Will you neglect the chance?" Rosecrans, being informed of the great Union victories at Gettysburg and Vicksburg, felt his efforts were slighted. He responded to Halleck, "You do not appear to observe the fact that this noble army has driven the rebels from Middle Tennessee, of which my dispatches advised you. I beg in behalf of this army that the War Department may not overlook so great an event because it is not written in letters of blood." He hastened to note he was near the Alabama state line and that Bragg had retreated to Chattanooga.[4] But Rosecrans' days were numbered. General Lovell Rousseau and Colonel J.P. Sanderson traveled to Washington to discuss with Stanton and Halleck the plan of reenlisting veterans. Stanton was overheard stating he would rather they had asked to command the Army of the Cumberland themselves. Making reference to Rosecrans, he said, "He shall not have another damned man."[5]

Rosecrans would not be forced to move until he was ready and his delay set off another series of demands from Washington to move. Rosecrans remained in Middle Tennessee for six weeks as he prepared his army for the next move against Bragg. On July 24, Henry Halleck wrote to Rosecrans stating, "You must not wait for Johnston to join Bragg, but must move forward…. There is great disappointment felt here at the slowness of your advance. Unless you can move more rapidly, your whole campaign will prove a failure, and you will have both Bragg and Johnston against you." In a personal and confidential letter from Halleck to Rosecrans, Halleck, in the role of offering personal advice to a friend, urged, "[Y]our army should remain no longer inactive. The patience of the authorities here has been completely exhausted, and if I had not repeatedly promised to urge you forward, and begged for delay, you would have been removed from the command. It has been said that you are as inactive as was General Buell, and the pressure for your removal has been almost as strong as it has been in his case."[6]

Rosecrans responded to Halleck on July 25 about the concerns in Washington regarding the lack of progress of his army, a lack he believed was justified due to the obstacles he faced. To Halleck's credit, he knew the low regard many in Washington had for Rosecrans and he knew if Rosecrans was to remain in command he needed to move. After receiving Rosecrans' reply of July 25, Halleck gave up his attempt to advise Rosecrans to begin an advance and simply wrote that he would not again refer to the matter.[7]

From Rosecrans' standpoint, he faced thirty miles of the Cumberland Mountains between Tullahoma and the Tennessee River. This was barren ground with little hope as a source of forage for his army or his animals. He needed to rely on the Nashville and Chattanooga Railroad for his daily supplies, which amounted to sixty railcars per day for the army. Before Rosecrans could realistically advance, as Washington urged, this lifeline needed to be secure and fully operational.[8]

Rosecrans wanted to build the railroad to Bridgeport to support any advance made on the other side of the river as the Army of the Cumberland inched forward toward the Tennessee River. There were ferries and fords also along the Tennessee River but the other side was guarded, generally, with detachments of Confederate infantry. Alexander McCook had three regiments at Stevenson, and Sheridan approached Bridgeport with a construction train on July 19. Colonel Daniel Ray, commanding the 2nd Tennessee Cavalry, worked with McCook's corps to protect the existing bridges and rails from further damage.[9]

Rosecrans gained intelligence on July 23 that Bragg's army was at Chattanooga, Forrest's cavalry stretched from Chattanooga to Ringgold, and Wheeler's cavalry was southwest of Chattanooga at Will's Valley. Wheeler's cavalry was positioned on the left flank of Bragg's army from Chattanooga along the Tennessee River extending as far west as Decatur, Alabama. Forrest was positioned on the right flank and stretched from Chattanooga toward Kingston, Tennessee. While the Union commanding general was having problems, the situation for the Confederate commanding general was no better. Bragg was an unpopular general among his subordinates and his relationship with Wheeler also became strained in July. Bragg reprimanded Wheeler at that time for his inaccuracies in reports and later stated that some of Wheeler's efforts at Cherokee Springs were causing "more harm than good." The relationship between the two generals declined throughout the summer, but much of the fault was not with Wheeler. Bragg was very concerned Rosecrans would combine with Ambrose Burnside's Union troops near Knoxville and march toward Chattanooga. As a result, Bragg neglected Wheeler and stretched his cavalry over too much geography while concentrating his focus on Forrest's flank.[10]

In late July Rosecrans remained stationary across Middle Tennessee. He positioned his army with Thomas's Fourteenth Corps at Decherd, and McCook had headquarters at Winchester. Stanley moved his headquarters to Salem, and Mitchell's division was at Fayetteville. Crittenden, whose headquarters was at Manchester, had a division at Pelham and three divisions at McMinnville. It was good news for the Union army that the railroad was open and carrying supplies, to Bridgeport and Tracy City, and the engineers sent pontoons forward. Phil Sheridan's report that Bragg destroyed the bridges over the Tennessee River saved the cavalry much effort. Rosecrans had contemplated sending Stanley on an expedition after the retreating Confederate army but concluded that without the bridges in place the effort would be futile.

Union Cavalry Activities in July

While Rosecrans and Washington argued about the next advance on Bragg, the Union cavalry remained busy with day-to-day activities. On July 8, Stanley reorganized the First Cavalry Division to include a third brigade. While no new cavalry regiments were added to the corps, Colonel Louis D. Watkins was given command of the Third Cavalry Brigade, which consisted of the 4th, 5th, 6th, and 7th Kentucky cavalries. Less than a month later, a third brigade was added to the 2nd Division, commanded by Colonel William Lowe of the 5th Iowa Cavalry. Lowe's brigade included the 5th Tennessee, 5th Iowa, and 10th Ohio cavalries.

After the Tullahoma Campaign, Stanley was troubled by the discipline in the Union army. He also tried to maintain the peace as much as possible, and in some cases, he resorted to fear tactics. He even tried to scare some citizens to keep the peace by "my savage threats,"

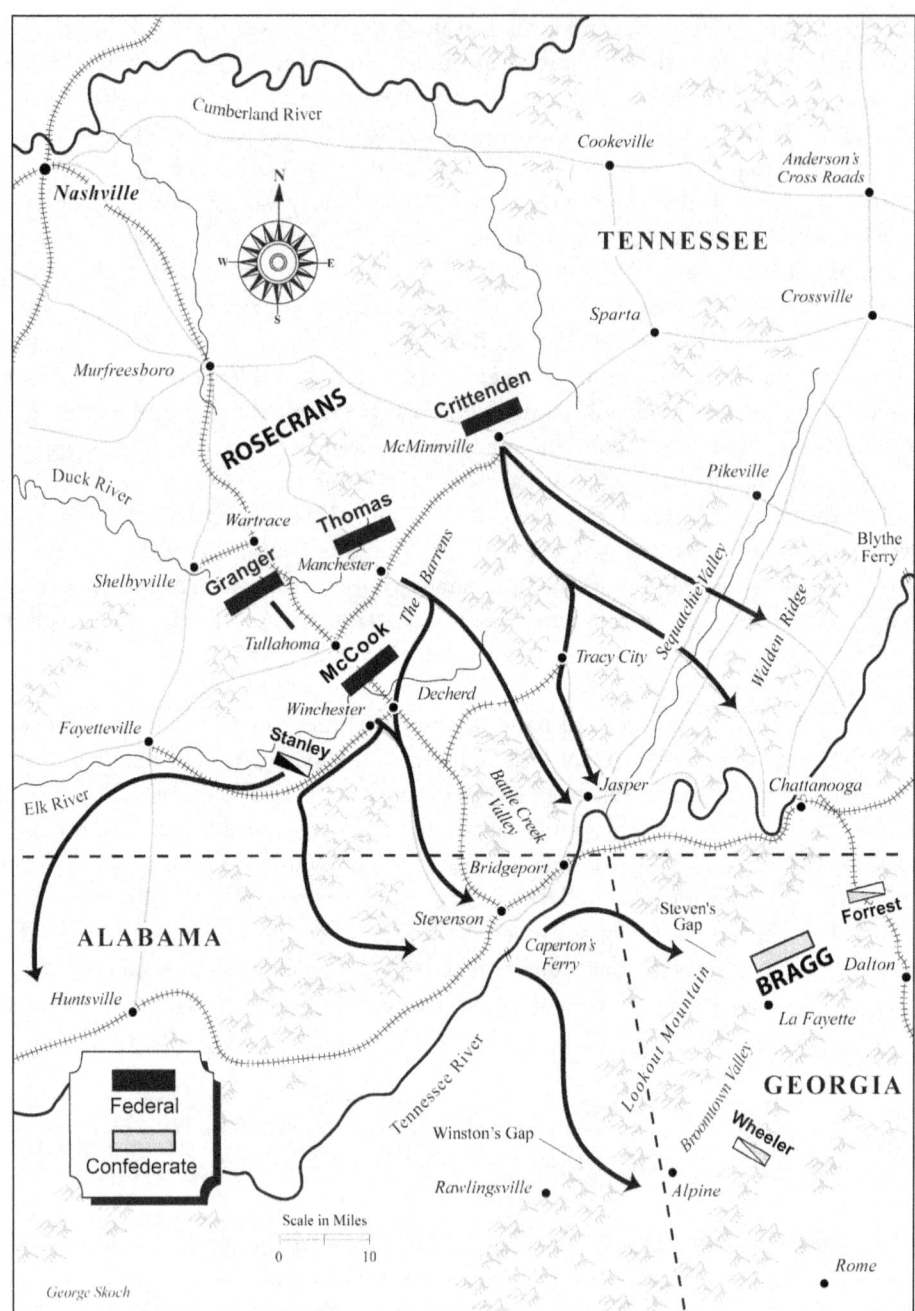

The Advance on Chattanooga (August 1863)

but he observed the local citizens generally opposed the actions of the bushwhackers and guerrillas. Overall, he recognized there were many who held a strong allegiance to the Union in eastern Tennessee and northern Alabama.[11]

Stanley, while he strove to make life as good as possible for his men, was a strict disciplinarian and was ever aware that lack of discipline could quickly turn into chaos and pillaging.

To demonstrate that he would not allow this type of behavior on the part of his troops, he endorsed the verdict of the court-martial of Corporal George W. Mercer, 1st Ohio Cavalry, who had been found guilty of setting fire to a cotton factory.[12] Stanley's mandate for discipline was communicated to his subordinates. He reminded his two division commanders, Mitchell and Turchin, of the importance of maintaining a tight rein on their soldiers. He wrote in a very thinly veiled jab at Turchin, who was involved in the "Rape of Athens" in 1862, "Irregularities and insufferable outrages in the war of foraging having been practiced by soldiers on former expeditions." He issued orders that if a soldier was found inside a civilian's house or acquiring a horse or mule in a method that was not according to regulations, the soldier would "be whipped, the uniforms stripped from him, and be drummed out of camp." In addition, he said, "The attention of subordinate officers was especially called to the order, and violations on the part of the soldiers detected in two instances, resulted in the dangerous wounding of one, and the sentencing of another, but a Drumhead Commission, of two years' confinement in the Penitentiary at Jeffersonville, after having one half of his head shaved as a mark of disgrace." While Stanley was not as severe a disciplinarian as Gordon Granger, he required his men to act like soldiers and not like bandits.[13]

David Stanley had long felt discipline was essential to the efficiency of his command, a belief that stemmed from whipping some of his soldiers who stole food prior to the war in the Dakota Territory. Julius Thomas, 1st Tennessee Cavalry, recorded at least one unpleasant event that probably prompted Stanley to reinforce discipline after the Tullahoma Campaign. Thomas wrote, "[A] complaint was given in by two women that some of our men had ravished them the charge was laid to the Col of the 7th Penn and a Capt. of the 4th regular Cav. in consequence of which very stringent order was issued by Gen Stanley." General Robert Mitchell heartily joined Stanley in enforcing discipline on the troops and was called a rigid disciplinarian by some of his subordinates.[14]

Discipline was not pleasant, as many of the men did violent and unacceptable acts. George Kryder, 3rd Ohio Cavalry, recorded, "Last Friday there was a man hung in Murfreesboro for deserting and murder. He deserted our army and went to bushwhacking and robbed a union man of his money and then shot him in the face and then cut the man's tongue out before he was dead. Horrible! Horrible!" John McLain, 4th Michigan, also noted in February "5 of our soldiers were whipped, heads shaved, and drummed through camp" for violating military regulations.[15]

W.R. Carter, 1st Tennessee Cavalry, wrote of a violation of ignoring the "lights out" rule: "And if a soldier was found with a light burning in his tent, he was taken to the provost-marshal's headquarters and there either tied up by the thumbs or made to carry a rail from three to five hours."[16] Charles Goodrich, 1st Wisconsin Cavalry, noted:

> We are subjected to a much more severe discipline than we were in Missouri. We are on the march, and no one is allowed to fall out of the ranks to get water or for any other purpose, without permission from the General. In a column of five to eight miles in length, he cannot be everywhere present to give permission, if he were so disposed. If one does fall out, he is in danger of being dismounted and performing a day's march on foot. No soldier is allowed, on pain of severe punishment, to enter any house…. All this strictness is right and necessary. In the army there are so many undisciplined and evilly disposed men to prevent our army from being converted into a marauding rabble, scattered all over the country, committing the most brutal and disgraceful outrages.

Both Stanley and Robert Mitchell would have been pleased with Goodrich's letter.[17]

Huntsville, Alabama, Expedition

On July 10, Rosecrans ordered Stanley to limit his expeditions and prepare the Union cavalry horses for future action. Three days later the cavalry rode to Huntsville, Alabama, and from July 13 through July 22 were to collect as much forage, horses and mules as could be found. Stanley was also ordered by Rosecrans to "impress every able bodied colored man I could find to use as teamsters and for work upon the fortifications of Nashville and Murfreesboro. My provost marshal arranged to capture the congregations of the negro churches as they were emptied after service on Sundays." Stanley collected 600–1,000 ex-slaves during various cavalry expeditions. Brigadier General John Beatty recorded in his diary, "General Stanley has returned from Huntsville, bringing with him about one thousand North Alabama negroes. This is a blow at the enemy in the right place. Deprived of slave labor, the whites will be compelled to send home, or leave at home, white men enough to cultivate the land and keep their families from starving." From the Southern point of view, Stanley's actions seemed to be achieving the desired effect. Local Huntsville resident Mary Jane Chadwick wrote, "They are stealing all the Negroes and confining them in the Seminary building. Seventy have just passed by under a strong guard. All the good horses have been taken." Stanley promised the local civilians that he would keep the ex-slaves overnight and if any wanted to return to their old masters, he would allow them to do so. None chose to return.[18]

While Stanley was confiscating mules as well as ex-slaves, he came in contact with many of the local citizens. A correspondent of the *Chicago Times* recorded one incident involving a Mrs. Pruitt, whose husband was a volunteer in Colonel A.A. Russell's Confederate cavalry. Mrs. Pruitt approached headquarters staff with a request for cornmeal and for the return of her confiscated mules. The lady began the encounter by being submissive and weak:

> [W]hich, together with a fluency of well-selected words, and a beauty of feature that would stir the feelings of an anchorite, would have plead her cause with partial success at least. But a casual reference to the proverbial cowardice of the command to which her husband is attached roused the dormant hostility that she had artfully concealed and partially denied, and she showered upon the authorities a perfect volume of vituperation, couched in terms as opprobrious as though it had been her business to vilify and denounce. The success that her feigned gentleness of disposition and excellency of character was about to secure, was swept away by this violent disclosure of her true character, and the General informed her that he would retain the mules and meal. Though she was left destitute of provisions almost, she continued furious, and, displaying an abundance of gold, proposed to purchase the property refused her.[19]

The troopers of the Union cavalry also met some of the local citizens. Trooper George Wood, 2nd Michigan Cavalry, recorded on July 23 his enjoyment of talking to the young women in Tennessee: "They are all full of fire (p___s & vinegar) for the southern cause. If I wished to know the sentiments of the people, I would talk to the female portion. They seldom keep anything back." Stanley also captured a Confederate captain who had just been married the day of his capture. The captain pleaded with Stanley to parole him, which Stanley did. The captain, true to his word, returned within two weeks and was sent to Johnson's Island until he was exchanged.[20]

Finally John Turchin was relieved of duty with the cavalry on July 29. The historian of the 7th Pennsylvania Cavalry wrote of Turchin, "General Turchin, as a cavalry officer, was not a success. He was personally brave, and had a good deal of dash in his mental make-up, but was physically out of place on horseback, the circumference of his body being equal to his height. His failure as a commander of cavalry was due, more than anything else, to the fact that he marched with too long a tail, orderlies and escort numbering nearly four hundred men." George Crook, a West Point classmate of Stanley, assumed command of the Second Cavalry Division upon Turchin's removal. Crook served early in the war in western Virginia, at the Second Battle of Bull Run and the Battle of Antietam. He and his division had been transferred west, and he had commanded an infantry brigade in the Fourteenth Corps during the Tullahoma Campaign.[21]

Brigadier General John Beatty's diary entry for July 31 recorded some important observations about the recent changes in the cavalry:

> Met General Turchin for the first time since he was before our court-martial at Huntsville. He appeared to be considerably down in spirit…. General Crook, hitherto in command of a brigade, succeeds Turchin as commander of a division. In short, Crook and Turchin just exchange places. The former is a graduate of the West Point Military Academy, and is an Ohio man, who has not, I think, greatly distinguished himself thus far…. General R.B. Mitchell is, with his command, in camp a little over a mile from us. He is in good spirits, and dwells with emphasis on the length and arduousness of the marches made by his troopers since he left Murfreesboro. The labor devolving upon him as the commander of a division of cavalry is tremendous; and yet I was rejoiced to find his physical system had stood the strain well. The wear and tear upon his intellect, however, must have been very great.[22]

The month began with the Union army pressing Bragg at Tullahoma and ended with the same army firmly in place in central Tennessee. The cavalry finished July with Mitchell's cavalry division scouting toward Sparta, Tennessee, where Forrest was reportedly concentrating some cavalry. Eli Long's brigade moved to Fayetteville to replace Mitchell. Long, who was returning from an expedition where he had citizens sign loyalty oaths, wrote he could not "make out oaths and bonds as fast as the rebs want to take them." He felt 75 percent of the citizens in the area supported the Union.[23]

August 1863

"What the intended movements of this are is impossible for me to grasp. Why we do not push on to Chattanooga and Atlanta and still farther down, I cannot see," wrote Charles Goodrich, 1st Wisconsin Cavalry. Henry Halleck would have approved of Goodrich's sentiments.[24]

The month of August began with a series of communications between Rosecrans and Halleck. Rosecrans began by outlining the seven problems he faced. These included the base of his supplies being 264 miles away and he being 83 miles from his closest depot at Nashville. His basest needs had to be transported overland or by raft. Next, he pointed out that the mountains to his front were difficult to travel, with poor roads and little hope of forage opportunities. Once he made it to the Tennessee

Brigadier General George Crook replaced John Turchin as division commander of cavalry (Library of Congress).

River, he faced an obstacle 600–1,000 yards wide defended by Confederates. Rosecrans also faced an undefeated foe that was likely to be reinforced by Johnston's army. Finally, he noted, "We must so advance as never to recede. The citizens say, and not without justice, 'Whip our armies, and then, when we no longer fear their return to power, we will show you that we are satisfied to be in the Union; but until you do that, we are not safe from proscription.'"[25]

The geography around Chattanooga, an important manufacturing center and transportation hub connecting the South to Virginia, proved an impressive obstacle for an advancing army. Chattanooga had been built on the south side of the Tennessee River and was nestled at the foot of Walden's Ridge and just to the west of Missionary Ridge. The dominating Lookout Mountain, 2,900 feet high, lay just southwest of the town. The mountains around the town were a hindrance for any military operation in regard to mobility and ability to observe the enemy.

At last a message from Halleck on August 5 included a preemptory order to march on Chattanooga and to furnish the War Department with daily updates of the movement of the various troops. Halleck added a personal, unofficial, message to Rosecrans on August 9 that stated that despite orders from the War Department, those in Washington wanted only success for Rosecrans' army. Halleck directly stated, "It is said that you 'do not draw straight in the traces, but are continually kicking out or getting one leg over.' No one doubts your good intentions and your great interest in the cause, and your desire to secure its success."[26]

Rosecrans began his initial movement toward the Tennessee River on August 9. Along the Union left flank, Minty's First Brigade was involved in the first skirmish of the campaign on Chattanooga on August 5 and again on August 9 with Colonel George Dibrell's 8th Tennessee Cavalry of Forrest's command. Minty was dispatched to Sparta, Tennessee, to screen and protect the flank of the Army of the Cumberland. Although the reports of the skirmish are vastly different between Dibrell and Minty, the encounter marked the first combat of the new campaign. Minty, receiving intelligence of Dibrell's position, sought to surprise him, which resulted in a hard-fought engagement.[27] Rosecrans boasted to Washington of Minty's success against Dibrell: "Minty's cavalry whipped General Dibrell's brigade of rebels out of Sparta." But, Dibrell remained ensconced around Sparta until the end of August. Robert Minty's brigade continued to protect the Union left flank and screened the forward positions of the army after his brush with Dibrell.[28]

Soon some of Wheeler's cavalry

Colonel Edward McCook, the personification of the "good officer," commanded Mitchell's division during much of the advance on Chattanooga (Library of Congress).

moved to Athens, Alabama, and Louis Watkins' Kentucky (U.S.) brigade rode after them on August 6. Edward McCook, commanding the First Cavalry Division due to Robert Mitchell's illness and absence from the army, moved his brigades toward the Tennessee River on August 11. McCook's division moved to Larkinsville, Alabama, on August 12, about twenty miles southwest of Bridgeport on the north side of the Tennessee River, with orders to protect the railroad and keep watch on any potential flanking movement by Wheeler.

For the Union cavalry from East Tennessee, the initiation of the campaign brought them closer to home. The members of the 1st Tennessee Cavalry had ridden hard for the past twelve months and by chance the army marched past Marion County, Tennessee. Company F requested permission for a week's leave to visit their families, who had suffered under the attacks of Southern sympathizing raiders who had burned the house of 2nd Lieutenant James Roulston. George Crook approved the request and allowed the men to travel home for a short visit.

CAVALRY CORPS, AUGUST 31, 1863[29]
Major General David S. Stanley

Escort
4th Ohio Cavalry, Company D, Captain Philip H. Warner

FIRST DIVISION
Colonel Edward M. McCook

First Brigade
Colonel Archibald P. Campbell
2nd Michigan, Maj. John C. Godley
9th Pennsylvania, Lt. Col. Roswell M. Russell
1st Tennessee, Lt. Col. James P. Brownlow
1st Wisconsin, Lt. Col. Henry Pomeroy

Second Brigade
Colonel Oscar H. La Grange
2nd Indiana, Maj. Joseph B. Presdee
4th Indiana, Col. John A. Platter
2nd Tennessee, Col. Daniel M. Ray

Third Brigade
Colonel Louis D. Watkins
4th Kentucky, Col. Wickliffe Cooper
5th Kentucky, Lt. Col. William T. Hoblitzell
6th Kentucky, Maj. Louis A. Gratz
7th Kentucky, Lt. Col. Thomas T. Vimont

Artillery
1st Ohio, Light, section Battery D (2nd Brigade),
Lieutenant Nathaniel M. Newell

SECOND DIVISION
Brigadier General George Crook

First Brigade
Colonel Robert H.G. Minty
3rd Indiana (battalion), Lt. Col. Robert Klein
4th Michigan, Maj. Horace Gray
7th Pennsylvania, Maj. James J. Seibert
4th United States, Capt. James B. McIntyre

Second Brigade
Colonel Eli Long
2nd Kentucky, Col. Thomas P. Nicholas
1st Ohio, Lt. Col. Valentine Cupp
3rd Ohio, Lt. Col. Charles B. Seidel
4th Ohio, Lt. Col. Oliver P. Robie

Third Brigade
Colonel William W. Lowe
5th Iowa, Maj. Alfred B. Brackett

10th Ohio, Lt. Col. William E. Haynes
5th Tennessee (1st Middle), Col. William B. Stokes
Artillery
Chicago (Illinois) Board of Trade Battery, Capt. James H. Stokes

Rosecrans Begins His Advance

"It begins tomorrow morning," wired Rosecrans to the War Department. The Union cavalry moved into position on August 15 in preparation for the beginning of the campaign. Rosecrans set his army in motion to accomplish a tremendous feat: he was faced with the challenge of moving his army over the Cumberland Mountains while his meager rail supply line was stretched. Then he faced an even more formidable obstacle in crossing the Tennessee River, several hundred yards wide, with no bridges and what was thought to be a strong Southern defense at the ferries and fords. He also faced an unbeaten foe that had had six weeks to entrench around Chattanooga.[30]

In the initial detailed orders given by Rosecrans to his corps commanders, he identified the specific lines of march. Great similarities can be drawn from this advance compared to the Tullahoma Campaign. The Twenty-first Corps advanced along the left, Thomas's Fourteenth Corps moved in the center, and McCook's Twentieth Corps marched on the right. The Union cavalry duties were very similar to the Stones River and Tullahoma advance. The cavalry on the left was to work closely with infantry command and was responsible for screening, protecting the flank and reconnaissance. The bulk of the cavalry was placed on the right and would be assigned a more offensive role. Rosecrans' initial orders detailed some specific duties for the cavalry. Much of Colonel William Lowe's Third Brigade (5th Tennessee, 10th Ohio and 5th Iowa cavalries) were detailed to protect the rear from guerrilla actions. As the army moved forward, Robert Minty's brigade was placed under the command of Brigadier General Horatio Van Cleve in a feint to make Bragg believe Rosecrans would attack Chattanooga from the north when he really planned to cross the river near Bridgeport. Minty again rode toward Sparta, with orders to completely move the Confederates out of the area as the army advanced. Meanwhile, Rosecrans shackled Stanley with these orders: "The chief of cavalry with the reserve brigade will follow the general headquarters, and will have special instructions for the remainder of the cavalry, which will be given him by the general commanding." This plan for the cavalry had worked well at Tullahoma, and Rosecrans—and presumably Stanley—hoped it would again be successful.[31]

Stanley, with the reserve brigade, was to follow Rosecrans' headquarters and act under his direct command as the situation developed. Edward McCook's division was ordered to the right flank and screened for Alexander McCook's Twentieth Corps. This command model put much of the cavalry (two of six brigades) away from the direct control of Stanley and many of the orders came directly from Rosecrans and Garfield and infantry commanders, as in the case of Minty. This order assigning Stanley near headquarters but without specific objectives set the stage for a confrontation between Rosecrans and Stanley later in the campaign. During the advance on Chattanooga, Stanley operated without the ability to use his own initiative. In addition, Rosecrans erased much of the progress Stanley had made by establishing an independent cavalry arm.

In another move also reminiscent of the Tullahoma Campaign, Rosecrans advanced on Bragg's entrenchments around Chattanooga while being forced to march through difficult geographic obstacles. Rosecrans wanted to feint a direct crossing near Chattanooga while moving his army across the expansive Tennessee River at Stevenson and Bridgeport. Then while Bragg expected a direct attack on Chattanooga Rosecrans hoped to implement a large wheeling movement, similar to the one used at Manchester, to cut Bragg off from his primary escape route and to be able to fight him removed from strong entrenched defenses. Crittenden's corps, with the efforts of John T. Wilder's mounted infantry along with Minty's First Cavalry Brigade, were the tools to provide the feint. Rosecrans wrote confidently to Halleck, "The rebels expect us above Chattanooga."[32]

The Union cavalry prepared to fulfill Rosecrans' orders. By mid–August, Louis Watkins' brigade quickly moved back to Huntsville guarding the extreme right flank. Watkins was ordered to protect the bridges but the environment around

Brigadier General James A. Garfield, Rosecrans' chief of staff and future United States president (Library of Congress).

Brownsborough, the location of his initial headquarters, was so unhealthy he was forced to move.[33] Minty was near Van Cleve's division on August 16, and Van Cleve watched Minty begin an expedition (to Pikeville) according to Rosecrans' campaign orders. Van Cleve wrote of Minty, "He is certainly an able and efficient officer." The bespectacled and thoughtful Van Cleve was one of the oldest generals in the Union army at the age of 54. He was a New Jersey native and lived in Minnesota before the war. A West Point graduate, class of '31, he was the past colonel of the 2nd Minnesota Infantry. Van Cleve, a seasoned veteran, suffered a leg wound and was removed from the field at the Battle of Stones River.[34]

Minty had sparred twice with George Dibrell's cavalry near Sparta and now, as Rosecrans began his advance, it was imperative for the Federal movement that the Confederate cavalry be pushed across the Tennessee River. On the afternoon of August 17 Robert Minty intended to complete what he had not been able to do before. Minty's 1,400-man brigade rode in the direction of Pikeville, Tennessee, and his route took him through Sparta, Dibrell's hometown. Minty found Dibrell's 1,200 Confederate troopers positioned along Calfkiller Creek near Sperry's Mill. With the 7th Pennsylvania and 4th Michigan cavalries in advance, the Union cavalry drove Dibrell's men across the creek and as Dibrell moved to the rear the 3rd Indiana and 4th U.S. Cavalry rode across the creek hoping to block the retreat. But, Dibrell had no problem escaping the trap Minty had set for him. Minty pursued his quarry to Yankeetown before disengaging and riding for Sparta to bivouac for the night, but the hunter became the hunted.[35]

As the Union cavalry rode for Sparta, the road curved by a creek bordered by a high, wooded bluff. As the column proceeded, Minty rode with his staff at the head of the column.

He was asked, "'Colonel, this is the first time I ever knew you to move without an advanced guard.'" Minty replied, "'It is scarcely necessary—we will go into bivouac almost immediately.'" As the column approached the creek, 200 Confederate troopers ambushed the column. The Confederate ambushers fired into the head of the column. The volley left four holes across the shoulder of Captain Joseph Vale, adjutant general, a ball to the thigh of Sergeant Birch, who also had a broken leg, Minty's horse with three bullet holes, and two orderlies' horses killed beneath them. Troopers of the 4th Michigan and 4th U.S. Cavalry dismounted and returned fire. The Confederate cavalry had chosen their ambush well because the creek was impassable upstream and resulted in one Union trooper drowning and a few others being wounded. Finally, the 7th Pennsylvania and 3rd Indiana were able to cross the creek from the other direction and flanked the ambushers, who quickly withdrew.[36]

Minty camped for the night and set out the next morning in search of Dibrell's cavalry, only to find them gone. Minty estimated Dibrell had 1,200 troopers, but local citizens estimated there were 1,500 Confederate cavalry. The engagement ended in a draw, but Minty was finally able to drive Dibrell from his base of operations. Minty claimed 14 prisoners and an unknown number of enemies killed and wounded. He reported one killed and 15 wounded of his command.[37]

The Southern-sympathizing Chattanooga newspaper erroneously reported that the ambush had killed "General" Minty, but when Captain Vale read the article, he swore to shave his beard. He said he didn't mind being killed as a captain, but he wasn't ambitious enough to assume the rank of general.[38]

Rosecrans was pleased with Minty's efforts: "Minty's cavalry had a fight with Dibrell's brigade, of Forrest's, at Sparta, on Monday night; whipped and drove them to Yankeetown and Kingston." While some of the cavalry performed well, Stanley received a message from Gordon Granger regarding the 5th Tennessee Cavalry: "Colonel Galbraith's command has left Shelbyville. I will send them back in a few days. They are terribly lax in their discipline." Of course, Granger, notorious for the level of discipline he required, had already alienated many in the Union army.[39]

On August 18, Archibald Campbell's First Brigade of McCook's cavalry division was in position at the various fords and ferries along the Tennessee River and reported no problems from the enemy. The 9th Pennsylvania Cavalry guarded the railroad bridge across Mud Creek, Bellefonte Ford, Gunter's Ford, and the mouth of Mud Creek. The 2nd Michigan and 1st Tennessee Cavalry defended Caperton's Ford, Cox's Ford, and Shallow Ford.

A puzzling order was transmitted on August 18 from Henry Halleck to Ulysses Grant at Vicksburg ordering George Crook, Stanley's Second Division commander, to duty in West Virginia. While Crook was actually part of the Army of the Cumberland, this order was obviously misdirected. However, the order would mark the relatively short, but valuable, tenure of Crook in the cavalry of the Army of the Cumberland. He would transfer to the Department of West Virginia in February 1864. Crook was a welcome addition as division commander. Not only was he a West Point graduate and classmate of Stanley, he had many of the same traits as Stanley in regard to the regular soldier. T.F. Dornblaser, 7th Pennsylvania Cavalry, recalled, "Crook is a gentleman and a soldier. He had the same respect for a private as he had for an officer. His orderly would not ride behind him, unless the road was too narrow for the two to ride side by side."[40]

The next day Minty continued his duty in conjunction with Crittenden's infantry. Van

Cleve reported that Minty had divided his command. One battalion was at Rock Island and another was positioned near the ardent secessionist stronghold of Sparta. Already Minty's brigade was being worn down by the action along the left flank and horses were already being worn out. Minty had only 1,200 troopers in total and he planned to make his next expedition with 1,000 men to Kingston, where a strong concentration of rebels were reported to be.[41]

In addition to the toll of the campaign on the men and mounts, the need for supplies was great and affected the ability of the cavalry to perform its assigned tasks. Van Cleve wrote to corps headquarters of Minty's woes in obtaining forage for his horses and asked how long Minty was expected to guard the left flank alone. While Minty should have returned for his forage, Crittenden interpreted Rosecrans orders as "required you to remain in the valley of the Tennessee until further orders." Minty would be required to send to the rear from supplies and forage what he could in the countryside.[42]

Despite a shortage of provisions, Minty had the situation along the left flank in good order. His scouts rode to Blythe's Ferry and found two Mississippi regiments entrenching along the other side of the Tennessee River, about 700 to 800 yards wide at that location. The continued problem for Minty, who was required to stay constantly in motion along the left, was the lack of forage and supplies. Minty's rations would last only until the next morning (August 22), and there was little to find in the countryside. He wrote, "Forage is not so plentiful as you appeared to think.... The position here is not good." Van Cleve's discovery of the dire situation of Minty's command resulted in the immediate dispatch of five days' rations and he concluded Minty would need to forage his horses in the countryside. While Minty worked well with Van Cleve, Crittenden proved to be a cruel master.[43]

Throughout this campaign the traditional cavalry and mounted infantry were challenged with the distances and duties of their roles. Fortunately, John Wilder's remarkable mounted infantry brigade also was on the move and provided concentrated firepower, striking the enemy when the opportunity presented and also providing intelligence that he promptly forwarded to General J.J. Reynolds. One of Wilder's first actions was the shelling of two steamboats, which sank one and disabled the other, on the Tennessee River at Chattanooga on August 21.[44]

By August 21 Edward McCook was in good control of his flank but reported he had a forage party bushwhacked by some irregulars. His Third Brigade, positioned at Maysville, guarded the Flint River and Hurricane River bridges. Watkins patrolled the Huntsville, Whitesburg, and Lemon's ferries and provided couriers for McCook's headquarters. Daniel Ray, temporarily in command of the Second Brigade, had the 4th Indiana Cavalry at Paint Rock Bridge. The 2nd Indiana and 1st Wisconsin were positioned at McCook's headquarters. Ray's brigade patrolled Larkin's Landing, the Guntersville and Fort Deposit roads and along the line of the railroad. Archibald Campbell's 9th Pennsylvania was at Mud Creek Bridge, also guarding the Bellefonte and Meltonsville fords. The 2nd Michigan and 1st Tennessee continued to guard Caperton's, Cox's and Shallow fords.[45]

On to the Tennessee River, August 23–September 1

On August 23, the Confederates crossed the river at Blythe's Ferry and Minty withdrew toward the main body of the army at Poe's Tavern—much to the unhappiness of Crittenden, who immediately dispatched Minty back to his position on the flank. Crittenden wrote, "I am much annoyed at this movement of Minty's." He was also disappointed that Minty gave no report of the size of the force that moved across the river. Van Cleve replied, "Colonel Minty has every available man and horse with him, and urges sending him more." Van Cleve continued to support Minty's actions throughout this campaign and he respected the cavalry officer. Being Minty's commanding officer for much of this campaign, Van Cleve knew intimately that Minty's duty was fraught with danger.[46]

Minty explained that on August 23 he held the extreme left flank of the army with a small number of men, and his scouts reported Forrest's cavalry was crossing the Tennessee at Sale Creek, which placed the enemy between his cavalry and Crittenden's infantry. As an experience officer, Minty recognized the vulnerability of his command, which could be attacked in the front as well as the flank and rear by Forrest's cavalry. Minty's reason for moving toward Poe's Tavern was to prevent the enemy from cutting him off and surrounding him with a superior force. However, his appeal fell on deaf ears, and he was ordered back into position with the admonition, "He has acted very imprudently and must return to watch the enemy." But again, Van Cleve came in support of Minty, stating the order was received and would be communicated to Minty. Van Cleve added that Minty "no doubt found it absolutely necessary to save his command."[47]

On August 25, while responding to Crittenden's concerns, Minty reported he had not abandoned his position on the left. Van Cleve came to his defense in a message to Crittenden, stating, "I have every confidence in Colonel Minty's vigilance and judgment, and believe you will be perfectly satisfied with his movements." While Minty was moving before what he perceived as a threat to his command, this was good news for Rosecrans. If Bragg was moving to meet the Union advance north of Chattanooga, Rosecrans' objective of crossing his army at Stevenson was likely to meet much less resistance.[48]

George Dibrell's cavalry, which had proved so troublesome, was finally confirmed across the Tennessee River on August 25. Local citizens reported that the remainder of Forrest's cavalry had moved to the Kingston area. So effective was Rosecrans' feint that Forrest had been dispatched there to block the Federal crossing of the river. On the right, Edward McCook obtained intelligence that Wheeler's cavalry was concentrating around Rome, Georgia.[49]

Meanwhile, on the west flank, the 4th Indiana Cavalry, at Paint Rock Bridge, skirmished with a group of Confederates at the ferry opposite Fort Deposit. The Confederates fired on the Union cavalry from a ferryboat and the southern shore. The 4th Indiana returned fire and drove off the raiders, capturing six prisoners. In another action, McCook noted five troopers of the 6th Kentucky Cavalry were taken prisoners by bushwhackers near Maysville. McCook retaliated by burning property in the vicinity and sent the 4th Kentucky in pursuit of the irregulars.[50]

As the month drew to a close, Rosecrans completed preparations for crossing the Tennessee River by identifying fords and moving pontoons into place. Van Cleve ordered the 3rd Indiana Cavalry, which had been positioned at Rock Island, closer to the main infantry line. Minty, chafing under infantry control, appealed to Crittenden: "I have made my pickets as small as possible—12 men on each road, except Blythe's, and there only 24—but yet the picket duty is very heavy. Can you not send me the men of my brigade that you have in Sequatchie Valley?" Minty's patience had finally run out on August 27 when he wrote to the Twenty-first Corps headquarters: "Rations ran out last night. You ought to keep me supplied with coffee, sugar, and salt. The men are constantly at work, and should be fed." Minty suffered from the same disregard which had been alleviated by placing the cavalry under Stanley's control. Now, the same old problems and misuse had reemerged. While Minty worked well with Van Cleve, there was almost total disregard from corps headquarters.[51]

While the cavalry guarded the advance of the Army of the Cumberland as it approached the Tennessee River, Gordon Granger's Reserve Infantry Corps began a slow advance forward. The Third Brigade of Crook's cavalry division continued protecting the supply lines in central Tennessee. On August 27, Galbraith's 5th Tennessee Cavalry moved into position at Shelbyville; two battalions of the 10th Ohio Cavalry moved to Athens, Alabama, and the 5th Iowa Cavalry remained in Murfreesboro.[52]

Stanley and Crook were remarkably quiet during the entire movement of the cavalry through the end of August. Perhaps this is because they were without the routine command duties which had been taken from them. This is one of the unknown aspects of this campaign. Most unfortunate would be the fact that Stanley would never write a record of the campaign. Much is unknown in regard to Stanley's opinions regarding the command decisions and the use of the cavalry during this advance. The cavalry continued working diligently in assisting in the monumental advance of the army toward the Tennessee River. As the month ended, Stanley directed the cavalry to assist in preparing and identifying fords which could be used to move the army across the river.[53]

The Confederate forces in the countryside struck back at the Union advance whenever they could. Louis Watkins's Third Cavalry Brigade, posted near Huntsville, found the destruction of three bridges by Southern guerrillas on August 26. The destruction occurred over a twenty-five-mile front and nothing could be done. Again, Watkins dispatched the 4th Kentucky Cavalry to the Maysville, Alabama, area to search for the perpetrators, but he was unable to find those responsible. The army continued to move ahead and, likewise, Watkins moved his brigade forward and left the defense of the bridges and railroads in northern Alabama to the following infantry.

At last the army was in position along the Tennessee River. The cavalry pushed across the fords on the evening of August 28 and the infantry corps followed soon afterward. The 2nd Michigan Cavalry crossed at Bridgeport to drive off the sharpshooters delaying the construction of the bridge at that location and Rosecrans ordered two cavalry regiments of Crook's division across at Hart's Bar to protect that ford. In the meantime, the two eastern regiments of Louis Watkins' Third Brigade again rode westward to protect the bridges and railroad around Huntsville even though Edward McCook objected to this move. Edward McCook's other two brigades of cavalry also crossed the river despite a 200-yard swim by the horses and troopers. Pontoon bridges were moved into place and some of the cavalry crossed the river on August 29. Soon thereafter, Rosecrans ordered Crittenden to move his various commands southward to the river in preparation of crossing. Minty still tried, unsuccessfully, to gain command of the 3rd Indiana Cavalry, part of his own brigade, as he joined the southward advance.[54]

Once across the river, the cavalry began its work of reconnaissance and screening. Eli Long's cavalry brigade crossed the river and scouted to Trenton, Georgia, on August 28–31. Long spooked the enemy's cavalry pickets that rode toward Rome, Georgia, but met little resistance. Long sent a detachment of three officers and fifty-two soldiers to secure Island Creek Ford before sunrise on August 31. As the group moved across the ford one of the officers accidentally discharged his revolver, wounding one of his own soldiers. The gunshot alerted the defenders, but no one else was injured in the crossing. Soon the 1st Ohio, 3rd Ohio, 4th Ohio and 2nd Kentucky were in position at the ford.[55]

Rosecrans pulled together his monthly returns of men available for duty. He had 76,071 men in his army, which included artillery, infantry and cavalry. What is somewhat surprising is the number of cavalry available for duty. Stanley recorded only 9,642 men present for duty and this included his artillery. The effort of keeping an effective number of cavalry was very difficult and maintaining serviceable horses was important to keeping the cavalry functioning. For example, on August 27 Archibald Campbell reported the 2nd Michigan Cavalry and the 1st Tennessee Cavalry had 124 men without horses and another 129 men mounted but on "nonserviceable" horses.[56] While constantly on the move during this campaign, it was important to keep the horses in top condition. Throughout the campaign, it was difficult to handle the routine duties while called upon to be ever on the move. In certain cases the men and horses were pushed to the point of exhaustion.[57]

One final and yet significant event occurred in August. On August 30, Secretary of war Stanton announced he was sending one of his assistants, Charles A. Dana, to Rosecrans. Earlier in 1863 Dana had been sent to observe Grant during the Vicksburg Campaign. Little did Rosecrans or Stanley know that having this person in their midst would affect both their careers in the Army of the Cumberland. Stanton wrote, "Mr. Dana is a gentleman of distinguished character, patriotism, and ability, and possesses the entire confidence of the Department. You will please afford to him the courtesy and consideration which he merits, and explain to him fully any matters which you may desire, through him, to bring to the notice of this Department." The purpose of Charles Dana with the Army of the Cumberland was not fully known, but the army received him as a "bird of ill-omen."[58]

Rosecrans ended August full of confidence, and his soldiers shared in that confidence. John Lynch, a trooper in the 2nd Michigan Cavalry, wrote in a letter on August 21, "We are satisfied that 'old Rosy' knows best when to move & when he starts we have no fears for the result." Just as he had done at Tullahoma, Rosecrans moved his army through difficult geographic obstacles and maneuvered easily around Bragg's strength. Rosecrans set Wilder to work carrying much of the offensive duty for the Army of the Cumberland, but it was a different matter for the Union cavalry. Stephen Starr, author of the *Union Cavalry in the Civil War*, noted, "The work the cavalry was given little to do from August 16 to September 4, the day the last of the Union infantry crossed the Tennessee, was completely inconsequential." He noted Stanley was given the task of "picket" duty, courier service, marking fords and driving bushwhackers away. The quietness on the part of Stanley likely reflected the fact that his cavalry had played such a small part in the campaign thus far and also because the cavalry was again placed under the control of infantry commanders despite the almost universal agreement that the cavalry worked better as a cohesive unit with defined objectives. Stanley's assessment of Rosecrans' use of the cavalry was an emphatic—he "had no idea of the use of cavalry."[59]

The assessment of the actions of the Union cavalry was correct. So far, it had seen almost no action in the campaign. Minty had sparred with George Dibrell's cavalry at Calfkiller River near Sparta on August 17, and the 4th Kentucky had two expeditions at Maysville, Alabama, on August 21 and 28, to try to control the guerrilla activities in the area. The 2nd Tennessee Cavalry performed reconnaissance action at Shellmound on August 30–31; and Eli Long's brigade explored the area around Trenton, Georgia, on August 28–31. The efforts of twenty-

Charles Dana, assistant secretary of war and a "bird of ill omen" (Library of Congress).

two regiments resulted in secure communications and flanks secure from marauding enemy cavalry, but overall they had unremarkable duty. Perhaps, the most notable service of the Union cavalry was the role of Minty's brigade in successfully misleading Bragg into believing Rosecrans intended to attack Chattanooga from the north.

It should be noted that while the Union cavalry was relegated to the feint along the left flank and supporting the advance of the infantry corps across the Tennessee River in August, the Confederate cavalry fared little better. Wheeler had been stretched across a fifty-mile front on picket duty, much as Stanley had. As Rosecrans marched toward Chattanooga, Wheeler withdrew most of his men to Rome, Georgia, and Alexandria, Alabama, and left only two regiments to guard the river. Meanwhile, Forrest had been deployed along the Union left flank in an attempt to impede what Bragg incorrectly assumed was Rosecrans' primary advance. Frustration was high for Union and Confederate cavalrymen alike at the end of August.

At the end of that month David Stanley wrote a long letter to Major General George Stoneman, chief of the U.S. Cavalry Bureau, in Washington and summarized the condition of the cavalry corps of the Army of the Cumberland. He outlined his need for more uniform firearms. He mentioned two of his regiments were armed with Colt revolving rifles, which, while effective when the trooper dismounted, were hardly cavalry rifles. Some of the regiments had "half a dozen different patterns of carbines." He focused much of the letter on the needs regarding the horses. The saddles which had recently been exposed to the rainfall of the Tullahoma Campaign were almost totally useless. Of importance was that he was in need of 1,300 mounts. Stanley concluded the letter by mentioning his pride in his troopers: "Some of them are all that could be expected of a volunteer cavalry and perhaps quite equal to any regular cavalry now in service. They are equal to any emergency and do not hesitate to charge anything sabre in hand." But he expressed his concern about the decision to mount so many of the Tennessee soldiers. Stanley wrote, "[The] men are brave and willing but the officers lack education and are wanting in industry." The letter concluded with an appraisal of the division commanders, Crook and Mitchell. Mitchell's health was a concern for Stanley and he asked Stoneman to contemplate a good officer to replace him.[60]

The March into Georgia, September 1–September 7

September was to prove a defining month for Rosecrans, Stanley and his cavalry, and the Army of the Cumberland. Rosecrans had again proved to be the master of moving his army against Bragg. It successfully crossed the Tennessee River, which had been a monumental task but one that occurred without a significant incident. Bragg, who was waiting for the development of the enemy at Chattanooga, failed to prevent the Army of the Cumberland from gaining a land approach on Chattanooga from the west. In part because of Wheeler's decision to remove the Confederate cavalry to the rear, the movement of the Army of the Cumberland across the Tennessee River came as a surprise to Bragg, who became aware of the crossing only after a resident of Stevenson told him of it. The Union infantry was successfully across the Tennessee River by September 4.[61]

The actions of the cavalry from September 1 through September 15 were important to the upcoming Battle of Chickamauga, but it is one of the most difficult periods to trace the movements, the twenty-two Union regiments being constantly in motion. The mountains and valleys around Chattanooga made the actions appear disjointed and confusing. To complicate matters, command issues and the interpersonal relations of the primary commanders were severely stressed during this period, which served as the preamble to the Battle of Chickamauga. For the most part, William Lowe's Third Brigade of Crook's Second Cavalry Division had little active participation in the cavalry actions during the advance on Chattanooga during September 1–17. Lowe's three-regiment brigade protected communications and supplies in Middle Tennessee and northern Alabama. This was difficult and important duty but duty that kept these regiments away from the front. Also, the 7th Kentucky Cavalry of Louis Watkins's Third Brigade was initially given the duty of protecting the fords and bridges along the Tennessee, because if Bragg was successful in defeating Rosecrans at Chattanooga, Rosecrans would be in the perilous position of having such a restricted route of retreat. With Minty also detached, this left fourteen regiments in four brigades of cavalry for work along the Union front and right flank.[62]

September began as a hot, dry and dusty month and many in the Union cavalry were sick. Captain Marshall Thatcher, 2nd Michigan Cavalry, estimated that nearly one-third of the troopers were ill. Thatcher recalled that sick soldiers were found wandering away from their beds. As they were gently returned to the hospital he thought that "rough soldiers sometimes have hearts of women." Trooper George Healy, 5th Iowa Cavalry, also reported the

Tennessee River near Chattanooga (National Archives).

extensive illnesses in the cavalry: "There are a great many sick nowadays—fevers of all kind and ague."[63]

Illness struck the high and the low. On September 3, Alexander McCook sent Stanley an important message. The purpose of the letter was to define the exact route Garfield had identified for Stanley's advance, but McCook closed his letter with, "I hope you are better. Have you any news?" This message is important as the point that marks the beginning of David Stanley's illness. The next two weeks would be detrimental to his reputation because of the impact of the illness on his performance. If McCook asked about Stanley's health on September 3, it was likely he had been ill for some days prior to this message. With Robert Mitchell's absence and Stanley's inability to command, Stanley felt he could not afford to be sick.[64]

Union Cavalry Operations Around Chattanooga (September 5–17, 1863)

Robert Mitchell, Stanley's second-in-command, was already on sick leave and missed much of the campaign. General John Beatty recorded in his diary his thoughts about Mitchell's absence: "The papers state that General R.B. Mitchell has gone home on sick leave. Poor fellow! He must have been taken suddenly, for when I saw him, a day or two ago, he was the picture of health. It is wonderful to me how a fellow as fat as Bob can come the sick dodge so successfully. He can get sick at a moment's notice." Mitchell was not an unlikeable commander and had the support of many in his command. A politician, he was simply not prepared to command the entire cavalry corps in the mountains around Chattanooga. George Crook, Stanley's other division commander, would have been a better choice but Mitchell's tenure in the cavalry corps and date of promotion superseded that of Crook. Neither of these commanders equaled Stanley's command ability.[65]

Bragg still occupied Chattanooga. Even though Rosecrans had moved his army over the Tennessee River, he still faced a dangerous enemy; but his confidence was growing. While Rosecrans advanced on Chattanooga, Major General Ambrose Burnside was marching on Knoxville. Although the two generals often exchanged communications, there was only a weak attempt to coordinate their advances. Burnside marched with the Army of the Ohio, which included the Ninth and Twenty-third corps. Occasionally Minty's cavalry extended far enough to the north and Burnside pushed far enough south for the two Union forces to work together. Robert Minty's troops rode into Kingston on September 2 along with Ambrose Burnside's troops in one of the rare cooperative efforts between these two Union forces. During his reconnaissance efforts, Minty also confirmed that Forrest was still on the other side of the Tennessee River. The Confederates had not abandoned the fords on this portion of the river and those and the ferries remained strongly defended.[66]

On September 3, Garfield issued marching orders to the corps commanders: "General Crook will communicate with General [Alexander] McCook on his route. General Stanley will send such force from Rawlingsville as he may deem sufficient for the purpose to Rome, Ga., or as far in that direction as practicable, to ascertain the position and intentions of the enemy. This force should push forward with audacity, feel the enemy strongly, and make a strong diversion in that direction." These orders set the stage for the first of two clashes Stanley would have with headquarters in the next ten days. The bulk of the Union cavalry moved to Will's Valley about thirty miles south of Bridgeport with orders to ride to Rome as a diversion and to "feel" the enemy. In the meantime, the 3rd Indiana Cavalry of Minty's cavalry was assigned directly to Thomas Crittenden and the remainder of Minty's cavalry reported to William B. Hazen.[67]

While moving to Will's Valley, the Union cavalry advanced over Sand Mountain, a large sandstone plateau about 1,000 feet above the surrounding geography. William Carter of the 1st Tennessee Cavalry recalled the sun shone

> on the long lines of blue marching slowly along the winding, zig-zag road that led up the mountain side. Sometimes the line was visible in a half-dozen places, so short were the crooks in the road. Heavy details were made to aid the teamsters in getting the heavily loaded wagons to the summit. The drivers shouted and yelled themselves hoarse, yes, and "cussed" a little, too, at the ever-willing, ever ready, patient government mule, who, unmindful of the surroundings, was so faithfully tugging away at the loaded wagons.

Despite the conditions and the hard work getting over the mountain, the view on the valley below was breathtaking for the troopers.[68]

While the 1st Ohio Cavalry moved over the mountain, the troopers discovered a manufacturer of peach brandy. W.L. Curry humorously noted that he could well understand why the rebel cavalry had made such a strong resistance for the mountain. The possession of the brandy provided an excellent incentive to fight. Soon many of the regiment had their canteens filled with the brandy and enjoyed their ride over the mountain that night. Curry noted that by the next morning "those that could not ride down or walk down, just fell down."[69]

Elbert Squire, 4th Michigan Cavalry, reported a humorous event and the advance on Chattanooga continued. A trooper in his regiment shot a pig and paid the owner for the animal belatedly. Squire found most of the civilians loyal Confederates despite their comments to the contrary. He questioned a young man about the various generals, Johnson Island (a Union POW camp) and Lake Erie. When asked about Lake Erie, the young man earnestly exclaimed "he did not know him." Squire more seriously summarized his feelings: "The more I see of Slavery, the more do I despise the system. I judge it to be fully debasing and injurious to the whites as to the blacks."[70]

As the Union advance progressed over Sand Mountain and the Union cavalry settled into Will's Valley the progress of the Federal advance sounded alarm bells for the Confederate cavalry. William Martin's cavalry passed through Summerville on September 2 and sent a report about the Union advance to Bragg's headquarters in Chattanooga. The presence of Union troops south of Chattanooga was of great concern to Bragg. The Confederates' primary fear was being flanked, and second was the threat to the Western and Atlantic Railroad, which ran from Rome and provided supplies to Bragg's army in Chattanooga.[71]

By the end of September 3, David Stanley established cavalry headquarters five miles from Winston's, about twelve miles from Rawlingsville. Edward McCook's First Division camped one mile west of Davis and George Crook's Second Brigade encamped at Winston's. The local citizens reported the close proximity of Wheeler and his Southern cavalry. Wheeler, Crew's brigade, was reported to be at Alpine, Georgia, with 2,000 troopers, about twenty-four miles from Stanley's location. Also during the day, Stanley acknowledged Garfield's order, replying, "As soon as I get the cavalry well together I will move Wheeler." Wharton's Confederate cavalry was reported to be in Rome. The Union cavalry on the Union right flank faced two divisions of cavalry with four brigades. To complicate matters, the maps of the area were of poor quality. Stanley noted that the Union maps were in error because Winston's was twenty miles from Trenton, not the ten miles shown on the Union maps. The next day Alexander McCook irritably wrote, "There is no such place as Winston's Gap." A citizen by the name of Winston lived at the foot of an eight-mile trek up Lookout Mountain.[72]

On September 4, Stanley moved ahead with some of his cavalry, feeling for the Confederates before him. Part of Eli Long's brigade rode with Stanley over Lookout Mountain intending to ride to Summerville and then to LaFayette. Morale was good within the cavalry corps and Alexander McCook reflected this in a message to Garfield: "I do not know what Stanley's instructions are, but he wrote me that he could carry them out as well on that side of Lookout Mountain. He has 5,800 sabers and can whip all before him."[73]

The Union cavalry was busy during the day after so much lethargy of the previous two weeks. George Crook set up his headquarters at Winston's and took possession of Winn's Gap. Edward McCook ordered Campbell's First Division to Rawlingsville. Stanley also observed there was little, if any, gap at Winston's Gap. Edward McCook located a trace over the mountain, described as a "bad road," about four miles from Rawlingsville, Stanley ended the day promising Garfield that he would send an expedition the next day into Broomtown

Panoramic view from Lookout Mountain. The view on the valley below was breathtaking for the troopers (Library of Congress).

Valley, the valley east of Winston's over Lookout Mountain. Stanley, grasping the magnitude of the geography to his front, emphasized in his report "Rome 48 miles; Dalton 45 to 50; and La Fayette 25." He also noted to Garfield that Rome was still seventy miles away from army headquarters down Broomtown Valley.[74]

While the Army of the Cumberland closed in on Bragg at Chattanooga, Bragg felt he was only in a defensive position, unable to take the fight to Rosecrans. Bragg wrote to Jefferson Davis that he was prepared to meet Rosecrans at whatever point he "assails." Bragg wrote, "My position is to some extent embarrassing in regard to offensive movements." But Bragg was not consistent in his messages. While he was talking about a defensive position with Davis, with his infantry commanders he contemplated crossing the Tennessee River and "crushing this corps," referring to Crittenden's Twenty-first Corps, while Rosecrans slowly marched over the mountains.[75]

Stanley easily moved over Sand Mountain and much of this was due to the lack of enterprise on the part of Wheeler's cavalry. Wheeler lightly defended the gaps over the mountain, causing very little delay for the Union cavalry and "surrendering both Lookout Valley and the chance to develop the enemy's intentions early on," noted historian Peter Cozzens. Facing the Union cavalry was Wheeler's command, which consisted of Wharton's and Martin's divisions and Roddey's brigade. Martin's cavalry, about 1,200 men, guarded the passes from the Tennessee River to Neal's Gap, and Wharton's cavalry was assigned from Neal's Gap to Gadsden. Stanley had faced Wheeler, Martin and Wharton in battle previously. Only Brigadier General Phillip Dale Roddey was a new adversary. Roddey was a native Alabaman who ran a steamboat before the Civil War. He was the first colonel of the 4th Alabama Cavalry and had served in various engagements, including the Battle of Shiloh and the advance on Corinth and was active in the capture of Abel Straight's abortive mounted infantry expedition earlier in the year.[76]

While Wheeler protected the Confederate left flank, the formidable Nathan Bedford Forrest occupied the Confederate right. Forrest's command included Brigadier General Frank Armstrong's and Brigadier General John Pegram's divisions. On September 5, the enemy was very active along Minty's front on the Union left flank. More Confederate defenders suddenly appeared at Blythe's Ferry, about twenty miles northeast of Chattanooga, but no move was made across the Tennessee River.

On September 5, the first friction between Stanley and headquarters occurred as George Crook moved into Broomtown Valley with the 1st Ohio and 3rd Ohio cavalries. Stanley, contemplating his orders to move against Wheeler, wrote to Garfield: "I do not want to start to interrupt the enemy's communications until Minty joins, unless the general desires me to go sooner. Ask the general to let me know tomorrow by cipher how far I am to regulate my movements by those of the infantry." Stanley was getting his cavalry ready to carry out his orders to move toward Rome, Georgia "to ascertain the position and intentions of the enemy." Stanley prepared to carry out his orders as he interpreted them, but he wanted all his cavalry present to do this. He could be facing Wheeler and Forrest by the time he returned from his raid. He also wanted to know to what extent he was tied to the infantry. The cavalry couldn't effectively do both—raid the enemy's rear and screen for the infantry—without compromising one or the other.[77] Garfield responded to Stanley's message that Rosecrans "hopes that your instructions in regard to the movement on Rome can be successfully carried out." He also gave Stanley what intelligence he had on Wheeler, who was still thought to be near Chattanooga, and Forrest, who had withdrawn from Kingston, also in the proximity of Chattanooga.[78]

Also on September 5, only one regiment of Louis Watkins' Third Brigade was present with McCook's main force. The 7th Kentucky guarded the crossing along the Tennessee River and the 5th and 6th Kentucky cavalries were still en route. The 4th Kentucky Cavalry scouted across Lookout Mountain and, finding enemy pickets, charged them, capturing thirteen. McCook's First Brigade, commanded by Archibald Campbell, also in the saddle, scouted south of Rawlingsville, where Colonel James Brownlow's 1st Tennessee Cavalry encountered some Southern cavalry but was unable to catch them. Campbell rode toward Lebanon and found no enemy. The whole scout totaled about thirty miles. Oscar La Grange's Second Brigade was still moving toward Winston's and would not arrive until the next day. The 2nd Tennessee Cavalry, which had been detached, was ordered to rejoin the brigade and reached La Grange's troops as Stanley pulled his commands together.[79]

The troopers of the 1st Tennessee Cavalry found catching the Confederate pickets at Rawlingsville to be a difficult task. Trooper Julius Thomas wrote. "[B]ut could not catch any of them succeeded in dismounting two of them and taking four horses we ran our horses about three miles it was so dusty you could not see a man the length of a horse. On nearing the town of Lebanon we made another charge but with no better success than before when we arrived there were no rebs."[80] George Crook's Second Brigade scouted into Broomtown Valley and found only 150–200 of the enemy, who scattered, and Crook returned to his headquarters that night.

On September 5, William Sinclair alerted Edward McCook, who was to lead the raid on Rome, that he needed "claw-hooks, crowbars, or any other means of tearing up a railroad track," as well as "torpedoes ... for blowing up railroad bridges, culverts." Sinclair told McCook these tools would be necessary, as the expedition to the enemy's rear was anticipated. Stanley planned to be battling Wheeler and Forrest and destroying the railroads also. McCook did not have the tools needed to complete this work because the cavalry trains would not arrive at Winston's until September 7. But McCook promised to send a reliable man back to Stevenson for the material he needed to complete this task. McCook, while fulfilling his orders, sent the 2nd Indiana and 4th Indiana cavalries along the Rome Road to within twenty-eight miles of Rome. No resistance was encountered from the enemy but the expedition was observed by enemy scouts. McCook proudly noted that his probe would draw some of the infantry from Chattanooga to protect Bragg's rear.[81]

Meanwhile, Robert Minty's brigade, which Stanley had requested from Garfield, was still on duty north of Chattanooga attached to Crittenden's Twenty-first Corps. Minty's reconnaissance determined the Confederates still strongly guarded the fords along the Tennessee River. He also reported that the slave labor of the Confederate army was shipped to Macon to work on fortifications there.

While the three Union infantry corps converged on Chattanooga Bragg had a pontoon bridge on the south bank ready to deploy across the Tennessee River. When this was discovered, a wave of concern rippled through Crittenden's troops on the north side of the river and concerned Rosecrans, who had anticipated Bragg would remain behind his defenses in the town. At the same time, Rosecrans received reports that suggested Forrest was preparing to break through the Union line north of the town to swing into the rear of the Federal army. Both of these situations were new threats that had not been anticipated. Fortunately, neither resulted in action on the part of Bragg.[82]

These new Confederate threats caused confusion among the Union commanders. Confusion was the order of the day on September 6, and confusion seemed to be taking hold of the entire Union advance on Chattanooga, as explained by historian Paul Shelton:

> In two hours Rosecrans and Garfield had painted three distinctly different pictures of the enemy. They prompted Sheridan, the demonstrated master of intelligence collection, to find out what was going on. They then tasked Stanley to break the enemy's communications as the Confederates prepared to make a stand. Halleck was told the enemy had concentrated considerable force in the area and left to draw his own conclusion regarding the enemy course of action, and Crittenden was told the enemy was preparing to fall back to Dalton!

Shelton suggested two explanations for these various messages. One was that Garfield and Rosecrans were so exhausted they could no longer keep up with intelligence reports coming into headquarters. The other was that they were using projected or anticipated movements as a basis to deliver orders to the commanders in the field.[83]

The Union cavalry on September 6 spent most of the day preparing for the raid toward Rome and received the anticipated supply train from Stevenson and Bridgeport. The next day some scouts of La Grange's Second Brigade rode toward Alpine and found the enemy firmly defending the town with infantry, cavalry and artillery. La Grange skirmished with the defenders and then fell back to his headquarters.

On the morning of September 7, David Stanley awoke to bad news from Garfield in a message written at 10:00 the evening before. Rosecrans ordered Stanley to "rush the enemy sharply, and if possible strike the railroad." He also told Stanley that Minty would not be able to join him for another week, which was too long for Stanley to wait before he started toward Rome. Rosecrans felt Bragg was preparing to make a stand at Chattanooga and rumors abounded that General Joseph Johnston had reinforced him. The situation was becoming tense for Rosecrans. Breaking the railroad south of Chattanooga was imperative for the Union advance, exclaimed Garfield. He also wrote that Forrest and a part of Wheeler's cavalry were in Chattanooga, so Stanley should be able to strike Rome with "impunity." Garfield concluded his message: "The general commanding hopes soon to hear that you have struck a heavy blow." For the common soldier, this was a tense time also. Trooper Joseph Shelley, 2nd Indiana Cavalry, knew this to be a time when Bragg could strike back. Expressing his trust in the Divine and General Rosecrans, he wrote on September 7, "You might, before this letter reaches you, hear of a battle, because the rebels will likely try to drive us back, but our hope is in God and old Rose."[84]

While Stanley wanted Minty's service, Minty's command stretched along the Union left flank dealing with the constant requests of Crittenden's corps. Minty reminded headquarters on September 7 "that my entire effective force consists of about 1,100 men, out of which over 100 are constantly on picket—some of them as far out as 8 miles—and that escorts to forage trains, patrols, and scouts reduce the force under my command which would be available for any sudden movement to about 500 men." Minty was scouting along the front and picketing: Thatcher's Ferry, Cross Ford, Sale Creek Ford, Dougherty's Ferry, Blythe's Ferry, and Belt's Ferry.[85]

The evening of September 7 was also a decisive one for Bragg. Observing the strong Union force that extended past his left flank and anticipating Rosecrans' intention of moving between Chattanooga and Rome, he decided to leave Chattanooga. Bragg concluded to move away from Chattanooga and fight Rosecrans, in detail, as he moved past Lookout Mountain.

Conflict Within Watkins' Third Brigade

While the Union cavalry was performing its duty, the command situation between Colonel Louis Watkins and the commander of the 5th Kentucky Cavalry deteriorated to such an extent Watkins arrested Lieutenant Colonel William Hoblitzell. Hoblitzell was appointed lieutenant colonel and commander of the 5th Kentucky Cavalry over objections of the officers of the regiment. He had served on the staffs of several high ranking generals and was given the opportunity to command a regiment. Lieutenant Colonel Thomas Vimont was also be given command of the 7th Kentucky Cavalry under similar circumstances and in both cases the results were unsuccessful.

Hoblitzell was an unpopular commander of the 5th Kentucky Cavalry. Some of the officers of regiment tried to prevent him from gaining command of the regiment before they were aware the final decision had been made. Major Christopher Cheeks had circulated a petition, signed by several of the officers, asking that Hoblitzell not be given the command. One incident resulted in the court-martial of Hoblitzell due to an altercation between him and Captain John B. Riggs, 5th Kentucky, an officer who had not signed the petition opposing Hoblitzell's promotion. Hoblitzell was observed pulling off his coat and threatening to fight Riggs. Hoblitzell was heard exclaiming, "[T]hrow rank to the devil!" He then shook his fist in the face of Riggs, who walked away.[86]

The altercation came about because of charges assigned to Riggs' company account. There was a discrepancy over two saddles charged to the company and when he objected, Hoblitzell took a pen and changed the number, increasing it by two. Riggs refused to accept the charges until the accounts were corrected. At that point Hoblitzell became angry and started cursing Riggs. Hoblitzell exclaimed "he would be damned if he made the corrections." Riggs stated that otherwise the receipts were forged. This resulted in Hoblitzell's continued bluster about fighting Riggs—"That any man who accused him of forgery—he could whip.... [H]e would be God damned if he couldn't whip anyone who accused him of forgery." Riggs made a statement about Hoblitzell's shoulder straps. Hoblitzell walked outside and took off his coat and prepared to fight Riggs. Riggs placed his hand on a knife at his waist but never drew the knife. At that point, the adjutant of the 5th Kentucky intervened and stopped the altercation.[87]

Watkins also found Hoblitzell disobeying standing orders to have civilian livestock returned to them in July and August 1863 and he had Hoblitzell arrested. Ultimately Hoblitzell was also charged with disregarding his arrest. The court found Hoblitzell guilty of some specifications but not guilty on the charges during his first court-martial in the summer of 1864. He was sentenced to be reprimanded in the General Orders of the army. General George Thomas recorded in these orders that Hoblitzell "had allowed himself to become involved in a personal altercation with an officer of his regiment of inferior rank," which could destroy the "discipline in his regiment and detract from the dignity of his position."[88]

Hoblitzell and Watkins were to become bitter enemies and their hatred peaked during the Battle of Chickamauga. Hoblitzell was previously under arrest, but as the battle became imminent an order by Rosecrans released him from arrest and placed him in command of his regiment again. The conflict between the two officers exploded during the Battle of Chickamauga.

Conditions Worsen for Stanley

On the evening of September 7, Rosecrans ordered Alexander McCook to send a brigade to hold the hold mountain passes as Stanley began his expedition to cut railroad communications between Chattanooga and Atlanta. The order explained that the cavalry was ordered to cut the communications between Bragg's army and Rome, although Stanley's own orders were never this explicit. Finally, McCook's infantry was ordered to march to Alpine to cover the return of the cavalry.[89]

Rosecrans ordered Stanley to strike the rear of the Confederate army at Rome on September 8, in the large wheeling movement of the Army of the Cumberland designed to capture the Confederate army at Chattanooga. The Union cavalry was important to this movement, but Stanley seemed to be an unwilling participant in the plan to close the door on Bragg and preventing his retreat from Chattanooga. Stanley still had much of his cavalry on duty screening the flanks, and he did not have access to the much-valued Robert Minty and his brigade. He seemed to be pleading that if only Rosecrans knew the correct status of the cavalry, he would not give this order. His responded to Garfield on September 7:

> I will start in the morning and endeavor to strike the railroad. I regret exceedingly that I cannot have the aid of Minty's brigade, as I deem my present force entirely inadequate to the work to be performed. I fear the general is not aware that I have but thirteen small regiments here, reduced by battalions guarding the Nashville and Huntsville Railroad. To seriously affect the railroad we should be able to hold it for at least half a day. My force is so small that I cannot make proper detachments for striking the road and at the same time fight the force of the enemy. The entire force of Wharton's and Martin's divisions lies between me and the railroad. I will do the best I can.[90]

Garfield replied later that night and denied Stanley's request to wait:

Alexander McCook, West Point classmate of Stanley, worked closely with him during the advance on Chattanooga (Library of Congress).

> Your dispatch of 10.30 a.m., 7th, is received. The general commanding thinks it practicable for you to make a successful expedition against the enemy's line of communication. Considering the relative strength of the enemy's cavalry and our own, and the additional fact that Forrest's whole force and nearly all of Wheeler's are in the neighborhood of Chattanooga and cannot be brought to bear against you, he has the more confidence in your ability to succeed in the expedition. Even should you fail in thoroughly breaking the railroad, you would at least make a strong diversion in that direction.... The general commanding directs you to push forward rapidly and with audacity. The severing of the enemy's railroad communication with Atlanta will be the most disastrous to him.[91]

Seeking to comply, Stanley ordered Edward McCook's division to prepare to march at daybreak on September 8, but for the first time in his career Stanley did not move. Whether he rescinded the orders or McCook was unable to comply is not known. Records show Stanley ordered the raid, but the failure to execute the order was Stanley's responsibility. Trooper Robert S. Merrill, 1st Wisconsin Cavalry, wrote in his diary on September 7, "Rec'd orders to march in the morning." The next day he wrote, "Saddled up but waiting most of the forenoon we did not move. We drew new horses this P.M."[92]

On the afternoon of September 8, Rosecrans informed general in chief Henry Halleck that the Confederates did not fight at Chattanooga but had evacuated the town, avoiding the trap Rosecrans hoped to spring. Rosecrans' great wheeling movement of his army had missed its prey. Stanley and Alexander McCook would be in pursuit the next morning. While Rosecrans calmly wrote to Halleck, he was livid about Stanley's lack of action on September 8, and told Stanley:

> The messenger brings nothing from you, but I learn from him that your command lies at the foot of the mountain on this side, intending to move in the morning. I am sorry to say you will be too late. It is also a matter of regret to me that your command has done so little in this great movement. If you could do nothing toward Rome, nor toward the railroad, you might at least have cleared the top of Lookout Mountain to Chattanooga and established a patrol and vedettes line along it, which I should have ordered had I not trusted to your discretion, expecting something more important to be done. But what is worse than this, you had peremptory orders to move, which were reiterated yesterday, expecting you would move this morning. It appears that the enemy have sent a large infantry and cavalry force to Alpine. Your cavalry ought to have full control from your position to that place. This you do not appear to have done. Had you gone according to orders you would have struck the head of their column, and probably inflicted on them irreparable injury. So far your command has been a mere picket guard for our advance.[93]

Stanley replied to Rosecrans in a weak and conciliatory message in which he stated he could not to start his expedition to Rome because he had a "deficiency of horseshoes." In a side note, Stanley replied that by delaying he gained 600 men who had been away on duty elsewhere. He promised to post Crook's brigade to guard the mountain passes and that the next morning McCook's division would strike Alpine, where a strong concentration of Confederate cavalry was to be found: "I expect to fight them at Alpine. Wharton has with him a full battery. If he can get them on good ground you need not fear the result." None of the cavalry reports provided insight about the failure to move against Rome on September 8. Interestingly, Stanley's itinerary of the cavalry recorded that September 7 was spent horseshoeing the command after the cavalry trains arrived. McCook's headquarters records show a request was made to Stanley on September 7 to continue the shoeing of the horses in his command. On September 8, Crook's command moved up Lookout Mountain and those troopers without horses returned to Nashville to obtain new mounts.[94]

After the rebuke from Rosecrans, there was still the question about the assignment for the cavalry, especially as the Confederates withdrew from Chattanooga. Rosecrans decided to return the cavalry to the picket duty for which he had just criticized Stanley. He directed the cavalry to again reconnoiter the retreat of Bragg's army.

Several questions arise about Stanley's failure to act. Clearly Rosecrans was disappointed with Stanley in regard to the expedition to Rome. It is unclear why Stanley did not advance on the morning of September 8 when orders had been given the night before to prepare for the raid; and Rosecrans was justified in his anger at Stanley. Rosecrans was probably overly harsh when he wrote, "So far your command has been a mere picket guard for our advance." In fact, the cavalry had been assigned just that duty. Rosecrans' criticism may reveal a more deep-seated unhappiness with Stanley, or it may just reveal the pressure Rosecrans faced seeking a deadly enemy in the mountains around Chattanooga. Stanley was ill and it was commendable he was trying to keep the cavalry going. However, if he was too ill to handle the job it was incumbent on him to step aside. In addition, Stanley asserted in his initial reply, and in his apologetic follow-up message, that he did not have enough troopers to successfully fulfill the mission.[95]

Stanley's cavalry advanced on Summerville on September 8 and 9 with support from a division of McCook's infantry. The Union cavalry and the Twentieth Corps also advanced on Alpine. These actions were a direct threat to Bragg's flank and put a large Union force in position to sever a direct route to the south. Before the Federals could swing into place trapping Bragg in Chattanooga, Bragg realized the threat, abandoned the town and moved twenty miles south. Although neither Stanley nor Rosecrans was aware of this, Stanley's raid on Bragg's rear might have been for naught; but Rosecrans felt if Stanley had followed orders he would have done great injury to the retreating Confederates.[96]

It is interesting to speculate on the outcome of Stanley's expedition to Rome on September 8 if it had been executed. First of all, Stanley's objective was fifty miles south of Chattanooga and any potential of striking the flank of a retreating demoralized army was not realistic. The Confederates did not withdraw that far south. Brigadier General States Rights Gist's brigade—reinforcements from Johnston and 1,800 men strong—was already diverted to Rome. Forrest had been ordered toward Rome in anticipation of the exact expedition Rosecrans ordered for September 8. Forrest wrote at 8:00 a.m., "I have arrived here with one of my brigades and six pieces of artillery; the other brigade will be up by 12 m. Please let me know what is going on in front. I am instructed by General Bragg to impede their advance on Rome as much as possible." Most likely Forrest would have joined Wheeler with artillery and two brigades of cavalry as McCook advanced with two brigades of Union cavalry. The confrontation had the potential of being an exciting engagement, although that far to the enemy's rear would probably have compelled Edward McCook to break off any engagement.[97]

Rosecrans, famous for his rages, had never before directed them at Stanley in this manner. Brigadier General George Crook offered his firsthand account of the receipt of the letter rebuking Stanley on September 8:

> The officers were together when Gen. Stanley received a letter from Gen. Rosecrans, accusing him unmercifully of procrastination, unnecessary delays, and of want of appreciation of situation, etc. stating that the enemy was in full retreat, and that instead of his cavalry being on their flanks, destroying them, he had by his delays lost the fruits of all the campaign, etc. Gen Stanley was taken sick. In fact, he was sick then. He was shortly afterwards compelled to go off duty.[98]

The Cavalry Returns to Duty

On the morning of September 9, the Stars and Stripes flew over Chattanooga. Rosecrans had again maneuvered Bragg out of his defenses and forced him to retreat southward. The tension that had been so palpable just the day before was gone, and Stanley and the cavalry were back on track. Edward McCook told his commanders to aggressively follow the orders by starting reveille at 2:30 a.m. and to be in the saddle at 4:00 a.m. Crook's troopers were already on Lookout Mountain with artillery. After the rebuke by Rosecrans, Stanley was back in control of the cavalry and ready to fulfill his orders by riding toward Alpine and Summerville in Broomtown Valley. The Rome expedition would take place, but not until September 10.

With Bragg's retreat from Chattanooga, the pursuit was on. Alexander McCook, being on the southern flank, marched forward in an attempt to strike Bragg's army as it moved southward. McCook confirmed his orders and replied to Garfield regarding Stanley:

> The dispatches for General Stanley were at once forwarded to him. He moved his artillery and ambulances on to Lookout Mountain last night, so that he could commence the ascent with his command at daylight this morning. Before your order reaches him modifying his movements he may have a portion of his force in Broomtown Valley. It will be as well, I think, for him to go over and drive the rebel cavalry back upon their infantry, if they are moving southward toward LaFayette. Stanley, with the infantry support, can certainly ascertain what they are doing, and certainly where they are. I fear the force engaged in making the reconnaissance ordered may prove too small, as I believe all of Wheeler's cavalry is in the vicinity of Summerville.

Unbeknownst to Rosecrans, the actions of Stanley's cavalry and Alexander McCook's corps had a major impact on the decisions made by Bragg. Bragg was very concerned about being blocked from a direct route to Rome even without a raid being made. One of Rosecrans' scouts, James Pike, 4th Ohio Cavalry, noted what Bragg was keenly aware of: "Gen. Stanley was threatening La Fayette from Broom Town valley, almost in rear of the rebel army."[99]

Crook's brigade camped on top of Lookout Mountain on September 8, and the next morning led the Union cavalry advance on Alpine, which scouts had determined was defended by infantry, cavalry and artillery. As Crook approached Henderson's Gap, he drove enemy pickets to his front. Immediately he found the gap, which was narrow and obstructed with timbers felled across the road and boulders that had been rolled onto the road. After an hour of clearing the road, Crook continued down into Broomtown Valley. As he approached Alpine across a large field, his command engaged the enemy occupying the tree line. Crook returned the fire and a bloody fight resulted. The arrival of McCook's division decided the contest. McCook flanked the defenders, who were "forced to retire, fighting us, however, from the time we struck them in the valley until we drove them through Alpine, some retreating on the Rome road, but most of them on the road to Summerville," as Robert Mitchell recorded.[100]

Meanwhile on the Union left flank, Minty's brigade crossed the Tennessee River and cooperated with Wilder's brigade to begin the pursuit of Bragg. Minty soon found a large concentration of Forest's Confederate cavalry at Hiwassee.[101]

September 10–12: The Rome Expedition, the Skirmish at Summerville, Mitchell Returns to Duty

As the Union infantry moved in pursuit of Bragg, the Confederate cavalry provided efficient screening duty, stalling the Federal advance. This was reported by Colonel William Palmer, 15th Pennsylvania Cavalry, which remained detached to army headquarters since its reorganization after the Battle of Stones River. Palmer also collected intelligence from a wounded prisoner that Bragg was not falling back to Dalton or Rome but that two brigades of Forrest's cavalry were camped along the LaFayette Road. The prisoner also revealed there were two divisions of infantry, Cheatham's and Hindman's, near Crittenden's corps position at Gordon's Mill about thirteen miles south of Chattanooga.[102]

For the cavalry, Rosecrans personally ordered two cavalry brigades to "picket duty," for which he had just criticized Stanley so severely. Crook was ordered to move his "division" (an error in the order, as he only had one brigade available to him) to Bridgeport because of

Officers of the 15th Pennsylvania Cavalry, detached to army headquarters (Library of Congress).

a report of the presence of Confederate cavalry. At the same time, Minty (part of Crook's division) moved to the Hiwassee River to secure abandoned steamboats, but the boats were burned by the Confederates before Minty received the orders. These orders were received while Stanley was in the process of ordering the delayed raid on Rome that Rosecrans had stated he so desperately needed. The lack of specific objectives for the cavalry resulted in an uncoordinated, reactive effort by an otherwise invaluable part of Rosecrans' army.[103]

While the movements of the army focused on Bragg, who appeared not to be in full retreat as expected and while Rosecrans was making demands along the left flank and the rear, half of the full Union cavalry corps on the right flank rode thirty miles toward Rome. Edward McCook commanded the raid, which included Archibald Campbell's and Oscar La Grange's brigades. After bivouacking near Alpine of the evening of September 9, the cavalry rode through Summerville and skirmished with Confederate cavalry along the way. Recalled north on September 8, Forrest ordered Frank Armstrong's cavalry back north of LaFayette as Pegram's division provided a screen between Chattanooga and Bragg's army. Wheeler's cavalry still screened the Confederate left flank and before Stanley were John Wharton's and William Martin's divisions.

The raid, or more realistically the reconnaissance, on Rome began—tentatively—on September 10. Archibald Campbell's First Brigade and Oscar La Grange's Second Brigade rode to Melville along the Rome Road on reconnaissance and bagged four prisoners. Then McCook returned that evening to Alpine after riding only fifteen miles. On September 11, McCook made a hard ride toward Rome with the First Division only, this time approaching to within twelve miles of the town. Campbell's brigade ran into a strong force of infantry and artillery at the junction of Chattooga and Coosa rivers. Private John Vogel, 2nd Michigan Cavalry, noted, when the Union cavalry reached Rome, "[W]e found the enemy ... waiting for us strongly entrenched and ready to do battle." The 1st Tennessee Cavalry scouted forward and reached as close as twelve miles from Rome. Colonel James Brownlow sent half the regiment to Rome and the other half rode to Dirt Town, but the enemy was too strong. The expedition did surprise the captured pickets, who did not believe that the 1st Tennessee was Union cavalry until they were shown the United States flag. Then they asked simply, "What are you doing down in 'Dixie?'" However, Brownlow's Tennesseans stirred up a nest of hornets as they heard Wheeler's cavalry bugle "boots and saddles" and had a running battle for about two miles. The 1st Tennessee Cavalry rode back toward friendly lines into the night and was finally challenged with, "Who goes there?" The response was, "Friends, without the countersign." They had reached the friendly pickets of the 2nd Indiana Cavalry, never so happy to be there.[104] The remainder of Campbell's command continued to scout and found no further concentrations of the enemy. There is no record of destruction to rails during this expedition, and ultimately the raid yielded no significant results.

While Campbell and La Grange operated near Rome, the 5th and 6th Kentucky cavalries under command of Louis Watkins had a stiff skirmish with two companies of the 3rd Georgia Cavalry on September 10. Watkins claimed Summerville after capturing one captain and eleven privates. Upon discovering another regiment of enemy cavalry positioned along the LaFayette Road, he ordered the 5th and 6th Kentucky in pursuit. The Kentuckians found the Confederate cavalry guarded a large storehouse filled with baled cotton, barrels of flour, vinegar, a small amount of bacon, and some hard bread. The Federal cavalry chased away the Confederates in a skirmish in which the 6th Kentucky lost one man killed and four slightly wounded. Watkins recorded two Confederates were killed.[105]

On the right flank of the Union army, Alexander McCook's Twentieth Corps were concentrated near Alpine when George Thomas opened communications with him on September 11. Meanwhile, Crittenden marched from Lee and Gordon Mills toward LaFayette, and Garfield told Thomas late on September 11 that Bragg was not in full retreat and was, in fact, concentrating his army. McCook was ordered to position his corps to support Thomas's as Rosecrans started to pull his scattered army together.

On the morning of September 11, Major General James Negley, 2nd Division, Fourteenth Corps, marched toward LaFayette. Bragg decided to launch his first offensive move of the campaign as he planned to strike Negley's division at McLemore's Cove located at the southern end of the Chickamauga Valley. Negley planned to march from Steven's Gap, cross the valley and cross the Pigeon Mountain through Dug Gap. Negley was isolated and twelve hours ahead of his nearest reinforcements.

Bragg ordered Major General Thomas Hindman's division south through the valley while Cleburne's division was positioned on Pigeon Mountain defending Dug Gap. Through a series of blunders, D.H. Hill did not move Cleburne's division into the valley and Hindman failed to attack despite being reinforced with two additional divisions. Due to these delays, Negley was able to withdraw his vulnerable division at McLemore's Cove with minor losses. Significantly, Bragg had just shifted from a defensive to an offensive strategy, in spite of this misstep.

Crittenden's reconnaissance during the day also conclusively determined Bragg was not in full flight and that perhaps only some cavalry had moved to Macon. Again the situation was tense for Rosecrans, who ordered Crittenden to take up a defensive position along the LaFayette Road near Gordon's Mill. Wood's division was ordered hastily forward to connect with the rest of Crittenden's corps. Brigadier General Thomas Wood sounded one of many alarms when he wrote as follows to Garfield: "Colonel Harker says that not only was General Bragg here yesterday, but also Generals Polk and Hill, with a large force of infantry and cavalry." Part of Minty's brigade quickly moved forward to guard the left flank of Crittenden's Corps.[106]

On the same day, Alexander McCook appealed to David Stanley to provide some cavalry assistance to Colonel Harrison's 39th Indiana Mounted Infantry, which had only 300 men. Harrison was stopped by a strong defense in his attempt to scout the area around LaFayette. Stanley complied with the request and Watkins's Kentucky cavalry brigade with Newell's artillery rode for LaFayette at 5:30 p.m. Watkins missed Colonel Harrison along the way and had to wait until he arrived about midnight. Watkins sent out a scout for two miles around their bivouac and found no enemy. Watkins and Harrison both concluded they did not have the firepower to push through the force they opposed. Bragg's concentration of force was so evident that Harrison and Watkins were ordered back to the Union lines.

At 10:45 p.m. Garfield ordered Stanley to close up on the flank of McCook's Twentieth Corps. Garfield also included a comment which would set the stage for the second, and perhaps most severe, rebuke of Stanley: "It is now of the utmost importance that the general commanding should be informed as soon as possible of the force and position of the enemy. Take measures to ascertain this as soon as possible." Garfield also told Stanley about Minty's detached First Brigade, which finally crossed the Tennessee River; but still Minty was not released to Stanley's command. The 4th U.S. Cavalry hastened forward to Crittenden's location at Gordon's Mill and the remainder of the brigade followed. Maybe most important, Stanley's second-in-command, Robert Mitchell, had returned to duty as Garfield noted: "General Mitchell is here."[107]

Robert Mitchell was in the saddle and arrived at Negley's headquarters that evening. Negley wrote to Thomas that Mitchell had just arrived from Rosecrans' headquarters with orders directing Thomas: "Order General McCook, and Stanley with his cavalry, to move at once within supporting distance of your corps, with a view of moving upon the enemy at the earliest practicable moment. General Rosecrans complains of a want of information in regard to your movements and position, and of the numbers and position of the enemy." Mitchell also brought word of the extent of the trap Negley had just avoided.[108]

Edward McCook's cavalry, which had just ridden to Rome, bivouacked that evening at the junction of the Gaylesville-Summerville and Rome-Chattanooga roads. McCook reported that Polk's Infantry Corps was at Trion Factory about twelve miles away and John Wharton's cavalry was only two miles away at Mitchell's. George Crook ordered McCook to scout the enemy positions before returning to Alpine. Crook, who had a more active role in commanding the cavalry corps because of Stanley's deteriorating health, ordered McCook to "occupy their attention" if he encountered the enemy.[109]

Early on the morning of September 12, Edward McCook relayed the activities of Colonel James Brownlow's 1st Tennessee Cavalry, which had scouted Dirt Town the day before to headquarters. Brownlow noted no troops retreating southward and John Wharton's cavalry, which had been positioned close to Rome, was riding toward LaFayette. McCook concluded, "The information I regard as definite and reliable is, that Bragg has not gone to Rome; that none of his force has passed over the Dalton road."[110]

Alexander McCook confirmed that Stanley was sending his entire cavalry toward LaFayette to definitely find out where Bragg was positioned. McCook cautiously noted,

> I am not desirous of fighting Bragg's whole army, and in case he is concentrated at La Fayette. I am in a false position, for I could not reach you. Where is Crittenden's corps? I will keep my wagon train on top of Lookout Mountain and my troops in the valley. La Fayette is the strategic position for Bragg; he then has his road open to Dalton, or to points farther south on the railroad. His object will be to oppose his whole force to our fractions as they debouch from the mountain.[111]

David Stanley's time with the cavalry during this campaign was over. He was again censured by Rosecrans, in perhaps the harshest tones yet, in aide-de-camp Major Frank S. Bond's September 12 message in which both Alexander McCook and David Stanley were taken to task:

> The general commanding directs me to say that after the most explicit order to connect with and keep open courier lines, he finds that neither your own nor General McCook's headquarters are connected with the headquarters of the department or of General Thomas. He directs me to say there is no military offense, except running from the enemy, so inexcusable as a neglect to keep up communications with headquarters. Our lines are now much extended, and we must husband our resources.[112]

Stanley was so ill he was either unaware of the message or could not respond; however, Alexander McCook struck back on both their behalves. McCook retorted to Garfield that the lack of communication was a result of Rosecrans' headquarters being moved to Chattanooga without McCook or Stanley being informed. He went on to put the blame on Rosecrans' 15th Pennsylvania Cavalry, which served as Rosecrans courier service, for the delay in informing the army of the movement of headquarters.[113]

W.R. Carter, historian of the 1st Tennessee Cavalry, noted, "General Stanley was unable to communicate with Rosecrans by the valley road, it being held by Bragg." This fact adds a dimension to this incident that perhaps reflects the stress and tension at headquarters rather than a failure on the part of Stanley to perform his duties. This is a historical uncertainty because Stanley never responded in his own defense or acknowledged any blame.[114]

With Mitchell back with the cavalry and the illness taking such a toll on Stanley's health, Stanley decided to relinquish command. He wrote to Garfield, "My dysentery, which has been working on me for a week, has completely prostrated me, so that I am not able to be out of bed but a few minutes at a time."[115] The day ended with George Crook ordering Edward McCook's division to proceed to LaFayette the next day if the horses were still fit after the long expedition to Rome.[116]

September 13–15: The Charge at Lafayette, Minty on the Left Flank, Stanley Cedes Command

Captain J.C. Van Druzer, superintendent of telegraph for Rosecrans, summarized the situation on September 13 in a communication to the War Department: "The enemy are between Thomas and McCook on the south and Crittenden and Granger on the north, and day before yesterday gave Negley a thrashing. Today Crittenden has been engaged. Rosecrans went down this P.M., and by day after to-morrow or Wednesday you may look to hear of Bragg getting hurt. We are in a ticklish place here, but hope to come out with whole skin. Can do nothing but wait." The Army of the Cumberland was in a ticklish place, indeed. Rosecrans' three corps were separated and maneuvering in the mountains, where the gaps could be easily defended. It was imperative for the three infantry corps to be able to support each other, and still the location and intent of Bragg was unclear.[117]

Bragg was very frustrated at the missed opportunity at McLemore's Cove when Negley's division barely missed a crushing blow. Bragg saw great opportunity if he could defeat Rosecrans' scattered corps in detail. While the focus of Rosecrans was on the Confederates at LaFayette, Bragg intended next to strike Crittenden's Twenty-first Corps. Bragg directed Leonidas Polk to move Cheatham's division, reinforced by Hindman's and Walker's divisions, to crush at least John Palmer's Union division. The morning of September 12 was selected as the time for the attack. Again the attack never came because, instead of just facing Palmer's division, Polk faced Crittenden's entire corps. Bragg urged Polk to make the attack on Crittenden in a late night message: "General, The enemy is approaching from the south, and it is highly important your attack in the morning should be quick and decided. Let no time be lost." Once again on the morning of 13th no attack came.[118]

For the Union side it appeared Bragg intended to make his stand at LaFayette, but his location had yet to be determined. He had not retreated to Rome and he wasn't at LaFayette. Alexander McCook wrote to Thomas on the morning of September 13: "General Crook sends word, from the information he has, that the enemy have evacuated La Fayette with their infantry." Crook's intelligence was wrong. In the meantime, McCook promised to move forward by way of Dougherty's Gap to establish contact with Thomas's corps that day.[119]

September 13 was a day of fighting for the Union Cavalry under Crook's command. Crook ordered all four active cavalry brigades on the right flank to advance on LaFayette. He planned for two brigades under his command and two brigades under McCook's command to ride abreast in a show of force. But McCook discovered a large Confederate force near the Chattooga River and swung his command to meet the threat. As Crook proceeded on to LaFayette he encountered enemy pickets of John Wharton's cavalry and dashed them to the rear. Outside of LaFayette, Crook found the main Confederate line. Archibald Campbell charged the 9th Pennsylvania Cavalry into the defenders' line, gathering all the pickets in front while receiving volleys from the defenders. The charge of the 9th Pennsylvania was concealed by the dust but the dust also caused problems for the Union cavalry. The first set of four fell during the charge because the dust concealed an obstacle across the road. As the remainder of the column charged forward the "enemy opened a withering enfilading fire, killing 1 man, mortally wounding 2 others, and disabling 8 horses," wrote Lieutenant Colonel Roswell Russell, commanding the 9th Pennsylvania. The Confederate defenders held their ground and fired away at the Union cavalrymen. Captain Marshall Thatcher, 2nd Michigan Cavalry, recalled the cavalry charge when the Confederate artillery opened up on the column: "There was no stopping to deploy and skirmish, not time for throwing away flankers; but the brigade, led by the Second Michigan with Colonel Campbell and staff at their head, grasping their rifles, revolvers or sabers in one hand, and reins in the other, dashed forward, on and over the pickets, yelling like wild Comanches." Captain Thomas McCahan, 9th Pennsylvania, explained the charge revealed a hidden Confederate artillery battery that opened upon Union attack. The first charge resulted in seven horses being killed and a second charge was ordered. Russell ordered the fences torn down in anticipation of another charge being prepared by the 2nd Michigan Cavalry when Crook ordered the Union cavalry to withdraw. Due to the heavy dust, the 9th Pennsylvania lost only five men in the charge but claimed 17 prisoners in the action.[120] The reconnaissance determined the Confederates at LaFayette were from John C. Breckinridge's command, which confirmed that Bragg was indeed determined to stand and fight and defeat Rosecrans in detail if possible.[121]

Crook was not pleased with Edward McCook and his actions on September 13. Crook wrote that the commands rode side by side for some distance but McCook broke away and pursued another Confederate force, much to the disgust of Crook. Crook sent a squadron to determine the enemy McCook faced. He found just a handful of enemy at a well. Crook's command continued on the mission and rushed a camp of infantry in a gutsy charge led by Campbell. In reference to McCook, Crook wrote, "He was simply showing his behavior in its true light, so I let it go at that." Crook held Edward McCook in low regard.[122]

Trooper Charles Goodrich, 1st Wisconsin Cavalry, wrote of the action of his brigade under McCook's command on September 13 and did little to ameliorate Crook's assessment of actions during the day. Goodrich wrote that he rode past Summerville to a point about fourteen miles east of Alpine and found the enemy across the Little Black Warrior River. He noted, "After a little firing cross the river, we returned and marched back rapidly."[123]

After the attack at LaFayette, George Crook, in command of the cavalry in the saddle on September 13, directed McCook to move his division to join Crook's men. McCook sent the 4th Indiana to LaFayette as far as they could advance and planned to join Crook in the afternoon. McCook wrote, "I thought it better to send only this small force the other side of the river, because the country there is bad to handle a large force in, and the force in front of me as I stated in my last dispatch—is larger than I could whip."[124]

The result of the reconnaissance toward LaFayette led to the discovery of Wheeler's cavalry at the Ringgold and LaFayette roads. "I cannot, of course, drive them off. They made a stand 3 miles from here, the regiment I spoke of attacking them." McCook agreed with Crook that combining the two divisions might result in greater success of pushing closer to LaFayette; but the fighting was finished for the day.[125]

While Crook was fighting the Confederate left flank, the 4th U.S. Cavalry detached to Crittenden performed reconnaissance from Gordon's Mill toward LaFayette via the Cove Road for about six miles and to within six miles of LaFayette. Captain James McIntyre, commanding the regiment, found no concentration of the enemy, only occasional pickets. Bragg's concentration was still unknown.

Back at cavalry headquarters, the close relationship between Stanley and Alexander McCook was noted in an interesting exchange of messages, with a personal tone, on the evening of September 13. Stanley wrote, at 6:00 p.m., "Do not send dispatch to General Rosecrans until I get one ready to send him. Will you send dispatch by way of General Thomas?" McCook replied thirty minutes later: "Will send to General Thomas, but it will go by Winston's." Stanley clearly wanted to increase his communication to Garfield and Rosecrans. McCook knew Stanley was very ill and probably knew he was too ill to continue. At 9:15 p.m., McCook requested a summary of intelligence Crook had been able to collect about the Confederate withdrawal from LaFayette and ended the message with, "Have one of your staff write me fully of all Crook saw."[126]

In the meantime, Stanley sent a message to Garfield: "I am still confined to my bed, and have had to ride in an ambulance today coming over the mountain. Unless I get better I shall have to turn over the command to General Mitchell and go where I can have rest and quiet. General Mitchell is here and will take command of his division in the morning." Rosecrans was increasingly irritated with all his corps commanders. "Thomas used the day to form a defensive position at Steven's and Cooper's Gaps. Rosecrans continued to express irritation with his senior corps commander due to Thomas's lack of information regarding his position and that of the enemy.... McCook ... remained huddled around Alpine," noted historian Larry Daniel.[127]

Unknown to Rosecrans, the actions by Alexander McCook's infantry advance and Crook's Union cavalry actions were enough to convince Bragg that his left flank was still too vulnerable, so he ordered his army to LaFayette. Bragg had unsuccessfully attempted to attack Rosecrans twice in the past few days and decided to disengage, as he feared his left flank was being turned. The outcome of this withdrawal allowed Rosecrans the time he needed for the next two days to pull his army together.

On September 14 Minty's brigade, which had crossed the Tennessee River a couple of days before, joined the advance of J.J. Reynolds' division toward Pond Springs. Next, Crook's cavalry moved to protect Dougherty's Gap after the near disaster with Negley's division. The commanders of the Union army realized the importance of controlling the gaps to avoid any unpleasant surprises.[128]

Rosecrans took to his horse and rode to Thomas's headquarters as he desperately attempted to concentrate his army. Alexander McCook continued his communication with Garfield, who responded to McCook's sharp retort to Major Bond's letter complaining of the lack of communication from McCook and Stanley and headquarters. Garfield responded, "I have not seen the dispatch of Major Bond to General Stanley, complaining that lines of communication were not kept up with department headquarters, but I am assured by the general commanding that he did not intend to censure you in that communication." The tone of this message implied the rebuke from Rosecrans was intended for Stanley alone.[129]

The underappreciated Union cavalry worked hard during these days and had little to show for it. On September 14, for example, Minty's brigade—now with just two regiments because the 4th U.S. Cavalry was detached to Crittenden and minus the 3rd Indiana, also detached—was ordered to accompany Reynolds' division southward, only to have Crittenden request that a contingent of Minty's cavalry be posted at Rossville. Crittenden asked Garfield, "Had you not better order Minty, if he is near you, to leave some force at Rossville? I am afraid cavalry may come in from toward Ringgold, and cut off my communication." At the same time, Garfield ordered Alexander McCook to send a brigade of Stanley's cavalry back to Winston's to protect from a Confederate raid.[130]

Garfield, acting directly in charge of Minty's brigade, ordered, "Post Minty so as to guard the approaches from Ringgold and La Fayette, and hold him responsible for your safety in that direction." Fortunately, Granger's Reserve Corps was across the river following the other infantry corps. Granger moved three brigades into the Rossville area, alleviating Minty of the sole responsibility for that flank.[131]

Stanley moved his headquarters back to Winston's on September 14; his illness had drained his ability to command. He wrote to Garfield at 9:00 p.m. and acknowledged Crook was on his way to seize Dougherty's Gap as ordered. Edward McCook's division camped at Little River and planned to rejoin the rest of the Union cavalry on the right flank the next day. McCook faced a problem of moving his cavalry through Winston's Gap; because of the trains in advance of him it promised to be a slow movement. Stanley was too ill to continue and prepared Garfield for the transition of command: "I am still confined to my bed, and have had to ride in an ambulance to-day coming over the mountain. Unless I get better I shall have to turn over the command to General Mitchell and go where I can have rest and quiet. General Mitchell is here and will take command of his division in the morning." This would be the last day with Stanley in command of the cavalry during this campaign. The illness had finally claimed Stanley, who agreed to be transported to the hospital in the rear.[132]

Stanley's last dispatch was sent on the morning of September 15, in which he confirmed Crook's movement to Dougherty's Gap. Stanley warned Garfield that the cavalry had worked hard and that the horses could not stay on the mountain due to lack of forage, the closest a four-hour ride. He also told Garfield the cavalry needed a day of rest for the animals. As promised, Edward McCook moved his division to Alexander McCook's right flank.[133]

Robert Mitchell formally assumed command of the cavalry from Stanley and wrote to Garfield on September 15: "General Stanley will go to the rear tomorrow. He is very sick, and I am fearful that he will have a serious time. Give me specific directions with regard to cavalry movements, and I will endeavor to carry them out. The cavalry are badly used up, both men and horses."[134]

Summary

By September 15, the Union cavalry had performed its defensive duty well. Minty had done his assigned tasks, working diligently for the past month alone and under the command of Crittenden's corps headquarters. His part in deceiving Bragg about Rosecrans' intended line of advance was important and successful. He forced Dibrell's cavalry back across the Tennessee River and prevented any penetration of the Union left flank. Meanwhile on the right flank the Union cavalry was effective at reconnaissance and also provided excellent protection from any breakouts by Wheeler's cavalry. The Union cavalry was unsuccessful in locating the bulk of Bragg's army in the days prior to the Battle of Chickamauga.

However, any real offensive operations were reluctantly done and accomplished little. The objective of disrupting Bragg's communications was not successful. Only Edward McCook's Rome expedition on September 10–11 could really be considered an attempt to take the action to the enemy. Certainly, Crook's charge at LaFayette and Louis Watkins's action at Summerville resulted in good, if limited, results. Edward McCook's raid, by the time it took place, was not productive. He reached Rome and met a determined Confederate defense and then returned to the main line. The half-hearted attempt to cut the Confederate communications yielded little results. Unfortunately, Rosecrans outlined only two objectives for his cavalry—the actions of Minty of the left flank and the Rome raid on the right flank. Otherwise, Rosecrans was too involved with the unfolding events to address the actions of the cavalry. Cavalry headquarters was too far from Rosecrans to get prompt, detailed communications and agreed-upon objectives from Rosecrans. The problem of Rosecrans' insistence upon direct control of the cavalry was now evident.[135]

Stanley failed to accomplish the one real assignment given to him—the raid on Rome. Rosecrans imagined Bragg's army streaming in a column toward Rome and that Stanley's cavalry would have been effective in causing havoc among this imagined demoralized Confederate army. In fact, Bragg's army was not marching to Rome. It had retreated to just south of Chattanooga, but Bragg had decided to go on the offensive. If Stanley had made the attack on September 8, he would have faced not only Wheeler's cavalry and the infantry near Rome, but Forrest had moved south of Chattanooga with orders to resist any Union movement on Rome. In addition, Rome had just received infantry reinforcements. On the very day the attack was ordered, Stanley faced not only Wheeler but probably Forrest swinging down on his flank or rear. The imperative for Stanley to strike worked only if Bragg remained in Chattanooga or if Bragg was in full retreat toward Rome. Neither of these scenarios was real. Afterwards, Rosecrans reactively assigned the cavalry fragmented and uncoordinated duties. He also failed to use his cavalry as a screen for the advance of his army. In addition, the organization Stanley had worked so hard to establish when he assumed command of the cavalry was discarded and the duties were assigned in a piecemeal way.[136]

Historically, Stanley's reputation and his relationship with his superior officer deteriorated during September. Stanley kept his cavalry in a defensive role and waited for a real opportunity to shift to a more offensive posture. It is important to note that the cavalry action at LaFayette and Summerville, along with Alexander McCook's Twentieth Corps, was of constant concern for Bragg and had effectively caused him to move from Chattanooga and then to move south again toward LaFayette after the two abortive Confederate attacks planned for Crittenden's Corps near Gordon's Mill and Negley's division at McLemore's Cove. Unknown to Rosecrans, the more conservative offensive actions of the cavalry were yielding results. Stanley's illness and the extreme stress under which Rosecrans operated were contributing factors to the reactions of both these commanders.

It is unclear when the illness, dysentery, began with Stanley, but Alexander McCook inquired about Stanley's health on September 3. The surgeon's certificate issued September 21, when Stanley entered the hospital, recorded he had been suffering from his illness for three weeks, which would be on or about September 1. Stanley was so ill he was confined to his bed and had to be moved in an ambulance. Even Robert Mitchell, who was not well liked by Stanley, wrote, "He is very sick, and I am fearful that he will have a serious time." Stanley had no confidence Mitchell could lead the cavalry in the complex campaign in the mountains around Chattanooga, and he was correct.[137]

William Rosecrans and David Stanley had been working long and hard to make the cavalry arm of the Army of the Cumberland a force equal or superior to that of the Confederate cavalry. Despite David Stanley's medical problems for three weeks in September, the Union cavalry was a formidable force and worked diligently in August and September 1863. On the eve of the Battle of Chickamauga, Brigadier General Robert Mitchell commanded the cavalry in one of the greatest battles of the Civil War.

PART II: BRIGADIER GENERAL ROBERT B. MITCHELL,
ACTING CHIEF OF CAVALRY

6. The Battle of Chickamauga

But consider what would have been the consequences had we, I refer to our brigade, and General Wilder's, failed to hold in check the overwhelming Confederate forces.—Charles Greeno

Brigadier General Robert Byington Mitchell now commanded the cavalry of the Army of the Cumberland. Mitchell was born in 1823 in Richland County, Ohio. He eventually prepared with Miller and Morgan Attorneys and practiced law at Mt. Vernon, Ohio, in the 1850s. As a second lieutenant in the 2nd Ohio Volunteers he served in the Mexican War. In 1856, he moved to Linn County, Kansas Territory, and served in the territorial legislature as a member of the Free Soil Party from 1857 to 1858. He was appointed territorial treasurer of the Kansas Territory in 1859 and served until 1861. In 1860 he was appointed adjutant general of Kansas. At the beginning of the Civil War, he recruited a company of infantry in the 2nd Kansas Infantry and was elected captain. He was soon elected colonel when the regiment was organized. During the Battle of Wilson's Creek, he was badly wounded and his regiment earned the nickname "Bloody Second." Mitchell, appointed brigadier general in April 1862, commanded a division at the Battle of Perryville and the Union garrison at Nashville until he was appointed to command the First Cavalry Division in April 1863.[1]

David Stanley was not pleased with Mitchell's command and later in life he was still adamant about Mitchell's unsuitability. In 1863, Stanley preferred Mitchell over Turchin. Mitchell had an ability to ingratiate himself with his superiors and was a politician, not a professional solider. But this made him similar to many other commanders in the volunteer army. Mitchell was not apt to make dramatic military moves, but he would fight and he would follow orders. He did not, and would not, ambitiously seek a higher rank and as chief of cavalry he was a reluctant commander. It can be said in his defense that his health (asthma and a wound) caused him many problems and prevented him from participating in the advance on Chattanooga. Now he needed to seize the reins of the cavalry on the eve of the Battle of Chickamauga.

Mitchell's headquarters was at Valley Head as he began the duty of commanding the cavalry. When he assumed command, he found George Crook firmly in control of Dougherty's Gap after having driven away enemy pickets. Next, Mitchell ordered the First and Second brigades of McCook's division to the right of Alexander McCook's Twentieth Corps, while Watkins's Third Brigade remained at headquarters. Unfortunately for Mitchell, the day he took command Braxton Bragg decided to resume his offensive against Rosecrans. Bragg planned to quickly march north and then turn west, separating Rosecrans from Chattanooga and hoping the action would result in a retreat by the Federal army. Bragg's attack would come on Crittenden's flank north of Gordon's Mill, and a strong Confederate infantry column would move west at Reed's Bridge as it cut the link to Chattanooga. Bragg's army was to cross the Chickamauga Creek and capture Rossville from Granger's Reserve Corps in its push west; but Bragg again hesitated. Finally, he sent the orders to the various commanders on the evening of September 16 to attack, only to hesitate again. The Confederate commanders were poised to strike but waited for orders to advance.[2]

Robert Minty's lonesome First Cavalry Brigade (4th Michigan and 4th U.S. cavalries) remained, underappreciated, at the whim of Thomas Crittenden as the sun rose on September 17. Minty's brigade camped along Pea Vine Ridge near Reed's Bridge after a hard day's skirmishing on the 16th. After the skirmishing, Minty sent his intelligence to Crittenden, reporting, "The force at Ringgold is, I believe, Scott's brigade. Pegram is at Leet's [Tanyard], with an outpost at Pea Vine Church." Although the *Official Records* show Crittenden took Minty's concerns seriously, Minty later noted Crittenden disregarded his report, exclaiming, "It is nothing but dismounted cavalry." Crittenden's response, Minty recorded, was that "all this would indicate infantry, which the major-general commanding cannot believe." On September 17 Minty pushed back the enemy along his front, collecting twenty-three infantrymen, but again Crittenden discounted the threat remarking, "They are only some stragglers you picked up." Minty concluded that he returned to his command at Reed's Bridge "with heavy heart," being unable to convince Crittenden and Rosecrans of the threat to the Union left flank. On the 16th, Minty believed he faced a serious Confederate threat to his front and again requested his regiments—the 3rd Indiana and 7th Pennsylvania cavalries. Robert Burns of Minty's staff confirmed in a letter that Minty was aware he faced a large concentration of enemy troops for a couple of days. Minty was in position to receive a heavy blow if Bragg could ever mount his attack.[3]

The action along Minty's front caused a ripple of concern throughout the Union army. Rosecrans' headquarters was at Crawfish Springs, a small village about two miles west of Lee and Gordon's Mill. The Confederate activity along his front was deeply concerning to him and he sent messages to his commanders asking for an accounting of their current positions. Crook continued to protect Dougherty's Gap and the area around Alpine with Eli Long's brigade. Upon receiving the orders from Garfield, Mitchell sent McCook with two brigades to Crawfish Springs and left Louis Watkins's Third Brigade at Winston's.[4]

The sun set on September 17, with the soldiers of the Army of the Cumberland anticipating an attack from Bragg. Rosecrans was finally drawing his army together and ominous clouds of dust were observed to the east. Minty's brigade remained posted near Reed's Bridge and John Wilder's mounted infantry settled in at Alexander's Bridge that evening. Meanwhile, Edward McCook began to move his two cavalry brigades to Crawfish Springs but decided to remain near Stephen's Gap, still about 10 miles from Crawfish Springs, for the night.[5]

Day 1, September 18: The Battle at Reed's Bridge

On September 18, Bragg sent his army forward and the Battle of Chickamauga began.[6] Fortunately for Rosecrans, two of his most able colonels were in two of the toughest spots on September 18. John Wilder's mounted infantry was located at Alexander's Bridge and

Lee and Gordon's Mills (National Archives).

Robert Minty's cavalry was protecting Reed's Bridge. Both of these commands were exhausted after a month in the saddle. In regard to Wilder's brigade, it seemed all the infantry commanders had work for him to do. Minty's underappreciated brigade had been slowly dismantled. Only the day before, Minty had command of the 2nd Michigan and the 4th U.S. Cavalry. Luckily, the 7th Pennsylvania had just returned to his command. In all, he had less than one thousand men. In addition, Minty's one section of the well-regarded Chicago Board of Trade Battery was positioned on Pea Vine Ridge along Reed's Bridge Road. Minty had chafed under Crittenden's command and he felt many of his reports had been disregarded by Crittenden.[7]

Early on September 18, Minty had pickets and patrols out looking for the enemy he believed was nearing his position. He sent one hundred troopers of the 4th U.S. Cavalry toward Leet's Tanyard and the same number of 4th Michigan and 7th Pennsylvania cavalries to Ringgold looking for the enemy. The latter patrol was commanded by Captain Heber Thompson, a Yale graduate who began his Civil War Service in what was termed "The First Defenders," the Washington Artillery of Pottsville. Thompson subsequently joined the 7th Pennsylvania Cavalry when it was organized. During the reconnaissance on the morning of September 18, he found the head of Brigadier General Bushrod Johnson's Confederate column slowly marching past Peeler's Mill only short a short distance to the east of Chickamauga Creek. Thompson sent a rider back to Minty explaining that he saw a large column of infantry marching in his direction. After sending messages to Gordon Granger, John Wilder, Thomas Wood, and Thomas Crittenden, Minty strengthened his pickets along the LaFayette Road and rode forward with the 4th Michigan, 7th Pennsylvania, a battalion of the 4th U.S. and section of the Chicago Board of Trade Artillery. Minty established his defensive line of about 600 troopers along the eastern slope of Pea Vine Ridge and prepared to meet Johnson's advancing column of 5,000 men. The movement of the Confederate column pushed Thompson's men back toward Minty's hastily prepared defensive line. Johnson's column included Brigadier General John Gregg's brigade of seven regiments, Brigadier General Evander McNair's five regiments, and Colonel John Fulton's four Tennessee regiments.[8]

Once the Confederate column got within range, Minty opened with an artillery barrage that caused Johnson to deploy into battle line. Minty noticed another column of dust moving to the north. Fearing he was about to be flanked and facing more Confederates than he could handle, he appealed to John Wilder for troops to protect Dyer's Bridge, a few miles north, which Minty thought was the objective of the Confederate column to the north. Wilder sent two regiments, the 123rd Illinois and the 72nd Indiana with a section of Lilly's Battery, to Dyer's Bridge to stop any attempt to flank Minty by that route. The remainder of Wilder's brigade held Alexander's Bridge. But Minty and Wilder had secured the key bridges, which prevented a rapid advance of Bushrod Johnson's and William H.T. Walker's Confederates. These two Union colonels were in for a long day.[9]

Little did Minty know that Nathan Forrest had ordered Colonel John Scott's cavalry brigade to guard the Old Federal Road leading to Rossville. As Scott's Confederate cavalry advanced, it ran into Brigadier General Walter Whitaker's First Brigade of James Steedman's Union reserve division at Red House Bridge. The dust Minty observed had been Scott's Confederate cavalry riding toward Whitaker's position. As a result, Wilder's two regiments that had been hastily sent to Dyer's Bridge would see no action during the day.[10]

Alfred R. Waud sketch of Robert Minty's cavalry brigade defending against the Confederate attack at Reed's Bridge, September 18, 1863 (Library of Congress).

Fortunately for Minty, Johnson's advance was delayed from the start of the day and it was not rushing to the front. Johnson was delayed by an outdated set of orders directing him to move to Leet's Tanyard instead of Reed's Bridge. Once the confusion was sorted out, Johnson's column marched forward. Nathan Forrest caught the column about 11:00 a.m. and he rode with about 240 troopers of Martin's Detachment, a fragment of survivors of John Hunt Morgan's July raid into the north.[11]

Captain Heber Thompson's 7th Pennsylvania troopers skirmished with Bushrod Johnson's advanced infantry units near Peeler's Mill, with more Southern infantry support following behind. Next, Forrest arrived on the scene and assumed command of the small Southern cavalry contingent, which pushed Thompson's men slowly westward. Johnson's infantry quickly moved forward and slowly advanced. Minty reinforced Thompson's men but the numbers were on Johnson's side and he pushed Minty back toward Reed's Bridge, "a narrow, frail structure, which was planked with loose boards and fence-rails." Lieutenant Jacob Sigmund, 7th Pennsylvania Cavalry, was in charge of some of Minty's skirmishers, and as Johnson's troops started moving forward Lieutenant Sigmund held his line but was slowly overwhelmed. To his left a soldier was killed, and Captain May, Company K, rode ahead to order Sigmund to fall back, but May was killed before he could give the order. The adjutant yelled to Sigmund, "Sigmund, why don't you fall back?" "'My instructions were to hold this hill,'" replied the lieutenant, "and I meant to hold it until I was ordered to fall back."[12]

Johnson deployed three brigades of infantry, supported by a fourth, and pushed the Union cavalry back toward Reed's Bridge. Nathan Forrest had joined Johnson's column but subsequently left in search of what he thought was another Union force. Upon his return around 1:00 p.m., Forrest took command of the advance on Minty's position and borrowed elements of the 17th and 44th Tennessee infantries. Reed's Bridge, while serving as a choke point for the Confederate advance, also made it necessary that Minty complete a tenuous maneuver to extract his command still on the east side of the Chickamauga Creek.

As the Southern infantry closed in, Minty had positioned much of his brigade on the east side of the creek while trying to delay Johnson's advance. He had hidden one section of artillery in bushes near the creek supported by one battalion of the 4th U.S. Cavalry. The rest of the regulars he sent to the other side of the creek in order to provide covering fire once the remainder of the brigade needed to cross the bridge. As the Confederate infantry advanced, the 4th Michigan and 7th Pennsylvania cavalries provided the first line of defense.[13]

Henry Albert Potter, 4th Michigan Cavalry, recorded the intense action as Johnson pushed Minty rearward:

> I could see them when they loaded, as soon as the smoke cleared away—order came to fall back—which we did—rejoined the regiment & moved through the woods—our skirmishers soon saw the rebels infantry—we dismounted half of the men and moved upon them—a smart skirmish ensued—but were obliged to fall back by overpowering numbers—formed in line again—again were driven back—passed thro' our camp and past the "Regulars"—towards the river—which we succeeded in crossing without loss. Formed in a line to cover the retreat of the 4th [Regulars] [and] presently crash! came the artillery in the midst of us.[14]

Minty began his withdrawal across the bridge as the Southern infantry pressed in on his position. After firing on the advancing Confederates, he ordered the cannons across the creek and they were unlimbered on the west side of the creek covering the withdrawal. Next, the 4th Michigan withdrew across the bridge and then the 7th Pennsylvania followed. Finally a squadron of the 4th U.S. regulars moved across and stopped long enough on the bridge to pull up the planks, making a quick crossing difficult for their enemy.[15] But not all of Minty's command had made it across the creek; a squadron of the 4th Michigan had been guarding the Harrison Road and was cut off due to the rapid advance of the Confederates. Lieutenant John Simpson, commanding the detail, made a determined stand against the Confederates closing on his position and finally his troopers escaped by swimming the creek.[16]

Once across the creek, Minty resisted the crossing until late afternoon, but he was being flanked on all sides. Also, he received a message from an officer in charge of his supply train which stated, "Colonel Wilder has fallen back from Alexander's Bridge to Gordon's Mills and the enemy are crossing at all points in force." Other reports suggest Minty fell back before Wilder did. About 4:00 p.m., Minty sent a message to Wilder's troops at Dyer's Bridge to fall back and join him as he retreated to Gordon's Mill.[17]

Aware of the action taking place on his left flank, Rosecrans dispatched Brigadier General James Steedman to send infantry from the Reserve Corps to support Minty's left flank, but Steedman could not get Dan McCook's infantry brigade on the road until 3:30. The first Confederates along Minty's front crossed Chickamauga Creek at 3:00 p.m. just as John Bell Hood's division arrived on the scene. Minty was forced to retire when he was informed that Brigadier General Henry B. Davidson's cavalry brigade of John Pegram's division found and forded Fowler's Ford, about a half-mile south of Reed's Bridge. Minty began falling back after 3:00 p.m., and Wilder, who had battled Major General William Walker's column at Alexander Bridge, held on until 4:00. At 3:30 p.m. John Wilder sent Rosecrans word of the situation: "Colonel Minty has fallen back, after being re-enforced by two regiments and two pieces of artillery of mine. A rebel infantry force has crossed Chickamauga between Alexander's Bridge and Reed's Bridge, getting in my rear. I held the rebels at Alexander's Bridge until they outnumbered me on every side. I got off my artillery, and am falling back on General Wood." Brigadier General Thomas Wood, Crittenden's Corps, First Division, rode to the front after hearing the noise of the battle and smugly discounted the initial reports that Minty and Wilder were under heavy attack. After observing the scope of the Confederate advance, he exclaimed, "By ____, they are here." Then, he ordered his infantry forward to meet the threat. Johnson's slow advance and Minty and Wilder's actions delayed the Confederate advance for almost a day, giving Rosecrans a chance to prepare for Bragg's move.[18]

As Minty and Wilder retired, they combined their commands and formed a single line near the LaFayette Road. As the Confederate infantry continued forward it was greeted by the combined firepower of Wilder and Minty. The fight continued for over an hour and the Union line held. Wood advanced his infantry, which met the advancing Confederate infantry, and as night fell the fighting ended for the day.[19]

During the day, Rosecrans had not been idle and pulled his army together. He recognized Bragg's attack was designed to strike his left flank, and he hastened his commands northward. The action around Reed's Bridge and Alexander's Bridge precipitated a second order for Steedman to send another brigade to bolster the Union left flank. Interestingly, David Stanley's and William Rosecrans' close friend Father Jeremiah Trecy was the bearer of the message about the movements of Minty and Wilder. Thomas Wood was greeted at 4:40 p.m. by Trecy, who informed him the two commands had merged into a single line resisting the Confederate advance. The Union line had been pushed back almost to the Chattanooga and Rossville Road, and the Confederates were pushing forward with infantry, artillery, and cavalry.[20]

While the fighting began on the Union left flank, the bulk of Robert Mitchell's cavalry was still guarding the Union right flank. Mitchell received his orders during the evening of September 18 directing his cavalry to close up on Alexander McCook's Twentieth Corps' right flank, abandoning Dougherty's Gap and Valley Head, which he had been guarding.

At the end of September 18, Rosecrans' army was being pulled together and the morrow would bring vicious fighting, the likes of which many in the army had never seen. During the day, most of the Union cavalry had the inglorious but important duty of protecting the gaps and the flanks. Robert Minty and John T. Wilder and their commands had performed immeasurably valuable service to the Army of the Cumberland as they did their jobs well. Luck as well as skill had been important in Minty's and Wilder's important efforts. Halfway between their positions was Lambert's Ford. The two Union colonels were already facing overwhelming odds, and had the Confederates chosen to utilize this crossing either colonel could have easily been flanked. Also, for the most part the Confederate cavalry played little part in the morning's attack, which allowed Minty and Wilder to focus on the Confederate Infantry. The only other active engagement with cavalry was Scott's fighting with Whitaker's infantry. Nevertheless, Minty and Wilder saved Rosecrans' left flank and gave him time to meet what could have been a crushing blow. Whatever happened the next day, they had given Rosecrans what he needed—time.[21]

Day 2, September 19: The Cavalry Moves to Crawfish Springs and Retreat

The morning began early and bloody. Colonel John Croxton led his infantry brigade close to Jay's Mill near the north side of the developing Union line in search of what was thought to be an isolated Confederate infantry brigade. Instead, he found Forest's dismounted cavalry and the battle began. Throughout the day Rosecrans and Bragg threw their armies into the field in a piecemeal fashion and the lines ebbed and flowed. The formidable Confederate cavalry was ordered by Braxton Bragg to "develop the enemy" on the morning of September 19. For Forrest, the "development" resulted in extensive fighting with the Union infantry throughout the day; no involvement from the Union cavalry occurred on the Union left flank. The day before, Wheeler had been ordered to move into McLemore's Cove through Dug and Catlett's gaps, to demonstrate against the enemy and to occupy the attention of the Union command while Bragg's right flank attack was implemented. On the morning of September 19, Wheeler moved to Owen's Ford, on Chickamauga Creek, after leaving a substantial force to protect the mountain gaps.[22]

Robert Minty's cavalry, which had fought so hard the day before, spent a fretful and "bitterly cold" night without any campfires. Minty held his position and welcomed John Palmer's infantry division the next morning. Then the cavalry moved to the rear to forage horses and obtain rations for the men. Minty's brigade spent the day guarding the supply trains coming and going from Chattanooga, and he would finish the day near Rossville without participating in the battle. For the bulk of the Union cavalry scattered fifteen miles south along the valleys, Rosecrans' orders drew them back to the main Union concentration forming along the LaFayette Road. Robert Mitchell's order, early on the 19th, sent the cavalry corps riding toward Crawfish Springs, Rosecrans' headquarters. Eli Long's Second Brigade of

Crook's division moved from Rape's Gap into McLemore's Cove during the day and toward Crawfish Springs that evening. McCook's First Division fought off a half-hearted attack of Wheeler's cavalry on the division's supply train during the advance northward.

Of the skirmishes during the day, Campbell's First Brigade of 1,200 troopers had light duty. Campbell rode from Pond Springs to Crawfish Springs and had slight clash with Wheeler's cavalry on his right flank, "but without loss [and t]he enemy's skirmishers retreated rapidly." Upon approaching Cowan's Ford on the Chickamauga Creek, Lieutenant Colonel Roswell Russell, 9th Pennsylvania, crossed the creek, chasing away a squad of Wheeler's cavalry posted at the edge of a cornfield.[23]

Major Leonidas R. Scranton, 2nd Michigan, noted that Wheeler's cavalry made a "dash" on the supply train but no loss in men or of supplies was suffered. It was Colonel Daniel Ray's Second Cavalry Brigade of about 1,300 troopers that had a tense experience on September 19. Ray's brigade followed behind Campbell's First Brigade and handled the repulse of the attack on the Union supply train. Wheeler attacked the supply train about a mile from Stevens Gap and four miles south of Crawfish Springs with four cavalry regiments and a section of artillery. Wheeler had been looking for an opportunity to seize the supply train, and Major David Briggs, 2nd Indiana Cavalry, found himself in a bad position when Wheeler's attack cut off the 2nd Indiana from the main column. The only hope for the train and the regiment was to get reinforcements. Briggs sent two riders to try to reach the main column. Three dismounted companies were placed within the train. The remainder of the regiment surrounded the train, still on horseback. Luckily, the riders reached the main column and the 2nd Indiana held off the Confederate cavalry until help arrived. The 2nd Indiana Cavalry repulsed the first attack on the trains and Wheeler tried again to attack the train in a heated engagement. The 1st Wisconsin Cavalry and 4th Indiana Cavalry returned to Briggs' position and the subsequent skirmish lasted about an hour. Colonel Oscar La Grange, 1st Wisconsin, riding to assist the 2nd Indiana, dismounted one-half of the regiment and exchanged fire with Wheeler's troopers, who fell back to a wooded area. La Grange sent the remainder of the regiment to find the Confederate cavalry's flank, and Wheeler finally broke off the attack and retired. La Grange lost one man severely wounded and one man missing, the 4th Indiana had two troopers missing, and the train was undamaged. Wheeler's only reference to the action was, "About 2 p.m. I learned the enemy's cavalry were moving up McLemore's Cove. I moved across the river and warmly assailed their flank, dividing the column and driving the enemy in confusion in both directions."[24]

Major Leonidas Scranton's 2nd Michigan Cavalry battled Wheeler's cavalry at Glass Mill (*History of Michigan at Chickamauga*, 1899).

The 2nd Michigan Cavalry also had some light action during the afternoon engaging the enemy along the front and right of Crawfish Springs and claiming possession of the fords along Chickamauga Creek. The action of the 2nd Michigan set the stage for a bloody fight the next day.

At the end of the day, Archibald Campbell had two

regiments of his brigade protecting ammunition and supply trains in Dry Valley, the 2nd Indiana was positioned on the left of John Wilder's mounted infantry, the 9th Pennsylvania was along the right of Wilder's command, with the remainder of McCook's division positioned in the front and left of Crawfish Springs. Ray's cavalry also formed a battle line around Crawfish Springs. Meanwhile, Crook's cavalry arrived just south of Crawfish Springs, having had a greater distance to ride during the day.

Captain Thomas McCahan's 9th Pennsylvania skirmished with Confederates on the way to Crawfish Springs. McCahan dismounted his company and he took a carbine from one of the troopers who held the horses. As he walked behind his line, he stepped on a dry twig, which cracked very loudly. Then McCahan humorously noted in his diary, "I jumped, the boys say, 20 feet to the rear and threw the carbine to my face." McCahan brought some needed levity to a serious situation. When the twig cracked, McCahan thought an enemy had fired at him, but fortunately no further fighting took place and McCahan led his company to Crawfish Springs. Meanwhile, Rosecrans fought to a draw on September 19 but successfully formed a solid north-south line along LaFayette Road. The day's fighting was hard, but Rosecrans was in a familiar position. His situation was similar to the Battle of Corinth and the Battle of Stones River. He fought hard the first day and developed a strong defensive position, a pattern that had yielded successes in the past. He felt confident the next day's battle would end as his previous battles had.[25]

Finally, McCook's Third Brigade, commanded by Colonel Louis Watkins, moved 400 sick soldiers to the rear. Watkins moved the sick through Stevens Gap and upon his arrival he was ordered to Crawfish Springs. This order was to result in a tough fight for Watkins on September 21.

The Final Day, September 20: The Engagement at Glass Mill

September 20 would be a pivotal day in the life of William Rosecrans and a disastrous day for the Army of the Cumberland. For the Union cavalry, the day held one important engagement between Joseph Wheeler's cavalry and George Crook's Second Brigade under the command of Colonel Eli Long.

Robert Mitchell had been successful in pulling his cavalry corps together. Louis Watkins' brigade, still separated from the main cavalry column, moved toward Crawfish Springs after escorting the sick to Steven's Gap the day before. Robert Minty's brigade protected the Union left flank. This left three Union brigades, Campbell's, Ray's, and Long's, in position around Crawfish Springs. Campbell and Ray's brigades were part of Edward McCook's First Division, but during the day, McCook commanded only part of Daniel Ray's Second Brigade. The 9th Pennsylvania (left), 1st Wisconsin (right), and 2nd Indiana (reserve) cavalries were stationed along the left of the Union defense near Crawfish Springs and connected with John Wilder's mounted infantry. Mitchell placed one of Archibald Campbell's regiments, the 2nd Michigan Cavalry, under his command. Campbell rode with the 1st Tennessee and 4th Indiana cavalries a mile to the rear of Crawfish Springs, presumably on Lookout Mountain to protect the flank, rear and fords across the Tennessee River. The 2nd Michigan was placed in front of Crawfish Springs and would be involved in a fight later in the day. Crook, with Long's brigade, had yet to arrive at Crawfish Springs.[26]

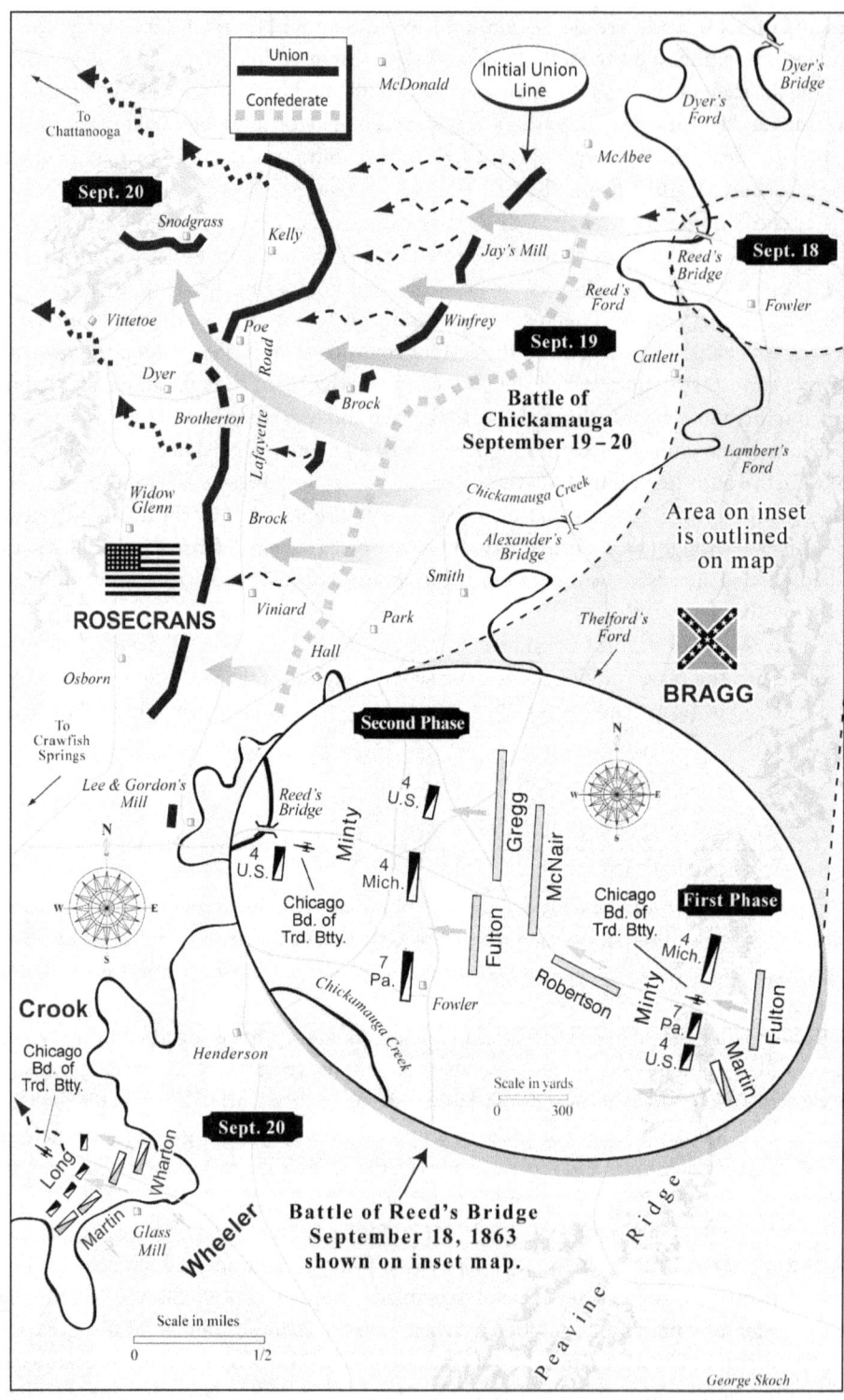

Union Cavalry Actions During the Battle of Chickamauga (Reed's Bridge and Glass Mill; map courtesy of Dave Powell and David Friedrichs)

During the evening of September 19, John C. Breckinridge's infantry division, which had been near Crawfish Springs, moved closer to the battle and Wheeler replaced him along the Confederate left flank. Wheeler had been given orders to connect with Longstreet's left flank and "to attack the enemy at every opportunity which presented itself." These orders set the stage for a significant cavalry fight on September 20 near the ford at Glass Mill just over a mile southeast of Crawfish Springs. Glass Mill was located on the Chickamauga Creek about two miles south of Gordon's Mill at a series of deep bends in the creek. The Union cavalry protected the north side of the creek where the land jutted forward and was vulnerable to enfilading fire from the flanks should there be any enemies on the other side.[27]

The 2nd Michigan Cavalry was in line at daylight on September 20 and skirmished with Colonel Thomas Harrison's Confederate cavalry brigade at the ford. The second and third battalions claimed the ford from the 8th Texas Cavalry and exchanged fire with the enemy throughout the morning. The 2nd Michigan's First Battalion guarded another ford about three-quarters of a mile west, but the Second and Third battalions were to have a busy day.

The men of the 2nd Michigan thought all was quiet and were satisfied they had repulsed the Southern attempts at capturing the ford. Sergeant Henry Mortimer Hempstead, 2nd Michigan Cavalry, was settling down for breakfast when Wheeler pushed his cavalry toward the Union position near Glass Mill. Hempstead recorded in his diary, "I got our mess coffee pot filled and nearly boiled when just as the Captain was inquiring if my coffee was done we were saluted with three or four shells in rapid succession from a battery at very short range, being located just back of the mill and evidently aiming at our camp fire…. [We] had retreated a few steps after the company when another shell burst close to or directly in the fire scattering the brands in every direction."[28]

About 10:00 a.m., the Confederates reappeared, intent on claiming the ford near Glass Mill. A battery of Southern artillery was unlimbered and the Union cavalry skirmishers were driven back to the main line under a hail of grape and canister. Major Leonidas R. Scranton, 2nd Michigan, observing his Second Battalion being flanked as a group of 100 Confederates crossed the creek, sent forward the Third Battalion and was able to drive the Texans back across the creek. Then he found he was receiving enfilading fire from the artillery on the left and the same from musket fire on the right. Due to a large bend in the river, the Union cavalry was vulnerable from fire on three sides. Wheeler had just begun an attack with Martin's and Wharton's cavalry divisions.[29]

While Scranton was fighting for his life, George Crook rode in his direction with reinforcements. The day began early for Crook. William Sinclair sent orders at 2:00 a.m. directing him to hurry his command to Crawfish Springs. Crook's Second Brigade was commanded by Eli Long, and unfortunately both of these commanders provided woefully inadequate reports of their actions on September 20, Wheeler succeeding in sending them to the rear. Equally unfortunate, none of the regimental commanders of this brigade filed an after action report.[30]

When Crook arrived at Crawfish Springs he met with Robert Mitchell, a commander he had little respect for; but Mitchell "wasn't afraid to fight," exclaimed Crook. Mitchell immediately ordered Crook to Glass Mill, about two miles from headquarters at Crawfish Springs, to reinforce Scranton's Michigan cavalry. Mitchell remained at Crawfish Springs. Crook took a section of the Chicago Board of Trade Artillery over his objection and went by the road around a juniper thicket to find the 2nd Michigan hotly engaged and falling back.[31]

George Crook arrived at Crawfish Springs at 9:00 a.m. with the 1st Ohio, 3rd Ohio, 4th Ohio, 2nd Kentucky and a section of artillery. The 2nd Kentucky Cavalry's Lieutenant Colonel Elijah Watts recalled he was "rested, hopeful, expectant, with an effort to be buoyant." Upon his arrival at Crawfish Springs he was astonished to find the cavalry in columns standing "to horse" and not in battle line, but waiting. When Long's brigade was ordered forward, Watts turned to see the remaining cavalry still calmly waiting by their horses. Watts recalled that Stanley was sick and in an ambulance. Watts wrote, "[I]f he was in command things would have been different." While riding to Glass Mill, the 2nd Kentucky found the Michigan cavalry moving to the rear, and as they passed the Michigan troopers they remarked they were in for a hot time.[32]

Crook found the 2nd Michigan being pressed as Wheeler brought the weight of his cavalry to bear on Scranton's command. Scranton's First Battalion moved to join the rest of the regiment as the fight intensified. Once Crook arrived the Union advance began again pushing toward the ford. Wheeler noted "warm skirmishing commenced." Crook and Long mistook the dismounted cavalry as Hindman's infantry but Wheeler's dismounted cavalry advanced on the Union position. Wheeler believed he tricked Long and Crook into thinking the Confederate cavalry was going to attack the flank. Wheeler saw "the enemy wavered [and] ... charged him" and drove the Union cavalry back to Crawfish Springs. The 2nd Michigan was positioned away from the point of Wheeler's attack. Scranton observed that the reinforcements on his left—Long's brigade—fell back, leaving him in his original predicament. He began falling back and ordered the First Battalion, still firing away, to move back also, but two companies failed to receive the order. Companies A and F unleashed a vicious enfilading volley into the pursuing Confederates, who were intent on pushing forward. Soon these two companies hurried to the rear and the entire regiment retreated to Crawfish Springs.[33]

William Crane, 4th Ohio Cavalry, recorded in his journal that the cavalry dismounted and advanced to meet the oncoming Confederate attack. The 4th Ohio was greeted with an intense fire from the enemy and the other three regiments advanced. The 1st Ohio was given the duty of guarding the section of the Chicago Board of Trade Artillery. Crane wrote, "It was tough work, the enemy was very strong, and our lines were slowly driven back." He observed that the 4th Ohio and 2nd Kentucky cavalries took the brunt of the attack.[34]

Much of the result of the fight was due to a confusing order. Sergeant John Chapin, 1st Ohio Cavalry, was dismounted and watched as the Confederates charged forward. At about 300 yards, a lieutenant from Crook's staff rode to the 1st Ohio and exclaimed, "Prepare to charge!" Lieutenant Colonel Valentine Cupp immediately ordered the 1st Ohio to "sling carbines and draw sabres." The 1st Ohio Cavalry prepared for a suicidal charge into a much superior force. Chapin told a fellow trooper, "If the charge is made not a man can come alive." Crook saw something was wrong with the 1st Ohio and rode to Cupp and explained the order was to "prepare to *resist* the charge," not to make a charge. By the time the real order was received, the 1st Ohio was some thirty yards in front of the artillery. The regiment was ordered to turn and ride back to the original line, which resulted in two turns, during which time the Confederates were constantly firing and charging. The Union artillery fired until the Confederates were 50 yards away then quickly limbered and made its escape. With the artillery safely away, Cupp ordered, "Fours, left about, march!" But before the turn was complete a shot struck Cupp in the lower abdomen, mortally wounding him. As for Chapin, he wrote that just as the about face was made "a Confederate officer had the impudence to shoot me with a revolver."[35]

Crook was just outmanned as he engaged Martin's and Wharton's divisions. Long's command of 900 was no match for four Confederate cavalry brigades. Crook lost 100 of his men in a fifteen-minute interval and many were lost trying to save the guns of the Chicago Board of Trade, which Crook had not wanted on the field. He had been overruled by Mitchell, who insisted the artillery be moved forward. Eli Long, who was generally not given to discussing his actions on the field, recorded in his autobiography that he was ordered to protect the artillery battery, which caused his cavalry to be placed in a position of facing overwhelming odds unsupported by the remainder of Mitchell's cavalry division.[36]

The Ohio regiments dismounted around the Chicago Board of Trade battery and the 2nd Kentucky was ordered to the left of the battery while remaining mounted. Elijah Watts rode into position in the raging battle and later remarked, "[O]nly God knows what was before us." He soon found the Rebel battery hammering with "shot and shell" on his position and Confederate soldiers steadily marching forward in the attack. The Kentuckians leveled their carbines and the Chicago Board of Trade fired double canister, momentarily staggering the advance. Then Watts noticed Troops B and D were forced back and instead of backing up they attempted to turn to fall back. When they turned they found they were more vulnerable to Confederate attack and were doubled back and the line "folded like a knife." With this, the Confederate attack flanked the 2nd Kentucky and reached its rear. There was nothing left to do but attempt to save as many troopers as possible. Watts also recorded he received Crook's order to prepare to charge Wheeler's cavalry just as his regiment was overrun. Henry Hempstead, 2nd Michigan, wrote that the 2nd Kentucky Cavalry was sent retreating from the battlefield, "Our 'brave' Kentuckians had after short resistance fled in confusion. I attempted to reach Capt. Johnson again but he had already comprehended the situation and the whole Company were breaking for the woods and liberty." The 2nd Kentucky recorded the greatest losses of the day, suffering eleven men killed, another fifty wounded and two missing.[37]

Crook rode to the rear with Long's retreating cavalry looking for help, but he got none from Mitchell. Crook found the remainder of the cavalry in a field at Crawfish Springs. Crook's cavalry fell in line with the rest of the Union cavalry and hastily formed a battle line at the rear of the field, providing an excellent field of fire in anticipation of Wheeler's attack, which never came. While the fight at Glass Mill was taking place, the Confederate infantry penetrated Rosecrans' main line and rolled up the brigades on both sides. Bragg had just won the Battle of Chickamauga. Wheeler received orders to ride to Lee and Gordon's Mill and to attack the enemy, sparing Crook and Mitchell what promised to be a bloody fight. This fight resulted in a loss of 122 men killed, wounded or missing, including the death of Lieutenant Colonel Valentine Cupp, commanding the 1st Ohio Cavalry.[38]

While Eli Long was having a bad day, Lieutenant Colonel Roswell Russell, 9th Pennsylvania, had a relatively uneventful time, only occasionally exchanging shots with the enemy. Captain Thomas McCahan's company was on picket duty and skirmished with Confederates until they were pushed backed. McCahan rallied the skirmishers and fell back when the enemy advanced in force. Also at Crawfish Springs was Daniel Ray's Second Cavalry Brigade, which had a fairly uneventful day as well. Ray remained in line of battle throughout the day until the withdrawal of the entire army later in the day. Charles Perry Goodrich, 1st Wisconsin, wrote to his wife, revealing the disparity of the action of the Union cavalry: "As usual our cavalry was found in line, in the rear."[39]

Mitchell had been ordered to guard Crawfish Springs at all costs. The location had recently been Rosecrans' headquarters and seven of the army's nine hospitals were located near the springs. About 3:00 p.m. Mitchell still held the cavalry in battle line waiting for another Confederate attack. Throughout the day along the main battle lines a vicious battle raged as the Confederates broke the Union line and focused the battle at Snodgrass Farm, where George Thomas pulled together a determined defense. The 9th Pennsylvania Cavalry was sent to find Sheridan's infantry and discovered the way north blocked by the enemy. Finally the information about the situation with the rest of the army was relayed to Mitchell, who realized he was separated from the main concentration of the army. He learned the right flank had been turned and the entire Union army was retreating to Chattanooga. Now Mitchell made a very difficult decision. He protected the seven hospitals but he needed to remain connected with the army. A more difficult moral, ethical decision is hard to imagine. He was unable to get orders from Rosecrans or Alexander McCook, and he decided to move with the army, abandoning the wounded in the hospitals.[40]

The Union cavalrymen understood the orders but didn't like leaving the wounded behind. Initially, the 1st Tennessee troopers let the wounded ride on their horses and the troopers walked. Colonel James Brownlow soon put an end to that and explained the importance of having the troopers in the saddle despite the sadness of the wounded having to walk. Lieutenant John Andes, 2nd Tennessee, wrote in his diary that "I shall never forget the piteous cries of hundreds of our men, as we would ride by."[41]

At 4:00 p.m. the cavalry started to move away with Colonel Sidney Post's First Brigade of infantry, which had just arrived, and Long's cavalry brigade led the way, escorting as many of the walking wounded as possible. An hour later the column was gone, and Wheeler's cavalry soon followed, capturing the hospitals filled with Union wounded. Edward McCook's First Division was placed in charge of the rearguard action as Mitchell moved west and then northward and bivouacked between six and nine miles south of Chattanooga. Lieutenant Colonel Roswell Russell, 9th Pennsylvania, manned the rear guard when a regiment of Wheeler's cavalry half-heartedly attacked the rear of Mitchell's column and was handily repulsed.[42]

On the left flank of the Army of the Cumberland remained Robert Minty's lone brigade of cavalry. As usual Minty operated under the command of an infantry commander, this time Gordon Granger in command of Rosecrans' Reserve Corps. Granger ordered Minty to advance to Missionary Mills and then send patrols to Chickamauga Station and Graysville while avoiding a fight.[43]

In the afternoon Minty took up Granger's position on the Rossville and Ringgold Road. Granger had left this position before Minty arrived. The irascible Granger was making one of his greatest decisions and he committed his Reserve Corps to reinforce George Thomas, who was making a desperate defense at Snodgrass Farm and Horseshoe Ridge. After the intense fighting over the past three days, Minty was determined not to be surprised and sent out reconnaissance patrols. One of the patrols rode to Red House Bridge and found Colonel John Scott's Confederate cavalry brigade, which was estimated to be about 1,500 men strong. Minty recorded he had an hour-long skirmish but Scott did not mention any cavalry action during the afternoon in his report. Minty recorded, "I drove Scott's brigade over the river on this road this P.M." Minty's actions were described by John McLain, 4th Michigan Cavalry, in his diary; McLain exclaimed the Confederate cavalry was driven over a creek just before dark and two men in his company were wounded.[44]

The actions of the day revealed a hard time for Eli Long's brigade and the 2nd Michigan

Cavalry, while the remainder of the Union cavalry was unengaged. Crook who made no secret of his dislike for Mitchell and wrote in his autobiography, "I was present when Gen. Mitchell made his verbal report to Gen. Rosecrans and to hear him recount the valorous deeds of his command. How he could have the cheek; after what had passed, surpassed by understanding. It was humiliating to see persons wearing the uniforms of general officers be so contemptible."[45]

The events of the day generate many questions. If one examines David Stanley's career, one of his maxims was "march to the sound of the guns." It is difficult to second guess events, especially with the spotty records that exist from the events of September 20 for the Union cavalry. Some of the more important questions revolve around Rosecrans' and Mitchell's decisions. On the morning of September 20, Mitchell had parts of three brigades of cavalry around Crawfish Springs, but he utilized only one brigade in the action there. It can be argued that events developed so quickly Mitchell didn't have time to reinforce Crook and Long. This certainly is true with Mitchell two miles in the rear. Hindsight strongly suggests that Mitchell would have been more effective if he had taken the initiative and ridden with Crook to the fighting. Instead, much of his command remained idle while Long was cut to pieces.

Next, Mitchell appears to have totally forgotten Louis Watkins' brigade as he left Crawfish Springs. There is no suggestion that a rider could not have reached Watkins to inform him of the situation and give him new orders upon his withdrawal from Crawfish Springs. This failure to consider an important part of his corps, and at the least his division, resulted in the loss of over 200 in casualties the next day.

Finally, one can question the use of the entire cavalry corps to simply guard hospitals around headquarters. The Union cavalry had essentially no offensive role during the battle and had lost communications with the main body of the Union infantry until late afternoon. Certainly, guarding the flanks and fords was important, but most of the Union cavalry had no part in the fighting on September 20, except for Eli Long's brigade at Glass Mill.

Retreat to Chattanooga: September 21, Watkins at Cooper's Gap and Minty's Actions

Early on the morning of September 21, Mitchell ordered his two division commanders to remain where they were and to maintain guard on the Union right flank. Mitchell ordered, "Prevent the enemy from penetrating our line by way of this valley or along Missionary Ridge." Rosecrans had fallen back during the late afternoon and evening and formed a line resembling a lazy "L." Crittenden's Twenty-first Corps held the left flank on Missionary Ridge, Thomas's Fourteenth Corps held the ground near the Rossville Gap and McCook's Twentieth Corps connected with Thomas and formed an east-west line into the Chattanooga Valley. Mitchell's cavalry extended the Union line to Lookout Mountain.[46]

Mitchell kept the cavalry in line of battle throughout the day, with some skirmishing occurring with Wheeler almost all day. Edward McCook opened communications with Alexander McCook and George Thomas and dispatched the 2nd Michigan to the Tennessee River to guard Harrison's Ferry, located about 14 miles from Chattanooga. Henry Hempstead, 2nd Michigan Cavalry, was exhausted after the previous day's battle and the continued retreat. He wrote in diary, "I was too tired and exhausted to care whether I ever had anything to eat again, so made no effort to stay the pangs of hunger."[47]

The Union cavalry had a very large flank to protect and Mitchell wrote, "We have a hell of a front here. We will do the best we can." Daniel Ray fought off an attempt to cut the cavalry from McCook's Twentieth Corps at 10:00 a.m., but the attack failed as the 1st Wisconsin Cavalry stymied two or three attacks. McCook observed that the enemy wanted to gain possession of the Chattanooga Valley, which if successful would have finished the Army of the Cumberland. This would have isolated the army along Missionary Ridge, placing it in a difficult position. Edward McCook noticed a large cloud dust to his front at 4:00 p.m. and he repulsed "a more determined attempt" to breach his line at 5:00 p.m. The 1st Wisconsin Cavalry and the 2nd Tennessee Cavalry "promptly repulsed" the attack and the Union line held.[48]

Mitchell wrote to Garfield on the morning of September 21: "I have not been able to open communication with Colonel Watkins, and am at a loss to know what has become of him." Mitchell appeared to realize that his final brigade had yet to rejoin his command, and it is unknown what attempts Mitchell made to contact Watkins. The situation at Crawfish Springs the day before suggested no obvious reason Mitchell could not have sent a rider to Watkins informing him of the decision to evacuate the town.[49]

As a result, it was Louis Watkins' lone Third Brigade, the 4th, 5th, and 6th Kentucky cavalries, and cavalry train which would have the hardest duty of the Union cavalry on September 21. Watkins was not with the remainder of Mitchell's command the day before because he escorted the sick to Steven's Gap. Upon completing his task, he was ordered to ride to Crawfish Springs, which had since fallen into enemy hands but was unknown to Watkins. Watkins was following his original orders when he ran into enemy pickets about three miles from Steven's Gap. He pushed the pickets aside and proceeded toward Crawfish Springs as ordered. Watkins rode to within a mile of Crawfish Springs when he encountered more enemy pickets. Suspecting the situation was not as he supposed, he sent forward twenty men under command of Lieutenant Joseph Cowell, 4th Kentucky, to scout forward to the town. They returned within an hour and reported the Confederates had possession of the town. Then Watkins rode about four miles west to the Chattanooga Road. Once gaining the road, Watkins waited for his train to catch up to him. While he waited, his scouts reported Wharton's and Martin's cavalry divisions were hurriedly advancing upon him.[50] Watkins determined his closest escape route was through Cooper's Gap over Lookout Mountain and he hurried his train in that direction, about four miles away. Watkins sent Lieutenant Colonel W.T. Hoblitzell with his 5th Kentucky Cavalry to hurry to the gap to cover the retreat of the train and the other two regiments. The chase was on.

Watkins had the unpleasant task of trying to hold off 3,000 experienced Confederate cavalry hot on his heels with about 400 men of the 4th and 6th Kentucky cavalries. But Watkins advanced to meet the threat, hoping to give his train a chance to escape. The 6th Kentucky Cavalry was placed on the left of the road and the 4th Kentucky on the right. The regiments sent forth skirmishers as the Confederates rapidly approached. Outmanned, the two regiments slowly withdrew. Watkins wrote, "Being flanked on both sides by overwhelming numbers, the Fourth Kentucky Cavalry was compelled to fall back slowly, fighting with desperation, and rallied on the Sixth Kentucky Cavalry, when the two regiments combined held the enemy in check for fully twenty minutes." Then, the 4th Kentucky and 6th Kentucky retreated and a running battle ensued as the Kentucky cavalry rode for their lives. Finally, the two cavalry regiments reached the base of the mountain only to find the wagons "blockaded the road and threw all into confusion. All efforts of the officers to form and rally the men proved only partially successful."[51]

Watkins had expected the 5th Kentucky in line preparing to cover the retreat, but the 5th Kentucky was not to be found. Watkins was enraged at the commander of the 5th Kentucky. If the 5th Kentucky had been line, he felt they could have halted the pursuit. Watkins noted in his after action report that Hoblitzell "had retreated through Cooper's Gap at a very rapid rate." The Confederates had caught their prey at the base of the mountain and Watkins noted that the Confederate cavalry caught up with the Fourth and Sixth Kentucky cavalries and "after considerable slaughter on both sides captured a large number of prisoners." Watkins was able to re-form the remainder of his command on the mountain and sent a rider to return Hoblitzell's 5th Kentucky to what was left of the brigade. When Hoblitzell returned, Watkins sent him to ride the rest of the way to Chattanooga at the rear of the train. Watkins' command suffered the greatest loss of the Union cavalry during the Battle of Chickamauga in this fight that resulted in 6 officers and 211 enlisted men recorded as missing, presumably captured at the entrance of Cooper's Gap. A total of 53 wagons were lost to the Confederate cavalry.[52]

The feud between Watkins and Hoblitzell, which began in the summer, peaked at Cooper's Gap. Louis Watkins would prefer charges against Hoblitzell for cowardice for his actions at Cooper's Gap. The court-martial began on July 26, 1864. Louis Watkins testified he had ordered Hoblitzell to take the 5th Kentucky Cavalry and hold the entrance of Cooper's Gap, a narrow and easily defended position. Later, he sent a lieutenant with the same orders to Hoblitzell to make sure there was no confusion. Watkins told the court if the entrance of the gap could have been held for fifteen minutes longer the supply train and the 4th and 6th Kentucky cavalries could have been saved. When Watkins arrived, he found none of the 5th Kentucky Cavalry present. About halfway up the mountain, he found part of the regiment, Major James Wharton and about 70 troopers, which had been stopped by Watkins' officers. At the top of the mountain, the remaining troopers of the 4th and 6th Kentucky cavalries dismounted and drove off the attacking Confederate cavalry. Watkins dispatched an orderly from the 4th Kentucky Cavalry to bring Hoblitzell back to him. When Hoblitzell was returned to Watkins, Watkins demanded to know where he had been. Hoblitzell, who had his saber in his hand, replied, "I could not stop my men, and had to draw my sabre upon them." Watkins told Hoblitzell that most of his command was on top of Lookout Mountain with the 4th and 6th Kentucky and demanded to know why he wasn't with his men. Hoblitzell replied that he thought the Union infantry was approaching up the west side of the mountain and he had ridden to speed them along. In addition, the brigade color guard reported that as soon as the troopers of the 5th Kentucky Cavalry present were ordered into line they moved swiftly and bravely.[53]

As is common in many trials, there were various accounts of the events. Most serious was the charge of cowardice, and Hoblitzell's defense centered on the confusion of whether the order meant the 5th Kentucky Cavalry should defend the trail at the base of the mountain or on top of the mountain. Hoblitzell interpreted the order to mean the top of the mountain and Watkins obviously meant the foot of the mountain. By all accounts, Hoblitzell remained at the rear of his command, away from the fighting, and his account stressed he was attempting to rally the troopers and personally seeking assistance from a small group of infantry on the west side of the mountain. The court found Hoblitzell not guilty, but not before Hoblitzell sought to have Watkins dismissed by accusing him of returning an ex-slave to his master against his will. The charge was untrue, but Hoblitzell appealed to James Garfield, the War

Department, and other politicians for Watkins' dismissal. Hoblitzell was subsequently superseded by Oliver Baldwin as colonel and commanding officer of the 5th Kentucky Cavalry early in 1864. Hoblitzell would later be transferred to a position in Missouri.[54]

The Battle Ends

Meanwhile, on the left flank of the Union line there remained the ever-vigilant Robert Minty and his brigade of cavalry. On the morning of September 21, Minty's brigade was two miles in front of Thomas's Fourteenth Corps, screening the Confederate advance. Minty observed the advance of three Confederate columns, Walker, Hill, and Polk, which moved from Missionary Mills, Red House Bridge and Dyer's Ford. Pegram's cavalry division advanced and pushed Minty's cavalry back to the Union main line. After the fight at Reed's Bridge, Minty was becoming skilled in the "fight, retreat, fight" method of delaying an advance. At 5:00 p.m., George Thomas informed Minty of his intention to move to Chattanooga and asked Minty to deceive the enemy by taking his place in line. Minty skirmished for a couple of hours and then fell back to Rossville. He lost 10 killed and another 14 wounded in the heated skirmishes.

On the evening of September 21, Robert Mitchell reassured James Garfield that Brigadier General James Spears' brigade of infantry was expected at any moment and would be used to extend the cavalry line on the right flank. Mitchell, a reluctant commander at best, sought the opportunity to shift the command of the defense to Spears, as he noted Spears ranked him by a day or two and he suggested the transfer of command to him.[55]

On the morning of September 22, Mitchell ordered the cavalry to Chattanooga under orders from Garfield. Edward McCook's division covered the retreat of the infantry to Chattanooga. Archibald Campbell's First Division screened the withdrawal of James Spears' brigade. The 2nd Indiana Cavalry had a hard-fought skirmish when Dibrell's cavalry attempted to cutoff Spears' retreat to Chattanooga. The fire was so hot the 1st Wisconsin Cavalry was ordered to join in a successful defense.[56] Next, Robert Mitchell ordered his cavalry which was desperately in need of forage, to the north of the Tennessee River. Also of importance, John Wilder's brigade was attached to the Union cavalry reporting to Mitchell.[57]

Casualties of the Cavalry Corps, Battle of Chickamauga[58]

FIRST DIVISION, Colonel Edward M. McCook

Command	Killed Officers	Killed Men	Wounded Officers	Wounded Men	Missing Officers	Missing Men	Total
First Brigade, Colonel Archibald P. Campbell							
2nd Michigan	1	1	0	6	1	2	11
9th Pennsylvania	0	0	0	0	0	3	3
1st Tennessee	0	0	0	0	0	1	1
Total First Brigade	**1**	**1**	**0**	**6**	**1**	**6**	**15**
Second Brigade, Colonel Daniel M. Ray							
2nd Indiana	0	1	0	4	0	0	5
4th Indiana	0	0	0	2	0	7	9
2nd Tennessee	0	1	0	2	0	0	3

Command	Killed Officers	Killed Men	Wounded Officers	Wounded Men	Missing Officers	Missing Men	Total
1st Wisconsin	0	0	0	2	0	4	6
Total Second Brigade	**0**	**2**	**0**	**10**	**0**	**11**	**23**
Third Brigade, Colonel Louis D. Watkins							
4th Kentucky	0	0	0	1	4	90	95
5th Kentucky	0	0	0	0	2	18	20
6th Kentucky	0	2	1	6	2	120	131
Total Third Brigade	0	2	1	7	8	228	246
Total First Division	**1**	**5**	**1**	**23**	**9**	**245**	**284**
SECOND DIVISION, Brigadier General George Crook							
First Brigade, Colonel Robert H. G. Minty							
3rd Indiana (battalion)	0	0	0	3	0	0	3
4th Michigan	0	1	1	11	0	6	19
7th Pennsylvania	1	4	0	13	0	1	19
4th United States	0	1	0	5	0	1	7
Total First Brigade	**1**	**6**	**1**	**32**	**0**	**8**	**48**
Second Brigade, Colonel Eli Long							
2nd Kentucky	0	11	5	45	0	2	63
1st Ohio	1	1	0	13	0	7	22
3rd Ohio	0	2	0	7	0	8	17
4th Ohio	1	3	0	9	2	19	34
Total Second Brigade	**2**	**17**	**5**	**74**	**2**	**36**	**136**
Total Second Division	**3**	**23**	**6**	**103**	**2**	**44**	**184**
Total Cavalry Corps	**4**	**28**	**7**	**129**	**11**	**289**	**468**

Summary

An analysis of the Union cavalry actions at the Battle of Chickamauga must highlight the remarkable Robert Minty, who performed the most commendable service of the cavalry corps. Charles Greeno, 7th Pennsylvania, wrote, "But consider, what would have been the consequences had we, I refer to our brigade, and General Wilder's, failed to hold in check the overwhelming Confederate forces." Minty's extraordinary actions at Reed's Bridge are important to the opening phase of the Battle of Chickamauga, which blocked Bragg's objective of cutting Rosecrans from Chattanooga while giving Rosecrans the time he needed to prepare a proper defense. Minty, cool under fire, maneuvered his command with the utmost skill during the difficult battle. Unfortunately, he was detailed to Crittenden's control and acted without any other cavalry support. Under the command of a capable superior, such as Crook or Stanley, in conjunction with Long's brigade, Minty could possibly have produced even better results. Perhaps Minty under the command of Stanley or Crook instead of Crittenden might have been successful in determining the location of Bragg's army before the attack on September 18.[59]

Eli Long, Crook's other brigade commander during the campaign, performed well. Long provided almost no personal thoughts about the actions of the campaign. His most important engagement was at Glass Mill, in which his brigade faced overwhelming odds. Crook's Third

Brigade, commanded by William Lowe, had no direct involvement during the campaign. Edward McCook's division also had little notable involvement in the Battle of Chickamauga with the exception of the 2nd Michigan Cavalry at Glass Mill. In addition, Louis Watkins' Third Brigade performed well during the Summerville expedition and was unpleasantly surprised at Cooper's Gap through no fault of Watkins' own.

Rosecrans wrote of General Mitchell's excellent service covering the right flank of the army while protecting the trains, artillery, caissons and wagons. Rosecrans continued: "On the 21st the cavalry still covered our right as securely as before, fighting and holding at bay very superior numbers. The number of cavalry combats during the whole campaign have been numerous, the successes as numerous, but the army could not have dispensed with those of the 19th, 20th, and 21st."[60]

Mitchell's actions appeared to have met Rosecrans' expectations, but the utilization of the Union cavalry, in excess of 5,000 men, detailed to guard the hospitals when Rosecrans needed the firepower on the battlefield has to be questioned. Historian John Londa noted, "If Mitchell could have massed the cavalry, he could have attacked Bragg's flank at the critical moment of the battle on the 20th. Mitchell could have caused Bragg's army great difficulty." In addition, Mitchell's lethargy at Glass Mills and mishandling of Watkins' brigade were serious mistakes.[61]

Peter Cozzens wrote an excellent summary of the interactions between Rosecrans and Stanley during the campaign and explained the apparent reconciliation of the two after the battle:

> Rosecrans might as well have been lecturing his horse. Stanley's health had taken a turn for the worse, and he was so sick with fever and dysentery that he could barely stand up. Mitchell had not yet reported in, however, and Stanley was apparently unwilling to relinquish command to either of his division commanders. Rosecrans must not have known of Stanley's incapacity, if he had, he presumably would have peremptorily ordered the Ohioan to the rear rather than issue him a reprimand that he was probably too sick to read.

Stanley understood the pressure Rosecrans experienced and he knew how Rosecrans pushed himself. Perhaps this understanding helped Stanley remain so amiable in his relations with Rosecrans. Stanley explained that a commander could push himself only so far, and in describing Rosecrans he wrote,

> Rosecrans habitually used himself badly in time of excitement. He never slept, he overworked himself, he smoked incessantly. At Iuka, at Corinth and Stone River, the stress of excitement did not exceed a week. His strong constitution could stand that, but at Chickamauga, this strain lasted a month and Rosecrans' health was badly broken.

This is supported by others who analyzed the Chickamauga Campaign. Military historian Robert Richardson noted Rosecrans was assuming too much direct control over the myriad duties required in commanding the Army of the Cumberland during this campaign, concluding Rosecrans also selected, trained, and poorly utilized his staff officers. The adverse environment within the staff was the responsibility of Rosecrans. However, the inability of his chief of staff to remove the administrative burden from the commander, coupled with the numerous distractions created by the inefficient staff significantly and directly contributed to Rosecrans' loss at Chickamauga.

In many ways, Rosecrans and Stanley were functioning in the same manner by taking all the responsibilities on their own shoulders rather than giving up control to their subordinates.[62]

Stephen Starr agrees in his *The Union Cavalry in the Civil War*: "The duties given General Stanley and the bulk of the cavalry—five of the six brigades of the Cavalry Corps—go a long way to justify Stanley's previously quoted opinion that Rosecrans 'had no idea of the use of cavalry.'"[63]

In John Londa's analysis of the Union cavalry during the Chickamauga Campaign, he asserted the Union right wing of the cavalry was less successful than the left commanded by Minty. He also stated the "problems that the cavalry suffered through were in a large measure caused by the initial plan for the cavalry's employment.... Rosecrans preferred to give directions rather than missions. He robbed the commanders of the latitude to make decisions on the employment of their forces.... The blame of the dispersal of the Cavalry Corps must rest with Rosecrans."[64]

Stanley never produced an official report for the cavalry during this campaign. Rosecrans reconsidered his initial report in January 1864, and rewrote his report of the actions of the cavalry. Whatever demons had possessed Rosecrans and Stanley during the campaign had departed. Of the cavalry and of Stanley, Rosecrans' reconsidered report noted,

> I cannot forbear calling the special attention of the General-in-Chief and the War Department to the conspicuous gallantry and laborious services of this arm. Exposed in all weather, almost always moving, even in winter, without tents or wagons, operating in a country poorly supplied with forage, combating for the most part very superior numbers, from the feeble beginnings of one year ago, when its operations were mostly within the infantry lines, it has become master of the field, and hesitates not to attack the enemy wherever it finds him. This great change, due chiefly to the joint efforts of both officers and men, has been greatly promoted by giving them arms in which they had confidence, and by the adoption of the determined use of the saber. To Maj. Gen. D.S. Stanley is justly due great credit for his agency in bringing about these results, and giving firmness and vigor to the discipline of the cavalry. It requires both nature and experience to make cavalry officers, and by judicious selections and promotions this arm may become still more useful and distinguished.[65]

Finally, the Union cavalry provided effective defensive service, but it must be concluded that it was very underutilized during the Chickamauga Campaign. Rosecrans relied totally on the infantry to do the fighting during the battle and appears to have seen the cavalry as an ineffective fighting force. Throughout the campaign, he failed to recognize the value of his cavalry past the need for an expedition to Rome and Minty's duty on the left. He saw the cavalry as a "mere picket guard" and reconnaissance arm and criticized Stanley for its use in this manner. The strategy Rosecrans had used in the Tullahoma Campaign over a one-week period in a concentrated area failed over the extended campaign over great distances at Chickamauga. Captain Marshall Thatcher explained the frustration in the cavalry during this critical campaign: "To guard the right flank was important, but they were ready and anxious to do more, and were kept further to the right than were actually needed."[66]

7. The Union Cavalry Guards the Tennessee River; Wheeler's Raid

You are dangerous and have left material proof of it upon many a field.
—Major General David S. Stanley

As Rosecrans entrenched his recently defeated army in Chattanooga, in Washington, Halleck and Stanton immediately began to mobilize reinforcement for the Army of the Cumberland. Over the next month, Henry Slocum's Twelfth Corps and Oliver O. Howard's Eleventh Corps would be dispatched from the east to reinforce the Army of the Cumberland. In addition, part of the Army of the Tennessee under command of William T. Sherman would also join Rosecrans' army at Chattanooga with parts of the Fifteenth and Seventeenth corps.

Shortly after the Battle of Chickamauga, the Union cavalry moved to the north side of the Tennessee River to provide reconnaissance, prevent raids, and guard the fords. With the army besieged at Chattanooga, supplies immediately became a critical issue and the cavalry had to find any forage possible for the remaining livestock in the town.[1] Fortunately, John Wilder's mounted infantry became part of the cavalry divisions and this provided extra firepower to the cavalry. In return, the benefit to Wilder's brigade was the ability to forage the horses on the north side of the Tennessee River. But the recent campaign had taken its toll on John Wilder, who left the army and returned home to recuperate.

Brigade command fell to Colonel Abram O. Miller, 72nd Indiana Mounted Infantry, who was a physician before the war. Miller, a native of Madison County, Indiana, was raised on a farm at Twelve Mile Prairie in Clinton County, Indiana. He studied medicine at the University of Louisville and graduated in 1856. He helped raise a company for the 10th Indiana Infantry as the war began. An experienced commander who had fought at the Battle of Rich Mountain, the Battle of Mills Springs, and the siege of Corinth, he was appointed colonel of the 72nd Indiana Infantry in August 1862. Miller was an able replacement for Wilder.[2]

Although it seemed like a short time since the Army of the Cumberland had reached Chattanooga, reports of a large concentration of Confederate cavalry forming north of the town were received. It was disturbing to contemplate a large raid of Confederate cavalry in light of the condition of the Union cavalry, which was not in top condition due to the activity during the recent campaign. The Second Brigade Cavalry inspector, Captain Chris Beck, reported the poor condition of the cavalry:

> In consequence of the arduous duties recently performed by the brigade, it is not in a very efficient condition. The horses are very much run down, principally from a want of forage, which, under the circumstances, could not be had. Quite a large number of the men reported fit for duty are hardly so, but which

a little rest and medical attendance will soon remedy.... The command is very much in need of clothing, especially boots.

If the Second Brigade was representative of the entire corps, Mitchell had barely 8,000 men ready for duty and in poor overall condition.[3]

The various Union cavalry regiments reported the number of men present for duty:

2nd Indiana Cavalry	392
4th Indiana Cavalry	328
4th and 6th Kentucky cavalries	355
5th Kentucky Cavalry	260
7th Kentucky Cavalry (Nashville)	290
1st Wisconsin Cavalry	406
2nd Tennessee Cavalry	407[4]

The Union cavalry fell into line. On the right flank, Colonel William T. Hoblitzell, 5th Kentucky Cavalry, watched across the Tennessee River near Jasper and reported seeing 3,000 Confederate horsemen on the south shore. Crook had the responsibility of the Union left flank and moved his headquarters to Washington, Tennessee, and the various regiments in his first two brigades guarded the numerous fords. Archibald Campbell patrolled even farther west, into Alabama on the extreme right flank.[5]

Mitchell feared the Confederate cavalry planned to break out into the rear of the Army of the Cumberland. Bragg had shown a threat from his cavalry on the Union right flank and Garfield responded by shifting over half of the cavalry in that direction. With threats on the right and the left, the Union cavalry was stretched thin across the wide front, which was Bragg's and Wheeler's plan.[6]

Union Cavalry Positions, September 23, 1863

Command	*Commander*	*Station*[7]
First Division	**Col. E.M. McCook**	**Sevely Springs***
First Brigade	*Colonel A.P. Campbell*	Sevely Springs
2nd Michigan Cavalry	Maj. John C. Godley	Dallas
9th Pennsylvania Cavalry	Lt. Colonel Russell	Sevely Springs
1st East Tennessee Cavalry	Lt. Colonel J.P. Brownlow	Sevely Springs
Second Brigade	*Colonel D.M. Ray*	Sevely Springs
2nd Indiana Cavalry	Maj. J.B. Presdee	Sevely Springs
4th Indiana Cavalry	Lt. Colonel Deweese	Sevely Springs
2nd East Tennessee Cavalry	Lt. Colonel W.R. Cook	Jasper
3rd East Tennessee Cavalry	Colonel W.C. Pickens	Nashville
1st Wisconsin Cavalry	Colonel O.H. La Grange	Sevely Springs
Section Batt. D, 1st Ohio Artillery	Lt. N.M. Newell	Sevely Springs
Third Brigade	*Colonel L.D. Watkins*	Sevely Springs
4th Kentucky Cavalry	Colonel Wickliffe Cooper	Sevely Springs
5th Kentucky Cavalry	Lt. Colonel W.T. Hoblitzell	Near Kelley's Ford
6th Kentucky Cavalry	Lt. Colonel Roper	Sevely Springs
7th Kentucky Cavalry	Lt. Colonel J.K. Faulkner	Nashville
Second Division	**Brig. Gen. George Crook**	**Near Island Ferry**
First Brigade	*Colonel R.H.G. Minty*	On scout in search of forage
7th Pennsylvania Cavalry	Colonel James J. Seibert	On scout in search of forage
4th Michigan Cavalry	Maj. Horace Gray	On scout in search of forage
4th U.S. Cavalry	Capt. J.B. McIntyre	On scout in search of forage
3rd Indiana Cavalry (detachment)	Lt. Colonel Robert Klein	Pikeville, Tennessee

Command	Commander	Station
Second Brigade	Col. Eli Long	
1st Ohio Volunteer Cavalry	Major Patten	Island Ferry, Tennessee
3rd Ohio Volunteer Cavalry	Lt. Colonel Seidel	Island Ferry, Tennessee
4th Ohio Volunteer Cavalry	Lt. Colonel O.P. Robie	Island Ferry, Tennessee
2nd Kentucky Cavalry	Colonel T.P. Nicholas	Island Ferry, Tennessee
Third Brigade	Col. William W. Lowe	
5th Iowa Cavalry	Lt. Colonel Patrick	McMinnville, Tennessee
10h Ohio Volunteer Cavalry	Colonel C.C. Smith	Stevenson, Tennessee
1st Middle Tennessee Cavalry	Lt. Colonel Galbraith	Stevenson, Tennessee
Stokes Battery, Illinois Artillery	Capt. James H Stokes	Island Ferry, Tennessee

*Sevely Springs is "near Chattanooga"

By September 25, there was little doubt the Confederate cavalry had something planned and Bragg's feint had worked. Although some cavalry movement was observed north of Chattanooga, much of the new activity was observed near Bridgeport. Garfield sent orders for McCook's cavalry division to ride immediately to Bridgeport and prepare to repel an attempted crossing. This left Crook to guard the Union left flank alone and on September 26 his troopers drew five days' rations in preparation for action with the enemy.[8]

Wheeler and Roddey, Middle Tennessee Raid

Wheeler struck, and he struck where Mitchell was the weakest, on the Union left flank. George Crook sent a message to Mitchell at 10:00 a.m. on September 30: "The enemy are endeavoring to cross at Cotton Port Ford, 3 miles from Washington. They are in very heavy force. I am fighting them." Crook subsequently determined from prisoners Wheeler's success in crossing was cleverly achieved by selecting a point on the Tennessee River without a known ford, in a location without a cavalry guard. Wheeler's men also carried five days' rations and the prisoner told Crook the raid was to be carried to the west over the mountains.[9]

When Wheeler began his raid through the rear of Rosecrans' defeated army, his move left only one brigade with Bragg's army around Chattanooga. Three brigades of Forrest's cavalry accompanied Wheeler's force, but Wheeler disparagingly referred to these brigades as mere "skeletons," totaling about 1,500 troopers on worn-out horses. However, Wheeler's numbers were impressive, as 5,600 Confederate cavalry rode west.[10] In addition, the assignment of Forrest's cavalry to Wheeler was the foundation of an explosive situation between Forrest and Bragg. The order from Bragg simply told Forrest, "The general commanding desires that you will without delay turn over the troops of your command previously ordered to Major General Wheeler." One can imagine how this order was received by Forrest, who then determined to resign from the army, living up to his vow never to serve under Wheeler. To appease Forrest, he was given a new command in western Tennessee and Mississippi; but Wheeler, after his October raid, gained complete control of his cavalry corps, plus Forrest's cavalry corps.[11]

Crook, with his division scattered at the various locations along the river, was no match for Wheeler's cavalry. He had less than 2,000 cavalry to defend the entire flank. He fought with Wheeler about an hour on September 30 before withdrawing, miraculously saving his supply train. He made his crossing, crashing into Eli Long's brigade, which had suffered a defeat at Glass Mill the week before. The brigade lost 136 of the 900 troopers in that fight and again faced the overwhelming numbers of Wheeler's horsemen. The 1st Ohio Cavalry guarded the Cotton Port Ford and the regimental command had fallen to Major Thomas J. Patten, known in the cavalry as "Rough and Ready" Tom after the death of Valentine Cupp at Glass Mill. Patton was never so happy as when he was in a mêlée, but on that day the 1st Ohio was thrown back as Wheeler crossed the river, losing 20 men wounded or captured. In addition, the 4th Ohio Cavalry, north of the Cotton Port Ford crossing, was temporarily cut off but made its escape. Wheeler sent an officer demanding the surrender of the Union cavalry, but Crook declined to surrender.[12]

Once across the river, Wheeler sent one column with 1,500 troopers south through the Sequatchie Valley and claimed a 32-wagon supply train while a second column, commanded by John Wharton, moved directly west. Next, Wheeler discovered an 800-wagon supply train, which he handily captured. After selecting the supplies he needed, he set fire to the remainder. The supply train was desperately needed for Rosecrans' defeated army and this was a severe loss. As Wheeler rode through the countryside, the Union cavalry and infantry, in close proximity, were mobilized to stop the raid. Colonel Oscar La Grange's 1st Wisconsin Cavalry and Major David Briggs' 2nd Indiana Cavalry, riding in advance of McCook's column, caught Wheeler while he was pillaging the train at Anderson's Crossroads.

As is often the case, the various reports of the actions are vastly different. As Wheeler was leaving the train, the two Union regiments surged ahead. Wheeler merely reported the skirmish: "Fortunately, the enemy was repulsed." La Grange recorded his pursuit, which resulted in the capture of a Confederate lieutenant and 10 skirmishers and the recapture of a Union surgeon and four other Union prisoners. La Grange described the scene of the Union wagon train: "Passing the burning train the explosion of ammunition was terrific, and farther on sutlers' goods were strewn." Riding another few miles ahead, La Grange found the rear guard of General W.T. Martin's column. La Grange pushed the Confederate rear guard for two miles, killing twelve of the enemy and wounding several others. When the chase was delayed by a more concentrated resistance, La Grange dismounted his troops and utilized his repeating rifles to deliver more effective fire than the enemy who remained in their saddles. When confronted with a group of five sharpshooters, La Grange charged their position, and the enemy was overtaken. La Grange attacked the Southern defenders "a few rods from their column, killed 2 with their sabers and wounded and captured 2 others, whom they brought back to our advance, escaping unharmed a heavy volley from the astonished rebels." The surprised column swung around preparing to meet the 1st Wisconsin when a reserve of cavalry charged into the defenders. La Grange exclaimed he "scattered his wavering ranks in the wildest rout. Thirty-seven of the enemy were killed and wounded, and 42 made prisoners.... The general himself was closely pursued and narrowly escaped. Nearly all the wounds were inflicted with the saber." Outnumbered, La Grange and Briggs broke off their pursuit.[13]

Captain Thomas McCahan, 9th Pennsylvania Cavalry, described La Grange in the attack as a "tall heavy man and striking whilst his horse was in the act of jumping, threw him." While La Grange was temporarily and ingloriously unsaddled, he had performed an extraordinary attack on a larger Confederate force.[14]

Meanwhile, Crook pulled his Second Division together and set off in pursuit but rode only about ten miles before darkness ended the first day. This would be the only short day Crook's cavalry would have until October 8 and Crook, in single-minded, relentless pursuit, chased Wheeler at a severe cost to his horses and men. On October 1, Edward McCook's First Division accompanied by Wilder's mounted infantry mobilized and also began the chase.

McCook lagged behind Crook for much of the pursuit but Wilder's (now Miller's) brigade reached Crook at Walden's Ridge. By the time the Union cavalry was organized for the pursuit, Wheeler had a twelve- to fourteen-hour headstart over Crook and even longer over McCook. Robert Mitchell, cavalry corps commander, joined McCook's division later. Mitchell, whose health was failing, was to have a difficult ride over the next week.[15]

Much of Crook's personality can be observed in his actions during Wheeler's raid. Crook, born on the family farm near Dayton in 1828, was a West Point graduate, class of 1852. He finished near the bottom of his class, 38th in a class of 43. Crook served in the 4th U.S. Infantry in the western United States after the war and returned east at the beginning of the Civil War, commanding a brigade of infantry in the Battle of South Mountain and at Antietam. The tenacity that he demonstrated in this pursuit of Wheeler revealed a part of his personality that would make him one of the best commanders in the western United States after the war. Crook caught the rear of Wheeler's cavalry at Robinson's Trace, resulting in a small skirmish on October 2. On October 3, Crook caught the rear guard of Martin's cavalry, in possession of Hill's Gap near Beersheba, and a heated skirmish resulted. Minty's cavalry began the skirmish, but the advantage of having mounted infantry attached to the cavalry was now apparent as Crook ordered Miller's mounted infantry to advance and moved Minty into position to support the advance. The 98th Illinois and 17th Indiana led the attack, and the 72nd Indiana and 123rd Illinois followed in reserve. A "brisk engagement ensued," recorded Abram Miller.[16]

The Union mounted infantry charged and broke the Confederate line, propelling the defenders back and capturing four guns. Crook almost surrounded the entire Confederate defense, but darkness fell before he could complete the encirclement and the Confederates slipped away, but not before Crook was able to draw blood in this heated engagement. He reported, "My loss was 46 killed and wounded. The enemy's loss is not definitely known. We found some 10 of their dead close by the road, and a good many of their wounded scattered along the road in houses." Abram Miller claimed the 4th Alabama Cavalry's colors during the fight. On the Confederate side of the fight, Wheeler recognized General William T. Martin; Colonel Isaac Avery, 4th Georgia; and Lieutenant Colonel J.C. Griffith, 3rd Kentucky Cavalry (CSA), for their actions in this hard-fought engagement. Darkness ended the fight and Wheeler withdrew.[17]

The hard-riding troopers soon exhausted the rations they received on September 26 as the cavalrymen pressed ahead with little sleep. The entire pursuit tested the endurance of horse and man alike. "It seems almost incredible that soldiers could have stood such service. At points during the advance the troopers cut down chestnut trees to collect the nuts to eat," wrote Lucien Wulsin, historian of the 4th Ohio Cavalry.[18]

Still Wheeler rode west—uniting his two columns, which had been advancing along different routes—and captured the Union garrison and stores at McMinnville on October 3. Wheeler captured almost 600 men, 200 horses and a large quantity of supplies. The day was spent destroying the commissary and military stores, a locomotive, railcars and the Hickory Creek Bridge. But the Union pursuit was intensifying.[19]

When Crook reached McMinnville he found the devastation of Wheeler's actions and that the garrison had surrendered without a fight. Crook continued his pursuit and two miles outside of McMinnville on the Murfreesboro Road encountered Wheeler's rear guard concealed at the edge of some woods. Crook had no time for the delay and he ordered Colonel Eli Long to charge the enemy. Long, with his favorite pipe clenched firmly between his teeth,

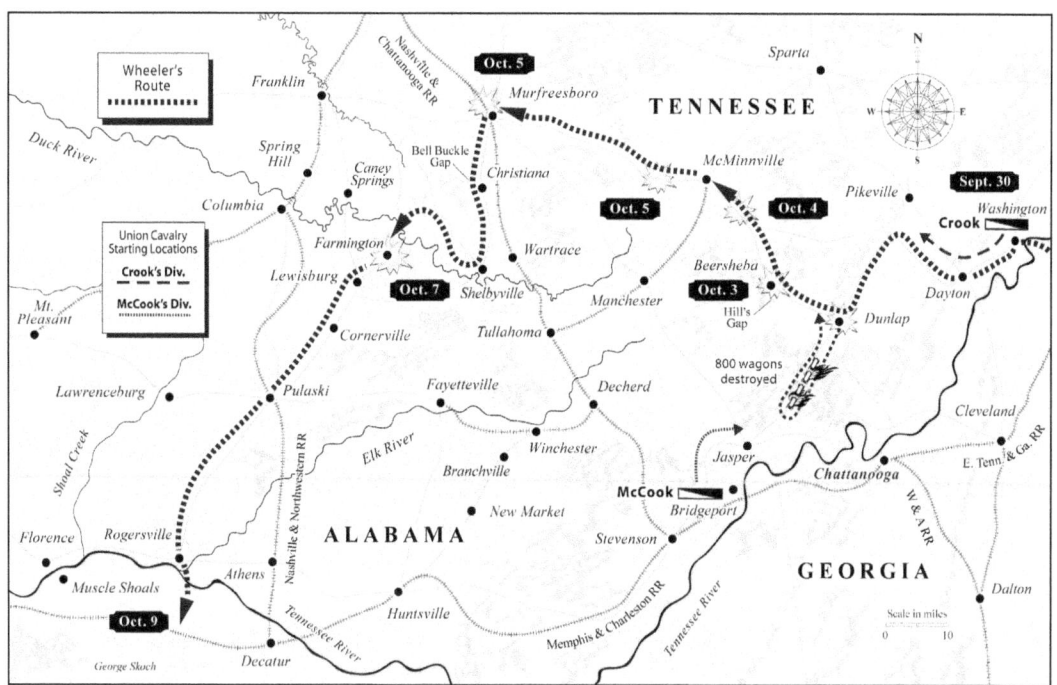

Wheeler's Raid and the Union Cavalry Pursuit (September 30—October 9, 1863)

rode at the head of the 2nd Kentucky Cavalry and "made a most gallant charge of some 5 miles, breaking through his lines ... driving the remainder into the main column, compelling him to turn round and give me fight."[20]

During the day's action Captain William Scott, 1st Ohio Cavalry, paid back some ill treatment by his temporary Confederate hosts. Scott had been captured during Wheeler's breakout over the Tennessee River and had been forced to run beside the Confederate cavalry under threat of death for his unrepentant remarks about the Confederacy. Scott escaped and now rode with Long's cavalry. During the action, the Confederate captain who had made Scott run was captured and fell under Scott's control. Scott took charge of the captain and ordered him to dismount. W.L. Curry, 1st Ohio Cavalry, recorded, "It is safe to say that the Texan had to take his turn at hoofing it that day."[21]

Having pushed the skirmishers aside, Crook met a defensive line at the edge of some woods. He called up his mounted infantry, unlimbered his artillery and pushed ahead. The fight lasted about two hours before he pushed the enemy to the rear. Crook's weary cavalrymen lay down for a night's sleep without supper, although the horses were able to graze. Crook recognized the Chicago Board of Trade Battery for another exemplary performance, as its fire knocked out the Confederate artillery during the exchange.[22]

The momentum of Wheeler's raid seemed to have slowed by October 5. He was unable to cause destruction at Murfreesboro, settling instead for a "demonstration." On October 6, he swung south, destroying bridges and railroads on his way to the pro–Union town of Shelbyville which he promptly sacked. When Crook rode through Murfreesboro, he "found every person at Murfreesborough in great consternation, and overjoyed to see us." The citizens of the town feared an attack from Wheeler, and the horsemen in blue were a welcome sight.[23]

The Union Pursuit and the Fight at Farmington

On October 6, the 5th Iowa Cavalry, which had been serving in Middle Tennessee during the previous campaign, got into action under command of the very capable Colonel William Lowe. Lowe initially moved the regiment from Winchester to Wartrace and as the pursuit continued the 5th Iowa passed through Tullahoma on the way northward, reaching the Duck River at 3 p.m. The group of Union infantry reported that the enemy cavalry were causing destruction near Wartrace. Lowe's fresh regiment found the group of raiders, belonging to Martin's Confederate Cavalry Division, burning a bridge and sent them scampering back to the main body of Confederate cavalry.

On the evening of October 6, Wheeler bivouacked south of the Duck River and ordered his division commanders to keep an eye out for the pursuing Union cavalry. Wheeler rested his command after sacking the town of Shelbyville. According to Wheeler, Brigadier General H.B. Davidson, commanding one of Forrest's brigades, was informed of the Union cavalry position and was ordered to keep scouts out to watch for any movement. Davidson would be blamed by Wheeler for the results of the fight that occurred the next day near Farmington. Wheeler wrote:

> Unfortunately, he failed to comply with this order, and on the following morning was attacked by a superior force of the enemy. I received two consecutive dispatches [following] from General Davidson which indicated that he was moving down Duck River, but on questioning his couriers I ascertained that he was moving toward Farmington. I immediately started at a trot toward Farmington with Martin's division, ordering General Wharton and the wagons to follow me. I reached Farmington just in time to place five regiments of Martin's command in position when the enemy appeared. I had ordered General Davidson to form in column by fours on the pike and to charge the enemy when they were repulsed by Martin's division, General Davidson having officially reported to me that only three regiments of the enemy had been seen during the day. The engagement commenced warmly, but the enemy was soon repulsed. General Davidson had failed to form as stated, and instead had moved for some distance. The enemy soon after came up in strong force with a division of infantry and a division of cavalry. We fought them with great warmth for twenty minutes, when we charged the line and drove it back for some distance.

Wheeler concluded his report by claiming 188 losses for the Union cavalry while he suffered losses one-quarter that number.[24] Certainly military commanders during the Civil War embellished the outcome of various engagements, but perhaps Wheeler took excessive liberties in this report. A more realistic report can be found in the Union cavalry reports and also in the only other Confederate report of this engagement, written by Colonel George B. Hodge.

General Robert Mitchell finally reached Crook's Second Cavalry Division on the evening of October 5 and with the combined Union cavalry corps rode in pursuit of Wheeler on October 6. Mitchell ordered Edward McCook's First Division of Cavalry to ride west for Unionville, George Crook's Second Division plus Miller's mounted infantry toward Farmington, and the remainder along the Unionville Road on October 7.[25]

Appropriately, it was Crook's column that participated in the heaviest fighting of the day. Crook rode for Farmington on the south side of the Duck River and ran into John Scott's Confederate cavalry brigade about three miles from Shelbyville. Crook sent Miller's mounted infantry forward on horseback, pushing the enemy cavalry into a cedar thicket. Next, Eli Long's cavalry brigade charged the Confederate cavalry. Long led "a most gallant saber charge, driving the enemy 3 miles, killing and capturing a great many rebels," exclaimed Crook. The enemy made another attempt to halt the Union attack, and the mounted infantry again rode to the front and drove the enemy to Farmington. Long, who had his horse shot from under him at McMinnville a few days before, was wounded by a ball in his side and his horse was shot during the attack. During the charge Colonel Charles Siedel, 3rd Ohio Cavalry, was hurled to the ground when his horse was killed beneath him. When the horse fell, it pinned Siedel to the ground, where he lay until some troopers could lift the horse from him.[26]

The Confederates again found refuge in a thicket, about three-quarters of a mile from Farmington. With the mounted infantry in the front and the cavalry on the flank, Crook advanced again. A portion of the retreating Confederates during the morning had swung to Crook's right and Crook was concerned this column would attack his flank. He sent a rider to bring Minty's brigade to the front. As Crook continued his fight, he assumed Minty had followed his orders, but he soon found Minty was not at the front with the rest of Crook's troops. This enraged Crook, because Minty's absence left him with only 1,500 men. Crook now found himself in a precarious position. He had advanced into Farmington against Wheeler's main body of cavalry with what he thought was his entire division only to find one of his brigades was missing. Wheeler moved his cavalry into a defensive line at Farmington and the battle intensified. Wheeler's artillery soon opened on the Union column with canister, grape and shell. Crook ordered the Chicago Board of Trade Battery forward and returned the fire on the Confederate artillery. Captain Stokes ordered the Union artillery to fire and "in three shots he disabled one of their pieces, blowing up a caisson, and throwing their ranks into confusion." In return, one of the Chicago Board of Trade guns was disabled by the fire of the Confederate battery, but the Union guns continued to fire. The Confederate cavalry, outnumbering Crook, also moved into position to charge his line, but the Union artillery shifted and began firing on the cavalry.[27]

Crook ordered his mounted infantry forward. Henry Campbell, 18th Indiana Artillery, recorded the "brisk engagement" in his diary: "The firing now became terrible—one constant roll—the 7 shooters carrying death & destruction into the Rebel ranks. The woods were so thick that the lines approached within 30 yards of each other. Rebs stood bravely—holding their position in spite of the dreadful fire." Wheeler's and Crook's reports vary on the outcome of the fight. Wheeler claimed he forced Crook to retreat "some distance," while Crook claimed his mounted infantry broke the Confederate line. Regardless of the truth of it, the two forces apparently fought to a standstill. Wheeler, realizing he had nothing to gain in a prolonged fight, withdrew.[28]

Crook wrote, "That night after the fighting had ceased, Colonel Minty with his brigade came up, stating that he had no orders to march with me. From this, together with a disposition manifested during the whole expedition to frustrate my designs in a covert manner, I deprived him of his command and sent him to the rear." The highly regarded Minty obviously had run afoul of his division commander and the disagreement resulted in Minty's court-martial.[29]

Colonel George B. Hodge's Third Confederate Cavalry Brigade after action report revealed a significantly different version of the action than Wheeler's report. Hodge had the unenviable task of providing the rearguard action for Davidson's cavalry. Hodge wrote, "For five hours and a half, over 7 miles of country, the unequal contest continued. My gallant brigade was cut to pieces and slaughtered. I had informed the officers and men that the sacrifice of their lives was necessary and they manfully made the sacrifice." Again the losses claimed by Wheeler and Crook were quite different. Crook reported he lost a total of 111 men for the entire expedition and Abram Miller recorded his loss at 96 for the campaign. Miller also recorded 86 enemy dead and another 270 prisoners during the engagement on October 7 alone. Wheeler claimed a loss of 40–50 men, apparently, for just the engagement at Farmington of his command on October 7 and not that of Hodge's, and perhaps all of Forrest's detached cavalry.[30]

The Union cavalry took up the pursuit of Wheeler as he rode for the Tennessee River. George Kryder, 3rd Ohio Cavalry, described the pursuit as fresh troops joined in the chase: "The next day we did not see them but the second day the 5th Iowa Cavalry was in advance and they took about 50 prisoners killing three and did not lose a man." Edward Walter, 5th Iowa Cavalry, recorded the action of his regiment as it caught up with Wheeler's rearguard the next day: "No sooner had we reached a creek when Whiz came a volley from a whole brigade ... but you can be assured we soon returned the compliment, and had a sharp little fight ensued until the Rebs broke and ran."[31]

Henry Albert Potter, 4th Michigan, also recorded the action of the 5th Iowa:

> Started out early—came on Col. Lowe of the 5th down in advance—came upon their rear guard—charged upon them—captured 50 of them—killed 3 or 4 when within 2 miles of Rodgersville we charged with drawn sabers—thro' town & on to the river four miles farther but the bird had flown—traveled about 35 miles this day—made the longest charge on our record—six miles—came back & encamped two miles from river—thus endeth Wheeler's great cavalry Raid.

The 5th Iowa fought the 6th Texas Cavalry, at Wartrace, serving as rearguard in a heated skirmish. Eugene Marshall recorded, "Within fifteen minutes, four horses & three men had been hit, all of them within twenty feet of me ... the bullets fell ... so thick that I could compare them to nothing but a shower of rain."[32]

Wheeler wrote that, having accomplished his objective, he rode to the safety of his lines. For the Union cavalry, it was the case that they had finally caught up with Wheeler, who rode for his life. Wheeler claimed, in his after action report, "During the trip we captured in action 1,600 prisoners, and killed and wounded as many of their cavalry as would cover our entire loss." Certainly the destruction of the bridges, the capture and destruction of the supply depot in McMinnville, and the destruction of the wagon trains all were notable accomplishments for the Confederate cavalry during this raid.[33]

Brigadier General Philip D. Roddey's Confederate cavalry brigade moved across the Tennessee River on October 7 in an attempt to assist Wheeler in his raid. Roddey soon found things were not working well for Wheeler. Roddey wrote from the Elk River, "At the same point I met several wounded men and stragglers from General Wheeler's corps.... All agreed in the statement that Wheeler had been severely repulsed at Farmington; that he had a valuable wagon train, and was trying to save it by sending it across the river below Decatur; that he was hard pressed." Roddey attempted to unite his column with Wheeler's but was unsuccessful.[34]

After the Union cavalry pursued Wheeler across the Tennessee River, Rosecrans ordered Mitchell to keep the cavalry away from Chattanooga. There was little chance of forage for the horses and to keep the cavalry in good shape it needed to be at another location. Half of the cavalry moved to the Flint River near Huntsville and the other half was posted at Winchester, Tennessee. The previous two months of hard duty had taken a severe toll on the cavalry, and Wheeler's raid had severely tested the horses and men. Mitchell wrote, "My command is, of course, very badly used up. Hard marches, scarcity of shoes (although each man carried two at starting), and miserable, worthless saddles that never should have been

Colonel George B. Hodge, commanding a cavalry brigade, reported, "My gallant brigade was cut to pieces and slaughtered. I had informed the officers and men that the sacrifice of their lives was necessary" (Library of Congress).

bought by the Government, or put on a horse's back after they were bought, have ruined many of the horses." Also, Colonel Thomas Jordan, 9th Pennsylvania Cavalry, arrived in Middle Tennessee recuperating from an illness and found the troopers sleeping without tents. Jordan wisely noted, "For one who dies by the bullet, another 20 die due to exposure and hard service."[35]

Results of Wheeler's Raid

The most notable operations on the part of the Union cavalry during the raid were by the 1st Wisconsin and 2nd Indiana cavalries at Anderson's Crossroads, the skirmish near McMinnville with the charge of the 2nd Kentucky, and the actions of the brigades of Eli Long and Abram Miller at Farmington. The really hard fighting often fell to the mounted infantry, commanded by Abram Miller, which contribution was immeasurable. Mitchell noted the Union cavalry's efforts outweighed any long-term impact of the raid. Mitchell recorded, "We captured six pieces of artillery, and, including killed, wounded, prisoners, and deserters, I think they re-crossed the Tennessee River with between 2,000 and 3,000 less men than they started out with."[36]

At the end of the campaign, Colonel Robert Minty lost command of his brigade and was court-martialed for failure to follow orders. The trial took place from February 2 through February 16, 1864. In light of the pressure the Union cavalry had been under for the entire year, it is not surprising that tempers flared, particularly during the intense pursuit of Wheeler. Crook believed that Minty's failure to participate in the action on October 7 at Farmington stemmed from a series of insubordinate actions starting on October 5. On that day, Minty requested his brigade be given an opportunity to forage the horses, a request Crook denied, citing the need to stay on Wheeler's heels. The next morning Minty encountered a wagonload of horseshoes and stopped his brigade and allowed his men to shoe the horses that needed it. He did not catch up to the main column until 11:30 a.m. That evening he and Crook met and Crook told Minty the command needed to be in the saddle at daybreak the next morning. Crook sent written orders to his other brigade commanders but did not send written orders to Minty. When the command rode out the next morning, Minty did not join the column. The crux of the problem revolved around the question of whether or not Minty had orders to move forward. The court-martial found Minty not guilty. Ultimately, Crook's decision to place this very popular colonel under arrest made him very unpopular with Minty's brigade.[37]

Union Cavalry Casualties, October 1–14, 1863[38]

	Killed	Wounded	Missing	Total
Headquarters cavalry	–	–	1	1
First Division, McCook	–	5	4	9
Second Division, Crook	14	103	–	117
Total	14	108	5	127

Wheeler's raid, after months of relative inactivity for the Confederate general, provided a great deal of excitement and accomplished the destruction of some important infrastructure in Middle Tennessee. The destruction of George Thomas's 800-wagon supply train caused a great deal of hardship for the hungry Union soldiers in Chattanooga, and Wheeler's raid pulled the entire Union cavalry corps from the Chattanooga area. In addition, the Union cavalry, which had labored since mid–August, was left in absolute exhaustion at the end of the raid and was stationed at Winchester and Decherd away from Chattanooga.

From the Union standpoint, little long-term damage occurred as a result of this raid. At the end, the morale of the Union cavalry was better than before. They felt they had defeated Wheeler's cavalry, and this was a needed boost after the Union army defeat at Chickamauga. Although Mitchell had failed to draw Wheeler into a prolonged cavalry fight, many felt they had severely repulsed Wheeler. The fight at Farmington with only 1,500 Union soldiers was viewed as a Union victory and Wheeler precipitately rode for the friendly confines of the Confederate line. Even within the Confederate ranks, there were those who felt the raid did more damage than good, including Colonel George Brent and Brigadier General Arthur Manigault.[39]

End of Mitchell and Stanley's Commands

Perhaps what was more important, the end of Wheeler's raid marked the beginning of a period of transition for the cavalry corps of the Army of the Cumberland. David Stanley missed the battle of Chickamauga and during the subsequent actions he had been moved to a Union hospital and returned to his home in Ohio while he recuperated from dysentery. He was transported to Wooster, Ohio, where his wife had been staying with Stanley's old teacher, Dr. Leander Firestone. He was away from the army for about a month.

While Stanley was away from the army, on October 9, 1863, Rosecrans relieved both Alexander McCook and Thomas Crittenden of their commands, and the infantry and artillery components of the army were reorganized. The next day, Brigadier General James A. Garfield left the army to serve in Congress, and although Garfield was praised by Rosecrans, David Stanley detested him as a politician. Military historian Robert Dalessandro wrote, "Although generally loyal to Rosecrans, Garfield made the unforgivable military faux pas of voicing his displeasure to his friends in Washington, particularly Secretary of the Treasury Chase. Garfield's criticisms of Rosecrans would ultimately be a contributing factor to Rosecrans relief as army commander."[40]

Stanley still held the position of chief of cavalry for the Army of the Cumberland in October, even though Robert Mitchell had served in that capacity since Stanley's illness in September. Mitchell's days were also numbered as chief of cavalry. Mitchell wrote on October 14, 1863, "I am out of rations and my horses are breaking down, but will do the best I can. I am as near a dead man on horseback as you ever saw." On October 18, Mitchell again appealed to Rosecrans to be relieved of duty: "The severe service devolving on me since having been on duty in this arm of the service has rendered the state of my health much worse than formerly, and the chances of my ultimate recovery more remote, and I feel that in justice to myself I should not expose myself any longer as I have been obliged to do for the last four months." After only a month in command of the cavalry, Mitchell had had enough and sought to give up command. He left the cavalry corps by the end of the month.[41]

On October 18 Major General Joseph Hooker inquired about the cavalry under Mitchell's command: "I have good reason to believe that Roddey is still on the north side of the Tennessee, and have so informed General Crook in the hope that he will be able to strike his trail, follow, and destroy him. Colonel Stokes was here on the 16th, and informed me that General Mitchell knew but little of the cavalry and its late operations, as he had not been with the command. I don't know how this is." Despite Stanley's failings during this campaign, he was right in trying to keep the cavalry from Mitchell's control. Subsequently, Mitchell was also taken to task during the court of inquiry of Alexander McCook's actions during the Battle of Chickamauga for failing to move his cavalry to assist in the battle.[42]

Finally, on October 19, 1863, Major General William S. Rosecrans was relieved of command of the Army of the Cumberland and replaced by Major General George H. Thomas. Two days later Brigadier General Washington Lafayette Elliott was ordered to report for duty in Chattanooga, and three days later Elliott was given command of Mitchell's cavalry division. On November 12, 1863, David Stanley was officially relieved of command of the cavalry and assigned to command the First Division of the Fourth Army Corps, serving under Major General Gordon Granger. Stanley would later write of his demotion, "I did not regret being relieved of the command of the cavalry. It was most unsatisfying and annoying." Stanley's reassignment to the infantry was decided by Major General George Thomas, who had been Stanley's instructor at West Point.[43]

On November 20, Stanley sent a message to the troopers of the Cavalry Corps:

> In parting with you, your late commander takes occasion to express his regrets that the changes of services should separate his fortunes from your own. For a year we have served together most pleasantly, and I am happy to congratulate the Cavalry upon their achievements in that time. My poor efforts to render you

efficient have been zealously seconded by both officers and men. As to our success, the testimony of our enemies is the more flattering to you, it being forced from them, they now admit you are dangerous and have left material proof of it upon many a field. Though separated from you, I shall serve in the same army with you and shall always watch your course with confident pride. Your success and glory is assured.

Stanley left a strong legacy with the cavalry. He had taken an outnumbered, demoralized group and transformed it into an excellent fighting corps.[44] There is no clear reason for Stanley's removal as head of the cavalry. Perhaps Stanley's performance during the advance on Chickamauga was deemed inadequate, or Grant felt all of Rosecrans' corps commanders needed to be relieved of duty during the October purge. Perhaps Assistant Secretary of War Charles Dana's rumors influenced the decision.

It is unknown if Grant wanted to relieve all of Rosecrans' corps commanders in this purge. Stanley had once served under Rosecrans in Grant's Army of the Mississippi. Certainly, the close ties of Stanley to Rosecrans were widely known and Grant's dislike of Rosecrans was also widely known. All that is known is from Stanley's memoirs: "It is frightful to think what havoc a set of scandal mongers who have access to the ears of the officers, may produce. Had not General Thomas known these men were falsifiers, I should have been left out of the reorganization."[45] The final possibility is innuendo from assistant secretary of war Charles Dana, who wrote two letters to Washington disparaging Stanley. The first was on October 16:

I learn, on the best evidence, that a few months ago General Stanley defeated an important operation by being drunk at the critical moment, and that he has repeatedly been guilty of that offense while in the discharge of most important duties in the field, yet General Rosecrans has never taken any notice of the fact. He cannot bear to hurt Stanley's feelings, and prefers, instead, to jeopardize the cause of the country.

The second came on November 20, after Stanley had been relieved of command:

Thomas has been much embarrassed by Stanley, who gets drunk and is lazy and careless. Still, he is a major-general assigned to this department by the Administration, and Thomas has not felt himself at liberty to order him away. Accordingly, he has very reluctantly appointed him to command a division. Can I tell Thomas that he must follow his own judgment in such cases?

Dana was seen as a "bird of ill omen," a spy, and a man intent on seeing Rosecrans relieved of command. Dana's influence was immense at this time, but historically there is no evidence that Stanley was drinking to excess at this time in his life.[46] Most likely seven days of illness, his failure to hand over command to his subordinates and his close relationship with Rosecrans cost Stanley the command of the Union cavalry of the Army of the Cumberland.

Mitchell was relieved of duty through his own request. Because Elliott was senior in rank he was initially given temporary command of the cavalry and in November he was named chief of cavalry of the Army of the Cumberland. On the other side of the line, Nathan Bedford Forrest was transferred to western Tennessee and would no longer cause trouble for the Army of the Cumberland. Joseph Wheeler was in command of the entire Confederate cavalry corps with four divisions of cavalry.

PART III. BRIGADIER GENERAL WASHINGTON LAFAYETTE ELLIOTT, CHIEF OF CAVALRY

8. The Knoxville Campaign and Campaigning in East Tennessee: A New Beginning

> *Take no prisoners!*
> —Colonel James P. Brownlow

The military was in Washington Lafayette Elliott's blood. Born in Carlisle, Pennsylvania, March, 31, 1825, he was the son of distinguished naval officer Commodore Jesse Elliott. Washington Elliott enrolled at the United States Military Academy in 1841, but resigned at the end of his third year. During the Mexican War he was commissioned second lieutenant in the Mounted Rifles, which later became the 3rd United States Cavalry, and in 1847 he was promoted to the rank of first lieutenant. Elliott was promoted to the rank of captain in 1854 and served in various locations in the western United States before the Civil War, including Arizona, Texas, New Mexico, and Wyoming.[1]

In September 1861, Elliott was appointed colonel of the 2nd Iowa Cavalry. He served with David Stanley during the Siege of New Madrid and Island Number 10 and the Siege of Corinth. He was promoted to the rank of brigadier general and was made chief of cavalry in Major General John Pope's Army of Virginia in the summer of 1862. Wounded at the Second Battle of Bull Run, he accompanied Pope to the northwest when Pope was reassigned after that battle.[2]

Elliott regained his health and, in March 1863, was given brigade command in the Eighth Corps in the disastrous Shenandoah Campaign in the summer of 1863. Elliott served under Major General Robert Milroy, who was soundly defeated at the Second Battle of Winchester. Milroy lost about 4,500 men (4,000 captured) in the battle compared to only 250 by Richard Ewell's Confederates. Elliott was then assigned command of the cavalry with the Army of the Cumberland in October 1863.

Grant Takes Command of the Armies in the West

Ulysses S. Grant assumed command of the Departments of the Ohio, Cumberland, and Tennessee on October 16, 1863. Edwin Stanton told Grant it would be his decision to keep Rosecrans in command of the Army of the Cumberland or replace him with George Thomas. When Grant was promoted, Rosecrans' fate was sealed. On the day Grant assumed command,

Rosecrans was replaced. Rosecrans had just barely escaped being relieved of duty by Grant before he assumed command of the Army of the Cumberland. In fact, Grant concluded to relieve Rosecrans of command of the Army of the Mississippi on the very day he was given command of the Army of the Cumberland. In addition to the removal of Rosecrans, many other changes were on the way for the Union army at Chattanooga, but perhaps the most positive benefit was the ability of Grant to coordinate the actions of all the Union armies in the West.[3]

While David Stanley was present with cavalry in the recent Middle Tennessee campaign, he did not officially assume command of the cavalry corps until November 9. Thomas allowed Stanley to return from his convalescence before he reassigned him. When Elliott assumed command, morale was high but he had a corps that was exhausted and in dire need of horses and equipment. To make matters worse, Roddey and Wheeler united their forces in northern Alabama and threatened another raid in Middle Tennessee. Fortunately, nothing resulted from the threat other than some small skirmishes. In early November Wheeler moved back to Chattanooga to join Bragg's army and the Union cavalry went back to duty protecting the flanks of the army as it regained its strength.[4]

On November 10 the Second Division of the Cavalry Corps was reorganized. The First Brigade was placed under the command of Colonel William Lowe, 5th Iowa Cavalry, replacing Robert Minty, who was under arrest for the incident during Wheeler's raid in October. Wilder's Mounted Infantry Brigade was formally organized into the division.[5]

REORGANIZED SECOND DIVISION[6]
Brigadier General George Crook

First Brigade	Second Brigade	Third Brigade
Colonel William W. Lowe	**Colonel Eli Long**	**Colonel John T. Wilder**
3rd Indiana Cavalry (battalion)	2nd Kentucky Cavalry	17th Indiana Mounted Infantry
5th Iowa Cavalry	1st Ohio Cavalry	72nd Indiana Mounted Infantry
4th Michigan Cavalry	3rd Ohio Cavalry	98th Illinois Mounted Infantry
7th Pennsylvania Cavalry	4th Ohio Cavalry	123rd Illinois Mounted Infantry
4th United States Cavalry	10th Ohio Cavalry	92nd Illinois Mounted Infantry

Artillery
Chicago Board of Trade Battery, Captain James H. Stokes

The remaining unassigned regiment of the old Third Brigade, the 5th Tennessee Cavalry, was moved to Nashville to reorganize and complete its muster.

Colonel Edward McCook permanently assumed command of the First Division after Elliott formally became the chief of cavalry. McCook moved his headquarters from Winchester to Alexandria, about 40 miles east of Nashville. Crook's Second Division remained near Huntsville, Alabama. The total of men present for duty at the end of November was 5,145 in McCook's First Division and 7,028 in Crook's Second Division, which included Wilder's and Miller's mounted infantry brigade.[7]

Colonel Louis Watkins' Third Brigade, McCook's Division, remained in camp near Stevenson, Alabama, serving as a reserve during the month of November. Watkins, who had previously had issues with William Hoblitzell of the 5th Kentucky Cavalry, arranged to have the regular army officer, Colonel Oliver Baldwin, recently of the 2nd Kentucky Infantry, promoted to the command the 5th Kentucky Cavalry. Baldwin, who had been wounded in the

West Point graduate, class of 1841, General Washington L. Elliott became the third chief of cavalry in November 1863 (MOLLUS-MASS Civil War Collection, United States Army Heritage and Education Center, Military History Institute, Carlisle, Pennsylvania).

jaw at Chickamauga provided a more steady hand on the regiment.

The rest of the cavalry remained unchanged as Elliott familiarized himself with the men and the remainder of the army. The Union cavalry stretched across Middle Tennessee in anticipation of another cavalry raid by Wheeler or Roddey. Bragg had, for a time, succeeded in closing the primary resupply routes to the Army of the Cumberland; but by the end of October, George Thomas, through the plans of Brigadier General W.F. "Baldy" Smith, had established a route, the "cracker line," around the Confederate blockade. Soon Hooker's Eleventh and Twenty-second Corps arrived at Chattanooga, and Sherman, with part of the Army of the Tennessee, moved slowly to reinforce George Thomas's command.

When Grant assumed command of the Military Division of the Mississippi, all the western military departments, Ohio, Cumberland, and Tennessee, were united under his control. As a result, the various cavalry commands formally fell under the control of the chief of the cavalry of the Military Division of the Mississippi, William Sooy Smith. This change was in many ways very efficient and allowed a conservation and concentration of force when needed, but the command structure was somewhat confused. The confusion could easily result from which order to follow, Smith's, Elliott's or that from army headquarters. Practically, Elliott commanded the cavalry of the Army of the Cumberland, but when called to cooperate in joint operations the command he could, and would, be under another commander. This would be the case in the upcoming East Tennessee Campaign when Elliott would be subordinate to Samuel Sturgis.

The Union cavalry began increasing its duties as fresh horses arrived from the Quartermaster Department. On November 18, Eli Long's 1,500-man Second Brigade began a raid to destroy the railroad near Cleveland, Tennessee. Long, headquartered at Woodville, Tennessee, about halfway between Chattanooga and Knoxville, rode to Chattanooga with his four regiments, plus the 17th Indiana and 98th Illinois Mounted Infantry from Wilder's brigade. At 3:00 a.m. on November 25, Long's column moved toward Cleveland, beginning the thirty-five mile ride as quietly as possible. Bypassing a large ammunition train, the Union column reached Cleveland and found it guarded by the 2nd Kentucky Cavalry (CSA), which retreated before the advance of the 1st Ohio Cavalry. For the remainder of the day, the Union cavalry destroyed railroad tracks and railcars.[8]

Long's cavalry bivouacked at the Cleveland Masonic Female Institute and observed a large Confederate force as it arrived near Cleveland on the evening of November 26. The next morning the Union pickets alerted Long to an advancing Confederate force supported by artillery. The Union column formed a defensive line and held off the attack. Along the Federal right flank was a rolling-mill used to manufacture shells and percussion caps, and Long ordered it burnt, which set off an explosive effect. Long chose not to prolong the battle behind enemy lines and rode back to Chattanooga.[9] He successfully destroyed twelve miles of railroad between Cleveland and Chattanooga and between Cleveland and Dalton. In addition, Long's success made it impossible for Bragg to recall Longstreet from East Tennessee. Long also destroyed the large rolling-mill and captured 233 prisoners. To top off a successful raid, he burned Confederate Brigadier General Marcus Wright's baggage and headquarters train on his way back from Cleveland. The 5th Ohio Cavalry had joined Long's brigade's actions in east Tennessee, but this regiment was detached from the Fifteenth Corps.[10]

While Long raided Cleveland, the rest of the Second Cavalry Division conducted an expedition from November 14 to 17 from Maysville to Decatur, Alabama, with the objective of disrupting Confederate efforts to move supplies from Union-held territory to the Confederate line. The expedition of 400 men from the 5th Iowa Cavalry, 4th U.S. Cavalry, and 72nd Indiana Mounted Infantry caused a great response from the Confederates and skirmishing occurred throughout the four-day Union raid. The Federal troops captured several of the boats used to transport livestock and other supplies to the Confederate-held south bank of the river. Major J. Morris Young, 5th Iowa Cavalry, humorously reported, "Rather amused than otherwise at so unexpectedly stirring up so much trouble for the rebels."[11]

The Knoxville Campaign

When Rosecrans advanced on Chattanooga in September, his advance was supposed to have been closely coordinated with Ambrose Burnside's advance on Knoxville, but the movements were rarely coordinated. Rosecrans' advance drew much of the Confederate presence in Knoxville southward to meet his army, and as a result Burnside met little resistance as he marched into Knoxville on September 3 and captured the Cumberland Gap on September 9.

While Rosecrans struggled with Bragg in Chattanooga, he requested help from Burnside to assist in covering the area between the two armies. There was some limited mutual action between the two Union commanders during this time, but Burnside was unable to provide support to Rosecrans either before or for two months after the Battle of Chickamauga.

While the Union armies made their preparations at Chattanooga, Bragg was unable to develop a strategy to finish off the Army of the Cumberland, now being reinforced. So he shifted his attention to Major General Ambrose Burnside's Army of the Ohio at Knoxville, and at the same time he was able to rid himself of the troublesome James Longstreet. If Bragg could defeat Burnside at Knoxville, he could at least prevent one additional source of reinforcements for the Union armies in Chattanooga. He saw an opportunity to bag an isolated concentration of Union troops while regaining control of the Cumberland Gap. Bragg detached Lieutenant General James Longstreet with McLaw's, Hood's (commanded by Brigadier General Micah Jenkins), and Buckner's (commanded by Brigadier General Bushrod

Johnson) divisions to deal with Burnside. He also sent William T. Martin's, John Wharton's, Frank Armstrong's, and Jenkins' cavalry divisions under the command of Joseph Wheeler. Longstreet had the support of Ransom's Division, which included Corse's Brigade and Jackson's Brigade of infantry and Jones's, Williams's, and Jackson's cavalry brigades. Longstreet commanded in total about 10,000 infantry and 5,000 cavalry.

On the Union side, Burnside had the Ninth Corps (two divisions), the Twenty-third Corps (two divisions) and two divisions of cavalry initially under the command of Brigadier General James Shackelford. Burnside outnumbered Longstreet with a total 12,000 infantry and 8,500 cavalry.

The start of Longstreet's march was slowed through a series of delays, but he soon found Burnside's infantry after he constructed two bridges across the Tennessee River at Loudon. He crossed on November 14 and advanced toward Knoxville. Wheeler remained in command of the Confederate cavalry until November 24, when he was summoned back to Chattanooga. William T. Martin commanded the Confederate cavalry afterward in the Knoxville area.

Burnside's plan called for a prolonged delaying action as he slowly retreated toward Knoxville, but Longstreet marched his infantry quickly forward and nearly cut Burnside from the town as the two enemies raced for Campbell's Station. Burnside narrowly escaped from being trapped and then slowly withdrew to his entrenchments at Knoxville on November 17. This began the siege of Knoxville, which lasted through December 2.

On November 27, Elliott's First Cavalry Division was ordered to join in the defense of Knoxville. Although campaigning was miserable in November and December, there was one Union cavalry regiment that could not be more pleased to be in East Tennessee. The 1st Tennessee Cavalry, originally designated the 1st East Tennessee Cavalry, was at home and looked forward to action with the enemy. Guerrillas and Confederate regulars were a constant problem in eastern Tennessee. On November 25, the 1st Tennessee and 9th Pennsylvania skirmished with the enemy commanded by Colonel John Hughes, 25th Tennessee Infantry (CSA), near Sparta. Colonel James Brownlow commanded the expedition to drive the Confederates out of the area of Yankeetown. The skirmishes took place with Confederates shooting from behind trees and the Union cavalry in pursuit. Brownlow's troopers pushed forward into Sparta, which was staunchly pro–Confederate, and received a cold welcome from the citizens. Brownlow was ordered to hold Sparta until the rest of the Federal column reached the location. Because "bushwhackers" were a threat, Brownlow was on watch and sent patrols into the countryside to reconnoiter. One such patrol was ambushed by a large Confederate force, reported to be 200–300 men, and was routed. The patrol came running toward their friendly line and Brownlow sent his regiment and a battalion of the 9th Pennsylvania in pursuit. This engagement demonstrated the bloodthirstiness of the divided sentiments in East Tennessee. When the Union patrol was attacked, no quarter was given; and Brownlow now returned the favor, exclaiming, "Take no prisoners!" Brownlow overtook the Confederates a few miles from town and set about the grim work. He claimed his command killed nine and wounded twenty and his losses were four killed and five wounded (one mortally). On November 30, Captain Thomas McCahan, 9th Pennsylvania Cavalry, recorded that he found the bodies of six little boys who had served as buglers for the Union cavalry, their heads caved in. They had been captured and the local citizens explained that their captors had smashed their skulls with the butt of a musket.[12] McCahan described a rare detailed account of a running, hand-to-hand fight with the enemy cavalry at Sparta:

I, at once, charged them. I came up with their rear guard commanded by Major Wash Wragan, 25 men, they tried to get away, we gained on them. Coming to a house a woman opened the gate, they passed through the yard around the house, as the last rebel passed through she shut the gate against the breast of my horse. I had a notion to shoot her. I struck my horse with my spurs, he jumped against the gate and went through. This took but a moment and I was at the heels of the rebels. G.W. Thomas shot at this woman with his carbine, cut her apron strings off. I came up to a rebel at the foot of the yard, a high pair of bars there. Our horses jumped them together, lighting on the opposite side I halted him. He threw his gun around, striking me in the breast. As it struck me, it went off, the ball passing under my arm, skin deep. Had I been back three inches, he would have killed me. I shot him below the ear through the neck, he fell off his horse. Our horses were running fast. I came up to a rebel Lieut[enant]. He tried to strike me over the head. I tried to shoot him but my gun would not go off and I threw it at his head.... The horse jumping the bars broke the strap of my holsters and they turned under his breast so I could not draw a second pistol.... I then drew my old sabre. I tried to strike him, but he was striking at me with his gun. I struck the horse with my sabre and he jumped in front of the rebel lieutenant. I turned in the saddle and struck back (the hardest stroke a man can make) hitting him over one side of the head, cutting the upper (illegible) off slanting down between his eyes, killing him dead. By this time the boys were up and went up to the Rebs all a fence corner.... This Major Wash Wragan (a very large man) made for me throwing his pistol out. I struck it on the end knocking it down over the head of the horse. It going off, shot me on the top of my instep—of left foot. He threw it up the 2nd time. I struck it again knocking it out of his hand. I then struck him twice with my sabre, cutting him up and down the face. At this time, I noticed a rebel about 15 feet away raising his carbine to shoot me. I made for him. He banged away, but missed me. He threw his gun at me, missed again.... [I] struck him with my old sabre, cutting through the head down to his ears. By this time they had got the fence down (what was left) and broke for the woods.[13]

Colonel Thomas Jordan wrote to his wife on November 27: "I am not able to mount more than 300 men.... We will be pushed to East Tennessee, as the rebels are playing the devil with Burnside." Archibald Campbell's and Oscar La Grange's First Division brigades were sent to handle this duty. These commands arrived at Sparta on November 30. But the cavalry stopped at Caney Fork, which was unfordable and the ice made ferrying almost impossible. Seven men of the 2nd Indiana Cavalry drowned while trying to ferry across the icy water.[14]

While Longstreet was outside Knoxville, the Battles of Lookout Mountain and Missionary Ridge were fought and Bragg was soundly defeated. The Union cavalry played no part in these battles. After the battles, Grant ordered a relief force under William Sherman to march to Burnside's assistance. Bragg initially ordered Longstreet to rejoin him after his defeats but changed his mind and wrote to Longstreet that he must depend upon his own resources. In fact, Bragg resigned command of the army on December 2, after the defeat, and General Joseph Johnston was given command of the Army of Tennessee. Upon arrival, Johnston, shocked at the condition of the Southern army, immediately began to rebuild it by improving discipline, rations, and supplies, and granting furloughs.[15]

Longstreet decided to continue the siege, until he intercepted a message from Grant to Burnside that outlined the details of Sherman's relief column. Realizing Sherman's column, plus the size of Burnside's command, made the siege impossible, he withdrew from Knoxville on December 2. Sherman's relief column included Gordon Granger's Fourth Corps; Major General Oliver Howard's Eleventh Corps; Brigadier General Jefferson C. Davis's Division, Fourteenth Army Corps; Major General Frank Blair's two divisions of the Fifteenth Army Corps; and Eli Long's Second Brigade of cavalry. The column totaled about 11,000 soldiers in addition to Burnside's command already at Knoxville.[16]

As the column marched forward, Long's cavalry kept out of sight of the Confederate scouts as Sherman's column neared Sweetwater, Tennessee. Long hoped he could quickly claim the important bridge over the Holston River. He was successful and drove the defenders to Loudon. Then, on the afternoon of December 2 as the column approached Loudon, Long's cavalry again charged, hoping to surprise Longstreet's men guarding the bridge. However, the bridge was supported by artillery and infantry, and it was Long who was surprised by Confederate infantry protecting the bridge. Dismounting his command, he decided to charge the infantry on foot. He ordered the charge, to the dismay of his troopers, but wisely recalled his men when they reached within 150 yards of the bridge. Long would not have been able to capture the bridge with the number of cavalry he had on hand with just carbines. By the time Major General Oliver O. Howard's Eleventh Corps arrived, the bridge and public stores were burned and three locomotives and forty-eight cars were pushed into the river.[17]

The Union cavalry pushed forward and Long ordered his brigade to swim the icy Tennessee River. Afterward, Long's cavalry rode ahead of the infantry column through the "gauntlet" of Confederates and reached Knoxville the next morning. Sherman was reported to have said, "If Long succeeds in doing it, he will have earned his star." Long's cavalry was tired, exhausted, cold and wet. The tired and hungry Captain John Rea, 1st Ohio Cavalry, recalled, "I remember but little of the incidents of the day." Long was successful in his attempt to reach Knoxville but would have to wait several months before receiving his promotion. With Longstreet withdrawing to Virginia, Long pursued an enemy wagon train headed for North Carolina, but he was unable to find the train. For the most part he had little additional action in December. He arrived at Calhoun, Tennessee, on December 15 and relieved the 3rd U.S. Cavalry there. The 3rd Ohio Cavalry moved to Columbus, Tennessee, to guard the fords at that point and the adjacent fords.[18]

After Longstreet withdrew from Knoxville, Captain John Rea, 1st Ohio Cavalry, recalled that during one of the patrols, his cavalry passed a log house and they noticed an elderly woman kneeling and praying on her front porch. When they investigated, she told Rea a group of Confederate raiders had stopped by her house two nights before and pulled her husband out of the house and hanged him for supporting the Union cause. He was still hanging when the Union cavalry arrived. They cut him down and buried him for the woman. As disgusting as the hanging was, the retribution might have been worse. Long's command captured several prisoners during its daily patrols who were turned over to the provost guard. A few days after encountering the old woman, the 1st Ohio Cavalry awakened at dawn to the sound of gunshots. When the troopers investigated, they found two young men lying in a field in Confederate uniforms. They found a drum-head military court had been convened and the two young men were executed as a result. Rea said he was convinced of their innocence, but it was an "application of the ancient savagery, *Lex talinois.*"[19]

The First Engagement at Mossy Creek

On December 14, Edward McCook's First Division marched to Knoxville to harass Longstreet's army, which retreated into Virginia. But the advance of Edward McCook's two brigades—Campbell's and La Grange's—went anything but smoothly. Elliott reached the Holston River about seven miles from Knoxville but was unable to ford. Colonel Thomas Jordan recorded the dismal work of riding in the winter in the mountains of East Tennessee: "[M]arched through one of the coldest rain storms I was in through sixteen miles of mountains." Elliott, who accompanied McCook, was unable to find a ford until December 18, and even then he had to leave his train behind. Campbell's brigade crossed at McKinney's Ford during the day, but the river rose four feet overnight, preventing La Grange's brigade from crossing. La Grange's brigade and Lilly's artillery were unable to cross until December 23.[20]

On December 22, Longstreet's army established their winter quarters near Russellville, about 30 miles from Strawberry Plains. Major General William Martin commanded the Confederate cavalry when Wheeler had been ordered back to Chattanooga in November and provided the security for the Confederate army. On the Union side Samuel Sturgis, commanding all the Union cavalry in East Tennessee, provided reconnaissance and screening for the Union advance, which included Campbell's and La Grange's brigades. Sturgis intended to disrupt foraging activities of the enemy and attack if he found an opportunity.

As the Union cavalry searched for Confederates, Sturgis ordered Archibald Campbell's brigade to attack Colonel Alfred A. Russell's Confederate cavalry brigade at Dandridge if he could find them. On December 24, Campbell's brigade rode to Dandridge accompanied by cavalry of the Army of the Ohio in an expedition aimed at cutting off Russell's retreating brigade. Campbell advanced about one-half mile from the main column down Bull's Gap Road and Colonel Israel Garrard's cavalry brigade of the Army of the Ohio advanced along his left flank hoping to intercept Russell's cavalry. Campbell attacked and surprised Russell's troopers; but the Confederates quickly assembled a strong defense and repulsed Campbell. Campbell expected help from Colonel Garrard that never came. Elliott recalled his brigade to move back toward New Market. When Campbell advanced across Mossy Creek, he left a section of artillery to cover his advance. As he was returning, he was attacked in the rear by two brigades of Confederate cavalry—Crew's and Russell's. Campbell's train made a mad dash from its place in the rear with "pots and frying pans, coffee cups, tin

Brigadier General Samuel Sturgis served as chief of cavalry for the Army of the Ohio (Library of Congress).

dishes and all the rattle-traps of a company cook's paraphernalia flying in the air," noted Lieutenant Marshall Thatcher, 2nd Michigan Cavalry. This was a humorous sight but one with danger in its trail. Thatcher continued: "The situation was truly appalling." The Confederate attack captured a section of Union artillery, but the 9th Pennsylvania and 2nd Michigan countercharged and reclaimed the guns. Then a running retreat followed.[21]

At Hay's Ferry, Campbell charged the enemy but was compelled to fall back. The Confederate cavalry again charged but the 2nd Michigan provided good covering fire while the 9th Pennsylvania countercharged the enemy. The Union cavalry found it was nearly surrounded except for a path through some woods that was promptly put to use. Colonel Israel Garrard was supposed to be moving in a coordinated advance but Campbell never received any support from him during the skirmish. Campbell bitterly recorded, "Being now surrounded by the enemy, one brigade in front and one in my rear, I sent to Colonel Garrard for support, which he did not send. I then ordered my artillery, ambulances, and led horses into the woods to the left of the original front, and marched them by a path as rapidly as possible toward the New Market road." Garrard explained his command was also attacked, which resulted in Garrard asking for help from Sturgis. Obviously, Sturgis's plan did not work out as he had hoped.[22]

During Campbell's retreat, one gun of Lilly's 18th Indiana Battery was spiked and abandoned because an axle broke. Campbell commended his commands for their cool defense and complimented the 1st Tennessee Cavalry for an effective saber charge that ended the day. Campbell noted, "Accompanying this charge the Second Michigan and Ninth Pennsylvania Cavalry opened a galling fire, which closed the fight. The enemy seeming to be satisfied with what they had received, fell back, and I marched to New Market at dark." It was a hard

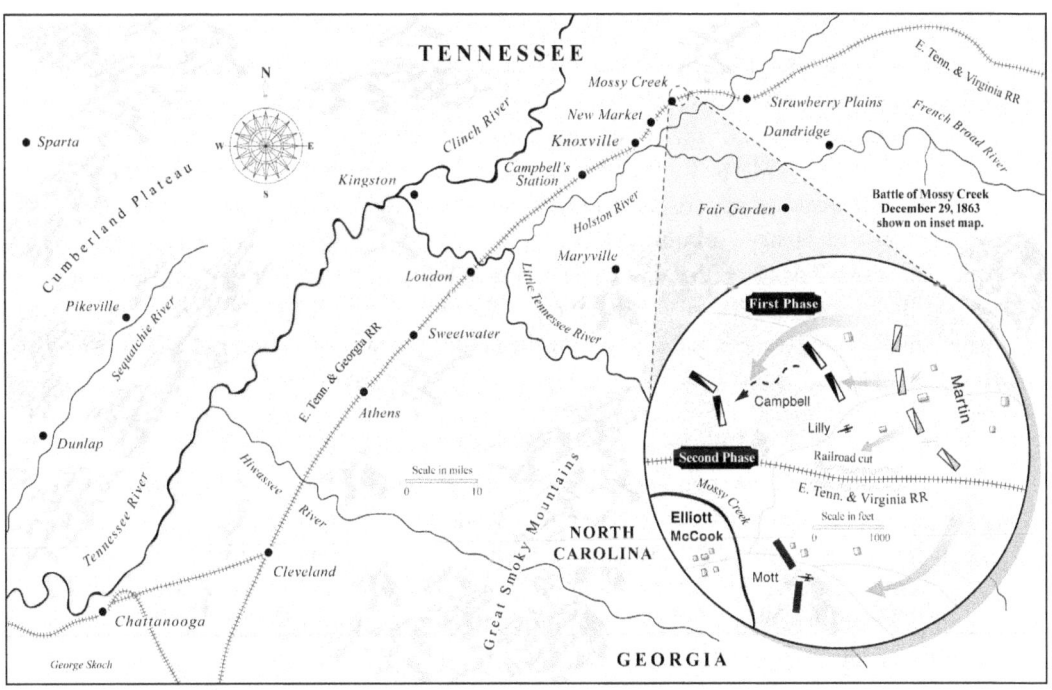

East Tennessee, 1863–1864, and the Battle at Mossy Creek, December 29, 1863

fight for Campbell, who recorded over sixty casualties. He claimed the killing and wounding of 100 of the enemy, including killing Major Alfred Bale of the 6th Georgia Cavalry. He also claimed thirty prisoners.[23]

Casualties of Engagement at New Market, Tennessee, December 24, 1863[24]

Command	Killed	Wounded	Missing	Total
2nd Michigan Cavalry	1	9	15	25
9th Pennsylvania Cavalry	3	8	5	16
1st Tennessee Cavalry	3	9	7	18
Section 18th Indiana Battery	–	1	–	1
Total	7	27	27	61

Brigadier General Martin claimed the Confederate victory on December 24:

> I have never witnessed greater gallantry than was displayed by Colonel Crews and the officers and men of the First, Second, Third, and Sixth Georgia Cavalry.... The enemy, mounted, three times charged our dismounted men in open field and were as often repulsed, but not until, mingling in our ranks, some of his men were brought to the ground by clubbed guns.[25]

The revolving rifles of the Union cavalry were important in making the engagement less disastrous than it already was. The local citizens told Marshall Thatcher that the Confederates didn't like fighting the 2nd Michigan: "They loaded their guns all night, and fired them all day."[26]

The Battle of Mossy Creek

From December 25 through December 28, skirmishing occurred daily between the Union cavalry and Martin's Confederate cavalry as the Federals clashed with Longstreet's army. A significant clash of cavalry occurred on December 29 at Mossy Creek. On this day McCook would repay Martin for the attack on Campbell on December 24. Sturgis commanded the joint Union cavalry actions, much to the disappointment of the cavalry of the Army of the Cumberland. Henry Campbell, 18th Indiana Artillery (Lilly's Artillery), recorded in his diary that Sturgis's decision that day "came very near being fatal to us." Sturgis sent La Grange's Second Brigade with the cavalry of the Army of the Ohio cavalry to pursue what was thought to be a lone Confederate brigade near Dandridge. In the meantime, Campbell's First Brigade, with the 9th Pennsylvania Cavalry, protected the flank at Mossy Creek. W.R. Carter, 1st Tennessee Cavalry, described Sturgis's expedition as a "Tom Fool" trip because the whole of Martin's cavalry Sturgis sought was bearing down on Archibald Campbell's First Brigade. Campbell, who held the ground west of Mossy Creek, had been ordered, if he was attacked, to fall back across the creek. Again Campbell was destined for a long day near the site of his fight just five days before. At 10:00 a.m., more than 2,000 troopers of Armstrong's and Morgan's Confederate divisions fell on Campbell's brigade and Colonel Samuel Mott's infantry brigade. Campbell's cavalry tried to hold the Confederate advance with Mott's support and the 18th Indiana Artillery. Mott moved the 118th Ohio to the left of the Union line while the remainder of his infantry held the right. The Union line began to bow under the pressure of Martin's attack, forming a horseshoe of defenders. The 18th Indiana Artillery and the cavalry held the center, and the right and left flanks were pushed rearward. The 118th Ohio Infantry charged the Confederate artillery, which was firing accurately and effectively into the Union troops, but was unsuccessful. Campbell was pushed back across Mossy Creek and set up another defensive line and unlimbered three guns of Lilly's artillery and held his position until 3:00 p.m., when he could no longer hold the line.[27]

Eighteenth Indiana artilleryman Henry Campbell recorded in his diary, "As soon as the Rebel line came within good range, we opened with our three guns. The first gun fired about 11 o'clock...." Lilly's artillery had fired about a dozen rounds when the Confederates unlimbered a four-gun battery about a thousand yards directly in the front of the Union artillery. As other Confederate batteries were unlimbered, Lilly's three 3-inch Rodmans fired away, but they were outnumbered by Martin's artillery. "Their shells burst all round & amongst us, in a perfect shower.... The boys stood up in that terrible storm of death without a falter."[28]

William Thomas, 9th Pennsylvania, recorded in his diary, "We fell back to Mossy Creek where the fighting became heavy.... Our artillery suffered today." Martin wisely anticipated Sturgis's expedition and the Confederate attack took advantage of the smaller Union force defending Mossy Creek. Although many of the Union infantry were green troops, Campbell was fortunate to have the 118th Ohio Infantry along his flank in a wooded area. As the Confederates charged Campbell, the 118th Ohio unleashed furious volleys into the attackers, but the Confederates extended their lines beyond Campbell's flanks. In a desperate attempt to stem the Confederate advance, Campbell sent the 1st Tennessee Cavalry to charge the flanking force, which successfully halted their advance for a time.[29]

Edward McCook accompanied Campbell as he fell back into a wooded area across Mossy Creek. As Lilly's artillery unlimbered, three Union guns met the fire of eight Confederate guns. McCook wrote that Lilly's artillery blasted for two and one-half hours, during which time many of horses and men were wounded. Finally, exhausted and suffering high casualties, the battery retired, leaving one gun on the field. The Confederate cavalry quickly moved ahead and captured the gun, but they were charged by a group of Union scouts who reclaimed the gun and returned it to the Union lines. Afterward the Confederates intensified the attack on Campbell's cavalry and the Union infantry which supported Lilly's artillery. "The enemy were repulsed with great loss, and upon making a demonstration of preparing for another charge, the First East Tennessee (Colonel Brownlow commanding), by a dashing saber charge, threw their columns into confusion and drove them back, capturing a lieutenant and 25 other prisoners," wrote McCook.[30]

Colonel James Brownlow and Colonel Archibald Campbell met to discuss the charge of the 1st Tennessee Cavalry. Brownlow asked to make the attack, but Campbell resisted, stating the enemy was too strong for Brownlow to be able to stop. So tense was the situation that Brownlow insisted this was the only way the Union force was going to survive. Brownlow quietly said, "Desperate diseases require desperate remedies." The situation deteriorated rapidly and Brownlow insisted the charge had to be done immediately. Campbell acquiesced. Brownlow drew the 1st Tennessee Cavalry into a line, and ordered, "Draw Sabers!" With a yell, he charged home. "The spirit, the boldness, and the audacity with which the charge was made" was scarcely equaled, noted W. L. Carter. The charge successfully pushed the attackers back to the tree line before the 1st Tennessee Cavalry returned to Campbell's line. The remainder of Campbell's command advanced toward the Confederate attack in support of the 1st Tennessee's charge. Yelling, "You have fallen back far enough—Forward!" Campbell spurred his horse and rode with the 1st Tennessee in the charge. The whole of Campbell's force temporarily pushed forward, granting the wavering Federal line a few critical moments.[31]

Meanwhile, more of the enemy were moving to the right, only partially covered by Colonel William Palmer's detached 15th Pennsylvania Cavalry. The 9th Pennsylvania Cavalry moved to assist Palmer once Lilly's artillery withdrew. McCook exclaimed that the 15th and 9th Pennsylvania fought so close they used pistols and held the large columns of the enemy in check. Colonel Thomas Jordan recorded that from the first firing of the cannon until dark "the fight was one of crash of artillery and small arms. The enemy fought well and was double our number drove us to a hand to hand fight." The actions of the 118th Ohio infantry were critical as it moved to face Martin's cavalry. McCook found his cavalry in an uncomfortable situation and recalled, "At this time the enemy were before us in force far exceeding our own, and by reason of their superior force had pressed us at every point. In our center was an uncovered space of a quarter of a mile." This situation looked hopeless but at that point columns of blue-coated cavalry came charging forward. Henry Campbell exclaimed the artillerymen heard a "loud ringing cheer … from our men which was the death knell to the rebel hopes that day." McCook's Second Brigade with Colonel Oscar La Grange's "gleaming sabres" came dashing forward. Now the numbers were more equal and Edward McCook ordered his command to charge forward. McCook recorded, "The enemy were driven steadily and rapidly before us, with great loss." Martin's troopers did not give up without a fight but McCook steadily pushed the enemy to the rear until dark. Archibald Campbell had done a hard day's work holding Martin's Confederates at bay until reinforcements arrived.[32]

The Federals held their position at Mossy Creek, having inflicted possibly four hundred casualties on the Confederate side compared to over a hundred of their own.[33] Fortunately, La Grange's brigade rode to the rescue. Elliott wrote that La Grange's brigade, the 15th Pennsylvania, the 118th Ohio, and one of Colonel Samuel Mott's Twenty-third Corps infantry brigades

> struck the enemy on the flank and signally routed them, driving them beyond Talbott's Station and pushing the pursuit until after dark. The casualties in this affair were 4 commissioned officers wounded, 12 enlisted men killed, and 36 men wounded severely. The enemy being much more exposed in his attacks doubtless lost more…. The cavalry of the Army of the Ohio took no part in the battle.

McCook was able to find many of the enemy's dead on the battlefield, and citizens reported that more than twenty wagon-loads of the enemy's dead and wounded were carried away from the fight. The nine-hour engagement left Martin's cavalry without ammunition by the time the battle was completed.[34] Afterward, Sturgis's cavalry remained at Mossy Creek until active operations resumed at Dandridge during the middle of January.

Final Actions of 1863

Colonel Eli Long had one last assignment on December 28 when Colonel William B. Wade, riding at the head of the 8th Confederate Cavalry, attacked a wagon train moving from Chattanooga to Knoxville. This action, while appearing to be a minor event, was important because it demonstrated the low morale of the Southern cavalry after months of campaigning. Eli Long arrived at the skirmish with only a reserve of cavalry and drove off the raiders near Calhoun, Tennessee, in a very easy fight. Many in the Union cavalry were reluctant to tell the

Union cavalry counterattacked at Mossy Creek. La Grange's "gleaming sabres" came dashing forward (from Frank Leslie's Illustrated *Famous Leaders and Battle Scenes of the Civil War* [New York: Mrs. Frank Leslie, 1896], p. 424).

story of this charge, fearing no one would believe them. Captain John Rea, 1st Ohio Cavalry, recalled the charge was effective only because Eli Long hid his force before he charged. As Long reached the wagon train, he found a small group of infantry to assist in the counterattack and ordered the column of fours of his small cavalry detachment to ride from their concealment. He ordered everyone to yell at the top of their lungs and they charged the raiders. Rea believed the Confederates heard the clatter and saw the head of a column of cavalry and guessed a large force was attacking. In reality, about 200 troopers spooked a much greater Confederate force through sheer audacity. But one must understand the exhaustion and the suffering from the elements that both sides experienced during this campaign, and there is no doubt the Union cavalry had better living conditions. Even so, Sergeant Croft, 3rd Ohio, recalled that the Union cavalry lived almost exclusively on "corn dodgers" fried in pork fat for most of the campaign. As the Union cavalry rode past a grist mill, the troopers said they could smell the meal as it was ground. When asked how long they thought they could eat it, one response was, "Until I starve."[35]

While the First Division of cavalry was busy in East Tennessee, Nathan Bedford Forrest began his new command in western Tennessee and Mississippi with a vengeance. His presence in Jackson, Tennessee, on December 6 resulted in an immediate response by the Union forces, which mobilized to stop his raids. To this end, George Crook's Second Division, excluding Long's brigade active in East Tennessee, moved westward in Tennessee. Despite Crook's concerns about the condition of his cavalry, he moved to Pulaski, Tennessee, by the end of the month. Crook's movement was part of several Union forces converging on Forrest. But the wily Forrest easily slipped through the noose set for him by riding through Collierville and then on to Holly Springs, Mississippi. At the end of the year, Elliott's headquarters was located at Talbott's Station in East Tennessee. Edward McCook's First Division was also there and a total of 3,916 men were present for duty. Crook's Second Division was headquartered at Pulaski with 7,464 men present for duty.[36]

As the year ended, the cavalry of the Army of the Cumberland stretched over a two-hundred-and-fifty-mile gap. The corps had a new commander and his leadership style was yet to be determined. McCook's division had heavy fighting while Crook's had little, but Crook had exhausted his division in the pursuit of Wheeler a few months before. The leadership abilities of Campbell and La Grange were at their peak and the experienced cavalry under Elliott's command was an effective fighting corps. There was little doubt McCook's cavalry chafed under the command of Sturgis and the complaints of Campbell, Elliott, McCook and La Grange were obvious from the reports of these officers. Campbell was unsupported at a key point when support was promised at New Market. Sturgis's expedition to find Martin resulted in the Battle of Mossy Creek, which almost cost the Union cavalry dearly. McCook pointedly remarked the cavalry of the Army of the Ohio played no part in the battle nor provided reinforcements later in the day. All hoped 1864 would be a better year and the war would soon be over. But the cavalry would fight wherever they were needed.

Othniel Gooding, 4th Michigan Cavalry, wrote a letter from Pulaski, Tennessee, at the end of the year with the thoughts of many of the cavalrymen who seemed to live in their saddles: "shant be here long. I dont no whare we are a going. thare is a rumore that we are fixing for a raid some whare. our officers dont no our destination yet. it dont make much odds to me whare we go."[37]

9. Preparation for the Atlanta Campaign: Two Divisions Divided

If this is generalship, then I have yet to learn the art of war.
—Colonel Thomas Jordan

As the new year began, Washington Elliott's two divisions were two hundred fifty miles apart facing vastly different threats. Elliott may have desired to command a corps of cavalry, but he was destined to be frustrated. The collegiality which existed between David Stanley and William Rosecrans was gone, and while Elliott served in George Thomas's Army of the Cumberland, Ulysses Grant was the overall commander. Elliott was described by Brigadier General James H. Wilson as a "cavalryman of high character"; but historian David Evans wrote, "He rarely ventured far from his headquarters and never accompanied his troops in the field." It is unclear if the new cavalry commander desired to command in this manner or whether the situation dictated this command style. Whichever it was, Elliott would chafe under Grant and later under Sherman.[1]

The fighting in Tennessee had reached a deplorable state. Civilians were terrorized and various units were offering no quarter in battles. Early in January the situation continued to deteriorate. Southern guerrillas captured part of a foraging party near Fayetteville, Tennessee, and the prisoners were returned to the camp of their captors: "The hands of the prisoners were then tied behind them, and they were robbed of everything of value about their persons. They were next drawn up in line, about 5 paces in front of their captors, and one of the latter, who acted as leader, commanded, 'ready,' and the whole party immediately fired upon them." Fortunately, the officer and one other soldier escaped the execution, but three soldiers were murdered. Afterward, George Thomas imposed a levy of $30,000 on the citizens living in a ten-mile radius of the event and divided the money among the families of the three murdered men. Retribution came quickly whenever guerrillas were found. George Kryder, 3rd Ohio Cavalry, wrote in his diary, "Our men caught a Bushwhacker and they took him out to a tree and tied him up and shot him dead."[2]

Action in East Tennessee

By January 9, Confederate expeditions moved closer to the Union lines, and the Union commanders feared Longstreet was again moving toward Knoxville. Conditions for the cavalry were poor because supplies were perilously low and the temperature hovered near zero in the evening. Having moved to East Tennessee in the late fall, Edward McCook's cavalry had no tents and inadequate winter clothing. To complicate matters, rumors abounded that Longstreet, reportedly with a division from Ewell's Corps, advanced on Knoxville, but Grant prepared to move additional troops to meet the threat.[3] Minor skirmishes occurred on January 5, 10, 12, 14, and 16 at Mossy Creek, Chucky Road, and Maryville as the Union cavalry encountered the enemy.

On January 14, the Union cavalry fell back from Mossy Creek about ten miles west to Dandridge in anticipation of a Confederate attack. Two days later, McCook's cavalry came to the assistance of a brigade of Colonel Frank Wolford's Army of the Ohio cavalry division, which was attacked by a strong Confederate infantry force. When McCook's cavalry fell in line, the Confederate advance halted. Edward McCook was ill on January 16 and Archibald Campbell commanded the division while Thomas Jordan assumed command of the First Brigade. Campbell received a dispatch from Colonel Israel Garrard that his command was being driven back by a superior Confederate force. General James Longstreet noted that Wolford got into trouble while attempting to attack his rear, the infantry driving the Union cavalry "back in some confusion." Campbell rushed ahead with the First and Second brigades of his command when he received a second message that he should support one of Colonel Wolford's brigades. Jordan's First Brigade had been riding at the rear and turned and led the relief column. Jordan found Wolford's division about a mile and a half from Dandridge, driven back in "disorder." To make matters worse, Wolford was cut off from Dandridge by a line of the enemy. Jordan dismounted and moved his brigade into line to charge and ordered Lilly's artillery to unlimber. By the time La Grange's Second Brigade reached Wolford, Jordan had ordered a charge into the enemy; La Grange quickly ordered his troopers to follow in a second dismounted charge. The enemy held a steady and heavy fire into Campbell's troopers, but with the addition of La Grange's troopers the Union cavalry succeeded in turning the enemy's flank and forcing it to the rear.[4]

First on the scene was the 2nd Michigan Cavalry, which Jordan ordered to dismount and fire into the enemy's flank. The 2nd Michigan unleashed a volley and then tried to hold on until the remainder of the brigade had moved forward. Next, the 9th Pennsylvania fell in line on the left of the 2nd Michigan, doubling the number of guns in the fight. As the 9th Pennsylvania moved into line it was struck with a volley from the enemy that dropped two troopers. Jordan noted, "While these formations were being made the Second Michigan Cavalry was hotly engaged, and, though outnumbered five to one, by steady, unflinching bravery held the enemy, though flushed with their victory over Wolford, in check." Then Lilly's artillery opened up on the Confederates. Next, the 2nd Indiana Cavalry fell into line to the left of the 9th Pennsylvania and unleashed a volley of its own. Finally, Jordan ordered his men to advance, driving the Confederate flank about a mile, which ended the action for the day.[5]

List of Casualties of the First Cavalry Division, Department of the Cumberland, in the Engagement of January 16, 1864, Near Dandridge, Tennessee[6]

Command	Killed	Wounded	Total
First Brigade (Campbell)	1	4	5
Second Brigade (La Grange)	1	1	2
Total	2	5	7

The next day, January 17, at 4:30 p.m. the enemy infantry again advanced "heavy columns" and met Colonel Oscar La Grange's Second Brigade on the right of Morristown Road. Colonel Thomas Harrison's Confederate cavalry attacked one of La Grange's pickets about two miles from Dandridge. La Grange ordered the 1st Wisconsin forward at a trot to investigate. He dismounted the regiment and moved to take possession of a hill but was struck with a volley in the flank before the hill could be occupied. La Grange ordered up the remainder of his brigade when the 1st Wisconsin was attacked by a charge of the 8th and 11th Texas cavalries. The Confederates ran for the Union horses and a mêlée between the two enemies resulted. Fortunately, the 2nd and 4th Indiana cavalries arrived in time to charge the Texans and drove them to the rear. Afterward the Indiana regiments formed on the left of the 1st Wisconsin. Meanwhile, the 7th Kentucky made a desperate but unsuccessful charge trying to regain the original Union position. Then three columns of Confederate infantry advanced across an open field toward the Union cavalry line. Oscar La Grange recorded:

> Disregarding our fire, which fell steadily upon them, [the enemy infantry] moved within 30 yards of our front, passing heedlessly over the bodies of their fallen comrades, planted their battle-flag, and began to deploy. Without waiting so hopeless a contest as must have taken place between dismounted cavalrymen and a superior force of trained infantry, our line was withdrawn in good order to its original position, where breast-works of rails were hastily erected, while the mounted men were properly posted for supports with the expectation that the enemy would advance and renew the contest. The First Brigade now arrived and promptly took position on our left.

The cavalry remained in line and withdrew at 11:00 p.m.[7]

After three attacks by the enemy, one of which resulted in three Confederate color bearers being shot, La Grange's cavalry held its line and the advance halted. Then the Confederates again advanced and the fighting was so intense that La Grange struggled to hold his line. McCook recorded, "Their solid, heavy columns suffered severely from the deliberate, well-directed fire of our men. This was the first occasion upon which the division had met the enemy's infantry." Once Longstreet's infantry fell into line the Union cavalry could make not more progress and retired after dark. McCook's casualties were a total of 48 killed, wounded, and missing.[8]

Charles Perry Goodrich, 1st Wisconsin, explained his regiment was initially in the forward position. Then, the Confederate cavalry lined up to charge into the 1st Wisconsin, which headed to the rear for support from the rest of the Union cavalry rushing forward:

> The 4th (Indiana) came and dismounted. We, the 1st Wisconsin, rallied on them and we again rushed to the onset…. At this point we saw a column of infantry march up and wheel into line four deep. They poured into us a fire that no single line of dismounted cavalry with short carbines could withstand. We broke and fled in dismay.[9]

A few days later, on January 21, Washington L. Elliott was relieved of duty in East Tennessee, and he traveled to Chattanooga to be closer to George Thomas's headquarters. Elliott was then in a location where he was not close to either of his divisions. It is unclear whether this was the new command style of the chief of cavalry or he needed to plan the upcoming campaign. Certainly, Elliott had had almost no time to discuss the cavalry with George Thomas since his appointment.[10]

The records of the cavalry reveal much about Elliott's style of command. His cavalry letterbook is a litany of complaints and instructions for his commanders to send him the required reports on time. He complained the reports were not prepared properly. He even requested that Colonel Louis Watkins, commanding the Third Brigade of the First Division, have his pay suspended because he returned to Kentucky on furlough with his veteran cavalry without completing his reports. Elliott seemed more comfortable with the administration of the cavalry corps rather than active field duty. But while Elliott was worrying over the reports, Watkins accompanied the 4th and 6th Kentucky cavalries to Kentucky as the regiments were mustered in as veterans. The local newspaper humorously cautioned the young women in Kentucky: "We take occasion to caution the young ladies of Kentucky, that although the officers of the 4th and 6th are veteran warriors, that there is scarcely one of them married."[11]

McCook's division moved to Knoxville on January 19 and performed various reconnaissance missions through January 26. The 1st Tennessee Cavalry captured a 25-wagon enemy supply train near Muddy Creek on January 22. What was thought to be a determined advance on Knoxville by Longstreet fizzled by January 24, much to the relief of the Union cavalry. Longstreet decided the shortage of troops and the difficultly of movement made such a move impractical until spring. Traveling in the eastern Tennessee Mountains was terrible and this caused Edward McCook to write, "The roads over here are the worst I ever saw."[12]

In addition, many in Elliott's cavalry were unhappy with their situation. Colonel Thomas Jordan, 9th Pennsylvania, complained that his command was moved closer to Knoxville fearing an advance by Longstreet and that the Confederates had successfully captured 800 cattle belonging to the Union army. He wrote his wife, "If this is generalship then I have yet to learn the art of war." He wanted away from the command of Samuel Sturgis. Since being assigned to the Army of the Ohio, he lamented his men "have been almost starved," often existing on half rations. The problems of the cavalry of the Army of the Cumberland continued as it served under the command of the Army of the Ohio. Michael Brown, 2nd Indiana Cavalry, wrote his brother about the poor treatment of McCook's cavalry under Colonel John Foster, commanding the second brigade of cavalry in the Army of the Ohio. Edward McCook had had enough and came to the defense of his men. Brown wrote, "Col. Foster treated us so meanly that Col. McCook told him to go to hell." Brown referred to Foster as a coward, ordering the Union troopers to fall back before the enemy, and he had high praise for the command of McCook, who continued the fight in east Tennessee.[13]

Battle of Fair Garden, January 27–28

On January 26, one of the Union scouts discovered a concentration of Confederate troops near Fair Garden, Tennessee, and the Confederates opened on the Union cavalry with artillery. One of the primary objectives of the cavalry in January was the disruption of foraging activities by the Confederate cavalry. As bad as conditions were in the Union army in East Tennessee, the conditions were at least as bad on the Confederate side. Samuel Sturgis sent orders to Edward McCook: "You will please attack the enemy in your front vigorously at daylight." The next day, Archibald Campbell's First Brigade and Oscar La Grange's Second Brigade went in search of the source of the artillery fire, moving along the Pigeon River in dense fog. Campbell and La Grange were seeking two brigades of General William T. Martin's cavalry. The Union cavalry found the two Confederate brigades about two miles from Fair Garden and a fairly balanced engagement resulted. The 2nd Michigan Cavalry dismounted and rushed around the flank of Martin's troops. Major Leonidas Scranton's regiment moved a little too far ahead of the other regiments and found his men all alone and ran into a "strong double line of the enemy extending far beyond us on both flanks." The enemy held their fire until the 2nd Michigan was about 100 yards away and "opened heavily." The cavalry hastened to the rear to the support of the rest of the brigade with the enemy in pursuit. As the battle unfolded, McCook's cavalry found a determined and strong resistance from the enemy. Once the 2nd Michigan reached the line of the brigade, it re-formed and advanced, slowly pushing Martin's cavalry to the rear throughout the day. At 4:00 p.m., McCook decided it was time to end the slow advance and ordered the 2nd and 4th Indiana cavalries to charge the Confederate position with sabers drawn.[14] On charged the Indianans and broke the line of the Confederate defenders.

Next, Oscar La Grange's cavalry charged a section of enemy artillery that had fired, killing two horses and wounding two men of the 4th Indiana. The 1st Wisconsin Cavalry moved to the extreme right and unleashed a volley into the flank of the enemy. Henry Campbell, Lilly's Artillery, recorded in his journal, "LaGrange's Brigade got away round on the flank of the Rebels and pitched into them with his usual dash." The enemy artillery shifted its attention to the new threat and, observing the advance of the Union line, started to limber and head to the rear. Then the Indiana cavalry charged in column of fours supported by the dismounted cavalry, who ran forward with "wild cheers." The attack caused the Confederates to precipitously retreat. Major Joseph Lesslie, 4th Indiana Cavalry, was killed in the charge. Private Solomon Glick watched Lesslie's death and closed in on the soldier who had fired the shot that killed him. "Glick brushed aside the rebel's rifle and calmly blew his brains out, shouting, 'You killed my colonel, you ___ rebel, and die you must.'" Lesslie commanded the First Battalion of the 4th Indiana Cavalry and was second in command of the regiment.[15]

McCook observed columns of infantry advancing and decided he had enough fighting for the day and retired. The Indiana cavalry claimed two 3-inch Rodman cannons, the battle flag of Confederate General John T. Morgan, the capture of his aide, and several other prisoners. In addition, the Indianans also actively participated in the attack of the Southern artillery and the troops in the battle. The Union cavalry also recaptured the colors of the 31st Indiana Infantry and an American flag. McCook's division captured 112 prisoners in total, including eleven officers. McCook concluded, "Morgan's rebel division was thoroughly broken, routed, and dispersed.... The enemy left a large number of dead and wounded in our hands, and their loss must have been over 350." McCook's total casualties amounted to twenty-eight.[16]

While Martin's cavalry was retreating, the 1st Tennessee Cavalry pursued. Brownlow charged the 8th and 11th Texas cavalries, but he had pushed too far ahead of his support, about a mile to his rear. Martin rallied his troopers and Brownlow's men were close to be being cut off. Brownlow, sensing his danger, unleashed a volley from his troopers into the re-forming Confederate cavalry and charged, sending the Confederates again into a retreat. Darkness was approaching and Brownlow ordered his troopers to withdraw to the main Union column. However, in the darkness Brownlow became separated from his regiment and was captured by some Texas cavalrymen. By using his wits and trading a gold watch, Brownlow, wearing a Scottish Glengarry hat tipped sideways on his head, was able to make his escape. He rode into the 1st Tennessee camp the next morning amidst the cheers of the regiment.[17]

A Confederate soldier was captured during the fight and was almost torn apart by the troopers of the 2nd Michigan. As the prisoner was being marched past the Union cavalry, someone noticed he was wearing the boots of the regiment's Captain Jim Smith, who had been wounded and left on the field. The Confederate had stripped the captain of his boots while leaving him to die. Although the troopers grumbled, "the prisoner was not molested except by scoffs and jeers from the whole regiment," exclaimed Sergeant Henry Hempstead.[18]

The next day McCook's division joined in Sturgis's pursuit of the Confederate cavalry and on this day Sturgis chose to attack Frank Armstrong's cavalry, which was three or four miles away from Fair Garden. Sturgis ordered Garrard's and Wolford's Union cavalry divisions of the Army of the Ohio to take the lead. Oscar La Grange's brigade was sent in support. This time Sturgis was surprised. Armstrong was much better prepared than Martin the day before. He had prepared heavy fortifications and had three infantry regiments as support. Armstrong, supported by Longstreet's infantry, handily repulsed Sturgis's attack. La Grange had little role in the attack and recorded six casualties.

But La Grange had much to say about Colonel Frank Wolford and his cavalry in a thinly veiled indictment. La Grange sent the 7th Kentucky, 4th Indiana and 2nd Indiana cavalries to try to drive the Confederates who had stalled Sturgis's advance. The 4th Indiana advanced to within 200 yards of the Confederate line only to find abates and received an explosive volley from Confederates concealed in dense woods. The 1st Wisconsin and 7th Kentucky covered the withdrawal of the two Indiana regiments. An unfortunate event occurred as the 2nd Indiana Cavalry was moving forward. Lieutenant William Stover was killed within sixty yards of the Confederate defenses by one of the Union troops in the rear. La Grange charged, "Thousands of rounds were fired in this skirmish by men who did not see the enemy. The habit of allowing cowards to fire over the heads of their own party from a safe distance in the rear is one of the most reprehensible, and officers who cannot prevent it ought to be shot themselves." Edward McCook's response to La Grange's report was that the gunshot which killed Stover was not from his cavalry and left the readers to draw their own conclusion. During the fighting at Fair Garden the Union troops recorded losses of 100 men compared to 165 for the Confederates.[19]

Meanwhile, there was much dissatisfaction with the way the Confederate cavalry was being handled by the commanding general. Longstreet had little confidence in W.T. Martin's ability to lead the Confederate cavalry in East Tennessee. He wrote of the action on January 27 and acknowledged the importance of McCook's cavalry: "General Martin had a severe cavalry fight on the 27th. He was driven back 4 miles, with a loss of 200 killed, wounded, and missing, and 2 pieces of artillery. The enemy's cavalry has been greatly increased by the cavalry from Chattanooga." Longstreet wanted someone better to lead the cavalry and concluded, "We can do but little while this superior cavalry force is here to operate on our flank and rear. Do send me a chief of cavalry."[20]

After the fight at Fair Garden, McCook's First and Second Brigades moved to Wear's Cove, just west of Fair Garden and between two forks of the Pigeon River, with orders to guard fords and watch for the enemy. At the end of the month McCook joined the remainder of Sturgis's cavalry and rode to Maryville on account of "starvation." The Third Brigade commanded by Colonel Louis Watkins was detached from his command, but the 7th Kentucky Cavalry was under McCook's command in East Tennessee and shared the hardship of the rest of McCook's troopers. Meanwhile, the 4th and 6th Kentucky were furloughed until March, the reward granted to troopers who reenlisted.[21]

Not all the conflicts within the Union cavalry were with their Confederate foes. One particularly bitter fight happened while the 7th Kentucky Cavalry was moving toward Dandridge. Lieutenant Colonel Thomas Vimont decided to pick on one of his officers, nineteen-year-old Lieutenant Andrew Jones. To complicate matters, Jones was the ward of Major William W. Bradley of the same regiment. Vimont rode up to a group of officers on January 14 between Dandridge and Mossy Creek and started to verbally abuse Jones in front of the group. Vimont exclaimed, "There is a Lieutenant that asked for a position in a nigger regiment. It is to be hoped that all such would get out of the regiment for they are a disgrace to the white race of people." Vimont continued to verbally prod the young lieutenant, additionally accusing him of seeking a commission in the Confederate army. Vimont continued, "You are not worth hell room nor none of your friends." Major Bradley stepped in to defend Jones from Vimont's tirade and cursing. Bradley asked Vimont to withdraw the statement about Jones wanting to join the Rebel army. Vimont shouted, "I do not retract anything. I am a lone Kentuckian and owe allegiance neither to Abe Lincoln or any of his God damned followers. And you are a liar." Vimont continued to be abusive toward Bradley, who drew his gun but did not point it at Vimont. He then reholstered his weapon and the argument calmed. When Bradley demanded Vimont take back what he said, Vimont declared, "Who are you, God damn you?" Then the argument heated up again and Vimont called Bradley a coward and exclaimed, "Why didn't you shoot, you God damned cowardly son of a bitch?" Vimont even ran his fist under Bradley's nose. Then Vimont slapped his hand on his revolver but Bradley pulled his revolver and shot Vimont. Vimont's horse spun as he tried to raise his revolver and Bradley shot twice more. Vimont died the next day. Apparently, Vimont intended to humiliate Bradley, who was a well-respected officer. Prior to the altercation, a petition had been circulated by the officers in the regiment asking that Bradley replace Vimont, but Vimont bragged he received his appointment through the influence of his powerful allies. Bradley was subsequently acquitted at his court-martial in May 1864. Vimont's orderly testified that the lieutenant colonel was intoxicated and Colonel John Faulkner, commander of the 7th Kentucky Cavalry, offered strong supporting testimony on Bradley's behalf. Bradley was later promoted to the rank of lieutenant colonel.[22]

Crook's Division at Pulaski

While Edward McCook's two brigades worked under the command of General Samuel Sturgis, George Crook's Second Division began the year at Pulaski under orders of the chief of cavalry for the Military Division of the Mississippi, William Sooy Smith. Crook had ridden his division into the ground chasing Joseph Wheeler through Tennessee. He was improving the condition of his command as new mounts arrived from the Quartermaster Department, but the opportunities to forage the horses of Crook's command were hard to find.

The year ended with Crook preparing to join Smith in an expedition to force Forrest out of Tennessee, and, if possible, inflict some major injury to his command. Instead, Forrest eluded the Union net that was being drawn around his command. Smith initially told Crook to settle his command around Pulaski and Huntsville and prepare for campaigning in the spring. William Sherman changed the plans of Smith when he decided to march on Meridian, Mississippi. Sherman had multiple objectives, including, destroying the Confederate rail system, eliminating the regular and irregular military attacks on the Union Army in Mississippi, and preventing the Confederates from receiving forage and food. The expedition did not begin until early February, but one part of Sherman's plans included Smith's leading a large cavalry column from Memphis against railroads and other Confederate infrastructure. To assist in the raid, Smith pulled the 4th U.S. Cavalry, 5th Kentucky Cavalry, 2nd Tennessee Cavalry and 72nd Indiana Mounted Infantry from Crook's Division and assigned them to the Cavalry Division of the Sixteenth Corps, officially removing them from the Army of the Cumberland until March 1864.[23]

On January 28, William Sooy Smith ordered Crook to make a demonstration on Decatur, Alabama, to hold the attention of Phillip Roddey's Confederate cavalry while Smith began his cavalry raid as part of the Meridian Campaign. Crook's actions were designed to divert as many of the enemy's cavalry as possible while Smith and Sherman advanced into Mississippi.[24]

Little action resulted from this demonstration, and for the month of January the Confederates in Crook's area remained quiet. Only Abram Miller's Third Brigade of mounted infantry was involved in fighting in January 1864. On January 26, Miller discovered Colonel William A. Johnson's Confederate cavalry crossing the Tennessee River about six miles from Huntsville at Bainbridge Ferry. Miller speculated that the cavalry was crossing to unite with a concentration of Southern infantry. When the Union mounted infantry arrived, Johnson's cavalry was stalled by Miller's vedettes. Miller dismounted his command and ordered the 92nd Illinois Mounted Infantry forward. Upon the arrival of the 92nd Illinois, the size of the Confederate force was determined and Miller decided he needed the entire brigade sent forward. The exchange of musket fire from both sides soon stopped as Johnson quickly withdrew. Miller discovered a set of orders on a dead Confederate. After talking with some prisoners and examining the orders, it was clear to Miller that Athens was to be attacked. This information was sent to the Union garrison at Athens, and an attack was made the next day by 600 Confederate troopers of the 1st Confederate Cavalry supported by artillery. Due to the advance notice, no damage was done to Athens, and only minor casualties occurred in the aborted attack.[25]

Reorganization of the Cavalry Corps of the Army of the Cumberland

When Grant assumed control of all the Union armies in the west, the organizational distinctions between the various cavalry divisions became blurred. As mentioned, McCook's division served with the cavalry of the Army of the Ohio under command of General Samuel Sturgis, and some of Crook's division was parceled out to the Army of the Tennessee. One advantage of Grant's unification of command was that cavalry and other resources could be used where most needed, whether East Tennessee or Mississippi, but many felt that command relationships and unit identity suffered as a result.

In addition, there can be little doubt that the relationship between Grant and George Thomas was strained and that Rosecrans' removal affected the cavalry corps. Grant concluded Thomas was "slow and argumentative, an opinion that time would not mellow." Grant held no better judgment of the Army of the Cumberland, and Grant's conclusions would influence Sherman, who would subsequently assume command of the western armies.[26]

The relationship between Grant and Thomas regarding the cavalry was chronicled through a series of messages in January 1864. Invariably, whatever Thomas requested, Grant had reason to deny. On January 15, Thomas requested Elliott's cavalry in East Tennessee to be sent to the Army of the Cumberland so that the cavalry could "demonstrate on the enemy's position at Dalton and completely occupy his attention." Grant responded that it was impossible to move Elliott's cavalry until Longstreet was subdued in East Tennessee. Next, Grant agreed to transfer Crook to West Virginia, a request that had lingered since September.[27]

Grant also began looking for an appropriate officer to replace Crook. In an interesting set of communications, it was a request from assistant secretary of war Charles Dana that decided Crook's replacement; however, the decision was apparently made without consultation with Thomas or Elliott. Dana requested James H. Wilson, who had served as inspector general for Grant. "It is a question of saving millions of money and rendering the cavalry arm everywhere efficient," remarked Dana. The result was essentially a swap, Wilson for Brigadier General Kenner Garrard. Garrard had been running the Cavalry Bureau, and when Wilson went to Washington, Garrard was assigned command of the Second Cavalry Division in the Army of the Cumberland.[28]

Kenner Garrard, a native of Bourbon County, Kentucky, was thirty-six years old when he was transferred to command the Second Cavalry Division. He was the grandson of the second governor of Kentucky, James Garrard. His two brothers were also in the Union Army. Garrard was a graduate of the United States Military Academy, class of 1851. Like many of the professional soldiers of the Union army, Garrard served on the western frontier, first in the dragoons, and then he transferred to the 2nd U.S. Cavalry. He had been promoted to the rank of captain in 1861 and had served with various individuals who were members of the both the Union and Confederate armies, including John Bell Hood, Albert Sidney Johnston, George Thomas, and William Hardee. Garrard was serving in Texas at the beginning of the war and was captured by Confederates. He was paroled in September 1861 and appointed commandant at West Point. He was officially "exchanged" in September and was free to enter the war. He began his active participation in the war by serving as colonel of the 146th New York Infantry and saw extensive action in the eastern theater. He fought at Fredericksburg, Chancellorsville and Gettysburg. He received a commendation for "Gallant and Meritorious Services" at Gettysburg when he assumed command of a brigade after Brigadier General Stephen Weed was killed at Little Round Top. Garrard had a short stay as chief of the Cavalry Bureau and requested field assignment after only two months in that position "in despair at the graft and corruption he had found there."[29]

Brigadier General Kenner Garrard left Washington due to his "despair at the graft and corruption he had found there" (MOLLUS-MASS Civil War Collection, United States Army Heritage and Education Center, Military History Institute, Carlisle, Pennsylvania).

February 1864

Little action occurred in February with McCook's First Division, which had seen hard duty for the prior two months in the mountains of East Tennessee. A respite was long overdue, as the men and horses were exhausted. The war was taking a toll on the regiments. Thomas Jordan lamented that the 9th Pennsylvania Cavalry had only 257 men and officers ready for duty. The division was mainly occupied with scouting, some light skirmishing, and capturing Confederates.[30]

Colonel William Stokes' 5th Tennessee was turning things around near Sparta as he received more of his men mounted on new horses. He was now the pursuer of Colonel John Hughes and his men. Stokes was so effective that the Confederates could not organize and remained scattered as a way to survive the relentless pursuit of the 5th Tennessee troopers.[31]

Probably the biggest scare of the month for those in East Tennessee was another abortive advance upon Knoxville. By all indications Longstreet was again marching on Knoxville, but he was frustrated and unhappy. And he didn't care who knew it. His actions caused a series of actions among the Union troops who prepared to meet his advance; but Longstreet decided not to continue with the plan.

For the commanders of the Army of Tennessee and the Army of the Cumberland, the detached cavalry fighting in East Tennessee caused many problems. Both Confederate general Joseph Johnston and Union general George Thomas wanted their cavalry back. Thomas felt he needed his cavalry, as the spring campaigns were approaching. In February, he succeeded in getting McCook placed under Gordon Granger's control and away from Sturgis. Next, he needed to get the First Division under Elliott's command, and he used Longstreet's retreat from Knoxville as the reason. Thomas was pressing ahead at Chattanooga and needed cavalry. On the Confederate side, Joe Johnston felt the same, but Longstreet was not cooperating. Johnston observed that over two-thirds of Wheeler's cavalry was under Longstreet's control, and he wasn't giving them up. As the winter advanced, Johnston complained that Longstreet was overusing the cavalry, which would be needed in the spring by the army around Dalton. Longstreet retorted the cavalry was in excellent condition and didn't need a rest. He wanted what Johnston feared. Longstreet wrote, "I think that the cavalry now here should be transferred to this army." Next, he took off the gloves and stated he was unhappy with the command of his cavalry: "General Martin has not had experience enough to give him confidence in himself or his men. Without confidence a cavalry leader can have no dash, and without either he cannot be the leader we need." Not only was Longstreet unhappy with the cavalry, so was Colonel Bolling Hall, 59th Alabama infantry: "All goes on quietly & will probably continue to do so until the enemy thrash out our cowardly cavalry again & we then will be forced to go out & recover their lost ground for them. It certainly is a fact that the cavalry arm of our service has accomplished very little & is dwindling away to nothing." Wheeler appealed directly to Longstreet for the release of the cavalry in East Tennessee, but Longstreet responded that he was faced with challenges of his own: "I concluded to keep it, at the time at least."[32]

Then Longstreet's frustration increased. He decided to move on Knoxville but complained that much of the Union army from Chattanooga had been moved to Knoxville. He asked Johnston to make some action to draw the reinforcements back to Chattanooga. Johnston appealed to Jefferson Davis in response to Longstreet's request, and he used the cavalry as a trump. "Weakness in cavalry has prevented me," wrote Johnston, and in a direct response to Longstreet, Johnston applied the pressure back on Longstreet: "I cannot move nearer to you. Can you move nearer to me?" Johnston suggested that he really couldn't do anything to help Longstreet without the return of his cavalry.[33]

Fortunately for the Union forces in East Tennessee, Longstreet finally just gave up. Without assistance from Johnston and outnumbered, he felt he could not advance against the Union forces at Chattanooga. He moved back toward Virginia. Longstreet also gave up Wheeler's cavalry and sent it to Wheeler. When the Confederate cavalry was sent to Johnston, George Thomas argued there was no longer any need for Edward McCook's division to remain in East Tennessee.[34]

Meanwhile on the Union right flank, Kenner Garrard arrived and assumed command of the Second Cavalry Division at Huntsville, Alabama, on February 10, 1864. He found four of his regiments on duty in Mississippi. The 4th U.S. Cavalry, 72nd Indiana Mounted Infantry, 2nd Tennessee and 5th Kentucky Cavalry participated in Sherman's Meridian Campaign. The latter three regiments served in the brigade commanded by Colonel Lafayette McCrillis, and the 4th U.S. Cavalry was unattached during the campaign. Although Forrest intercepted Smith's cavalry at West Point, Mississippi, and then soundly defeated the Federals at Okolona, the troopers of the 4th U.S. Cavalry, 72nd Indiana Mounted Infantry, 5th Kentucky Cavalry, and 2nd Tennessee were identified as performing exemplary duty. While the cavalry regiments from the Army of the Cumberland performed well, the performance of William Sooy Smith further jaded Sherman's outlook on the cavalry. Sherman wrote his wife, "I am down on William Sooy Smith.... He could have come to me, and I know it."[35]

Back in Tennessee, the 5th Tennessee set up its headquarters near Sparta, Tennessee, and continued its arduous duty of fighting local guerrillas. The Union cavalry immediately killed "17 of the worst men in the country" and captured another twelve. Colonel William B. Stokes, commanding the regiment, claimed the

William B. Stokes's 5th Tennessee Cavalry killed "17 of the worst men in the country" when it arrived at Sparta (Library of Congress).

men were responsible for murder, rape, and other unnamed "outrages." Stokes' 5th Tennessee set up camp in the notoriously pro–Southern community, home of Confederate cavalry colonel George Dibrell. He estimated the irregulars in the area totaled as many as 600 men.[36]

Stokes' duty was difficult as he faced the war-hardened Confederates in East Tennessee. The 5th Tennessee Cavalry was in poor condition, with many of the regiment still in Nashville awaiting horses. The regiment faced good news and bad news. The good news was the enemy had stopped stealing and terrorizing the local citizens; but the bad news was they had focused their attention on destroying Stokes' cavalry. A member of the 1st Wisconsin stated that the Confederates had a propensity for capturing unsuspecting Union cavalry: "[T]he way our thrifty Northern housekeepers have to catch unwary mice and rats—to set a trap for them" On February 22, Colonel Hughes attacked two companies of the 5th Tennessee Cavalry. The companies were surrounded and "overwhelmed" by men wearing Union uniforms. Only six officers and forty-five men returned from the fight. Later, Stokes' pickets were tricked when six troopers in Union uniforms rode hard to their location with a group of gray-clad troopers close on their heels. Four of the pickets were killed when they discovered the ruse. The first six men were also Confederates, dressed in blue uniforms. One Union picket was killed and the other three were murdered after they surrendered. Stokes acknowledged that Colonel Hughes did not allow such "barbarity" but his men did. Stokes also recorded that the local citizens near Sparta were "thoroughly and decidedly disloyal."[37]

The Reconnaissance to Dalton, Georgia

In February, George Thomas ordered an advance on Dalton to deter the Confederates from sending troops to oppose Sherman's advance on Meridian. Thomas's delayed advance was too late to prevent the dispatch of two divisions towards Mississippi, but they were quickly recalled when Confederate scouts detected the move. Thomas ordered Brigadier General Charles Cruft's First Division, Fourth Corps, to move from Cleveland, Tennessee, to Red Clay, Georgia, and then advance as far as possible toward Dalton. Eli Long's Second Cavalry Brigade met with Cruft at Red Clay and provided reconnaissance and secured the infantry's flanks during the advance, which began on February 22. Long's command consisted of about 600 men, of which 250 were cavalry and the remainder was mounted infantry. The majority of Long's cavalry had been granted furloughs as a reward for reenlisting.

General Jefferson C. Davis's division moved to Ringgold, Georgia, and Brigadier General Charles Matthies' brigade reinforced Cruft's advance. Long met Cruft and Matthies on February 23 and advanced to Spring Place Road, pushing the enemy's vedettes to within four miles of Dalton. The sight of Long's cavalry startled Joseph Wheeler's cavalry, Hardee's infantry, and Joe Johnston, all headquartered at Dalton. Long's attack crashed into a regiment of infantry and sent them scampering to Dalton with news that the Union cavalry had arrived. Long captured twelve prisoners during this engagement. While Cruft and Matthies moved forward, Jefferson Davis's division successfully pushed the Confederates a mile past Tunnel Hill. By the morning of February 24, Absalom Baird moved his division near Ringgold, Richard Johnson's division joined Davis's division in the forward position, Cruft was at Lee's House, Harrison's mounted infantry was leading the advance on Tunnel Hill and Long's cavalry was at Varnell's Station, accompanied by William Grose's infantry brigade.[38]

The Union infantry moved forward in three columns. The center column came under heavy artillery fire and stopped, but the right and left columns succeeded in their advance, forcing the artillery to retire. Davis sent his division in pursuit. He advanced as far as Mill Creek Gap, a pass in Rocky Face Ridge, which runs for about ten miles and is located northwest of Dalton. The ridge presented an impressive obstacle, as it rose seven hundred feet above the valley floor in a very steep incline. While the main Union force was marching towards Rocky Face Ridge, Long's cavalry and Grose's infantry were in Crow Valley, about three miles north of Dalton on the east side of the ridge. Long dismounted his men to meet a Confederate counterattack but soon found they were outnumbered and retired.

Distaining a frontal assault on Rocky Face Ridge, Thomas dispatched Baird's division towards Crow Valley to join Cruft's division and Long's cavalry brigade on February 25. Davis's and Johnson's divisions remained on the western side of the ridge. It was hoped the two Union columns would dishearten the Confederates on the ridge, forcing them to abandon their position. This plan failed when Cruft and Baird ran into a determined Confederate defense. The column skirmished throughout the day. Long simply noted in his after action report that "after advancing half a mile, the enemy was found and engaged." Cruft and Baird could not accomplish the plan, and fearing Confederate reinforcements from Dalton they withdrew during the night.[39]

Killed and wounded at the Battle of Buzzard Roost, near Dalton, on February 24 and 25, 1864[40]

Command	Killed Officers	Killed Men	Wounded Officers	Wounded Men	Total
Fourth Army Corps Cruft	–	5	1	51	57
Fourteenth Army Corps Davis, Johnson, Baird	–	9	6	185	200
Cavalry Long	1	2	1	28	32
Total	1	16	8	264	289

March–April 1864

The cavalry of the Army of the Cumberland spent March and April scouting northwest Georgia for the upcoming campaign. At long last, Edward McCook's First Cavalry Division was returned to Thomas after serving the Army of the Ohio for the four months. McCook moved his cavalry to Cleveland, Tennessee, with orders to protect the army's left flank and was instructed to get his horses in proper condition for campaigning. Eli Long's cavalry brigade was assigned duty at Calhoun, Tennessee, with the same instructions. Private David Ayers, 4th Ohio Cavalry, wrote his wife in March that the Union line was only two miles from the enemy and the enemy was visible every day. He also noted Confederate desertions were common.[41]

Probably the biggest concerns during March and April were raids made by Forrest's cavalry. General Kenner Garrard's Second Cavalry Division at Huntsville was alerted to Confederates moving northward in March, but Forrest veered west and moved into western Tennessee and Kentucky. Forest left his camp on March 15 and reached Jackson, Tennessee, on March 23 and Paducah, Kentucky, on March 25. This left little action for Garrard, although he did move his cavalry westward to Columbia, Tennessee, in hopes of cutting Forrest off from Mississippi when he returned southward. On his return, Forrest bypassed the Union obstacles, and Garrard's cavalry saw little action. Forrest raided again to the north in April and stormed Fort Pillow, resulting in the infamous slaughter of Union defenders there on April 12.

The biggest changes for the cavalry came in the form of reorganizations. The first major change was the promotion of Ulysses Grant to the rank of lieutenant general and his move east to become general in chief of all Union armies. On March 12, William Sherman succeeded to the command of the Military Division of the Mississippi, but not everyone was pleased with Sherman's ascension. Andrew Johnson, governor of Tennessee, wrote to Lincoln: "I feel satisfied from what I know and hear that placing the command of the department under General Sherman, over Thomas, will produce disappointment in the public mind and impair the public service."[42]

Thomas gave orders for Garrard's cavalry to move eastward in preparation for the campaign that was planned to begin on May 2, but he was delayed until May 7 so Major General James McPherson's Army of the Tennessee could get into place. Upon McPherson's arrival, Sherman ordered the campaign to begin, which coincided with the opening of Grant's campaign in the East. On April 11, Thomas reorganized the cavalry of the Army of the Cumberland into four divisions, which were commanded by Colonel Edward M. McCook (promoted to brigadier general on April 27), Brigadier General Kenner Garrard, Brigadier General Judson Kilpatrick, and Brigadier General Alvan C. Gillem. Each division was generally composed of three brigades with three regiments per brigade.

CAVALRY CORPS, APRIL 30, 1864
Brigadier General Washington Lafayette Elliott[43]

FIRST DIVISION
Brigadier General Edward M McCook

First Brigade	*Second Brigade*
Colonel Joseph B. Dorr	**Colonel Oscar H. La Grange**
8th Iowa, Col. Horatio Barner	
2nd Michigan, Maj. Leonidas S. Scranton	2nd Indiana, Lt. Col. James W. Stewart
9th Pennsylvania, Maj. Edward G. Savage	4th Indiana, Lt. Col. Horace P. Lamson
1st Tennessee, Lt. Col. James P. Brownlow	1st Wisconsin, Maj. William H. Torrey

Third Brigade
Colonel Louis D. Watkins
4th Kentucky, Col. Wickliffe Cooper
6th Kentucky, Maj. William H. Fidler
7th Kentucky, Capt. Charles C. McNeely

Artillery
Indiana Light, 18th Battery, Lieut. William B. Rippetoe

SECOND DIVISION
Brigadier General Kenner Garrard

First Brigade	*Second Brigade*
Colonel Robert Minty	**Colonel Eli Long**
4th Michigan, Lt. Col. Josiah B. Park	1st Ohio, Col. Beroth B. Eggleston
7th Pennsylvania, Col. William B. Sipes	3rd Ohio, Lt. Col. Horace N. Howland
4th United States, Capt. James B. McIntyre	4th Ohio, Lt. Col. Oliver P. Robie

Third Brigade
Colonel John T. Wilder

17th Indiana Mounted Infantry, Lt. Col. Henry Jordan
72nd Indiana Mounted Infantry, Col. Abram O. Miller
98th Illinois Mounted Infantry, Lt. Col. Edward Kitchell
123rd Illinois Mounted Infantry, Lt. Col. Jonathan Biggs

Artillery
Chicago (Illinois) Board of Trade Battery, Lt. George I. Robinson

THIRD DIVISION
Brigadier General Hugh Judson Kilpatrick

First Brigade	Second Brigade
Colonel William Lowe	**Colonel Charles C. Smith**
3rd Indiana (battalion), Lt. Col. Robert Klein	8th Indiana, Col. Thomas J. Harrison
5th Iowa, Lt. Col. Matthewson T. Patrick	2nd Kentucky, Lt. Col. Elijah S. Watts
9th Pennsylvania, Col. Thomas J. Jordan	10th Ohio, Maj. Thomas W. Sanderson

Third Brigade
Colonel Eli Murray

92nd Illinois Mounted Infantry, Col. Smith Adkins
3rd Kentucky, Maj. Lewis Wolfley
5th Kentucky, Lt. Col. Oliver L. Baldwin

FOURTH DIVISION
Brigadier General Alvan C. Gillem

First Brigade	Second Brigade
Lieut. Col. Duff G. Thornburgh	**Lieut. Col. George Spalding**
2nd Tennessee, Lt. Col. William F. Prosser	5th Tennessee, Maj. William J. Clift
3rd Tennessee, Maj. John B. Minnis	10th Tennessee, Lt. Col. George W. Bridges
4th Tennessee, Lt. Col. Jacob M. Thornburgh	12th Tennessee, Maj. John S. Kirwan
1st Tenn. Light Artill, Batt A, Capt. Albert F. Beach	1st Kansas Battery, Capt. Marcus D. Tenney

Third Brigade
Colonel John K. Miller

8th Tennessee, Col. Samuel K. N. Patton
9th Tennessee, Maj. Etheldred W. Armstrong
13th Tennessee, Maj. George W. Doughty

The 9th Pennsylvania Cavalry was furloughed in May. It participated in actions in Kentucky in June and July, and was assigned to the Military District of Kentucky until September 1864.

On April 30, Thomas reported the strength of his cavalry and location of the various divisions.

Cavalry Corps (Elliott): Men Present for Duty[44]

Command	Men Present	Location
Headquarters	7	Chattanooga, Tennessee
First Division (E. McCook)	4,660	Cleveland, Tennessee
Second Division (K. Garrard)	7,514	Columbia, Tennessee
Third Division (H. Kilpatrick)	4,247	Ringgold, Georgia
Fourth Division (A. Gillem)	6,103	Nashville Tennessee
Detached (Palmer)	431	Rossville, Georgia
Total Cavalry Corps	22,962	

In addition to the cavalry of the Army of the Cumberland, Major General George Stoneman's four brigades of cavalry of the Army of the Ohio were also preparing for the campaign. Stoneman reported about 4,600 troopers present for duty on April 30. McPherson's Army of the Tennessee reported about 700 cavalry present for duty near Chattanooga. These components of the Union cavalry, totaling about 26,000, now faced the cavalry of Joseph Johnston's Army of Tennessee under the command of Joseph Wheeler. Wheeler had three divisions plus two brigades of cavalry, which totaled about 10,000 troopers present for duty at the end of April. For the first time since the organization of the Army of the Cumberland, the Union cavalry had a clear dominance in numbers over its Confederate counterparts.[45]

Most of the regiments of the Union cavalry remained unchanged during the reorganization, with one important addition, the Fourth Division. This division comprised Tennessee cavalry. Only the artillery that was assigned to this division came from states other than Tennessee. The division was commanded by Brigadier General Alvan C. Gillem, a 33-year-old native of Tennessee and West Point graduate, class of 1851. He finished eleventh in his class and was commissioned lieutenant in the United States Artillery, beginning his career battling the Seminoles in Florida. From 1853 to 1858 he served at various forts in the eastern United States before he was sent to Texas. At the beginning of the Civil War, his command surrendered to the newly formed Confederate army, but he was not captured. His next assignment was at Fort Taylor in Key West, where he was promoted to captain. At the beginning of the war, he served as George Thomas's quartermaster. In spring 1862, he became Major General Don Carlos Buell's quartermaster for the Army of the Ohio. In May 1862, he was appointed colonel of the 10th Tennessee Infantry and later was assigned provost marshal duties in Nashville. This assignment was not successful, and he was relieved of those responsibilities. But while in Nashville, Gillem developed a personal friendship with the governor of Tennessee, Andrew Johnson, and in June 1863 he was appointed adjutant general for the state. A promotion to the rank of brigadier general soon followed. Next, he commanded troops responsible for protecting the Nashville and Northwestern Railroad. While Gillem, a professional soldier, had served in various commands before and during the war, he had no cavalry experience. Almost certainly his relationship with Andrew Johnson aided him in the appointment to command the Tennessee cavalry division. On June 6 Sherman summed up his impression of Gillem's command: "I have always regarded General Gillem's command as a refugee hospital for indolent Tennesseans. I never dreamed of their being a part of my military command, and have never reckoned them anything but a political element." In reality, Gillem and the Tennessee cavalry had a very important job protecting Sherman's supply line and preventing the numerous Confederate troops in Tennessee from causing havoc in the state as Sherman advanced on Atlanta.[46]

Brigadier General Alvan Gillem commanded the Tennessee Cavalry Division, which protected Sherman's supply line (Library of Congress).

Those regiments Sherman criticized were not

pleased with their role, either. Some of the Tennessee cavalry regiments were quickly called into service but incompletely organized. Among these were the 4th and 5th Tennessee regiments. Both of these regiments had served since 1862 but were formally reorganized later. For the 4th Tennessee Cavalry, this reorganization resulted in the de facto colonel of the regiment, Richard M. Edwards, being denied command. In his case, some politicians questioned his loyalty because he endorsed a speech made by Samuel Cox of Ohio that criticized Lincoln's war policies. Edwards, also a politician, was a veteran of the Mexican War. A contributing factor to Edwards's denial of command was the infighting in the 4th Tennessee Cavalry under his tenure. He graciously offered his farewell to the regiment on July 6, 1863. A 27-year-old attorney and Jefferson County Tennessee native, Lieutenant Colonel Jacob Thornburg, assumed command of the regiment. The 4th Tennessee Cavalry went on to participate in the Meridian Campaign, Rousseau's Raid and McCook's Raid before giving up its horses to Kilpatrick's cavalry in August. Thornburg was a Tennessean displeased by the comment made by Sherman and was not happy about the assignment given his regiment. He exclaimed that his brigade had been "placed in a condition [that] could do little service—reflect little credit to the state" and then carried the stigma of being placed in the rear of the entire campaign. Thornburg was to prove an effective commander of the 4th Tennessee. He was a strict disciplinarian but one who deeply cared for his men. He made a point to be among them each day.[47]

While eyebrows were raised at Gillem's appointment, the decision to give command of the Third Cavalry Division to Hugh Judson Kilpatrick was more controversial. Kilpatrick had served in the cavalry in the East, but his most recent actions resulted in his being dispatched to the West. Kilpatrick, long known to be brash, impulsive and reckless, had earned the nickname "Kill-Cavalry Kilpatrick." Ironically, he had found a place in the Atlanta Campaign because Sherman wanted just such a person to command a division of cavalry.

Left: **Colonel Jacob Thornburg, 4th Tennessee Cavalry, felt being away from the front reflected "little credit to the state."** *Right:* **Brigadier General Hugh Judson Kilpatrick, long known to be brash, impulsive and reckless, assumed command of the Third Cavalry Division (Library of Congress).**

Kilpatrick was a native of Deckertown, New Jersey, and was born on January 14, 1836. He received his education in preparatory schools and entered West Point in 1856, graduating in the class of 1861. He received his commission in the United States artillery but soon was elected captain in the 5th New York Volunteer Infantry, Duryée's Zouaves. He had the dubious honor of being the first regular army officer wounded in the war at the Battle of Big Bethel in June 1861. Returning to the army after his wound, he was commissioned lieutenant colonel of the 2nd New York Cavalry. Kilpatrick served in the Shenandoah Valley Campaign and at Second Bull Run. He was arrested and incarcerated for three months in late 1862 for confiscating civilian property but was freed after the charges could not be proven. Next, he was promoted to colonel of the 21st New York Cavalry and was soon in command of a brigade under Alfred Pleasonton. Kilpatrick fought at the Battle of Brandy Station and participated in the Gettysburg Campaign. However, it was the "Dahlgren Affair" that caused his exile from the Army of the Potomac. He led a raid toward Richmond in an attempt to free Union prisoners at Libby Prison and Belle Isle beginning on February 28, 1864. He planned to move against Richmond from the north while Colonel Ulric Dahlgren with 500 troopers planned to approach Richmond from the east. Dahlgren intended to free the Union prisoners at Belle Isle and move back through Richmond and unite with Kilpatrick's main column. Both Dahlgren and Kilpatrick met strong Confederate resistance. Dahlgren was killed while at the head of his column. On Dahlgren's body were two documents that revealed plans to burn Richmond and murder Jefferson Davis and his cabinet. Allegations were made that Kilpatrick had endorsed these orders, although this was vehemently denied. Although he was able to cause much destruction during his raid, the loss of 324 troopers killed and wounded and another 1,000 captured, in addition to death of Dahlgren and questions, both North and South, about the plan to burn Richmond and murder Confederate officials made the raid a disaster.[48]

The Cavalry Prepares for the Spring Campaign

New cavalry regiments arrived as the campaign began. The 8th Indiana, 8th Iowa, 3rd, 4th, 8th, 9th, 10th, 12th and 13th Tennessee cavalries regiments had been added to the Army of the Cumberland. Only the 8th Indiana and 8th Iowa would advance with Sherman's army. The 8th Iowa joined the First Brigade of McCook's division and was jokingly referred to as the "Persimmon Knockers" by the 1st Tennessee Cavalry. The 8th Indiana Cavalry was a veteran regiment commanded by Colonel Thomas Harrison and the regimental name was previously the 39th Indiana Mounted Infantry. This regiment had been part of the cavalry of the Army of the Cumberland in 1863. As the 8th Indiana joined, the chief of cavalry was growing unhappy because Sherman personally assigned missions removing the authority from Elliott. Clearly, the Army of the Cumberland had the largest cavalry contingent of the three Union armies beginning this campaign, but that distinction held little importance. His cavalry had been parceled out to various commands without his orders. Elliott wrote to Thomas on March 9: "I request that copies of all orders relating to the cavalry be furnished me or given through me."[49]

The might of the North was evident with the resupply of the cavalry. As the war continued, the North's ability to replace men, equipment, and mounts was superior to that of the South. The 1st Ohio Cavalry was given new mounts and each company was assigned a particular color horse. There were three companies with bay horses, two with sorrel, and one each with black, gray, white, dun, and light sorrel. That did not mean the upcoming campaign would be easy. Sherman's armies were about to begin one of the most important, exhausting, and difficult campaigns of the war. It would take four months, with fighting almost daily and many miles of marching.

One additional item that improved the spirits of the veteran cavalry troopers was the distribution of seven-shot Spencer repeating rifles, which were highly prized, to many of the regiments. Previously, the regiments had various weapons[50]:

2nd Michigan	Sharps Rifles and Colt Revolving Rifles
9th Pennsylvania	Sharps Rifles and Burnside Carbines
2nd Indiana	Colt revolving rifles and Smith Carbines
4th Indiana	Smith Carbines
1st Wisconsin	Sharps Rifles, Merrill Carbines and Maynard Carbines
1st Tennessee	Sharps Rifles, Gallagher Carbines, and Enfield Muskets
7th Kentucky	Sharps Rifles and Burnside Carbines
11th Ohio	Sharps Rifles[51]

Elliott requested Spencer repeating rifles be provided for all the cavalry but this was never fully accomplished. The Spencer was a more appropriate and effective weapon, and the advantage of maintaining an inventory of only one type of ammunition was highly desirable. He also requested sabers be issued to the cavalry but felt that pistols were not important if the troopers had Spencer rifles.[52]

A few more changes were in store for the Union cavalry. From the fall of 1863 through the beginning of the campaign, many regiments had given their three years of service. While this resulted in men leaving and some regiments being disbanded, in many regiments almost all of the men reenlisted. George Kryder, 3rd Ohio Cavalry, happily recorded in his diary that the entire company reenlisted. The 7th Pennsylvania returned to service after the troopers reenlisted and gained new troops, swelling in size to 1,300 men. However, two excellent regiments were lost to the cavalry corps. The 9th Pennsylvania Veteran Cavalry reenlisted but as it was returning to service it was assigned to the Military Department of Kentucky and did not participate in the Atlanta Campaign. The same occurred with the 2nd Michigan Veteran Volunteer Cavalry, which was garrisoned near Franklin, Tennessee. The 2nd Michigan Cavalry began the campaign with only 300 troopers. The 5th Iowa also experienced difficulty during its process of being "veteranized." The 5th Iowa was composed of companies from various states. During its reenlistment, three companies were assigned to Minnesota and formed an independent battalion no longer part of the 5th Iowa.[53]

Finally, Colonel Archibald Campbell, commander of McCook's First Brigade, left the war and returned to Michigan. Campbell was ill with consumption and died the next year. The citizen soldier who had boldly taken over of the reins of one of the premier Union cavalry brigades and proved himself worthy of following in the footsteps of Gordon Granger and Phil Sheridan was lost to the service.[54]

Campbell was replaced by Colonel Joseph Bartlett Dorr, son of a shipbuilder. He was born in 1825 in Hamburg, New York. Dorr's education was completed at Hamburg Academy and at the Westfield Seminary in Chautauqua, New York. The family moved to Jackson County, Iowa, in the 1840s. Dorr began working as a clerk in a store owned by the governor of Iowa,

Ansel Briggs. Next he started a newspaper, the *Democrat*, in Andrew, Iowa. Dorr made a career as a newspaperman and was an important political voice for the state, even surviving an assassination attempt. At the beginning of the war, he was elected first lieutenant of the 12th Iowa Infantry. He participated in the attack on Fort Donelson and was captured at the Battle of Shiloh. He escaped in May 1862, and early the next year he began recruiting a cavalry regiment over the objections of the governor of Iowa. Most of the 1,200-man 8th Iowa Cavalry regiment came from the two southern-most tiers of counties in the state, and the regiment was officially organized in October 1863.[55]

The first four months of 1864 were ones of preparation. The Union cavalry was rested and many new mounts replaced the worn out horses from the fall, particularly for the Second Cavalry Division. Of importance, the cavalry of the Army of the Cumberland now had four divisions with some new faces. George Crook was transferred and the solid Kenner Garrard commanded the Second Division. The reckless Judson Kilpatrick, an unknown for Elliott, commanded the Third Division, and the politically influential Alvan Gillem commanded the Tennessee division, the Fourth Division. Most of Gillem's Fourth Division remained in Tennessee protecting the rear from guerrillas and marauding Confederate cavalry. As Sherman's campaign to destroy Johnston's army began, Elliott, Garrard and Gillem had never commanded cavalry in an active campaign. Their abilities were yet to be proven.

Colonel Joseph Dorr, first colonel of the 8th Iowa Cavalry, assumed command of the First Brigade after Archibald Campbell left the cavalry (Special Collections, State Historical Society of Iowa, Des Moines).

10. Rocky Face Ridge to the Chattahoochee River, May–July 9, 1864

May God help them for man will not.
—First Sergeant John Bennett

May 7, 1864, marked the start one of the grandest and bloodiest campaigns of the Civil War, as Sherman began his march that would ultimately lead to Atlanta. Sherman's objective in May 1864 was the destruction of Johnston's army wherever it was located. Ultimately, Johnston would withdraw to Atlanta, but the city was not Sherman's objective as this campaign began. Sherman outnumbered Johnston about two-to-one. Sherman marched with about 100,000 men compared to 55,000 for Johnston, but Johnston would benefit from reinforcements throughout the campaign. Johnston had the advantage of a direct and short supply route and if he was fortunate he could choose the terrain on which to fight Sherman. Johnston had chosen his first line of defense well. He spent the winter and spring fortifying the area around Dalton, which would cost Sherman dearly if he chose to attack.

Sherman issued orders for the cavalry's initial advance on the Confederates at Dalton in Special Orders No. 35 on April 25. Major General George Stoneman commanded the Union cavalry for the Army of the Ohio on the left (east) flank of Sherman's forces, and Brigadier General Kenner Garrard was ordered to protect the Army of the Tennessee (commanded by Major General James McPherson) on the right flank since the Army of the Tennessee's cavalry was still in the Mississippi Valley. Then Sherman ordered George Thomas to organize McCook's and Kilpatrick's divisions of cavalry in the center of the advance. In addition, Sherman revealed his philosophy regarding the cavalry. He prohibited the practice of officers selecting companies of cavalry to serve as their escorts and personal bodyguards, stating it was "very ruinous to the cavalry arm of the service." He also outlined his thoughts about the value of cavalry, exclaiming, "Cavalry is most effective when appearing suddenly on the flank or rear of the enemy, as it usually is the advance of a column of infantry, and thus appearing it causes that idea, but if it hesitates in acting the effect is lost."[1]

As the Army of the Cumberland prepared for the campaign, Edward McCook's division moved to Cleveland, Tennessee, to protect the left flank of Major General Oliver Howard's Fourth Corps and also Schofield's Army of the Ohio, until Stoneman's cavalry, still in eastern Tennessee, arrived for that duty. La Grange's Second Brigade was assigned duty with Howard, and Dorr's First Brigade worked with Schofield. The cavalry's initial actions were designed to develop the positions of the enemy. Kenner Garrard's Second Division was also in the saddle with orders from Sherman to unite with McPherson's army on May 6 or 7 at LaFayette, Georgia. Kilpatrick's division was ordered to screen for Hooker's Twentieth Corps. In addition, Elliott ordered Alvan Gillem to place two Tennessee cavalry regiments on the railroad from Murfreesboro, Tennessee, to Stevenson, Alabama. Sherman had several months of provisions sitting in Nashville and the railroad was very important in getting those supplies to the army as it began its advance through enemy territory. The regular flow of supplies would prove to be a major issue during the entire Atlanta Campaign.[2]

Schofield was on the left flank, Thomas was in the lead in the center, and McPherson was on the right flank. The advance was to be coordinated with Grant's offensive in the east, but rain hampered Sherman's movements, and the tactical advance didn't start until May 7. With two great Union armies marching simultaneously, striking the "head" and the "heart" of the Confederacy, the Confederates would not be able to shift reinforcements from one location to the other.[3]

The first obstacle in the advance was Tunnel Hill through Chetoogeta Mountain, with a 1,400-foot railroad tunnel, about four miles south of Ringgold. Sherman ordered George Thomas to capture Tunnel Hill while Schofield moved to Varnell's, about seven miles east of Ringgold. Then Schofield and Thomas would advance toward Dalton. This would be only a demonstration, as Sherman's plan called for McPherson's Army of the Tennessee to march through Snake Creek Gap thirteen miles south of Dalton. The advance on Resaca through this gap could cut Johnston's supply and escape route to the south. Sherman hoped for a quick fight and planned to flank Johnston from the south and west while he remained behind his strong defenses at Dalton and Rocky Face Ridge.[4]

Sherman wanted his army nimble and not burdened down with baggage, and he ordered his

Major General William T. Sherman stated, "Cavalry is most effective when appearing suddenly on the flank or rear of the enemy" (Library of Congress).

commanders to march forward with as little encumbrance as possible. This decision would cause hardships to his troops during the campaign, but he needed to be able to act quickly. As ordered, Thomas successfully seized Tunnel Hill on May 7 without a fight and then marched on Rocky Face Ridge and Mill Creek Gap. On the Confederate side, Johnston had known for some days that Sherman was massing his troops and that a Union advance was imminent. When no movement was detected toward Rome, Johnston surmised Sherman's intent was along Rocky Face Ridge but he was unsure where the attack would come.[5]

As the campaign began, Elliott's cavalry corps marched with two important brigades left behind. Eli Long's veteran Ohio brigade was in Nashville being refitted and would not reach the army until June 6, and Louis Watkins' Kentucky brigade was stuck in Chattanooga without serviceable horses. Due to the lack of mounts, Watkins was given the unenviable task of trying to rehabilitate enough horses to be able to move with the army. He remarked, "The great majority of them being nothing but skin and bone, and the very best of them unfit for any kind of use." Unfortunately, Watkins' brigade would remain at the rear of the army through the entire campaign.[6]

Cavalry During the Atlanta Campaign, Army of the Cumberland
(c = captured, w = wounded, dis = discharged, k=killed)

BRIGADIER GENERAL WASHINGTON LAFAYETTE ELLIOTT—Chief of Cavalry

FIRST DIVISION
Brigadier General Edward M. McCook

First Brigade
Colonel Joseph B. Dorr (Command until 7/20; c. 7/30)
Colonel John Croxton (7/20)
Colonel James P. Brownlow (7/30–8/12)
Brigadier General John Croxton (8/13)

8th Iowa	Col. Horatio Barner
	Col. Joseph B. Dorr
	Maj. Richard Root
	Maj. John H. Isett
	Maj. Richard Root
4th Kentucky Mounted	Col. John Croxton
(Joined Division July 18)	Lt. Col. Robert M. Kelly (7/20)⁺
	Capt. James H. West (c. 7/31)
	Lt. Granville C. West
	Capt. James I. Hudnall
(⁺Kelly, c. 7/30)	
2nd Michigan	Maj. Leonidas S. Scranton
(Ordered to Franklin, TN June 29)	Lt. Col. Benjamin Smith
1st Tennessee	Lt. Col. James P. Brownlow

Third Brigade (at the rear of the army)
Colonel Louis D. Watkins
Colonel John Faulkner (7/5–8/10)

4th Kentucky	Col. Wickliffe Cooper
6th Kentucky	Maj. William H. Fidler

Second Brigade
Colonel Oscar H. La Grange (c. 5/9)
Lt. Col. James W. Stewart (c. 5/26)
Lt. Col. Horace P. Lamson
Lt. Col. William H. Torrey (7/21–30, w., c. 7/30)
Lt. Col. Horace P. Lamson

2nd Indiana	Lt. Col. James W. Stewart
	Maj. David A. Briggs
4th Indiana	Lt. Col. Horace P. Lamson
	Maj. George H. Purdy
	Capt. Albert J. Morley
1st Wisconsin	Maj. Nathan Paine (k. 5/9)
	Capt. H. Harnden (w. 5/26)
	Capt. Lewis M. B. Smith
	Maj. William H. Torrey
	Maj. N. Paine (k. 7/28)
	Capt. Lewis M. B. Smith

7th Kentucky	Col. John K. Faulkner
	Maj. Robert Collier
	Col. John K. Faulkner

Artillery
| Indiana Light, 18th Battery | Lt. William B. Rippetoe |
| | Capt. Moses Beck (9/7) |

SECOND DIVISION
Brigadier General Kenner Garrard

First Brigade		*Second Brigade (In N. Alabama until June 6)*	
Colonel Robert Minty		**Colonel Eli Long** (w. 8/20)	
4th Michigan	Lt. Col. Josiah B. Park	**1st Ohio**	Beroth B. Eggleston
	Maj. Frank W. Mix (w. 8/20)		Lt. Col. Thomas J. Patten
	Capt. L. Briggs Eldridge		
		3rd Ohio	Col. Charles B. Seidel
7th Pennsylvania	Col. William. B. Sipes		
	Maj. James F. Andreas	**4th Ohio**	Lt. Col. Oliver P. Robie
	Maj. William H. Jennings		
4th United States	Capt. James B. McIntyre		

Third Brigade (Mounted Infantry)
Colonel John T. Wilder (sick from June 14)
Col. Abram O. Miller

98th Illinois Mounted Infantry	Lt. Col. Edward Kitchell
123d Illinois	Lt. Col. Jonathan Biggs
17th Indiana Mounted Infantry	Lt. Col. Henry Jordan
	Maj. Jacob G. Vail
72nd Indiana Mounted Infantry	Col. Abram O. Miller
	Maj. Henry M. Carr
	Capt. Adam Pinkerton
	Lt. Col. Samuel C. Kirkpatrick

Artillery
| Chicago (Illinois) Board of Trade Battery | Lt. George I. Robinson |

THIRD DIVISION
Brigadier General Hugh Judson Kilpatrick (w. 5/13; resumed command 7/23)
Col. Eli H. Murray (5/13–5/21), Col. William W. Lowe, Brig. Gen. Judson Kilpatrick

First Brigade		*Second Brigade**	
Colonel William Lowe		**Colonel Charles C. Smith**	
Lieut. Col. Robert Klein		Maj. Thomas W. Sanderson (7/2–8/6)	
Lieut. Col. Matthewson T. Patrick		Lieut. Col. Fielder A. Jones	
Maj. J. Morris Young			
3rd Indiana (battalion)	Maj. Alfred Gaddis	**8th Indiana**	Col. Thomas J. Harrison
			Lt. Col. Fielder A. Jones.
			Maj. Thomas Herring
5th Iowa**	Maj. Harlon Baird		
Maj. J. Morris Young.	Maj. Thomas Graham		
	Capt. Martin Choumee		
		2nd Kentucky	Maj. William H. Effort
			Maj. Owen Star
		10th Ohio	Maj. Thomas W. Sanderson
			Maj. William Thayer
			Lt. Col. Thomas W. Sanderson

*Col. Thomas Harrison, commanding the brigade was captured July while in command of a provisional brigade of the 8th Indiana, 2nd Kentucky, 5th Iowa, 4th Tennessee, and Battery E, 1st Michigan Artillery. **5th Iowa in the field from July 2.

Third Brigade
Colonel Eli Murray
Col. Smith D. Atkins (5/13–5/21)
Col. Eli H. Murray

92nd Illinois Mounted Infantry	Col. Smith D. Atkins
	Capt. Matthew Van Buskirk
	Col Smith D. Atkins
	Maj. Albert Woodcock
	Col. Smith D. Atkins
3rd Kentucky	Maj. Lewis Wolfrey
	Lt. Col. Robert H. King
5th Kentucky	Lt. Col. Oliver L. Baldwin
	Maj. Christopher T. Cheek
	Col. Oliver L. Baldwin

Artillery
10th Wisconsin Battery	Capt. Yates V. Beebe

Opening Moves

By May 8, McPherson's Army of the Tennessee marched toward Snake Creek Gap, about ten miles west of Resaca. Garrard's Second Division, advancing from Tennessee, still had not reached him, and Sherman urged Garrard to hurry to McPherson. In the meantime, Edward McCook protected the left flank of Schofield's and Howard's infantry while George Stoneman's cavalry hurried forward from Kingston, Tennessee. Howard's infantry reached the summit of Rocky Face Ridge and attacked the Confederate position from the north along the ridge. John Newton's division successfully pushed the defenders to within a mile of Mill Creek Gap before he was stopped. Hooker's Twentieth Corps also unsuccessfully attacked at Dug Gap a few miles south of Buzzard's Roost while the Fourth and Fourteenth corps infantry demonstrated along the ridge. But the important line of march was that of McPherson, who seized Snake Creek Gap by the end of the day. But McPherson had only limited reconnaissance as he moved toward Resaca and only the 9th Illinois Mounted Infantry screened his advance. Because Kenner Garrard's cavalry lagged behind, much to Sherman's irritation, Sherman ordered Kilpatrick's Third Cavalry Division, which had been screening Hooker's corps, to McPherson's army. Sherman wrote, "Write to General Garrard at all events to keep up with infantry." Garrard, who had been guarding the railroads in central Tennessee, began his march to the front from Decherd, Tennessee, on May 4 and was not intentionally lagging. He was initially delayed with rain and mud, but since reaching Bridgeport he was moving as quickly as possible under the direction of Sherman's appointed guide, John Corse.[7]

Thomas and Schofield pressed the enemy on May 9, trying to keep Johnston's attention at Rocky Face Ridge and Buzzard's Roost while McPherson's Army of the Tennessee pushed toward Resaca with orders to destroy the Western & Atlantic Railroad. Kilpatrick happily worked with McPherson by scouting to the south and east of McPherson's advance and reported no surprises. McPherson reported that the Confederates were trying to rally to deal with his surprise arrival near Resaca. The 4th Georgia Cavalry resisted his advance without success and Wheeler began moving more cavalry from the north. McPherson exclaimed, "I think that Kilpatrick will attend to any cavalry that crosses the mountain from the north." At the end of the day, Garrard was still lagging and was at LaFayette, about ten miles to the west of Snake Creek Gap. In regard to the cavalry, McPherson wrote, "General Kilpatrick is very anxious to make the attempt to cut the railroad. General Garrard is in La Fayette tonight; says his horses are very much fatigued and short of forage; desires to remain there until his forage train comes down from Chattanooga." But Garrard's desire to rest his horses was not the message Sherman wanted to hear, and this began a conflict that would last for the entire campaign.[8]

As the sun rose on May 9, Johnston still believed Sherman's intention was to move against Rocky Face Ridge and Dalton, so he placed his heaviest defenses in these areas. McCook's cavalry, while awaiting the arrival of George Stoneman's cavalry, faced the heaviest threat along the Union left flank. McCook's cavalry skirmished daily with the enemy as the campaign began, and the fighting intensified on May 7 when Colonel Joseph Dorr's First Cavalry Brigade screened the Union infantry which advanced to Varnell's Station. Dorr met a determined defense and was being pushed back when La Grange's Second Brigade arrived and stabilized the line.

The next day La Grange's brigade scouted toward Dalton without incident, but May 9 was to prove a hard day for the Union cavalry. Schofield ordered Edward McCook to make a strong demonstration toward Dalton, and McCook selected Oscar La Grange's brigade to carry out the order. La Grange was repulsed by a strong Confederate defense during the day and initially Elliott received a message that La Grange was killed during the fighting. Fortunately, La Grange was just taken prisoner. McCook ordered La Grange to advance and develop the enemy's position. La Grange complied and rode ahead with the 4th Indiana Cavalry. After a two-mile ride, enemy pickets were found and driven to the rear.

But awaiting La Grange was a strong concentration of dismounted Confederate cavalry, Brigadier General William Wirt Allen's Alabama brigade and Colonel George Dibrell's Tennessee brigade. Two regiments, the 8th Confederate and 8th Texas, remained in the saddle. La Grange's brigade was stopped and the Confederate line moved forward. The attack of dismounted Confederate cavalry quickly sent the Union skirmishers back to their lines just as Lieutenant Colonel James Stewart arrived with the 2nd Indiana Cavalry, forming on the left of the 4th Indiana. The two regiments firing with their repeating Spencer rifles temporarily halted the Confederate advance.

Major General James McPherson commanded the Army of the Tennessee and worked well with Kenner Garrard (Library of Congress).

The 1st Wisconsin formed on the right of the Union cavalry's line and became the next target of the attack along that flank. The numbers were against La Grange's troopers and he ordered his men to move to the rear. The mounted Confederate cavalry, watching the situation, "rushed forward in overwhelming numbers, with an impetuosity not to be checked by our single line…. It was in the midst of this confusion that the gallant La Grange was captured, after two horses being shot under him," recorded Lieutenant Colonel Horace Lamson, 4th Indiana Cavalry. Sergeant Daniel Ferrier, 2nd Indiana Cavalry, came to La Grange's assistance as the first horse was killed. As La Grange rode with the Indiana cavalry, he was attacked by a young Confederate officer who demanded his surrender, but La Grange responded by shooting the officer, who in turn shot La Grange's horse. Ferrier rode up at that point and offered his horse to the colonel but La Grange declined saying, "I can run faster than you can, let me get hold of his tail." They tried to get away in this manner as the Confederates closed in on them.

The Union cavalry was taking fire and became disorganized. Ferrier saw the Union troops were being cut off and leapt from his horse and exclaimed, "Here! Take this horse—you can do ten times as much as I can, see how our men are jammed in that gate." La Grange was riding and trying to gain control of the situation when the second horse was killed and he was taken prisoner. Ferrier was also taken prisoner and was subsequently awarded the Medal of Honor for his sacrifice. Lieutenant Colonel James Stewart, 2nd Indiana Cavalry, assumed command of the brigade and extracted the remainder of the men, who rode back to Varnell's Station. The Second Brigade recorded five men killed, forty-two wounded, and ninety-three missing, including eleven officers. This was a bitter present for Edward McCook, who was informed he had just been promoted to the rank of brigadier general. Perry Goodrich, 1st Wisconsin Cavalry, wrote that La Grange was "naturally impetuous and daring, this time he was too heedless and headstrong." Sergeant Ferrier made an escape from his captors and ultimately made it back to the Union lines.[9]

The next day, May 10, Sherman refined his strategy. McPherson advanced to within sight of Resaca, but he was unable to reach the railroad. Sherman's new plan held Schofield and Howard in their current positions and moved the remainder of his troops to support McPherson. Sherman was close to achieving his objective of cutting Johnston from a direct southerly route to Atlanta. He saw an opportunity and exclaimed that the defenses at Dalton would do Johnston no good if the Union army was at Resaca. He also noted that it was as difficult to march out of Buzzard's Roost as it was for the Union infantry to march in.

During the day, Edward McCook's division maintained its vigil on Schofield's left flank and Kilpatrick continued his duty with McPherson. Stoneman and Garrard still had not arrived. The five-day delay in these two divisions reaching Sherman's infantry reinforced many of his negative opinions about the cavalry. Kilpatrick was at the front where Sherman needed him and he urged McPherson to allow his division to make an independent raid on the railroad near Resaca. This initiative was exactly what Sherman wanted and one the cavalry of the Army of the Cumberland had lacked so far. Sherman explained his opinion of the remainder of the cavalry in a message to Schofield on May 10: "I am mistrustful of cavalry; it moves so slow." Stoneman, who had a tarnished reputation based on actions at Chancellorsville, missed much of Sherman's scorn. Stoneman assumed command of the cavalry of the Army of the Ohio after Samuel Sturgis was dispatched to Kentucky to command cavalry there. Garrard, who had stopped to rest at LaFayette, was the commander who received most of Sherman's attention. Sherman needed Garrard with McPherson and ordered Thomas to demand that Garrard's division "proceed without delay" to McPherson's army. Sherman openly revealed his impressions of Garrard to McPherson: "Garrard has moved so slow that I doubt if he has the dash we need in a cavalry officer." But Garrard responded that McPherson had ordered him to remain in LaFayette and he had not been idle while there. He replied that he had a brigade scouting toward Rome and was awaiting its return. As a result he was forced to remain in place for the rest of the day and vowed to ride for McPherson as soon as possible.[10]

While Garrard was confused about the conflicting orders, Confederate general Joseph Johnston was confused about Sherman's intent. Joseph Wheeler's cavalry made a reconnaissance near Ringgold to find out where Sherman was concentrating his army. While Wheeler was having success against McCook's cavalry division the day before, he and Johnston missed the opportunity to discover McPherson's advance. Johnston had erroneously concluded any Federal advance on Resaca would be only from cavalry; instead, he was more concerned about the vulnerability of Rome and ordered the advance elements of Polk's infantry there. As Johnston received reinforcements at Rome, infantry units marched toward Dalton and two Confederate brigades were at Resaca when McPherson marched through Snake Creek Gap. In addition, an erroneous order sent a brigade of Confederate cavalry scouting in the wrong direction. Brigadier Warren Grigsby discovered the error in the order and his brigade of Confederate Kentucky cavalry collided with McPherson's infantry near Resaca.

Next, Sherman ordered Edward McCook and the recently arrived George Stoneman, along with Oliver Howard's Fourth Corps, to occupy the Confederates in Crow Valley and on Rocky Face Ridge while the remainder of the Union troops moved west and south toward Resaca on May 12. But on the day Sherman hoped to close the noose on Johnston, Johnston started evacuating Dalton and moved south to Resaca. On May 13, Kilpatrick, who had so boldly desired to cut the railroad, was pushed back toward the Union infantry line after a reconnaissance mission was met by a strong Confederate force. He complained that he was "constantly being flanked." While one of Kilpatrick's brigades fell back, Kilpatrick ordered reinforcements to stem the retreat. While rallying his troops he was shot in the groin and the ball exited his hip without damaging any of the large vessels. "The little brigadier commanding the division, always impatient and always brave, dashed ahead, riding into the thicket, and was shot by a Confederate not ten feet distant," wrote Colonel Sam Atkins, 92nd Illinois Mounted Infantry. Afterward, Colonel William Lowe was ordered forward to command the Third Division, and Colonel Eli Murray, 3rd Kentucky Cavalry, commanded until his arrival. Kilpatrick's wound would keep him away from the cavalry until July 23.[11]

Garrard's cavalry finally arrived and was also present for duty on May 12. He ordered his troopers to push toward Rome to challenge the concentration of Confederates there.

Within the first week of the campaign, the losses in the command of the Union cavalry were great. The

Major General George Stoneman commanded the cavalry of the Army of the Ohio (Library of Congress).

highly regarded Oscar La Grange, Second Brigade commander, was captured and Judson Kilpatrick was wounded and would be absent for two months. La Grange would be exchanged in August and would effectively miss the remainder of the Atlanta Campaign.

In addition, two organizational casualties occurred. Kenner Garrard was considered an ineffective cavalry commander by Sherman and if Garrard was to succeed, he needed to demonstrate he could push his cavalry as Sherman needed them. Finally, the stage was set for Washington Elliott, who was a commander without the ability to command. He had titular command but was disregarded. If the first week of the campaign was an example of the next four months, Elliott was in for an extended period of unhappiness. In his report of the campaign, he wrote that McCook served under the command of Schofield and he himself could not comment on the actions of Garrard since he received none of the orders that were sent to him. Elliott unhappily sat at cavalry headquarters as Sherman directed the cavalry as he needed, the only input coming from his army commanders.[12]

For the most part, the Union cavalry that was present for duty performed well during the opening phase of the campaign. Sherman was better served by his cavalry, despite some of his remarks, than was Johnston. Wheeler was generally blamed for the failure to develop Sherman's movements and communicate the threat to Resaca; however, other scholars conclude Johnston was negligent in ignoring the Union threat to Resaca. Sherman almost achieved a singular success during the first week of the campaign, but McPherson could not penetrate the Confederate line at Resaca. As a result, the campaign would extend for four months.[13]

Total Present for Duty, Army of the Cumberland and Army of the Ohio (Cavalry and Artillery)[14]

	April 30	May 31	June 30	July 31	Aug 31
Garrard's division	4,798	5,155	4,352	3,992	3,184
McCook's division	2,426	2,804	2,408	1,817	1,928
Kilpatrick's division	1,759	1,887	2,717	2,618	2,526
Stoneman's cavalry division*	2,951	2,891	Incomplete**	1,899	1,936
Total (Sherman's Records)***	12,455	12,908	12,039	10,517	9,394

*Army of the Ohio. ** Records are incomplete. Record show only 128 officers and no men present for duty. ***There is no explanation for the differences in Sherman's total and the cavalry division total. Sherman's total may include cavalry with the Army of the Tennessee, or more likely, detached cavalry, e.g., 15th Pennsylvania Cavalry.

The Battle of Resaca

While McCook contended with the enemy on the Union left flank, Sherman sent orders directly to Kenner Garrard to send his entire division southward toward Rome, destroying the railroad along the way. Sherman, who did not think Johnston would stay and fight at Resaca, wrote,

> Do this in your own way, but do it thoroughly and well. I will commence crossing McPherson about Lay's Ferry near the mouth of Snake Creek today; he will move on the Rome road; communicate with him but do not wait for him. If it be impossible to cross the Oostenaula with even a raiding force, then threaten Rome, and the Coosa below Rome ... the less wheels you have, the better; but I leave it to you—only act with the utmost possible energy and celerity.

Sherman believed Johnston was retreating. He also thought the Confederates were accompanied by wagon trains and would be vulnerable to a cavalry attack.[15]

Garrard pushed his division to Rome but Robert Minty's First Brigade could advance only to a point where Rome was in sight. Minty occupied the attention of the Confederates at Rome until he came under concentrated artillery fire. While Minty was involved in this action, Garrard attempted to cross the Oostenaula River and was unable to do so. A few days later communications were still confusing from Garrard's flank. Garrard was two days late crossing the Oostenaula but Sherman assumed he had crossed the river. He sent infantry to cross the river only to find Garrard still positioned at a tributary. However, Garrard was successful through the actions of Abram Miller's cavalry brigade of cutting the railroads, albeit a couple of days late.[16]

Garrard's initial failure at Rome was not taken well by Sherman. Also, in Garrard's report of his action to Sherman, he reported an inaccuracy about Nathan Bedford Forrest's being present in Rome and used this as an excuse for his failure. Sherman wrote sharply to Garrard on May 15:

> I regret exceedingly you did not avail yourself of the chance I gave you to cut the railroad. At the time you reached the bridge, Martin's cavalry was all that was on that flank, and they widely scattered. Forrest on the 6th was retreating before Sam. Sturgis, in Mississippi, toward Tupelo. In person he may be at Rome, but if his horses are there they can outmarch ours.... I want you to dash in and strike the retreating masses in flank and all round. Leave your artillery at the bridge, or better still, throw it into the Oostanaula, and operate rapidly against the enemy retreating by all roads for Atlanta.... Now, do not spare horse-flesh, but strike boldly on the flank of the retreating columns.

Sherman continued to communicate directly with cavalry commanders without the benefit of Washington Elliott.[17]

McPherson, fearing that his command could be cut off from the rest of Sherman's forces, did not aggressively attack the Confederate troops stationed at Resaca. McPherson's inability to take Resaca gave Johnston the time he needed to move his army southward. During May 13, Johnston's army prepared their defenses around Resaca as Sherman's armies converged on the town. Johnston's left flank rested on the Oostanaula River and the right flank reached the Connasauga River about two miles north of Resaca.

When Sherman arrived at Villanow, he chided McPherson for his caution and told him, "Well, Mac, you have missed the opportunity of a lifetime." General Johnston disagreed. He wrote that had McPherson attempted to take Resaca alone he would have faced all of Johnston's army the next morning. Meanwhile, David Stanley's division of Howard's corps slowly marched into Mill Creek Gap only to find the enemy gone. Howard telegraphed Sherman of the situation and Sherman ordered the Fourth Corps to march southward to Resaca. As Stanley marched into Dalton, he remarked, "I do not see how we could have forced his line at Dalton. It was the strongest military position I saw during the war." Stanley and others later questioned whether Sherman would have been more successful if the Army of the Cumberland, which was considerably larger, had been initially ordered to Snake Creek Gap.[18]

On May 13, McPherson's army pushed toward Resaca and Thomas ordered the Army of the Cumberland to push ahead. Schofield's Army of the Ohio followed Howard's Fourth Corps south toward Resaca. The fighting at Resaca began in earnest on May 14 as the Union infantry moved against the entrenched soldiers of Johnston's army. During the day, the battle was a bloody affair and no major gains being made by Sherman.

David Stanley's First Division of the Fourth Corps marched along the extreme left flank of the Union armies, and he encountered only a few Confederate pickets to slow his march. While Joseph Wheeler's cavalry had missed Sherman's movement to Snake Creek Gap, he was back on duty on May 13–14 slowing the Union advance and allowing the Confederate infantry time to prepare strong defenses at Resaca. By 2:00 p.m. Stanley's three brigades had formed a battle line about two miles north of Resaca. Being the left flank of the army, he began to build defenses and had orders to hold the line along the Dalton Road. Before the defenses were completed, Stanley observed Confederate infantry massing for an attack. He wasted no time in reporting his observations to the Fourth Corps commander, Howard, who rode in person to George Thomas to report the situation. Wisely, Stanley withdrew his artillery commanded by Captain Peter Simonson to a position that would cover the open ground in front of his lines. Wheeler reported to Johnston that Stanley's flank was vulnerable to a concentrated attack of infantry. John Bell Hood unleashed a vicious attack on the Union left flank, which was saved by Stanley's unwillingness to yield, Simonson's superb skill with artillery, and the timely arrival of reinforcements from Hooker.[19]

The fiery surgeon of the 2nd Michigan Cavalry, Dr. George Ranney, a twenty-four-year-old native of New York, assisted with Stanley's wounded as his lines were broken by the Confederate attack. Ranney, who had a reputation of doing dangerous acts to aid the wounded, again lived up to his reputation. While the battle was raging between the Union and Confederate troops, he ran through the hail of lead from both sides to rescue a wounded soldier. For this action specifically, and for numerous other selfless acts, Ranney was awarded the Medal of Honor.[20]

Two Federal mistakes led to the attack on Stanley. One revealed the unfamiliarity of the Union command with the geography near Resaca. It was hoped that the Union line would stretch to the Connasauga River, but Howard observed, "The bend of the river was so great that an entire corps, thrust in, could hardly have filled the opening." The other issue was the missing cavalry support on the left flank. Edward McCook received a late order and had his hands full during the day and simply couldn't reach Stanley's flank. He explained in a message to Washington Elliott the evening after the attack:

> I received your dispatch directing me to move with my column to support a brigade and battery at 10:30 p.m. It was dated 4:30. No brigade or battery has passed on the road indicated as yet. I have sent a note to General Stanley about it. My command was engaged several times today and lost about 40 killed and wounded. I drove the enemy to the ridge on General Stanley's left, but could not dislodge them. I am doing all I can to cover the left and have every road regularly patrolled.[21]

But Johnston did not retreat from Resaca as Sherman expected. On May 15, the fighting continued along the Union and Confederate lines in another bloody day. At nightfall the casualties of the two armies were relatively equal—Sherman reported 2,747 and Johnston 2,800 losses at the two-day battle. During the night of May 15, Johnston did withdraw and marched for Adairsville. After the previous day's battle, the Union soldiers were surprised on the morning of May 16 to find Johnston gone. They soon saw smoke billowing up in the town and realized the bridge across the river was afire.

On to the Etowah River

On May 16, Sherman wired Henry Halleck in Washington that Resaca was in Union hands and that Johnston's army was retreating toward the Etowah River. He exclaimed that

Garrard, who commanded two elite brigades—Robert Minty's First Brigade and John Wilder's Third Brigade—and Stoneman's cavalry divisions were pushing ahead attempting to cut off Johnston's retreat. Facing the Union advance was Wheeler's cavalry, contesting the pursuit and giving Johnston time to find his next place to make a stand. Garrard, who hoped to change Sherman's impression of him as a commander, captured a bridge over the Oostanaula River about eight miles from Rome. Edward McCook's and Eli Murray's divisions of Union cavalry marched in front of Sherman's column of infantry developing the route of the Confederate retreat.[22]

The Union infantry marched south through and around Calhoun and then toward Adairsville, about fifteen miles south of Resaca. General Joseph Johnston decided to make his next stand at Adairsville, but he found the valley where he planned to fight too wide to defend against the number of Union troops he was facing. So, again the march proceeded southward, toward Cartersville. Johnston, after consulting with his commanders, decided to march to Cassville, about ten miles north of the Etowah River, by two roads, one via Kingston and the other directly over the Gravelly Plateau. He hoped to induce the Union armies also to divide and march down each of the roads. He also wanted to make Sherman believe the majority of his army was entrenched at Kingston. His intent was to strike the Union column marching down the Cassville Road and destroy it before the other column marching via Kingston came to its aid. As Johnston had hoped, Sherman hurried his three armies forward. He ordered Stoneman and Garrard to strike the railroads to the east and west of Kingston, limiting Johnston's route of retreat and source of supplies and reinforcements; but he sacrificed the important intelligence gathering role of the cavalry.

Robert Minty's cavalry brigade rode toward Kingston on May 17 and the 4th Michigan Cavalry successfully drove the Confederate pickets. Minty's cavalry fought to within a mile of Kingston. Joseph Vale, 7th Pennsylvania Cavalry, recorded, "The boys of the Fourth Michigan had an idea that they could whip the whole rebel army if they only had a fair chance." Minty knew McPherson's infantry was marching in support and he decided to allow the 4th Michigan to charge forward. They "boldly attacked the whole rebel force" in front of them, but their impetuosity was too much. The Confederate infantry was firmly in place behind barricades with cavalry support. When Minty's attack was stopped by the Confederate defenses, the Confederate cavalry charged, surrounding the 4th Michigan. The regiment used their sabers to cut their way out but not before having thirteen officers and men killed or mortally wounded and another eighteen wounded.[23]

Meanwhile, Kenner Garrard was trying to carry out his orders to destroy the railroad into Rome. Sherman had no expectation that Johnston would fight north of the Etowah but he was puzzled by Johnston's retreat toward Kingston. He wanted his cavalry to limit any rapid movement of Confederates to or from Kingston via the railroad. Sherman wrote to Schofield on May 18: "All the signs continue of Johnston's having retreated on Kingston, and why he should lead to Kingston, if he designs to cover his trains to Cartersville, I do not see." Nonetheless, Sherman fell for the ruse. Minty's brigade entered Kingston on May 18 and found the enemy was gone, but Abram Miller's mounted infantry brigade was involved in a fight with Confederate cavalry. Alva Griest, 72nd Indiana Mounted Infantry, recorded in his journal, "Had just time to complete these arrangements when the Rebels drove our pickets in and charged us to the number of near 1,000 with demoniac yells. Our boys lay quiet, until they were within 200 yards, then for a few moments our Spencers shot forth a stream of blazing fire. This was more than the poor fellows could stand." In fact, by May 19 Johnston redeployed the bulk of his army near Cassville while Sherman converged on Kingston.[24]

Johnston concluded he had retreated enough and he turned to face part of Sherman's army. He hoped to find Howard's Fourth Corps, Hooker's Twentieth Corps, and the Twenty-third Corps marching toward Cassville. He also hoped McPherson's three corps and Thomas's Fourteenth Corps were still marching toward Kingston. Johnston had assembled more than 70,000 troops—Hood's, Hardee's, Polk's, and Wheeler's corps—as he prepared to crush Sherman's left flank.

On May 19 the ever-present Confederate cavalry pickets slowed the march of the Union infantry converging on Cassville. Wheeler's cavalry served as rear guard, as it would throughout the campaign, a task at which it was adept. The Confederate cavalry laid obstructions in the road about every thousand yards and posted skirmishers behind the barricades. The Union infantry had to push the defenders from each obstruction, only to find another barricade in their front.

The Twentieth Corps and the Twenty-third Corps marched on the road directly to Cassville over the Gravelly Plateau. The rest of Sherman's troops followed Hardee's corps down the Hall Mountain Road that paralleled the Western & Atlantic RR. Hardee made the intended demonstration at Kingston and then withdraw toward Cassville with Union infantry columns following. The Confederate main line was soon found in the hills east of Cassville and the Union line marched toward it. The Fourth Corps moved down the Western & Atlantic Railroad track in an attempt to push Hardee's Confederate infantry back into the main Confederate line. After some stiff skirmishing the Confederates withdrew toward Cassville. Then David Stanley saw what was before him: "[T]he enemy was discovered, formed in three lines of battle perpendicular to the road, and very soon after the appearance of the head of the column the entire rebel line advanced toward us." The Union infantry column deployed in battle line and the enemy began withdrawing. As the infantry marched forward, they were puzzled by the actions of the Confederate army. The withdrawal resulted due to the arrival of the Union cavalry, which caused Johnston to change his plan of attack.[25]

Johnston had positioned Polk's corps north of Cassville with Hood's corps to Polk's right. The plan called for the Federal advance to encounter Polk, and then Hood would attack the flank. After Hood was in position, he was surprised by reports of Union troops behind him. It was part of Edward McCook's First Division that generated the alarm. McCook had gotten lost by turning too soon on the Canton Road, but his emergence behind Hood was fortuitous for the Federals. Several thousand Union cavalrymen converging on Hood's exposed flank caused him to postpone his attack. McCook and Stoneman, through this serendipitous encounter, saved many lives at Cassville. The Union cavalry happened on the scene because they were following orders to destroy the railroad between Cass Station and the Etowah River. Edward McCook reported to Washington Elliott, "I have had General Stoneman's advance all day, and met large bodies of the enemy's infantry. Their force was too formidable to do anything more than skirmish with." Historian Albert Castel remarked, "It is the most valuable service that will be performed by Sherman's cavalry during the entire campaign."[26]

At the time, Edward McCook was unaware of the significance of the service he had provided. He was tired and correctly felt he had carried the majority of the cavalry duty on the Union left flank. He had skirmished all the way to Cassville but never reached the town. As he got closer, he saw the rows of Confederate infantry. He dismounted his troopers and fell into line and exchanged fire throughout the day. He was pushed back when Major General Carter Stevenson's infantry moved toward his position. Later, Stoneman ordered McCook to charge the enemy. McCook was incredulous and wrote to Elliott there was nothing but infantry to his front. McCook recorded some successes: "I drove them from two lines of rifle-pits. The Second Indiana in a saber charge captured one entire company of Eighteenth Alabama. Part of the Eighth Iowa in a charge also killed and captured a number of the enemy." Daniel Bischard, 8th Iowa, recorded some spectacular luck as his regiment charged:

> Made a charge at Cassville and in the charge our company lost two men killed dead and one wounded and 4 horses killed dead. We charged the rebel Cavalry out from behind a row of breastworks and while we was making a charge the rebel infantry shot into us and also six rebel batteries was a pouring the shot and shells to us. It looks to me as if they would have killed us all but they overshot us and the batteries couldn't get range of us as we moved over the ground so fast they didn't have time.

McCook "performed admirably" in his assigned mission from Stoneman. McCook's artillery destroyed one of the enemy's cannons and caisson, which had to be abandoned. After the action, he concluded, "Both men and horses of my division need rest. They have been in the saddle from eighteen to twenty hours each day since the 2d of this month."[27]

Reacting to reports that cavalry was in his rear, Hood moved his corps to address this threat and thereby ruined the chance to launch a flank attack on Union infantry approaching the town from the north. Still, Union infantry approached the veterans of Hardee's corps, who felt capable of making their own attack against the Federals approaching from the west; however, Hood's failure to spring the trap caused Johnston to pull the Confederate line—including Hardee's corps—onto the hills east and south of Cassville.[28]

Johnston extended his army along a three-mile front with Hood on the right, Polk in the center, and Hardee on the left. In the meantime, the Union infantry corps converged on Johnston's army and fell into a battle line. Then 40 Union cannons opened fire that continued until after dark. During the evening, Polk and Hood convinced Johnston of the vulnerability of the Confederate position and Johnston decided to withdraw again.

While the lines of infantry faced each other, Robert Minty's Cavalry Brigade rode hard for Gillem's Bridge over the Etowah River on May 19. Minty rode five miles to the bridge at the cost of 300 of horses being rendered unsuitable for further duty. Realizing the value the bridge held in the pursuit of Johnston, Minty built barricades and breastworks and held the bridge until Colonel Eli Murray's Third Cavalry Division moved forward to take over as guards. Benjamin Nourse, Chicago Board of Trade Battery, recorded in his diary that his artillery was unlimbered and covered the approaches to the bridge. Nourse wrote that Confederates advanced on the bridge but found it too well guarded and broke off the attack.[29]

May 19 was also a good day for Kenner Garrard and his division, which was performing good service on the Union right flank. Garrard captured two bridges and two fords over the Etowah River, and these would be used by Sherman's armies. Garrard also established communications between McPherson and the Union troops that had recently occupied Rome.[30]

By the end of May 20, the Confederates were across the Etowah and deploying along the Allatoona Range, destroying bridges as they retreated. George Stoneman, commanding the cavalry for the Army of the Ohio, had failed to destroy the railroads as Sherman had ordered and really had not performed notable service in the campaign. Stoneman wrote to Sherman and provided several excuses for his failure to accomplish his tasks. Stoneman, who always seemed to be able to blame someone else, wrote, "One great difficulty I have to contend against is the utter incompetency of subordinate officers. I have to post and put in every regiment myself and send out every party. I know that my movements appear tardy, but I can't help it; it is next to impossible to get up a trot even on the field." Stoneman complained that he had only 1,200 horses that could make an aggressive march, due to the poor overall condition of his division; but he acknowledged he had 2,500 troopers he could bring into battle if they could be moved to the right location. Then Stoneman revealed a strategy that would save his division from much activity at the expense of Edward McCook's division:

> McCook, with a much stronger and older force than mine, is withdrawn from the flank to the center. I don't say this in any spirit of complaint; I will take what is given me, and do the best I can with it, both for my own sake and that of the service. No one, not even yourself, has been more anxious to strike the railroad than I have.[31]

Fortunately for all, Sherman ordered a rest of three days, May 20–22, for his troops. The men had marched hard for over two weeks and needed a rest. Captain Daniel Wait Howe, 79th Indiana Infantry, wrote to his mother about the how the Confederates felt about facing the three armies Sherman commanded:

> I won't say how many men we do have but we had so many at Resaca that thousands were not brought into action simply because there was no room to put them. A rebel writing from Dalton speaks of Sherman as giving commands like this, "Attention: Creation; by Kingdoms right-wheel."[32]

By the time Sherman's armies reached the defenses along the bluffs of the Etowah River, Edward McCook remarked, "both men and horses of my division need[ed] rest" (Library of Congress).

New Hope Church, Pickett's Mill, Dallas

On May 23, Sherman began the next phase of the campaign as his armies crossed the Etowah River. He expected Johnston to move his army to Allatoona, a formidable geographic obstacle. Several years earlier Sherman had participated in an army survey of the area and he now concluded he would not try to assault Johnston at this location. Instead, he decided to advance on Dallas, Georgia, about fifteen miles south of the Etowah River and west of Allatoona. Next, he planned to advance on Marietta, fifteen miles east of Dallas. He decided to maneuver around the Allatoona Mountains, then swing east and cut Johnston off from Atlanta, just as he had planned at Resaca.

Meanwhile, Sherman ordered Major General Francis Blair's Seventeenth Corps, accompanied by Colonel Eli Long's cavalry brigade, to the front from their duty in Alabama and Tennessee. And when Sherman crossed the Etowah River Colonel William Lowe, commanding the Third Cavalry Division, remained in Kingston with orders to protect the Union supply line and to hold the various fords and bridges across the river. The Union cavalry would move toward Dallas with three cavalry divisions—Stoneman on the left, McCook in the center, and Garrard on the right.[33]

Johnston countered Sherman's advance by marching two-thirds of his army—Hardee and Polk—to Dallas but he initially retained Hood at Allatoona. He also sent Wheeler's cavalry north of the Etowah River to reconnoiter the Union advance on May 23. Ironically, not everyone wanted the cavalry near their command, Major General Daniel Butterfield wrote to Hooker: "McCook's cavalry command is camped on my left [and] ... their presence here will only lead to confusion." Butterfield felt in case of attack, the cavalry would throw his division into disorder.[34]

Butterfield didn't have to worry long, because the next day Edward McCook moved forward to cover the advance of the Hooker's Twentieth Corps as it demonstrated toward Allatoona while Garrard rode west and south of Dallas reconnoitering the town. Garrard skirmished throughout the day. Captain Heber Thompson, 7th Pennsylvania Cavalry, recorded the Confederate cavalry resisted their reconnaissance: "Rebs came up handsomely several times and each time driven back." Also, during the day Wheeler's cavalry attacked a supply train north of the Etowah River, burning twenty wagons and carrying off several others. In response, Colonel William Lowe sent his Third Cavalry Division to protect the other supply trains from further attacks.[35]

On the morning of May 25, the three Confederate infantry corps moved to establish a line east of Dallas. Hood's corps arrived first as Hardee marched toward Dallas and Polk had yet to arrive. Hood covered the line near New Hope Church, about two miles northeast of Dallas. That afternoon Joseph Hooker's Twentieth Corps advanced and a bloody fight erupted between Hood and Hooker's troops which ended with Hooker withdrawing after suffering about 1,600 casualties.

The next day, Edward McCook's cavalry clashed with the enemy at Burnt Church and claimed eighty of the enemy killed and another fifty-two as prisoners. McCook reported,

> I attacked Wheeler's whole cavalry force at 4:30 this afternoon, inflicting severe loss upon him and taking 52 prisoners. On being attacked he retreated with a train toward Acworth. I have lost Lieutenant-Colonel Stewart, commanding Second Brigade, who is missing, and about 25 men and officers killed and wounded. I propose pushing him still farther tonight. After breaking their cavalry line I struck their infantry. I have turned their cavalry force toward Acworth. General Stoneman has arrived with one brigade.[36]

10. Rocky Face Ridge to the Chattahoochee River　　　227

View of the countryside at New Hope Church, Georgia, where the bloody battle was fought on May 25, 1864 (Library of Congress).

Lieutenant Colonel Horace Lamson, commanding McCook's 2nd Brigade on May 26, moved his brigade to within a mile of the Ackworth and Dallas Road and discovered a column of Confederate cavalry moving ahead accompanied by a supply train. Lamson attacked into the flank of the enemy at 4:00 p.m. and surprised the Southern troopers. The Union cavalry won the day in a hard fight in which several Confederate troopers were killed, wounded and captured. Captain Lewis Smith, 1st Wisconsin, recorded that the 1st Wisconsin and the 4th Indiana charged the 4th Georgia Cavalry near Burnt Church about seven miles northeast of Dallas. Smith supported the claim of a Union victory during the skirmish. Lieutenant Colonel James Stewart, 4th Indiana Cavalry, who had commanded the brigade since Oscar La Grange had been captured earlier in the campaign, was wounded during the fighting and taken prisoner. Stewart, a merchant and hotel owner from Terre Haute, was held as a prisoner and would not be exchanged until September. In addition, Captain Henry Harnden, 1st Wisconsin Cavalry, was shot in the shoulder while leading the charge of his regiment.[37] Meanwhile, on McPherson's flank Garrard found the flank of the enemy with Robert Minty's brigade and diverted four regiments of Confederate cavalry to fight Minty along the flank instead of resisting McPherson's advance.[38]

　　The next day, May 27, the bloody fight at Pickett's Mill occurred about three miles east of New Hope Church when Oliver Howard was ordered to assault the Confederate position. The terrain was so densely wooded it was difficult to maneuver and observe the enemy. Howard assumed he was attacking an exposed flank of Johnston's army, only to find a strong

Confederate defensive line manned mostly by Cleburne's division. As Howard tried to find the Confederate right he was also strongly resisted by Kelly's Confederate cavalry division. As Howard attacked, he did so in a piecemeal fashion when each brigade ran into resistance; others moved to the left to try to turn the flank. Cleburne responded each time with his own moves to his right. The Union loss in the disastrous attack totaled 1,600 men in Brigadier General William Hazen's, Colonel William Gibson's and Colonel Frederick Knefler's brigades. Cleburne recorded about 500 casualties among his defenders.

On May 28, Edward McCook's cavalry held the Marietta Road and repulsed a determined attack by dismounted Confederate cavalry. Stoneman's cavalry was to his right, but McCook formed the end of the line. In regard to the Confederate attack, McCook reported, "The most stubborn and persistent one I have seen them make during this campaign." He observed infantry and cavalry to his front and left. When he asked for support from the infantry, he was told he would not receive any help. McCook had grown into an excellent and underappreciated cavalry officer. He ended his communication to Elliott bitterly remarking, "Privately, this thing of covering the flank of the infantry seems to be a one-sided affair; if they are attacked I am to pitch in, while, if I was attacked by a superior force I can expect no assistance." During the fight, James Brownlow's 1st Tennessee was ordered to take a hill where Confederate artillery was shelling McCook's men. Brownlow fought for much of the morning before capturing it and then repulsed an attempt to retake the hill. Fortunately, McCook was able to hold on throughout the day and night.[39]

While McCook held his line, Johnston took two important actions during the day. First, he sent Hood to attempt to flank the Federal left, but Hood did not attack when he found he faced a strongly entrenched position. Next, Johnston sent two cavalry brigades and Major General William Bate's infantry division to develop McPherson's position along the Union right flank. In what was to be called the Battle of Dallas, Bate pushed forward but was unsuccessful in a bloody fight, with estimated losses of 2,400 for the Union forces and 3,000 for the Confederates. Garrard's cavalry provided protection along the right flank of McPherson's army and fought the Confederate cavalry along that flank. All of William Jackson's Confederate cavalry division was involved in this attack. Armstrong and Ross attacked, with the latter taking the Union line in the flank. Ferguson's brigade moved into the rear where it fought Miller's mounted infantry brigade, which played a significant role in repulsing the attack.

While the fighting was taking place, Eli Long's Second Brigade of veteran Ohio cavalry rode from Tennessee toward Rome, Georgia. Phillip Roddey's Confederate cavalry attacked Long at Moulton, Alabama, while in camp early on May 29. George Kryder, 3rd Ohio Cavalry, wrote to his family about the incident:

> The next day we started for Moulton, that is our brigade, and the infantry went back towards Decatur and the Rebs followed us up and thought [they] would capture our brigade. There were 5 regiments and four companies of them and only three Regts of us, the 1st, 3rd, and 4th Ohio, and we had two pieces artillery with us and they had 8 pieces ... [and] just about daylight they advanced in force and we had to fall back. They brought their artillery and shelled us but done us no damage and on they came with their yells and cheers but they could not scare the 2nd Brigade. Unexpected as they came upon us it did not take Col. Long a great while to form his line and when the Rebs came down to our lines they run against a circumstance and quit their yelling and our boys commenced yelling and drove them back with a loss of 13 killed and about 60 wounded and 32 prisoners.[40]

After a severe fight, Roddey was driven off with about equal casualties on both sides. One of the Confederate prisoners revealed that Roddey told his men that the attack would be successful because these were green recruits heading for the front. Thomas Crofts, 3rd Ohio Cavalry, replied, "It's the same old regiment, only it had got new clothes." Roddey chose the most experienced brigade in the Union cavalry of the Army of the Cumberland to attack. The attack did not stop Long from reaching the Union columns in early June.[41]

Disturbing was a report from the 7th Pennsylvania Cavalry about the hard service the cavalry was performing in May 1864. Major William Jennings recorded many of the horses actually starved to death in May. On May 22, the officers of the regiments reported that 76 horses died of starvation due to daily movements and inability to find forage. From May 26 through June 2, another 134 were lost in one battalion, 101 of this number due to starvation. The same situation occurred throughout the corps. Just as soldiers and troopers were lost, so the horses were lost to attrition. Colonel Joseph Dorr, commanding the First Brigade, reported the horses died by the hundreds, generally through starvation, and they were not being replaced fast enough. Edward McCook echoed the other messages when he reported horses were dying on duty. He wrote to Elliott saying "five from one company dropped on picket this morning, totally exhausted for want of something to eat." Consequently, some of the cavalry regiments were rotated across the Etowah River to forage. The cavalry was following the brutality of Sherman's orders not to "spare the horseflesh." Sherman was never in the cavalry and perhaps it was this unfamiliarity with the requirements of the mounts that caused him to push the animals beyond their limits. There were not enough horses to replace those lost and this loss would greatly reduce the effectiveness of the cavalry later in the campaign.[42]

On to the Chattahoochee

General Joseph Johnston successfully stopped Sherman's advance near Dallas when he moved his army from Allatoona and formed an arc in front of Sherman. Sherman needed to find a way around this Confederate line, and concluded if the Confederate army was at Dallas then Allatoona was undefended. Sherman initially wanted to bring Major General Frank Blair's Seventeenth Corps to Rome and then onto Allatoona to seize this important location. On May 31, Blair's infantry and cavalry still lagged several days behind, so Sherman ordered Kenner Garrard's cavalry division to ride to Allatoona and capture the pass. Sherman told Garrard if he found the enemy along the way to ride over them and seize the pass. Sherman stressed the importance of the mission, "Do not be deterred by appearances, but act boldly and promptly; the success of our movement depends on our having Allatoona Pass." Sherman also sent George Stoneman's division to Allatoona Pass while Edward McCook engaged the enemy in a diversion in his front. Stoneman claimed one end of the pass and Garrard the other. Of great importance at Allatoona was the railroad that Sherman needed.[43]

The capture of Allatoona gave hope to Sherman's armies that they would soon be back to a more permanent supply line and away from what they called the "hell hole." The name had a special meaning for the local population caught in the struggle between Sherman and Johnston. First Sergeant John Bennett, 4th Michigan Cavalry, wrote to his wife the sadness he saw among the local citizens:

> Whenever we have a fight, we can see women & children cowering nearby scared to death, praying to God to protect them & holding up both hands to us not to hurt them. Little children crying with fear & hunger. This, you know, is hard, even to the wicked. There is thousands of women & children crying for bread.... I really believe they will die of hunger.... May God help them for man will not.[44]

Sherman wired to Henry Halleck that, despite some bloody fights that had taken place, no real battle had occurred, only a "universal skirmish" all along the front. The Union armies were now called on to perform the tricky maneuver of extricating McPherson's troops from the enemy they faced, and performing an eastward movement. The movement began well. McPherson moved the Army of the Tennessee from Dallas to New Hope Church by June 2 as both Thomas and Schofield shifted to the east.[45]

During this shift, Captain James McIntyre did "some big swearing" as his 4th U.S. Cavalry rode toward the Union infantry line near Dallas. Union troops began firing on his men and he couldn't understand this until he turned in his saddle and saw that his men had ridden for so long their blue uniforms were covered with a light brown dust, making them appear to be Confederate cavalry. Fortunately, the fire was so poor only one horse was killed and another was wounded.[46]

The shift of the Union Army toward the east continued through June 4, and Johnston moved his army to Lost Mountain, about six miles southeast, to meet the redeployment of Sherman's armies. The Confederate line, ten miles long, stretched from Lost Mountain to Brushy Mountain. Sherman knew the line was too long for Johnston to adequately defend. Sherman revealed on June 5 that he expected Johnston would next fight at Kennesaw Mountain and he was determined not make any frontal assaults on entrenched Confederate lines. Sherman's armies were positioned to march in a more southerly direction with Allatoona and the railroad in the rear, but he paused again. He wanted the bridge over the Etowah River to be rebuilt to carry supplies and he wanted Major General Frank Blair's infantry and Eli Long's cavalry ready for the action before he marched again.[47]

On June 10, Sherman pushed forward. With the shifts in Sherman's infantry, Kenner Garrard rode on the left flank of the army with McPherson, and Stoneman covered the right flank with Schofield's Army of the Ohio. Thomas's Army of the Cumberland advanced in the center and Edward McCook protected the rear of the column. Just as Sherman's advance began on June 10, he sent Kenner Garrard a message urging his increased aggressiveness. Sherman had just received a message that his supply line had been attacked near Calhoun and he asked why, if the enemy could make such progress, his cavalry could not do the same. The threats to McPherson's flanks kept Garrard posted on duty near Sherman's infantry, but the seed was there for future cavalry actions in the campaign.[48]

The damage at the rear of the Union armies resulted from the Confederates placing a torpedo on the rail tracks, which caused an engine and two cars to be derailed. William Lowe's Third Cavalry Division drove off the raiders and saved a building being threatened by the raiders at Calhoun. Once Lowe organized a pursuit, the raiders dissolved into the countryside. By June 11, the Union armies converged on a line of defenses and fell into line about 500 yards from the bases of Brushy Mountain, Pine Mountain and Lost Mountain. Sherman's advance was blocked when he found Johnston's army behind firm entrenchments. The railroad running through Allatoona reopened and continued to resupply Sherman's armies, despite the temporary setbacks.[49]

McCook, Garrard, Stoneman and Lowe continued to scout and guard the armies' flanks. All had extensive territory to guard. Kenner Garrard's troopers covered from north of the Etowah to the flank of his army, about ten miles. On June 14, Garrard was ordered to try to establish a foothold on the ridge between Brushy Mountain and Kennesaw Mountain and McCook and Stoneman were ordered to reconnoiter Lost Mountain to do the same. Sherman probed the center at Gilgal Church and Lattice's Farm while he used the cavalry to turn the Confederate line at Lost Mountain, causing Johnston to swing part of his line back to Mud Creek. The Confederate defenders at Lost Mountain were still too strong for the cavalry on the Union right and repulsed any attempt to claim the mountain. The 4th Indiana and 1st Tennessee reached the first line of barricades on the west side of the mountain but could not proceed farther. However, by June 17, Johnston had again withdrawn and McCook and Stoneman claimed Lost Mountain.[50]

Eli Long's cavalry on the left flank had a tough fight on June 15: "At 2 p.m. I attacked General Wheeler's cavalry command, and fought him for about an hour, but was at length compelled to fall back, Wheeler being well fortified, and intrenched beyond our power to drive him out. In this engagement we lost 2 killed, 16 wounded, and 2 missing."[51]

The timbre of the communications within the Union cavalry revealed that the perception of the organization and its performance were not favorable. Sherman's direct control of the cavalry, which he had little experience with and little confidence in, caused tensions throughout his army. He wrote to Ulysses Grant on June 18: "Our cavalry is dwindling away. We cannot get full forage and have to graze, so that the cavalry is always unable to attempt anything. Garrard is over cautious and I think Stoneman is lazy.... Each has had fine chances of cutting in but is easily checked by the appearance of an enemy." Only Edward McCook escaped Sherman's criticism. But McCook had trouble of his own with Elliott, and only McCook and Lowe regularly reported directly to Elliott, who was hypercritical of his most effective cavalry commander. A few days before, McCook had misinterpreted an order from Elliott and apologized for the error, although nothing significant had occurred. On June 17, McCook sent an overly formal reply to an order from Elliott directing McCook to deal with some Confederate cavalry near Moon's Station. Despite the fact Major General Stoneman had troopers on the way to Moon's Station, McCook also had to send troopers of his own. He appeared to be nearing the end of his rope when his sent his reply to Elliott: "I sent a force out, fearing that General Stoneman's taking the responsibility might not be sufficient reason in your eyes for not obeying your order should anything happen." McCook's response revealed a superior officer who appeared to have little to do and who was unfamiliar with the situations McCook faced.[52]

Kennesaw Mountain, Noonday Creek and Frustration for the Cavalry

Cavalry actions centered at Noonday Creek continued for two weeks as Sherman's infantry advanced toward Kennesaw Mountain. Garrard had not been idle on the left flank and began his actions in this area, about four miles northeast of Kennesaw Mountain, on June 9 when his cavalry charged Confederate cavalry at Rocky Hill and drove them to the hill in front of Big Shanty. The efforts of Miller's mounted infantry brigade again played an important role in the Union actions. Heber Thompson, 7th Pennsylvania, noted in his diary, "Wilder's men do fight splendidly. They hesitate at nothing." Benjamin Nourse, Chicago Board of Trade Artillery, wrote in his diary the Confederates made three attempts to stop the Union advance and were unsuccessful each time. The attack succeeded in driving the Confederates back to their main lines. Garrard made another determined charge into three lines of Confederates: two lines of Martin's cavalry, supported by a third line of infantry near Summers House. The attack was repulsed and Garrard fell back. On June 10, the rain continued to fall, for the seventh straight day. Garrard pushed ahead, driving the Confederates away from McAfee's Crossroads on June 11. The rain continued into June 18 and Noonday Creek, which separated Garrard's cavalry from the Confederate line, became a swamp four hundred yards wide. Sherman, in a letter to Grant during this time of frustration due to the wet weather, expressed he was dissatisfied with all his commanders except for McPherson. During his frustration, he decided to focus on Garrard's cavalry along Noonday Creek. Along with the much of the Union line, the area around Noonday had been a site of several actions over the previous ten days as Johnston established an impressive line at Kennesaw Mountain.[53]

Garrard's cavalry scouted along the left flank of the army on June 17 and reported directly to Sherman the best way for the infantry to cross Noonday Creek. Garrard also provided intelligence about enemy positions and sent details about rebuilding some bridges that could be used to effectively make a rapid crossing. But Sherman continued to be unhappy with what he judged to be Garrard's timid performance. Despite Garrard's actions over the prior week, Sherman wrote to George Thomas on June 20,

> I have sent peremptory orders for Garrard to cross Noonday and attack the enemy's cavalry, and if he don't do it I must get another to command the cavalry. McPherson has a good position and could have advanced today, but we cannot try to turn both flanks at once.... I will in the morning go to that flank and see that Garrard crosses the creek and ridge, and that he threatens the enemy's right flank and attacks any cavalry there.

Garrard was not a novice to the cavalry but a well-respected (at least, by others than Sherman), brave and efficient commander. He had even coauthored a book on the training of the cavalry in 1862, *Nolan's System for Training Cavalry Horses*.[54] Sherman's order to Garrard follows:

> I do not wish to extend the infantry on that flank for good reasons. But the enemy has detached a great part of his cavalry back to our line of railroad where they are doing mischief. Now, if they can cross the Etowah, the Oostenaula, and Connesauga—large streams—it does seem to me you can cross the little Noonday. I therefore order you to cross and advance against the enemy's cavalry toward the Chattahoochee, keeping as far north of Marietta as you please. Take no artillery or wagons with you, and leave all dismounted and ineffective men, but with the balance attack the enemy's cavalry and drive it back and interpose between the enemy and their detached cavalry. We will press the enemy at all points. Stoneman's cavalry is at and beyond Powder Springs.[55]

Garrard promised to make a demonstration the next day to develop the positions of the enemy. Dr. George Parry, veterinary surgeon for the 7th Pennsylvania Cavalry, wrote in his diary that June 20 was "a very exciting day ... severe fighting." Minty's brigade moved across Noonday Creek and pushed the Confederate pickets aside. The Union cavalry chased the pickets about two miles but found the main Confederate defensive line. A heated fight resulted in the loss of twenty men in Minty's cavalry. One of the wounded in the fight at Noonday Creek was Private Jarratt Johnston, 1st Ohio Cavalry, who lost a leg when a shell hit him. He pleaded to be taken back to the Union line, but he was left behind. Sherman had left strict orders: "First whip the enemy, and then your wounded are safe."[56]

Minty's cavalry crossed Noonday Creek on the old Alabama Road, fell into line and remained there throughout the day. At 3:00 p.m. Minty's brigade was attacked by a heavy force of Confederate cavalry and the 7th Pennsylvania was pushed back. The Pennsylvanians were reinforced with the 4th U.S. Cavalry on the left flank and held their position near Noonday Church. The 4th Michigan and a battalion of the 7th Pennsylvania held the center. Two

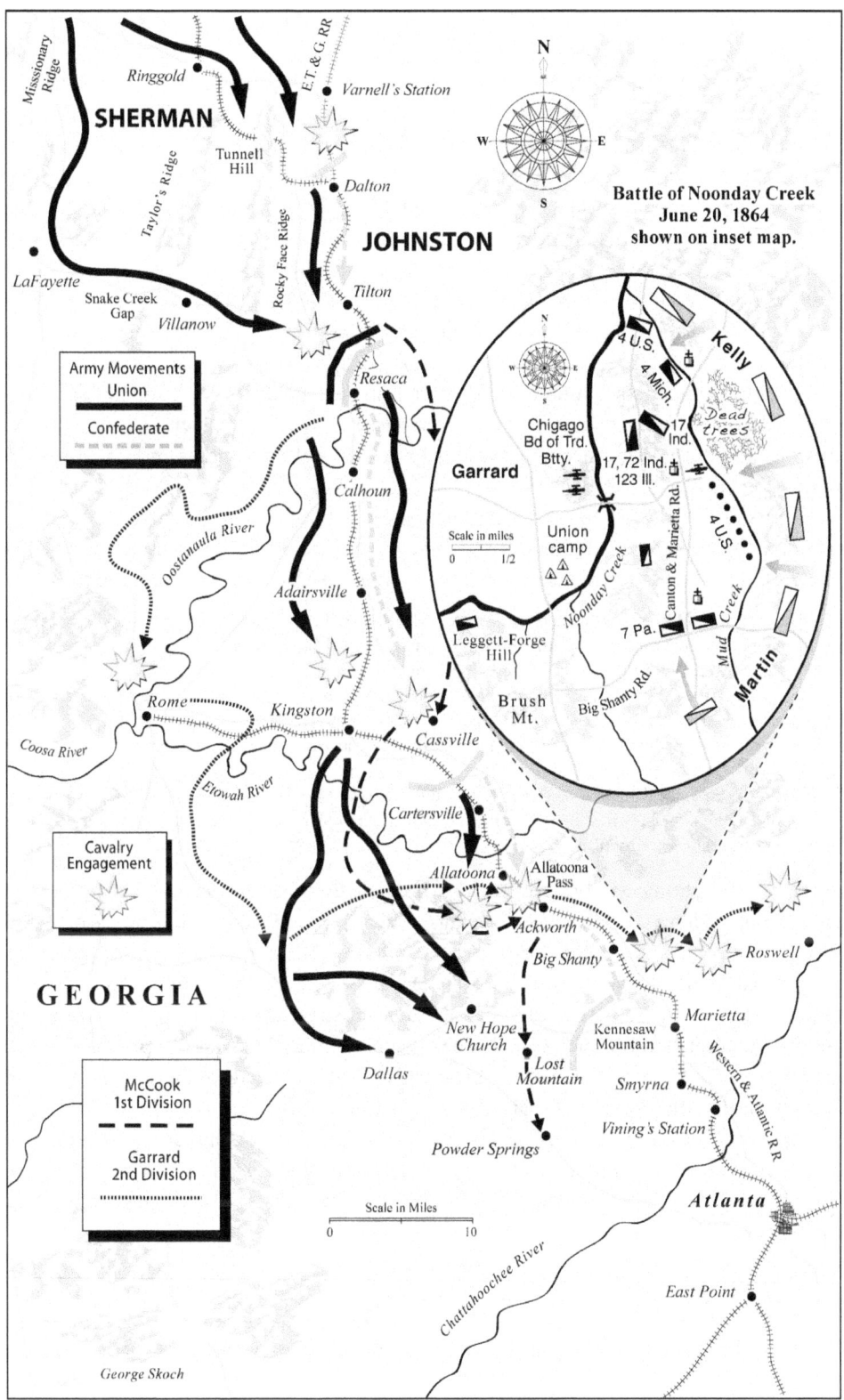

The Atlanta Campaign (May—July 9, 1864) and the Cavalry Battle of Noonday Creek, June 20, 1864

battalions of the 7th Pennsylvania were positioned on the right flank. Minty's line held through three Confederate charges from six Confederate cavalry brigades that began flanking the Union troopers. Minty called for a section of the Chicago Board of Trade battery to delay the Confederate flanking action on his line and artillery began shelling the advancing cavalry. Lieutenant Griffin, commanding the section, told Minty he was afraid he would lose his guns as the Confederates pushed forward. Minty replied, "Those men need to be checked—pour in your canister." Griffin again expressed his concern for his guns and asked permission to withdraw. Minty exclaimed, "No sir, you will not; give them another round or two." At that point, a charge wedged in one of the guns making it inoperable, but the other cannon continued to fire and successfully stopped the attack. Next, Miller's mounted infantry provided support and reinforced the Union troopers already in line. As Miller's men fought, the attacks ended and Miller's support allowed Minty to withdraw from the field with a loss of 65 men. Johnston's line was just too strong for Garrard's cavalry, but the action temporarily silenced Sherman's criticisms.[57]

Garrard had to have been particularly unhappy with Sherman's remarks about his cavalry's efforts. He had ordered Minty's brigade across Noonday Creek on June 20 only to have him attacked by several brigades of Confederate cavalry. We have Minty's record of the action:

> Was attacked by Wheeler with six brigades, viz: Allen's, Iverson's, Anderson's, Hannon's, Williams's, and Dibrell's. About 500 men of Seventh Pennsylvania and Fourth Michigan, with Lieutenant Griffin's section of Chicago Board of Trade Battery, fought Williams's, Hannon's, and Anderson's brigades for over two hours. The Seventh Pennsylvania and Fourth Michigan each made one saber charge, and two battalions of Fourth Michigan repulsed three saber charges made by Anderson's brigade of regular cavalry. Colonel Miller reported to me with three regiments from his brigade. I directed him to form on the hills around the bridge over Noonday. One battalion Fourth U.S. Regulars checked the advance of Allen's and Iverson's brigades on my right flank and enabled me to fall back on Colonel Miller. The six brigades of rebels dismounted and charged my new line. The artillery, which I had placed in position across the creek, opened on them and they were repulsed.

After the heavy fighting, Minty knew he could not hold his position and returned to the north side of the creek. John C. McLain, 4th Michigan Cavalry, described the importance of Miller's brigade, which waited for Confederate cavalry to follow Minty's troopers. McLain wrote in his diary that night, "Wilders [Miller's]brigade were waiting for them behind a rail barrack and it was dark by the time they came up and did not see what was in front and for a short time it was a warm place." General Jacob Cox exclaimed the action was "one of the most hotly contested cavalry fights of the war," and Joseph Johnston referred to this as the "most considerable cavalry affair of the campaign."[58]

Kenner Garrard struck back directly at Sherman after the fight at Noonday Creek. Sherman had made him a whipping boy thus far in the campaign. Garrard wrote his impression of the situation at Noonday Creek and his willingness to abdicate his command if Sherman found his performance unsatisfactory.

> Please inform the major-general commanding the army that his communication of last night has been received. His instructions to cross Noonday Creek have, in anticipation, been complied with four times, and attempted another, within the last ten days. I have in that time attacked the enemy's cavalry five times, and have always found it superior to me in numbers, and always they have had the advantage in position. Yesterday I lost 65 men in the fight.

Garrard was positioned within four miles of the main force of Confederate cavalry, and he flatly told Sherman if he was unsatisfied with his command to replace him:

I regret exceedingly that on several occasions the major-general commanding has seen fit to write as if he were dissatisfied with my activity and zeal. It is impossible to do all that might be desired, but the same consideration should be had for the cavalry, which cannot advance over natural advantages and a strong enemy, that is given to the infantry, which has not overcome the numerous difficulties before them. The cavalry is a special arm of the service, and the commander of [a] division, situated on one of the flanks like mine, should possess the full confidence of the commanding general. Unless such is the case his sphere of usefulness is materially injured and the real good of the service is affected. My service with the cavalry this campaign has been very unsatisfactory, for I have been made to feel more than once that it was not equal to the occasion, when I feel confident that both men and officers of the command have been earnest and zealous in the discharge of their duties and have well and faithfully done all in their power to accomplish what was asked of them. Should the general commanding desire a change in the command of this division, I will most cheerfully yield it and take command of a brigade of infantry. The Noonday is not the obstacle to my advance on these roads, but the superior force of the enemy in strong positions.[59]

Next, Garrard updated McPherson on the conditions along his flank. He planned to carry out Sherman's orders for June 21, but this would leave McPherson's flank exposed. For Garrard to complete the orders, he would have to move his division away from McPherson and swing around the eastern flank of the enemy. To accomplish this maneuver, Garrard had to ride north and then east. But McPherson knew the service Garrard had provided to his army and interceded on his behalf. McPherson returned to Garrard with new orders and gave him the reassurance he needed: "The general is well satisfied with your operations yesterday, and what he wants and expects is that you will keep the rebel cavalry in your front occupied, and be certain that they do not send a large force to our rear."[60]

The maps showed Noonday Creek as a small and insignificant obstruction, but that was only part of the picture. The problem was the approach to the creek, which was 700 yards of swamp, according to James Larson, 4th U.S. Cavalry, who described the terrain: "So soft a man could not walk on it, far less a horse." The swampy area around the creek had to be covered with rails if any artillery or wagons were expected to move.[61]

Secrets were never secret for very long in the army. Even Garrard's subordinates knew Sherman was dissatisfied with him. Captain Heber Thompson, 7th Pennsylvania Cavalry, wrote,

It is evident that the authorities (Sherman and McPherson) are dissatisfied with Genl. Garrard and disposed to find fault with him without occasion. Sherman yesterday wrote to General Garrard making great complaint of our inactivity and inefficiency, forsooth!... Such an absurd letter as that, one would not expect from Genl. Sherman, though lately it must be confessed, our confidence in his Generalship has been greatly weakened.[62]

Garrard followed Sherman's orders on June 21 with satisfactory results. The extent of Sherman's acknowledgement of the action was in a message to George Thomas, which reported Garrard had crossed Noonday Creek. While Garrard was fighting Confederates in front and Sherman at headquarters, McCook and Stoneman pressed the Confederate withdrawal along the Union right flank, which resulted in a brisk skirmish. Wesley Templeton, 8th Iowa Cavalry, recorded the fight at Lost Mountain as "shurely one of the hardest battles ever recorded in history." In addition, Edward McCook still attempted to fulfill the order Elliott had sent him to find and subdue a group of 300 enemy cavalry. McCook reported this was a wild goose chase. He sent 250 troopers toward Powder Springs, the direction of Sherman's attempt to turn Johnston's left flank, only to find a strong Confederate defense. McCook recorded Stoneman's cavalry had already ridden in the same direction, and Johnston's Confederates had sent the Union cavalry scampering to the rear, despite Sherman's belief Stoneman was beyond Powder Springs.[63]

Alfred Waud sketch of Lost Mountain, where McCook's cavalry skirmished with Confederate defenders (Library of Congress).

As the Union infantry marched through the mud of the recent heavy rains, it came under fire from a formidable Confederate defense. This was an unfortunate turn of events for Sherman, and Johnston selected a very difficult position for Sherman to attack along the apex of Kennesaw Mountain. Next, Sherman began to move around Johnston's flanks. Sherman ordered McPherson to demonstrate along with Garrard on June 21 toward Marietta along the Union left flank; but Sherman didn't believe he could turn both of Johnston's flanks at once. He wanted the primary push to be on the Union right flank with Hooker's Twentieth Corps and Schofield's Army of the Ohio.

As Sherman's infantry advanced along the Union right flank in an attempt to turn Johnston's flank and threaten the Western & Atlantic Railroad, it found Hood's Confederate corps ready for a fight at Kolb's Farm on the morning of June 22. Hood carried the initiative of the attack but Hooker and Schofield had time to entrench. The terrain in this area made Hood's attack difficult. The Union line entrenched, and being supported by artillery, made the attack a bloody affair for Hood's corps. At the end of the day the Union army recorded about 350 casualties compared to over 1,000 for Hood.[64]

By June 23, Edward McCook had had enough. He was ordered to pursue another small group of Confederate cavalry in George Stoneman's vicinity, and McCook was seven miles away. There can be little argument that of all the Union cavalry command McCook's had worked the hardest and Stoneman was willing to let McCook continue to do so. McCook struck back in a message to Elliott:

> It is impossible for me to cover all the roads leading in that direction; all I can do is to scout and patrol the country as thoroughly as my force will admit of. I would like to attack those three brigades the other side of Powder Springs, and will do so if any possibility of success offers. They are now behind barricades, and it would be folly to attempt it. I am so tired of taking my share of this fight in little skirmishers and

scouting parties that I would risk cheerfully the lives and wind of the few anatomical steeds I have left for the purpose of getting my proportion of the glory, if there is any for the cavalry, of this campaign. I recognize the certainty that whatever is done must be done quickly, if we do it mounted. The party I sent to cut the railroad failed. The Chattahoochee was so high it was impossible to cross except at the public ferries, which are well guarded. The rebels have a complete chain clear to the river.

He concluded in the message that he would send troopers to fulfill his orders. But McCook was to lose this battle, as Stoneman complained to Schofield that he could not keep that area clean of Confederate raiders because Edward McCook was refusing to cooperate with him. Stoneman continued to show a knack for blaming someone else when things went wrong.[65]

Meanwhile, McPherson and Garrard were working well together. Although there are no records of the conversation McPherson had with Sherman on Garrard's behalf, it appears McPherson supported Garrard's actions along his flank. After McPherson's conversation with Sherman, Sherman stopped the direct communications with the commander of the Second Cavalry Division for a time, and McPherson took over with much better results. Garrard had not been idle along McPherson's flank. To the contrary, he was doing good service and had had six engagements with the enemy cavalry, on "the 11th, 15th, 19th, 20th, 23d, and 27th of June. The enemy had in every instance the advantage of position, and, as far as I could learn, a superior force," he recorded. McPherson recognized this, even if Sherman did not.[66]

McPherson was much more collegial and supportive of Garrard. On June 23, he wrote to Garrard that his actions were very "satisfactory" for the day. Garrard had stopped a Rebel attack along McPherson's flank during the day. W.L. Curry, 1st Ohio Cavalry, reported the Confederates "wheeled into line and with a yell charged down the hill.... Our whole division was lying in line dismounted, and at the command they raised up, rushed forward with a yell, opened up with their carbines, and the volleys were deafening ... volley after volley ... poured into them." McPherson then informed Garrard that his cavalry would be needed to support a movement for the Seventeenth Corps the next day. Garrard had found a friend in McPherson.[67]

On June 24, Edward McCook had regained his composure after his previous message to Elliott. McCook wrote, "General Stoneman had demoralized me by a dispatch a few minutes before." On June 24, McCook's ever diminishing number of troopers had cleared the area around Powder Springs of Confederate cavalry but he found William H. Jackson's three brigades of Confederate cavalry southeast of the town. McCook wrote, "I have refrained from attacking these fellows in the works, not from inclination, but want of men." McCook, who began the campaign with over 2,400 men, reported just greater than 1,000 men available for duty on his weekly returns.[68]

While the situation intensified near Kennesaw Mountain, the Confederates attacked the rear of Sherman's armies. It should be recalled that Colonel Louis Watkins's horseless Third Cavalry Brigade of Kentucky regiments followed the army while providing protection to Sherman's supply line. On June 24, Major General James Steedman, who commanded the Military District of the Etowah, reported Brigadier General Gideon Pillow attacked LaFayette, Georgia, with 3,000 men, only to be repulsed by Watkins's cavalry. Pillow began his attack at 3:00 a.m. by "charging furiously" into LaFayette. The attack was so sudden that about forty troopers of the 7th Kentucky Cavalry were cut off and captured. Watkins' entire command amounted to about 450 men. He organized his command despite the suddenness of the attack but the Confederates had superior numbers and surprise on their side. Watkins withdrew and made a stand at the courthouse, barricading the doors and stacking bags of grain as defenses. Pillow sent a formal demand of surrender, threatening to level the courthouse with artillery and set it afire. Watkins declined to surrender and the fight raged for three hours. Colonel John Croxton's 4th Kentucky Mounted Infantry (U.S.) arrived on the scene the next morning and the Confederates hastily withdrew. Croxton noted, "They left their dead on the field, also a number of wounded. We captured about 78 prisoners, including lieutenant-colonel of the Ninth Alabama Cavalry, and several commissioned officers." (Croxton was given command of the First Cavalry Brigade in July after patrolling the rear for enemy cavalry.) Sherman's response was a rousing, "Good for Watkins."[69]

By the end of June 24, Garrard's cavalry pushed to within two miles of Marietta and Sherman's infantry inched steadily closer to Johnston's Confederates entrenched in an arc around Marietta. The stage was set for the Battle of Kennesaw Mountain on June 27. The battle would be carried by McPherson and Thomas. Garrard and one division of infantry were ordered to feint toward Marietta with orders to contain Johnston's cavalry, and Schofield and Stoneman were to feint to the extreme west end of the Union line. The Union advance began at 8:00 a.m. and by 11:30 a.m. the attack had stalled. At the end of the day the Union casualties were about three times that of the Confederate defenders—about 3,000 Union losses compared to about 1,000 Confederate losses in this Confederate victory.[70]

Johnston Moves Across the Chattahoochee River

Sherman decided any further frontal assaults on Johnston's lines would be futile. He decided to supply his armies and again try to flank Johnston by swinging his right flank around Kennesaw Mountain in an attempt to isolate Johnston from the south. On the evening of June 30, Edward McCook was again ordered to cooperate with George Stoneman in the flanking action along the Union right flank toward Campbellton. Sherman ordered Stoneman, supported by McCook's division, to move across Sweetwater Creek to Sweetwater Town. The cavalry's objective was to hold the crossing and once the crossing was secure, McCook was ordered to return to Lost Mountain. Sherman reasoned, "If Johnston holds on to the Kenesaw then we must strike some point on the railroad between Marietta and the bridge, but if he lets go of Marietta then we swing across the railroad to a position that gives us again the use of the railroad."[71]

The two armies remained in place for a few days and on July 1 Sherman began to maneuver his flanks around Kennesaw Mountain toward the Chattahoochee River. Stoneman's and McCook's cavalry divisions claimed the village of Sweetwater Town, about ten miles south of Kennesaw Mountain, on July 2. In the meantime, Garrard's cavalry division protected the flanks and rear of McPherson's and Thomas's armies, which were moving forward along the Union left flank. Johnston had temporarily stopped Sherman's advance, but he was slowly being swallowed by the Union armies in front of his lines. To his rear were the Chattahoochee River and his line of retreat. The Chattahoochee River was also the last significant geographic obstacle before Atlanta.[72]

At 10:00 the next morning, Sherman wired Halleck that he had possession of Kennesaw Mountain and Johnston had withdrawn because of the flanking movement to the west. Immediately Garrard and McCook, who was still cooperating with George Stoneman, were ordered

View across the Chattahoochee River. By July 9, Sherman had made three crossings over the Chattahoochee River and was only eight miles from Atlanta (Library of Congress).

to push for the Chattahoochee River. By the end of the day, Marietta was in the hands of the Union army, but Johnston stopped at Smyrna to give his wagons time to move south. After two days of relatively minor fighting, Johnston withdrew again to the well-prepared defenses north of the Chattahoochee. To get around Johnston, Garrard's cavalry was ordered to Roswell, site of the next bridge upriver from Johnston's river line. McCook was ordered to scout the river between the Federal left and Garrard's right and to be prepared to join Garrard should he run into trouble. The advantage of numbers was now apparent. Should Wheeler try to strike Sherman's rear from the east, he would face two Union cavalry divisions with infantry support. In addition, if the Confederate cavalry focused on the Union left flank, George Stoneman, who was already near the Chattahoochee River near Campbellton on the Union right, was prepared to cross the river and attack Johnston's rear and communications.[73]

In the meantime, the infantry advance moved forward, engaging the Confederates along the Smyrna line on July 4 when Sherman ordered Howard's Fourth Corps to continue the advance in the face of an entrenched Confederate line of infantry and was repulsed. The Federals collapsed part of the Confederate line, but the Confederates successfully delayed the Federals long enough to get their wagons across the river.

On July 5, Garrard's Second Division approached Roswell, about ten miles east of Marietta. The Confederate defenders withdrew from the town and burned the bridge over the

Chattahoochee. The next day, Garrard's troopers burned wool and cotton mills and machine shops. Edward McCook joined Garrard on the left flank on July 6, while along the Union right flank George Stoneman had not yet reached the Chattahoochee River because of the enemy entrenchments.[74]

Garrard's success at Roswell, in which he burned over one million dollars' worth of Confederate factories, made a favorable impression on Sherman. When Garrard arrived in Roswell, he found a French flag flying over some of the mills and a claim by a French citizen, Theophile Roche, that he owned the mills. This was a lie perpetrated by the mill owners, for whom Roche worked. Garrard discovered the material being produced in the mills was used to make blankets and Confederate uniforms. Despite Roche's protestations that he was not part of the Confederacy but a French citizen, the factories were burned. The more distressing part of the event related to the women who worked in the factory. Sherman ordered Garrard "to arrest for treason all owners and employees, foreign and native, and send them under guard to Marietta, whence I will send them North. Being exempt from conscription, they are as much governed by the rules of war as if in the ranks." Records show approximately 400 women from Roswell and 100 women from the New Manchester Mill at Sweetwater (burned by Stoneman's troopers on July 9) were deported to various locations in the north.[75] In addition, Garrard secured positions the Union infantry would use to cross the river. Sherman, finally addressing Garrard's expressed willingness to be relieved of command, wrote a conciliatory message to him, but he did subtly suggest Garrard should be more aggressive in his action: "I assure you, spite of any little disappointment I may have expressed, I feel for you personally not only respect but affection, and wish for your unmeasured success and reputation, but I do wish to inspire all cavalry with my conviction that caution and prudence should be but a very small element in their characters."[76]

On July 8 and 9, Schofield, Garrard, and McCook crossed the Chattahoochee River. Edward McCook had regained enough of his sense of humor to report the actions of the 1st Tennessee Cavalry in crossing the Chattahoochee: "Brownlow performed one of his characteristic feats today. I had ordered a detachment to cross at Cochran's Ford. It was deep, and he took them over naked, nothing but guns, cartridge-boxes and hats." As the troopers forded the river, their feet were cut by sharp stones. Brownlow, who joined the expedition, was the son of a minister and upon cutting his foot, he proclaimed, "The occasion is worthy of considerable profanity, but cuss low, cuss low!" Upon reaching the other side of the river, they surprised the enemy pickets and captured four men and two boats. McCook commented, "They would have got more, but the rebels had the advantage in running through the bushes with clothes on. It was certainly one of the funniest sights of the war, and a very successful raid for naked men to make." One of the captured Confederates told his captors it was good they were successful, because if the Confederates had captured Brownlow's Tennesseans they would have been shot as spies because they were out of uniform.[77]

Despite McCook's humor, the grueling campaign was taking its toll on both armies. William Allen Clark of the 72nd Indiana Mounted Infantry wrote, "I am getting tired of this Campaign. We have been either in the saddle or on the skirmish line almost every day since the 10th of May."[78]

Once Sherman crossed the Chattahoochee River, he was past all the natural obstacles around Atlanta and was poised to advance on the city. Thus far in the campaign, Sherman was less than satisfied with the performance of the cavalry that had performed reconnaissance

General Kenner Garrard's actions at Roswell secured a ford for Federal infantry to cross the Chattahoochee River on July 10 (from Frank Leslie's *Illustrated Famous Leaders and Battle Scenes of the Civil War*, 1896).

and security for his armies. In fact, his cavalry was successful in its duties thus far and worked very hard, even to the point of exhausting the men and horses Sherman desperately needed, even though the quartermaster records reflect that enough horses and mules were sent to replace every one of the animals in Sherman's armies. Moreover, the bond between rider and horse was often strong. Private Benjamin Pike, 2nd Michigan Cavalry, described this bond in letter written on June 30: "I could not think of parting with Old Bob, that is my horse's name. I have rode him ever since I came in the service both up & down mountains, waded & swum rivers & rode him in & out battle & [no] money can not get him from me."[79]

Sherman wanted more aggressive action from the cavalry. He envisioned his cavalry raiding deep in the rear of the Confederate army, causing havoc on the enemy's communications and drawing off enemy resources to deal with the threat. The cavalry's biggest problem might have been Sherman himself. He clearly did not trust the cavalry, and by all appearances his cavalry commanders knew it. He assumed direct control over the cavalry, essentially bypassing the chain of command and totally ignoring his chief of cavalry. Sherman had too much on his hands to manage his three armies and command four divisions of cavalry. Kenner Garrard had been disregarded by Sherman as too tentative, but McPherson judged Garrard's performance to be creditable. When Sherman chastised Garrard on June 20, Garrard had already taken the initiative several times but failed to gain the objective Sherman had set for him. In fact, the day before Sherman's negative comments, Garrard had been involved in what one of Sherman's infantry commanders described as one the hottest cavalry fights in the war. Sherman just did not have time to command three armies and know in detail what each cavalry division was doing.

The cavalry performed the duty Sherman ordered it to do. If he was unhappy with the cavalry, it was due to his own orders. Heber Thompson, 7th Pennsylvania Cavalry, wrote in his diary the cavalry's unhappiness with him in return: "Many of us wish Rosecrans was in Sherman's place now."[80]

By July 9, Sherman had made three crossings over the Chattahoochee River and was only eight miles from Atlanta. He had been given authority to make his actions independent of any concerns about keeping the enemy occupied as a way to support Grant's actions in the east. What was more important, he had new plans for his cavalry.

11. Chattahoochee River to Atlanta, July 10–August 7, 1864

> *Tell your general that as soon as I get ready I will walk out of here.*—Colonel Israel Garrard

On July 10, Sherman's headquarters was at Vinings Station along the Western & Atlantic Railroad just north of the Chattahoochee River, with Atlanta within striking distance. Both Sherman and Johnston understood that although Sherman had a larger army it was vulnerable and deep in enemy territory. If his tenuous supply line was severed, Sherman could be in trouble. As commander of the Military Division of the Mississippi, he used two additional military actions to occupy the attention of Confederate troops in Mississippi, Alabama and Tennessee.

In Sherman's eyes, Nathan Bedford Forrest was the most disruptive enemy force and he felt it was imperative to keep Forrest away from the vulnerable Union supply lines. In early June, Sherman sent Brigadier General Samuel Sturgis to deal with this threat. Sturgis, who had previously commanded the Union cavalry in the East Tennessee Campaign, had been shuffled off to Kentucky to rehabilitate portions of the Union cavalry. When he went to Kentucky, he had been replaced by Major General George Stoneman. In June, Sturgis was selected to command 8,500 troops, greatly outnumbering Forrest, to pursue Forrest in western Tennessee and northern Mississippi. Sherman felt Sturgis could keep Forrest occupied while the Union armies advanced toward Atlanta. Sturgis's pursuit ended on June 10 at the Battle of Brice's Crossroads. The Union losses totaled over 2,200 men killed, wounded or missing compared to slightly less than 500 for Forrest. Certainly Sherman was not happy with the result of this expedition. Next, he sent Major General A.J. Smith and Brigadier General Joseph Mower on an expedition to deal with Forrest. These two generals are two of the least known but best generals in the western theater, and their expedition ended quite differently. Lieutenant General Stephen Lee and Forrest were defeated at the Battle of Tupelo on July 14 and 15. The Union expedition marched from La Grange, Tennessee, on July 5, 1864, in temperatures described by one Union soldier as "so hot here that it appears as though the earth will burn." Unfortunately, after the battle A.J. Smith found his rations had rotted in the Mississippi sun and he was compelled to return to La Grange. The Union infantry held Forrest's attention and even wounded the famed Confederate general on July 15. Both of these expeditions had the twofold objective of trying to destroy Forrest and diverting the enemy's resources away from Sherman's supply line.[1]

Sherman alerted Henry Halleck regarding his next steps. Instead of directly attacking Johnston's entrenchments, he proposed to destroy all the railroads leading to Atlanta, thereby starving Johnston into abandoning the city. This was a tricky maneuver but it would save many lives. Sherman had hinted at this strategy, and now he proposed to put his cavalry to work to accomplish the task. The months of July and August would signal a beginning of Sherman's decision to use his cavalry in a much more offensive series of raids behind enemy lines.[2]

Union Cavalry Raids, July and August 1864

Raid	Date	Location	Outcome
Rousseau's Raid	July 10–22, 1864	Loachapoka and Opelika, Alabama	Success
Stoneman's Raid	July 10–15, 1864	Atlanta and West Point	Failure
Garrard's Raid	July 21–24, 1864	Covington, Georgia	Success
McCook's Raid	July 27–August 3, 1864	Lovejoy's Station, Georgia	Failure
Stoneman's Raid	July 27–August 6, 1864	Macon, Georgia	Failure
Kilpatrick's Raid	August 18–22, 1864	Jonesborough, Georgia	Failure

Rousseau's Raid

Major General Lovell Rousseau commanded the Union forces in Nashville of the District of Tennessee while Sherman advanced on Atlanta. The forty-five-year-old Rousseau, a native Kentuckian, was an attorney and politician in Kentucky and Indiana before the war. He began the war as colonel of the 5th Kentucky Infantry and had served in many of the important battles in the west. As Sherman moved on Atlanta, Rousseau offered his services to lead a cavalry raid deep into enemy territory in Alabama to cut the West Point and Montgomery Railroad, which brought supplies to Johnston in Georgia. Sherman had known Rousseau since the beginning of the war and held him in high regard. This was just the aggressive spirit Sherman desired for his cavalry.[3]

On June 19, Rousseau wrote to Sherman offering a plan to strike into the heart of Alabama: "[I]t would afford me a fine opportunity of paying my long desired visit to Selma. Roddey's forces are strong along the road from a point within seven miles of Decatur toward Moulton and beyond. Forrest was at Fulton a few days ago." Rousseau concluded that with 3,000 cavalry he could destroy up to one hundred million dollars' worth of Confederate property. More important to Sherman, Rousseau intended to destroy the railroad leading from Alabama to Atlanta. Rousseau identified some very large bridges that could be destroyed and thereby ensure that the rail system would be ineffective for months. Also, he wanted to destroy some key ironworks used by the Confederate army. On June 30, Sherman replied to Rousseau that such a plan would be very useful for the outcome of the campaign. He replied that the expedition should begin near Decatur, Alabama, and then proceed to Blountsville or Ashville, crossing the Coosa River near Ten Islands. After destroying the bridge after them, the raiders would continue to Talladega or Oxford and then cross the Tallapoosa River. The real objective was the railroad between Tuskegee and Opelika. Sherman stressed the raid should destroy the railroad completely, including heating the rails and twisting them into useable pieces of metal. Once the destruction was completed, Rousseau would join Sherman's armies along the Chattahoochee River.[4]

Major General Lovell Rousseau commanded the first of six cavalry raids in the summer of 1864 (Library of Congress).

Rousseau's expedition began near the same time A.J. Smith's Sixteenth Corps marched toward Tupelo and when Major General Edward Canby was taking action at Mobile. Sherman hoped the other two expeditions would leave Rousseau with a high chance of success and the outcome would be favorable for his armies at Atlanta. Rousseau selected three regiments from the Third Cavalry Division: 8th Indiana Cavalry, Colonel Thomas Harrison; 2nd Kentucky, Colonel Elijah Watts; 5th Iowa, Lieutenant Colonel Matthewson Patrick; one regiment from the Fourth Cavalry Division: 4th Tennessee, Major Mashack Stephens; and the 9th Ohio, Colonel William Hamilton, from the Army of the Ohio. Due to the lack of horses, all but the 4th Tennessee Cavalry were dismounted; but Rousseau found enough horses to mount two brigades for this expedition. John Brandon, 5th Iowa Cavalry, wrote to his father on June 15 that his regiment had to give up all their horses for Sherman's cavalry at the front and they had received condemned horses instead; but Rousseau provided his command with good horses for the expedition. Thomas Harrison was in command of the First Brigade and Matthewson Patrick commanded the Second Brigade. One section of the First Michigan Artillery was also part of the expedition.[5]

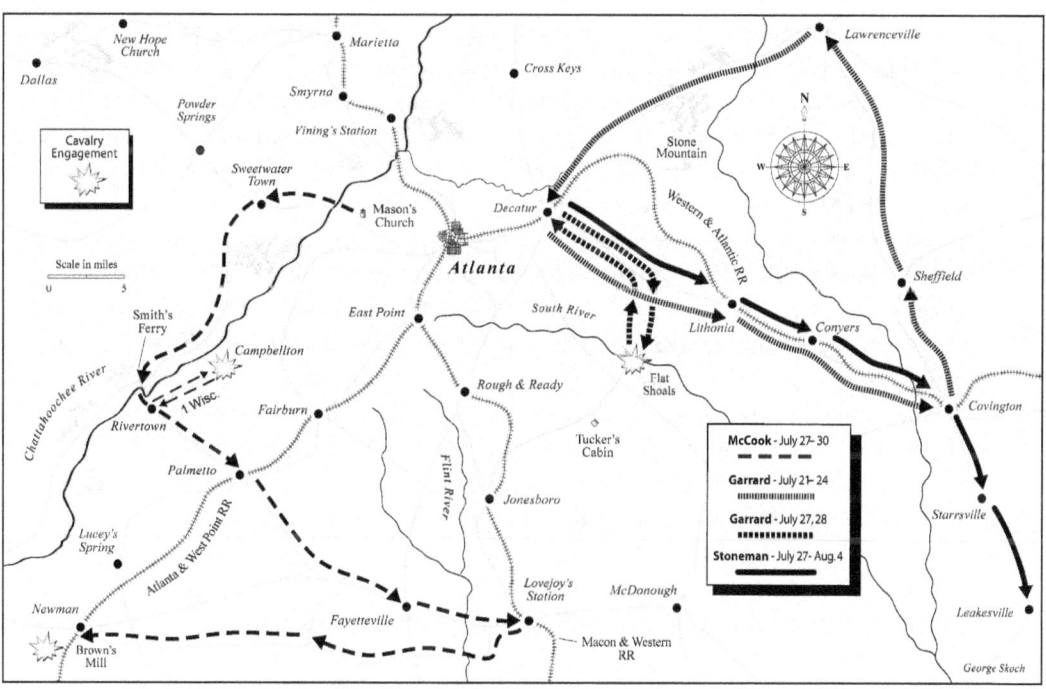

Union Cavalry Raids in Georgia (July 1864)

Rousseau struggled to assemble his command and finally marched from Decatur to Somerville, Alabama, on July 10. The Union column then rode through Blountsville and Ashville, and one trooper reported a little fun with a local secessionist newspaper, the *Ashville Vidette*. The Union troopers took control of the press and ran an article on their raid announcing "the arrival of distinguished gentlemen, Major General Rousseau and staff," but it added that it "was uncertain how long they would stay." The Union cavalry ran into its first resistance near Greensport on the Coosa River on the evening of July 13. Rousseau dispatched two hundred 8th Indiana troopers over the river to secure a crossing at Green's Ferry. A section of the 1st Michigan Artillery also unlimbered on the east side of the river. The next morning Rousseau ordered the 8th Indiana Cavalry to ride four miles south and secure the crossing at Ten Islands Ford, while the remainder of his column marched on the west side of the river. The 8th Indiana Cavalry ran into trouble on the east side of the river when it clashed with the 6th and 8th Alabama cavalries, commanded by Brigadier General James H. Clanton. Two additional companies reinforced the 8th Indiana, which skirmished with Clanton's troopers. As the resistance intensified, Matthewson Patrick's 5th Iowa and Major Mashack Steven's 4th Tennessee crossed to islands in the middle of the river, fired into the flank of the enemy and drove the Confederate cavalry away from its attack on the 8th Indiana. (Lieutenant Colonel Patrick, thirty-three years old, was an experienced veteran of the 5th Iowa Cavalry. A businessman in Omaha before the war, he had enlisted in the 1st Nebraska Cavalry, which was consolidated into the 5th Iowa Cavalry.) Once the fighting stopped, the advance was described by a journalist on the expedition: "The long array of horsemen winding between the green islands and taking a serpentine course across the ford ... guidons fluttering about the column."[6]

Only three days into the expedition, 300 unserviceable horses and the wounded were sent to the rear. On the morning of July 14, Rousseau recorded 2,200 men present for duty in his column.[7] Five miles past the Coosa River, Rousseau destroyed the large Janney Furnace used by Confederates to manufacture cannonballs and sheet metal that went to the Selma arsenal. On July 15, Rousseau started the grim task of destroying the large quantity of supplies at Talladega. In addition, two gun factories, railroad cars, and a depot were burned. Rousseau feinted toward Montgomery, the first capital of the Confederacy and the state capital of one of the most staunchly supportive states in the Confederacy, and then moved to his primary objective—the West Point and Montgomery Railroad at Loachapoka. The Union cavalry was forty-eight miles from Montgomery on July 17 when the destruction of the railroad began.[8]

Along the way Rousseau, seeking water and mules, rode onto a plantation and encountered the owner on the porch of his house. The planter replied he had already donated liberally to the Southern cause and then he noticed the uniforms. "The planter got to his feet uneasily. 'Ain't you on our side?' he asked. Rousseau told him that he was a general in the United States Army and that the long line of soldiers were Federal cavalrymen. 'Great God,' the planter gasped, 'whoever would have thought that the Yankees could come way down here in Alabama.'"[9]

The Union regiments dispersed in different directions with orders to destroy the railroad on July 18. Fortunately, Rousseau's feint toward Montgomery was effective and delayed the movement of Confederates troops to his location. Those in Montgomery, fearing a Union raid, quickly began to prepare defenses against the Union cavalry, but local forces were soon dispatched toward the Union raiders along the railroad. In the meantime, the efforts of the

Union troopers were generally unopposed, although the 9th Ohio Cavalry did some light skirmishing near Auburn and the 5th Iowa and 4th Tennessee battled a force of about 500 young men at Chehaw Station. Many of the Confederate troops that advanced on Chehaw Station were 16- and 17-year-old boys from of H.C. Lockhart's Battalion. In addition, about 50 University of Alabama cadets and some newly drafted men were sent to stop Rousseau. The initial clash of Confederate troops and the 5th Iowa cavalry at Chehaw resulted in a call for reinforcements. Rousseau quickly sent the 8th Indiana Cavalry to support Major Harlon Baird's Iowans and pushed the defenders away from the railroad. The Confederates found a strong defensive position in a ravine and fired at the Union cavalry. Thomas Harrison ordered the 8th Indiana to the flank and rear of the Confederate force and with the superior firepower of the Spencer rifles succeeded in driving them away. The 4th Tennessee Cavalry was dispatched to ride about five miles westward to give the impression that Rousseau planned to attack Montgomery.

The next day the Union expedition moved to Opelika and a large quantity of supplies was claimed or destroyed, and six railcars full of commissary stores were also burned. On July 20, the Union cavalry continued to destroy the railroad into the night. Colonel William Hamilton, 9th Ohio Cavalry, exclaimed, "We continued the work of tearing up the track and twisting the rails until twelve o'clock that night, leaving a line of blazing light behind us as far as we could see." Rousseau was thoroughly successful in the raid and arrived at Marietta on July 22. He claimed the destruction of thirty miles of railroad and this raid caused the cessation of arms, munitions and food to the Confederate army around Atlanta from Montgomery, during which time the important Battle of Peach Tree Creek, the Battle of Atlanta and the Battle of Ezra Church were all fought. The *Montgomery Weekly Advertiser* wrote of the raid, "We doubt whether any other raiding party since the commencement of hostilities, comprising no more men, has penetrated as far into the country, done as much damage, and succeeding in escaping with so little loss."[10]

Private George Healy, 5th Iowa Cavalry, wrote his family after returning from the raid that he had slept no more than four hours on any night and that he had lived on mush and meat. He concluded with a comment about the importance of the raid: "We have cut the Railroad in the rear of Johnson's Army and it is impossible for the Rebs to get supplies."[11]

Along the Chattahoochee River: Stoneman's First Cavalry Raid

While Rousseau was making his successful foray deep into Alabama, Sherman revised his strategy regarding Atlanta. He ordered George Stoneman to take his cavalry across the Chattahoochee River and destroy the railroad "below" Atlanta. If Stoneman failed to destroy the railroad, Rousseau was on a mission Sherman was confident would succeed. Sherman felt Stoneman would return from the raid, which began on July 10, within five days and then he planned to feint to the right and swing his army to the left (east). Sherman reasoned he would weaken Johnston's center and left flanks with the move, and if Johnston moved his army to the east, then Sherman would rush Atlanta. If Johnston, took the offensive Sherman was prepared to use Peach Tree Creek as a formidable defensive obstacle.[12]

While waiting for Stoneman to return from his raid, the Union army rested until Sherman was informed on July 15 that Stoneman's attempt to destroy the railroad "below" Atlanta had failed. Stoneman tried to capture a bridge to cross the Chattahoochee at Newnan (ten miles from the railroad) but was met with artillery fire. Rather than force a crossing, he burned the bridge and camped at Villa Rica, where he reshoed his horses. Sherman's entire command was awaiting the return of Stoneman's cavalry, which had not shown much cooperation or energy in its assignment. Sherman, however, showed no obvious concern about the abortive raid and was confident Rousseau would accomplish the task. Afterward, McCook and Stoneman were assigned duty protecting the crossings along the Chattahoochee River and Garrard was ordered to operate in cooperation with the movement of McPherson's army, which was being shifted to the left of the army in the direction of Stone Mountain. But Sherman still held Kenner Garrard in low regard, as he counseled McPherson into ensuring Garrard was committed to any mission he was assigned. Sherman felt Garrard passively resisted orders and could be relied upon only for those missions he thought were worthwhile.[13]

While the two armies were on the banks of the Chattahoochee River, the soldiers could yell across the river. Sergeant Daniel Bischard, 8th Iowa Cavalry, recorded a conversation he had with the enemy. When a voice asked from across the river which general commanded, Bischard replied, "Sherman." The Confederate replied that was odd, because Sherman commanded him also. He said, "When he tells us to git out of a place, we are sure to do it." Then another voice from across river warned Bischard to be prepared because the Southern army had just been reinforced. When Bischard asked who reinforced them, the reply was "Sherman."[14]

Sherman began his movement southward on July 17 and brought the Fourteenth and Twentieth corps across the Chattahoochee. Garrard's cavalry screened McPherson's advance during the day and found little opposition. In addition, Garrard observed the tracks of a large Confederate cavalry force that led south to Buckhead or Atlanta. Sherman ordered Garrard to push forward and destroy the railroad between Decatur and Stone Mountain in cooperation with McPherson's infantry.[15]

Garrard began fulfilling the orders and on the evening of July 18, Sherman reported, "General Garrard's cavalry at once set to work to break up road and was re-enforced by Brig. Gen. Morgan L. Smith's division of infantry, and they expect by night to have five miles of road effectually destroyed." Sherman had to be pleased with Garrard's performance during that day. By the end of July 18, Sherman's armies moved two to five miles with their right flank under Thomas on the Chattahoochee River. McPherson was on the left flank and Schofield held the center.[16] The next day, Garrard pressed east to destroy the railroad towards Augusta. On July 20, Sherman ordered a general advance on Atlanta, and Garrard was pulled from railroad destruction and ordered to protect the left flank and rear from any actions of the Confederate cavalry. McCook and Stoneman maintained position along the Chattahoochee and also screened the right flank.[17]

George Stoneman's reputation was dealt another blow on July 20. This time it was from George Thomas, who responded to a concern Stoneman had regarding the infiltration of Confederates. Thomas wrote, "The Stoneman raid turns out to be a humbug. I sent you his last report yesterday afternoon and hope it was received. It seems that when twenty-five of the enemy are seen anywhere, they are considered in force." However, Sherman thought it might be time for Stoneman and McCook to strike in the rear of Hood's army in a determined raid.[18]

Meanwhile, on the Confederate side of the line big changes were taking place. On the evening of July 17, a telegram relieving Johnston of command arrived at his headquarters. In Johnston's place, President Davis appointed John Hood and promoted him to full general. Prior to being relieved of command, Johnston concluded to vigorously resist any further advance on Atlanta. Hood was selected in part because Jefferson Davis correctly believed he was more likely to take action than many of the other possible commanders.

Garrard's Raid, July 21–24

Jefferson Davis thought Hood would take action, and on July 20 the new commander of the Army of Tennessee attacked Thomas's Army of the Cumberland after it crossed Peachtree Creek. Although the Union infantry was hard pressed, it successfully repulsed the attack of the aggressive Hood, which resulted in a loss of 2,600 men compared to 2,100 for Thomas. While the battle was being fought, McPherson pressed within a couple miles of Atlanta, but Sherman was frustrated that none of his subordinate army commanders could break through for a quick victory, so he began the process of isolating the city. Over the night of July 20–21, he ordered Garrard to destroy more thoroughly the railroad to Augusta. Garrard was ordered to proceed to Covington, about thirty miles east of his headquarters at Decatur. He was to destroy the Georgia Railroad at Lithonia, ten miles west of Covington, and then destroy the railroad at the Yellow River Bridge, a 555-foot trestle about five miles west of Covington. Next, he was ordered to destroy the railroad and bridge over the Ulcofauhachee River. By destroying this section of railroad Sherman ensured no supplies or reinforcements could be moved quickly from Virginia by way of Augusta, a rumor Grant had just communicated to Sherman. Then Sherman chided Garrard: "I want you to put your whole strength at this, and to do it quick and well. I know it can be done." Sherman reminded Garrard he had met with little resistance along his flank and concluded the enemy cavalry was a long way to the west of the armies. Then, he stressed the importance of the mission and specifically told Garrard the loss of 25 percent of his command should be contemplated and expected. Finally, Sherman told him to start on July 21 and gave him two days to complete his task.[19]

But Sherman's orders to begin a raid at Covington angered McPherson and were abrupt for Garrard. McPherson, who had been attacked during the day, felt he should have some input before pulling his cavalry away, and retorted, "[I] will simply remark in closing, that I have no cavalry as a body of observation on my flank, and that the whole rebel army, except Georgia militia, is not in front of the Army of the Cumberland." Garrard, on the other hand, received Sherman's orders at 1:30 a.m. directing him to begin this raid the next day. Garrard replied that he had regiments strung along a ten-mile front and he would have to pull his command together, which also had skirmished throughout the day. He replied, "I desire to succeed, as you place so much importance in having it done, and I will endeavor to do it." Garrard decided to start for the bridges with five regiments at 5:00 that morning and wait for the remainder of his command to catch up before starting the destruction of the railroad.[20]

The condescension in Sherman's orders was obvious to Garrard. Sherman was aware Rousseau had been successful in his raid and felt he had to find a way to convince his cavalry commanders to follow up with successes of their own. But Sherman still had little confidence in his cavalry. He wrote to Thomas on July 22 that Garrard was off on a raid to Covington and that he wanted to push McPherson's army to the right flank. Then he wanted to swing

Stoneman and McCook around the rear of Hood, but he remarked he had little hope Stoneman could lead the raid. He wrote, "[B]ut I hate to base any calculations on the cavalry. McCook might attempt it, but he is not strong enough, for I take it the main cavalry force of the enemy is now on that flank."[21]

Garrard was to have a successful three days in the saddle. He began his raid by scattering the Confederates at McAfee's Bridge and then he rode east. True to his word, Garrard rode for the 555-foot trestle bridge over the Yellow River, and the 92nd Illinois Mounted Infantry burned it. Then, the 250-foot covered bridge over the Ulcofauhachee (or Alcovy) River was burned. Next, part of the column rode through Oxford and captured a train and locomotive at Conyers before setting both afire. The depot was also burned as the column rode away. The Union column descended on Covington and burned the depot. Garrard proceeded to claim the quartermaster and commissary stores and burned what his troopers couldn't carry. Another two trains were burned there also, and by destroying the bridge over the Yellow River another two trains were stranded along the railroad. Garrard also burned 2,000 bales of cotton and turned his attention to a new, thirty-building hospital, which was set afire.[22]

Garrard's troopers encountered civilians who were fleeing before the Union cavalry who thought their personal possessions were not safe from the marauding cavalry. "Garrard's men emptied all the barns and smokehouses along their route." Over 1,000 sick and wounded Confederate soldiers were in hospitals at Oxford and Covington and many escaped into the woods and hills. At Oxford, the civilians were treated well:

> [T]hey treated the citizenship ... if not as well as they had a right to expect, certainly much better than they had feared. Their officers were invariably civil and polite; and Gen. Garrard ... showed himself the gentleman. Private property was generally respected, and yet there were few houses that were not robbed of articles of one kind or another by lawless soldiers as opportunity offered.... [T]here was not the first indignity offered to any of our ladies; nor do I know of an instance in which any gentleman was treated with rudeness or injury. Several were deprived of their watches ... but no personal violence was used.

Those who remained in the hospitals were undisturbed by the raiders.

Then Garrard's troopers began destroying the railroad for six miles, as ordered by Sherman and within the time frame given. Garrard's division rode ninety miles and had two men killed during the raid. Garrard's only real resistance came at Loganville, where fifty hastily assembled Confederate soldiers awaited Robert Minty's brigade. The small band was quickly dispersed once Minty advanced. When Garrard returned to the Union line he found the Battle of Atlanta had been fought while he was gone. He also was greeted with what he needed most—praise from Sherman: "I am rejoiced to hear that you are back safe and successful.... I will give you time to rest and then we must make quick work with Atlanta. I await your report with impatience, and in the meantime tender you the assurance of my great consideration." Sherman so welcomed Garrard's return that he ordered Major General Grenville Dodge to make a demonstration on Wheeler's cavalry to distract him so that Garrard would be unimpeded on his return.[23]

While Garrard followed Sherman's orders to destroy the Georgia Railroad at Covington, Hood attacked McPherson's exposed left flank. The terse message McPherson sent to Sherman regarding lack of cavalry support on the evening on July 21 was prophetic, and a coordinated attack by Hardee's corps and Wheeler's cavalry began around noon on July 22. Garrard's absence along McPherson's flank prompted McPherson to convince Sherman to forego, at least, temporarily, using part of McPherson's infantry to further destroy the railroad. Instead,

McPherson put two brigades on his left flank, preventing a disaster when Hardee's infantry appeared unexpectedly. Although there were delays in launching the attack, Hood outmaneuvered Sherman on July 22 and launched a furious attack, with Benjamin Cheatham's corps making a frontal assault. The Union line was tested by this attack, but held. Meanwhile, Joseph Wheeler's cavalry attacked John Sprague's Union infantry brigade at Decatur. Wheeler's cavalry approached the Federal wagon trains parked around Decatur, where Sprague had the unenviable duty of guarding the Union supply train. Sprague was successful in withdrawing to avoid being encircled by the Confederate cavalry and prevented Wheeler from swinging into the rear of McPherson's infantry. He was outnumbered three to one and fought the dismounted Southern troopers. He had two batteries to assist in the repulse, one of which was the Chicago Board of Trade Battery, which played an important role in stemming the attack. Benjamin Nourse of the battery described it: "[W]e gave the rebs canister fearfully, which checked them and allowed the Michigan battery to bring off two guns." The battery fell back 100 yards under Wheeler's dismounted cavalry attack and again fired canister, hoping to stop the attack. But the Confederates converged on the artillery without infantry or cavalry support and "shot our men like dogs." The battery again fell back and found infantry support and fired into attackers throughout the remainder of the day. The Chicago Board of Trade Artillery's actions allowed Colonel John Sprague time to prepare a defense against the attack. Nourse's section lost about 25 percent of the men and he bitterly remarked in his diary, "Col. Sprague told us we could go. So we left him after saving his brigade and artillery—for all this, he did not so much as thank us or express the least regret at our loss.... Shall we ever receive any credit for yesterday's work? I doubt." Nourse was glad to return to his duty with Garrard's cavalry. However, Sprague recorded in his report that the Chicago Board of Trade "served and worked with admirable skill and rapidity during the action." Wheeler, who had pushed into the center of town, finally withdrew and went to the aid of Hardee's infantry. Almost 30 years later, Sprague was awarded the Medal of Honor for organizing the defense of Decatur on July 22.[24]

The toll was heavy, with over 3,700 Union casualties and 5,500 Confederate casualties. Hood replaced Joseph Johnston because it was thought he would fight, and fight he did; but he was losing more men than Sherman, men he could ill afford to lose. Certainly one of the biggest losses for the Sherman's command was the death of James McPherson. McPherson had shown, perhaps, a unique ability to work with Sherman and had served as a buffer between Garrard and Sherman.

Preparation for McCook's and Stoneman's Raids

Sherman had, so far, called for three cavalry raids in July. Rousseau and Garrard had been very successful. Only Stoneman had failed to find the Chattahoochee River crossing that would have enabled him to strike the Atlanta & West Point Railroad. An added benefit from Rousseau's raid on the railroad was the addition of 2,000 cavalry to Sherman's armies. Sherman's reward for Garrard's "perfectly successful" expedition was an opportunity for his men to recuperate from the three-day raid, and Stoneman was ordered to take Garrard's position on the Union left flank while Rousseau's provisional division assumed responsibility for the Union right flank in cooperation with McCook.[25]

After the Battle of Atlanta on July 22, Hood moved his army into the inner defenses of Atlanta and Sherman asked a rhetorical question of General John Logan, who temporarily commanded the Army of the Tennessee after McPherson's death: "What next?" On July 25, Sherman revealed what was next for the cavalry. Sherman put together a plan which would send an infantry column to the south of the city to occupy the attention of the Confederates and then swing much of his cavalry south of the city, cutting off the railroad coming into Atlanta from Macon. The Atlanta & West Point and the Macon & Western railroads united at East Point and continued to Atlanta on a single track. If the Union cavalry could destroy the railroad at East Point and move southward, the last rail line into Atlanta would be closed. Edward McCook, who would lead a column from the Union right flank, was informed on July 25 to prepare for a "big raid" starting on July 27.[26]

On July 25, Sherman issued his orders. Kenner Garrard's and Rousseau's former division, now commanded by the 8th Iowa's Colonel Thomas Harrison, were included in the raid, but because both commands had seen hard duty, their roles were initially planned only as support. Only Edward McCook's and Stoneman's divisions would attempt to cut the railroads. McCook, positioned on the right (west) flank, would travel west and then swing south and rendezvous with Stoneman at Lovejoy's Station, well south of East Point. Stoneman, on the left (east) flank, would begin his raid at Decatur and feint toward Augusta. He would then swing south and meet McCook at Lovejoy's Station. It was later decided that Harrison's cavalry would accompany McCook. Garrard was to occupy the Confederate cavalry's attention south of Decatur but not participate in the raid. Sherman wanted two to five miles of rails destroyed during the raid.[27] Sherman wrote to Halleck of his strategy:

> At the same time I send by the right a force of about 3,500 cavalry, under General McCook, and round by the left about 5,000 cavalry, under Stoneman, with orders to reach the railroad about Griffin. I also have consented that Stoneman (after he has executed this part of his plan), if he finds it feasible, may, with his division proper (about 2,000), go to Macon and attempt the release of our officers, prisoners there, and then to Anderson[ville] to release the 20,000 of our men, prisoners there. This is probably more than he can accomplish, but it is worthy of a determined effort.

Sherman's exact orders for Stoneman were as follows:

> [H]ave received your letter of July 26, asking permission after breaking good the railroad below McDonough to push on [to Macon], release the officers there, and afterward to go to Anderson[ville] and release the men, confined there. I see many difficulties, but, as you say, even a chance of success will warrant the effort, and I consent to it. You may, after having fulfilled my present orders, send General Garrard back to the left flank of the army, and proceed with your command proper to accomplish both or either of the objects named.

It was these orders that caused so much confusion and controversy after the raid was over.[28]

On the eve of the cavalry raids, several important command changes occurred within the Army of the Cumberland. Fourth Corps commander Oliver Howard was promoted to command the Army of the Tennessee after McPherson's death. This decision caused some dissension within the command of the Union army. Some felt John Logan should have been offered command. The other officer particularly unhappy was Joseph Hooker, who had performed well after arriving in the west in the fall of 1863, and he complained that Howard was his junior in rank. Hooker immediately asked to be relieved of command of the Twentieth Corps and his request was granted. In the cavalry, Judson Kilpatrick recuperated from his wound and returned to command the Third Cavalry Division of the Army of the Cumberland.

McCook's Raid: The Advance

McCook's command included only his First and Second brigades because his Third Brigade was still in northern Georgia guarding the supply lines. The First Brigade, under the command of Colonel John Croxton, included the 8th Iowa Cavalry, the 4th Kentucky Mounted Infantry, and the 1st Tennessee Cavalry. The 4th Kentucky Mounted Infantry replaced the longtime First Brigade regiment, the 2d Michigan Veteran Cavalry, which had been assigned duty guarding the railroad in Tennessee. The Second Brigade was commanded by Lieutenant Colonel William H. Torrey and was composed of the 2nd Indiana, 4th Indiana, and 1st Wisconsin cavalries. Colonel Thomas Harrison's provisional division joined the raid and contained the 8th Indiana, 5th Iowa, 2d Kentucky, and 4th Tennessee Cavalry regiments and one section of 1st Michigan Light Artillery. A detachment of 9th Ohio Cavalry and the non-veteran 2nd Michigan also accompanied the expedition. As the raid began, McCook had 1,500 men, Stoneman 2,000, Garrard 4,500, and Harrison about 2,000.[29]

While the cavalry was riding toward Lovejoy's Station, Sherman kept his promise to keep Hood occupied at Atlanta. He ordered Howard's Army of the Tennessee from the east to west of the city. As Howard was on the march, Hood sent two divisions each from Stephen D. Lee's (formerly Hood's) corps and A.P. Stewart's corps to attack the Federals near Ezra Church on July 28. Howard was able to quickly throw up barricades to meet the attack. The battle was lopsided in favor of the Union troops, which sustained about 600 casualties compared to about 3,000 for the Confederates.

McCook began his raid by swinging west to Campbellton and then moving south, turning the flank of the Confederate cavalry. McCook began his march on the morning of July 27, leaving from Mason Church. Along with McCook was the provisional cavalry division under forty-year-old Colonel Thomas J. Harrison. Harrison was a man of "large and commanding presence" and he was greatly liked by his men as an effective and efficient commander. A native of Shelby County, Kentucky, he had moved to Crawfordsville, Indiana, when he was six years old. He attended Wabash College but did not complete his program of study. He left college in 1849 and moved to Kokomo and began teaching school. While teaching, he began studying law under the supervision of Judge Nathaniel Linsday, his future father-in-law. He completed his studies and joined a partnership with Judge Linsday. In 1858, he was elected to the state legislature and was one of the first to enlist when the war began. After serving in a three-month regiment, he raised the 39th Indiana Infantry and was commissioned colonel. He led the regiment at the Battle of Mill Springs and Stones River. Harrison succeeded in mounting the regiment in the spring of 1863, and the regiment subsequently became the 8th Indiana Cavalry in October 1863.[30]

McCook was immediately delayed. The pontoon bridge he planned to use to cross the Chattahoochee River was not in place due to the poor condition of the mules moving the pontoons. McCook was finally able to get his command over the river by the afternoon of July 28 at Riverton, about seven miles downriver from Campbellton. He rode directly for Palmetto, a small village about thirty miles southwest of Atlanta, but he sent the 1st Wisconsin Cavalry toward Campbellton to occupy the attention of Confederate cavalry there. He did not want his cavalry bogged down in a running fight at the start.[31]

Major Nathan Paine, commanding the 1st Wisconsin, was ordered to strike the Confederates at Campbellton, then turn east to cut the railroad at Fairburn, if possible. Paine was a graduate of Lawrence University in Appleton, Wisconsin, and completed law school at Albany. Immediately upon his graduation, he enlisted in the 1st Wisconsin Cavalry and shortly thereafter was married. Now, after his action at Campbellton, he planned to ride and meet the main Union column at Fayetteville. The 1st Wisconsin pushed the Confederate vedettes toward Campbellton. Once the regiment reached the lightly defended town, the one hundred or so defenders retreated to the east. Paine rode in pursuit about two miles east of the town when he found the enemy behind barricades and protected on the flank by an impassable swamp. Paine ordered sabers drawn and charged the barricade. A volley from the defenders stopped the charge, killing Paine, Lieutenant John Warren and nine enlisted men. It was reported that Paine exclaimed, "I am shot—Forward!" Unable to move ahead, the 1st Wisconsin backtracked through the town and returned to Marietta. A few troopers of the regiment who had not accompanied Paine remained with McCook's main column.[32]

Although the 1st Wisconsin completed its objective, the action alerted the Confederate commanders that Union cavalry was across the river. Commanding the Confederate cavalry were Brigadier General William Hicks "Red" Jackson, West Point graduate in 1856, along the Confederate left flank and Joseph Wheeler on the right flank. Jackson, under orders from Hood, sent Brigadier General Lawrence Sullivan "Sul" Ross and Colonel Thomas Harrison (not to be confused with the Federal colonel of the same name) to take up the pursuit of McCook's column.

Upon arriving at Palmetto on July 28, McCook began destroying the Atlanta & West Point Railroad. He destroyed three small trestles, two and one-half miles of telegraph, the same distance of rails, and a large quantity of commissary stores. While the Union cavalry was at Palmetto, Red Jackson's cavalry was assisting the Confederate infantry in resisting Howard's advance to Ezra Church. His and Brigadier General William Y.C. Humes' cavalry were the closest to McCook, and Harrison's and Ross's Confederate cavalry brigades were dispatched to pursue the Union cavalry until the Ezra Church fight was concluded. Wheeler was already occupied east of Atlanta with Stoneman and Garrard, who began their actions on July 27.

On July 29, McCook's column reached Fayetteville, another twenty miles closer to Lovejoy's Station, and wrecked several railcars. At 5:00 a.m., the cavalry rode for Lovejoy's Station. Colonel James Brownlow rode at the head of the 1st Tennessee Cavalry and was supported by the 8th Iowa Cavalry. Along the way over 500 wagons of Hardee's supply train were captured and also 100 bales of cotton, which were torched. The Union cavalry then killed 800–2,000 mules, depending upon which report was accurate. As the column advanced, Confederate guards at the Flint River Bridge attempted to burn the bridge, but the 1st Tennessee Cavalry was able to

William "Red" Hicks Jackson, 1856 West Point graduate, commanded Confederate cavalry during McCook's Raid (MOLLUS-MASS Civil War Collection, United States Army Heritage and Education Center, Military History Institute, Carlisle, Pennsylvania).

capture it. McCook reached the Macon & Western Railroad about one-half mile north of Lovejoy's Station at 7:00 a.m, and his men worked at destroying the railroad and the telegraph until 2:00 p.m. When McCook arrived at Lovejoy's Station a day late, he expected to find an angry George Stoneman awaiting him, but Stoneman wasn't there. Alone, McCook's command was able to destroy two and one-half miles of tracks and five miles of telegraph during the day.[33]

Leading McCook's First Brigade was the able Colonel John Thomas Croxton. The thirty-five-year-old Croxton, a Kentucky native, was a graduate of Yale, class of 1857. He began studying law and teaching in Mississippi after graduation and in 1859 had returned to Paris, Kentucky, where he established his law practice. He helped raise the 4th Kentucky Infantry and commanded a brigade at the Battle of Chickamauga when he was severely wounded in the leg. He recovered from his wound and again commanded the 4th Kentucky Infantry when it was mounted in June 1864 and joined McCook's division. When Croxton joined the cavalry he was given command of the First Brigade.[34]

McCook sent out scouts to reconnoiter the territory around Lovejoy's Station and look for Stoneman. At 2:00 p.m. the scouts reported that cavalry was approaching, but it was Wheeler and not Stoneman. Wheeler had concluded the Confederate cavalry facing McCook needed reinforcements, but Wheeler was faced with three Union cavalry columns. Wheeler sent Brigadier General Alfred Iverson's three brigades in pursuit of Stoneman, while Colonel George G. Dibrell's Brigade was placed near Garrard, who had returned to the Union lines. Then Wheeler rode with the remaining three brigades to help Jackson at Lovejoy's Station.

Alfred R. Waud sketch of Union cavalry destroying the railroad, which Sherman desperately needed, June 20–25, 1864 (Library of Congress).

In addition, General Philip D. Roddey's 600-man cavalry brigade was ordered to Palmetto and later to Newnan to try to stop McCook's escape.[35]

McCook called his commanders together to discuss what to do next. William Torrey voted to return along the same route, while John Croxton, James Brownlow and others wanted to march around the east flank of Hood's army and back to the Union lines, hoping to meet Stoneman along the way. McCook decided to return the way he had come, with scouts ahead of the column to find a crossing across the Chattahoochee. Thomas Harrison's 5th Iowa Cavalry led the column out of Lovejoy's Station, followed by Lieutenant Colonel William Torrey's Second Brigade. McCook waited until 3:00 p.m., hoping for some sight of Stoneman, now over two days late for the rendezvous. Then things began to go terribly wrong.

McCook's Raid: Retreat and Fight at Brown's Mill

John Croxton's First Brigade was the last to leave Lovejoy's Station and crashed into Jackson's Confederate cavalry, which was attempting to cut off the Union cavalry. McCook placed some dismounted troopers north of Lovejoy's Station, directing the regiments to take the Panhandle Road back to the west. These troopers first observed the enemy cavalry. Colonel Joseph Dorr, 8th Iowa Cavalry, was riding with one battalion as Jackson's cavalry arrived. Croxton ordered Dorr to charge the enemy to keep the crossroads open. Croxton had three regiments yet to reach Panhandle Road. Dorr was readying his regiment when he was charged by the 9th Texas Cavalry, but he held his position and rode to the fight, charging with revolvers. In what was described as "fiercer hand to hand fight never occurred," the 8th Iowa pushed the Texans back. During the fight, Dorr was shot in the right side but remained with his command, continuing the fight with them. Just then, the 6th Texas arrived and dismounted. The Confederates formed a line while the 9th Texas re-formed. Dorr, with his one battalion, faced both enemy regiments while Croxton moved the remainder of the 8th Iowa, 1st Tennessee, and 4th Kentucky onto the Panhandle Road. Then the rest of the 8th Iowa and 1st Tennessee formed a line along the Panhandle Road, which allowed Dorr to extract his battalion and back toward the forming Union line. Once Dorr fell into line, his medic stitched his wound closed.[36]

The fight along the intersection of the Panhandle Road intensified. Just as Croxton had committed the 4th Kentucky Mounted Infantry to the line, he received a message that the enemy had captured the Panhandle Road in his rear. He was being cut off. The last two companies of the 4th Kentucky out of Lovejoy's Station arrived at that moment and Croxton sent them quickly to his rear, explaining the necessity of keeping the road open. He advanced his entire line toward the Texas cavalry and then planned to make a hasty withdrawal. As things were looking bleak for Croxton, a column of blue amid a cloud of dust appeared from the west. Torrey's Second Brigade was riding hard to his position, opening the road. He was able to withdraw to the west over the Glass Road and along a road south of his original route. But now McCook was in a bad position. His command was deep in enemy territory and the enemy had found him. He was encumbered by a large mule train and burdened with several hundred prisoners he had picked up along the way.[37]

Fight and withdraw, fight and withdraw, was the order for the Union column, which stretched over eight miles. The column crossed the Flint River just before sunset, where the

4th Indiana Cavalry waited to burn the bridge as the last horse crossed, then rode to the west. Harrison's command was in the lead, Torrey's brigade was in the center, and Croxton's First Brigade rode in the rear. After midnight on July 29, Wheeler caught the Union column and "the raiders were battered by unceasing attacks, day and night, front, rear, and flanks." The route the column had been forced to take to avoid the Confederate cavalry slowed its progress. Croxton observed, "The road was a narrow, devious path, crossing innumerable ditches and bogs." One of McCook's staff officers met Croxton with orders to hurry forward. Croxton "simply pointed to the train of pack-mules passing." Several times the rear of the column was ordered to hurry forward only to find the road clogged with the retreating troopers. Finally, the column stopped entirely and one of Croxton's staff found the problem. The mule train was fast asleep. He finally got the column moving again only to be attacked by Confederate cavalry striking the rear of his column. Croxton fought a determined rear guard, detaching parts of his command to hold off the pursuit as the Confederate cavalry narrowed in on its prey. He left one company of the 4th Kentucky Mounted Infantry with orders to hold the bridge over Whitewater Creek until daylight under command of his lifelong friend Lieutenant Colonel Robert Kelly. The 4th Kentucky had a vicious fight with Wheeler's cavalry, which included Ross's and Humes' brigades. As Croxton moved his brigade forward, he found he had been cut off from the main column but was able to break through. Three miles ahead, he placed the remainder of the 4th Kentucky Mounted Infantry in a line along the road. After a three-hour fight and with the rear guard's ammunition depleted, the Union column again moved forward, riding hard for Newnan. During the fighting, the Kentuckians fought off five "desperate charges" by Humes' Confederate cavalry. But two companies, G and I, of the 4th Kentucky were surrounded before they could leave. Kelly estimated 150–200 men were captured before the regiment made its escape and another 40–50 were killed or wounded along the road. The 4th Kentucky was being whittled away.[38]

The Confederate cavalry was now converging on McCook from almost every direction. Wheeler had ridden hard from the north with three brigades and was nipping at McCook's heels, while Jackson's cavalry moved to head off the Union column and attack its flanks. The rearguard actions by Croxton's brigade damaged Wheeler's pursuing cavalry, but it was exactly what Wheeler had hoped. If McCook was stopping to fight, Wheeler might have time to get Jackson's and Roddey's cavalry between McCook and the river.[39]

On the 30th, the Federal column advanced toward Newnan, intending to cross the river beyond the town at Moore's Bridge, about ten miles west of McCook's original crossing of the Chattahoochee. McCook and Croxton knew the 4th Kentucky Mounted Infantry had been overwhelmed and the Confederate cavalry was on their heels. Hoping to slip past the Confederate cavalry at Newnan, McCook was frustrated to find infantry and Roddey's cavalry waiting for him.

Lawrence "Sul" Ross commanded a brigade of Texas cavalry during McCook's Raid (MOLLUS-MASS Civil War Collection, United States Army Heritage and Education Center, Military History Institute, Carlisle, Pennsylvania).

James Brownlow, 1st Tennessee Cavalry, recorded, "Here we were attacked at 8 a.m. by two divisions of cavalry and one division of infantry. The fighting was desperate during the entire day." Lieutenant Colonel H.P. Lamson, Second Brigade, observed the Confederate infantry filing off train cars at Newnan. McCook ordered the 8th Indiana, 5th Iowa and 4th Tennessee Cavalry to hold off Roddey's command arriving at Newnan while the remainder of his column arrived.[40]

Being unable to march north from Newnan, the Union column headed west again, bypassing Newnan to the south. McCook sent his Second Brigade, commanded by Lt. Colonel William Torrey, ahead while Croxton's and Harrison's brigades formed a rear guard. The mule train and the rest of Torrey's Second Brigade were ordered forward. Their pace was slowed with the pack animals, ambulances, and prisoners, and while Torrey plodded ahead Harrison and Croxton protected the rear.[41] After riding about five miles south of Newnan, McCook ordered the column to advance west in a wooded area onto the Ricketyback Road. Any hope of an organized escape ended here, near Brown's Mill, where McCook found he was surrounded by Wheeler, Roddey and Jackson. The 2nd Kentucky Cavalry led the advance, and after traveling about three miles down the road they found the intersection with the Corinth Road blocked by Confederates.[42]

As the 2nd Kentucky advanced, it received a furious volley from the Confederates ahead. George Purdy, commanding the 4th Indiana, exclaimed, "They retreated promiscuously." The 2nd Kentucky had run headlong into Colonel Henry M. Ashby's 1st and 9th Tennessee Battalion, about two hundred men. Wheeler hoped Ashby could stop the column while he attacked the flank. Upon recovering from the surprise, the 4th Indiana and 2nd Kentucky formed a line to face the threat. Torrey's remaining regiment, the 2nd Indiana, was still detailed to guard the prisoners. The fight at the Corinth Road intersection lasted one-and-a-half hours before the Confederate reinforcements began to push the Union cavalry off the road. Torrey threw all his men into the effort—5th Iowa, 2nd Indiana, 4th Indiana and 2nd Kentucky—to keep the Corinth Road open for the trailing brigades, which had closed to within a half a mile. But they were also heavily engaged with the Confederate flank attack. Torrey held out as long as he could until his regiments were charged by reinforcements of Roddey's and Anderson's Confederate cavalry, which broke his line, Torrey being killed during the fighting.[43]

With Torrey's death, command transferred to Major George H. Purdy. Purdy, who had just criticized the 2nd Kentucky, did no better and his brigade fell apart. Purdy was observed by one of the troopers as he led the

Kentuckian John Croxton commanded McCook's First Brigade in a determined rearguard action during the raid (Library of Congress).

panicked troopers trying to escape the Confederate attack. One officer and 100 men were able to charge through the Confederate line and break out and they were soon joined by Purdy's 4th Indiana and another 180 men. Only 283 men of the Second Brigade were able to ultimately reach the river and cross over after scrambling through the countryside.[44]

The trailing brigades soon found themselves attacked from the right flank as well as cut off from the front. Croxton ordered the 1st Tennessee, 8th Iowa and what remained of the 4th Kentucky wheeled to the right to face the Confederates coming from the north. Harrison's brigade was also wheeling right. McCook informed Croxton and Harrison that Torrey had been stopped ahead and the Confederates were advancing on the right. Croxton moved his troops ahead about 100 yards and battled the Confederates. In the meantime, Harrison also dismounted the 5th Iowa and 4th Tennessee and met the Confederate attack. As the Union lines were being surrounded, the 8th Iowa was ordered to protect the line while the other regiments withdrew. Lieutenant Cornelius Bennett, 8th Iowa, explained: "The 8th was wheeled into line of battle on the crest of the hill, as calmly as if on dress parade, though by the changed expression of countenance, I saw the boys regarded themselves as doomed." The 8th Iowa held the line as the others moved away from the battle.[45]

After the other regiments moved away, Croxton ordered the 8th Iowa to try to break out ahead and connect with Torrey's brigade. The 8th Iowa charged ahead into Ross's Texas brigade, forcing the Texans backward and temporarily capturing Brigadier General Sul Ross in the process. Major Richard Root, commanding the 8th Iowa, observed, "The fighting all along the line was terrific." (Root had joined the 8th Iowa after serving in the 19th Iowa Infantry. The 30-year-old major was a Maryland native and lived in Mt. Pleasant, Iowa, before the war.) The 8th Iowa continued to push ahead, losing men all along, and being surrounded three times only to fight their way out each time. As the Confederate reinforcements pushed ahead, Root was compelled to retreat. Then he ordered the men to disperse and find their way back to the river as best they could. Root, two officers and ten privates found McCook and rode with his column back to the river. For the remainder of the 8th Iowa, which had some of the hardest fighting during the morning, the day resulted in a bitter end as they found themselves surrounded and forced to surrender. Three hundred sixteen men started the raid in the 8th Iowa Cavalry and only twenty reached the safety of the Union lines. Colonel Joseph Dorr, wounded, was also captured.[46]

Meanwhile Croxton was still trying to hold off the Confederate attack. He formed a line with the 1st Tennessee, the remainder of the 4th Kentucky, and a detachment of the 2nd Indiana. Harrison's command was forced back after a determined counterattack by Wheeler's cavalry. Soon Harrison's brigade joined Croxton's and tried to force its way through the Confederate encirclement but was unsuccessful. With McCook's approval, Croxton agreed to take his brigade and try to find a way out. He rode with the 1st Tennessee and after a battle with the enemy, found a bridge. Croxton ordered the brigade to move ahead. Colonel Brownlow, 1st Tennessee, exclaimed as they rode to break out, "Boys, take care of yourselves, and the devil take the hindmost man!" While trying to move the rest of his brigade forward, Croxton and two orderlies were separated and forced to find their own way out. Croxton was not able to reach Union lines until August 12.[47]

McCook decided to try to lead Harrison's command out of the encirclement in the absence of Harrison, who had become separated from his troops. Harrison directed his orderly to follow with his horse. When the 5th Iowa and 4th Tennessee saddled up and rode away,

Harrison could not find the orderly and was trapped on foot and subsequently captured. McCook was able to break through near Franklin by a charge in a column of 1,200 troopers. McCook noted the sacrifices of some his men: "Some of the men of the Second and Eighth Indiana remained in stockades on the river bank to cover our crossing, and fought until their last cartridge was exhausted. Not one of them escaped. They cheerfully sacrificed themselves to insure the safety of their comrades."[48]

Brownlow's adventure was not over. He assumed command of the Second Brigade of about 600 men when Croxton was separated from the column. Brownlow was able to cross 250 men near Rotherwood using two canoes at 1:00 a.m. while the 4th Tennessee Cavalry served as rear guard. Unfortunately, the crossing was discovered and was attacked on both sides of the river. Brownlow exclaimed, "[T]he remainder killed, wounded, and captured. I believe more would have escaped if the brigade had moved in the direction suggested by General McCook."[49]

McCook finally made it to the Union lines on August 3 and his preliminary report concluded, "Colonel Dorr, Colonel Torrey, Major Austin wounded; Major Paine, killed; Harrison missing, supposed a prisoner. My loss very heavy. No co-operation from Stoneman." In addition, Croxton was missing and eventually returned with one orderly. When Major Owen Starr, 2nd Kentucky Cavalry, reported, he had only 95 troopers left in his command, a loss of about 50 percent of his command. The 5th Iowa recorded 119 casualties. Of Harrison's provisional division, only 500 were in the Union lines by August 11.[50]

On the positive side, McCook claimed,

> Two and a half miles of the Atlanta and West Point Railroad and telegraph destroyed near Palmetto; the same amount of Macon and Western Railroad and five miles of telegraph destroyed at Lovejoy's Station; 1,160 wagons burned; 2,000 mules killed or disabled; 1,000 bales cotton destroyed; 1,000 sacks of corn; 300 sacks of flour, and large quantities of bacon and tobacco.

McCook concluded his report:

> I regard the raid as a brilliant success, and had the forces of General Stoneman been able to unite with mine near McDonough, as I understood was contemplated by the general commanding the military division, I think we might have successfully carried our arms wherever desired, and accomplished more magnificent results than any raid in the history of this war.

The cost was his division:

> Since reaching Cartersville the division has been much scattered; parts of some regiments have been mustered out, many men are dismounted, and those who have succeeded in obtaining horses have already seriously impaired their usefulness in a long pursuit after Wheeler. Its line extends from Cartersville, Ga., to Franklin, Tenn. The constant calls upon it for scouting parties preclude the idea of recruiting its old horses, and the frequent forced gaps in its communications prevent anything like unity of action. It is my earnest hope that the interests of the service will soon permit the consolidation of, and thus restore its usefulness to, my command."[51]

The stories from McCook's Raid ranged from highs to lows, as in the case of Private George Healey, 5th Iowa Cavalry. The expedition began well for Healey, on July 29, when he ran into a group of Confederates and captured five of them single-handedly, an act for which he would receive the Medal of Honor. After capturing a Confederate, Healy and a fellow trooper, Oscar Martin, discovered the following:

> As we were about to resume our march, we heard men talking. We got behind a tree and the next minute four Confederates came, trailing in Indian fashion, toward us. Martin and I stepped from behind the trees

and covered them. I ordered: "Halt! Drop those guns!" but had to repeat the command before they obeyed. I then marched them some fifty feet, halted them, and ordered one man to advance at a time, when Martin and I relieved them of their revolvers, holsters and belts. Next, while Martin kept guard, I went back, removed the cartridges from the rifles they had dropped and returned the empty guns to them.

The exultation of the act of July 29 quickly faded because Private Healey was captured near Newnan during the raid and sent to Andersonville. Fortunately for Healey, he was exchanged in September.[52]

It took some time for all the stragglers to return to the Union lines. The overall loss was claimed to be approximately 500–600 casualties for the expedition, or about 20 percent of the original expedition, though other accounts indicate McCook lost around two-thirds of his 3,500 men (his own division plus Harrison's division). For McCook's Raid, Sherman and the newspapers declared this a success. McCook actually did accomplish the orders Sherman set for him—the destruction of two to five miles of rail south of Atlanta—and more. He had expected to find Stoneman but was disappointed. However, the cessation of supplies via railroad to Atlanta was short, as the railroad was quickly put back into working condition. The raid provided some boost in the morale of the soldiers facing Hood's lines at Atlanta. The message to the common soldier was that McCook had cut the railroad and captured several hundred prisoners. Those on the raid knew the truth, and one member of the 1st Wisconsin wrote to a local newspaper and exclaimed, "I don't want any more raids, if they please.... Curse the packs mules. Whoever heard of a pack train going on a raid. The d—d fools!" Peter Williamson, 1st Wisconsin Cavalry, wrote his wife that McCook now promised to ease up on the troopers who "had done all the hard knocks of this campaign."[53]

Garrard's Support of Stoneman's Raid

George Stoneman began his raid the same day McCook planned to begin his raid. Stoneman was to swing around the east side of Hood's army and meet with McCook near Lovejoy's Station. Kenner Garrard served under orders from Stoneman, but Sherman, temporarily pleased with Garrard's latest action, ordered Stoneman not to overuse Garrard's exhausted horses. Stoneman rode with three brigades totaling about 2,000 men, while Garrard's division of 3,500 men served under Stoneman's command.

On July 27, Stoneman met Garrard's division and ordered them to Flat Rock, or Flat Shoals, to occupy the Confederate cavalry there. William E. Crane wrote sarcastically of the role Garrard's cavalry was to play: "[W]e attract the enemy's attention toward ourselves— Stoneman to do the raiding & we the fighting." This plan would allow Stoneman to start his raid unencumbered and divert the enemy's attention away from his march in their rear. Garrard spent the first day without much resistance and reached his destination at 2:00 p.m. He ordered his command to form a horseshoe-shaped defensive line on the north side of the South River. Brigadier General Alfred Iverson's three brigades of Confederate cavalry rode to meet Garrard's command and attacked about 10:00 p.m. that evening when a few picket shots erupted into an explosive fight. About midnight Joseph Wheeler arrived to take command of the Confederate forces.[54]

Despite Garrard's diversion, Wheeler was aware that Stoneman continued his march across the South River intent on destroying the railroad somewhere south of Atlanta. Wheeler ordered one brigade to stay in Garrard's front while the other two brigades pursued Stoneman. Confederate reinforcements, brigades of Colonel George Dibrell's and Colonel Robert Anderson's, converged on Garrard's position. At 8:00 a.m. on July 28, the Confederates opened with two 12-pound howitzers in the Union rear. The Chicago Board of Trade Artillery returned fire. The author of *Sherman's Horsemen*, David Evans, wrote, "Everyone knew they were in a tight place. A captured Confederate intimated Garrard was surrounded by seven brigades of Wheeler's cavalry." Rebel infantry might already be closing in from Atlanta. At 10:00 a.m. a Confederate officer approached the Union line under a flag of truce demanding Garrard's unconditional surrender. After an extended conversation, Garrard, whom Sherman thought timid, replied, "Tell your general that as soon as I get ready I will walk out of here." Then the Confederate officer was escorted across the lines.[55]

Next, Garrard formed a skirmish line, placed Abram Miller's brigade of mounted infantry in the center, Minty's cavalry on the flanks, and Eli Long's cavalry behind. Then the line of blue surged forward, pushing back north toward Latimer's Crossroad. In twenty minutes, it was done. Garrard had cut his way out and the Confederates did not pursue. On the evening of July 30, Garrard's column returned to the main Union lines, having fulfilled his orders and providing time for Stoneman to initiate his raid.[56]

But Stoneman was not destined to be successful in his raid despite Sherman's initial conclusion that the railroad was cut south of Atlanta. Sherman notified Henry Halleck that Stoneman had two days' headstart on the Confederates. Sherman was wrong in his supposition. The rails cut south of Atlanta were the result of McCook's efforts and not Stoneman's. He was correct, however, that Garrard had given Stoneman a headstart. After Minty's return from Flat Shoals, he talked with Kilpatrick. Kilpatrick spoke of Stoneman: "Mark me, Minty, I know Stoneman like a book. He will go to the proper spot like a cannon ball, but when he gets there, like a shell, he will burst."[57]

As the days dragged on, Sherman began to worry about McCook and Stoneman. He wrote on July 31,

> I think I appreciate General Garrard's good qualities, but he is so cautious that if forced to make a bold move to the relief of General McCook I doubt if he would attempt it. General Stoneman went with a full knowledge of his risk; but General McCook will have reason to expect co-operation from about McDonough, and may be disappointed when he finds his bridge gone and a new road ahead closed by Wheeler. He has, however, a bold and well-appointed force and can fight his way back; still, for his sake, we must occupy the attention of the enemy as much as possible.[58]

Sherman's fickleness toward Garrard continued. His irritability about the cavalry focused on Garrard, who, just days before, was in his good graces for his success at Covington and Yellow River. Now he was in the doghouse again. Despite the fact Garrard reported he was surrounded by superior Confederate force (which was not actually true), Sherman focused on the small losses of his command and the fact he had not destroyed any of the railroad even though Garrard acted properly under Stoneman's and Sherman's own orders. This manner of evaluation of military effort recalled William Rosecrans' communication to Henry Halleck, who disregarded the achievements of the Tullahoma Campaign because they were not "written in letters of blood." Sherman's unhappiness during the day resulted in a letter to Thomas and Howard: "I must have a bolder commander for General Garrard's cavalry and want General Thomas to name to me General Kilpatrick or some good brigadier for the command." Thomas came to Garrard's defense, urging Sherman to reconsider: "I think if you will bear with Garrard you will find in a short time he will be the best cavalry commander you have."[59]

Perhaps Sherman would have been more tolerant of Garrard's actions if he was aware of orders given to him by Stoneman. Sherman seemed to have expectations that Garrard would have a more active role in Stoneman's raid despite orders and was frustrated that Garrard made no further progress than Flat Rock. Sherman expected Garrard to accompany Stoneman to McDonough, but Stoneman had no such intentions. Stoneman, in his haste for glory, followed what he perceived to be Sherman's orders of assigning Garrard to light duties since he had so recently been on a raid of his own. To round out this lack of understanding, Garrard was equally frustrated and said so in his after action report: "On the 27th the division was placed under General Stoneman, who ordered it to Flat Rock, and abandoned it to its fate."[60]

Sherman's greater concern was the fate of McCook, whom he believed was stranded at Lovejoy's Station waiting for Stoneman, who was not to arrive. Perhaps Sherman's frustration was just focused on Garrard. In Sherman's message about the cavalry raid, he clearly and correctly envisioned McCook with no bridge to recross the river, facing Wheeler, deep in enemy territory and alone.

Historians do not agree about Stoneman's decisions during his raid and the ultimate outcome. He had imagined a greater raid than originally planned by Sherman. Sherman's original plan was to destroy the last railroad from the south leading into Atlanta, but Stoneman imagined sweeping through enemy territory releasing Union prisoners at Macon and then Andersonville. Sherman had agreed, but Stoneman needed to destroy the railroad first. Bypassing his obligations at Lovejoy's Station, Stoneman reached the outskirts of Macon on July 30, about 90 miles south of Atlanta, but a determined defense of militia, citizens and reserves prevented his entry into the town. He initially considered riding to Florida but then headed north. He ran into Wheeler's cavalry north of Macon on July 31, and he ordered two of his brigades to break out on their own while he and the last brigade covered the escape. Stoneman was forced to surrender with 700 of his men.[61]

Stoneman would ultimately blame his Kentucky brigade for causing his defeat, which was overly harsh but typical of his pattern of assigning blame. Certainly, he had ownership of his unfortunate situation this far behind enemy lines despite the actions of his Kentuckians. Lieutenant Colonel R.W. Smith, assistant inspector general, wrote the report of the cavalry operations during this raid and did not refer to any bad behavior from Colonel Silas Adams' Kentucky cavalry. Perhaps the fate of Colonel Horace Capron's Third Brigade was the most tragic of the expedition. Capron's command reached King's Tanyard, very close to Union lines, only to be attacked by a group of Confederates on August 2. His command was shattered and most of them captured. When Lieutenant Colonel Smith wrote his report on August 7, only one hundred of this command had reached the Union lines. Sherman reported he believed Stoneman's losses would total 1,300. William Clark, 72nd Indiana Mounted Infantry, wrote in a letter to his parents on August 7, "Stoneman's Cavalry reported captured, cant think it. But nothing impossible here."[62]

It is also important to note the exceptional performance of the Confederate cavalry during the McCook and Stoneman raids. Wheeler and Jackson were drawn in three different directions and still effectively contained the Union raids. This is a testament to the Southern cavalry and their commanders. This was one of the premier defensive actions of the war and the result was saving the last lifeline to Atlanta and the destruction of two full Union cavalry divisions along the way. Certainly, this was one of Joseph Wheeler's best actions of the war.

Sherman's summed up the cavalry expeditions beginning on July 27 and 28:

> General McCook is entitled to much credit for thus saving his command, which was endangered by the failure of General Stoneman to reach Lovejoy's. But on the whole the cavalry raid is not deemed a success, for the real purpose was to break the enemy's communications, which though done was on so limited a scale that I knew the damage would soon be repaired.

The newspapers generally gave McCook credit for a successful raid. McCook, who personified the "good officer," fulfilled his orders by destroying more of the railroad than Sherman asked and as a result had slightly more than 1,000 troopers remaining, only about half of them mounted. Stoneman, on the other hand, yielded no significant positive results in his raid and his failure to reach McCook at Lovejoy's Station contributed to McCook's unfortunate results. Stoneman's attitude toward those who were captured intensified the dislike many held for him. Lieutenant Henry Belfield, 8th Iowa Cavalry, who had been captured, wrote in reference to Stoneman at a Charleston prison: "In the Charleston prison he occupied a room or rooms which I think had been the quarters of the superintendent of the prison. In this he secluded himself, and never mingled with those who bore no stars on their shoulders."[63]

Sherman, ever the practical general, with half of his cavalry essentially gone ordered Garrard to the left flank and ordered up Kilpatrick's Third Division to the right flank. What remained of McCook's cavalry was sent to the Marietta area for garrison duty. After all the efforts, Sherman still had to find a way to cut the last railroad to Atlanta, and now Wheeler was looking at the vulnerable supply line in the rear of the Union armies. Sherman temporarily reviewed the use of his cavalry and wrote to Henry Halleck: "I will use my cavalry hereafter to cover the railroad, and use infantry and artillery against Atlanta." Sherman was not to follow his own advice.[64]

The Union cavalry, despite its successes and failures, was in the South to stay for the remainder of the war. Some of the local citizens were absolutely amazed by the fact that blue-coated troopers were riding through the countryside. A group of troopers of the 4th Tennessee Cavalry was riding near Sand Mountain, Georgia, and asked a lady for some water. She inquired who the soldiers were and they replied they were "Yankees." She was astounded and she said, "I know you'ns ain't no Yankees." The soldiers persisted, declaring they were most certainly Union cavalry from Tennessee. She paused then seemed to understand, but exclaimed, "[Y]ou'ns haint got no horns." Then a trooper clarified the problem. "We are young Yankees, our horns haven't sprouted yet. The horned Yankees are in the rear and will be up directly."[65]

12. Atlanta to Lovejoy's Station, August 8–October 26, 1864

It was a glorious sight, with horses stamping, and champing the bits as if eager for the fray, standards and guidons flung to the breeze.—W.L. Curry

While Stoneman's and McCook's raids were in progress in late July, Sherman moved his armies back to the west and attempted to get around Hood's flank. Schofield's Army of the Ohio moved from the left to the Union right flank, Howard's Army of the Tennessee held the center and Thomas's Army of the Cumberland held the left flank. When Schofield moved, Sherman assigned the duty of occupying the vacated trenches east of the city to Kenner Garrard's cavalry. This was hapless duty for cavalrymen, but the Confederate cavalry had been manning the lines with the infantry for many months. Fortunately, not all of Garrard's cavalry was destined for the trenches. Much of his cavalry remained in the trenches for only two weeks, and the rest for the horses was needed.[1]

After three years of war, the country (North and South) was running out of horses. Since the beginning of Sherman's advance toward Atlanta some of the Union cavalry had been without horses. After McCook's and Stoneman's raids the shortage of horses was sorely felt. Sherman found 2,000 horses in St. Louis and requested the mounts for his army. Henry Halleck sent the unpleasant response that only 1,000 would be sent. He concluded, "The country is nearly exhausted of cavalry horses, and unless there is a greater economy in their use the men must very soon go afoot."[2]

Brigadier General Washington L. Elliott was only slightly more visible after the cavalry raids in July. It is remarkable the small presence he had on the operations of cavalry of the Army of the Cumberland. On August 8, he reported on the condition of the cavalry for Sherman's armies at Atlanta.

Strength of the Cavalry (Army of the Cumberland)—August 8, 1864[3]

Total Present for Duty	Officers	Men	Total
McCook's Division	67	949	1,016
Garrard's Division	199	4,177	4,376
Kilpatrick's Division	162	2,826	2,988

After McCook's and Stoneman's raids, McCook's division was dismounted and sent to join Louis Watkins' brigade in the rear to protect the supply line at Kingston and Cartersville, Georgia, and Calhoun, Tennessee. When horses became available, McCook's troopers were

Troopers from Garrard's division manned the trenches near Atlanta for two weeks (Library of Congress).

sent to Nashville to be remounted. In the meantime, Sherman found John Schofield supported his low opinion of all the cavalry commanders. Schofield garnered the approval of his superiors while he ambitiously furthered his own career; and in light of the less than positive results of the two recent cavalry raids it was easy to turn on the cavalry. In an interesting set of messages between Schofield and Sherman, both men expressed their disdain for officers in the cavalry. Only Thomas seemed to have moral fiber to support his subordinates. Sherman asked Schofield on August 9 who would command the cavalry for the Army of the Ohio while Stoneman was a prisoner of war. Schofield responded, "I have no good cavalry commander." Schofield suggested bringing someone in from another department. Sherman replied, "I have no cavalry commander at all. All the cavalry of the old Army of the Tennessee are back in Mississippi, and General Thomas's cavalry is not well commanded." Even so, the two generals finally decided on Colonel Israel Garrard, Kenner Garrard's brother, to command Schofield's cavalry while Stoneman remained a prisoner.[4]

On August 10, the fear that the Confederate cavalry would strike the Union supply line was realized. Wheeler began a raid that would challenge the reserves and defenses in the rear of Sherman's armies. Wheeler's raid would stretch from August 10 until September 9. He initially raided toward Dalton and then headed into Tennessee. Sherman rallied his troops in the rear to deal with Wheeler and believed the raid to be more of a nuisance than a threat. The removal of Wheeler and the majority of Confederate cavalry from the Atlanta area and Schofield's reluctance to send his infantry on an expedition to cut the railroad south of Atlanta helped persuade Sherman to allow another cavalry raid. Kilpatrick, whose aggressive tendencies found favor with Sherman, was able to persuade him to try another raid. Not everyone supported this raid, and George Thomas questioned, "I think it better to pursue Wheeler with our cavalry than to attempt another raid with it on the enemy's communications during Wheeler's absence." Sherman replied that Garrard and Kilpatrick should be able to act with impunity with Wheeler gone. Thomas asked, "But do you think it prudent to risk any more cavalry on their communications until our force is materially increased?"[5]

Washington Elliott issued orders for both Kilpatrick and Garrard on August 14 to develop the Confederate positions. Garrard was ordered to push hard on the left flank and to give battle with the Confederate cavalry "without too much risk." Kilpatrick was also ordered, "You will make a bold reconnaissance in the direction of Fairburn to the railroad if you can reach it." But before any raid was ordered Sherman wanted to hear from both Garrard and Kilpatrick about what they were facing.[6]

Sherman was tired of what he perceived as the reluctance of Garrard to ride boldly against the enemy. He wrote to secretary of war Edwin Stanton on August 16 and sealed Garrard's fate as commander of the Second Division of Cavalry: "I need a good cavalry brigadier very much, and recommend Col. Eli Long ... [as] the cavalry is not commanded to my satisfaction." Sherman should have made this decision much earlier in the campaign, not because Garrard was not a good commander but because Sherman had no confidence in him. He treated Garrard poorly and condescendingly. The conservative nature of Garrard's actions in mid–August caused Sherman to decide on Eli Long to command the Second Division. Sherman had just lost the bulk of two of his four cavalry divisions on ill-fated raids on Hood's communications, but Garrard's performance was supported by both army commanders (Thomas and McPherson) he had served. Garrard's actions were also supported by his immediate commanding officer, Elliott. Elliott wrote to Garrard on August 15: "I say, if the enemy won't come out and fight you, you can't make him, but can drive him to his works. If, in connection with your reconnaissance, you think you cannot strike the railroad, I would not attempt it." Both Elliott and Thomas were reluctant about another cavalry raid. Elliott also wrote to Thomas about pulling Garrard's cavalry into another raid: "Would not our trains be in danger if Garrard's entire division should go, with a brigade or division of rebel cavalry in front of our left?" Thomas finally wrote to Sherman: "If you think a cavalry raid can destroy the Macon road sufficiently to force Hood to retreat, I think now would be a good time to send against it." Thomas was right. If Sherman was bound to make the raid, the time was right, with much of the Confederate cavalry in the rear; but this message revealed anything but a rousing endorsement of another raid.[7]

Kilpatrick's fighting spirit convinced Sherman to make the final decision to attempt to break the railroad south of Atlanta. The Kilpatrick Raid would take place from August 18 through August 22. Prior to the raid, Sherman explained his reasoning to allow Kilpatrick to lead: "[H]e will fight. I do believe he, with his own and General Garrard's cavalry, could ride right round Atlanta and mash the Macon road all to pieces, but I don't want to risk our cavalry." Sherman, who had no confidence in Garrard, chose to send Garrard's best two brigades while not including Garrard himself in the raid. Captain George Robinson, commanding the Chicago Board of Trade Battery, related that during the planning of the raid Garrard told Sherman he did not think the raid would be successful unless all of the cavalry was used to destroy the railroads. Sherman was not prepared to commit all of his cavalry and Garrard's reluctance gave Sherman the opportunity to exclude him from the raid.[8]

Kilpatrick's Raid: The Advance

Kilpatrick left the Union lines on the evening of August 18. He rode with over 4,500 troopers from his own Third Cavalry Division and two brigades of Garrard's Second Cavalry Division, under command of Brigadier General Eli Long, who was probably not aware he had been promoted to the rank of general that day. In light of Stoneman's failed raid, Sherman specifically described this action: "It is not a raid, but a deliberate attack for the purpose of so disabling that road that the enemy will be unable to supply his army in Atlanta." Once the expedition was completed, Kilpatrick planned to return to the Union right flank. Kilpatrick's objective was to destroy enough track to put the railroad out of commission for two weeks. Neither Sherman nor Kilpatrick had any doubts this could be accomplished.[9]

Long, who on paper commanded Garrard's cavalry brigades, rode with 871 men and 54 officers of Colonel Robert Minty's brigade (4th Michigan, 7th Pennsylvania, 4th U.S.) and another 1,308 men and 73 officers of Colonel Beroth Eggleston's brigade (1st, 3rd, and 4th Ohio cavalries). Eggleston assumed command of Long's brigade upon Long's promotion to command Garrard's cavalry during the expedition. The forty-six-year-old Eggleston was a native of Saratoga County, New York, whose family moved to Ohio when he was fifteen. He was a businessman, postmaster and farmer before the war near Chillicothe, Ohio. The veteran Eggleston joined the 1st Ohio Cavalry and was promoted to the rank of major in 1863 and colonel in 1864. The highly regarded Chicago Board of Trade Artillery (four guns) also accompanied the expedition. Kilpatrick sent a communication to each of the regiments outlining the objective of the raid and concluded, "Let each soldier remember this & resolve to accomplish this, the great object for which so much is risked, or die trying."[10]

Kilpatrick left the Union lines on August 18 and ran into pickets of the 6th Texas Cavalry at Camp Creek, about three miles south of Sandtown. At 12:30 a.m. on August 19, he pushed General "Sul" Ross's 400 troopers aside at East Point. Ross's cavalry was held off the road by Lieutenant Colonel Fielder Jones's Second Brigade (8th Indiana, 2nd Kentucky, 10th Ohio) as the rest of the Union column passed. Kilpatrick reached Red Oak, about eight miles south of the Chattahoochee River, at daylight and destroyed a section of the Atlanta & West Point Railroad. General Ross pulled his command together and attacked Kilpatrick while he was attending to the destruction of the rails. However, Ross was greatly outnumbered, and the Union cavalry repulsed his attack. Then Kilpatrick marched for his real objective—Jonesborough. He was in his element, as described by Captain William E. Crane, 4th Ohio Cavalry: "I found

12. Atlanta to Lovejoy's Station 269

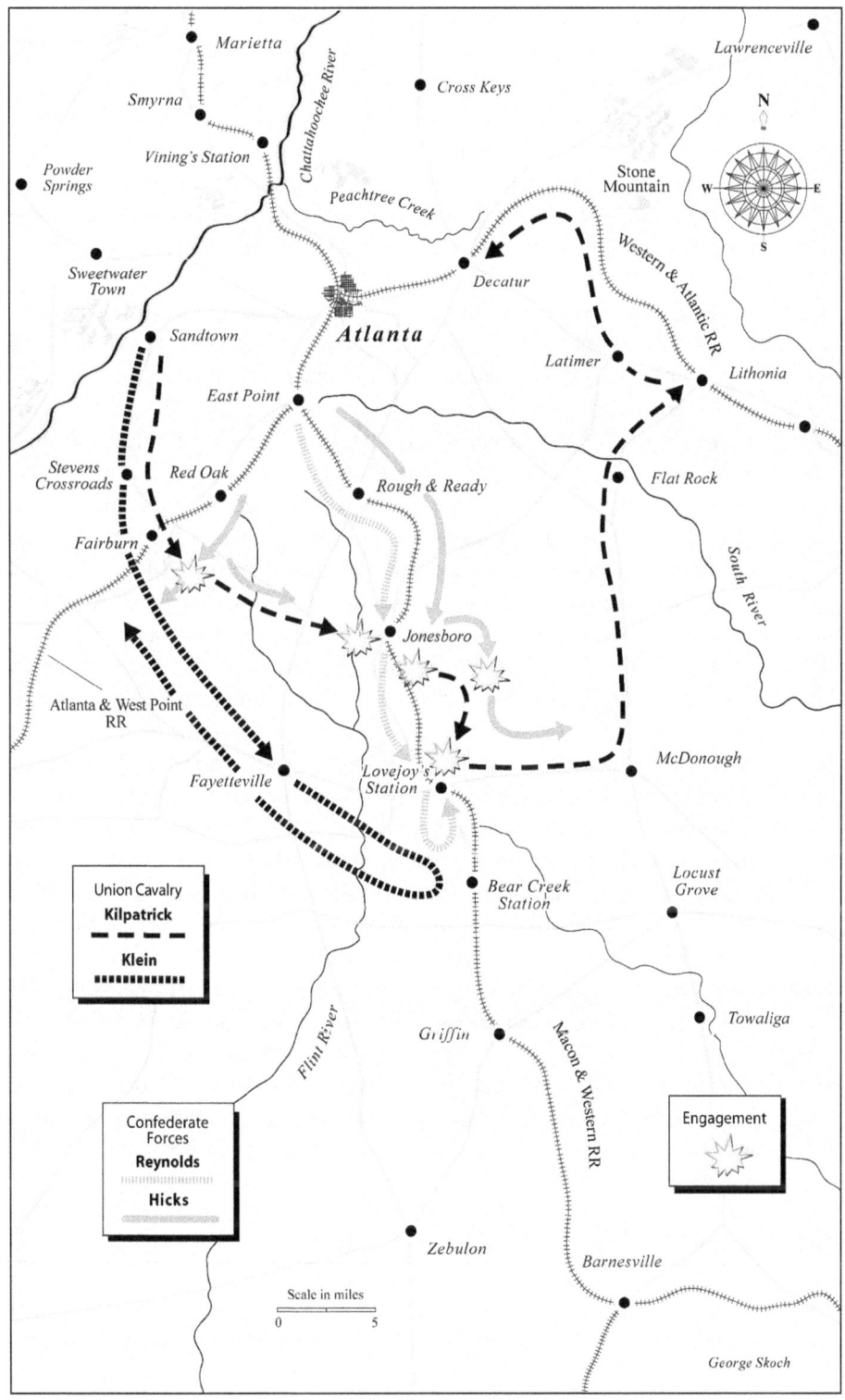

Kilpatrick's Raid During the Atlanta Campaign (August 18–22, 1864)

Kilpatrick flying about in lively style, swearing at everything & issuing half a dozen orders in a breath." As Kilpatrick rode for Jonesborough, he found Ross had ridden ahead of his column and tried to slow the Union advance by fighting and withdrawing over and over again. Ross made his first determined resistance at the Flint River Bridge. He attempted to burn the bridge over the river while trying to delay the Union column. Long's cavalry rode across the Flint River and drove the Confederate line defending the bridge and approach to the river. The Chicago Board of Trade Artillery was involved in a duel with Confederate artillery during the fight at the river. Kilpatrick repaired the bridge, and his command reached Jonesborough at 5:00 p.m. on August 19.[11]

While on the way to Red Oak, Kilpatrick decided he needed a diversion to keep the Confederates from focusing all their efforts on the main column. He ordered his 309-man, two-regiment First Brigade (3rd Indiana and 5th Iowa) under command of the veteran Lieutenant Colonel Robert Klein to ride to Fairburn, five miles west of Red Oak, and destroy the railroad there. The 5th Iowa Cavalry totaled only 90 troopers and had the dubious honor of also having participated in the McCook raid, where it lost about 50 percent of its men. Upon completing this task, Klein was to rejoin Kilpatrick at Griffin. Klein's ruse worked perfectly. Frank Armstrong's Confederate cavalry was posted at Jonesborough and rode to meet Klein's feint, leaving Jonesborough lightly defended. When Kilpatrick reached Jonesborough, he found the telegraph and railroad at Bear Creek Station, 10 miles south of Jonesborough, were already destroyed by Klein's command. Brigadier General Frank Armstrong's and Brigadier General Samuel Ferguson's cavalry had ridden through Jonesborough at 1:00 p.m. to attack Klein. Klein destroyed about 300 yards of track at Bear Creek Station and after setting a train afire rode northward destroying sections of track along the way. Two miles south of Lovejoy's Station, a train filled with Confederates was observed heading in his direction. Facing infantry and cavalry and not finding Kilpatrick, Klein decided it was time to try to get his two regiments back to the Union lines. He rode west for Fayetteville and when he was within two miles of the town, he saw Confederates, part of Frank Armstrong's Mississippi Cavalry, across the road in front of him. He had been cut off. Klein, a former Prussian soldier, decided his only hope lay ahead. He ordered "charge" and the column slammed into and then through the thin Southern line. Klein reached the Union lines on August 20.[12]

The main column of the Union cavalry spent the next six hours destroying the railroads around Jonesborough. Minty's 4th U.S. and 4th Michigan moved north of the town, guarding the crossroads and forming a screen to prevent any attacks from Atlanta. W.L. Curry, 1st Ohio Cavalry, described the scene around Jonesborough: "The sky was lighted up with burning timbers, buildings and cotton bales; the continuous bang of carbines, the galloping of staff officers and orderlies up and down the streets carrying orders and dispatches, the terrified citizens peering out their windows, the constant marching of troops changing positions." All this was accompanied by Kilpatrick's headquarters band playing patriotic Union music. At 11:00 p.m., Colonel Eli Murray's Third Brigade of Kilpatrick's division (92nd Illinois Mounted Infantry, 3rd Kentucky, and 5th Kentucky) was attacked a mile south of the town by Brigadier General Daniel Harris Reynolds' Arkansas infantry, which had been carried part of the way by railcars. Reynolds was joined with Brigadier General William "Red" Jackson's cavalry. It was the 10th Ohio Cavalry's turn to be surprised as they rode along the track southward and were hit by a volley from Reynolds' infantry. Kilpatrick suspended his rail destruction and sent his entire command to face the Confederate force converging on his position. The two

Kilpatrick destroyed a section of railroad at Jonesborough, but only a day after Kilpatrick's return Sherman wrote, "I think the rebels have already repaired the Macon [rail]road" (Library of Congress).

lines faced each other as a heavy rain began, which made the situation even worse for both sides. Kilpatrick in his own particular style worsened the situation as artillery from the Southern guns and the Union side counter-fired. Due to the darkness, it was somewhat difficult to locate the various guns, but Kilpatrick insisted that his band play Union songs while positioned near the Union artillery. J.A. Nourse, Chicago Board of Trade Artillery, recorded, "Our cannoneers were quite indignant and used their ramrods to drive the band out of the battery."[13]

Kilpatrick faced cavalry and infantry from the south, and train whistles were heard coming from the north. If Kilpatrick was forced into a pitched battle, he knew it would not end well. He called his commanding officers to a meeting on the porch of a house and discussed his escape route. He would feint on a northerly route and then ride west. Unknown to Kilpatrick, in addition to Reynolds's infantry, Ferguson's, Ross's and Armstrong's Confederate cavalry brigades were also riding toward him. He made the decision to extract his command and begin moving east on the Stockbridge Road, then turned south and west on the Fayetteville Road.[14]

Kilpatrick's Raid: Fight at Nash Farm

The Union column was riding south toward the Fayetteville Road when the 3rd Texas Cavalry attacked the 3rd Ohio Cavalry, which was serving as rear guard, sending it rushing for the Union column. The 3rd and 4th Ohio cavalries formed a solid line and stopped the Confederate attack and then moved to regain the column. But General Ross had discovered the true route of Kilpatrick's retreat. He was not riding north, he was riding south. Ross sent this information to Reynolds, who ordered his infantry back down the railroad to Lovejoy's Station, correctly anticipating Kilpatrick would turn west.[15]

The men of Garrard's brigade were uncomfortable under Kilpatrick's command. Private Lucien Wulsin, 4th Ohio Cavalry, commented on the excessive duty of Long's and Minty's cavalry: "When the boys found that we were again moving from our lines there was some tall swearing done and remarks made that 'Kill-Horse' was bound to get into a muss before going back." Intentionally misquoting Kilpatrick's nickname, Wulsin's prediction was about to come true.[16]

Kilpatrick, in his movement to the west, struck the railroad about a mile north of Lovejoy's Station at 11:00 a.m. on August 20. As he moved south toward the station he ran into Reynolds' infantry. What ensued is known at the Battle of Nash Farm. Kilpatrick was engaged in battling infantry in his front, and cavalry was attacking his rear in this hard-fought battle.

ORDER OF BATTLE, AUGUST 20, 1864[17]
UNION FORCES
Major General Judson Kilpatrick

SECOND CAVALRY DIVISION
Brig. General Eli Long

1st Cavalry Brigade,	2nd Cavalry Brigade,
Colonel Robert H. G. Minty	**Colonel Beroth B. Eggleston**
4th Michigan Cavalry, Major Frank Mix	3rd Ohio Cavalry, Colonel Charles B. Seidel
7th Pennsylvania Cavalry, Major Wm. Jennings	4th Ohio Cavalry, Lt Colonel Oliver P. Robie
4th U.S. Cavalry, Captain James B. McIntyre	1st Ohio Cavalry, Colonel Beroth B. Eggleston

Chicago Board of Trade Battery, Lieutenants Henry Bennett and George Robinson

THIRD CAVALRY DIVISION
Brig. General Judson Kilpatrick

1st Cavalry Brigade,	2nd Cavalry Brigade,
Lt. Colonel Robert Klein	**Lieutenant Colonel Fielder Alsor Jones**
3rd Indiana Cavalry, Major Alfred Gaddis	8th Indiana Cavalry, Major Thomas Herring
5th Iowa Cavalry, Major John Morris Young	2nd Kentucky Cavalry, Major Owen Starr

10th Ohio Cavalry, Lt Colonel Thomas Wakefield Sanderson

3rd Cavalry Brigade, Colonel Eli Houston Murray
92nd Illinois Mounted Infantry, Colonel Smith D. Atkins (Major Albert Woodcock)
3rd Kentucky Cavalry, Lt Colonel Robert H. King
5th Kentucky Cavalry, Colonel Oliver L. Baldwin
10th Wisconsin Battery Light Artillery, Captain Yates V. Beebe

CONFEDERATE FORCES
Cavalry Division, Brigadier General William Hicks Jackson

Armstrong's Brigade, Brig. General Frank Armstrong
1st Mississippi Cavalry, Col. R. A. Pinson
2nd Mississippi Cavalry, Major J. J. Perry
28th Mississippi Cavalry, Major Joshua T. McBee
Ballentine's (Mississippi), Lt Colonel William L. Maxwell
Company "A" 1st Confederate Cavalry, Captain James Ruffin

Ross's Brigade, Brig. General Lawrence S. Ross
1st Texas Legion, Colonel Edwin R. Hawkins
3rd Texas Cavalry, Lt Colonel Jiles S. Boggess
6th Texas Cavalry, Lt Colonel Peter F. Ross
9th Texas Cavalry, Colonel Dudley W. Jones

Ferguson's Brigade, Brig. General Samuel Wragg Ferguson
2nd Alabama Cavalry, Colonel John N. Carpenter
56th Alabama Cavalry, Colonel William Boyles
9th Mississippi Cavalry, Colonel H. H. Miller
11th Mississippi Cavalry, Colonel R. O. Perrin
12th Mississippi Cavalry Battalion, William M. Inge

Artillery, Captain John Waties
Croft's Battery, Georgia Light Artillery (Columbus Artillery), 1st Lt Alfred J. Young
Farris Battery, Missouri Light Artillery (Clark Artillery), Captain Houston King
3rd Battalion, South Carolina Light Artillery (Palmetto Battalion), Lt R. B. Waddell

Confederate Infantry Brigade, Brigadier General Daniel Harris Reynolds
1st Arkansas Mounted Rifles (dismounted)
2nd Arkansas Mounted Rifles (dismounted)
4th Arkansas Infantry
9th Arkansas Infantry
25th Arkansas Infantry
48th Tennessee Infantry (Attached to Reynold's brigade)

As Kilpatrick's column approached Lovejoy's Station, he faced a line of Reynolds' infantry. A volley from the pickets of Jackson's cavalry stopped the Union advance. Reynolds' brigade charged ahead as Minty and Long deployed their regiments, dismounted, into a battle line. One volley killed Minty's horse under him and the Union cavalry was pushed backed through a 400-yard-long cornfield. The 9th Pennsylvania Cavalry was hit particularly hard during the fight. T.F. Dornblaser recorded the Confederate infantry poured a volley into his company, killing four and wounding several others, including Dornblaser. Many in the company were captured. Long deployed his cavalry as Minty's forward command was roughly pushed to the rear, but they rallied on Long's position. Long's troopers began throwing up hastily prepared barricades. The cornfield gave the Chicago Board of Trade Artillery a field of fire and the gunners began to fire double-loaded canister. In fifteen minutes, the artillery fired seventy rounds and then pulled back. In the fight, one of the guns had a broken trail and could not fire. The battle with the infantry took a heavy toll on the Union battery as men began to fall and over 75 percent of the horses were killed in the first few minutes of the fight. As the battery began to pull back, they could not withdraw the damaged gun. Then the 3rd Ohio Cavalry charged ahead and temporarily stopped the infantry advance and pulled the gun off the field by hand.[18]

A creditable Union defensive line took shape. A battalion of the 4th Michigan held the right flank of the Union line and, left to right, were the 3rd Ohio, 1st Ohio, and 92nd Illinois. The 3rd and 5th Kentucky cavalries fell into line behind. Finally Fielder Jones's 8th Indiana, 2nd Kentucky and 10th Ohio completed the Union defense in a third defensive line. As all the Union regiments joined in the fight, the Confederate infantry began to push ahead. So close were the two lines the cavalry resorted to using their revolvers, but the Union defense stopped Reynolds' advance.[19]

When things seemed to be working out for the Union cavalry, an explosion of gunfire was heard in their rear as General Sul Ross's Texas cavalry attacked the 10th Ohio Cavalry which was assigned duty of protecting the Lovejoy–Lee's Mill Road. The battle thus far had been hard fought and rapid. The fight in the rear and in the front made a continuous roar.

Kilpatrick wrote, "In twenty minutes I found that I was completely enveloped by cavalry and infantry, with artillery." He called for Minty to discuss the situation and said, "[W]e are surrounded. You know what is in our front; Jackson with 5,000 cavalry is in rear of our left, and Pat Cleburne with 10,000 infantry is closing on our right." Despite Kilpatrick's exaggeration of the number of troops he faced, he decided he wanted Minty and Eli Murray's brigades to charge side-by-side and cut through Ross's cavalry on the east. Minty agreed to follow any orders but suggested a charge by column of fours. Kilpatrick replied, "Form in any way you please." Facing the Union cavalry were three lines of defenders, formed about fifty yards apart behind hastily constructed barricades.[20]

Leaving a line of skirmishers facing the infantry to the south, the Union cavalry again got into their saddles and formed north of the cornfield. George Robinson, Chicago Board of Trade Artillery, described the preparation for the charge:

> Col. Minty rides to the front and center of the first brigade and gives the command, 'Draw, sabre!' and as the twelve hundred blades leaped and swung into the air, the flash of sunlight upon each one of them seemed to reflect the courageous countenance and confident expression of him who now more tightly grasped its hilt.

At 2:00 p.m., three Union cavalry brigades, all riding in columns of fours, charged Ross's Texans. W.L. Curry, 1st Ohio Cavalry, wrote,

> It was a glorious sight, with horses stamping, and champing the bits as if eager for the fray, standards and guidons flung to the breeze, with the dashing here and there of staff officers carrying orders, the serious faces of the commanders, the stern, quick commands of the officers as the squadrons are forming.

As they charged, the Confederate artillery boomed, but the distance was quickly covered by the charging horses. Minty led the Union charge and the Union horsemen riding with sabers drawn raced forward. They were irresistible.[21] "Into the jaws of death, Into the mouth of hell," quoted the 3rd Ohio's Thomas Crofts as he used Tennyson's *Charge of the Light Brigade* to describe the actions at Nash Farm.[22]

The Texans fell under the onslaught of the Union cavalry, and those who could run did so. Kilpatrick would claim four guns, three of which were destroyed and one captured, three battle flags captured and ordinance train seized, in addition to a large number of enemy killed and captured. Also, much to Kilpatrick's credit, he acknowledged that the command was saved through the "prompt and daring" actions of Minty, Long, and Captain Estes, Kilpatrick's assistant adjutant general.[23]

T.F. Dornblaser, 7th Pennsylvania, observed the 4th U.S. Cavalry in their charge:

> At this point, the writer saw Captain McIntyre, commanding the Fourth Regulars, leading his regiment against the battery. His white horse struck an artillery carriage in the road, throwing horse and rider against the fence, behind which a number of rebel horsemen were sitting; in their saddles, with revolvers in hand, but too badly frightened to do any shooting.

McIntyre remounted and continued the fight.[24]

The Union cavalry had successfully punched a hole through the encirclement, but the charge had disorganized the regiments, which took some time to get back into shape. Luck is important, and Kilpatrick was lucky. As his command re-formed a few miles away, Brigadier General Frank Armstrong's cavalry arrived at Lovejoy's Station. If he had arrived sooner, the results of the charge might have been quite different; however, Armstrong did mount a determined pursuit. The 1st, 3rd and 4th Ohio cavalries formed the rear guard and Eli Long placed the 3rd Ohio as the rear-most regiment along a road on the banks of Walnut Creek, a few miles northeast of Lovejoy's Station. The Ohioans faced the 1st Mississippi Cavalry which crossed the creek and then charged across a cornfield. The 3rd Ohio fired their Spencer rifles, but this did not stop the Mississippians, who threw the Ohio cavalry into disorder. During the fight, Long was wounded and his horse was killed under him and the horse of the 3rd Ohio's commanding officer, Colonel Charles Seidel's, was also killed.[25]

To their rear were two of Minty's regiments, the 4th Michigan and 7th Pennsylvania. The Ohioans passed through this line. Minty's regiments greeted the Confederate cavalry with a volley from their Spencer rifles and what followed what was described as "the hardest fighting that we had seen during the raid." The Chicago Board of Trade Artillery and King's Battery exchanged fire as the cavalry battle continued. During the battle, one the guns of the Chicago Board of Trade exploded, cutting all the spokes above the wheel hub, and all the cannoneers were thrown to the ground but no one was seriously injured. All that remained of the gun was a small piece of the breach. The remainder of the cannon was thrown out of sight. Minty's men repelled three different charges before he was forced to give way. After a one-hour-and-forty-minute fight, Minty and Long ordered their men back into the saddle and rode after Kilpatrick, who was leading the rest of the column northward. Almost immediately heavy rain drenched the troopers.[26]

Kilpatrick abandoned any thoughts of continuing west and his weary Union cavalry rode for Covington, near the eastern-most Union lines. Many of the men had not slept for sixty hours. The column continued northward, across muddy roads, through unfriendly towns and across rain-swollen streams; all the while with Confederate cavalry on their heels. The Union cavalry column had a difficult crossing at the rain-swollen Cotton River. Kilpatrick abandoned his wagons in getting the cavalry across. George Robinson clashed with Kilpatrick when he was ordered to throw his damaged cannon into the river. Robinson wrote some twenty years after the war; "Some of my men, dumped the gun from the wagon and into the river, cut down the wagon and set fire to it, and have frequently, though mentally, damned Kilpatrick from then till now." Kilpatrick finally reached David Stanley's Fourth Corps lines northeast of Atlanta on August 22, absolutely exhausted. Minty's brigade recorded 106 casualties and Long's 94. In Kilpatrick's division, his Second Brigade recorded 49 casualties and his Third Brigade only 15. Robert Klein's First Brigade, which had separated from Kilpatrick early in the raid, recorded only two casualties. Garrard's men did the hardest fighting during the expedition; regardless of that, the numbers were only a fraction of the losses recorded in McCook's and Stoneman's raids. Joseph Vale, 7th Pennsylvania Cavalry, sarcastically wrote of Kilpatrick, "Kilpatrick seemingly to be desirous of complimenting the Second Division by giving it the precedence whenever a fight was imminent, no matter whether in the front or rear!"[27]

Kilpatrick rode to Sherman's headquarters and explained the complete success of his raid. He exaggerated the ease with which he had pushed aside the Confederates and trumpeted the accomplishments of the expedition. He assured Sherman that the railroad was destroyed to such an extent it would take ten days to repair.

Sherman summed up his view of the mission on August 23, just one day after Kilpatrick's return: "I think the rebels have already repaired the Macon [rail]road." It is hard not to criticize Kilpatrick for his bravado, both prior to and following the mission. On August 17 Sherman noted that Kilpatrick had exclaimed how "comparatively easy" it would be to destroy the railroad "effectually." Kilpatrick himself said, "Such an opportunity to strike the enemy a terrible blow has never offered." In the end, this raid, like the two before it, proved to be ineffective. The practical and professional soldier Brigadier General Eli Long concluded that the raid was not a success. He stated that the railroad was unlikely to be destroyed by a raiding party such that Hood would be unable to rebuild it quickly: "[I]t would, under the circumstances, have been but a comparatively short time before it would have been rebuilt." Long's assessment applied to not only Kilpatrick but also Stoneman and McCook. The raids were ill-conceived and had only a minimal chance for success from the start.[28]

While the preparation for the raid was being made, Sherman concluded to remove Kenner Garrard from command of the Second Cavalry Division and replace him with Eli Long. Sherman's hand-picked favorite cavalry commander had just failed on a mission that could have saved many lives, but Sherman had little criticism for Kilpatrick. He liked the style of Kilpatrick and appeared to ignore the lack of substance. George Thomas defended Garrard in an accurate assessment to Sherman:

> I think Garrard's Services on the Augusta road show how thoroughly he performs his work when he undertakes what he has to do. By not rashly pushing on to the main road, regardless of the forces opposed to him, he has preserved to us his fine division, with which I believe he will yet do good service.

Sherman responded,

> I am willing to admit that General Garrard's excessive prudence saves his cavalry to us, but though saved, it is as useless as so many sticks. Saving himself, he sacrifices others operating in conjoint expeditions. I am so thoroughly convinced that if he can see a horseman in the distance with a spy-glass he will turn back, that I cannot again depend on his making an effort, though he knows a commander depends on him.

Because the other divisions had paid the butcher's bill, Sherman appeared to resent the fact Garrard had not done so.[29]

Finally, in regard to Eli Long, Thomas's impression of him was this: "I regard Long as a very efficient officer, who, by his services during this war, has dearly earned his promotion, not only for gallantry, but on account of his administrative ability and experience." Sherman agreed with Thomas's assessment, but he replied that he promised Long a promotion for his actions at Cleveland, Tennessee, and he was going to belatedly fulfill that promise. This wasn't a compelling reason to justify the promotion and command of a division of cavalry. Long and Minty were excellent commanders worthy of promotion, but not for the reason specified by Sherman.[30]

In fact, Garrard still had the best division in the cavalry and one Sherman desperately needed. But Garrard was a quiet and gentlemanly officer who did the job and hoped the results would speak for him. Of the two successful cavalry raids during the summer of 1864, Garrard commanded one of them, and he would receive a commendation for his actions at Covington. Kilpatrick would continue with Sherman in his "march to the sea." After Atlanta fell, Garrard would be relieved and assigned command of an infantry division in Major General A.J. Smith's Sixteenth Corps during the Battle of Nashville. He would receive another commendation for his actions during that battle and yet another at Mobile in 1865. In the meantime, Brigadier General Eli Long had been promoted, justly so. But he needed to recuperate from the wounds of the past expedition, where he had received a head wound, and wounds to his right arm and thigh.[31]

The Battle of Jonesborough

After cavalry raids failed to effectively cut the two railroads still supplying Atlanta, Sherman determined to accomplish the task using six of his seven infantry corps. He issued the orders for the movement twelve miles south of Atlanta to Jonesborough on August 25 and left Major General Henry Slocum's Twentieth Corps to guard the most important Chattahoochee River crossings northwest of Atlanta. The disappearance of the Federal infantry from the trenches north and west of Atlanta caused brief excitement among the Confederates and the few citizens remaining in the city, but Hood's remaining cavalry quickly discovered the mass movement of Federals. Hood could not defend the entire length of the railroads and determined that Jonesborough was a likely Federal objective. He dispatched both Lieutenant General William Hardee's and Lieutenant General Stephen Dill Lee's corps by rail and on foot to Jonesboro, with Hardee in overall command.[32]

The two remaining divisions (Garrard and Kilpatrick) of Union cavalry were placed along the flanks of Sherman's armies as the movement began. Kilpatrick's exhausted cavalry patrolled the right flank and Garrard's equally tired cavalry the left flank. Sherman ordered Thomas to have Garrard's cavalry, again, rip up the track again near Covington.[33]

On August 30, Howard's three corps (Fifteenth, Sixteenth, Seventeenth) stopped for the night near Renfroe's Place, northwest of Jonesborough. Confederate cavalry skirmished with Howard's advance. Kilpatrick's cavalry attempted to reach the railroad near Jonesborough on August 30 but was forced back.[34]

Howard's infantry prepared defensive positions and at 2:00 p.m. the Confederates began forming for the attack. The Confederate line, 20,000 strong, stretched for about a mile and a half, roughly the length of Jonesborough. On the afternoon of August 31, the Confederate artillery began to pound the Union forces. Around 3:00 p.m., Lee's corps on the right and Hardee's corps on the left attacked, but they were handily repulsed. Several Confederate officers remarked that the spirit of attack seemed to be gone from their troops. The Southerners were forced to withdraw with heavy losses of 2,200 men, almost ten times as many as Howard's.[35]

Because Kilpatrick made a display on the Confederate left, some of the Southern attack during the day was directed at the Union cavalry near Anthony's Bridge rather than the main Union line. Kilpatrick repulsed two attacks and then was forced to the west side of the Flint River. He was not pursued farther.[36]

After Cleburne (commanding Hardee's corps while Hardee was in overall command of the two corps defending Jonesborough) and Lee were repulsed on the 31st, Hood realized at last that Atlanta could be lost, and he prepared to abandon the city. He still wanted to hold Atlanta but he needed a miracle at Jonesborough to do this. During the night, he ordered Lee's corps back to Atlanta and Hardee realized he was outnumbered and alone; but he needed to hold off as many as five Federal corps to save his one corps.[37]

On September 1, Hardee constructed a defensive line in a fish-hook shape, with the shank running roughly south to north then curving around to the east. The Union army found itself in a reverse role of the action of the previous day. Now it would be attacking heavily fortified positions.[38] As the Yankees advanced in the afternoon, they came under tremendous musket and canister fire from the defenders. The first assault was repulsed, but Major General Jefferson C. Davis realized the Confederate line was vulnerable and could be broken. The Fourteenth Corps had pushed forward without support and received enfilading fire from other Southern units. Davis added Colonel George P. Este's brigade to the fight, which broke the point of resistance on the salient of the Confederate defenses.[39]

Jonesborough was a decisive victory for the Federals and forced Hood to abandon Atlanta, but the principal objective of the campaign—destruction of the Confederate army—remained unmet. Although Sherman had six corps within range of Hardee, he failed to bring the full might of his armies on the defenders at Jonesborough. Instead, he blamed David Stanley for being late, despite Sherman's own orders assigning Stanley's corps to completely destroy the railroad. As a result, Hardee was able to withdraw from Jonesborough.[40]

Wheeler's Raid

Since August 10, Joseph Wheeler's cavalry had been attempting to disrupt Sherman's communications. One of Wheeler's biographers wrote of the August-September raid:

> General Sherman's new war method of raid had fallen miserably. He wrote home to his government of his deep mortification. He now turned his attention to his main army to circumvent Atlanta. We shall see that General Hood lost his head. He put out his eyes and stopped his ears by sending his cavalry hundreds of miles away on a raid.[41]

Wheeler initially converged on Dalton, while Sherman concentrated on the task at Atlanta. Sherman allowed the commanders in his rear to deal with Wheeler. In north Georgia, those commanders were Major General James Steedman (commanding the District of the Etowah) and Brigadier General John E. Smith (commanding a Fifteenth Corps division assigned to guard the railroad), along with Edward McCook and his less than 600 cavalrymen. Sherman knew he had enough resources in his rear to deal with the cavalry raid and, even though Wheeler could do some minor damage to his supply line, the absence of the Confederate cavalry gave him the opportunity to unleash Kilpatrick on his raid in August.[42]

Steedman was able to fend off Wheeler at Dalton and force him to the northeast toward Spring Place. Wheeler detached Brigadier General William T. Martin to capture a small post at Tilton and ordered him to rejoin the main column at Dalton. Due to a misunderstanding,

Martin failed to do so and the Confederate attack on Dalton failed. Wheeler was so angered that Martin wasn't there when he needed him that he relieved him of command and arrested him. Rufus Clason, 1st Wisconsin Cavalry, reported from Cartersville that Wheeler caused no problems to Sherman's supply line near Dalton: "Old Wheeler came back and tried to cut the road he made out to tear up two or three miles of the road and tried to get into Dalton but got beautifully whipped. The cars have come through here this morning so he did but little damage."[43]

Next, Wheeler sent Brigadier General John Williams to attack the Union garrison at Strawberry Plains in East Tennessee. But Williams lost contact with Wheeler and was unable to rejoin the column. Wheeler began to feel the pressure as the slow but numerous Union commands converged on his cavalry. The Union units attacked Wheeler when they could find him, but Wheeler continued westward. He broke the Alabama & Tennessee Railroad south of Nashville and had to fight his way through Rousseau's troops. On August 20 at Franklin, he lost another valued commander, Brigadier General John H. Kelly.[44]

Alvan Gillem's Tennessee Union Cavalry protected the vital supply line to Sherman's armies in Atlanta during the summer campaign and sparred with Southern sympathizing irregulars and Confederate cavalry. When Wheeler moved north in mid–August, the Tennessee cavalry regiments prepared to meet him. Colonel W.F. Prosser's First Brigade (2nd, 3rd, 4th Tennessee) operated from its headquarters in Huntsville, Alabama. Colonel George Spalding's Second Brigade (5th, 10th and 12th Tennessee) was posted near Pulaski. Colonel John Miller's Third Brigade (8th, 9th, 13th Tennessee) was near Knoxville in East Tennessee. Miller's cavalry actively engaged Williams' cavalry and Spalding worked to prevent Wheeler from doing damage in the central part of the state. The Tennessee cavalry regiments skirmished with Southern cavalry during the raid and in Wheeler's retreat.[45]

John Croxton's First Brigade of McCook's cavalry also participated in the actions in Middle Tennessee against Wheeler as he tried to advance on Nashville. The 1st Tennessee Cavalry took the lead in conjunction with Rousseau's overall effort to expel Wheeler from Tennessee. Colonel James Brownlow led the 1st Tennessee Cavalry in a skirmish with Wheeler near La Vergne on September 1 and then in a more severe fight at Franklin on September 2. Wheeler and Croxton raced for position at Franklin and Croxton won the race. Wheeler then tried to turn the Union right flank held by the 1st Tennessee Cavalry and capture the Union artillery firing at his troopers. Croxton's cavalry dismounted as the Confederate cavalry tried to dislodge the Union troops resulting in a bloody fight. The orders for the 1st Tennessee Cavalry were, "Hold the hill, and don't give it up until ordered to do so." The 1st Tennessee held as long as it could and then was forced to withdraw until Rousseau's reinforcements arrived. During this fight Brownlow was shot through both of his legs but surgeons were able to stop the loss of blood and he survived. One on the most efficient officers of the cavalry of the Army of the Cumberland had just barely missed death. After this severe battle, Wheeler again headed south. Croxton charged Wheeler near Campbellsville a few days later during the pursuit. The fight was severe and Othniel Gooding, 2nd Michigan Cavalry, wrote, "[H]ave heard it was about 150 killed wounded & prisoners thar is only about seven hundred left in the Brigade now."[46]

Wheeler's raid ended on September 10 when the Confederate column crossed the Tennessee River at Tuscumbia. Wheeler failed to cause significant damage to the Union infrastructure during his month-long action. He returned south with a demoralized and exhausted command. He also faced the criticism he shared with Hood for sending his cavalry on a raid when they were needed at Atlanta. Nathan Bedford Forrest met with Wheeler ten days after his raid and reported, "His command is in a demoralized condition. He claims to have about 2,000 men with him; his adjutant general says, however, that he will not be able to raise and carry back with him exceeding 1,000, and in all probability not over 500."[47]

At the end of Wheeler's raid Colonel Thomas Jordan's 9th Pennsylvania got back into action after garrison duty in Kentucky. Jordan's cavalry routed Colonel George Dibrell's cavalry near Readyville, Tennessee, on September 6. Dibrell, with only 130 men, was also detached by Wheeler and sent to Sparta, Dibrell's home. Dibrell was able to increase the size of his command to 1,000 men through recruitment. Dibrell rode toward Wheeler's column but various Union infantry and cavalry commands blocked any attempt to combine his troops with Wheeler's. As Dibrell advanced toward Murfreesboro, he picked up another 200 stragglers. His entire command was armed but poorly trained and with little ammunition. He camped between Readyville and Woodbury on September 5.[48]

Just as Dibrell was breaking camp on September 6, his command was attacked by the 9th Pennsylvania Cavalry. Jordan split his command into a dismounted group and a second group that charged with sabers drawn. Jordan wrote, "I charged them without firing a shot.... [M]y sabers were flashing in the uncertain light of the morning." The surprise thoroughly unnerved the untrained group Dibrell had assembled and they were routed. Dibrell said, "I used every effort to rally the men, but owing to the large number unarmed, quite a stampede took place and it was with difficulty that they could be rallied and checked." Then Dibrell realized any further advance into Middle Tennessee was futile and he led the part of the group he could reassemble back to the mountains. The 5th Tennessee Cavalry and Jordan's 9th Pennsylvania pursued him as he withdrew.[49]

Final Events

During the campaign, Sherman failed to force Johnston or Hood into a decisive battle nor was he able to trap the Confederate Army, but he had succeeded in capturing Atlanta. Many historians have criticized Sherman for allowing Hood to escape Atlanta, but Sherman appreciated the psychological importance of capturing the city and the difficulty of destroying Hood's army. In mid–November, Sherman would begin his "march to the sea," for which he reorganized his armies. The reorganization of the cavalry would take place on October 24 when the cavalry of the Military Division of the Mississippi, including that of the Army of the Cumberland, was placed under the direct command of Major General James H. Wilson. Officially, the cavalry of the Army of the Cumberland ceased, though the troopers had more campaigning to do.[50]

Before the reorganization, Edward McCook's First Division was split. His First Brigade was stationed at Cartersville, his Second Brigade was sent to Franklin and Nashville for remounting, and his Third Brigade was at Calhoun, Georgia. Kenner Garrard's Second Division was sent to picket duty at Rossville, Georgia; and Judson Kilpatrick's Third Division served on picket duty on the Chattahoochee River, near Campbellton. Alvan Gillem's Fourth Division still protected the supply line from Nashville to Decatur and Stevenson, Alabama.[51]

Hood met with Jefferson Davis on September 25–27 and the decision was made for

Hood to strike northward into Tennessee. The Confederates thought Sherman could operate in Georgia only as long as his supply lines were intact. If Hood could destroy these supply lines and threaten Nashville, Sherman would be forced to retreat. Hood, with 40,000 troops, started his campaign on September 29. Sherman recognized the threat to his supply line and ordered George Thomas, with David Stanley's Fourth Corps and John Schofield's Twenty-third Corps, to Tennessee to deal with Hood and Forrest. Stanley and Schofield moved to Johnsonville and Pulaski, Tennessee, in October and screened Hood's advance toward Nashville. Much of the cavalry of the Army of the Cumberland assisted in the action of the infantry by reconnaissance and by protecting the flanks but no major battles occurred through the end of October.

Special Field Orders Number 103

Unlike William Sooy Smith and Richard Johnson, who had preceded him in the role, Wilson took direct command of the cavalry, doing away with the designations of cavalry attached to the various armies. Operationally, this was something long overdue and should have been implemented in the fall of 1863 when Grant took command of all the armies in the west.[52] When Wilson took command the Union cavalry was a wreck. Of the three Army of the Cumberland cavalry divisions—McCook's, Garrard's and Kilpatrick's—only 4,500 men were mounted and twice this number were dismounted. Wilson's new direction was: "Cavalry is useless for defense; its only power is in a vigorous offensive; therefore I urge its concentration south of the Tennessee and hurling it into the bowels of the South in masses that the enemy cannot drive back as it did Sooy Smith and Sturgis."[53] The new organization of the Military Division of the Mississippi cavalry is shown below:

First Division	Edward McCook
Second Division	Eli Long
Third Division	Hugh Judson Kilpatrick
Fourth Division	Benjamin Grierson
Fifth Division	Edward Hatch
Sixth Division	Emory Upton
Seventh Division	Edward Winslow
Eighth and Ninth Divisions	Two Tennessee divisions
An independent brigade in the District of Vicksburg[54]	

Garrard and Elliott were reassigned command in the infantry. The chiefs of cavalry were abolished and Wilson took direct control of the cavalry. Much still remained ahead for the cavalry that had been assigned to the Army of the Cumberland: the Battles of Spring Hill, Franklin, Nashville, Selma, and Bentonville; Sherman's march to the sea; raids in Mississippi and Georgia; and the capture of Jefferson Davis. But these actions would be accomplished by the Military Division of the Mississippi.

By the end of 1864, the war was personal for soldiers and civilians alike. An incident was recorded by Doctor James Comfort Patten, 58th Indiana Infantry, that brought the devastation of the war into focus. He had recorded that the women around Atlanta were trying to trade whatever goods they had for food. Patten wrote,

The women still come in to trade but our stock is rather short and we will soon have nothing to trade. A little girl wanted to sell me some muscadines yesterday. I offered her the money for them but she said she could not eat money, and as I had nothing else, we did not trade. I shall be glad when we get out of this for I am tired of war and all its sights and sounds.[55]

Atlanta Campaign Conclusion

Historians often refer to the poor performance of the Union cavalry during the Atlanta Campaign and expound on how the cavalry failed Sherman. This is, at the least, a too-simple conclusion.

When the Atlanta Campaign began Sherman had two primary objectives for his cavalry—security and reconnaissance for his armies and protection for his very vulnerable supply line. In regard to the supply line, Alvan Gillem's 4th Tennessee Cavalry Division and William Lowe's and Judson Kilpatrick's Third Cavalry Division were charged with this responsibility in cooperation with the various infantry units. Although the Confederate cavalry would break the supply line at various times, at no time was there a serious interruption of matériel and supplies for Sherman's armies, thanks in large part to the underappreciated efforts of Colonel William Wright, who commanded a special brigade that maintained the railroads, and Colonel Adna Anderson, who oversaw scheduling and operation of the railroads. The biggest threat came from Wheeler's raid in August and September but this failed to cause significant problems.

In regard to security and reconnaissance for the three Union armies, while the Union cavalry did not always operate at top performance it would be difficult to identify specific instances when the Confederate cavalry or infantry surprised Sherman. In a way, an exception was at Cassville when the cavalry had been ordered away from its reconnaissance duties to break the railroads from the east and Rome in the west, thereby preventing reinforcements or supplies from reaching the enemies. The serendipitous arrival of McCook and Stoneman prevented a furious attack by Hood. Otherwise, the three cavalry divisions of McCook, Garrard and Stoneman performed exemplary service protecting the flanks of the advancing armies. Perhaps the best evidence of the unappreciated effort of the Union cavalry's duty on the flanks was the Battle of Atlanta. When Garrard was ordered away from flank duty to destroy the railroad at Covington, Hood took the opportunity to attack Sherman in a coordinated infantry and cavalry attack that failed, but in which James McPherson was killed. In summary, the objectives Sherman set for the cavalry at the beginning of the campaign were met by the cavalry.

The claims of failure on the part of the Union cavalry generally point to the three raids that failed to effectively disrupt rail transportation from Macon, while the two successful raids, Rousseau's and Garrard's, are often overlooked. These two successful raids effectively stopped reinforcements and supplies from the east via Augusta and from the west via Montgomery.

The three failed raids require greater consideration. Since Stoneman's division was not part of the Army of the Cumberland, his raid falls outside the purview of this work, except for its impact on McCook's Raid. Stoneman's inability to unite with McCook near Jonesborough compromised McCook's ability to return to Union lines. Another 2,000 Union troopers would, most likely, have made the expedition too large to be contained and both divisions might have safely returned. However, the failure of the raids really falls at the feet of Stoneman and Sherman and not with the ability of the troopers to perform their duty. Sherman allowed himself to be seduced by Stoneman's unrealistic plan. This was just the spirit Sherman was looking for in his cavalry and he accepted the risk. In Robert Leach's analysis of the role of the Union cavalry during the Atlanta Campaign, he summarized as follows:

> After the Stoneman-McCook Raid failed, Sherman admitted Stoneman's scheme to liberate Andersonville and Macon was impracticable and should have been refused. Had the destruction of the Macon & Western Railroad been the raid's only purpose, it likely would have cut Atlanta's railroad communications for a long period and Sherman would have saved his cavalry. On August 7, Sherman told Halleck why he allowed Stoneman to move on Macon and Andersonville: "Nothing but the natural and intense desire to accomplish an end so inviting to one's feelings would have drawn me to commit a military mistake, at such a crisis, as that of dividing and risking my cavalry, so necessary to the success of my campaign. The Confederates gained one of the greatest cavalry victories of the war because of Wheeler's vigor, Iverson's enterprise, Stoneman's glory hunting and blunders, his men's lack of fighting spirit, and Sherman's chronic mishandling of mounted forces.

Kilpatrick's Raid also proved to have been an impractical exercise. The failure of the raids does not belong to the cavalry but to the commander who ordered such impractical expeditions.[56]

Sherman seemed to see what he desired rather than the reality of the situation. Railroads were the lifeline of the Confederates at Atlanta and Hood was not likely to give them up easily. The irony of how Sherman virtually ignored Wheeler's raid in August after Stoneman's and McCook's raids failed to disrupt Confederate communication cannot be overlooked. Sherman essentially ignored Wheeler, while he had expected his own cavalry raids to be effective enough to force Hood to evacuate Atlanta.

Many of the problems that occurred within the Union cavalry during the Atlanta Campaign stem from two causes—improper organization and an ineffective chain of command. Sherman had the foundation of a good cavalry organization. He had a chief of cavalry in the Army of the Cumberland who had overall command of four divisions. In addition, he had two additional divisions, Rousseau's and Stoneman's. It would have been beneficial for Sherman to place all six divisions, or at least five of the six excluding Gillem's, into a single cavalry corps with a chief of cavalry. The poor organization of the cavalry exacerbated the second major obstacle, an ineffective chain of command. Because Sherman did not have a single chief of cavalry, he chose to assume direct control over five divisions of cavalry while he also commanded the entire Military Division of the Mississippi. This was a disservice both to Sherman and those who served under him. It is also important to remember that communications during the Civil War were often slow. Sherman needed immediate answers about the locations and movements of the enemy, and so perhaps he felt he had reason to micromanage the cavalry. A single, effective chief of cavalry might have removed the need to communicate individually with cavalry division commanders.

The overall problem was that Sherman had little confidence in cavalry; but he actually had some good cavalry commanders. Edward McCook, while disparaged by some, was an effective commander of the First Cavalry Division and one that Sherman never criticized. McCook, while perhaps not a visionary commander, was always where he was needed and always intent on fulfilling his orders. If anything, others within the Union army took unfair advantage of McCook, who commanded an experienced and effective division. Because of this, he was promoted to brigadier general but was subordinate to George Stoneman. Stoneman,

McCook's superior officer for much of the campaign, was on record as being less than pleased with his own division and consequently overused McCook's division during the first two months of the campaign to such an extent that it was reduced by half. In the final analysis, McCook was sacrificed during his raid due to Stoneman's failure to reach McDonough.

Sherman's dissatisfaction with Kenner Garrard robbed Sherman of an effective division commander and his best cavalry division. Garrard made mistakes, just like every other commander at some time during the campaign. Garrard, an experienced cavalry commander, wanted to keep his mounts in good condition at the beginning of the campaign while Sherman was impatient to have Garrard on McPherson's flank. This set the stage for the conflict between the two. It is unknown if Sherman had developed a personal dislike for Garrard before the campaign, but he developed a dislike in the opening days of the campaign. Garrard was the antithesis to Sherman's hand-picked favorite, Judson Kilpatrick. Garrard was quiet, intelligent, gentlemanly, taking care for his men, and personally brave. Garrard lacked Kilpatrick's recklessness, which Sherman confused with boldness. Garrard protected the flanks of the army, successfully completed one of the two successful cavalry raids during the campaign, destroyed the railroad at Stone Mountain, destroyed the railroad west of Kingston when Stoneman failed to accomplish the same task east of the town, and provided two healthy brigades that did all the hard fighting during Kilpatrick's Raid. In fact, Garrard was the most effective cavalry commander in the destruction of railroads, an important objective for Sherman. Garrard was appreciated by McPherson and Thomas but disparaged by Sherman.

Hugh Judson Kilpatrick played a minimal role in the campaign due to his wound at Resaca on May 13. When Kilpatrick returned, he led a raid to Jonesborough and was fortunate to have the able commanders Robert Minty and Eli Long to do the fighting for his division. At one point, he had Minty's brigade leading his advance while Long's brigade covered the rear, effectively protecting his own division from attack from Confederates. His bravado to Sherman about the success of his raid was short-lived, as the trains immediately resumed their movements from the south; but Sherman still chose Kilpatrick to accompany his command into the Carolinas.[57]

Finally, the almost invisible member of the cavalry command in the Army of the Cumberland was Washington Lafayette Elliott, the titular chief of cavalry. Elliott was bypassed throughout the campaign and it is difficult not to draw conclusions about his silence. He was relegated to the role of a member of Thomas's staff who completed reports about the cavalry. If he made other contributions history does not record them.

Sherman had never served in the cavalry and this lack of experience could explain some of his unrealistic expectations. His insistence on direct command contributed to the loss of one of every three cavalrymen in the Atlanta Campaign. McCook's division recorded a loss of greater than half. In addition, the destruction of the mounts of the cavalry resulted in the additional ineffectiveness of the cavalry, much to the detriment of the armies. However, Sherman's greatest mistake in regard to the cavalry was his inability to immediately replace those in whom he had no confidence, namely Stoneman, Elliott and Garrard. Robert Leach declared, "Sherman had the responsibility to demonstrate confidence in Garrard or else relieve him." He also showed a lack of value for commanders who did not exhibit the type of personality he favored, even commanders who performed well, and denied the armies the contributions these commanders could have made. David Evans, author of *Sherman's Horsemen*, sums up the situation with the cavalry during the Atlanta Campaign well: "Instead of promoting capable subordinate officers within the ranks, the politics of command saddled Sherman's horsemen with outsiders who had already been tried elsewhere and found wanting." These commanders would include Kilpatrick, Stoneman, Elliott, and Garrard, four of the top five commanders in the Union cavalry. Evans asked the question many scholars asked: What would the cavalry have been like if Robert Minty, William Lowe, Louis Watkins, and Eli Long had been promoted to division commanders prior to this campaign?[58]

For the cavalry in the Atlanta Campaign, the question should not be whether the cavalry failed Sherman. It should be whether Sherman failed the cavalry.

Epilogue

The best cavalry officers I ever saw
—General James H. Wilson

The end of the cavalry of the Army of the Cumberland marked a new beginning, with James H. Wilson. The type of command Wilson would initiate was long overdue. Sherman had had chiefs of cavalry for his overall command, William Sooy Smith and most recently Richard Johnson. But Wilson assumed a more active role in the operations of the cavalry rather than serving just in an administrative capacity. Richard W. Johnson gave Wilson a summary of the state of the cavalry on October 15. Sherman had about 10,000 cavalry in the Military Division of the Mississippi that were armed and mounted. He had an equal number without mounts or arms or both, and another 6,000 dismounted cavalry "imperfectly armed" that protected the railroads. Specifically for the Army of the Cumberland, Garrard had about 2,500 cavalry, Kilpatrick 1,500, and McCook 600 available for duty as mounted cavalry. This was about half the cavalry that was present on April 30, 1864.[1]

Wilson assumed command of the cavalry when the balance of power had clearly shifted in favor of the Union. With the resources of the North and through Wilson's efforts, he rebuilt the cavalry. This allowed Wilson to state, "Cavalry is useless for defense; its only power is in a vigorous offensive." This was an appropriate statement for him to make at this time in the war and for cavalrymen this signaled a positive change. Had Wilson assumed command of the Union cavalry of the Army of the Cumberland in the fall of 1862, he could not have fulfilled this intent. The strides made in November 1864 reflected the efforts of those in the cavalry in 1862, 1863 and 1864.[2]

The Cavalry Divisions of the Army of the Cumberland

The cavalry of the Army of the Cumberland had a remarkable two-year record. The four divisions contributed to Wilson's cavalry from the Army of the Cumberland amounted to about one-half of his entire force: McCook's, Long's (recently Garrard's), Kilpatrick's and Gillem's divisions. This was a great stride from the seven regiments David Stanley found when he joined the Army of the Cumberland in November 1862. Stanley built two divisions—really three. The Third Division was not organized until the Atlanta Campaign, but that reorganization, for the most part, was just the reassignment of regiments already in the cavalry corps. Only the Fourth Division, Gillem's, was added after Stanley's departure.

Changes continued during the two years this cavalry corps existed. Officially the Army of the Cumberland never had a cavalry corps designation, even though the corps existed. The Union cavalry of the Army of the Cumberland was always designated as simply divisions and not a corps. The major changes that were made in the cavalry can be summarized into four major areas: organization, composition, tactics, and arms and training.

Certainly, the success of the chiefs of cavalry is directly linked to the commanding general of the army, or armies, in Sherman's case. Despite problems that developed during the Chickamauga Campaign, the relationship between Stanley and Rosecrans resulted in the strong cavalry component of the Army of the Cumberland and later to the Military Division of the Mississippi. While the role of the cavalry was to support the actions of the rest of the army, the change David Stanley made to the organization of the cavalry was critical to the Union cavalry successes in 1863 and 1864. Once Stanley was removed from command the cavalry of the Army of the Cumberland was often placed under control of commanders who were less effective or under control of infantry commanders, a model Stanley had been able to break. When the Union cavalry could operate as a corps, it could operate more like its Confederate counterparts. The operation of the cavalry under the restrictions of infantry commanders resulted in the misuse and depletion of this important component of the army. However, the generals commanding the army constantly reverted to a structure in which the cavalry was parceled out to infantry commanders. Without the critical mass of the Union cavalry operating at brigade and division size, the cavalry corps was much less effective. The greatest successes of the cavalry resulted when all the cavalry operated under a single cavalry commander.

The composition of the cavalry included 40 regiments supported by four artillery batteries by October 1864. The successes of the cavalry of the Army of the Cumberland showed an evolution from a small division facing superior enemy cavalry at Stones River. The situation at Murfreesboro was dire—the 15th Pennsylvania Cavalry had mutinied, the 2nd Tennessee Cavalry ran "like sheep." But a good commander working with the commanding general of the army built an excellent cavalry corps. At the Battle at Shelbyville, parity was reached when the Union cavalry defeated Wheeler and Martin. From that point, the Union cavalry was on equal footing with the enemy. While the enemy cavalry was still formidable, and would be through the end of the war, a balance had been achieved.

The addition of mounted infantry also changed the face of the cavalry of the Army of the Cumberland, primarily through the use of Wilder's (later Miller's) brigade. The mounted infantry must be counted one of the greatest experiments of Rosecrans' command. The mounted infantry performed exemplary work in numerous battles including the Tullahoma Campaign, the fight at Alexander's Bridge during Chickamauga, Wheeler's October 1863 raid and the Atlanta Campaign. When the mounted infantry was assigned to the traditional cavalry, the firepower of the cavalry increased dramatically.

The evolution of tactics within the cavalry changed over the course of the Civil War. The cavalry's primary offensive action was from the saddle in 1862. But by 1864, the cavalry fought more often dismounted than mounted. Just as infantry tactics changed, relying more on trenches and barricades, so the cavalry tactics changed. The infantry found frontal assaults to be suicidal later in the war. In fact, during the Atlanta Campaign only one frontal assault, Jonesborough, was successful in four months of fighting. While both mounted and dismounted skills were necessary for the cavalry, the technology of weapons made it more practical for the cavalry to fight dismounted in many situations. Reginald Stuart, in his analysis of the Union cavalry, noted that the Union "should not be glibly labelled 'mounted infantry' even though they displayed a distinct penchant for fighting on foot and an increased dependence on firearms.... [I]ts duties were still essentially cavalry duties." The traditional tactics, while not being discarded, were modified, i.e., old tactics were used and supplemented through the new demands of the Civil War. The cavalry continued in reconnaissance and security roles being the "eyes and ears" of the army, the traditional role of the cavalry. Despite many historians discounting the use of the saber, it was used by the Union cavalry of the Army of the Cumberland through its last mission. Many in the cavalry felt its use struck fear in the hearts of their Confederate opponents. Its use in hand-to-hand combat and when silence was needed made it an invaluable tool for the Union cavalry. Still, the saber was not the primary tool for the cavalrymen. The technologically superior Spencer repeating rifle and the Colt revolving rifle became the weapons of choice. From November 1862 through October 1864 it was a stated goal for all the cavalry to receive the Spencer rifle. The final weapon for the cavalry was the revolver, which many in the cavalry used despite some commanding officers discounting this weapon. For example, Washington Elliott wrote to army headquarters in Washington that revolvers weren't needed if Spencer rifles were given to the troopers; however, Colonel Joseph Dorr, 8th Iowa Cavalry, proudly fought the Texas cavalry primarily using revolvers south of Atlanta in 1864.[3]

The most controversial and yet usually unaddressed issue for the cavalry of the Army of the Cumberland was how to employ the cavalry. The chief of cavalry and the general commanding the army often disagreed on this. This set the stage for repeated conflict. It was the greatest argument between Stanley and Rosecrans, and was perhaps the basis of the Garrard—Sherman conflict. David Stanley would write,

> Neither Rosecrans, Sherman or Grant ever understood the true uses of cavalry. All these commanders were given to sending cavalry upon aimless raids, invariably resulting in using up their cavalry without accomplishing anything. Generals Thomas and Sheridan had more correct views of cavalry and used it to protect their flanks, to keep themselves in order of battle, and then ... threw the whole cavalry upon the enemy's flank at the critical time of the battle and crushed the opposing force.

Elliott and Garrard had the same West Point training and prewar experiences as Stanley and operated in a manner more congruent with this training. Some military historians refer to this method of operation as the "shield and dagger"—protect the flank, screen the advance, and strategically make offensive strikes. This was the model many of the West Point-trained officers used. Both Rosecrans and Sherman desired to change this paradigm, making the cavalry more offensive, without gaining the understanding or agreements of those commanding the cavalry. The result was disagreement and conflict.[4]

Successes of the Cavalry, Army of the Cumberland

Although an incomplete list, the following are the most important actions of the cavalry of the Army of the Cumberland:

Location	Date	Result
Hartsville, Tennessee	December 7, 1862	Confederate Victory
Stones River, Tennessee	December 31, 1862–January 2, 1863	Union Victory

Location	Date	Result
Rover, Tennessee	January 31, February 13, 1863	Union Victory
Bradyville, Tennessee	February 22, 1863	Union Victory
Thompson Station, Tennessee	March 5, 1863	Confederate Victory
Vaught's Hill, Tennessee	March 20, 1863	Union Victory
Brentwood, Tennessee	March 25, 1863	Confederate Victory
Woodbury, Tennessee	March 27, 1863	Confederate Victory
Snow Hill, Tennessee	April 2, 1863	Union Victory
McMinnville, Tennessee	April 17, 1863	Union Victory
Franklin, Tennessee	April 10, 1863	Union Victory
Middleton, Tennessee	May 21–22, 1863	Union Victory
Franklin, Tennessee	June 4, 1863	Inconclusive
Triune, Tennessee	June 7–9 1863	Inconclusive
Shelbyville, Tennessee	June 27, 1863	Union Victory
Sparta, Tennessee	August 9, 12, 17, 1863	Inconclusive/Union
Chickamauga, Georgia	September 18–20, 1863	Confederate Victory
Anderson's Crossroads, Tennessee	October 1, 1863	Confederate Victory
Robinson Trace, Tennessee	October 2, 1863	Union Victory
Farmington, Tennessee	October 7, 1863	Union Victory
Blue Springs, Tennessee	October 10, 1863	Union Victory
Maysville, Alabama	November 14–17, 1863	Union Victory
Cleveland, Tennessee	November 25–26, 1863	Union Victory
New Market, Tennessee	December 24, 1863	Confederate Victory
Mossy Creek, Tennessee	December 29, 1863	Union Victory
Dandridge, Tennessee	January 17, 1864	Confederate Victory
Fair Garden, Tennessee	January 27, 1864	Union Victory
Buzzard's Roost, Georgia	February 24–25, 1864	Confederate Victory
Varnell's Station, Georgia	May 9, 1864	Confederate Victory
Resaca, Georgia	May 13–15, 1864	Inconclusive
Adairsville, Georgia	May 17, 1864	Inconclusive
Kingston, Georgia	May 17, 1864	Confederate Victory
Cassville, Georgia	May 18, 1864	Union Victory
Rome, Georgia	May 18, 1864	Union Victory
Acworth, Georgia	May 25, 1864	Union Victory
Dallas, Georgia	May 28–29, 1864	Union Victory
Big Shanty/McAffee's Cross Roads, Georgia	June 9, 1864	Union Victory
Powder Springs, Georgia	June 20, 1864	Inconclusive
Noonday Creek, Georgia	June 20, 1864	Confederate Victory
Kennesaw, Georgia	June 27, 1864	Confederate Victory
Roswell, Georgia	July 5, 1864	Union Victory
Rousseau's Raid	July 10–22, 1864	Union Victory
Garrard's Raid	July 22–24, 1864	Union Victory
McCook's Raid	July 27–31, 1864	Confederate Victory
Flat Rock/Shoals, Georgia	July 28–30, 1864	Inconclusive
Kilpatrick's Raid	August 18–22, 1864	Confederate Victory
Jonesboro, Georgia	August 30–September 1, 1864	Union Victory
Readyville, Tennessee	September 6, 1864	Union Victory

The major successes of the cavalry of the Army of the Cumberland include the actions at Stones River, the actions prior to the Tullahoma Campaign, the cavalry battle at Shelbyville, Tullahoma Campaign, actions on the right flank during the advance on Chattanooga, the action at Reed's Bridge at Chickamauga, the pursuit of Wheeler in October 1864, the East Tennessee Campaign, Long's Covington Raid, the surprise of Hood at Cassville, securing bridges across the Chattahoochee and Etowah rivers, Rousseau's Raid, Garrard's Raid, and the rail destruction at Stone Mountain. These were all important contributions to Union successes.

For the Army of the Cumberland, the cavalry had three official chiefs of cavalry, but only one, Stanley, can be said to have been effective in that role. Robert Mitchell served as acting chief of cavalry for less than two months before resigning, and Washington Lafayette Elliott, although by all accounts a good officer, made no obvious contribution. David Stanley had a close and collegial relationship with William Rosecrans, his recent godfather. Both Stanley and Rosecrans wanted the other to succeed. Rosecrans secured an excellent command for Stanley and insured Stanley was promoted to the rank of major general, a rank rightly earned. From November 1862 through August 1863, these two generals worked diligently to create a cavalry corps that could meet the Confederate cavalry on the field of battle. Cavalry regiments were added, technologically superior arms acquired, mounted infantry introduced, training increased, and an effective organization implemented, all under the command of David Stanley and William Rosecrans. These two generals built the cavalry into the effective fighting force it came to be.

Robert B. Mitchell, while unsuitable in Stanley's eyes, was a good commander; but Mitchell was not an adequate chief of cavalry. He served only six weeks as chief of cavalry and demonstrated himself a fighter, although a reluctant commander. During that time, Crook was asked to handle the military operations at Crawfish Springs because Mitchell did not feel competent to complete the task.

The last chief of cavalry for the Army of the Cumberland was Washington Lafayette Elliott. A lack of information hinders an evaluation of his command ability, although he served as long as David Stanley as chief of cavalry. It was hardly noticeable that Elliott commanded the cavalry. He initially rode with McCook's division in Tennessee but under the command of Samuel Sturgis. Certainly another chief of cavalry was not needed to assist in the command of McCook's division, and Elliott traveled to Chattanooga. There are no records that Elliott attempted to assist Crook's or McCook's divisions in the field, and during the entire Atlanta Campaign he appeared to be an administrative officer on George Thomas's staff. He did not attempt to ride with any of his command. Instead, he remained at Thomas's headquarters.

Failures of the Cavalry, Army of the Cumberland

While there were many successes of the cavalry of the Army of the Cumberland, there were many difficulties and failures. These include supply and armament, army/district commanders, selection of cavalry officers, organization of the cavalry command and ineffective use of the cavalry divisions.

From the beginning, the supply and armament for the cavalry was a problem and would remain a problem through October 1864. While the Union cavalry was generally better armed and supplied than its Southern counterparts, the difficulty persisted. In the fall of 1862 and into the spring of 1863 a shortage of weapons and horses was common. Once weapons were furnished to the cavalry they were often not standardized. The Union cavalry would boast of the Colt or Spencer repeating rifles, but many of the regiments would never receive these weapons and would have a variety of weapons that created logistical problems of providing different ammunition. Finally, the country was just not prepared to meet the demand for serviceable horses. The toll of active campaigning was severe on horses. The horses were often ridden beyond endurance, in poor conditions with poor food or care. This was particularly true during the Atlanta Campaign when entire cavalry brigades were dismounted in the rear and horses simply died on picket duty. Two important command conflicts probably resulted from good cavalry commanders being unwilling to ride their horses to death—Minty during Wheeler's Raid and Garrard's advance toward Snake Creek Gap. When Wilson reorganized the cavalry in 1864 approximately half of the cavalry of the Army of the Cumberland was dismounted and inadequately armed.

Much has already been made in this book of the army or district commanders mishandling cavalry. Sherman saw the value of cavalry raiding and destroying railroads as the Atlanta Campaign progressed, but he destroyed two of three primary divisions (Stoneman's and McCook's) while accomplishing little in poorly planned raids around Atlanta. Kilpatrick's division was then brought forward to participate in a third unsuccessful raid. Sherman underestimated the capabilities of the Confederate cavalry and infantry in these poorly conceived missions. Despite the strides made by Rosecrans in improving the cavalry corps, during the Chickamauga Campaign, he also appeared to lose sight of the limitations of his cavalry in hopes of striking the rear of Bragg's army near Rome. His failure to give Stanley the ability to design, coordinate and execute missions resulted in an unremarkable performance by the cavalry during that campaign. Assigning cavalry to infantry corps and division commanders resulted in its being misused, as was Minty by Crittenden during the Chickamauga Campaign. When the chief of cavalry was given operational command of the cavalry, the overall performance was greatly enhanced.

The selection of cavalry officers for command was botched from the beginning. Rosecrans' and Garfield's selection of John Turchin and Robert Mitchell for division command was poor, and these selections were not made to improve the cavalry. Stanley believed the reason these men were selected was for political reasons and he was probably right. One must question why they were chosen, because Turchin was unable to ride and Mitchell's health would not permit it. Next, Elliott, Garrard, Stoneman (Army of the Ohio), and Kilpatrick were discarded from the eastern theater of the war and inserted into the Army of the Cumberland cavalry. Long, Minty, Croxton, Watkins, Lowe, and Miller were all fully capable to command cavalry and all would have been effective division commanders.

The organization of the cavalry worked well on paper; but in fact, after Stanley's departure the cavalry of the Army of the Cumberland was generally under command of someone other than the chief of cavalry. This began in the East Tennessee Campaign when McCook's division fell under control of Samuel Sturgis and continued into the Atlanta Campaign when McCook often fell under command of George Stoneman. Stoneman justified the misuse of McCook's division by complaining that his own officers and troops weren't very good. Stoneman is on record ordering McCook to charge entrenched Confederate infantry at Cassville and assigning McCook duty even when Stoneman's own troops were in the same general area. When McCook balked, Stoneman complained to his commanding officer than he wasn't successful in accomplishing his objectives because McCook wasn't cooperating. Likewise, the regiments of Crook's division were assigned to William Sooy Smith in the disastrous Meridian Expedition. The assignment of cavalry to infantry commanders and commanders from the Army of the Ohio was often fraught with misuse. As previously mentioned, the exclusion of the chief of cavalry in the chain of command resulted in much confusion and ineffective use of the cavalry.

Final Comments

After the Battle of Stones River, the Union cavalry of the Army of the Cumberland became a premier fighting force for the next two years in the central theater of the Civil War. The issues and problems are almost all related to command and supply. The regiments themselves were effective fighting units and while there was give and take between the Union and Confederate cavalry, the morale and fighting ability of the Union cavalry was excellent. These regiments knew how to fight and did so bravely, yielding any ground grudgingly. Perhaps the best compliment to the cavalry of the Army of the Cumberland was James H. Wilson's list of officers for promotion. These included Long, Croxton, McCook, Minty, and La Grange. Wilson exclaimed these were the "best cavalry officers I ever saw."[5]

It is sad that the names of Long, Croxton, McCook, Minty, Miller, La Grange, and others are not well known to many people today. Certainly, the list of important commanders of the cavalry must also include David Stanley, George Crook, and Archibald Campbell. The contributions of the cavalry of the Army of the Cumberland were numerous and a more hardworking and brave group is difficult imagine. Their two-year story is one of service, bravery and pride.

Appendix A: Biographical Notes

First Division

Major General Edward M. McCook

Edward Moody McCook, one of the "fighting McCooks," served throughout the war. James Wilson recommended McCook for the rank of major general and the recommendation was approved in 1865. McCook's division was slowly rebuilt after the July 1864 raid and defeat at Brown's Mill. He later led a cavalry division during Wilson's Raid in 1865. Afterward he proceeded to ride south and received the surrender of the Confederate troops in Georgia and Florida. He had the honor of reading Lincoln's Emancipation Declaration in Florida, officially ending slavery in that state. His division has the dubious honor of fighting what was considered by many to be the last battle of the Civil War, the Battle of West Point, on April 16, 1865. He stayed in Florida and served as military governor until 1866.

After the war was over, McCook moved to Colorado and was soon appointed minister to the Kingdom of Hawaii, where he served from 1866 to 1868. In 1869, he was appointed governor of the Territory of Colorado for two terms and played an important role in bringing the railroad to the state. He remained active in the mining and agriculture industries in Colorado after he served as governor. Edward McCook died in Chicago in 1909.[1]

First Division, First Brigade

Colonel Archibald Campbell

Campbell, a 36-year-old native Scotsman, left the cavalry in 1864 due to ill health. He had commanded one of the premier cavalry regiments, 2nd Michigan Cavalry, before assuming brigade command and demonstrated his worthiness in many situations while commanding the First Brigade. Unfortunately, he suffered from consumption and died on May 24, 1865, in Saint Clair County, Michigan.[2]

Colonel Joseph Dorr

Dorr, a politically connected newspaperman from Dubuque and was five feet eleven inches tall and of stocky build. Having assumed brigade and regimental command while with the cavalry his most notable service in it occurred early in the Atlanta Campaign at Varnell's and when he led the 8th Iowa Cavalry during McCook's raid. During this raid, Dorr was wounded while holding the Texas cavalry, allowing additional Union cavalry regiments escape to the west. Later, his regiment was selected to hold the Confederate cavalry at Brown's Mill, which allowed other regiments a chance to escape. Dorr's regiment was surrounded and he was captured during this selfless act. He was exchanged and returned to this regiment in the fall of 1864. In December 1864, he also fought in the Battle of Nashville.

Dorr clashed with some in his regiment as the war progressed. He and Major Richard Root clashed verbally and this resulted in Root's being court-martialed for various charges including drunkenness, neglect of duty, and insubordination. Root was tried in February 1865 and found not guilty of the charges and specifications, much to the disappointment of Dorr. In addition, the court made a point of chastising Dorr. The court decided to "severely censure Colonel Joseph B. Dorr for the arrest and confinement of Major Root" and determined that the "above sentence be read in front of each regiment in the 1st Division Cavalry Corps." Dorr continued actively campaigning with the 8th Iowa Cavalry until the end of the war, but he was never to reach home. He died of disease on May 24, 1865, at Macon, Georgia.[3]

Brigadier General John Croxton

Croxton continued in command of the First Brigade through the end of the war. He was brevetted major general in the Union Army at the end of the war. The Yale-educated attorney from Paris, Kentucky, became a provincial governor in the south after the war while learning to plant and cultivate cotton. He eventually returned to Kentucky and continued a successful law practice. Croxton had been severely wounded at Chickamauga and that lingering wound and the demands of his law practice caused his health to fail. In an attempt to regain it, he accepted a position as foreign minister to Bolivia. Croxton moved his family there in 1872 and died the next year in Bolivia at the age of 37.[4]

First Division, Second Brigade

Oscar La Grange

An ardent abolitionist who was fearless at the head of his cavalry, La Grange was exchanged in September 1864 after his capture during the first week of the Atlanta Campaign. He led his brigade in the Battle of West Point on April 16, 1865, a full week after Lee's surrender in Virginia. He had the pleasure of facing the "Nancy Harts," a militia group made up of women who lived near Lagrange, Georgia. The militia's captain, Nancy Morgan, told La Grange he was not going to be allowed to burn the homes of those in the town. La Grange agreed to the terms and had dinner with one of the Nancy Harts that evening. After the war he settled into a more traditional life. He studied law, was admitted to the bar and was appointed superintendent of the U.S. Mint in San Francisco. Then he became district attorney in Alameda County, California, before traveling to New York, where he served as fire commissioner for the city. Next, he became governor of the soldier's home in Santa Monica, California. He returned to New York in 1905 to practice law but his health began to fail; he died of pneumonia in New York in 1915.[5]

Colonel Horace P. Lamson

Lamson commanded the Second Brigade twice during the Atlanta Campaign and once again in 1865. Along with his 4th Indiana Cavalry he participated in Wilson's Raid in 1865. Mustered out of service July 3, 1865, he moved back to Indiana and had various occupations, including undertaker, cabinetmaker, and coroner in Kosciusko County, Indiana, in 1878 and 1879. In 1882, he moved to Washington, D.C., and worked as a U.S. Pension Office clerk. He died in Washington in 1900.[6]

First Division, Third Brigade

Brigadier General Louis D. Watkins

Although Louis Watkins spent much of the Atlanta Campaign at the rear of Sherman's armies, his contributions were recognized and he helped keep the supply line open. In June 1864, he received a promotion to the brevet rank of brigadier general and in 1865 he received a full promotion to that rank. Also in 1864, he married Mary E. Rousseau, the daughter of Major General Lovell Rousseau. In January 1865 his brigade was reorganized and he moved to Louisville, Kentucky, for garrison duty. He continued his service in the regular army after the war as lieutenant colonel of the 20th U.S. Infantry. He died of yellow fever while visiting New Orleans in March 1869 (or 1868) at the age of 34 or 35 years. His wife died only a short time later, in July 1869, in Minnesota.[7]

Colonel John K. Faulkner

Faulkner, who had temporary brigade command in 1864, served the remainder of the war in command of the 7th Kentucky Cavalry. A farmer before the war, he returned to Kentucky after the war. He served as a member of the Kentucky state legislature, circuit clerk for Garrard County and surveyor for the Port of Louisville before returning to farming near Lancaster, Kentucky. Faulkner had been severely wounded in the hip near Franklin, Tennessee, in June 1863 and the wound continued to plague him for years after the war. He died on January 7, 1895, of poisoning at his own hand. A note found near his bed indicated he felt he would die soon after a "paralytic attack" and due to the constant pain from his wound he decided to hasten the inevitable outcome.[8]

Second Division

Major General George Crook

After Crook left the cavalry of the Army of the Cumberland, he was ordered by Grant to command the Army of West Virginia and later the Eighth Corps of the Army of the Shenandoah. In 1865 he was promoted to the rank of brevet major general of volunteers, but he was embarrassed when he was captured by Confederate guerrillas at his headquarters in February 1865. Once he was exchanged a month later, he was assigned to again command cavalry, this time in the Army of the Potomac until the end of the war. Crook is probably most remembered for his action with Native Americans. In 1866, he was assigned the rank of lieutenant colonel in the U.S. Army and sent to Idaho to protect the settlers. He later was promoted to the rank of brigadier general and commanded the Military Department of the Platte. His new strategy of destruction of villages and economic warfare was implemented during his command. He most notably pursued the Chiricahua Apaches in Arizona in the 1880s. When Geronimo left the reservation in 1885, Crook was criticized "for his fair treatment of the Apaches" and Philip Sheridan transferred him back to the Department of the Platte. In 1888 he was promoted to major general and ordered to command of the Military Division of the Missouri and moved to Chicago. He died in Chicago suddenly in March 1890.[9]

Major General Kenner Garrard

Kenner Garrard was assigned command of an infantry division in October 1864 and received commendations for his actions during the Battle of Nashville and the actions at Fort Blakeley and Spanish Fort during the Mobile Campaign. He was also promoted to the rank of major general by the end of the war and commanded the Military District of Mobile. He resigned from the U.S. Army in November 1866 and moved to Cincinnati, where he made a living in the real estate business. He was a prominent member of the Cincinnati community and worked for the betterment of the city. Garrard died in 1879 in Cincinnati.[10]

Major General Eli Long

Professional soldier Eli Long was assigned command of a division in James Wilson's cavalry of the Military District of the Mississippi when Kenner Garrard was moved to the infantry. Long was wounded in the rearguard action during Kilpatrick's raid and recuperated. He rejoined the cavalry in November 1864 and participated in the Nashville Campaign and later in Wilson's Raid in 1865. He was wounded for the fifth time in the war during Wilson's Raid on Selma, this time a severe head wound. His skull was indented and his tongue, his right arm and right side were paralyzed as a result, which continued into 1868. Long was given command of the Military District of New Jersey after the war. He retired from the army in 1867 with the rank of major general, which was subsequently reduced to brigadier general, and practiced law in Plainfield, New Jersey. He also stayed involved with military affairs in Washington after his retirement. He died at a New York hospital from complications following surgery in 1903.[11]

Second Division, First Brigade

Major General Robert Minty

Sherman realized that Minty was one of the best cavalrymen in the Union army and also knew that Minty had little of the political influence that had allowed other less able commanders to be promoted to the rank of general. The oversight of Minty was recognized throughout the cavalry and prompted an article in the *Louisville Journal* that summarized this neglect: "He has been more than two years colonel commanding a brigade. His friends have long ceased to look for justice to this truly worthy officer. When this 'cruel war' is over, and history does justice to those who have fought it will be seen how little minds invested with temporary power, from motives of jealousy so mean that they can hardly be believed, have withheld that which was due honest merit, while blustering pretense and worthless impudence have stolen honors due better men. Impartial history will do justice to the soldier who has faithfully served his country and successfully led her armies during this her terrible struggle for life." Minty's accomplishments, in due time, were recognized and he was finally promoted to the brevet rank of major general after his actions at Selma, his action in the capture of Macon, Georgia, and his part in the capture of Jefferson Davis in 1865. After the war he was offered a commission as major in the 8th U.S. Cavalry but he declined the appointment and resigned from the army.

Minty raised ten children and moved west after the war. He was first appointed general manager of the Louisville and Nashville Railroad then he was hired as a traveling auditor for the Union Pacific Railroad in Utah. Next, he was named manager of the Jerome Railroad in Arizona. He was active in Grand Army of the Republic and made a living in the railroad business in Utah and Arizona in his later years. The premier Union cavalry brigade commander died on August 24, 1906.[12]

Brigadier General Beroth B. Eggleston

In March 1865, Beroth Bullard Eggleston was promoted to the brevet rank of brigadier general and remained an active member of the cavalry until the end of the war. He became the military commander for Macon and Atlanta for some time before traveling to Orangeburg, South Carolina, where he commanded the cavalry for the Department of the South until he mustered out of service in October 1865. He then moved to Mississippi and settled on a cotton plantation near Crawfordsville and subsequently was elected to the U.S. Senate from Mississippi. He later worked in the gas business in Columbus, Mississippi, for six years. In 1878 he moved to Kansas, where he farmed, and then to Wichita, where he became superintendent of the waterworks. Eggleston died in Wichita on May 27, 1891.[13]

Brigadier General John T. Wilder

Wilder, who had battled typhoid fever earlier in the war, suffered from chronic diarrhea. He was promoted to the rank of brigadier general in August 1864 but resigned due to ill health in October. He returned to Chattanooga in 1865 and made it his home, hoping the milder climate would aid in improving his health. In 1867, he established the Roane Iron Company and even built a railroad, with his partners, to carry the ore from Rockwood, Tennessee, to Chattanooga. Wilder continued to expand the business, adding the Roane Rolling Mill and then a foundry. In 1871 he served for a short time as mayor of Chattanooga. He later moved to Johnson City, Tennessee, and continued his activity with the railroad and mining. In 1897, he became a pension clerk in Johnson City. In 1913, he moved to Monterey, Tennessee, and continued with his business ventures. He died during a visit to Jacksonville, Florida, on October 20, 1917, after a life of business, military and civic contributions.[14]

Colonel Abram O. Miller

Miller continued to command the mounted infantry brigade throughout the remainder of the war and participated in Wilson's Raid and the capture of Jefferson Davis. He was mustered out of service with his regiment, the 72nd Indiana Mounted Infantry, in June 1865. Miller was severely wounded when he was shot through his thigh during the 1865 actions at Selma. He returned to civilian life in Lebanon, Indiana, where he continued his life as a physician; but he became interested in banking and in 1877 he was president of the First National Bank in Lebanon. Miller and others lost much of their financial worth when a railroad investment reversed. Afterward, he returned to the practice of medicine. He continued to practice medicine until his death in 1901.[15]

Third Division

Major General Hugh Judson Kilpatrick

Kilpatrick was selected by Sherman to command the cavalry for his "march to the sea" and his cavalry continued to battle the Confederate cavalry and infantry. His best action was, perhaps, at Waynesboro, where he defeated Wheeler's cavalry, and his worse action was at the Monroe Crossroads, where Wade Hampton's men nearly captured Kilpatrick while he was in bed with his mistress in March 1865. After this event, his "shirttail skedaddle" was added to his nickname "kill-cavalry."

In December 1865 Kilpatrick resigned from the army and became the U.S. Envoy Extraordinary and Minister Plenipotentiary to Chile. While living in Chile, Kilpatrick married Luisa Fernandez de Valdivieso, a wealthy lady from a politically influential family in that country. He returned to the United States in 1868 and briefly served as a director of the Union Pacific. He was also active on the lecture circuit. He was unsuccessful in a congressional election in 1880. In 1881, President James Garfield appointed him as minister to Chile. Kilpatrick became seriously ill from Bright's disease and died on December 2, 1881, at the age of 46.[16]

Brigadier General William W. Lowe

Lowe spent much of the second half of 1864 in Nashville in charge of remounting much of the cavalry of the Army of the Cumberland, an important but inglorious chore, until January 1865. Then he resigned from volunteer service and reentered the regular army, but not before he was promoted to the rank of brevet brigadier general. A West Point graduate, class of 1853, he was transferred to Fort Leavenworth, Kansas, where he was "Acting Asst. Provost Marshal General, Superintendent of Volunteer Recruiting service, and Chief Mustering and Disbursing Officer for Kansas, Nebraska, Dakota, and Colorado" from February 1865 through July 1866. He later moved to Nashville and then New Orleans until his resignation in June 1869. In civilian life he was in various occupations including superintendent of an Omaha smelting works, mining in Utah, president of a lubrication and soap company, and working in the construction industry. He died in Omaha in May 1898.[17]

Brigadier General Eli Houston Murray

After Wilson's reorganization of the Union cavalry, Eli Murray remained with Edward McCook's cavalry division in western Kentucky and received a promotion to the rank of brigadier general in 1865. After the war, he attended the University of Louisville Law School and graduated in 1866. He was appointed U.S. Marshall in Kentucky after graduation and from 1876 to 1880 he was the editor of the *Louisville Commercial*. He was appointed governor of the Utah Territory in 1880 and served in that role until 1886. During his time as governor he laid the foundation for the abolition of polygamy in Utah. After leaving the office of governor of Utah, he was a journalist in San Diego for a short time before returning to Bowling Green, Kentucky, where he died in 1896.[18]

Colonel Charles Smith

Charles Smith remained with the army until January 1865, when he resigned due to ill health. The engineer-turned-cavalryman returned home to Painesville, Ohio, and became involved in the life of the community. He turned to farming after the war and also served on the city council. He died after a short illness in February 1877.[19]

Chiefs of Cavalry

Brigadier Robert Byington Mitchell

Mitchell was shot in the hip during the Battle of Wilson's Creek and this injury continued to plague him throughout the war. When he asked to be relieved of command of the cavalry corps, he was placed on general court-martial duty until February 1864, when he was assigned to military duty in his home state of Kansas. Mitchell's long-term malady was asthma, which would remain with him throughout his life. He was mustered out of service from the army in January 1866 and was appointed governor of the New Mexico Territory in December 1866, holding that office until 1869. His administration was very controversial and he was charged with not taking his responsibilities seriously. The legislature called for his removal and declared acts not signed by Mitchell would be sent to Congress for approval. Unsuccessful as governor, he returned to Paola, Kansas. A Liberal Republican, he was nominated for a position in Congress but was not elected. He retired to Washington after his unsuccessful bid for Congress and died in January 1882 of pneumonia complicated by his asthma.[20]

Major General Washington Lafayette Elliott

Elliott was given command of an infantry division serving under David Stanley after James H. Wilson reorganized the cavalry in October 1864. He participated in the Nashville Campaign and the pursuit of Hood's army. In August 1865 he was assigned duty at Fort Leavenworth, Kansas, and reentered the regular army in 1866 as a lieutenant colonel in the 1st U.S. Cavalry; in 1878 he was promoted to the rank of colonel of the 3rd U.S. Cavalry. In 1879, after thirty years of service, he retired from the army and moved to San Francisco, where he became a vice president of the Safe Deposit and Trust Company. He died of heart disease in June 1888.[21]

Major General David S. Stanley

After Stanley was relieved of command of the cavalry corps he commanded a division of the Fourth Corps until July 1864, when he was given command of the entire corps. Stanley's command performed well in the Atlanta Campaign. He next marched to central Tennessee and participated in the Nashville Campaign. He considered his actions at the Battle of Spring Hill to be his most important duty of the war. In this remarkable action, he protected the escape route of Schofield's army, held Hood's army at bay, and extracted an 800-wagon supply train from under the noses of the Confederates. The next day his actions resulted in the award of the Medal of Honor as he was shot rallying his troops at Franklin. Next, Stanley's corps was sent to Texas to insure the peaceful transition to civil rule with the end of hostilities. He entered the regular army at the end of the Civil War as colonel of the 22nd U.S. Infantry, stationed in the Dakota Territory, until 1874. Then he was transferred to the Great Lakes garrison. He later moved with the 22nd Infantry to Texas and New Mexico. He was promoted to the rank of brigadier general in 1884 and given command of the military district in Texas. He retired in 1892 after forty years of service and died of kidney disease in 1902.[22]

Appendix B: Organization of the Cavalry of the Army of the Cumberland

Commanders, Chief of Cavalry

David S. Stanley	Major General	November 24, 1862 to September 9, 1863
Robert B. Mitchell	Brigadier General	September 9, 1863 to November 9, 1863
David S. Stanley	Major General	November 9, 1863 to November 20, 1863
Washington L. Elliott	Brigadier General	November 20, 1863 to October 29, 1864

FIRST DIVISION

1st Division, Commanders	Rank	Time of Command
John Kennett	Colonel, 4th Ohio Cavalry	October 24, 1862 to February 1863
Robert B. Mitchell	Brigadier General	March 1863 to September 9, 1863
Edward M. McCook	Colonel 2nd Indiana Cavalry	September 9, 1863 to October 29, 1864

1st Brigade, Commanders	Rank	Time of Command
Robert H.G. Minty	Colonel, 4th Michigan Cavalry	November 5, 1861 to March 1863
Archibald P. Campbell	Colonel, 9th Pennsylvania Cavalry	March 1863 to April 12, 1864
Joseph B. Dorr	Colonel, 8th Iowa Cavalry	April 12, 1864 to July 20, 1864
John T. Croxton	Colonel, 4th KY Mounted Infantry	July 20, 1864 to July 30, 1864
Joseph B. Dorr	Colonel, 8th Iowa Cavalry	July 30, 1864 to July 30, 1864
James P. Brownlow	Lt. Colonel, 1st Tennessee Cavalry	July 30, 1864 to August 12, 1864
John T. Croxton	Brigadier General	August 12, 1864 to October 29, 1864

1st Brigade, Regiments	Date of Inclusion	Transferred From
2nd Indiana Cavalry	October 1862	1st Brig. Cav. Div. Army Ohio
3rd Indiana Cavalry	October 1862	1st Brig. Cav. Div. Army Ohio
4th Michigan Cavalry	October 1862	1st Brig. Cav. Div. Army Ohio
7th Pennsylvania Cavalry	October 1862	1st Brig. Cav. Div. Army Ohio
3rd Kentucky Cavalry	October 1862	1st Brig. Cav. Div. Army Ohio
4th Kentucky Cavalry	March 1863	Dist. West KY Dept. Ohio
6th Kentucky Cavalry	March 1863	Unattached, Army KY Dept. Ohio
7th Kentucky Cavalry	March 1863	Post Gallatin, Tennessee
2nd Michigan Cavalry	March 1863	Dist. Central KY, Dept. Ohio
9th Pennsylvania Cavalry	March 1863	Dist. Central KY, Dept. Ohio
1st Tennessee Cavalry	March 1863	Dist. Central KY, Dept. Ohio
8th Iowa Cavalry	March 1863	Def. Nashville & N.W.R.R.
4th Kentucky Mounted Cavalry	June 1864	3-Brig. 3-Div. 14-Corps
2nd Michigan Cavalry	October 1864	Dist. Nashville, Tennessee

2nd Brigade, Commanders

Commanders	Rank	Time of Command
Lewis Zahm	Colonel, 3rd Ohio Cavalry	October 24, 1862 to January 9, 1863
Edward M. McCook	Colonel, 2nd Indiana Cavalry	January 9, 1863 to September 9, 1863
Oscar H. La Grange	Colonel, 1st Wisconsin Cavalry	September 9, 1863 to October 12, 1863
Edward M. McCook	Colonel, 2nd Indiana Cavalry	October 12, 1863 to November 20, 1863
Oscar H. La Grange	Colonel, 1st Wisconsin Cavalry	November 20, 1863 to April 1, 1864
Daniel M. Ray	Colonel, 2nd Tennessee Cavalry	April 1, 1864 to April 20, 1864
Oscar H. La Grange	Colonel, 1st Wisconsin Cavalry	April 20, 1864 to May 9, 1864
James W. Stewart	Lt. Colonel, 2nd Indiana Cavalry	May 9, 1864 to May 26, 1864
Horace P. Lamson	Lt. Colonel, 4th Indiana Cavalry	May 26, 1864 to July 21, 1864
William H. Torrey	Lt. Colonel, 1st Wisconsin Cavalry	July 21, 1864 to July 30, 1864
Horace P. Lamson	Lt. Colonel, 4th Indiana Cavalry	July 30, 1864 to October 29, 1864

2nd Brigade, Regiments

Regiment	Date of Inclusion	Transferred From
1st Ohio Cavalry	October 1862	2-Brig. Cav. Div. Army Ohio
3rd Ohio Cavalry	October 1862	2-Brig. Cav. Div. Army Ohio
4th Ohio Cavalry	October 1862	2-Brig. Cav. Div. Army Ohio
5th Kentucky Cavalry	January 1863	Cav. 4-Div. Centre 14-Corps
2nd Tennessee Cavalry	January 1863	Reserve Cav. Cumberland
2nd Indiana Cavalry	March 1863	1-Brig. 1-Cav. Div. Cumberland
4th Indiana Cavalry	March 1863	Dist. West Ky. Dept. Ohio
1st Wisconsin Cavalry	June 1863	Army S. E. Mo. Dept. Mo
3rd Tennessee Cavalry	June 1863	Post Nashville, Tennessee

3rd Brigade, Commanders
Organized July 8, 1863

Commanders	Rank	Time of Command
Louis D. Watkins	Colonel, 6th Kentucky Cavalry	July 8, 1863 to July 5, 1864
John K. Faulkner	Colonel, 7th Kentucky Cavalry	July 5, 1864 to August 10, 1864
Louis D. Watkins	Colonel, 6th Kentucky Cavalry	August 10, 1864 to October 29, 1864

3rd Brigade, Regiments

Regiment	Date of Inclusion	Transferred From
4th Kentucky Cavalry	July 1863	1-Brig. 1-Cav. Div. Cumberland
5th Kentucky Cavalry	July 1863	2-Brig. 1-Cav. Div. Cumberland
6th Kentucky Cavalry	July 1863	1-Brig. 1-Cav. Div. Cumberland
7th Kentucky Cavalry	July 1863	1-Brig. 1-Cav. Div. Cumberland

Artillery, 1st Division

Unit	Date of Inclusion	Transferred From
Battery D, 1st Ohio Artillery, Sect.	November 1862	33-Brig. 10-Div. 3-Corps Ohio
18th Indiana Batty	January 1864	Arty. 2-Cav. Div. Cumberland

Reserve Cavalry Brigade

Unit	Date of Inclusion	Transferred From
15th Pennsylvania Cavalry	November 1862	New Organization
2nd Tennessee Cavalry	November 1862	Dist. W. Va. Dept. Ohio
5th Tennessee Cavalry	November 1862	New Organization

Unattached Cavalry

Unit	Date of Inclusion	Transferred From
4th U.S. Cavalry	November 1862	Headquarters, Army of Ohio

SECOND DIVISION
Organized March 1863

2nd Division, Commanders

Commanders	Rank	Time of Command
John B. Turchin	Brigadier General	March 1863 to July 28, 1863
George Crook	Brigadier General	July 28, 1863 to February 3, 1864
Kennard Garrard	Brigadier General	February 3, 1864 to October 29, 1864

Appendix B: Organization of the Cavalry of the Army of the Cumberland

1st Brigade, Commanders	Rank	Time of Command
Robert H.G. Minty	Colonel, 4th Michigan Cavalry	March 1863 to December 1863
William B. Sipes	Colonel, 7th Pennsylvania Cavalry	Dec, 1863 to January 24, 1864
William W. Lowe	Colonel, 5th Iowa Cavalry	Jan. 24, 1864 to April 1, 1864
Robert H. G. Minty	Colonel, 4th Michigan Cavalry	April 1, 1864 to September 29, 1864
William H. Jennings	Major, 4th U.S. Cavalry	September 29, 1864 to October 29, 1864

1st Brigade, Regiments	Date of Inclusion	Transferred From
3rd Indiana Cavalry	March 1863	1-Brig. 1-Cav. Div. Cumberland
4th Michigan Cavalry	March 1863	1-Brig. 1-Cav. Div. Cumberland
7th Pennsylvania Cavalry	March 1863	1-Brig. 1-Cav. Div. Cumberland
5th Tennessee Cavalry	March 1863	Reserve Cav. Cumberland
4th U.S. Cavalry	March 1863	Headquarters, Dept. Cumberland
5th Iowa Cavalry	June 1863	Fort Donelson, Tennessee
8th Indiana Cavalry	October 1863	39th Ind. Mounted Infantry
5th Tennessee Cavalry	November 1863	3-Brig. 2-Cav. Div. Cumberland
5th Iowa Cavalry	November 1863	3-Brig. 2-Cav. Div. Cumberland
4th Michigan Cavalry	November 1863	2-Brig. 2-Cav. Div. Cumberland

2nd Brigade, Commanders	Rank	Time of Command
Eli Long	Colonel, 4th Ohio Cavalry	March 1863 to August 20, 1864
Beroth B. Eggleston	Colonel, 1st Ohio Cavalry	August 20, 1864 to October 29, 1864

2nd Brigade, Regiments	Date of Inclusion	Transferred From
2nd Kentucky Cavalry	March 1863	Cav. 1-Div. 14-Corps
1st Ohio Cavalry	March 1863	2-Brig. 1-Cav. Div. Cumberland
3rd Ohio Cavalry	March 1863	2-Brig. 1-Cav. Div. Cumberland
4th Ohio Cavalry	March 1863	2-Brig. 1-Cav. Div. Cumberland
10th Ohio Cavalry	March 1863	New Organization
4th Michigan Cavalry	November 1863	1-Brig. 2-Cav. Div. Cumberland
10th Ohio Cavalry	November 1863	3-Brig. 2-Cav. Div. Cumberland
17th Indiana Mounted Infantry	November 1863	3-Brig. 2-Cav. Div. Cumberland
98th Illinois Mounted Infantry	November 1863	3-Brig. 2-Cav. Div. Cumberland

3rd Brigade, Commanders	Rank	Time of Command
William W. Lowe	Colonel, 5th Iowa Cavalry	August 5, 1863 to November 8, 1863
John T. Wilder	Colonel, 17th Indiana Mount. Infy	November 8, 1863 to December 25, 1863
Abram O. Miller	Colonel, 72nd Indiana Mount. Infy	December 25, 1863 to January 28, 1864
Smith D. Atkins	Colonel, 92rd Illinois Mount. Infy	January 28, 1864 to February 20, 1864
John T. Wilder	Colonel, 17th Indiana Mount. Infy	February 20, 1864 to June 14, 1864
Abram O. Miller	Colonel, 72nd Indiana Mount. Infy	June 14, 1864 to October 29, 1864

3rd Brigade, Regiments	Date of Inclusion	Transferred From
5th Iowa Cavalry	August 1863	1-Brig. 2-Cav. Div. Cumberland
10th Ohio Cavalry	August 1863	2-Brig. 2-Cav. Div. Cumberland
5th Tennessee Cavalry	August 1863	1-Brig. 2-Cav. Div. Cumberland.
92rd Illinois Mounted Infantry	November 1863	Wilder's Mounted Infantry Brig
98th Illinois Mounted Infantry	November 1863	Wilder's Mounted Infantry Brig
123d Illinois Mounted Infantry	November 1863	Wilder's Mounted Infantry Brig
17th Indiana Mounted Infantry	November 1863	Wilder's Mounted Infantry Brig
72nd Indiana Mounted Infantry	November 1863	Wilder's Mounted Infantry Brig
18th Indiana Batty	November 1863	Wilder's Mounted Infantry Brig
17th Indiana Mounted Infantry	November 1863	2-Brig. 2-Cav. Div. Cumberland

3rd Brigade, Regiments

3rd Brigade, Regiments	Date of Inclusion	Transferred From
98th Illinois Mounted Infantry	November 1863	2-Brig. 2-Cav. Div. Cumberland
72nd Indiana Mounted Infantry	April 1864	3-Brig. 1-Cav. Div. 16-C. Tennessee

Artillery 2nd Division

	Date of Inclusion	Transferred From
Battery D, 1st Ohio Artillery, Sect.	March 1864	Arty. 1-Div. Cav. Cumberland
Board of Trade Illinois Battery	March 1864	Pioneer Brig. Cumberland

Unattached

	Date of Inclusion	Transferred From
39th Indiana Mounted Infantry	April 1863	1-Brig. 1-Div. 20-Corps

THIRD DIVISION
Organized April 2, 1864

3rd Division, Commanders	Rank	Time of Command
William W. Lowe	Colonel, 5th Iowa Cavalry	April 2, 1864 to April 17, 1864
Eli H. Murray	Colonel, 3rd Kentucky Cavalry	April 17, 1864 to April 26, 1864
Judson Kilpatrick	Brigadier General	April 26, 1864 to May 13, 1864
Eli H. Murray	Colonel, 3rd Kentucky Cavalry	May 13, 1864 to May 21, 1864
William W. Lowe	Colonel, 5th Iowa Cavalry	May 21, 1864 to July 23, 1864
Judson Kilpatrick	Brigadier General	July 23, 1864 to October 29, 1864

1st Brigade, Commanders	Rank	Time of Command
William W. Lowe	Colonel, 5th Iowa Cavalry	April 2, 1864 to May 21, 1864
Robert Klein	Lt. Colonel, 3rd Indiana Cavalry	May 21, 1864 to August 23, 1864
Matthewson T. Patrick	Colonel, 5th Iowa Cavalry	August 23, 1864 to August 26, 1864
J. M. Young	Major, 5th Iowa Cavalry	August 26, 1864 to September 5, 1864
Thomas J. Jordan	Colonel, 9th Pennsylvania Cavalry	September 5, 1864 to October 29, 1864

1st Brigade, Regiments	Date of Inclusion	Transferred From
3rd Indiana Cavalry, 4 Companies	April 1864	1-Brig. 2-Cav. Div. Cumberland
5th Iowa Cavalry	April 1864	1-Brig. 2-Cav. Div. Cumberland
9th Pennsylvania Cavalry	April 1864	1-Brig. 1-Div. Cav. Cumberland

2nd Brigade, Commanders	Rank	Time of Command
Charles C. Smith	Colonel, 10th Ohio Cavalry	April 2, 1864 to July 27, 1864
Thomas J. Harrison	Colonel, 8th Indiana Cavalry	July 27, 1864 to July 30, 1864
Charles C. Smith	Colonel, 10th Ohio Cavalry	July 30, 1864 to August 6, 1864
T.W. Sanderson	Major, 10th Ohio Cavalry	August 6, 1864 to August 10, 1864
F.A. Jones	Lt. Colonel, 8th Indiana Cavalry	August 10, 1864 to September 26, 1864
William Thayer	Major, 10th Ohio Cavalry	September 26, 1864 to October 29, 1864

2nd Brigade, Regiments	Date of Inclusion	Transferred From
8th Indiana Cavalry	April 1864	Dist. Nashville, Tenn.
2nd Kentucky Cavalry	April 1864	2-Brig. 2-Cav, Div. Cumberland
10th Ohio Cavalry	April 1864	2-Brig. 2-Cav. Div. Cumberland

3rd Brigade, Commanders	Rank	Time of Command
Eli H. Murray	Colonel, 3rd Kentucky Cavalry	April 2, 1864 to May 13, 1864
Smith D. Atkins	Colonel, 92nd Illinois Mount Inftry	May 13, 1864 to May 23, 1864
Eli H. Murray	Colonel, 3rd Kentucky Cavalry	May 23, 1864 to August 18, 1864
R.H. King	Lt. Colonel, 3rd Kentucky Cavalry	August 18, 1864 to Aug. 22, 1864
Eli H. Murray	Colonel, 3rd Kentucky Cavalry	August 22, 1864 to Oct. 29, 1864

Appendix B: Organization of the Cavalry of the Army of the Cumberland 303

3rd Brigade, Regiments	Date of Inclusion	Transferred From
92nd Illinois Mounted Infantry	April 1864	3-Brig. 2-Cav. Div. Cumberland
3rd Kentucky Cavalry	April 1864	3-Brig. 2-Cav. Div. Cumberland
5th Kentucky Cavalry	April 1864	3-Brig. 1-Cav. Div. 16-C. Tennessee

Artillery, 3rd Division

10th Wisconsin Battery	April 1864	Unassigned Arty. Dept. Cumberland

Unattached, 3rd Division

1st Alabama Cavalry	September 1864	Headquarters, 16-Corps Left Wing
9th Illinois Mounted Infantry	September 1864	2-Brig. 2-Div. 16-C. Tennessee

FOURTH DIVISION
Organized April 1, 1864

4th Division, Commanders	Rank	Time of Command
Alvan C. Gillem	Brigadier General	April 1, 1864 to August 16, 1864
George Spalding	Colonel, 12th Tennessee Cavalry	August 16, 1864 to October 29, 1864

1st Brigade, Commander	Rank	Time of Command
Duff G. Thornburg	Lt. Colonel, 3rd Tennessee Cavalry	April 1, 1864 to October 29, 1864

1st Brigade, Regiments	Date of Inclusion	Transferred From
2rd Tennessee Cavalry	April 1864	3-Brig. 1-Cav. Div. 16-C. Tennessee
3rd Tennessee Cavalry	April 1864	3-Brig. 1-Cav, Div. 16-C. Tennessee
4th Tennessee Cavalry	April 1864	3-Brig. 1-Cav. Div. 16-C. Tennessee
Battery A, Tennessee Artillery	April 1864	Decatur, Alabama

2nd Brigade, Commanders	Rank	Time of Command
George Spalding	Lt. Colonel, 12th Tennessee Cavalry	April 1, 1864 to August 16, 1864
W.J. Clift	Lt. Colonel, 5th Tennessee Cavalry	August 16, 1864 to Oct. 29, 1864

2nd Brigade, Regiments	Date of Inclusion	Transferred From
5th Tennessee Cavalry	April 1864	Dist. Nashville, Tennessee
10th Tennessee Cavalry	April 1864	Dist. Nashville, Tennessee
12th Tennessee Cavalry	April 1864	Def. Nash. & N.W.R.R.
1st Kansas Battery	April 1864	Def. Nash. & N.W.R.R.

3rd Brigade, Commander	Rank	Time of Command
J.K. Miller	Colonel, 13th Tennessee Cavalry	April 1, 1864 to Oct. 19, 1864

2nd Brigade, Regiments	Date of Inclusion	Transferred From
8th Tennessee Cavalry	April 1864	2-Brig. 2-Div. Cav. Corps Ohio
9th Tennessee Cavalry	April 1864	New Organization
13th Tennessee Cavalry	April 1864	New Organization

Wilder's Mounted Infantry Brigade

Assigned to Cav. Command Cumberland from 4-Div. 14-Corps, October 16, 1863; assigned to 2nd Cav. Division, November 8, 1863

Commander	Rank	Time of Command
John T. Wilder	Colonel, 72nd Indian Mounted Infy	October 16, 1863 to November 8, 1863

Wilder's Brigade, Regiments	Date of Inclusion	Transferred From
92nd Illinois Mounted Infantry	October 1863	1-Brig. 4-Div.14-Corps
98th Illinois Mounted Infantry	October 1863	1-Brig. 4-Div. 14-Corps
123d Illinois Mounted Infantry	October 1863	1-Brig. 4-Div. 14-Corps
17th Indiana Mounted Infantry	October 1863	1-Brig. 4-Div. 14-Corps
72rd Indiana Mounted Infantry	October 1863	1-Brig. 4-Div. 14-Corps
18th Indiana Battery	October 1863	Arty. 4-Div. 14-Corps

Source: Frederick H. Dyer, *A Compendium of the War of the Rebellion Compiled and Arranged from Official Records of the Federal and Confederate Armies Reports of the Adjutant Generals of the Several States, the Army Registers and Other Reliable Documents and Sources* (Des Moines: Dyer, 1908), 442, 460–462.

Chapter Notes

Chapter 1

1. James Edward Kelly, *Generals in Bronze: Interviewing the Commanders of the Civil War*, William B. Styple, ed. (Kearney, NJ: Bell Grove, 2005), 185.
2. Henry Halleck, *The War of the Rebellion: A Compilation of the Official Records of the Union and Confederate Armies*, Series I, Vol. 16, Part 2 (Washington, D.C.: U.S. Government Printing Office, 1880–1901), 640–642. [Hereafter designated as *Official Records*.]
3. William Rosecrans, *Official Records*, Series 1, Vol. 16, Part 2, 653.
4. *Ibid.*, 655.
5. William McClelland, *Official Records*, Series 1, Vol. 7, 931.
6. William Rosecrans, *Official Records*, Series 1, Vol. 20, Part 2, 27.
7. William Rosecrans, *Official Records*, Series 1, Vol. 20, Part 2, 31; Ulysses Grant, Special Order No. 15, Union Generals Records–David S. Stanley, Record Group 94, Entry 159, Box 28, National Archives, Washington, D.C., November 11, 1862.
8. George Thomas, *Official Records*, Series 1, Vol. 16, Part 2, 657; Henry Halleck, *Official Records*, Series 1, Vol. 16, Part 2, 663.
9. Arthur C. Ducat, *Official Records*, Series 1, Vol. 20, Part 2, 12.
10. J. B. Anderson, *Official Records*, Series 1, Vol. 20, Part 2, 14.
11. Alexander McCook, *Official Records*, Series 1, Vol. 20, Part 2, 15.
12. Arthur Ducat, *Official Records*, Series 1, Vol. 20, Part 2, 15.
13. Arthur Ducat, *Official Records*, Series 1, Vol. 20, Part 2, 19.
14. Arthur Ducat, *Official Records*, Series 1, Vol. 20, Part 2, 21.
15. Arthur Ducat, *Official Records*, Series 1, Vol. 20, Part 2, 23.
16. Thomas Crittenden, *Official Records*, Series 1, Vol. 20, Part 2, 28.
17. George Thomas, *Official Records*, Series 1, Vol. 20, Part 2, 39.
18. William Rosecrans, *Official Records*, Series 1, Vol. 20, Part 2, 45; George Thomas, *Official Records*, Series 1, Vol. 20, Part 2, 45–46.
19. George Thomas, *Official Records*, Series 1, Vol. 20, Part 2, 56; Arthur C. Ducat, *Official Records*, Series 1, Vol. 20, Part 2, 66.
20. Ulysses Grant, Special Order No. 15.
21. J. Garesche, *Official Records*, Series 1, Vol. 20, Part 2, 94.
22. Society of the Army of the Cumberland, *Twenty-seventh Reunion* (Cincinnati: The Robert Clark Company, 1898), 149–150.
23. William Rosecrans, *Official Records*, Series 1, Vol. 20, Part 1, 182.
24. David Stanley, *An American General: The Memoirs of David Sloan Stanley*, Samuel W. Fordyce IV, ed. (Santa Barbara, California: The Narrative Press, 2004), 150.
25. John Beatty, *The Citizen Soldier: The Memoirs of a Civil War Volunteer* (Lincoln: Bison Books, University of Nebraska Press, 1998), 235.
26. Lucien Wulsin, *The Fourth Regiment Ohio Veteran Volunteer Cavalry* (Cincinnati: Fourth Ohio Volunteer Cavalry Association, 1912), 8.
27. *National Cyclopedia of American Biography*, Vol. VI (New York: James T. White Co., 1896), 448.
28. George Hazzard, *Hazzard's History of Henry County, Indiana, 1822–1906, Vol. 1* (New Castle, Indiana: George Hazzard Publisher, 1906), 187; *The Daily Wabash Express*, "Cavalry," Terra Haute, Indiana, November 16, 1861, 3.
29. Edward Tullidge, editor, "Governor Murray and Family," *Tullidge Quarterly Magazine*, Vol. 1, No. 3 (1881), 496–501; David Evans, *Sherman's Horsemen* (Bloomington: Indiana University Press, 1996), 445.
30. William Henry Powell, editor, *Officers of the Army and Navy (Volunteer) Who Served in the Civil War* (Philadelphia: L. R. Hamersly, 1893), 313.
31. William Sipes, *History and Roster of the 7th Pennsylvania Veteran Volunteers* (Pottsville: Miners' Journal Print, 1905), 1–3; Chester Bailey, *The Mansfield Men in the Seventh Pennsylvania Cavalry, Eighth Regiment* (Mansfield: Published by Author, 1986), 1–6.
32. W. L. Curry, *Four Years in the Saddle: History of First Regiment Ohio Volunteer Cavalry* (Columbus: Champlin Printing Co., 1898), 20.
33. *Ibid.*, 28–29; Alexander C. McClurg, "An American Soldier, Minor Millikin," *Military Essays and Recollections: Papers Read Before the Commandery of the State of Illinois* (Chicago: A. C. McClurg and Company, 1894), 363–364.
34. Thomas Crofts, *History of the Service of the Third Ohio Veteran Volunteer Cavalry* (Toledo: Stoneman Press, 1910), 12–13, 239.
35. W. L. Curry, *Four Years in the Saddle*, 9–12.

36. *A Military Record of Battery D, First Ohio Veteran Volunteers, Light Artillery* (Oil City, Pennsylvania: The Derrick Publishing Co., 1908), 39, 57.

37. Ibid., 9, 58.

38. John Fitch, "Captain Elmer Otis," *Annals of the Army of the Cumberland* (Philadelphia: J. B. Lippincott and Co., 1864), 215–218.

39. *Official Register of the Officers and Cadets of the U.S. Military Academy* (West Point, NY: U.S. Military Academy, June 1852), 7.

40. David Stanley, *An American General: The Memoirs of David Sloan Stanley*, Samuel W. Fordyce IV, ed. (Santa Barbara, California: The Narrative Press, 2004), 49–50; Philip Sheridan, *Personal Memoirs of Philip H. Sheridan, General United States Army*, Vol. 1 (New York: D. Appleton and Company, 1902), 8–9.

41. Stanley, *An American General*, 98; Eli Long, Diary, July 29, 1857, United States Army Heritage and Education Center, Eli Long Papers—1855–1892, Carlisle, Pennsylvania; Crimmins (Martin Lalor) Papers, David S. Stanley, "David Stanley Diary, United States 2nd Dragoons of a March from Fort Smith, Arkansas, to San Diego, California, made in 1853," Briscoe Center for American History, University of Texas–Austin.

42. William S. Rosecrans, Letter, Undated, William S. Rosecrans Papers, Box 59, Folder 54, University of California–Los Angeles; Thomas M. Vincent, "David Sloane Stanley," *The Thirty-fourth Annual Reunion of the Association Graduates of the United States Military Academy at West Point, New York* (Saginaw: Seeman & Peters Printers and Binders, 1903), 62.

43. David Power Conyngham Papers (CON), "Soldiers of the Cross," University of Notre Dame Archives (UNDA), Notre Dame, IN, 26–27.

44. Ibid., 27–29.

45. William D. Bickham, *Rosecrans' Campaign with the Fourteenth Army Corps, of the Army of the Cumberland* (Cincinnati: Moore, Wilstach, Keys & Co., 1863), 81; David Stanley, *An American General: The Memoirs of David Sloan Stanley*, Samuel W. Fordyce IV, ed. (Santa Barbara, California: The Narrative Press, 2004), 150.

46. John Londa, "The Role of Union Cavalry during the Chickamauga Campaign," Master's Thesis, Command and General Staff College, Fort Leavenworth, Kansas, 1991, 28.

47. David Stanley, *An American General*, 150.

48. W. L. Curry, *Four Years in the Saddle: History of First Regiment Ohio Volunteer Cavalry*, 82.

49. George Thomas, *Official Records*, Series 1, Vol. 20, Part 2, 129.

50. Basil Duke, *Morgan's Cavalry* (New York: The Neale Publishing Co., 1909), 14–17.

51. Clement A. Evans, editor, *Confederate Military History*, Vol. I (Atlanta: Confederate Publishing, 1899), 699–702.

52. Ibid., 705–710.

53. *The Vevay Reveille*, "Necrology Col. Robert Klein," Vol. 85, no. 13, Thursday, 27 March 1902, page 5, columns 3 and 4; W. N. Pickerill, *History of the Third Indiana Cavalry* (Indianapolis: Aetna Printing Co., 1906), 40–46.

54. L. Wallace Duncan and Charles F. Scott, editors, *History of Allen and Woodson Counties, Kansas: Embellished with Portraits of Well-Known People of These Counties, With Biographies of Our Representative Citizens, Cuts of Public Buildings and a Map of Each County* (Iola, Kansas: Iola Registers, Printers and Binders, 1901), 880–894.

55. James Alex Baggett, *Homegrown Yankees: Tennessee's Union Cavalry in the Civil War* (Baton Rouge: Louisiana State University, 2009), 30, 46–47.

56. Samuel Bates, *History of the Pennsylvania Volunteers, 1861–65* (Harrisburg: B. Singerly, State Printer, 1870), 902–903.

57. Walter Hines Page and Arthur Wilson Page, editors, "Gen. William J. Palmer, Builder of the West," in *The World's Work: A History of Our Time, Vol. 15* (New York: Doubleday, Page, and Co., 1908), 9899.

58. Rosecrans, *Official Records*, Series 1, Vol. 20, Part 1, 45.

59. David Stanley, *Official Records*, Series 1, Vol. 20, Part 1, 76.

60. David Stanley, Edward McCook, John Wharton, *Official Records*, Series 1, Vol. 20, Part 1, 76–77.

61. Larry Daniel, *Days of Glory: The Army of the Cumberland 1861–1865* (Baton Rouge: Louisiana State University Press, 2006), 196.

62. Thomas Edison, *John Hunt Morgan and His Raiders* (Lexington: University Press of Kentucky, 1985), 65.

63. N. H. Davis, *Official Records*, Series 1, Vol. 20, Part 2, 346.

64. Ibid.

65. Ibid.

66. George Fobes, "An Account of the Mutiny in the Anderson Cavalry, at Nashville, Tenn., December 1862," in *Leaves of a Trooper's Dairy*, by John Williams (Philadelphia: Published by Author, 1869), 78–103.

67. Ibid.

68. N. H. Davis, *Official Records*, Series 1, Vol. 20, Part 2, 346.

69. Ibid., 347–348.

70. Ibid.

Chapter 2

1. William Rosecrans, *Official Records*, Series 1, Vol. 20, Part 2, 31.

2. Gerould Otis Gibson, Diary of Otis Gibson Gerould (1830–1918), January 1, 1862–February 11, 1863, Unpublished, Pennsylvania Regimental Files, Stones River National Park, Technical Information Center, Murfreesboro, TN.

3. Edwin Stanton, *Official Records*, Series 1, Vol. 20, Part 2, 64; William Rosecrans, *Official Records*, Series 1, Vol. 20, Part 2, 118.

4. William Rosecrans, *Official Records*, Series 1, Vol. 20, Part 1, 182.

5. D. S. Stanley, Letter, December 24, 1862. Simon Gratz Collection H250A. Historical Society of Pennsylvania, Philadelphia, Pennsylvania; David Stanley, *Official Records*, Series 1, Vol. 20, Part 1, 617; Gilbert Kniffin, *The Battle of Stone's River, Battles and Leaders of the Civil War*, Vol. 3 (New York: The Century Company, 1884, 1888), 61.

6. Terry L. Jones, *Historical Dictionary of the Civil War, Vol. 1* (Lanham, Maryland: Scarecrow Press Inc., 2011), 232–233, 1091; William Wharton Groce, "Major General John A. Wharton," *The Southwestern Historical Quarterly*, Vol. 19, No. 3 (Jan. 1916), 271–278.

7. John McLain, Diary entry, December 26, 1862,

McLain Papers (c.00111), Michigan State University Archives & Historical Collections, East Lansing, Michigan.
    8. Lewis Zahm, *Official Records*, Series 1, Vol. 20, Part 1, 633.
    9. Robert Minty, *Official Records*, Series 1, Vol. 20, Part 1, 623; N. M. Newell, *Official Records*, Series 1, Vol. 20, Part 1, 622.
    10. Edward G. Longacre, *A Soldier to the Last: Maj. Gen. Joseph Wheeler in Blue and Gray* (Washington: Potomac Books Inc., 2007), 73.
    11. Robert Klein, *Official Records*, Series 1, Vol. 20, Part 1, 646–647; Charles Kirk, "The Fifteenth Pennsylvania (Anderson) Cavalry at Stone's River," in *History of the Fifteenth Pennsylvania Volunteer Cavalry*, J. C. Reiff, ed. (Philadelphia: Society of the Fifteenth Pennsylvania Cavalry, 1906), 83.
    12. Peter Cozzens, *No Better Place to Die* (Urbana: University of Illinois Press, 1991), 58–59.
    13. Lewis Zahm, *Official Records*, Series 1, Vol. 20, Part 1, 635.
    14. David Stanley, *Official Records*, Series 1, Vol. 20, Part 1, 618; David Stanley, *An American General: The Memoirs of David Sloan Stanley*, Samuel W. Fordyce IV, ed. (Santa Barbara, California: The Narrative Press, 2004), 152.
    15. Edward Longacre, *A Soldier to the Last*, 75, 78.
    16. Robert Minty, *Official Records*, Series 1, Vol. 20, Part 1, 624.
    17. Alexander McCook, *Official Records*, Series 1, Vol. 20, Part 1, 256.
    18. David Stanley, *An American General*. 152.
    19. Edwin C. Bearss, *Cavalry Operations—Battle of Stones River*, Unpublished, Stones River National Park, Technical Information Center, Murfreesboro, TN, 1959, 59.
    20. Stanley, *An American General*, 153.
    21. Thomas Crofts, *History of the Service of the Third Ohio Veteran Volunteer Cavalry* (Toledo: Stoneman Press, 1910), 60.
    22. Lewis Zahm, *Official Records*, Series 1, Vol. 20, Part 1, 637.
    23. David Stanley, *Official Records*, Series 1, Vol. 20, Part 1, 618.
    24. Bearss, *Cavalry Operations*, 65.
    25. Lewis Zahm, *Official Records*, Series 1, Vol. 20, Part 1, 637.
    26. Lewis Zahm, *Official Records*, Series 1, Vol. 20, Part 1, 637.
    27. W. L. Curry, *Four Years in the Saddle: History of First Regiment Ohio Volunteer Cavalry* (Columbus: Champlin Printing Co., 1898), 83–84; *The Catalogue and History of Sigma Chi* (Chicago: Published by the Fraternity, 1890), 4.
    28. Lewis Zahm, *Official Records*, Series 1, Vol. 20, Part 1, 637.
    29. *Lancaster Daily Evening Express*, "The Story of a Cavalry Soldier The Fourth Regular Cavalry at Murfreesboro—Feeling the Position of the Enemy—A Brilliant Charge—A Brigade of Rebel Cavalry Routed—A Personal Adventure—A Hazardous Reconnaissance," January 28, 1863; Elmer Otis, *Official Records*, Series 1, Vol. 20, Part 1, 649.
    30. Robert Klein, *Official Records*, Series 1, Vol. 20, Part 1, 647.
    31. J. W. Paramore, *Official Records*, Series 1, Vol. 20, Part 1, 643.
    32. J. W. Paramore, *Official Records*, Series 1, Vol. 20, Part 1, 643.
    33. Bearss, *Cavalry Operations–Battle of Stones River*, 37; John Kennett, *Official Records*, Series 1, Vol. 20, Part 1, 621.
    34. John Kennett, *Official Records*, Series 1, Vol. 20, Part 1, 621; E. H. Murray, *Official Records*, Series 1, Vol. 20, Part 1, 627–628; John Kennett, "History of the First Cavalry Division From November 1, 1862, to January 1, 1863," in *G.A.R. War Papers* (Cincinnati: Fred C. Jones Post, 1891), 348.
    35. Edwin C. Bearss, "Cavalry Operations in the Stones River Campaign," in *The Battle of Stones River*, Timothy Johnson, editor, Vol. 4 (Nashville: Tennessee Historical Society, 2012), 37.
    36. John Wynkoop, *Official Records*, Series 1, Vol. 20, Part 1, 631–632.
    37. Stanley, *An American General*, 153.
    38. Kirk, *History of the Fifteenth Pennsylvania Volunteer Cavalry*, 93; Robert Minty, Letter to Backus, November 11, 1906, Robert Minty Papers, Civil War Collection, USAHEC, Carlisle, Pennsylvania.
    39. Robert Minty, *Official Records*, Series 1, Vol. 20, Part 1, 624.
    40. Stanley, *An American General*, 153; David Stanley, *Official Records*, Series 1, Vol. 20, Part 1, 618.
    41. Robert Minty, *Official Records*, Series 1, Vol. 20, Part 1, 624.
    42. Reiff, *History of the Fifteenth Pennsylvania Volunteer Cavalry*, 93.
    43. Robert Minty, *Official Records*, Series 1, Vol. 20, Part 1, 624–625.
    44. Robert Minty, "The Saber Brigade," *National Tribune*, August 11, 1892; Eugene Bronson, Letter, January 22, 1863, Eugene Bronson Collection, Kalamazoo College, Kalamazoo, Michigan.
    45. John Wharton, *Official Records*, Series 1, Vol. 20, Part 1, 968.
    46. William Lamers, *The Edge of Glory: A Biography of General William S. Rosecrans, U.S.A.* (New York: Harcourt, Brace & World, Inc., 1961), 235; Stanley, *An American General*, 154.
    47. Lamers, *The Edge of Glory*, 235.
    48. Braxton Bragg, *Official Records*, Series 1, Vol. 20, Part 1, 667.
    49. Lewis Zahm, *Official Records*, Series 1, Vol. 20, Part 1, 637–638.
    50. John Wharton, *Official Records*, Series 1, Vol. 20, Part 1, 968; Joseph Burke, *Official Records*, Series 1, Vol. 20, Part 1, 656.
    51. David Stanley, *Official Records*, Series 1, Vol. 20, Part 1, 618.
    52. Lewis Zahm, *Official Records*, Series 1, Vol. 20, Part 1, 638.
    53. Robert Minty, *Official Records*, Series 1, Vol. 20, Part 1, 623.
    54. David Stanley, *Official Records*, Series 1, Vol. 20, Part 1, 619.
    55. James Alex Baggett, *Homegrown Yankees: Tennessee's Union Cavalry in the Civil War* (Baton Rouge: Louisiana State University, 2009), 60; Richard Hall, *Patriots in Disguise: Women Warriors in the Civil War* (New York: Paragon House, 1994), 27.

56. William Rosecrans *Official Records*, Series 1, Vol. 20, Part 1, 214.

57. Reginald Stuart, "The Role of the Cavalry in the Western Theatre of the American Civil War from the Battle of Shiloh to the Tullahoma Campaign," Master's Thesis 1968, University of British Columbia, Vancouver, British Columbia, 132.

58. Frank Mix, Letter from Frank Mix, January 9, 1863, Elisha Mix Papers, 1818–1898, Bentley Historical Library, University of Michigan, Ann Arbor.

59. Nancy Pape-Findley, *The Invincibles: The Story of Fourth Ohio Veteran Volunteer Cavalry* (Tecumseh, MI: Blood Road, 2002), 112, 360; United States Census, 1860; C. S. Williams, *Williams' Cincinnati Directory* (Cincinnati: C. S. Williams Publisher, 1860), 254.

60. Alexander McCook, *Official Records*, Series 1, Vol. 20, Part 1, 258; William Rosecrans, *Official Records*, Series 1, Vol. 20, Part 1, 198.

61. David Stanley, *Official Records*, Series 1, Vol. 20, Part 1, 619–620.

62. Stanley, *American General*, 155.

63. William Rosecrans *Official Records*, Series 1, Vol. 20, Part 2, 6; Stephen Z. Starr, *The Union Cavalry in the Civil War: The War in the West*, Vol. III (Baton Rouge: Louisiana State University, 2007), 114.

64. William D. Bickham, *Rosecrans' Campaign with the Fourteenth Army Corps, of the Army of the Cumberland* (Cincinnati: Moore Wilstach, Keys & Co., 1863), 80.

65. Stanley, *American General*, 150.

Chapter 3

1. David Stanley, *An American General: The Memoirs of David Sloan Stanley*, Samuel W. Fordyce IV, ed. (Santa Barbara, California: The Narrative Press, 2004), 160.

2. Edwin Stanton, *Official Records*, Series 1, Vol. 20, Part 2, 307; Larry J. Daniel, *Days of Glory: The Army of the Cumberland, 1861–1865* (Baton Rouge: Louisiana State University Press, 2004), 226.

3. Michael Bradley, "Tullahoma: The Wrongfully Forgotten Campaign," *Blue and Grey*, Vol. XXVII, No. 1 (2010), 7.

4. Edwin Stanton, *Official Records*, Series 1, Vol. 20, Part 2, 306.

5. William Rosecrans, *Official Records*, Series 1, Vol. 20, Part 2, 328.

6. Stephen Z. Starr, *The Union Cavalry in the Civil War: The War in the West, Vol. III* (Baton Rouge: Louisiana State University, 2007), 225.

7. A. C. Sands et. al, Letter to Abraham Lincoln, December 1, 1862, David Stanley Personnel File ACP 000183, National Archives, Washington, D.C. 001-06-08.

8. William Rosecrans, *Official Records*, Series 1, Vol. 23, Part 2, 34.

9. Joseph Vale, *Minty and the Cavalry: A History of Cavalry Campaigns in the Western Armies* (Harrisburg: Edwin K. Myers, Printer and Binder, 1886), 182.

10. United States War Department, *Cavalry Tactics*, Vol.s 1–3 (Philadelphia: J. B. Lippincott, & Co. 1862), i–vii; John Londa, "The Role of Union Cavalry During the Chickamauga Campaign," Master's Thesis, Command and General Staff College, Fort Leavenworth, Kansas, 1991, 28–29; Moses Harris, "Some Thoughts on Equipment," *Journal of the United States Cavalry Association*, Vol. 4 (1891), 166.

11. John Andes and Will McTeer, *Loyal Mountain Troops, The Second and Third Tennessee Volunteer Cavalry* (Maryville, Tennessee: Blount County Genealogical and Historical Society, 1992), 42–46; C. M. Kiggs, Sergeant-Major, "Camp Life," in *Four Years in the Saddle: History of First Regiment Ohio Volunteer Cavalry*, W. L. Curry (Columbus: Champlin Printing Co., 1898), 275–279; Daniel Wait Howe, January 31, 1863 Diary Entry, Box 1, F 16, Army Diary of Captain (M148), Indiana Historical Society, Indianapolis, Indiana.

12. L. K. Dunn, January 19, 1863 Letter, Dunn Family Papers, 1854–1977 (D923, folder 4–6), Filson Historical Society, Louisville, Kentucky.

13. Daniel Prickitt, *3rd Ohio Cavalry*, February 24, 1863 diary entry, Colonel E. D. Stoltz, ed. (Archbold, Ohio: Edwin Stoltz, 1988), 72.

14. James Alex Baggett, *Homegrown Yankees: Tennessee's Union Cavalry in the Civil War* (Baton Rouge: Louisiana State University, 2009), 87.

15. Ibid., 88–89.

16. Elmer Otis, *Official Records*, Series 1, Vol. 23, Part 1, 17.

17. W. R. Carter, *History of the First Regiment of Tennessee Volunteer Cavalry* (Knoxville: Gaut-Ogden Co., Printers and Binders, 1902), 60.

18. William Rosecrans, *Official Records*, Series 1, Vol. 20, Part 2, 363–364; Francis Bernard Heitman, *Historical Register and Dictionary of the United States Army 1789–1903* (Washington, D.C.: U.S. Government Printing Office, 19030, 669; George W. Cullum, *Biographical Register of the Officers and Graduates of the US Military Academy*, Vol. 2 (New York: D. Van Nostrand, 1868–79), 559–560.

19. William J. Palmer, *Official Records*, Series 1, Vol. 20, Part 2, 376.

20. George Garrett, Letter, February 22, 1863, Stones River National Park, Technical Information Center, Murfreesboro, TN.

21. Joseph Vale, *Minty and the Cavalry*, 130.

22. Mary Pearre, Diary–February 9, 1863, Tennessee State Library and Archives, Nashville, Microfilm Accession Number: 1957.

23. Glenn W. Sunderland, *Lightning at Hoover's Gap* (New York: Thomas Yoseloff, 1969), 23–26.

24. Henry Halleck, *Official Records*, Series 1, Vol. 23, Part 2, 155.

25. Abner Harding, *Official Records*, Series 1, Vol. 23, Part 1, 34–35.

26. J. W. Paramore, *Official Records*, Series 1, Vol. 23, Part 1, 66–67; *New York Times*, "The Victory at Bradyville, Tenn.; Brilliant Conduct of Our Forces Under Gen. Stanley. The Army of the Frontier," March 8, 1863.

27. George Brent, *Official Records*, Series I, Vol. 23, Number 2, 701; Robert Lanier, *Photographic History of the Civil War* (New York: The Review of Reviews Co., 1911), 270.

28. William Henry Egle, A. S. Dudley, Harry Huber, R. H. Schively, editors, *Commemorative Biographical Encyclopedia of Dauphin County, Pennsylvania* (Chambersburg, Pennsylvania: J.M. Runk & Co., 1896), 1194–1195.

29. Marshall Thatcher, *A Hundred Battles in the West: The Second Michigan Cavalry* (Detroit: L. F. Kilroy, Printer, 1884), 115; Franklin Everett, *Memorials of the Grand*

River Valley (1878; Reprint, London: Forgotten Books, 2013), 617–618.

30. William M. Anderson, "The Union Side of Thompson's Station," in *The Battle of Stones River and the Fight for Middle Tennessee, Vol. IV* (Nashville: Tennessee Historical Society, 2012), 116–119; William Rosecrans, *Official Records*, Series 1, Vol. 23, Part 1, 75; Thomas Jordan, "Battle of Thompson's Station and the Trial of the Spies at Franklin, Tennessee," in *The United Service*, Vol. III (Philadelphia: L. R. Hamersly and Company, 1890), 300–314, 304–306.

31. Thomas Jordan, *Official Records*, Series 1, Vol. 23, Part 1, 81; William Rosecrans, *Official Records*, Series 1, Vol. 23, Part 1, 73–75; Stephen Z. Starr, *The Union Cavalry in the Civil War*, 230; Emerson Opdycke, *To Battle for God and the Right: The Civil War Letterbooks of Emerson Opdycke* (Urbana: University of Illinois Press, 2003), 63; *Ibid.* Jordan, 307; Anderson, *Ibid.*

32. Henry Albert Potter, March 8, 1863, Letter, MS 91–480 Henry Albert Potter Collection, Accession Box 461 Folder 2. Archives of Michigan. Historical Society of Michigan, Lansing.

33. Augustus Yenner, Diary March 9, 1863, Yenner, Augustus L., 1837–1924, Papers, Western Michigan University, Kalamazoo, Michigan; Joseph Vale, *Minty and the Cavalry*, 189.

34. Green Clay Smith, *Official Records*, Series 1, Vol. 23, Part 1, 180; John W. Rowell, *Yankee Cavalrymen* (Knoxville: University of Tennessee Press, 1971), 126.

35. Charles Seidel, *Official Records*, Series 1, Vol. 23, Part 1, 198; David Stanley *Official Records*, Series 1, Vol. 23, Part 1, 198; William Hazen, *Official Records*, Series 1, Vol. 23, Part 1, 197.

36. James Alex Baggett, *Homegrown Yankees*, 73–77; Henry Albert Potter, March 30, 1863, Letter from Henry Albert Potter; Daniel Prickitt, *3rd Ohio Cavalry*, April 29, 1863 diary entry; Frank Smith, "A Maine Boy in the Tenth Ohio Cavalry," *Maine Bugle* 4 (1897): 11–21.

37. Joseph Vale, *Minty and the Cavalry*, 188; John Andes and Will McTeer, *Loyal Mountain Troops*, 52.

38. Thomas Speed, *Union Regiments of Kentucky Vol. I* (Louisville: The Courier Journal Job Printing, Co., 1897), 120.

39. Frederick H. Dyer, *A Compendium of the War of the Rebellion* (Des Moines: The Dyer Publishing Co., 1908), 1189–1666.

40. H. Levin, editor, *Lawyers and Lawmakers of Kentucky* (Chicago: Lewis Publishing Co., 1897), 530.

41. *The Union Army, A History of Military Affairs in the Loyal States 1861–65*, Vol. 8 (Madison: Federal Publishing Co., 1908), 292.

42. Thomas Speed, *Union Regiments of Kentucky Vol. I*, 185.

43. *Ibid.*

44. Frederick H. Dyer, *A Compendium of the War of the Rebellion*, 1106; Roger Hunt, *Colonels in Blue—Indiana, Kentucky and Tennessee* (Jefferson, NC: McFarland, 2013), 102.

45. "Letter to Governor David Tod," June 3, 1862, in *Correspondence to the Governor and Adjutant General, 1861–1866, Vol. 34, Series 147–39: 90*, Ohio Historical Society, Columbus.

46. Joseph Vale, *Minty and the Cavalry*, 475; *Commemorative Biographical Encyclopedia of Dauphin County, PA* (Chambersburg, PA: J. M. Runk & Co., 1896), 1194–1195.

47. W. R. Carter, *History of the First Regiment of Tennessee Volunteer Cavalry*, 19–62; Myers E. Brown, *Tennessee's Union Cavalrymen* (Charleston: Arcadia Publishing Co., 2008), 27.

48. Leroy Graf and Ralph Haskins, editors, "Telegram from Rosecrans—April 12, 1863," in *Papers of Andrew Johnson*, Vol. 6 (Knoxville: University of Tennessee Press, 1983), 211; Julius Thomas Diary—June 4, 1863, Julius E. Thomas Diary, 1863–1864, Julius E. Thomas Collection, MS.2720, University of Tennessee, Knoxville; Carter, *History of the First Regiment of Tennessee Volunteer Cavalry, Ibid.*

49. W. L. Curry, *Four Years in the Saddle*, 307.

50. Earnest East, "Lincoln's Russian General," *Journal of the Illinois State Historical Society*, Vol. 52, No. 1 (1959), 106–122; Don Carlos Buell, *Official Records*, Series 1, Vol. 16, Part 2, 71.

51. David Stanley, *Personal Memoirs of Major-General D. S. Stanley USA* (Cambridge: Harvard University Press, 1917), 136–137.

52. James Edwin Love, Letter to Wife, May 20, 1863, James Edwin Love Papers (1859–1865) ARC A0940. Missouri Historical Society, St. Louis.

53. Marshall Thatcher, *A Hundred Battles in the West: The Second Michigan Cavalry*, 124.

54. Nancy Pape-Findley, *The Invincibles: The Story of Fourth Ohio Veteran Volunteer Cavalry* (Tecumseh, MI: Blood Road, 202), 135; *New York Times*, "Death of Gen. Eli Long," January 6, 1903; Absolom Mattox, *History of the Cincinnati Society of Ex-Army and Navy Officers* (Cincinnati: Peter G. Thompson Publisher, 1880), 184–185; Eli Long, "Autobiography," Eli Long Papers, Civil War Collection, Box 1, USAHEC, Carlisle, Pennsylvania.

55. Robert Minty, *Official Records*, Series 1, Vol. 23, Part 1, 207–208.

56. John Allan Wyeth, *The Life General Nathan Bedford Forrest* (New York: Harper Brothers, 1899), 177.

57. Gordon Granger, *Official Records*, Series 1, Vol. 23, Part 1, 224; David Stanley, *Official Records*, Series 1, Vol. 23, Part 1, 230–231.

58. David Stanley, *Official Records*, Series 1, Vol. 23, Part 2, 230–231.

59. Lewis Hanback, Letter, April 11, 1863, Hanback Collection—A H233, Filson Historical Society, Louisville, Kentucky.

60. Albert Potter, Letter, April 14, 1863; Gordon Granger, *Official Records*, Series 1, Vol. 23, Part 1, 227.

61. Joseph Vale, *Minty and the Cavalry*, 146–147.

62. Joseph Reynolds *Official Records*, Series 1, Vol. 23, Part 1, 267; Robert Minty, *Official Records*, Series 1, Vol. 23, Part 1, 271–272.

63. John Andes and Will McTeer, *Loyal Mountain Troops*, 50.

64. Lucy Virginia Smith, "Lucy Virginia French Diaries" entry for April 26, 1863, Tennessee State Library and Archives, Microfilm 1816, Nashville, Tennessee; John McLain, Diary entry April 21, 1863, McLain Papers (c.00111), Michigan State University Archives & Historical Collections, East Lansing, Michigan.

65. Eli Long, *Official Records*, Series 1, Vol. 23, Part 1, 275; Steven L. Wright, "*Louisville Daily Journal* April 27, 1863," *Kentucky Soldiers and Their Regiments in the Civil War*, Vol. III (Utica, Kentucky: McDowell Publi-

cations, 2009), 69; *Weekly Reporter*, "By Telegraph," Henderson, Kentucky, April 30, 1863, 2, column 3.

66. Jacob Piatt Dunn, *Memorial and Genealogical Record of Representative Citizens of Indiana* (Indianapolis: B. F. Brown Publisher, 1912), 657–66.

67. Henry Halleck, *Official Records*, Series 1, Vol. 23, Part 2, 256.

68. Montgomery C. Meigs, *Official Records*, Series 1, Vol. 23, Part 2, 289, 301–304; William Rosecrans, *Official Records*, Series 1, Vol. 23, Part 2, 289, 320–321.

69. Stanley, *An American General*, 156.

70. Thomas Jordan, Letter to Wife, May 5, 1863, Thomas J. Jordan Civil War Letters [2066] Box Number: 1, Folder 13, Historical Society of Pennsylvania, Philadelphia, Pennsylvania.

71. David Stanley, *Official Records*, Series 1, Vol. 23, Part 1, 334–335.

72. David Stanley, *Official Records*, Series 1, Vol. 23, Part 1, 335.

73. Stanley, *An American General*, 158–159.

74. William H. Sinclair, *Official Records*, Series 1, Vol. 23, Part 2, 568; Stanley, *An American General*, 159.

75. Nadine Turchin, "A Monotony Full of Sadness: The Diary of Nadine Turchin, May, 1863–April, 1864," Edited by Mary Ellen McElligott, *Journal of the Illinois State Historical Society*, Vol. 70 (1977), 27–89.

76. Stanley, *An American General*, 156.

77. Edward G. Longacre, *A Soldier to the Last: Maj. Gen. Joseph Wheeler in Blue and Gray* (Washington: Potomac Books Inc., 2007), 100.

78. Henry Halleck, *Official Records*, Series 1, Vol. 23, Part 2, 337; William Rosecrans, *Official Records*, Series 1, Vol. 23, Part 2, 351.

79. Peter Mathews, Letter to David Stanley, May 24, 1863, National Archives, Record Group 393, Part 2, Number 2469, Letters and Orders by the Chief of Cavalry, Washington, D.C.

80. Abraham Lincoln, *Official Records*, Series 1, Vol. 23, Part 2, 369.

81. Henry Halleck, *Official Records*, Series 1, Vol. 23, Part 2, 377, 383.

82. David Stanley, *An American General*, 162.

83. Theodore Clarke Smith, *The Life and Letters of James A. Garfield* (New Haven: Yale University Press, 1925), 309–310.

84. W. R. Carter, *History of the First Regiment of Tennessee Volunteer Cavalry*, 72.

85. *Historical Sketch of the Chicago Board of Trade Battery* (Chicago: The Henneberry Co. Publishers, 1902), 42–44.

86. *Twenty-Second Annual Reunion of the Association of the Graduates of the United States Military Academy: June 12th, 1891* (Saginaw: Seemam & Peters, Printers and Binders, 1891), 40–41.

87. Frederick H. Dyer, *A Compendium of the War of the Rebellion*, 1161–1162; Charles C. Nott, *Sketches of the War: A Series of Letters to the North Moore Street School of New York* (New York: Anson D. F. Randolph, 1865), 43–44; Kurt D. Bergmann, *Brackett's Battalion: Minnesota Cavalry in the Civil War and Dakota War* (St. Paul: Borealis Books, 2004), 56.

88. *Twenty-Ninth Annual Reunion of the Association of Graduates of the United States Military Academy at West Point* (Saginaw: Seemann & Peters, Printers and Binders, 1898) 83–83.

89. Edwin B. Quiner, "1st Cavalry," in *E. B Quiner's Military History of Wisconsin* (Chicago: Clark and Co., 1866), 884.

90. *Ibid.*, "Biographical Sketches," 1002.

91. Robert Minty, *Official Records*, Series 1, Vol. 23, Part 1, 356.

92. Marshall Thatcher, *A Hundred Battles in the West*, 128–129.

93. Thomas Jordan, Letter to Wife, June 7, 1863, Thomas J. Jordan Civil War Letters [2066] Box Number: 1, Folder 13, Historical Society of Pennsylvania, Philadelphia, Pennsylvania; *Western Citizen*, "Telegraphic News," Paris, Kentucky, June 12, 1863, 2, column 4.

94. James K. Magie, "Death by the Rope," *National Tribune*, September 26, 1889, 3; Richard Johnson, *A Soldier's Reminiscences in Peace and War* (Philadelphia: J. B. Lippincott and Company, 1886), 218–222; Thomas Jordan, "Battle of Thompson's Station and the Trial of the Spies at Franklin, Tennessee," 311–313.

95. Robert Mitchell, *Official Records*, Series 1, Vol. 23, Part 1, 375–376.

96. Michael Bradley, "Varying Results of Cavalry Fighting: Western Flank vs. Eastern Flank," *Blue and Grey*, Vol. XXVII, No. 1 (2010), 21.

97. *Ibid.*; W. L. Curry, *Four Years in the Saddle*, 22, 99.

Chapter 4

1. Michael Bradley, *Tullahoma: The 1863 Campaign for the Control of Middle Tennessee* (Shippensburg, PA: White Mane, 1999), 34–36; Robert S. Brandt, "Lightning and Rain in Middle Tennessee: The Tullahoma Campaign of June-July 1863," in *The Battle of Stones River and the Fight for Middle Tennessee*, Timothy D. Johnson, editor (Nashville: Tennessee Historical Society, 2012), 126–127.

2. C. Goddard, *Official Records*, Series 1, Vol. 23, Part 2, 395.

3. Larry J. Daniel, *Days of Glory: The Army of the Cumberland, 1861–1865* (Baton Rouge: Louisiana State University Press, 2006), 260; Williams Lamers, *The Edge of Glory: A Biography of General William S. Rosecrans, U. S. A.* (New York: Harcourt, Brace & World, Inc., 1961), 269; John Turchin, *Official Records*, Series 1, Vol. 23, Part 2, 396–397; Robert Mitchell, *Official Records*, Series 1, Vol. 23, Part 2, 418.

4. D. S. Stanley, Letter, June 9, 1863, Rosecrans Papers Box 8 Folder 73, University of California, Los Angeles.

5. Michael Bradley, "Tullahoma: The Wrongly Forgotten Campaign," *Blue & Gray*, Vol. XXVII, No. 1, (2010), 22; Lamers, *The Edge of Glory*, 275.

6. Charles Alley, "Civil War Diary of Lieutenant Charles Alley, June 23, 1863" (n.p., n.d.) Tennessee State Library and Archives, Nashville, TN.

7. Larry J. Daniel, *Days of Glory: The Army of the Cumberland*, 267; William Rosecrans, *Official Records*, Series 1, Vol. 23, Part 1, 404–405.

8. Henry Mortimer Hempstead, "Diary, June 23, 1863," Hempstead, Henry Mortimer, 1832–1916, Papers, Bentley Historical Library, University of Michigan, Ann Arbor; Michael Bradley, *Tullahoma: The 1863 Campaign*, 51–52; Thomas McCahan, Diary, June 24, 1863, Thomas McCahan Papers (Am. 6092) Historical Society of

Pennsylvania, Philadelphia; *National Tribune*, "Tullahoma Campaign," May 6, 1882; John Randolph Poole, *Cracker Cavaliers: The 2nd Georgia Cavalry Under Wheeler and Forrest* (Macon: Mercer University Press, 2000), 78.

9. David Stanley, *An American General: The Memoirs of David Sloan Stanley*. Samuel W. Fordyce IV, ed. (Santa Barbara, California: The Narrative Press, 2004), 164.

10. Michael Bradley, "Tullahoma: The Wrongly Forgotten Campaign," 23.

11. David Stanley, *Official Records*, Series 1, Vol. 23, Part 1, 538; Thomas Jordan, Letter to Wife, June 26, 1863, Thomas J. Jordan Civil War Letters [2066] Box Number: 1, Folder 12, Historical Society of Pennsylvania, Philadelphia, Pennsylvania.

12. Edward G. Longacre, *A Soldier to the Last: Maj. Gen. Joseph Wheeler in Blue and Gray* (Washington: Potomac Books Inc., 2007), 103.

13. Brandt, "Lightning and Rain in Middle Tennessee," 130.

14. Joseph Vale, *Minty and the Cavalry: A History of Cavalry Campaigns in the Western Armies* (Harrisburg, Pennsylvania: Edwin K. Myers, Printer and Binder, 1886), 174–175.

15. Michael Bradley, *Tullahoma: The 1863 Campaign*, 76; David Stanley, *Official Records*, Series 1, Vol. 23, Part 1, 539.

16. George Steahlin, "Stanley's Cavalry: Minty's Sabre Brigade at Guy's Gap," *National Tribune*, May 27, 1882, 1, col. 5.

17. Michael Bradley, "Tullahoma: The Wrongly Forgotten Campaign," 44; David Stanley, *Official Records*, Series 1, Vol. 23, Part 1, 540–541.

18. Michael Bradley, "Tullahoma: The Wrongly Forgotten Campaign," 44.

19. Ibid.

20. Stephen Z. Starr, *The Union Cavalry in the Civil War, Vol. 3: The War in the West, 1861–1865* (Baton Rouge: Louisiana State University Press, 1985), 246; John Allan Wyeth, *With Sabre and Scalpel: The Autobiography of a Soldier and Surgeon* (New York: Harper Brothers, 1914), 214.

21. Michael Bradley, "Tullahoma: The Wrongly Forgotten Campaign," 44; Walter F. Beyer and Oscar F. Keydel, *Deeds of Valor: How America's Heroes Won the Medal of Honor* (Detroit: The Perrien-Keydel Company, 1901), 216–217.

22. William B. Sipes, *Official Records*, Series 1, Vol. 23, Part 1, 565; Stephen Z. Starr, *The Union Cavalry in the Civil War*, 245.

23. William B. Sipes, *Official Records*, Series 1, Vol. 23, Part 1, 565; Henry Snyder, Letter to Mrs. Frances Reed—July 1863, Frances W. Reed Papers, Civil War Times Illustrated Collection, USAHEC, Carlisle, Pennsylvania.

24. George Steahlin, "Stanley's Cavalry," *National Tribune*, May 27, 1882, pp 1–2.

25. Frank Mix, *Official Records*, Series 1, Vol. 23, Part 1, 562.

26. David Stanley, *Official Records*, Series 1, Vol. 23, Part 1, 540–541.

27. Edward G. Longacre, *A Soldier to the Last*, 105; Michael Bradley, "Tullahoma: The Wrongly Forgotten Campaign," 47; Starr, *The Union Cavalry in the Civil War*, 246–247.

28. Bradley, *Tullahoma*, 79.

29. David Stanley, *Official Records*, Series 1, Vol. 23, Part 1, 540; C. Goddard, *Official Records*, Series 1, Vol. 23, Part 2, 472.

30. Stanley, *An American General*, 166.

31. Elbert J. Squire, Letter, June 27, 1863, Stones River National Park, Technical Information Center, Murfreesboro, TN.

32. W. L. Curry, *Four Years in the Saddle: History of First Regiment Ohio Volunteer Cavalry* (Columbus: Champlin Printing Co., 1898), 105.

33. Nancy Pape-Findley, *The Invincibles: The Story of Fourth Ohio Veteran Volunteer Cavalry* (Tecumseh, MI: Blood Road, 202), 146; Thomas Crofts, *History of the Service of the Third Ohio Veteran Volunteer Cavalry*, 103–104; Noel V. Bourasaw, "Arthur C. Seidell, Civil War Veteran and Builder in Old Woolley," *Skagit River Journal of History & Folklore*, 2000.

34. Elijah Watts, *Official Records*, Series 1, Vol. 23, Part 1, 570; Elijah Watts, "Biographical Note," Watts, Elijah S., Papers. 1861–1907, Mss./A/W349, Filson Historical Society, Louisville, Kentucky.

35. Richard J. Brewer, *The Tullahoma Campaign: Operational Insights*, Master's Thesis, U.S. Army Command and General Staff College, Leavenworth, KS (1978), 142; Stanley, *Official Records*, Series 1, Vol. 23, Part 1, 540–541; John Allan Wyeth, *With Sabre and Scalpel: The Autobiography of a Soldier and Surgeon* (New York: Harper Brothers, 1914), 232.

36. John Turchin, *Official Records*, Series 1, Vol. 23, Part 1, 554.

37. T. F. Dornblaser, *Sabre Strokes of the Pennsylvania Dragoons* (Philadelphia: Lutheran Publication Society, 1884), 118–119; Thomas Crofts, *History of the Service of the Third Ohio Veteran Volunteer Cavalry* (Toledo: Stoneman Press, 1910), 108.

38. Louis Watkins, *Official Records*, Series 1, Vol. 23, Part 1, 550; Robert Burr, "The Letters of Robert Burr," July 29, 1863, Monroe Ohio Historical Society, Woodsfield, Ohio.

39. William Rosecrans, *Official Records*, Series 1, Vol. 23, Part 1, 423–424.

40. William Rosecrans, *Official Records*, Series 1, Vol. 23, Part 1, 409.

41. Bradley, *Tullahoma: The 1863 Campaign*, 93–94.

42. Richard J. Brewer, *The Tullahoma Campaign*, 131.

43. Starr, *The Union Cavalry in the Civil War*, 237; James A. Garfield, *Official Records*, Series 1, Vol. 23, No. 2, 465; Richard J. Brewer, *The Tullahoma Campaign*, 73.

44. Thomas M. Vincent, "David Sloane Stanley," in *The Thirty-fourth Annual Reunion of the Association Graduates of the United States Military Academy at West Point, New York* (Saginaw: Seeman and Peters, Printers and Binders, 1903), 57.

45. James Connolly, *Three Years in the Army of the Cumberland*, Paul Angle, ed. (Bloomington: Indiana University Press, 1959), 98.

46. Robert J. Dalessandro, *Morale in the Army of the Cumberland During the Tullahoma and Chickamauga Campaigns*, Master's Thesis, U.S. Army Command and General Staff College, Leavenworth, KS, 1980, 74; Theodore Clarke Smith, *The Life and Letters of James Abram Garfield*, Vol. 1 (New Haven: Archon Books, 1968), 308.

47. Doyle D. Broome, "Intelligence Operations of the Army of the Cumberland During the Tullahoma and

Chickamauga Campaigns," Master's Thesis, U.S. Army Command and General Staff College, Leavenworth, KS, 1989, 80–83.

Chapter 5

1. Braxton Bragg, *Official Records*, Series 1, Vol. 23, Part 1, 584; David Stanley, *Official Records*, Series 1, Vol. 23, Part 1, 538, 541.
2. William Rosecrans, *Official Records*, Series 1, Vol. 23, Part 2, 573–574; Braxton Bragg, *Official Records*, Series 1, Vol. 23, Part 2, 920.
3. Robert S. Brandt, "Lightning and Rain in Middle Tennessee," in *The Battle of Stones River and the Fight for Middle Tennessee*, Timothy Johnson, ed. (Nashville: Tennessee Historical Society, 2012), 133; Phil Sheridan, *Official Records*, Series 1, Vol. 23, Part 2, 519.
4. Edwin Stanton, *Official Records*, Series 1, Vol. 23, Part 2, 518; William Rosecrans, *Official Records*, Series 1, Vol. 23, Part 2, 518.
5. William Lamers, *The Edge of Glory: A Biography of General William S. Rosecrans, U.S.A.* (New York: Harcourt, Brace & World, Inc., 1961), 295.
6. Henry Halleck, *Official Records*, Series 1, Vol. 23, Part 2, 552.
7. William Rosecrans, *Official Records*, Series 1, Vol. 23, Part 2, 555; Henry Halleck, *Official Records*, Series 1, Vol. 23, Part 2, 556.
8. John W. Taylor, *Official Records*, Series 1, Vol. 23, Part 2, 601.
9. David Stanley, *Official Records*, Series 1, Vol. 23, Part 2, 548.
10. George Thomas, *Official Records*, Series 1, Vol. 23, Part 2, 551; Kinloch Falconer, *Official Records*, Series 1, Vol. 23, Part 2, 938; Edward G. Longacre, *A Soldier to the Last: Maj. Gen. Joseph Wheeler in Blue and Gray* (Washington: Potomac Books Inc., 2007), 109.
11. James A. Garfield, *Official Records*, Series 1, Vol. 23, Part 2, 527; David Stanley, *Official Records*, Series 1, Vol. 23, Part 2, 548.
12. *Nashville Daily Press*, "Court-Martialed," July 16, 1863.
13. *Chicago Times*, "An Expedition into the Enemy's Country," July 22, 1863.
14. Julius E. Thomas, Diary—July 5. 1863, Julius E. Thomas Collection, MS.2720, University of Tennessee, Knoxville, Tennessee.
15. George Kryder, Diary, June 8, 1863, MS 163 George Kryder (1834–1925), William T. Jerome Library, Bowling Green State University, Bowling Green, Ohio; John McLain, Diary Entry, February 13, 1863, John McLain Papers (c.00111), Michigan State University Archives & Historical Collections, East Lansing, Michigan.
16. W. R. Carter, *History of the First Regiment of Tennessee Volunteer Cavalry* (Knoxville: Gaut-Ogden Co., Printers and Binders, 1902), 80.
17. Charles Perry Goodrich, "July 16, 1863," *Letters from Home from the First Wisconsin Cavalry*, Richard N. Larson, editor (Madison: State Historical Society of Wisconsin, not published).
18. David Stanley, *An American General: The Memoirs of David Sloan Stanley*, Samuel W. Fordyce IV, ed. (Santa Barbara, California: The Narrative Press, 2004), 167–168; John Beatty, *The Citizen Soldier: The Memoirs of a Civil War Volunteer* (Lincoln: Bison Books, University of Nebraska Press, 1998), 303; Mary Jane Chadwick, *Incidents of the War: The Civil War Journal of Mary Jane Chadwick*, Nancy Rohr, ed. (Huntsville, AL: SilverThread Publishing, 2005), 110.
19. *Chicago Times*, "The War in Tennessee, An Expedition into the Enemy's Country," August 4, 1863.
20. George D. Wood, Letter, July 23, 1863, Slayton Family Papers, Bentley Historical Library, University of Michigan, Ann Arbor; James Perry, Letter, July 14, 1863, MMS 1457 James H. M. Perry Papers, 1863, William T. Jerome Library, Bowling Green State University, Bowling Green, Ohio.
21. David Stanley, *Official Records*, Series 1, Vol. 23, Part 2, 549; William Sinclair, *Official Records*, Series 1, Vol. 23, Part 2, 568; Joseph Vale, *Minty and the Cavalry: A History of Cavalry Campaigns in the Western Armies* (Harrisburg, Pennsylvania: Edwin K. Myers, Printer and Binder, 1886), 196.
22. John Beatty, *The Citizen Soldier*, 306–307.
23. William Sinclair, *Official Records*, Series 1, Vol. 23, Part 2, 565.
24. Goodrich, *Letters Home*, August 3, 1863.
25. William Rosecrans, *Official Records*, Series 1, Vol. 23, Part 2, 585–586.
26. Henry Halleck, *Official Records*, Series 1, Vol. 23, Part 2, 602.
27. Robert Minty, *Official Records*, Series 1, Vol. 23, Part 1, 845–846, George Dibrell, *Official Records*, Series 1, Vol. 23, Part 1, 847–848.
28. William Rosecrans, *Official Records*, Series 1, Vol. 30, Part 3, 4.
29. William Rosecrans, *Official Records*, Series 1, Vol. 30, Part 3, 274–275.
30. William Rosecrans, *Official Records*, Series 1, Vol. 30, Part 3, 33.
31. C. Goddard, *Official Records*, Series 1, Vol. 30, Part 3, 37.
32. William Rosecrans, *Official Records*, Series 1, Vol. 30, Part 3, 11.
33. Edward McCook, *Official Records*, Series 1, Vol. 30, Part 3, 54.
34. Horatio Van Cleve, *Official Records*, Series 1, Vol. 30, Part 3, 92.
35. Robert Minty, *Official Records*, Series 1, Vol. 30, Part 1, 920–921.
36. Joseph Vale, *Minty and the Cavalry*, 206; Robert Minty, *Official Records*, Series 1, Vol. 30, Part 1, 920–921.
37. Minty, *Ibid*.
38. Joseph Vale, *Minty and the Cavalry*, 207.
39. William Rosecrans, *Official Records*, Series 1, Vol. 30, Part 3, 98–99; Gordon Granger, *Official Records*, Series 1, Vol. 30, Part 3, 105.
40. Henry Halleck, *Official Records*, Series 1, Vol. 30, Part 3, 65; T. F. Dornblaser, *Sabre Strokes of the Pennsylvania Dragoons* (Philadelphia: Lutheran Publication Society, 1884), 122.
41. Horatio Van Cleve, *Official Records*, Series 1, Vol. 30, Part 3, 79.
42. Horatio Van Cleve, *Official Records*, Series 1, Vol. 30, Part 3, 91; E. A Otis, *Official Records*, Series 1, Vol. 30, Part 3, 107.
43. Robert Minty, *Official Records*, Series 1, Vol. 30, Part 3, 125.
44. Thomas Crittenden, *Official Records*, Series 1,

Vol. 30, Part 3, 90; John Wilder, *Official Records*, Series 1, Vol. 30, Part 3, 100–101.
45. Edward McCook, *Official Records*, Series 1, Vol. 30, Part 3, 106.
46. Thomas Crittenden, *Official Records*, Series 1, Vol. 30, Part 3, 137; Horatio Van Cleve, *Official Records*, Series 1, Vol. 30, Part 3, 139.
47. P. Oldershaw, *Official Records*, Series 1, Vol. 30, Part 3, 140; Horatio Van Cleve, *Official Records*, Series 1, Vol. 30, Part 3, 140.
48. Horatio Van Cleve, Official Records, Series 1, Vol. 30, Part 3, 166.
49. Robert Minty, *Official Records*, Series 1, Vol. 30, Part 3, 178.
50. Edward McCook, *Official Records*, Series 1, Vol. 30, Part 3, 106.
51. Robert Minty, *Official Records*, Series 1, Vol. 30, Part 3, 191.
52. Gordon Granger, *Official Records*, Series 1, Vol. 30, Part 3, 192.
53. William Sinclair, *Official Records*, Series 1, Vol. 30, Part 3, 194.
54. Robert Minty *Official Records*, Series 1, Vol. 30, Part 3, 237; Horatio Van Cleve, *Official Records*, Series 1, Vol. 30, Part 3, 238.
55. Thomas Crofts, *History of the Service of the Third Ohio Veteran Volunteer Cavalry* (Toledo: Stoneman Press, 1910), 111.
56. Archibald Campbell Letter to Edward McCook, August 27, 1863, National Archives, Record Group 393, Part 2, Number 2469, Letters and Orders by the Chief of Cavalry, Washington, D.C.
57. Eli Long, *Official Records*, Series 1, Vol. 30, Part 3, 206.
58. Edwin Stanton, *Official Records*, Series 1, Vol. 30, Part 3, 229–230; *Milwaukee Journal*, "Eccentric Brother of Famous Editor," November 27, 1897, 11.
59. John Lynch, Letter, August 23, 1863, Morris Fitch Papers, Bentley Historical Library, University of Michigan, Ann Arbor; Stephen Z. Starr, *The Union Cavalry in the Civil War: The War in the West*, Vol. III (Baton Rouge: Louisiana State University, 2007), 263–264.
60. David Stanley, Letter to George Stoneman, August 24, 1863, National Archives, Record Group 393, Part 2, Number 2460, Letters Sent by the Chief of Cavalry, Washington, D.C.
61. Peter Cozzens, *This Terrible Sound: The Battle of Chickamauga* (Urbana: University of Illinois Press, 1992), 49.
62. Robert B. Mitchell, et. al., *Official Records*, Series 1, Vol. 30, Part 1, 890–927.
63. Marshall Thatcher, *A Hundred Battles in the West: The Second Michigan Cavalry* (Detroit: L. F. Kilroy, Printer, 1884), 138; George Healy, Letter, August 24, 1863, George Healy Papers, Box 006, Folder 22, State Historical Society of Iowa, Des Moines, Iowa.
64. Alexander McCook, *Official Records*, Series 1, Vol. 30, Part 3, 332.
65. John Beatty, *The Citizen Soldier: The Memoirs of a Civil War Volunteer* (Lincoln: Bison Books, University of Nebraska Press, 1998), 309.
66. Robert Minty, *Official Records*, Series 1, Vol. 30, Part 3, 307, 317.
67. John Garfield, *Official Records*, Series 1, Vol. 30, Part 3, 322–323.

68. W. R. Carter, *History of the First Regiment of Tennessee Volunteer Cavalry*, 83–85.
69. W. L. Curry, *Four Years in the Saddle: History of the First Regiment Ohio Volunteer Cavalry* (Columbus: Champlin Printing Company, 1898), 109.
70. Elbert J. Squire, Letter, August 28, 1863, Stones River National Park, Technical Information Center, Murfreesboro, TN.
71. David A. Powell, *Failure in the Saddle* (New York: Savas and Beatie, 2010), 47.
72. David Stanley *Official Records*, Series 1, Vol. 30, Part 3, 331; Robert Mitchell, 332; Alexander McCook, 344–345.
73. Alexander McCook *Official Records*, Series 1, Vol. 30, Part 3, 346.
74. David Stanley, *Official Records*, Series 1, Vol. 30, Part 3, 354.
75. Braxton Bragg, *Official Records*, Series 1, Vol. 30, Part 2, 21; Braxton Bragg, *Official Records*, Series 1, Vol. 30, Part 4, 594.
76. Peter Cozzens, *This Terrible Sound*, 54; Joseph Wheeler, *Official Records*, Series 1, Vol. 30, Part 2, 520.
77. David Stanley, *Official Records*, Series 1, Vol. 30, Part 3, 374; James Garfield, *Official Records*, Series 1, Vol. 30, Part 3, 322.
78. James Garfield, *Official Records*, Series 1, Vol. 30, Part 3, 374.
79. Edward McCook, *Official Records*, Series 1, Vol. 30, Part 1, 895.
80. Julius E. Thomas, Diary—Sept 5. 1863, Julius E. Thomas Collection, MS 2720, University of Tennessee, Knoxville, Tennessee.
81. William Sinclair, Alexander McCook, *Official Records*, Series 1, Vol. 30, Part 3, 375–376.
82. R. L. Kimberly, *Official Records*, Series 1, Vol. 30, Part 3, 399; William Hazen, *Official Records*, Series 1, Vol. 30, 392; William Rosecrans, *Official Records*, Series 1, Vol. 30, Part 3, 378.
83. Paul Shelton, "The Blame Game: Federal Intelligence Operations During the Chickamauga Campaign," Master's Thesis, Fort Leavenworth, KS, 2000, U.S. Army Command and General Staff College, 87.
84. James Garfield, *Official Records*, Series 1, Vol. 30, Part 3, 397–398; Joseph Frederick Shelly, "The Shelly Papers," Fanny Anderson, ed., *Indiana Magazine of History* 44, No. 2 (June 1948): 181–198.
85. Robert Minty, *Official Records*, Series 1, Vol. 30, Part 3, 427–428.
86. William T. Hoblitzell Court Martial, June, 1864, Record Group (RG) 153, Adjutant General's Office, Court Martial Case Files, 1809–1854, Case Number NN-3269, National Archives, Washington, D.C.
87. *Ibid.*
88. *Ibid.*
89. James Garfield, *Official Records*, Series 1, Vol. 30, Part 3, 412.
90. David Stanley, *Official Records*, Series 1, Vol. 30, Part 3, 431–432.
91. James Garfield, *Official Records*, Series 1, Vol. 30, Part 3, 432.
92. Robert Merrill, *Robert Sidney Merrill, Co. K. 1st Wis. Cav.* (Cedarsburg, WI: MSG Publishing, 1995), 52.
93. William Rosecrans, *Official Records*, Series 1, Vol. 30, Part 3, 468.
94. David Stanley, *Official Records*, Series 1, Vol. 30,

Part 3, 468; Edward McCook, National Archives, Letter, September 7, 1863, Record Group 393, Part 2, Number 2305, Correspondence, First Cavalry Division, National Archives, Washington, D.C.

95. Williams Lamers, *The Edge of Glory: A Biography of General William S. Rosecrans, U. S. A.* (New York: Harcourt, Brace & World, Inc., 1961), 303.

96. Lamers, *The Edge of Glory*, 307.

97. Nathan Forrest, *Official Records*, Series 1, Vol. 30, Part 4, 628; David A. Powell, *Failure in the Saddle*, 54.

98. George Crook, *General George Crook: His Biography* (Norman: University of Oklahoma Press, 1960), 104.

99. James Pike, *The Personal Adventures Corporal Pike Or The Fourth Ohio Cavalry* (Cincinnati: J. R. Hawley and Company, 1865), 297; Alexander McCook, *Official Records*, Series 1, Vol. 30, Part 3, 483.

100. Robert Mitchell, *Official Records*, Series 1, Vol. 30, Part 1, 891.

101. Robert Minty, *Official Records*, Series 1, Vol. 30, Part 3, 500–501.

102. William Palmer, *Official Records*, Series 1, Vol. 30, Part 3, 532–533; John M. Palmer, *Official Records*, Series 1, Vol. 30, Part 3, 518.

103. James Garfield, *Official Records*, Series 1, Vol. 30, Part 3, 521–522.

104. Frank Vogel, "Dairy of Frank Vogel," Frank L. Vogel Collection, MS 67-111: Accession Box 12 Folder 6, Michigan Historical Center, Lansing, Michigan, 6; W. R. Carter, *History of the First Regiment of Tennessee Volunteer Cavalry*, 87–88.

105. Louis Watkins, *Official Records*, Series 1, Vol. 30, Part 1, 914.

106. C. Goodard, *Official Records*, Series 1, Vol. 30, Part 3, 549; James Garfield, *Official Records*, Series 1, Vol. 30, Part 3, 546; Thomas Wood, *Official Records*, Series 1, Vol. 30, Part 3, 548.

107. James Garfield, *Official Records*, Series 1, Vol. 30, Part 3, 551.

108. James Negley, *Official Records*, Series 1, Vol. 30, Part 3, 567.

109. George Crook, *Official Records*, Series 1, Vol. 30, Part 3, 552–553.

110. Edward McCook, *Official Records*, Series 1, Vol. 30, Part 3, 569.

111. Alexander McCook, *Official Records*, Series 1, Vol. 30, Part 3, 570.

112. Frank Bond, *Official Records*, Series 1, Vol. 30, Part 3, 588.

113. Robert D. Richardson, "Rosecrans' Staff at Chickamauga: The Significance of Major General William S. Rosecrans' Staff on the Outcome of the Chickamauga Campaign." Master's Thesis, Command and General Staff College, Fort Leavenworth, Kansas, 1989, 135.

114. W. R. Carter, *History of the First Regiment of Tennessee Volunteer Cavalry*, 90.

115. David Stanley, *Official Records*, Series 1, Vol. 30, Part 3, 589.

116. George Crook, *Official Records*, Series 1, Vol. 30, Part 3, 589.

117. J. C. Van Druzer, *Official Records*, Series 1, Vol. 30, Part 3, 596.

118. Peter Cozzens, *This Terrible Sound*, 82–83; George Brent, *Official Records*, Series 1, Vol. 30, Part 2, 50.

119. Alexander McCook, *Official Records*, Series 1, Vol. 30, Part 3, 598–599.

120. Roswell Russell, *Official Records*, Series 1, Vol. 30, Part 1, 904; Marshall Thatcher, *A Hundred Battles in the West*, 141–142; Thomas McCahan, Diary, September 13, 1863, Thomas McCahan Papers (Am. 6092) Historical Society of Pennsylvania, Philadelphia.

121. W. R. Carter, *History of the First Regiment of Tennessee Volunteer Cavalry*, 89.

122. George Crook, *General George Crook*, 105.

123. Goodrich, *Letters Home*, September 24, 1863.

124. William Sinclair, *Official Records*, Series 1, Vol. 30, Part 3, 616; Edward McCook, *Official Records*, Series 1, Vol. 30, Part 3, 616.

125. Edward McCook, *Official Records*, Series 1, Vol. 30, Part 3, 616.

126. David Stanley, *Official Records*, Series 1, Vol. 30, Part 3, 615, 637; Alexander McCook, *Official Records*, Series 1, Vol. 30, Part 3, 615.

127. David Stanley, *Official Records*, Series 1, Vol. 30, Part 3, 637; Larry J. Daniel, *Days of Glory: The Army of the Cumberland, 1861–1865* (Baton Rouge: Louisiana State University Press, 2006), 305.

128. Alexander McCook, *Official Records*, Series 1, Vol. 30, Part 3, 628.

129. James Garfield, *Official Records*, Series 1, Vol. 30, Part 3, 629.

130. Thomas Crittenden, *Official Records*, Series 1, Vol. 30, Part 3, 632.

131. James Garfield, *Official Records*, Series 1, Vol. 30, Part 3, 633.

132. David Stanley, *Official Records*, Series 1, Vol. 30, Part 3, 637.

133. David Stanley, *Official Records*, Series 1, Vol. 30, Part 3, 652–653.

134. Robert Mitchell, *Official Records*, Series 1, Vol. 30, Part 3, 653.

135. John Londa, "The Role of Union Cavalry During the Chickamauga Campaign," Master's Thesis, Command and General Staff College, Fort Leavenworth, Kansas, 1991, 109.

136. Ibid., 110.

137. David Stanley, Union General Papers, surgeon's certificate, September 21, 1863; Robert Mitchell, *Official Records*, Series 1, Vol. 30, Part 3, 653.

Chapter 6

1. *Harper's Weekly*, "Brigadier General Robert B. Mitchell," April 4, 1863

2. Peter Cozzens, *This Terrible Sound* (Urbana: University of Illinois Press, 1992), 89.

3. Robert Minty, *Official Records*, Series 1, Vol. 30, Part 3, 679; Robert Minty, *Official Records*, Series 1, Vol. 30, Part 1, 922; Robert Minty and Horace Gray, "Michigan to her Fourth Regiment of Cavalry," *History of the Michigan Organizations at Chickamauga, Chattanooga, and Missionary Ridge*, Charles Eugene Belknap, ed. (Lansing: Robert Smith Printing Co., 1899), 276; Robert Burns, Letter, October 20, 1863, Robert Burns Letterbook, MSS M642, Minnesota Historical Society, St. Paul, MN.

4. James Garfield, *Official Records*, Series 1, Vol. 30, Part 3, 690.

5. Thomas Wood, *Official Records*, Series 1, Vol. 30, Part 3, 712.
6. George W. Brent, *Official Records*, Series 1, Vol. 30, Part 2, 31.
7. Charles Eugene Belknap, *History of the Michigan Organizations at Chickamauga*, 276–277.
8. Robert Minty, Official Records, Series 1, Vol. 30, Part 1, 923; David Powell, *Failure in the Saddle* (New York: Savas Beatie, 2010), 104; *Obituary Record of the Graduates of Yale University, Deceased from June 1910, to July 1915* (New Haven: Yale University Press, 1915), 40–43.
9. Peter Cozzens, *This Terrible Sound*, 104; Robert Minty, *Official Records*, Series 1, Vol. 30, Part 1, 923.
10. David Powell, *Failure in the Saddle*, 100–101.
11. Ibid.
12. Robert Minty, *Official Records*, Series 1, Vol. 30, Part 1, 923; T. F. Dornblaser, *Sabre Strokes of the Pennsylvania Dragoons* (Philadelphia: Lutheran Publication Society, 1884), 131–132.
13. Robert Minty, *Official Records*, Series 1, Vol. 30, Part 1, 923.
14. Henry Albert Potter, September 18, 1863, Diary Entry, MS 91-480 Henry Albert Potter Collection, Accession Box 461 Folder 2, Archives of Michigan. Historical Society of Michigan, Lansing.
15. Robert Minty, *Official Records*, Series 1, Vol. 30, Part 1, 923.
16. Ibid.
17. Ibid.; Joseph Vale, "Address of Captain Joseph Vale," in *Pennsylvania at Chickamauga and Chattanooga*, George W. Skinner, editor (Harrisburg, Pennsylvania: William Stanley Ray, State Printer of Pennsylvania, 1897), 304.
18. John Wilder, *Official Records*, Series 1, Vol. 30, Part 3, 724–725; Charles Eugene Belknap, *History of the Michigan Organizations at Chickamauga*, 278; Robert Minty, "Minty's Saber Brigade, The Part They Took in the Chattanooga Campaign," *National Tribune*, March 3, 1892.
19. Joseph Vale, *Minty and the Cavalry: A History of Cavalry Campaigns in the Western Armies* (Harrisburg, Pennsylvania: Edwin K. Myers, Printer and Binder, 1886), 230.
20. Thomas Wood, *Official Records*, Series 1, Vol. 30, Part 3, 728.
21. David Powell, *Failure in the Saddle*, 121.
22. Nathan Forrest, *Official Records*, Series 1, Vol. 30, Part 2, 524.
23. Joseph Wheeler, *Official Records*, Series 1, Vol. 30, Part 2, 520.
24. Archibald Campbell, Oscar La Grange David Briggs, G. H. Purdy, *Official Records*, Series 1, Vol. 30, Part 1, 899–909.
25. Thomas McCahan, Diary, September 19, 1863, Thomas McCahan Papers (Am. 6092), Historical Society of Pennsylvania, Philadelphia.
26. Edward McCook, Archibald Campbell, Daniel Ray, Louis Watkins, George Crook, Eli Long Reports, *Official Records*, Series 1, Vol. 30, Part 1, 895–926; Archibald Campbell, *Official Records*, Series 1, Vol. 30, Part 1, 900.
27. Joseph Wheeler, *Official Records*, Series 1, Vol. 30, Part 2, 520.
28. Henry Mortimer Hempstead, "Diary, September 20, 1863," Hempstead, Henry Mortimer, 1832–1916, Papers, Bentley Historical Library, University of Michigan, Ann Arbor.
29. L. S. Scranton, *Official Records*, Series 1, Vol. 30, Part 1, 902
30. William Sinclair, Letters, September 1863, Letters Sent, Chief of Cavalry, RG 393, Number 151 (2460) National Archives, Washington, D.C.
31. George Crook, *General George Crook: His Biography* (Norman: University of Oklahoma Press, 1960), 105.
32. Robert B. Mitchell, Letter, September 20, Letters Sent, Chief of Cavalry, RG 393, Number 151 (2460) National Archives, Washington, D.C.; Elijah S. Watts, Chickamauga Campaign (handwritten account, undated), Filson Historical Society, Mss. A W349, Folder 16, Louisville, Kentucky.
33. Joseph Wheeler, *Official Records*, Series 1, Vol. 30, Part 2, 521; L. S. Scranton, *Official Records*, Series 1, Vol. 30, Part 1, 902; Eli Long, *Official Records*, Series 1, Vol. 30, Part 1, 927.
34. Nancy Pape-Findley, *The Invincibles: The Story of Fourth Ohio Veteran Volunteer Cavalry* (Tecumseh, MI: Blood Road, 202), 162; William E. Crane, "William E. Crane's Daily Journal of Life in the Field during the War of the Rebellion," September 20, 1863 entry, Mss. 980, Cincinnati Historical Society, Cincinnati Museum Center.
35. John Chapin, "At Chickamauga," in *Reunions of the First Ohio Volunteer Cavalry* (Columbus: Landon Printing, Co., 1891), 15–17.
36. David Powell, *Failure in the Saddle*, 160; Eli Long, "Autobiography" and "Synopsis of the Military Career of Brevet Major-General Eli Long," Eli Long Papers, Civil War Collection, Box 1, USAHEC, Carlisle, Pennsylvania.
37. Henry Mortimer Hempstead, "Diary, September 20, 1863"; Elijah S. Watts, "Chickamauga Campaign."
38. George Crook, *General George Crook: His Biography*, 106; Joseph Wheeler, *Official Records*, Series 1, Vol. 30, Part 2, 521.
39. Charles Perry Goodrich, September 24, 1863 letter; Thomas McCahan, Diary, September 20, 1863.
40. David Powell, *Failure in the Saddle*, 170–171.
41. W. R. Carter, *History of the First Regiment of Tennessee Volunteer Cavalry* (Knoxville: Gaut-Ogden Co., Printers and Binders, 1902), 97; John Andes and Will McTeer, *Loyal Mountain Troops, The Second and Third Tennessee Volunteer Cavalry* (Maryville, Tennessee: Blount County Genealogical and Historical Society, 1992), 65.
42. David Powell, *Failure in the Saddle*, 171; Roswell Russell, *Official Records*, Series 1, Vol. 30, Part 1, 905.
43. Robert Minty, *Official Records*, Series 1, Vol. 30, Part 1, 924.
44. Ibid.; John McLain, Diary entry September 20, 1863, McLain Papers (c.00111), Michigan State University Archives & Historical Collections, East Lansing, Michigan.
45. George Crook, *General George Crook: His Biography*, 107.
46. William Sinclair, *Official Records*, Series 1, Vol. 30, Part 3, 768.
47. Henry Mortimer Hempstead, Diary, September 21, 1863.
48. Robert Mitchell, *Official Records*, Series 1, Vol.

30, Part 1, 155; Edward McCook, *Official Records*, Series 1, Vol. 30, Part 1, 896.
49. Robert Mitchell, *Official Records*, Series 1, Vol. 30, Part 1, 151.
50. Louis Watkins, *Official Records*, Series 1, Vol. 30, Part 1, 915.
51. Ibid.
52. Ibid., 916; C. H. Sowle, *Military Record of C. H. Sowle*, unpublished, Manuscript C. S., undated, Filson Historical Society, Louisville, Kentucky.
53. William T. Hoblitzell Court Martial, July 1864, Record Group (RG) 153, Adjutant General's Office, Court Martial Case Files, 1809–1854, Case Number NN-2774, National Archives, Washington, D.C.
54. Ibid.
55. Robert Mitchell, *Official Records*, Series 1, Vol. 30, Part 3, 767.
56. James Garfield, *Official Records*, Series 1, Vol. 30, Part 3, 783; Daniel Ray, *Official Records*, Series 1, Vol. 30, Part 1, 907.
57. C. Goddard, *Official Records*, Series 1, Vol. 30, Part 1, 166–167.
58. William Rosecrans, *Official Records*, Series 1, Vol. 30, Part 1, 178–179.
59. Charles Greeno, "Address of Lieut.-Col. Charles L. Greeno," in *Pennsylvania at Chickamauga and Chattanooga*, George W. Skinner, editor (William Stanley Ray, State Printer of Pennsylvania, 1897), 312.
60. William Rosecrans, *Official Records*, Series 1, Vol. 30, Part 1, 62; John Londa, "The Role of Union Cavalry During the Chickamauga Campaign," Master's Thesis, Command and General Staff College, Fort Leavenworth, Kansas, 1991, 67.
61. John Londa, "The Role of Union Cavalry during the Chickamauga Campaign," 103.
62. Peter Cozzens, *This Terrible Sound*, 64; *Twenty-Ninth Annual Reunion of the Association of the Graduates of the United States Military Academy, June 9th, 1898*, 70–71; Robert D. Richardson, "Rosecrans' Staff At Chickamauga: The Significance of Major General William S. Rosecrans' Staff on the Outcome of the Chickamauga Campaign," Master's Thesis, Command and General Staff College, Fort Leavenworth, Kansas, 1989, 183.
63. Stephen Z. Starr, *The Union Cavalry in the Civil War: The War in the West*, Vol. III (Baton Rouge: Louisiana State University Press, 1985), 263.
64. John Londa, "The Role of Union Cavalry During the Chickamauga Campaign," 118, 123.
65. William Rosecrans, *Official Records*, Series 1, Vol. 30, Part 1, 79–80.
66. Marshall Thatcher, *A Hundred Battles in the West: The Second Michigan Cavalry* (Detroit: L. F. Kilroy, Printer, 1884), 152.

Chapter 7

1. Robert Mitchell, Abram O. Miller, *Official Records*, Series 1, Vol. 30, Part 3, 804.
2. Samuel Harden and John Spahr, *Early life and times in Boone County, Indiana* (Indianapolis: Carlon and Hollenbeck, 1887), 453–454.
3. Chris Beck, *Official Records*, Series 1, Vol. 30, Part 3, 833–834.
4. Daniel Ray, *Official Records*, Series 1, Vol. 30, Part 3, 952; Louis Watkins, *Official Records*, Series 1, Vol. 30, Part 3, 900.
5. W. T. Hoblitzell, *Official Records*, Series 1, Vol. 30, Part 3, 920.
6. Daniel Ray, *Official Records*, Series 1, Vol. 30, Part 3, 952.
7. Robert Mitchell, *Official Records*, Series 1, Vol. 30, Part 3, 836.
8. William H. Sinclair, *Official Records*, Series 1, Vol. 30, Part 3, 857, 880.
9. George Crook, *Official Records*, Series 1, Vol. 30, Part 3, 952; Stephen Z. Starr, *The Union Cavalry in the Civil War: The War in the West*, Vol. III (Baton Rouge: Louisiana State University, 2007), 292.
10. Joseph Wheeler, *Official Records*, Series 1, Vol. 30, Part 2, 723.
11. Edward G. Longacre, *A Soldier to the Last: Maj. Gen. Joseph Wheeler in Blue and Gray* (Washington: Potomac Books Inc., 2007), 118–119; Thomas Jordan and J. Pryor, *The Campaigns of Lieut.-Gen. Nathan B. Forrest of Forrest's Cavalry* (New Orleans: Blelock & Co., 1868), 358–359; George W. Brent *Official Records*, Series 1, Vol. 30, Part 4, 710.
12. W. L. Curry, *The Raid of the Confederate Cavalry through Central Tennessee, October 1863* (Columbus: The Ohio Commandery of the Loyal Legion, MOLLUS, 1908), 4–6.
13. Joseph Wheeler, *Official Records*, Series 1, Vol. 30, Part 2, 723; Oscar La Grange, *Official Records*, Series 1, Vol. 30, Part 2, 683.
14. Thomas McCahan, Diary, October 3, 1863, Thomas McCahan Papers (Am. 6092) Historical Society of Pennsylvania, Philadelphia.
15. George Crook, *Official Records*, Series 1, Vol. 30, Part 2, 684–685.
16. Abram Miller, *Official Records*, Series 1, Vol. 30, Part 2, 693.
17. George Crook, *Official Records*, Series 1, Vol. 30, Part 2, 685; Joseph Wheeler, *Official Records*, Series 1, Vol. 30, Part 2, 723.
18. Lucien Wulsin, *The Fourth Regiment Ohio Veteran Volunteer Cavalry* (Cincinnati: Fourth Ohio Volunteer Cavalry Association, 1912), 40.
19. Joseph Wheeler, *Official Records*, Series 1, Vol. 30, Part 2, 724.
20. W. L. Curry, *Four Years in the Saddle: History of First Regiment Ohio Volunteer Cavalry* (Columbus: Champlin Printing Co., 1898), 137; George Crook, *Official Records*, Series 1, Vol. 30, Part 2, 685–686.
21. W. L. Curry, "The Raid of the Confederate Cavalry through Central Tennessee, October 1863," 9–10.
22. Ibid., 10; 21, W. L. Curry, "The Raid of the Confederate Cavalry through Central Tennessee," *Journal of the United States Cavalry Association*, Vol. 19 (1908/1909), 823.
23. Joseph Wheeler, *Official Records*, Series 1, Vol. 30, Part 2, 724; George Crook, *Official Records*, Series 1, Vol. 30, Part 2, 686.
24. Joseph Wheeler, *Official Records*, Series 1, Vol. 30, Part 2, 724.
25. Robert Mitchell, *Official Records*, Series 1, Vol. 30, Part 2, 670.
26. George Crook, *Official Records*, Series 1, Vol. 30, Part 2, 686; Thomas Crofts, *History of the Service of the Third Ohio Veteran Volunteer Cavalry* (Toledo: Stoneman

Press, 1910), 114; Whitelaw Reid, *Ohio in the War: Her Statesmen, Her Generals, and Soldiers*, Vol. I (New York: Moore, Wilstach & Baldwin, 1868), 861; John Stutsman, Letter, November 10, 1863, Civil War Times Illustrated Collection, USAHEC, Carlisle, Pennsylvania.

27. George Crook, *Official Records*, Series 1, Vol. 30, Part 2, 686–687; *Historical Sketch of the Chicago Board Of Trade Battery: Horse Artillery Illinois Volunteers* (Chicago: The Henneberry Company Printers, 1902), 26.

28. Henry Campbell, Diary Entry, October 7, 1863, *Three Years in the Saddle: a Diary of the Civil War*, Unpublished (n.d.), Wabash College, Crawfordsville, Indiana.

29. George Crook, *Official Records*, Series 1, Vol. 30, Part 2, 686–687.

30. George Hodge, *Official Records*, Series 1, Vol. 30, Part 2, 726; Crook, *Official Records*, Series 1, Vol. 30, Part 2, 686–687.

31. George Kryder, Letter to Wife November 2, 1863, George Kryder Papers—MS 163, Bowling Green State University, Special Collections, Bowling Green Ohio; Edward Walter Letter, November 19, 1863, McEwen Family Papers A 269, Missouri Historical Museum. Special Collections, St. Louis, Missouri; A. A. Stuart, "Colonel William W. Lowe," in *Iowa Colonels and Regiments Being a History of Iowa Regiments* (Des Moines: Mills & Company, 1865), 621–630.

32. Henry Albert Potter, Entry Diary—October 9, 1863. Henry Albert Potter papers, 1862–1908, Bentley Historical Library, University of Michigan, Ann Arbor, Michigan; Isaac Botsford, "Narrative of Brackett's Battalion of Cavalry," in *Minnesota in the Civil and Indian Wars, 1861–1865* by Minnesota Legislature, eds. (St. Paul: Pioneer Press Company, 1890), 579; Clark G. Reynolds, "The Civil and Indian War Diaries of Eugene Marshall, Minnesota Volunteer," Master's Thesis, Duke University, Durham, NC., 1963.

33. Joseph Wheeler, *Official Records*, Series 1, Vol. 30, Part 2, 725.

34. Phillip D. Roddey, *Official Records*, Series 1, Vol. 30, Part 2, 729.

35. Robert Mitchell, *Official Records*, Series 1, Vol. 30, Part 2, 673; Thomas Jordan, Letter to Wife—October 25, 1863, Thomas J. Jordan Civil War Letters [2066] Box Number: 1, Folder 13, Historical Society of Pennsylvania, Philadelphia, Pennsylvania; Charles Alley, Civil War Diary of Lieutenant Charles Alley, October 9, 1863 (Publisher [n.p., n.d.]) Tennessee State Library and Archives, Nashville, Tennessee.

36. Robert Mitchell, *Official Records*, Series 1, Vol. 30, Part 2, 673.

37. Paul Magid, *George Crook: From the Redwoods to Appomattox* (Norman: University of Oklahoma Press, 2011) 167–171; James Larson, *Sergeant Larson, 4th Cavalry* (San Antonio: Southern Literary Institute, 1935), 206.

38. Robert Mitchell, *Official Records*, Series 1, Vol. 30, Part 2, 673.

39. Peter Cozzens, *The Shipwreck of Their Hopes: The Battle for Chattanooga* (Urbana: University of Illinois Press, 1994), 19, 34–35.

40. C. Goddard, *Official Records*, Series 1, Vol. 30, Part 4, 249–250; Robert J. Dalessandro, "Major General William S. Rosecrans and the Transformation of the Staff of the Army of the Cumberland: A Case Study," Strategy Research Project, U.S. Army War College, Carlisle Barracks, Pennsylvania, 2002, 6.

41. Robert Mitchell, *Official Records*, Series 1, Vol. 30, Part 4, 371, 462.

42. Joseph Hooker, *Official Records*, Series 1, Vol. 30, Part 4, 466–467.

43. William McMichael, *Official Records*, Series 1, Vol. 31, Part 3, 126; David Stanley, *An American General: The Memoirs of David Sloan Stanley*. Samuel W. Fordyce IV, ed. (Santa Barbara, California: The Narrative Press, 2004), 171; Benson Bobrick, *Master of War: The Life of George H. Thomas* (New York: Simon & Schuster, 2009), 38.

44. David Stanley, Union General Papers, communication—November 20, 1863, Record Group 94, Entry 159, Box 28, Stanley, D., National Archives, Washington, D.C.

45. David Stanley, *An American General*, 172.

46. Charles Dana, *Official Records*, Series 1, Vol. 30, Part 1, 220; Charles Dana, *Official Records*, Series 1, Vol. 31, Part 2, 63.

Chapter 8

1. "Bvt. Maj. Gen. Washington Lafayette Elliott," in *Reunion of the Society of the Army of the Cumberland, Nineteenth Reunion: Chicago, Illinois* (Cincinnati: Robert Clarke & Co., 1889), 183.

2. *Ibid.*, 184.

3. Henry Halleck, E. D. Townsend, *Official Records*, Series 1, Vol. 30, Part 4, 404; Ulysses Simpson Grant, *Personal Memoirs of U. S. Grant* (New York: Charles L. Webster & Co., 1894), 249

4. David Stanley, Telegram Sent by David Stanley, November 9, 1863, National Archives, Record Group 393, Part 2, Telegrams Sent by Chief of Cavalry, Number 263, Vol. 19/31.

5. William McMichael, *Official Records*, Series 1, Vol. 31, Part 3, 109.

6. *Ibid.*

7. George H. Thomas, *Official Records*, Series 1, Vol. 31, Part 3, 291.

8. John Rea, "Four Weeks with Long's Cavalry in East Tennessee," in *Glimpses of the Nations Struggle*, J. C. Donahower, Silas Towler, David Kingsbury, editors (St. Paul: Review Publishing Co., 1908), 22–23; E. S. S. Rouse, "Colonel Longs Raid in Bragg's Rear," in *The Bugle's Blast*, MOLLUS (Philadelphia: James Challen & Sons, 1864), 283–285.

9. John Rea, *Ibid.*, 24.

10. *Ibid.*, 25–26.; Timothy M. Burke, *The Fifth Ohio Volunteer Cavalry: A Story of Citizen Soldiers, Civil War Politics and Southwest Ohio* (Raleigh: Lulu Publishing, 2010), 111.

11. J. Morris Young, *Official Records*, Series 1, Vol. 31, Part 1, 568.

12. W. R. Carter, *History of the First Regiment of Tennessee Volunteer Cavalry* (Knoxville: Gaut-Ogden Co., Printers and Binders, 1902), 110–111; W. L. Elliott, Letter, December 13, 1863, National Archives, Record Group 393, Part 2, Number 151 (2460), Letters Sent by the Chief of Cavalry, Washington, D.C.; Thomas McCahan, Diary, November 30, 1863, Thomas McCahan Papers (Am. 6092), Historical Society of Pennsylvania, Philadelphia.

13. Thomas McCahan, Diary, November 30, 1863;

Thomas McCahan, "History of the Relics of the War," Harrisburg Civil War Roundtable Collection, McCahan Family Papers, USAHEC, Carlisle, Pennsylvania.

14. W. L. Elliott, *Official Records*, Series 1, Vol. 31, Part 1, 437; Thomas Jordan, Letter to Wife—November 27, 1863, Thomas J. Jordan Civil War Letters [2066] Box Number: 1, Folder 13, Historical Society of Pennsylvania, Philadelphia, Pennsylvania.

15. James Longstreet, *Official Records*, Series 1, Vol. 31, Part 1, 461.

16. Ulysses Grant, *Official Records*, Series 1, Vol. 31, Part 3, 430.

17. Charles Dana, *Official Records*, Series 1, Vol. 31, Part 1, 262; Thomas Crofts, *History of the Service of the Third Ohio Veteran Volunteer Cavalry* (Toledo: Stoneman Press, 1910), 122; John Rea, "Four Weeks with Long's Cavalry in East Tennessee," 28–29.

18. Eli Long, *Official Records*, Series 1, Vol. 31, Part 1, 435; John Rea, "Four Weeks with Long's Cavalry in East Tennessee," 29–30.

19. John Rea, "Four Weeks with Long's Cavalry in East Tennessee," 32–35.

20. Thomas Jordan, Letter to Wife—December 13, 1863, Thomas J. Jordan Civil War Letters [2066] Box Number: 1, Folder 14, Historical Society of Pennsylvania, Philadelphia, Pennsylvania.

21. W. L. Shaw, Letter, December 24, 1863, National Archives, Record Group 393, Part 2, Number 151 (2460), Letters Sent by the Chief of Cavalry, Washington, D.C.; Marshall Thatcher, *A Hundred Battles in the West: The Second Michigan Cavalry* (Detroit: L. F. Kilroy, Printer, 1884), 163; Edward McCook, *Official Records*, Series 1, Vol. 31, Part 1, 635–636.

22. Archibald Campbell, *Official Records*, Series 1, Vol. 31, Part 1, 636–637.

23. John W. Rowell, *Yankee Cavalrymen* (Knoxville: University of Tennessee Press, 1971), 160–161; Archibald Campbell, *Official Records*, Series 1, Vol. 31, Part 1, 637–638.

24. Archibald Campbell, *Official Records*, Series 1, Vol. 31, Part 1, 638–639.

25. William Martin *Official Records*, Series 1, Vol. 31, Part 1, 547.

26. Marshall Thatcher, *A Hundred Battles in the West*, 165.

27. Edward McCook, *Official Records*, Series 1, Vol. 31, Part 1, 654–657; W. R. Carter, *History of the First Regiment of Tennessee Volunteer Cavalry*, 127; "Mossy Creek, A Desperate Battle Fought in East Tennessee," *National Tribune*, February 8, 1883, page 1.

28. Henry Campbell, Diary Entry, December 29, 1863, *Three Years in the Saddle: A Diary of the Civil War*, Unpublished (n.d.), Wabash College, Crawfordsville, Indiana.

29. John W. Rowell, *Yankee Cavalrymen* (Knoxville: University of Tennessee Press, 1971), 162.

30. Edward McCook, *Official Records*, Series 1, Vol. 31, Part 1, 653–656.

31. W. R. Carter, *History of the First Regiment of Tennessee Volunteer Cavalry*, 126–128; Marshall Thatcher, *A Hundred Battles in the West*, 17.

32. Thomas Jordan, Letter to Wife—January 2, 1864, Thomas J. Jordan Civil War Letters [2066] Box Number: 1, Folder 14, Historical Society of Pennsylvania, Philadelphia, Pennsylvania; Henry Campbell, Diary Entry, December 29, 1863, *Three Years in the Saddle: a Diary of the Civil War*; Edward McCook, *Official Records*, Series 1, Vol. 31, Part 1, 654–655.

33. W. L. Elliott, Letter December 31, 1863, National Archives, Record Group 393, Part 2, Number 151 (2460), Letters Sent by the Chief of Cavalry, Washington, D.C.

34. W. L. Elliott, *Official Records*, Series 1, Vol. 31, Part 1, 652–653; Edward McCook, *Official Records*, Series 1, Vol. 31, Part 1, 653–656.

35. Eli Long, *Official Records*, Series 1, Vol. 31, Part 1, 435–436; John Rea, "Four Weeks with Long's Cavalry in East Tennessee," 40; Thomas Crofts, *History of the Service of the Third Ohio Veteran Volunteer Cavalry*, 124.

36. Stephen Z. Starr, *The Union Cavalry in the Civil War: The War in the West*, Vol. III (Baton Rouge: Louisiana State University, 2007), 373.

37. Othniel Gooding, Letter, December 29, 1863, Othniel Gooding Letters (c.00275) Michigan State University Archives & Historical Collections, Michigan State University, East Lansing.

Chapter 9

1. James H. Wilson, *Under the Old Flag*, Vol. 2 (New York: D. Appleton and Company, 1912), 20; David Evans, *Sherman's Horsemen* (Bloomington: Indiana University Press, 1996), 3.

2. William Whipple, *Official Records*, Series 1, Vol. 32, Part 2, 38; George Kryder, Diary—June 15, 1863, MS 163 George Kryder (1834–1925), William T. Jerome Library, Bowling Green State University, Bowling Green, Ohio.

3. Samuel Sturgis, *Official Records*, Series 1, Vol. 32, Part 2, 52–53; George Thomas, *Official Records*, Series 1, Vol. 32, Part 1, 33–34; Ulysses Grant, *Official Records*, Series 1, Vol. 32, Part 2, 100–101.

4. James Longstreet, *Official Records*, Series 1, Vol. 32, Part 1, 93; Archibald Campbell, *Official Records*, Series 1, Vol. 32, Part 1, 86.

5. Thomas Jordan, *Official Records*, Series 1, Vol. 32, Part 1, 88.

6. Archibald Campbell, *Official Records*, Series 1, Vol. 32, Part 1, 86.

7. Oscar La Grange, *Official Records*, Series 1, Vol. 32, Part 1, 90–91.

8. Edward McCook, *Official Records*, Series 1, Vol. 32, Part 1, 85.

9. Charles Perry Goodrich, *Letters from Home from the First Wisconsin Cavalry*, Richard N. Larson, editor (Madison: State Historical Society of Wisconsin, unpublished), January 24, 1864.

10. Henry Curtis, *Official Records*, Series 1, Vol. 32, Part 2, 171.

11. W. L. Elliott, Letters—January 23, February 2, February 3, February 14, 1864, Record Group 393, Number 151, Letters Sent, Cavalry Forces of the Army of the Cumberland, National Archives Administration, Washington, D.C.; Steven Wright, *Kentucky Soldiers and Their Regiments in the Civil War*, Vol. IV (Utica, Kentucky: McDowell Publications, 2009), 12; *Daily Commonwealth*, "The Fourth and Sixth Kentucky Cavalry," Frankfort, Kentucky, January 23, 1864, 3, column 3.

12. Edward McCook, *Official Records*, Series 1, Vol. 32, Part 2, 154.

13. Thomas Jordan, Letter to Wife—January 25, 1864, Thomas J. Jordan Civil War Letters [2066] Box Number: 1, Folder 13, Historical Society of Pennsylvania, Philadelphia, Pennsylvania; Michael Brown, Letters—February 21, 1864, March 30, 1864, Michael Brown Letters, Box 16, Folder 13, USAHEC, Carlisle, Pennsylvania.

14. Samuel Sturgis, *Official Records*, Series 1, Vol. 32, Part 2, 231; George Thomas, *Official Records*, Series 1, Vol. 32, Part 1, 35; Henry Mortimer Hempstead, "Diary, January 26, 1864." Hempstead, Henry Mortimer, 1832–1916, Papers, Bentley Historical Library, University of Michigan, Ann Arbor.

15. Oscar La Grange, *Official Records*, Series 1, Vol. 32, Part 1, 144; Richard Reid, *Fourth Indiana Cavalry Regiment: A History* (Fordsville, Kentucky: Sandefur Offset Printing, undated), 116; Henry Campbell, Diary Entry, January 27, 1864, *Three Years in the Saddle: A Diary of the Civil War*, Unpublished, Wabash College, Crawfordsville, Indiana.

16. Edward McCook, *Official Records*, Series 1, Vol. 32, Part 1, 35.

17. W. R. Carter, *History of the First Regiment of Tennessee Volunteer Cavalry* (Knoxville: Gaut-Ogden Co. Printers and Binders, 1902), 141–2; Charles Perry Goodrich, *Letters from Home from the First Wisconsin Cavalry*, February 1, 1864.

18. Henry Mortimer Hempstead, Diary, January 27, 1864.

19. La Grange, *Official Records*, Series 1, Vol. 32, Part 1, 145–146.

20. James Longstreet, *Official Records*, Series 1, Vol. 32, Part 1, 149–150.

21. R. O. Selfridge, *Official Records*, Series 1, Vol. 32, Part 2, 275; Edward McCook, *Official Records*, Series 1, Vol. 32, Part 1, 34.

22. Lorien Foote, *The Gentlemen and the Roughs: Violence, Honor, and Manhood in the Union Army* (New York: New York University Press, 2010), 60–63; William Bradley, Bradley Court Martial, May 14–24, 1864, Record Group (RG) 153, Adjutant General's Office, Court Martial Case Files, 1809–1854, case number LL 2413, National Archives, Washington, D.C.

23. William Smith, *Official Records*, Series 1, Vol. 32, Part 2, 40.

24. William S. Smith, *Official Records*, Series 1, Vol. 32, Part 2, 250.

25. Abram Miller, *Official Records*, Series 1, Vol. 32, Part 1, 122.

26. Peter Cozzens, *The Shipwreck of Their Hopes* (Urbana: University of Illinois Press, 1994), 392.

27. George Thomas, *Official Records*, Series 1, Vol. 32, Part 2, 102–103; Ulysses Grant, *Official Records*, Series 1, Vol. 32, Part 2, 110.

28. George Thomas, *Official Records*, Series 1, Vol. 32, Part 2, 154; Charles Dana, *Official Records*, Series 1, Vol. 32, Part 2, 115–116.

29. *Harper's Weekly*, "General Kenner Garrard," February 11, 1865; Frances Densmore, "Garrard Family in Frontenac," *Minnesota History*, Vol. 14, No. 1 (March 1933), 31–43; David S. Evans, "Kenner Garrard's Georgia Romp," *America's Civil War*, Vol. 15, No. 1 (March 2002), 44–50.

30. Thomas Jordan, Letter to Wife—February 10, 1864.

31. William Stokes, *Official Records*, Series 1, Vol. 32, Part 1, 494.

32. Joseph Johnston, *Official Records*, Series 1, Vol. 32, Part 2, 510; James Longstreet, *Official Records*, Series 1, Vol. 32, Part 2, 597, 632, 711; Bolling Hall, February 7, 1864, Letter, Bolling Hall family papers; Box Number LPR39, Vault box 52; Folder Number 8; Folder Title: Bolling Hall (1813–1897) letters, 1864 January–March. Alabama Dept. of Archives and History, Montgomery, Alabama.

33. Joseph Johnston, *Official Records*, Series 1, Vol. 32, Part 2, 759.

34. James Longstreet, *Official Records*, Series 1, Vol. 32, Part 2, 789.

35. William Sherman, *Official Records*, Series 1, Vol. 32, Part 1, 172; Lafayette McCrillis *Official Records*, Series 1, Vol. 32, Part 1, 305; William T. Sherman, *Home Letters of General Sherman* (New York: Charles Scribner's Sons, 1909), 285.

36. William Stokes, *Official Records*, Series 1, Vol. 32, Part 1, 163.

37. William Stokes, *Official Records*, Series 1, Vol. 32, Part 1, 416–417; News Article, April 14, 1864 (no author or paper) "Quiner's Scrapbook, Vol. 10, Correspondence," Wisconsin Historical Society, Mss. 600; WIHVQ500-A, Madison, Wisconsin.

38. George Thomas, *Official Records*, Series 1, Vol. 32, Part 1, 10.

39. W. L. Elliott, *Official Records*, Series 1, Vol. 32, Part 1, 38; George Thomas, *Official Records*, Series 1, Vol. 32, Part 1, 10.

40. George Thomas, *Official Records*, Series 1, Vol. 32, Part 1, 14.

41. David Ayers, Letter March 27, 1864, David Ayers Papers, Civil War Collection, Box 3, Folder 19, USAHEC, Carlisle, Pennsylvania.

42. Andrew Johnson, *Official Records*, Series 1, Vol. 32, Part 3, 105.

43. George Thomas, *Official Records*, Series 1, Vol. 32, Part 3, 557.

44. George Thomas, *Official Records*, Series 1, Vol. 32, Part 3, 550.

45. John Schofield, *Official Records*, Series 1, Vol. 32, Part 3, 569; James McPherson, *Official Records*, Series 1, Vol. 32, Part 3, 561; Joseph Johnston, *Official Records*, Series 1, Vol. 32, Part 3, 866.

46. Chris Hartley, *Stoneman's Raid, 1865* (Winston-Salem: John F. Blair Publisher, 2010), 43–48; William Sherman, *Official Records*, Series 1, Vol. 39, Part 2, 80.

47. James Alex Baggett, *Homegrown Yankees: Tennessee's Union Cavalry in the Civil War* (Baton Rouge: Louisiana State University, 2009), 12, 40–41, 78, 82; Alexander Eckel, *History of the Fourth Tennessee Cavalry* (Johnson City, Tennessee: Overmountain Press, 2001), 28, 47, 106.

48. George E. Pond, "Kilpatrick's and Dahlgren's Raid to Richmond," in *Battles & Leaders*, Vol. 4 (New York: The Century Company, 1888), 95–96.

49. Washington Elliott, Letter to Whipple—March 9, 1864, Record Group 393, Number 151, Letters Sent, Cavalry forces of the Army of the Cumberland, National Archives Records Administration, Washington, D.C. [#2460]; Ron Seymour, *The Life of Col. Joseph B. Dorr and His 8th Iowa Cavalry* (self-published eBook, www.8thIowaCav.com, 2012), 91–96; W. R. Carter, *History of the First Regiment of Tennessee Volunteer Cavalry*, 149.

50. W. L. Curry, *Four Years in the Saddle: History of the First Regiment Ohio Volunteer Cavalry* (Columbus: Champlin Printing Company, 1898), 163; Mortimer Hempstead, Diary–March 6, 1864.

51. W. L. Elliott, Letter, February 29, 1864, March 1, 1864, NARA RG 393. Letters Sent.

52. Ibid., Letter sent to Brigadier General George Ramsay, March 9, 1864.

53. George Kryder, Letter to Wife, January 27, 1864, George Kryder Papers—MS 163, Bowling Green State University, Special Collections, Bowling Green Ohio; T. F. Dornblaser, *Sabre Strokes of the Pennsylvania Dragoons* (Philadelphia: Lutheran Publication Society, 1884), 148.

54. Marshall Thatcher, *A Hundred Battles in the West: The Second Michigan Cavalry* (Detroit: L. F. Kilroy, Printer, 1884), 152.

55. Ron Seymour, *The Enlisted Soldier*, 2–53.

Chapter 10

1. R. M. Sawyer, *Official Records*, Series 1, Vol. 32, Part 3, 497.

2. William Sherman, *Official Records*, Series 1, Vol. 38, Part 4, 29–30; Robert Ramsey, *Official Records*, Series 1, Vol. 38, Part 4, 46; William Whipple, *Official Records*, Series 1, Vol. 38, Part 4, 7; Washington Elliott, *Official Records*, Series 1, Vol. 38, Part 4, 14.

3. William Sherman, *Official Records*, Series 1, Vol. 38, Part 4, 26.

4. William Sherman, *Official Records*, Series 1, Vol. 38, Part 4, 38.

5. Albert Castel, *Decision in the West: The Atlanta Campaign of 1864* (Lawrence: University Press of Kansas, 1992), 127.

6. Louis Watkins, *Official Records*, Series 1, Vol. 38, Part 2, 792–793; Hiram Chapman, Letter, June 15, 1864, Hiram Chapman Papers, Box 22, Folder 6, Civil War Collection, USAHEC, Carlisle, Pennsylvania.

7. William Sherman, *Official Records*, Series 1, Vol. 38, Part 4, 85; Kenner Garrard, *Official Records*, Series 1, Vol. 38, Part 4, 29; John Corse, *Official Records*, Series 1, Vol. 38, Part 4, 53, 85.

8. H. Judson Kilpatrick, *Official Records*, Series 1, Vol. 38, Part 4, 96–97; James McPherson, *Official Records*, Series 1, Vol. 38, Part 4, 104–106.

9. Horace Lamson, *Official Records*, Series 1, Vol. 38, Part 2, 780–781; Charles Perry Goodrich, Letter, May 11, 1864, *Letters from Home from the First Wisconsin Cavalry*, Richard N. Larson, editor (Madison: State Historical Society of Wisconsin, not published); *Delphi Journal* (Delphi, Indiana), "Medal of Honor Well Bestowed," Thursday, July 27, 1905; John Schofield, *Official Records*, Series 1, Vol. 38, Part 4, 98, Joseph Wheeler, *Official Records*, Series 1, Vol. 38, Part 3, 944.

10. William Sherman, *Official Records*, Series 1, Vol. 38, Part 4, 123; Kenner Garrard, *Official Records*, Series 1, Vol. 38, Part 4, 129.

11. William Sherman, *Official Records*, Series 1, Vol. 38, Part 4, 133; J. D. Fessenden, *Official Records*, Series 1, Vol. 38, Part 4, 150; W. L. Elliott, *Official Records*, Series 1, Vol. 38, Part 4, 167; James Moore, *Kilpatrick and Our Cavalry* (New York: W. J. Widdleton, Publisher, 1865), 165; Sam Atkins, "With Sherman's Cavalry," *Military Essays and Recollections*, Vol. 2, Military Order of the Loyal Legion of the United States. Commandery of the State of Illinois (1894, reprint, London: Forgotten Books, 2013), 382–3.

12. W. L. Elliott, *Official Records*, Series 1, Vol. 38, Part 2, 746.

13. Stephen Davis, *Atlanta Will Fall: Sherman, Joe Johnston, and the Yankee Heavy Battalions* (Wilmington, DE: Scholarly Resources, 2001), 43.

14. William Sherman, *Official Records*, Series 1, Vol. 38, Part 1, 115–117.

15. William Sherman, *Official Records*, Series 1, Vol. 38, Part 4, 187.

16. Kenner Garrard, *Official Records*, Series 1, Vol. 38, Part 2, 803; Robert Minty, *Official Records*, Series 1, Vol. 38, Part 2, 811; Robert B. Leach, "The Role of Union Cavalry During the Atlanta Campaign," Master's Thesis, U.S. Army Command and General Staff College, Fort Leavenworth, Kansas, 1994, 39–40.

17. William Sherman, *Official Records*, Series 1, Vol. 38, Part 4, 198.

18. David Stanley, *An American General: The Memoirs of David Sloan Stanley*, Samuel W. Fordyce IV, ed. (Santa Barbara, California: The Narrative Press, 2004), 176; Rowland Cox, "Snake Creek Gap and Atlanta," *Personal Recollections of the War of the Rebellion*, ed. A. Noel Blakeman (New York: G. Putnam and Sons, 1897), 19; Joseph Johnston, "Opposing Sherman's Advance to Atlanta," *Battles and Leaders*, Vol. IV (New York: The Century Company, 1888), 266.

19. Marshall Thatcher, *A Hundred Battles in the West: The Second Michigan Cavalry* (Detroit: L. F. Kilroy, Printer, 1884), 333–336.

20. *Portrait and Biographical Album: Ingham & Livingston Counties* (Chicago: Chapman Brothers, 1891), 225–242; Frederick Mann, "Items and Notes," *The Medical Age*, Vol. 19, No. 10 (1901), 385.

21. Oliver O. Howard, *The Autobiography of Oliver Otis Howard* (New York: Baker & Taylor Company, 1907), 510; Edward McCook, *Official Records*, Series 1, Vol. 38, Part 4, 180.

22. William Sherman, *Official Records*, Series 1, Vol. 38, Part 4, 201; L. M. Dayton, *Official Records*, Series 1, Vol. 38, Part 4, 209.

23. Joseph Vale, *Minty and the Cavalry: A History of Cavalry Campaigns in the Western Armies* (Harrisburg, Pennsylvania: Edwin K. Myers, Printer and Binder, 1886), 285; Heber Thompson, Diary Entry–May 18, 1864, Heber Thompson Diary, Civil War Roundtable Collection, USAHEC, Carlisle, Pennsylvania.

24. William Sherman, *Official Records*, Series 1, Vol. 38, Part 4, 220, 232, 242–243; Robert Minty *Official Records*, Series 1, Vol. 38, Part 2, 811; Alva Greist, *Three Years in Dixie: Personal Adventures, Scenes and Incidents of the March—The Journal of Alva C. Griest*, May 18, 1864 Journal Entry, Alva Greist Collection, Folder 2, William Henry Smith Memorial Library, Indiana Historical Society, Indianapolis, Indiana.

25. Chesley D. Bailey Papers (1863–1864), Diary—June 19, 1864 entry, Bailey Papers, Call no.: Mss. A B155, Filson Historical Society, Louisville, Kentucky; David Stanley, *Official Records*, Series 1, Vol. 38, Number 1, 222.

26. Albert Castel, *Decision in the West: The Atlanta Campaign of 1864*, 198–202; Edward McCook, *Official Records*, Series 1, Vol. 38, Part 4, 255.

27. Edward McCook, *Official Records*, Series 1, Vol. 38, Part 2, 752; Robert B. Leach, "The Role of Union Cavalry During the Atlanta Campaign," Master's Thesis, U.S. Army Command and General Staff College, Fort Leavenworth, Kansas, 1994, 42; Ron Seymour, *The Life of Col. Joseph B. Dorr and His 8th Iowa Cavalry* (self-published eBook, www.8thIowaCav.com, 2012), 198; Daniel C. Bischard Letters, June 9, 1864 (005: F08; N17/8/4), State Historical Society of Iowa, Des Moines.

28. Larry J. Daniel, *Days of Glory: The Army of the Cumberland, 1861–1865* (Baton Rouge: Louisiana State University Press, 2006), 399.

29. Robert Minty *Official Records*, Series 1, Vol. 38, Part 2, 812; Benjamin Nourse, "Diary" Entry May 19, 1864, Duke University, David M. Rubenstein Rare Book & Manuscript Library, Durham, North Carolina.

30. William Sherman, *Official Records*, Series 1, Vol. 38, Part 4, 249–250; Jefferson C. Davis, *Official Records*, Series 1, Vol. 38, Part 4, 251.

31. George Stoneman, *Official Records*, Series 1, Vol. 38, Part 4, 268.

32. J. C. Van Duzer, *Official Records*, Series 1, Vol. 38, Part 4, 261; Daniel Wait Howe, Correspondence, May 21st, 1864, Daniel Howe Papers, M128, Box 1, F3, Indiana Historical Society, Indianapolis, IN.

33. W. L. Elliott, *Official Records*, Series 1, Vol. 38, Part 2, 747; Sherman, *Official Records*, Series 1, Vol. 38, Part 4, 278.

34. Daniel Butterfield, *Official Records*, Series 1, Vol. 38, Part 4, 296.

35. William D Whipple, *Official Records*, Series 1, Vol. 38, Part 4, 300; H. A. Hambright, *Official Records*, Series 1, Vol. 38, Part 1, 623; Heber Thompson, Diary Entry–May 24, 1864, Heber Thompson Diary.

36. W. L. Elliott, *Official Records*, Series 1, Vol. 38, Part 2, 746–747; Edward McCook, W. L. Elliott, *Official Records*, Series 1, Vol. 38, Part 2, 753.

37. Richard Reid, *Fourth Indiana Cavalry Regiment: A History* (Fordsville, Kentucky: Sandefur Offset Printing, undated), 129; Horace Lamson, *Official Records*, Series 1, Vol. 38, Part 2, 782.

38. James McPherson, *Official Records*, Series 1, Vol. 38, Part 4, 328–329.

39. Edward McCook, *Official Records*, Series 1, Vol. 38, Part 4, 335–336; James Alex Baggett, *Homegrown Yankees: Tennessee's Union Cavalry in the Civil War* (Baton Rouge: Louisiana State University, 2009), 238.

40. George Kryder, Letter, June 5, 1864, George Kryder Papers—MS 163, Bowling Green State University, Special Collections, Bowling Green Ohio.

41. Beroth Eggleston, *Official Records*, Series 1, Vol. 38, Part 2, 842; George Kryder letter June 5, 1864; Thomas Crofts, *History of the Service of the Third Ohio Veteran Volunteer Cavalry* (Toledo: Stoneman Press, 1910), 147.

42. Orr Kelly and Mary Davies Kelly, *Dream's End: Two Iowa Brothers in the Civil War* (Tokyo: Kodansha International, 1998), 206; Edward McCook, *Official Records*, Series 1, Vol. 38, Part 4, 387; Wesley Templeton, Letter, June 11, 1864, Wesley G. L. Templeton Collection, Vol. 1b, N16/2/4, State Historical Society of Iowa, Des Moines, Iowa; Benjamin Nourse, "Diary" Entry June 1, 1864.

43. William Sherman *Official Records*, Series 1, Vol. 38, Part 4, 367; W. L. Elliott, *Official Records*, Series 1, Vol. 38, Part 4, 378; Kenner Garrard, *Official Records*, Series 1, Vol. 38, Part 5, 60; David Q. Curry, Letter, June 6, 1864, David Curry Papers, Civil War Collection, Box 30, Folder 3, USAHEC, Carlisle, Pennsylvania.

44. John Bennett, June 5 letter to wife, Bennett, John, B. Papers, Bentley Historical Library, University of Michigan, Ann Arbor; Albert Castel, *Decision in the West: The Atlanta Campaign of 1864*, 249.

45. William Sherman *Official Records*, Series 1, Vol. 38, Part 4, 385.

46. James Larson, *Sergeant Larson, 4th Cavalry* (San Antonio: Southern Literary Institute, 1935), 246–247.

47. William Sherman, *Official Records*, Series 1, Vol. 38, Part 4, 408–409.

48. L. M. Dayton, *Official Records*, Series 1, Vol. 38, Part 4, 445–446; William Sherman, *Official Records*, Series 1, Vol. 38, Part 4, 449–450.

49. J. C. Van Duzer, *Official Records*, Series 1, Vol. 38, Part 4, 479; William Lowe, *Official Records*, Series 1, Vol. 38, Part 2, 865.

50. Kenner Garrard, *Official Records*, Series 1, Vol. 38, Part 4, 478; L. M. Dayton, *Official Records*, Series 1, Vol. 38, Part 4, 480; Edward McCook, *Official Records*, Series 1, Vol. 38, Part 4, 501; Edward McCook, *Official Records*, Series 1, Vol. 38, Part 2, 756.

51. Eli Long, *Official Records*, Series 1, Vol. 38, Part 2, 837.

52. William Sherman, *Official Records*, Series 1, Vol. 38, Part 4, 507; Edward McCook, *Official Records*, Series 1, Vol. 38, Part 2, 756.

53. Robert Minty, "The Saber Brigade: Incidents in the History of Minty's Cavalry in the Army of Cumberland," *National Tribune*, March 1, 1894, 1–2; Albert Castel, *Decision in the West: The Atlanta Campaign of 1864*, 284; Heber Thompson, Diary Entries June 9–11, 1864; Benjamin Nourse, "Diary" Entry June 9, 1864.

54. William Sherman, *Official Records*, Series 1, Vol. 38, Part 4, 535; Kenner Garrard and Lewis Edward Nolan, *Nolan's System for Training Cavalry Horses* (New York: D. Van Nostrand, 1862), 1–120.

55. William Sherman, *Official Records*, Series 1, Vol. 38, Part 4, 542.

56. Kenner Garrard, *Official Records*, Series 1, Vol. 38, Part 4, 505–506; W. L. Curry, *Four Years in the Saddle: History of First Regiment Ohio Volunteer Cavalry* (Columbus: Champlin Printing Co., 1898), 83–84; *The Catalogue and History of Sigma Chi* (Chicago: Published by the Fraternity, 1890), 169; George Parry, Diary Entry June 20, 1864, George F. Parry Family Vols., Collection 3694, Record Number: 10325, Historical Society of Pennsylvania, Philadelphia, Pennsylvania.

57. Robert Minty, "Noonday Church," *National Tribune*, January 31, 1895, 3; Heber Thompson, Diary Entry June 20, 1864.

58. Robert Minty, *Official Records*, Series 1, Vol. 38, Part 2, 812–813; Joseph Vale, *Minty and the Cavalry: A History of Cavalry Campaigns in the Western Armies* (Harrisburg, Pennsylvania: Edwin K. Myers, Printer and Binder, 1886), 318–319; John McLain, Diary Entry—June 20, 1864, John McLain Papers (c.00111), Michigan State University Archives & Historical Collections, East Lansing; Joseph Johnston, *Narrative of Military Operations Directed During the Civil War* (New York: D. Appleton, 1874), 339.

59. Kenner Garrard, *Official Records*, Series 1, Vol. 38, Part 4, 556.

60. James McPherson, *Official Records*, Series 1, Vol. 38, Part 4, 557; Kenner Garrard, *Official Records*, Series 1, Vol. 38, Part 4, 556; W. L. Curry, *Four Years in the Saddle: History of First Regiment Ohio Volunteer Cavalry* (Columbus: Champlin Printing Co., 1898), 170.

61. James Larson, *Sergeant Larson, 4th Cavalry*, 249; Benjamin Nourse, "Diary" Entry June 20, 1864.

62. Robert B. Leach, "The Role of Union Cavalry During the Atlanta Campaign," 54; Heber Thompson, Diary June 21, 1864.

63. Edward McCook, *Official Records*, Series 1, Vol. 38, Part 4, 539; Abram Miller, *Official Records*, Series 1, Vol. 38, Part 2, 848–849; James Larson, *Sergeant Larson, 4th Cavalry*, 254; Wesley Templeton, Letter, June 19, 1864, 8th Iowa; Wesley G. L. Templeton Letters, N16/2/4; State Historical Society of Iowa, Des Moines.

64. Albert Castel, *Decision in the West: The Atlanta Campaign of 1864*, 295.

65. George Stoneman, *Official Records*, Series 1, Vol. 38, Part 4, 576; Henry Stone, W. L. Elliott, Edward McCook, *Official Records*, Series 1, Vol. 38, Part 4, 575; George Stoneman, *Official Records*, Series 1, Vol. 38, Part 5, 60–61.

66. Kenner Garrard, *Official Records*, Series 1, Vol. 38, Part 2, 804.

67. James McPherson, *Official Records*, Series 1, Vol. 38, Part 4, 579; W. L. Curry, *Four Years in the Saddle*, 170.

68. Edward McCook, *Official Records*, Series 1, Vol. 38, Part 4, 583.

69. James Steedman, *Official Records*, Series 1, Vol. 38, Part 4, 586, 633; William Sherman, *Official Records*, Series 1, Vol. 38, Part 4, 586; Louis Watkins, *Official Records*, Series 1, Vol. 38, Part 2, 794; John Croxton, *Official Records*, Series 1, Vol. 38, Part 2, 778.

70. William Clark, *Official Records*, Series 1, Vol. 38, Part 4, 605; William Whipple, *Official Records*, Series 1, Vol. 38, Part 4, 602–603.

71. William Sherman, *Official Records*, Series 1, Vol. 38, Part 4, 645

72. William Sherman, *Official Records*, Series 1, Vol. 38, Part 5, 61–62.

73. W. L. Elliott, *Official Records*, Series 1, Vol. 38, Part 4, 643; William Sherman, *Official Records*, Series 1, Vol. 38, Part 4, 645; William Sherman, *Official Records*, Series 1, Vol. 38, Part 5, 24–25.

74. William Sherman, *Official Records*, Series 1, Vol. 38, Part 5, 29–30, 42.

75. Dianna Avena, *Roswell: History, Haunts and Legends* (Charleston, SC: History Press, 2007), 23–28; William Sherman, *Official Records*, Series 1, Vol. 38, Part 5, 73.

76. William Sherman, Official Records, Series 1, Vol. 38, Part 5, 77.

77. James Alex Baggett, *Homegrown Yankees: Tennessee's Union Cavalry in the Civil War* (Baton Rouge: Louisiana State University, 2009), 242; W. R. Carter, *History of the First Regiment of Tennessee Volunteer Cavalry* (Knoxville: Gaut-Ogden Co., Printers and Binders, 1902), 171; Edward McCook, *Official Records*, Series 1, Vol. 38, Part 2, 761; J. Brownlow, "More on 'Raw Courage," ed. Richard McMurry, *Civil War Times Illustrated* (Oct 1975), 36–38.

78. William Allen Clark, "Please Send Stamps: The Civil War Letters of William Allen Clark," Part IV, Edited by Margaret Black Taturn, *Indiana Magazine of History*, XCI (December 1995), 424.

79. Pike, Benjamin H. "I Have Commited [sic] a Wrong by Coming Here." *Civil War Times Illustrated* (June 2000): 16, 68–77.

80. Heber Thompson, Diary June 24, 1864.

Chapter 11

1. Charles Treadway, "The Letters of Charles Wesley Treadway," *Foot Prints: Past and Present*, Vol. 9 (Olney, IL: Richland County Genealogical and Historical Society, 1986), 140–141; Michael Ballard, *The Battle of Tupelo, Mississippi—July 14 & 15, 1864* (Tupelo, Mississippi: Northeast Mississippi Historical & Genealogical Society, 2009), 10–28.

2. William Sherman, *Official Records*, Series 1, Vol. 38, Part 4, 66.

3. Mark E. Fretwell, "Rousseau's Alabama Raid," *Alabama Historical Quarterly*, Vol. 18, No. 4 (Winter 1956), 528.

4. Lovell Rousseau, *Official Records*, Series 1, Vol. 38, Part 4, 530–531; William Sherman, *Official Records*, Series 1, Vol. 38, Part 2, 910; John Brandon, Letter June 15, 1864, John Brandon Papers, Civil War Collection, Box 14, Folder 8, USAHEC, Carlisle, Pennsylvania.

5. Lovell Rousseau, *Official Records*, Series 1, Vol. 38, Part 2, 905.

6. David Evans, *Sherman's Horsemen: Union Cavalry Operations in the Atlanta Campaign* (Bloomington: Indiana University Press, 1996), 106–107; Edwin Bearss, "Rousseau's Raid on the Montgomery and West Point Railroad," *Alabama Historical Quarterly*, Vol. 25, Nos. 1&2 (Spring and Summer 1963), 25; *Ohio Statesman*, "General Rousseau's Raid into Alabama and Georgia—Several Railroads and Millions of Property Destroyed," August 2, 1864 (Columbus); J. N. Jones, "Rousseau's Raid: Reminiscences of an 8th Ind. Cavalryman Who Followed the Daring General," *National Tribune*, May 2, 1901, pg. 5, col. 1–4; *New York Times*, "Gen. Rousseau's Raid," August 3, 1864; *Salt Lake Tribune*, "Colonel—Sudden End of Busy Life," February 26, 1899; Frank Moore, ed., "General Rousseau's Expedition," *Rebellion Record*, Vol. 11 (New York: Van Nostrand, 1868), 191.

7. Mark E. Fretwell, "Rousseau's Alabama Raid," 534.

8. Green Raum, "With the Western Army: Rousseau Raid," *National Tribune*, October 2 1902, page 7, col. 2.

9. Mark E. Fretwell, "Rousseau's Alabama Raid," 536; Edwin Bearss, "Rousseau's Raid on the Montgomery and West Point Railroad," 29; Alexander Eckel, *History of the Fourth Tennessee Cavalry* (Johnson City, Tennessee: Overmountain Press, 2001), 53.

10. Lovell Rousseau, *Official Records*, Series 1, Vol. 38, Part 2, 904–909; *New York Times*, "Gen. Rousseau's Raid," August 3, 1864; Mark E. Fretwell, "Rousseau's Alabama Raid," 942–944; *Montgomery Weekly Advertiser*, August 10, 1864; William Douglas Hamilton, *Recollections of a Cavalryman of the Civil War After Fifty Years 1861–1865* (Columbus: The F. J. Heer Printing Co., 1915), 38.

11. George Healy Papers, July 24, 1864 Letter, State Historical Society of Iowa, Des Moines (1F 006: F22; N14/3/4-B/HU).

12. William Sherman, *Official Records*, Series 1, Vol. 38, Part 5, 108.

13. William Sherman, *Official Records*, Series 1, Vol.

38, Part 5, 142; George Stoneman, *Official Records*, Series 1, Vol. 38, Part 5, 145–146; Alex Sackett, letter July 10, 1864, Private Alex Sackett Letters (N16/3/5; B/HF), State Historical Society of Iowa, Des Moines.

14. Daniel C. Bischard, Letter, July 20, 1864, Daniel C. Bischard Letters (005: F08; N17/8/4), State Historical Society of Iowa, Des Moines.

15. L. M. Dayton, *Official Records*, Series 1, Vol. 38, Part 5, 166–167; William Sherman, *Official Records*, Series 1, Vol. 38, Part 5, 167; William Clark, *Official Records*, Series 1, Vol. 38, Part 5, 168.

16. J. C. Van Duzer, *Official Records*, Series 1, Vol. 38, Part 5, 179; William Sherman, *Official Records*, Series 1, Vol. 38, Part 5, 169–170.p.

17. William T. Clark, *Official Records*, Series 1, Vol. 38, Part 5, 194.

18. George Thomas, *Official Records*, Series 1, Vol. 38, Part 5, 196. William Sherman, *Official Records*, Series 1, Vol. 38, Part 5, 198.

19. David Evans, *Sherman's Horsemen*, 177; William Sherman, *Official Records*, Series 1, Vol. 38, Part 5, 209; Robert Ramsey, *Official Records*, Series 1, Vol. 38, Part 5, 207.

20. Kenner Garrard, Official Records, Series 1, Vol. 38, Part 5, 221; James McPherson, *Official Records*, Series 1, Vol. 38, Part 5, 219.

21. William Sherman, *Official Records*, Series 1, Vol. 38, Part 5, 223.

22. Kenner Garrard, *Official Records*, Series 1, Vol. 38, Part 2, 809; William E. Crane, "William E. Crane's Daily Journal of Life in the Field During the War of the Rebellion," July 22, 1864 entry, Mss. 980, Cincinnati Historical Society, Cincinnati Museum Center.

23. William Clark, *Official Records*, Series 1, Vol. 38, Part 5, 240; Kenner Garrard, *Official Records*, Series 1, Vol. 38, Part 2, 809; William Sherman, *Official Records*, Series 1, Vol. 38, Part 2, 811; David S. Evans, "Kenner Garrard's Georgia Romp," *America's Civil War*, Vol. 15, No. 1, March 2002.

24. Benjamin Nourse, "Diary" Entry July 22–23, 1864, Duke University, David M. Rubenstein Rare Book & Manuscript Library, Durham, North Carolina; Joseph Wheeler, *Official Records*, Series 1, Vol. 38, Part 3, 952–953; John Sprague, *Official Records*, Series 1, Vol. 38, Part 3, 507; George I. Robinson, *Official Records*, Series 1, Vol. 38, Part 2, 854.

25. William Sherman, *Official Records*, Series 1, Vol. 38, Part 5, 240.

26. William Sherman, *Official Records*, Series 1, Vol. 38, Part 5, 238, 248–249.

27. L. M. Dayton, *Official Records*, Series 1, Vol. 38, Part 5, 255–256.

28. William Sherman, *Official Records*, Series 1, Vol. 38, Part 5, 260–261, 265.

29. Lovell Rousseau, *Official Records*, Series 1, Vol. 38, Part 2, 904–905; Robert B. Leach, "The Role of Union Cavalry During the Atlanta Campaign," Master's Thesis, U.S. Army Command and General Staff College, Fort Leavenworth, Kansas, 1994, 72.

30. Jacob Piatt Dunn, *Memorial and Genealogical Record of Representative Citizens of Indiana* (Indianapolis: B. F. Brown Publisher, 1912), 657–661.

31. William Sherman, *Official Records*, Series 1, Vol. 38, Part 5, 261; "Death of Major Paine of the First Wisconsin Cavalry," *Quiner's Scrapbook*, Vol. 10, Correspondence, Wisconsin Historical Society Wis. Mss. 600; WIHVQ500-A.

32. "McCook's Disaster Below Atlanta," and "Death of Major Paine of the First Wisconsin Cavalry," *Quiner's Scrapbook*, Vol. 10, Correspondence, Wisconsin Historical Society, Wis. Mss. 600; WIHVQ500-A; E. B. Quiner, *Military History of Wisconsin: A Record of the Civil and Military Patriotism of the State*, "1st Cavalry"(Chicago: Clarke and Company, 1866), 893.

33. Mary Davies Kelly and Orr Kelly, *Dream's End: Two Iowa Brothers in the Civil War* (New York: Kodansha International, 1998), 218–219; John Croxton, *Official Records*, Series 1, Vol. 38, Part 2, 770.

34. William Perrin, *The History of Bourbon, Scott, Harrison and Nicholas Counties, Kentucky* (Chicago: O. L. Baskin & Co., 1882), 457–458.

35. Robert B. Leach, "The Role of Union Cavalry During the Atlanta Campaign," 78.

36. Richard Root, *Official Records*, Series 1, Vol. 38, Part 2, 776.

37. John Croxton, *Official Records*, Series 1, Vol. 38, Part 2, 770.

38. Stephen Z. Starr, *The Union Cavalry in the Civil War: The War in the West*, Vol. III (Baton Rouge: Louisiana State University, 2007), 472; James Brownlow, *Official Records*, Series 1, Vol. 38, Part 2, 774; Granville West, *Official Records*, Series 1, Vol. 38, Part 2, 780; John Croxton, *Official Records*, Series 1, Vol. 38, Part 2, 771; David Evans, *Sherman's Horsemen*, 246–247.

39. Evans, *Sherman's Horsemen*, 249.

40. Horace Lamson, *Official Records*, Series 1, Vol. 38, Part 2, 783; James Brownlow, *Official Records*, Series 1, Vol. 38, Part 2, 774.

41. John Croxton, *Official Records*, Series 1, Vol. 38, Part 2, 787.

42. David Evans, *Sherman's Horsemen*, 256–260.

43. Horace Lamson, *Official Records*, Series 1, Vol. 38, Part 2, 783–784; George Purdy, *Official Records*, Series 1, Vol. 38, Part 2, 787.

44. Lamson, *Ibid.*; David Evans, *Sherman's Horsemen*, 260.

45. Ron Seymour, *The Life of Col. Joseph B. Dorr and his 8th Iowa Cavalry* (self-published eBook, www.8thIowaCav.com, 2012), 127.

46. Hiram Thornton Bird, *Memories of the Civil War* (n. p., 1925), Indiana State Library, Indianapolis, 22, 84; Mary Davies Kelly and Orr Kelly, *Dream's End*, 228; Homer Mead, *The Eighth Iowa Cavalry in the Civil War: Autobiography And Personal Recollections of Homer Mead* (Carthage, IL : S.C. Davidson, 1925), 39; John Croxton, *Official Records*, Series 1, Vol. 38, Part 2, 772; Richard Root, *Official Records*, Series 1, Vol. 38, Part 2, 776–777; Charles Marvin, Letter September 28, 1864, Charles Marvin Letter, Civil War Collection, Box 76, Folder 6, USAHEC, Carlisle, Pennsylvania.

47. John Croxton, *Official Records*, Series 1, Vol. 38, Part 2, 773; W. R. Carter, *History of the First Regiment of Tennessee Volunteer Cavalry* (Knoxville: Gaut-Ogden Co., Printers and Binders, 1902), 183.

48. Edward McCook, *Official Records*, Series 1, Vol. 38, Part 2, 764; Alexander Eckel, *History of the Fourth Tennessee Cavalry* (Johnson City, Tennessee: Overmountain Press, 2001), 62.

49. W. R. Carter, *History of the First Regiment of Tennessee Volunteer Cavalry*, 184–185; James Brownlow, *Official*

Records, Series 1, Vol. 38, Part 2, 775; James Alex Baggett, *Homegrown Yankees: Tennessee's Union Cavalry in the Civil War* (Baton Rouge: Louisiana State University, 2009), 258.

50. *Roster And Record Of Iowa Soldiers In The War of the Rebellion*, Vol. IV (Des Moines: Emory H. English, State Printer, E. D. Chassell, State Binder, 1910), 858; Edward McCook, *Official Records*, Series 1, Vol. 38, Part 2, 762–763; J. W. Bartmess, "Jacob W. Bartmess Civil War Letters," *Indiana Magazine of History*, Vol. 52, No. 2 (1956), 157–186.

51. Edward McCook, *Official Records*, Series 1, Vol. 38, Part 2, 762–764, 768.

52. Reprint of *Dubuque Times*, n.d.; and September 21, 1864 Letter, in George Healey Papers, State Historical Society of Iowa, Des Moines, 1F 006: F22 N14/3/4B/HU; Walter F. Beyer and Oscar F. Keydel, *Deeds of Valor: How America's Heroes Won the Medal of Honor* (Detroit: The Perrien-Keydel Company, 1901), 377–378.

53. Joshua Breyfogle Family Papers; MS 3124 to MS 3129, University of Georgia, Hargett Rare Book & Manuscript Library, Athens, GA, August 2, 1864 letter; *Quinter's Correspondence*, Vol. 10, "McCook's Disaster Below Atlanta," August 9, 1864; Peterson Williamson, "The Letters of Peter J. Williamson (II)," ed. Henry Lee Swint, *Wisconsin Magazine of History*, Vol. 26, No. 4 (June 1943), 443; Peter Williamson, Letter to Wife, August 8, 1864, Peter J. Williamson Letters (PJW—F, 59), Special Collections Division of the Nashville Public Library, 615 Church Street, Nashville, Tennessee, 37219.

54. William E. Crane, "William E. Crane's Daily Journal," July 27, 1864.

55. David Evans, *Sherman's Horsemen*, 213; James Larson, *Sergeant Larson, 4th Cavalry* (San Antonio: Southern Literary Institute, 1935), 267.

56. Kenner Garrard, *Official Records*, Series 1, Vol. 38, Part 2, 803–804.

57. William Sherman, *Official Records*, Series 1, Vol. 38, Part 5, 309; Robert Minty, "Picketing and Scouting," *National Tribune*, May 31, 1894, 1–2.

58. William Sherman, *Official Records*, Series 1, Vol. 38, Part 5, 309–310.

59. William Sherman, *Official Records*, Series 1, Vol. 38, Part 5, 310; George Thomas, *Official Records*, Series 1, Vol. 38, Part 5, 311.

60. Kenner Garrard, *Official Records*, Series 1, Vol. 38, Part 2, 804.

61. Robert W. Smith *Official Records*, Series 1, Vol. 38, Part 2, 916.

62. George Stoneman, *Official Records*, Series 1, Vol. 38, Part 2, 914; Robert W. Smith *Official Records*, Series 1, Vol. 38, Part 2, 915–919; William Sherman, *Official Records*, Series 1, Vol. 38, Part 5, 352; William Allen Clark "'Please Send Stamps': The Civil War Letters of William Allen Clark," ed. Margaret Black Tatum, *Indiana Magazine of History*, Vol. 91, No. 4 (1995), 429; Benjamin Nourse, "Diary" Entry June 20, 1864

63. William Sherman, *Official Records*, Series 1, Vol. 38, Part 1, 77; Henry H. Belfield, "My Sixty Days in Hades. In Hades, Not in Hell—Andersonville Was Hell," *Military Essays and Recollections Papers Read Before the Commandery of the State of Illinois, Military Order of the Loyal Legion of the United States*, Vol. III (Chicago: The Dial Press, 1899), 451–452; John McElroy, "The Atlanta Campaign," *National Tribune*, June 17, 1909, 2, column 4–5.

64. William Sherman, *Official Records*, Series 1, Vol. 38, Part 5, 340.

65. Alexander Eckel, *History of the Fourth Tennessee Cavalry*, 57.

Chapter 12

1. L. M. Dayton, *Official Records*, Series 1, Vol. 38, Part 5, 327; Joseph Vale, *Minty and the Cavalry: A History of Cavalry Campaigns in the Western Armies* (Harrisburg, Pennsylvania: Edwin K. Myers, Printer and Binder, 1886), 332–333; Robert Minty, "Picketing and Scouting," *National Tribune*, May 31, 1894, 2.

2. Henry Halleck, *Official Records*, Series 1, Vol. 38, Part 5, 368.

3. W. L. Elliott, *Official Records*, Series 1, Vol. 38, Part 5, 433.

4. William Sherman, *Official Records*, Series 1, Vol. 38, Part 5, 442; Schofield, *Official Records*, Series 1, Vol. 38, Part 5, 442.

5. George Thomas, *Official Records*, Series 1, Vol. 38, Part 5, 490; William Sherman, *Official Records*, Series 1, Vol. 38, Part 5, 489.

6. William Sherman, *Official Records*, Series 1, Vol. 38, Part 5, 507; W. L. Elliott, *Official Records*, Series 1, Vol. 38, Part 5, 494.

7. W. L. Elliott, *Official Records*, Series 1, Vol. 38, Part 5, 509; George Thomas, *Official Records*, Series 1, Vol. 38, Part 5, 524; William Sherman, *Official Records*, Series 1, Vol. 38, Part 5, 521.

8. William Sherman, *Official Records*, Series 1, Vol. 38, Part 5, 524; George I. Robinson, "With Kilpatrick Around Atlanta," *War Papers*, Commandery of Wisconsin MOLLUS, Vol. 1 (New York: Nostrand Van Allen, 1891), 207–209.

9. William Sherman, *Official Records*, Series 1, Vol. 38, Part 5, 551.

10. William E. Crane, "William E. Crane's Daily Journal of Life in the Field during the War of the Rebellion," August 18, 1864 entry, Mss 980, Cincinnati Historical Society, Cincinnati Museum Center; David Evans, *Sherman's Horsemen* (Bloomington: Indiana University Press, 1996), 407–408; *Portrait And Biographical Album of Sedgwick County, Kan.* (Chicago: Chapman Brothers, 1888), 469–471.

11. David Evans, *Sherman's Horsemen*, 412–413; William E. Crane, "William E. Crane's Daily Journal," August 19, 1864; Albert Castel, *Decision in the West: The Atlanta Campaign of 1864* (Lawrence: University Press of Kansas, 1992), 471.

12. *Roster and Record of Iowa Soldiers in the War of the Rebellion*, Vol. IV (Des Moines: Emory H. English, State Printer, E. D. Chassell, State Binder 1910), 858; Albert Castel, *Decision in the West*, Ibid.

13. David Evans, *Sherman's Horsemen*, 431, 432; W. L. Curry "Raid of the Union Cavalry by General Judson Kilpatrick Around the Confederate Army in Atlanta, August 1864," in *Sketches of War History 1861–1865*, Vol. VI, Theodore F. Allen, Edward McKee, and J Gordon Taylor, eds. (Cincinnati: Monfort & Company, 1908), 263–264; Robert Winn letter August 24, 1864, Winn-Cook Family: Papers, 1861–1875 (Mss. A W776), Filson

Historical Society, Louisville, Kentucky; J. A. Nourse, Letter to Minty–February 3, 1903, Robert Minty Papers, Box 1, Folder 3, Civil War Collection, USAHEC, Carlisle, Pennsylvania.

14. Hugh Judson Kilpatrick, *Official Records*, Series 1, Vol. 38, Part 2, 858–859.

15. David Evans, *Sherman's Horsemen*, 402–403; Hugh Judson Kilpatrick, *Official Records*, Series 1, Vol. 38, Part 2, 858–859.

16. Lucien Wulsin, *The Fourth Regiment Ohio Veteran Volunteer Cavalry* (Cincinnati: Fourth Ohio Volunteer Cavalry Association, 1912), 57.

17. Daniel T. Elliott and Tracy M. Dean, *The Nash Farm Battlefield: History and Archaeology* (Savannah, Georgia: The Lamar Institute, 2007), 10–11.

18. Eli Long, *Official Records*, Series 1, Vol. 38, Part 2, 839–840; Robert Minty, *Official Records*, Series 1, Vol. 38, Part 2, 814; David Evans, *Sherman's Horsemen*, 441; William E. Crane, "Bugle Blasts," *Sketches of War History 1861–1865* (MOLLUS, Ohio, Vol. 1) (Cincinnati: Robert Clarke, 1888), 233–51, 247; T. F. Dornblaser, *My Life Story for Young and Old* (Privately printed, 1930), 64; J. A. Nourse, Letter to Minty—February 3, 1903, Robert Minty Papers, Box 1, Folder 3, Civil War Collection, USAHEC, Carlisle, Pennsylvania.

19. W. L. Curry, "Raid of the Union Cavalry Commanded by General Judson Kilpatrick around the Confederate Army at Atlanta," 265.

20. David Evans, *Sherman's Horsemen*, 446; Hugh Judson Kilpatrick, *Official Records*, Series 1, Vol. 38, Part 2, 859; W. S. Scott, "Kilpatrick's Raid Around Atlanta, August 18–22, 1864," *Journal of the Association of the United States Cavalry*, Vol. 3 (1890), 268; Robert Minty, "Raiding Hood's Rear," *National Tribune*, January 22, 1903.

21. David Evans, *Sherman's Horsemen*, 438–450; W. L. Curry, *Four Years in the Saddle: History of First Regiment Ohio Volunteer Cavalry* (Columbus: Champlin Printing Co., 1898), 181; George I. Robinson, "With Kilpatrick Around Atlanta," 222–223.

22. Thomas Crofts, *History of the Service of the Third Ohio Veteran Volunteer Cavalry* (Toledo: Stoneman Press, 1910), 163.

23. Judson Kilpatrick, *Official Records*, Series 1, Vol. 38, Part 2, 859; John McLain, Diary Entry—August 20, 1864, John McLain Papers (c.00111), Michigan State University Archives & Historical Collections, East Lansing.

24. T. F. Dornblaser, *Sabre Strokes of the Pennsylvania Dragoons* (Philadelphia: Lutheran Publication Society, 1884), 181.

25. Joseph Vale, *Minty and the Cavalry*, 350–351; David Evans, *Sherman's Horsemen*, 458–9; L. K. Dunn, August 24, 1864 Letter, Dunn Family Papers, 1854–1977 (D923, folder 4–6), Filson Historical Society, Louisville; W. L. Curry, Letter to J. A. Nourse–March 10, 1903, Robert Minty Papers, Box 1, Folder 5, Civil War Collection, USAHEC, Carlisle, Pennsylvania.

26. James Thompson Diary, August 20, 1864, James Thomson Papers. 1861–1865 [VFM 2167] Ohio Historical Society, Columbus, Ohio; David Evans, *Sherman's Horsemen*, 458–459; J. A. Nourse, Letter to Minty–February 3, 1903, Robert Minty Papers, Box 1, Folder 3, Civil War Collection, USAHEC, Carlisle, Pennsylvania.

27. M. T. Patrick, *Official Records*, Series 1, Vol. 38, Part 5, 615; Joseph Vale, *Minty and the Cavalry*, 343; David Evans, *Sherman's Horsemen*, 467; George I. Robinson, "With Kilpatrick Around Atlanta," 225–226.

28. William Sherman, *Official Records*, Series 1, Vol. 38, Part 5, 641; Eli Long, "Letter from General Long," *Journal of the United States Cavalry Association*, Vol. 3, 1890, 430.

29. George Thomas, *Official Records*, Series 1, Vol. 38, Part 5, 526; William Sherman, *Official Records*, Series 1, Vol. 38, Part 5, 526.

30. William Sherman, *Official Records*, Series 1, Vol. 38, Part 5, 527; Thomas, *Ibid*.

31. George Thomas, *Official Records*, Series 1, Vol. 38, Part 5, 526.

32. Albert Castel, *Decision in the West*, 492.

33. William Sherman, *Official Records*, Series 1, Vol. 38, Part 5, 640.

34. Oliver Howard, *Official Records*, Series 1, Vol. 38, Part 5, 725; Albert Castel, *Decision in the West*, 497.

35. Albert Castel, *Decision in the West*, 498.

36. Judson Kilpatrick, *Official Records*, Series 1, Vol. 38, Part 2, 857.

37. Richard M. McMurry, *Atlanta 1864: The Last Chance for the Confederacy* (Lincoln: University of Nebraska Press, 2000), 172–173.

38. Albert Castel, *Decision in the West*, 510; Thomas H. Martin, *Atlanta and Its Builders: A Comprehensive History of the Gate City of the South*, Vol. 1 (Atlanta: Century Memorial Publishing Co., 1902), 669.

39. George Thomas, *Official Records*, Series 1, Vol. 38, Part 1, 166; Jefferson C. Davis, *Official Records*, Series 1, Vol. 38, Part 1, 513–515.

40. Richard M. McMurry, *Atlanta 1864: The Last Chance for the Confederacy*, 173–174

41. John Witherspoon DuBose, *General Joseph Wheeler and the Army of Tennessee* (New York: The Neale Publishing Co., 1912), 381.

42. William Sherman, *Official Records*, Series 1, Vol. 38, Part 1, 79.

43. Robert Black, *Cavalry Raids of the Civil War* (Mechanicsburg, PA: Stackpole Books, 2004), 66; Rufus Clason, Letter, August 18, 1864, Clason family letters (1862–1865), RG 409, Box 1 FF 1–17, Auburn University Libraries Special Collections & Archives Department. Auburn, Alabama.

44. Robert Black, *Ibid*.

45. James Alex Baggett, *Homegrown Yankees: Tennessee's Union Cavalry in the Civil War* (Baton Rouge: Louisiana State University, 2009), 260–264.

46. W. R. Carter, *History of the First Regiment of Tennessee Volunteer Cavalry* (Knoxville: Gaut-Ogden Co., Printers and Binders, 1902), 192–195; Othniel Gooding, Letter, September 15, 1864, Othniel Gooding Letters (c.00275) Michigan State University Archives & Historical Collections, Michigan State University, East Lansing.

47. Nathan Forrest, *Official Records*, Series 1, Vol. 39, Part 2, 859; Robert Black, *Cavalry Raids of the Civil War*, 68.

48. Thomas Jordan, *Official Records*, Series 1, Vol. 39, Part 1, 495.

49. Thomas Jordan, *Official Records*, Series 1, Vol. 39, Part 1, 495; George Dibrell, *Official Records*, Series 1, Vol. 39, Part 1, 496; Thomas Jordan, Letter to Wife—September 7, 1864, Thomas J. Jordan Civil War Letters

[2066] Box Number: 1, Folder 16, Historical Society of Pennsylvania, Philadelphia, Pennsylvania; F. W. Weatherbee, *The 5th (1st Middle) Tennessee Cavalry Regiment, USA* (Carrollton, MS: Pioneer Publishing Co., 1992), 47–48.
    50. W. L. Elliott, *Official Records*, Series 1, Vol. 39, Part 1, 724.
    51. John Andes and Will McTeer, *Loyal Mountain Troops, The Second and Third Tennessee Volunteer Cavalry* (Maryville, TN: Blount County Genealogical and Historical Society, 1992), 134–137; W. L. Elliott, *Official Records*, Series 1, Vol. 39, Part 1, 724.
    52. L. M. Dayton, *Official Records*, Series 1, Vol. 39, Part 3, 415.
    53. J. H. Wilson, *Official Records*, Series 1, Vol. 39, Part 3, 444.
    54. Ibid.
    55. James Patten, "An Indiana Doctor Marches with Sherman: The Diary of James Comfort Patten," Robert G. Atheurn, ed., *Indiana Magazine of History*, No. 49 (December 1953), 413.
    56. Robert B. Leach, "The Role of Union Cavalry during the Atlanta Campaign," 58, 95.
    57. James Harrison Wilson, *Under the Old Flag*, Vol. II (New York: D. Appleton & Co., 1912), 12–13.
    58. David Evans, *Sherman's Horsemen*, 475–478; Robert B. Leach, "The Role of Union Cavalry During the Atlanta Campaign," 54; W. R. Carter, *History of the First Regiment of Tennessee Volunteer Cavalry*, 187.

Epilogue

    1. William Sherman, *Official Records*, Series 1, Vol. 39, Part 3, 358; Ulysses Grant, *Official Records*, Series 1, Vol. 39, Part 3 , 63; Richard Johnson, *Official Records*, Series 1, Vol. 39, Part 3, 300.
    2. J. H. Wilson, *Official Records*, Series 1, Vol. 39, Part 3, 444.
    3. Reginald Stuart, "The Role of the Cavalry in the Western Theatre of the American Civil War from the Battle of Shiloh to the Tullahoma Campaign," Master's Thesis, 1968, University of British Columbia, Vancouver, British Columbia, 195; Stephen Z. Starr, "Cold Steel: The Sabre and Union Cavalry," in *Battles Lost and Won: Essays from Civil War History*, John T. Hubbell, ed. (Westport, Connecticut: Greenwood Press, 1975), 107–124.
    4. David Stanley, *An American General: The Memoirs of David Sloan Stanley*, Samuel W. Fordyce IV, ed. (Santa Barbara, California: The Narrative Press, 2004), 101; Reginald Stuart, "The Role of the Cavalry in the Western Theatre of the American Civil War from the Battle of Shiloh to the Tullahoma Campaign," 11.
    5. J. H. Wilson, *Official Records*, Series 1, Vol. 49, Part 2, 663.

Appendix A

    1. William Richard Cutter, ed., *American Biography: A New Cyclopedia*, Vol. 2 (New York: American Historical Society Inc., 1918), 196–197.
    2. Marshall Thatcher, *A Hundred Battles in the West: The Second Michigan Cavalry* (Detroit: L. F. Kilroy, Printer, 1884), 124, 152.
    3. Ron Seymour, *The Life of Col. Joseph B. Dorr and his 8th Iowa Cavalry* (eBook, www.8thIowaCav.com), 2012, 160–169, 179; A. A. Stuart, "Colonel Joseph B. Dorr," *Iowa Colonels and Regiments Being a History of Iowa Regiments* (Des Moines: Mills & Company, 1865), 639–650; Don Treichler, *Cold Steel, Raw Courage: Major John Dance and 8th Iowa Cavalry* (Charleston, SC: By the Author, 2012), 158.
    4. William Perrin, *The History of Bourbon, Scott, Harrison and Nicholas Counties, Kentucky* (Chicago: O. L. Baskin & Co., 1882), 457–458; Zachary F. Smith and Mary Rogers Clay, "The Clay Family," Filson Club Publications No. 14 (Louisville, Kentucky: Filson Club, 1899), 213.
    5. S. E. Lathrop, "A Tribute to His Old Commander, Gen La Grange," *Madison Democrat*, May 30, 1915; *Lagrange News*, "Event to Commemorate Nancy Harts," April 3, 2014; Muriel Phillips Joslyn, *Confederate Women* (Gretna, LA: Pelican Publishing, 2004), 49–51.
    6. Roger D. Hunt, *Colonels in Blue—Indiana, Kentucky, Tennessee: A Civil War Biographical Dictionary* (Jefferson, NC: McFarland, 2013), 76.
    7. Thomas Speed, *Union Regiments of Kentucky*, Vol. I (Louisville: The Courier Journal Job Printing, Co., 1897), 73–74; *National Tribune*, "Their Last Resting Place, the Remains of Gens. Rousseau and Watkins Buried at Arlington Cemetery," October 27, 1892, page 7.
    8. *Louisville Courier Journal*, "Col. Faulkner Dead," January 8, 1895, page 5; *Maysville Evening Bulletin*, "The Late Col. Faulkner," January 26, 1895; *Semi-Weekly Interior Journal* (Stanford, Kentucky), "Suicide," January 11, 1895.
    9. "George Crook, Biographical Sketch," George Crook Papers, GA-13, Rutherford B. Hayes Presidential Library, Fremont, Ohio.
    10. *National Tribune*, "Generals," November 5, 1903, 5; Ezra J. Warner, *Generals in Blue: Lives of Union Commanders* (Baton Rouge: Louisiana State University Press, 1992), 168.
    11. *New York Times*, "Death of Gen Eli Long, January 6, 1903"; Ezra J. Warner, *Generals in Blue: Lives of Union Commanders* (Baton Rouge: Louisiana State University Press, 1992), 283–284; Whitelaw Reid, *Ohio in the War: Her Statesmen, Her Generals, and Soldiers*, Vol. I (New York: Moore, Wilstach & Baldwin, 1868), 862.
    12. William Henry Powell, editor, *Officers of the Army and Navy (Volunteer) Who Served in the Civil War* (Philadelphia: Hamersly and Company, 1893), 313–314; *Salt Lake Tribune*, "General Minty at Rest," August 29, 1906, 3; *Salt Lake Herald*, "Another Veteran Gone: News Received in Ogden of the Death of General R. H. G. Minty," August 25, 1906, 7; "Col. R. H. G. Minty and the 4th Michigan Cavalry," Reprinted from the *Louisville Journal*, Othniel Gooding Letters (c.00275) Michigan State University Archives & Historical Collections, Michigan State University, East Lansing.
    13. Anonymous, *Portrait and Biographical Album of Sedgwick County, Kansas* (Chicago: Chapman Brothers, 1888), 469–471.
    14. Steven Cox, "Chattanooga Was His Town: The Life of General John T. Wilder," *Chattanooga Regional Historical Quarterly*, Vol. 7, No. 1 (2004), 1–19.
    15. *Lebanon Pioneer*, "Col. Abram O. Miller, Brief

Biography of the Man Who Is Being Honored Today," September 21, 1911, 12.

16. Spencer Tucker, editor, *American Civil War: The Definitive Encyclopedia and Document Collection*, Vol. 6 (Santa Barbara: ABC–Clio LLC, 2013), 1074; "Hugh Judson Kilpatrick," in Ohio Civil War Central, Retrieved June 30, 2014, from Ohio Civil Central: http://www.ohiocivilwarcentral.com/entry.php?rec=1028.

17. George W. Cullum, *Biographical Register of the Officers and Graduates of the United States Military Academy*, Vol. IV (Cambridge: The Riverside Press, 1901), 92; *Twenty-Ninth Annual Reunion of the Association I Graduates of the United States Military Academy* (Saginaw: Seemann & Peters, Printers And Binders, 1898), 83–84.

18. Rossiter Johnson, editor in chief, *The Twentieth Century Biographical Dictionary of Notable Americans* (Boston: Plimpton Press, 1904), n.p.

19. *Columbus Dispatch*, "Death of C. C. Smith," February 7, 1877.

20. Jack Welsh, *Medical Histories of Union Generals* (Kent: Kent State University Press, 1996), 233; Ralph Emerson Twitchell, *The Leading Facts of New Mexican History*, Vol. II (Cedar Rapids: The Torch Press, 1912), 410–412; William H. Powell, *Officers of the Army and Navy Who Served in the Civil War* (Philadelphia: R. J. Hamersly, 1893), 221.

21. "Bvt. Maj.-Gen. Washington Lafayette Elliott," *Reunion of the Society of the Army of the Cumberland, Nineteenth Reunion: Chicago, Illinois* (Cincinnati: Robert Clarke & Co., 1889), 184–185.

22. Anonymous, *The Union Army*, Vol. VIII (Madison: Federal Publishing Co., 1908), 252; Dennis W. Belcher, *General David S. Stanley, USA* (Jefferson, NC: McFarland, 2014), 217–239.

Bibliography

Primary Sources

Published Letters, Diaries, Journals and Other Manuscripts

Bartmess, J. W. "Jacob W. Bartmess Civil War Letters." *Indiana Magazine of History*, Vol. 52, No. 2 (1956), 157–186.

Beatty, John. *The Citizen Soldier: The Memoirs of a Civil War Volunteer*. Lincoln: Bison Books, University of Nebraska Press, 1998.

Chadwick, Mary Jane. *Incidents of the War: The Civil War Journal of Mary Jane Chadwick*. Nancy Rohr, ed. Huntsville: SilverThread Publishing, 2005.

Clark, William Allen. "'Please Send Stamps': The Civil War Letters of William Allen Clark." Part IV, ed. Margaret Black Tatum. *Indiana Magazine of History*, Vol. 91, No. 4 (1995), 407–437.

Fobes, George. "An Account of the Mutiny in the Anderson Cavalry, at Nashville, Tenn, December 1862." In *Leaves of a Trooper's Dairy*, John Williams. Philadelphia: Published by Author, 1869.

Graf, Leroy, and Ralph Haskins, eds. *Papers of Andrew Johnson*, Vol. 6. Knoxville: University of Tennessee Press, 1983.

Kelly, Orr, and Mary Davies Kelly. *Dream's End: Two Iowa Brothers in the Civil War*. Tokyo: Kodansha International, 1998.

Longacre, Glenn V., and John E. Haas, ed. *To Battle for God and the Right: the Civil War: Letterbooks of Emerson Opdycke*. Urbana: University of Illinois Press, 2003.

Nott, Charles C. *Sketches of the War: A Series of Letters to the North Moore Street School of New York*. New York: Anson D. F. Randolph, 1865.

Patten, James. "An Indiana Doctor Marches With Sherman: The Diary of James Comfort Patten." Robert G. Atheurn. *Indiana Magazine of History*, No. 49 (December 1953), 405–422.

Prickitt, Daniel. *3rd Ohio Cavalry, Diary*. Col. E. D. Stoltz, ed. Archbold, Ohio: Edwin Stoltz, 1988.

Reynolds, Clark G. "The Civil and Indian War Diaries of Eugene Marshall, Minnesota Volunteer." Master's Thesis, Duke University, Durham, NC, 1963.

Shelly, Joseph Frederick. "The Shelly Papers." Fanny Anderson, ed. *Indiana Magazine of History*, Vol. 44, No. 2 (June 1948): 181–198.

Sherman, William T. *Home Letters of General Sherman*. New York: Charles Scribner's Sons, 1909.

Smith, Theodore Clarke. *The Life and Letters of James A. Garfield*. New Haven: Yale University Press, 1925.

Smith, Theodore Clarke. *The Life and Letters of James Abram Garfield*, Vol. 1. New Haven, Connecticut: Archon Books, 1968.

Treadway, Charles. "The Letters of Charles Wesley Treadway." *Foot Prints: Past and Present*, Vol. 9. Olney, IL: Richland County Genealogical and Historical Society, 1986.

Turchin, Nadine. "A Monotony Full of Sadness, The Diary of Nadine Turchin, May, 1863–April, 1864." Mary Ellen McElligott, ed. *Journal of the Illinois State Historical Society*, Vol. 70 (1977), 27–89.

Williamson, Peter. "The Letters of Peter J. Williamson (II)." Henry Lee Swint, ed. *Wisconsin Magazine of History*, Vol. 26, No. 4 (June 1943) 433–448.

Unpublished Letters, Diaries, Journals and Other Manuscripts

Alabama Dept. of Archives and History, Montgomery
Bolling Hall family papers; Box Number LPR39, Vault box 52; Folder Number 8; Folder Title: Bolling Hall (1813–1897) letters, 1864 January–March.

Auburn University Libraries Special Collections & Archives Department Auburn, Alabama
Clason Family Letters (1862–1865), RG 409, Box 1 FF 1–17.

Bentley Historical Library, University of Michigan, Ann Arbor
John B. Bennett, Papers.
Henry Mortimer Hempstead, Papers and Diary (1832–1916).
Morris Fitch Papers.
Elisha Mix Papers, 1818–1898.
Slayton Family Papers.

Bowling Green State University, William T Jerome Library, Bowling Green, Ohio
George Kryder, Diary, MS 163 George Kryder (1834–1925).
James H. M. Perry Papers, MMS 1457.

Briscoe Center for American History, University of Texas at Austin
Crimmins (Martin Lalor) Papers, David S. Stanley, "David Stanley Diary, United States 2nd Dragoons of a March from Fort Smith, Arkansas, to San Diego, California, made in 1853," Accession No.: 1936; 1950.

Cincinnati Historical Society, Cincinnati Museum Center
Crane, William E. "William E. Crane's Daily Journal of Life in the Field during the War of the Rebellion," Mss. 980.

Duke University, David M Rubenstein Rare Book & Manuscript Library, Durham, North Carolina
Benjamin F, Nourse, Diary.

Filson Historical Society, Louisville, Kentucky
Chesley D. Bailey—Collection (1863–1864). Call no.: Mss. A B155.
Dunn Family Papers, 1854–1977 (D923, folder 4–6).
Lewis Hanback, Papers 1839–1897, A H233.
Sowle, *Military Record of C. H. Sowle*, unpublished, Manuscript C. S, undated.
Elijah Watts, "Biographical Note" and "Chickamauga Campaign" (hand written account, undated), Watts, Elijah S, Papers. 1861–1907, Mss./A/W349.
Winn-Cook Family: Papers, 1861–1875 (Mss. A W776).

Indiana Historical Society, William Henry Smith Memorial Library, Indianapolis
Daniel Wait Howe, January 31, 1863 Diary Entry, Box 1, F 16, Army Diary of Captain (M148).
Gresiet, Alva. "Three Years in Dixie: Personal Adventures, Scenes and Incidents of the March—The Journal of Alva C. Griest," Alva Griest Collection, Folder 2, Indiana Historical Society, Indianapolis, Indiana.

Kalamazoo College, Kalamazoo, Michigan
Eugene Bronson Collection.

Michigan Historical Society, Lansing
Henry Albert Potter Collection. MS 91–480, Accession Box 461 Folder 2.
Frank L. Vogel Collection, Diary, MS 67–111, Accession Box 12 Folder 6.

Michigan State University Archives & Historical Collections, Michigan State University, East Lansing
Othniel Gooding Letters (c.00275).
John McLain Diary and Papers (c.00111).

Minnesota Historical Society, St. Paul
Robert Burns Letters (Mss. M642).

Missouri Historical Society, St. Louis
James Edwin Love Papers (1859–1865) ARC A0940.
McEwen Family Papers A 269.

Monroe Ohio Historical Society, Woodsfield, Ohio.
Robert Burr, "The Letters of Robert Burr."

Nashville Public Library, 615 Church Street, Nashville, Tennessee
Peter J. Williamson Letters (PJW-F, 59), Special Collections Division.

National Archives, Washington, D.C.
Bradley, William. Bradley Court Martial, May 14–24, 1864, Record Group (RG) 153, Adjutant General's Office, Court Martial Case Files, 1809–1854, case number LL 2413.
Correspondence, First Cavalry Division, Record Group 393, Part 2, Number 2305.
General Orders, Cavalry. Record Group 393, Part 2, Number 2472.
Letters Sent by the Chief of Cavalry, Record Group 393, Part 2, Number 2460.
Letters and Orders by the Chief of Cavalry, Record Group 393, Part 2, Number 2469.
Letters Sent, Second Cavalry Division, Record Group 393, Part 2, Number 2500.
Letters Sent, First Cavalry Division, Record Group 393, Part 2, Number 2527.
Organization Charts, Record Group 393, Part 2, Number 2477.
Special Orders, Cavalry, Record Group 393, Part 2, Number 2473.
Stanley, David. Personnel Records ACP 000183, National Archives Microfiche.
Stanley, David. Union General Papers. Record Group 94, Entry 159, Box 28.
Telegram Sent by Chief of Cavalry, Record Group 393, Part 2, Number 2463, Vol. 19/31.
William T. Hoblitzell Court Martial, July 1864, Record Group (RG) 153, Adjutant General's Office, Court Martial Case Files, 1809–1854, case number NN-2774.
William T. Hoblitzell Court Martial, June, 1864, Record Group (RG) 153, Adjutant General's Office, Court Martial Case Files, 1809–1854, case number NN-3269.

Ohio Historical Society, Columbus, Ohio
David Tod, *Correspondence to the Governor and Adjutant General, 1861–1866, Vol. 34, Series 147–39: 90*, Ohio Historical Society, Columbus, Ohio.
James Thompson. Diary and Papers, 1861–1865 [VFM 2167].

Pennsylvania Historical Society, Philadelphia
George F. Parry Family Vols., Collection 3694.
Simon Gratz Collection H250.
Thomas J. Jordan Civil War Letters (2066).
Thomas McCahan Papers and Diary (Am. 6092).

Rutherford B. Hayes Presidential Library, Fremont, Ohio
George Crook Papers, GA-13.

State Historical Society of Iowa, Des Moines
Daniel C. Bischard Letters (005: F08; N17/8/4).
George Healy Papers (Box 006, Folder 22).
Private Alex Sackett Letters (N16/3/5; B/HF).
Wesley G. L. Templeton Collection (Vol. 1B, N16/2/4).

State Historical Society of Wisconsin, Madison
Charles Perry Goodrich, "Letters from Home from the First Wisconsin Cavalry," Richard N. Larson editor (Madison: State Historical Society of Wisconsin, not published).
Quiner's Scrapbook, Vol. 10, Correspondence, Mss. 600; WIHVQ500-A.

Stones River National Park, Technical Information Center, Murfreesboro, TN
Elbert J. Squire, Letters.
George Garrett, Letters.
Gerould, Otis Gibson. Diary of Otis Gibson Gerould (1830–1918), 1863 Unpublished, Pennsylvania Regimental Files.

Tennessee State Library and Archives, Nashville
Charles Alley. Civil War Diary of Lieutenant Charles Alley, October 9, 1863 (Publisher, [n.p., n.d.]).
Lucy Virginia Smith, "Lucy Virginia French Diaries" entry for April 26, 1863, Microfilm 1816.
Mary Pearre, Diary—February 9, 1863, Microfilm Accession Number: 1957.

U.S. Army Heritage and Education Center, Carlisle, Pennsylvania

Charles Marvin Letter, Civil War Collection, Box 76, Folder 6.
David Ayers Papers, Civil War Collection, Box 3, Folder 19.
David Q. Curry, Papers, Civil War Collection, Box 30, Folder 3.
Eli Long, Diary and Papers 1855–1892, Civil War Collection.
Frances W. Reed Papers, Civil War Times Illustrated Collection.
Heber S. Thompson, Diary, Harrisburg Civil War Roundtable Collection.
Hiram Chapman, Civil War Collection, Papers, Box 22, Folder 6.
John Brandon Papers, Civil War Collection, Box 14, Folder 8.
John Stutsman, Letters, Civil War Times Illustrated Collection.
Michael Brown Letters, Civil War Collection Box 16, Folder 13.
Robert Minty Papers, Civil War Collection, Box 1 and 2.
Thomas McCahan, "History of the Relics of the War," Harrisburg Civil War Roundtable Collection, McCahan Family Papers.

University of California Los Angeles Library, Department of Special Collections

William S. Rosecrans Papers: 1810–1920, Collection 66.

University of Georgia, Hargett Rare Book & Manuscript Library, Athens, Georgia

Joshua Breyfogle Family Papers; MS 3124 to MS 3129.

University of Notre Dame Archives (UNDA), Notre Dame

Conyngham, David Power, Papers (CON), "Soldiers of the Cross," (unpublished).

University of Tennessee, Knoxville

Julius E. Thomas Diary, 1863–1864, Julius E. Thomas Collection, MS.2720.

Wabash College, Crawfordsville, Indiana

Henry Campbell. "Three Years in the Saddle: a Diary of the Civil War," Unpublished.

Western Michigan University, Kalamazoo, Michigan

Augustus L. Yenner. Papers and Diary (1837–1924).

Regimental Histories

Andes, John, and Will McTeer. *Loyal Mountain Troops, The Second and Third Tennessee Volunteer Cavalry.* Maryville, Tennessee: Blount County Genealogical and Historical Society, 1992.
Bailey, Chester. *The Mansfield Men in the Seventh Pennsylvania Cavalry, Eighth Regiment.* Mansfield, Pennsylvania: Published by Author, 1986.
Bergmann, Kurt D. *Brackett's Battalion: Minnesota Cavalry in the Civil War and Dakota War.* St. Paul: Borealis Books, 2004.
Burke, Timothy M. *The Fifth Ohio Volunteer Cavalry: A Story of Citizen Soldiers, Civil War Politics and Southwest Ohio.* Raleigh: Lulu Publishing, 2010.
Carter, W. R. *History of the First Regiment of Tennessee Volunteer Cavalry.* Knoxville: Gaut-Ogden Co., Printers and Binders, 1902.
Crofts, Thomas. *History of the Service of the Third Ohio Veteran Volunteer Cavalry.* Toledo: Stoneman Press, 1910.
Curry, W. L. *Four Years in the Saddle: History of the First Regiment Ohio Volunteer Cavalry.* Columbus: Champlin Printing Co., 1898.
Dornblaser, T. F. *Sabre Strokes of the Pennsylvania Dragoons in the War of 1861–1865. Interspersed with Personal Reminiscences.* Philadelphia: Lutheran Publication Society, 1884.
Eckel, Alexander. *History of the Fourth Tennessee Cavalry.* Johnson City, Tennessee: Overmountain Press, 2001.
Historical Sketch of the Chicago Board of Trade Battery. Chicago: The Henneberry Co. Publishers, 1902.
Mead, Homer. *The Eighth Iowa Cavalry in the Civil War: Autobiography and Personal Recollections of Homer Mead.* Carthage, IL: S.C. Davidson, 1925.
A Military Record of Battery D, First Ohio Veteran Volunteers, Light Artillery. Oil City, Pennsylvania: The Derrick Publishing Co., 1908.
Pape-Findley, Nancy. *The Invincibles: The Story of Fourth Ohio Veteran Volunteer Cavalry.* Tecumseh, Michigan: Blood Road Publishing, 2002.
Pickerill, W. N. *History of the Third Indiana Cavalry.* Indianapolis: Aetna Printing Co., 1906.
Poole, John Randolph. *Cracker Cavaliers: The 2nd Georgia Cavalry under Wheeler and Forrest.* Macon: Mercer University Press, 2000.
Reiff, J. C. ed. *History of the Fifteenth Pennsylvania Volunteer Cavalry.* Philadelphia: Society of the Fifteenth Pennsylvania Cavalry, 1906.
Seymour, Ron. *The Life of Col. Joseph B. Dorr and His 8th Iowa Cavalry.* Self-published eBook, www.8thIowaCav.com, 2012.
Sipes, William. *History and Roster of the 7th Pennsylvania Veteran Volunteers.* Pottsville: Miners' Journal Print, 1905.
Treichler, Don. *Cold Steel, Raw Courage: Major John Dance and 8th Iowa Cavalry.* Charleston, SC: By the Author, 2012.
Vale, Joseph. *Minty and the Cavalry: A History of Cavalry Campaigns in the Western Armies.* Harrisburg, Pennsylvania: Edwin K. Myers, Printer and Binder, 1886.
Weatherbee, F. W. *The 5th (1st Middle) Tennessee Cavalry Regiment, USA.* Carrollton, MS: Pioneer Publishing Co., 1992.
Wulsin, Lucien. *The Fourth Regiment Ohio Veteran Volunteer Cavalry.* Cincinnati: Fourth Ohio Volunteer Cavalry Association, 1912.

Official Documents

United States Census

United States War Department, *Cavalry Tactics*, Vols. 1–3. Philadelphia: J. B. Lippincott, & Co. 1862.
The War of the Rebellion. A Compilation of the Official Records of the Union and Confederate Armies. Washington, D.C.: U.S. Government Printing Office, 1880–1901.

Journals

Bearss, Edwin. "Rousseau's Raid on the Montgomery and West Point Railroad." *Alabama Historical Quar-*

terly, Vol. 25, Nos. 1&2 (Spring and Summer 1963), 7–48.
Bourasaw, Noel V. "Arthur C. Seidell, Civil War Veteran and Builder in Old Woolley." *Skagit River Journal of History & Folklore*, 2000.
Bradley, Michael. "Tullahoma: The Wrongfully Forgotten Campaign." *Blue and Grey*, Volume XXVII, No. 1 (2010), 6–25.
Bradley, Michael. "Varying Results of Cavalry Fighting: Western Flank vs. Eastern Flank." *Blue and Grey*, Vol. XXVII, No. 1 (2010), 21.
Brownlow, J. "More on 'Raw Courage.'" McMurry Richard, ed. *Civil War Times Illustrated* (Oct. 1975), 36–38.
Cox, Steven. "Chattanooga Was His Town: The Life of General John T. Wilder." *Chattanooga Regional Historical Quarterly*, Vol. 7, No. 1 (2004), 1–19.
Curry, W. L. "The Raid of the Confederate Cavalry through Central Tennessee." *Journal of the United States Cavalry Association*, Vol. 19 (1908/1909), 815–835.
Densmore, Frances. "The Garrard Family in Frontenac." *Minnesota History*, XIV (Mar. 1933), 31–43.
East, Earnest. "Lincoln's Russian General." *Journal of the Illinois State Historical Society*. Vol. 52, No. 1 (1959): 106–122.
Evans, David S. "Kenner Garrard's Georgia Romp." *America's Civil War*, Vol. 15, No. 1 (March 2002), 44–50.
Fretwell, Mark E. "Rousseau's Alabama Raid." *Alabama Historical Quarterly*, Vol. 18, No. 4 (Winter 1956), 526–551.
Groce, William Wharton. "Major General John A. Wharton." *The Southwestern Historical Quarterly*, Vol. 19, No. 3 (Jan. 1916), 271–278.
Harris, Moses. "Some Thoughts on Equipment." *Journal of the United States Cavalry Association*, Vol. 4 (1891), 166–178.
Long, Eli. "Letter from General Long." *Journal of the United States Cavalry Association*, Vol. 3 (1890), 428–430.
Mann, Frederick. "Items and Notes." *The Medical Age*, Vol. 19, No. 10 (1901), 383–390.
Pike, Benjamin H. "I Have Commited [sic] a Wrong by Coming Here." *Civil War Times Illustrated* (June 2000): 16, 68–70 & 75–77.
Scott, W. S. "Kilpatrick's Raid Around Atlanta, August 18–22d, 1874." *Journal of the Association of the United States Cavalry*, Vol. 3 (1890), 263–270.
Smith, Frank. "A Maine Boy in the Tenth Ohio Cavalry," *Maine Bugle*, Vol. 4 (1897): 11–21.
Tullidge, Edward, ed. "Governor Murray and Family," *Tullidge Quarterly Magazine*, Vol. 1, No. 3 (1881), 496–501.

Newspapers

Chicago Times
Columbus Dispatch, Columbus, Ohio
Daily Commonwealth, Frankfort, Kentucky
The Daily Wabash Express, Terra-Haute, Indiana
Delphi Journal, Delphi, Indiana
Dubuque Times
Harper's Weekly
Lagrange Daily News, Lagrange, Georgia
Lancaster Daily Evening Express, Lancaster, Pennsylvania
Lebanon Pioneer, Lebanon, Indiana
Louisville Courier Journal, Louisville, Kentucky
Madison Democrat, Madison, Wisconsin
Maysville Evening Bulletin, Maysville, Kentucky
Milwaukee Journal
Mobile Register and Advertiser
Nashville Daily Press
National Tribune, Washington, D.C.
New York Times
Ohio Statesman, Columbus, Ohio
Salt Lake Herald
Salt Lake Tribune
Semi-Weekly Interior Journal, Stanford, Kentucky
The Vevay Reveille, Vevay, Indiana
Western Citizen, Paris, Kentucky

Other Sources

Anderson, William M. "The Union Side of Thompson's Station." *The Battle of Stones River*, Vol. 4, Timothy Johnson, ed. Nashville: Tennessee Historical Society, 2012.
Atkins, Sam. "With Sherman's Cavalry." In *Military Essays and Recollections, Volume 2. 1894*. Military Order of the Loyal Legion of the United States, Commandery of the State of Illinois. Reprint. London: Forgotten Books, 2013.
Avena, Dianna. *Roswell: History, Haunts and Legends*. Charleston, SC: History Press, 2007.
Baggett, James Alex. *Homegrown Yankees: Tennessee's Union Cavalry in the Civil War*. Baton Rouge: Louisiana State University, 2009.
Ballard, Michael. *The Battle of Tupelo, Mississippi—July 14 & 15, 1864*. Tupelo: Northeast Mississippi Historical & Genealogical Society, 2009.
Bates, Samuel *History of the Pennsylvania Volunteers, 1861–65*. Harrisburg: B. Singerly, State Printer, 1870.
Belfield, Henry H. "My Sixty Days in Hades. In Hades, Not in Hell—Andersonville Was Hell." In *Military Essays And Recollections Papers Read before the Commandery of the State of Illinois, Military Order of the Loyal Legion of the United States*, Vol. III. Chicago: The Dial Press, 1899.
Bearss, Edwin C. *Cavalry Operations—Battle of Stones River*, Unpublished. Stones River National Park, Technical Information Center, 1959.
Bearss, Edwin C. "Cavalry Operations in the Stones River Campaign." *The Battle of Stones River*, Vol. 4, Timothy Johnson, ed. Nashville: Tennessee Historical Society, 2012.
Belcher, Dennis W. *General David S. Stanley, USA*. Jefferson, NC: McFarland, 2014.
Beyer, Walter F., and Oscar F. Keydel. *Deeds of Valor: How America's Heroes Won the Medal of Honor*. Detroit: The Perrien-Keydel Company, 1901.
Bickham, William D. *Rosecrans' Campaign with the Fourteenth Army Corps, of the Army of the Cumberland*. Cincinnati: Moore Wilstach, Keys & Co., 1863.
Black, Robert. *Cavalry Raids of the Civil War*. Mechanicsburg, PA: Stackpole Books, 2004
Bobrick, Benson. *Master of War: The Life of George H. Thomas*. New York: Simon & Schuster, 2009.

Botsford, Isaac. "Narrative of Brackett's Battalion of Cavalry." In *Minnesota in the Civil and Indian Wars, 1861–1865* by Minnesota Legislature, eds. St. Paul: Pioneer Press, 1890.
Bradley, Michael. *Tullahoma: The 1863 Campaign for the Control of Middle Tennessee*. Shippensburg, Pennsylvania: White Mane Publishing Company, 1999.
Brandt, Robert S. "Lightning and Rain in Middle Tennessee: The Tullahoma Campaign of June-July 1863," *The Battle of Stones River*, Vol. 4, Timothy Johnson, ed. Nashville: Tennessee Historical Society, 2012.
Brewer, Richard J. "The Tullahoma Campaign: Operational Insights." Master Thesis, U.S. Army Command and General Staff College, Leavenworth, Kansas, 1978.
"Bvt. Maj.-Gen. Washington Lafayette Elliott." In *Reunion of the Society of the Army of the Cumberland, Nineteenth Reunion: Chicago, Illinois*. Cincinnati: Robert Clarke & Co., 1889.
Broome, Doyle D. "Intelligence Operations of the Army of the Cumberland During the Tullahoma and Chickamauga Campaigns." Master's Thesis, U.S. Army Command and General Staff College, Leavenworth, KS, 1989,
Castel, Albert. *Decision in the West: The Atlanta Campaign of 1864*. Lawrence: University Press of Kansas, 1992.
The Catalogue and History of Sigma Chi. Chicago: Published by the Fraternity, 1890.
Chapin, John. "At Chickamauga." In *Reunions of the First Ohio Volunteer Cavalry*. Columbus: Landon Printing Co., 1891.
Commemorative Biographical Encyclopedia of Dauphin County, PA. Chambersburg, PA: J. M. Runk & Co., 1896.
Connolly, James. *Three Years in the Army of the Cumberland*, ed. Paul Angle. Bloomington: Indiana University Press, 1959.
Cox, Rowland. "Snake Creek Gap and Atlanta." In *Personal Recollections of the War of the Rebellion*, A. Noel Blakeman, ed. New York: G. Putnam & Sons, 1897.
Cozzens, Peter. *No Better Place to Die: The Battle of Stones River*. Urbana: University of Illinois Press, 1991.
Cozzens, Peter. *The Shipwreck of Their Hopes: The Battle for Chattanooga*. Urbana: University of Illinois Press, 1994.
Cozzens, Peter. *This Terrible Sound: The Battle of Chickamauga*. Urbana: University of Illinois Press, 1992.
Crane, William E. "Bugle Blasts." *Sketches of War History 1861–1865* (MOLLUS, Ohio, Volume 1). Cincinnati: Robert Clarke, 1888.
Crook, George. *General George Crook: His Biography*. Norman: University of Oklahoma Press, 1960.
Cullum, George W. *Biographical Register of the Officers and Graduates of the US Military Academy*. New York: D. Van Nostrand, 1868–79.
Cullum, George W. *Biographical Register of the Officers and Graduates of the United States Military Academy*, Vol. IV. Cambridge: The Riverside Press, 1901.
Curry, W. L. *The Raid of the Confederate Cavalry through Central Tennessee, October 1863*. Columbus: The Ohio Commandery of the Loyal Legion, MOLLUS, 1908.
Curry, W. L. "Raid of the Union Cavalry by General Judson Kilpatrick Around the Confederate Army in Atlanta, August 1864." In *Sketches of War History 1861–1865*, Theodore F. Allen, Edward McKee, and J. Gordon Taylor eds. Vol. VI. Cincinnati: Monfort & Co., 1908.
Cutter, William Richard, ed. *American Biography: A New Cyclopedia*, Vol. 2. New York: American Historical Society Inc., 1918.
Daniel, Larry J. *Days of Glory: The Army of the Cumberland, 1861–1865*. Baton Rouge: Louisiana State University Press, 2006.
Dalessandro, Robert J. "Major General William S. Rosecrans and the Transformation of the Staff of the Army of the Cumberland: A Case Study." Strategy Research Project, U.S. Army War College, Carlisle Barracks, Pennsylvania, 2002.
Dalessandro, Robert J. "Morale in the Army of the Cumberland During the Tullahoma and Chickamauga Campaigns." Master's Thesis, U.S. Army Command and General Staff College, Leavenworth, Kansas, 1980.
Davis, Stephen. *Atlanta Will Fall: Sherman, Joe Johnston, and the Yankee Heavy Battalions*. Wilmington, DE: Scholarly Resources, 2001, 43.
Dornblaser, T. F. *My Life Story for Young and Old*. Privately printed, 1930.
DuBose, John Witherspoon. *General Joseph Wheeler and the Army of Tennessee*. New York: The Neale Publishing Company, 1912.
Duke, Basil. *Morgan's Cavalry*. New York: The Neale Publishing Co., 1909.
Dunn, Jacob Piatt. *Memorial and Genealogical Record of Representative Citizens of Indiana*. Indianapolis: B. F. Brown Publisher, 1912.
Dyer, Frederick H. *A Compendium of the War of the Rebellion*. Des Moines: The Dyer Publishing Company, 1908.
Edison, Thomas. *John Hunt Morgan and His Raiders*. Lexington: University Press of Kentucky, 1985.
Egle, William Henry, A. S. Dudley, Harry Huber, R. H. Schively, eds. *Commemorative Biographical Encyclopedia of Dauphin County, Pennsylvania*. Chambersburg, PA: J.M. Runk & Co., 1896.
Elliott, Daniel T., and Tracy M. Dean. *The Nash Farm Battlefield: History and Archaeology*. Savannah, Georgia: The Lamar Institute, 2007.
Evans, Clement, ed. *Confederate Military History*, Vol. 1. Atlanta: Confederate Publishing Company, 1899.
Evans, David. *Sherman's Horsemen*. Bloomington: Indiana University Press, 1996.
Fitch, John. *Annals of the Army of the Cumberland*. Philadelphia: J. B. Lippincott & Co., 1864.
Foote, Lorien. *The Gentlemen and the Roughs: Violence, Honor, and Manhood in the Union Army*. New York: New York University Press, 2010.
Garrard, Kenner, and Lewis Edward Nolan. *Nolan's System for Training Cavalry Horses*. New York: D. Van Nostrand, 1862.
Grant, Ulysses Simpson. *Personal Memoirs of U. S. Grant*. New York: Charles L. Webster & Co., 1894.
Greeno, Charles. "Address of Lieut.-Col. Charles L. Greeno." In *Pennsylvania at Chickamauga and Chattanooga*, George W. Skinner, ed. Harrisburg, Pennsylvania: William Stanley Ray, State Printer of Pennsylvania, 1897.
Hall, Richard. *Patriots in Disguise: Women Warriors in the Civil War*. New York: Paragon House, 1994.

Hamilton, William Douglas. *Recollections of a Cavalryman of the Civil War After Fifty Years 1861–1865.* Columbus: The F. J. Heer Printing Co., 1915.

Harden, Samuel, and John Spahr. *Early Life and Times in Boone County, Indiana.* Indianapolis: Carlon & Hollenbeck, 1887.

Hartley, Chris. *Stoneman's Raid, 1865.* Winston-Salem: John F. Blair Publisher, 2010.

Hazzard, George. *Hazzard's History of Henry County, Indiana, 1822–1906, Volume 1.* New Castle, Indiana: George Hazzard, 1906.

Heitman, Francis Bernard. *Historical Register and Dictionary of the United States Army 1789–1903.* Washington, D.C.: U.S. Government Printing Office, 1903.

Howard, Oliver O. *The Autobiography of Oliver Otis Howard.* New York: Baker & Taylor, 1907.

Hunt, Roger. *Colonels in Blue—Indiana, Kentucky and Tennessee.* Jefferson, NC: McFarland, 2013.

Johnson, Richard. *A Soldier's Reminiscences in Peace and War.* Philadelphia: J. B. Lippincott & Co., 1886.

Johnson, Rossiter, ed. in chief. *The Twentieth Century Biographical Dictionary of Notable Americans.* Boston: Plimpton Press, 1904.

Johnston, Joseph. *Narrative of Military Operations Directed During the Civil War.* New York: D. Appleton, 1874.

Johnston, Joseph. "Opposing Sherman's Advance to Atlanta." In *Battles and Leaders,* Vol. IV. New York: The Century Company, 1888.

Jones, Terry L. *Historical Dictionary of the Civil War,* Vol. 1. Lanham, Maryland: Scarecrow Press Inc., 2011.

Jordan, Thomas. "Battle of Thompson's Station and the Trial of the Spies at Franklin, Tennessee." In *United Service,* Vol. III. Philadelphia: L. R. Hamersly & Co., 1890.

Jordan, Thomas, and J. Pryor. *The Campaigns of Lieut.-Gen. Nathan B. Forrest of Forrest's Cavalry.* New Orleans: Blelock & Co., 1868.

Joslyn, Muriel Phillips. *Confederate Women.* Gretna, Louisiana: Pelican Publishing Company, 2004.

Kelly, James Edward. *Generals in Bronze: Interviewing the Commanders of the Civil War,* William B. Styple, ed. Kearney, NJ: Bell Grove, 2005.

Kennett, John. "History of the First Cavalry Division from November 1, 1862, to January 1, 1863." In *G.A.R. War Papers,* 337–359. Cincinnati: Fred C. Jones Post, 1891.

Kniffin, Gilbert. *The Battle of Stone's River. Battles and Leaders of the Civil War.* Volume 3. New York: The Century Company, 1888.

Lanier, Robert Lanier. *Photographic History of the Civil War.* New York: The Review of Reviews Co., 1911.

Lamers, William. *The Edge of Glory: A Biography of General William S. Rosecrans, U.S.A.* New York: Harcourt, Brace & World, Inc., 1961.

Larsen, James. *Sergeant Larson, 4th Cavalry.* San Antonio: Southern Literary Institute, 1935.

Leach, Robert B. "The Role of Union Cavalry during the Atlanta Campaign." Master's Thesis, U.S. Army Command and General Staff College, Fort Leavenworth, Kansas.

Levin, H., ed. *Lawyers and Lawmakers of Kentucky.* Chicago: Lewis Publishing Co., 1897.

Londa, John. *The Role of Union Cavalry during the Chickamauga Campaign.* Master's Thesis, U.S. Army Command and General Staff College, Leavenworth, Kansas, 1980.

Longacre, Edward G. *A Soldier to the Last: Maj. Gen. Joseph Wheeler in Blue and Gray.* Washington: Potomac Books Inc., 2007.

Magrid, Paul. *George Crook: From the Redwoods to Appomattox.* Norman: University of Oklahoma Press, 2011.

Martin, Thomas H. *Atlanta and Its Builders: A Comprehensive History of the Gate City of the South,* Vol. 1. Atlanta: Century Memorial Publishing Company, 1902.

Mattox, Absolom. *History of the Cincinnati Society of Ex-Army and Navy Officers.* Cincinnati: Peter G. Thompson Publisher, 1880.

McClurg, Alexander C. "An American Soldier, Minor Millikin." In *Military Essays and Recollections: Papers Read Before the Commandery of the State of Illinois.* Chicago: A. C. McClurg & Co., 1894.

McMurry, Richard M. *Atlanta 1864: The Last Chance for the Confederacy.* Lincoln: University of Nebraska Press, 2000.

Minty, Robert, and Horace Gray, "Michigan to her Fourth Regiment of Cavalry." In *History of the Michigan Organizations at Chickamauga, Chattanooga, and Missionary Ridge,* Charles Eugene Belknap, ed. Lansing: Robert Smith Printing Co., 1899.

Moore, Frank, ed. "General Rousseau's Expedition." In *Rebellion Record,* Vol. 11. New York: D. Van Nostrand, 1868.

Moore, James. *Kilpatrick and Our Cavalry.* New York: W. J. Widdleton, Publisher, 1865.

National Cyclopedia of American Biography, Vol. VI. New York: James T. White Co., 1896.

Obituary Record of the Graduates of Yale University, Deceased from June 1910, to July 1915. New Haven: Yale University Press, 1915.

Official Register of the Officers and Cadets of the U.S. Military Academy. West Point, NY: U.S. Military Academy, June 1852.

Page, Walter Hines, and Arthur Wilson Page, eds. *The World's Work: A History of Our Time, Volume 15.* New York: Doubleday, Page & Co., 1908.

Perrin, Henry. *The History of Bourbon, Scott, Harrison and Nicholas Counties, Kentucky.* Chicago: O. L. Baskin & Co., 1882.

Pike, James. *The Personal Adventures Corporal Pike of the Fourth Ohio Cavalry.* Cincinnati: J. R. Hawley & Co., 1865.

Pond, George E. "Kilpatrick's and Dahlgren's Raid to Richmond." In *Battles & Leaders,* Vol. 4. New York: The Century Company, 1888.

Portrait and Biographical Album: Ingham & Livingston Counties. Chicago: Chapman Brothers, 1891.

Portrait and Biographical Album of Sedgwick County, Kan. Chicago: Chapman Brothers, 1888.

Powell, David. *Failure in the Saddle.* New York: Savas Beatie, 2010.

Powell, William Henry, ed. *Officers of the Army and Navy (Volunteer) Who Served in the Civil War.* Philadelphia: L. R. Hamersly, 1893.

Quiner, Edwin B. *E. B Quiner's Military History of Wisconsin.* Chicago: Clark and Co., 1866.

Rea, John "Four Weeks with Long's Cavalry in East Tennessee." In *Glimpses of the Nations Struggle,* J. C. Donahower, Silas Towler, David Kingsbury, eds. St. Paul: Review Publishing Company, 1908.

Reid, Whitelaw. *Ohio in the War: Her Statesmen, Her Generals, and Soldiers*, Vol. I. New York: Moore, Wilstach & Baldwin: 1868.

Richardson, Robert D. "Rosecrans' Staff at Chickamauga: The Significance of Major General William S. Rosecrans' Staff on the Outcome of the Chickamauga Campaign." Master's Thesis, Command and General Staff College, Fort Leavenworth, Kansas, 1989.

Robinson, George I. "With Kilpatrick around Atlanta." In *War Papers, Commandery of Wisconsin MOLLUS*, Vol. 1. New York: Nostrand Van Allen, 1891.

Roster and Record of Iowa Soldiers in the War of the Rebellion, Volume IV. Des Moines: Emory H. English, State Printer, E. D. Chassell, State Binder, 1910.

Rouse, E. S. S. "Colonel Long's Raid in Bragg's Rear." In *The Bugle's Blast*, MOLLUS. Philadelphia: James Challen & Sons, 1864.

Rowell, John W. *Yankee Cavalrymen*. Knoxville: University of Tennessee Press, 1971.

Shelton, Paul. "The Blame Game: Federal Intelligence Operations during the Chickamauga Campaign." Master's Thesis, U.S. Army Command and General Staff College, Fort Leavenworth, Kansas, 2000.

Sheridan, Philip. *Personal Memoirs of Philip H. Sheridan. General United States Army. Volume 1*. New York: D. Appleton & Co., 1902.

Smith, Zachary F., and Mary Rogers Clay. *The Clay Family*, Filson Club Publications No. 14. Louisville, KY: Filson Club, 1899.

Speed, Thomas. *Union Regiments of Kentucky Volume I*. Louisville: The Courier Journal Job Printing, Co., 1897.

Stanley, David S. *An American General: The Memoirs of David Sloan Stanley*. Samuel W. Fordyce IV, ed. Santa Barbara, CA: The Narrative Press, 2004.

Stanley, David S. *Personal Memoirs of Major-General D. S. Stanley USA*. Cambridge: Harvard University Press, 1917.

Starr, Stephen Z. "Cold Steel: The Sabre and Union Cavalry." In *Battles Lost and Won: Essays from Civil War History*, John T. Hubbell, ed. Westport, CT: Greenwood Press, 1975.

Starr, Stephen Z. *The Union Cavalry in the Civil War, Volume 3: The War in the West, 1861–1865*. Baton Rouge: Louisiana State University Press, 1985.

Stuart, A. A. *Iowa Colonels and Regiments Being a History of Iowa Regiments*. Des Moines: Mills & Co., 1865.

Stuart, Reginald. "The Role of the Cavalry in the Western Theatre of the American Civil War from the Battle of Shiloh to the Tullahoma Campaign." Master's Thesis 1968, University of British Columbia, Vancouver, British Columbia.

Sunderland, Glenn W. *Lightning at Hoover's Gap*. New York: Thomas Yoseloff, 1969.

Tucker, Spencer, ed. *American Civil War: The Definitive Encyclopedia and Document Collection*, Volume 6. Santa Barbara: ABC-Clio LLC, 2013.

Twenty-Ninth Annual Reunion of the Association of Graduates of the United States Military Academy at West Point. Saginaw: Seemann & Peters, Printers and Binders, 1898.

Twenty-Second Annual Reunion of the Association of the Graduates of the United States Military Academy: June 12th, 1891. Saginaw: Seemam & Peters, Printers and Binders, 1891.

Twenty-seventh Reunion, Society of the Army of the Cumberland. Cincinnati: The Robert Clark Co., 1898.

Twitchell, Ralph Emerson. *The Leading Facts of New Mexican History*, Vol. II. Cedar Rapids: The Torch Press, 1912.

The Union Army, A History of Military Affairs in the Loyal States 1861–65, Vol. 8. Madison: Federal Publishing Co., 1908.

Vale, Joseph. "Address of Captain Joseph Vale." In *Pennsylvania at Chickamauga and Chattanooga*, George W. Skinner, ed. Harrisburg, PA: William Stanley Ray, State Printer of Pennsylvania, 1897.

Vincent, Thomas M." David Sloane Stanley." In *The Thirty-fourth Annual Reunion of the Association Graduates of the United States Military Academy at West Point, New York*. Saginaw: Seeman & Peters, Printers and Binders, 1903.

Warner, Ezra J. *Generals in Blue: Lives of Union Commanders*. Baton Rouge: Louisiana State University Press, 1992.

Welsh, Jack. *Medical Histories of Union Generals*. Kent: Kent State University Press, 1996.

Wilson, James H. *Under the Old Flag*, Vol. 2. New York: D. Appleton & Co., 1912.

Williams, C. S. *Williams' Cincinnati Directory*. Cincinnati: C. S. Williams Publisher, 1860.

Wright, Stephen. *Kentucky Soldiers and Their Regiments in the Civil War*, Vol. III & IV. Utica, KY: McDowell Publications, 2009.

Wyeth, John Allan. *The Life General Nathan Bedford Forrest*. New York: Harper Brothers, 1899.

Wyeth, John Allan. *With Sabre and Scalpel: The Autobiography of a Soldier and Surgeon*. New York: Harper Brothers, 1914.

Index

Page numbers in ***bold italics*** indicate illustrations.

Adairsville, Georgia 221–222, 289
Adkins, Col. Smith 205
Alabama Units 4th Cavalry 98, 126, 168; 6th Cavalry 246; 8th Cavalry 246; 14th Cavalry Battalion 64; 18th Infantry 224; 51st Cavalry 40, 62, 90, 98; 59th Infantry 200; H.C. Lockhart's Battalion 247
Alexander's Bridge 144, 146, 148–149, 287
Allen, Brig. Gen. William Wirt 216, 234
Alpine, Georgia 124, 128–129, 131–134, 136, 139–140, 144
Anderson, J.B. 13
Anderson, Col. Robert (CSA) 234, 258, 262
Anderson, Brig. Gen. Robert (U.S.) 28
Anderson Cavalry *see* Pennsylvania Units, 15th Cavalry
Anderson Troop 12, 16, 28, 30–31, 41, 51
Andes, Lt. John 60, 156
Antietam, Battle of 28, 30, 61, 109, 168
Arkansas Units: Wiggins Artillery 93–94
Armstrong, Brig. Gen. Frank 66, 85, 126, 133–134, 181, 186, 196, 228, 270, 272–273, 275
Army of Tennessee 3, 26, 36, 52, 64, 87–88, 103, 182, 200, 206, 249
Army of the Cumberland 2–3, 5–7, 9–12, 15–16, 18, 21, 23–24, 27–30, 32–33, 56–61, 68–71, 74, 77–78, 82–83, 103–104, 110, 114, 117–120, 125, 129, 137, 142–144, 164–165, 174–180, 186, 190–191, 198–201, 203, 204, 206, 208, 210–211, 286–292, 297, 299; Atlanta Campaign 212–285; Battle of Chickamauga 143–163; Battle of Stones River 33–56; Tullahoma Campaign 87–102
Army of the Mississippi 10, 176, 178
Army of the Ohio 9, 11–12, 23–24, 30, 35, 123, 180, 184, 186, 188, 190, 192, 194, 196, 198, 203, 206, 211, 291; Atlanta Campaign 212–285
Army of the Potomac 27, 33, 88, 208, 295
Army of the Tennessee 100, 164, 179, 198, 204, 206, 211–212, 215–216, 219, 230, 252–253, 265
Ashby, Col. Henry M. 258
Atlanta, Battle of 250–251
Avery, Col. Isaac 168

Baird, Brig. Gen. Absalom 202–203
Baldwin, Col. Oliver 160, 179, 205, 215, 273
Bale, Maj. Alfred 186
Bate, Maj. Gen. William 228
Bayles, Col. Jesse 68
Beatty, Brig. Gen. John 16, 108–109, 123
Beck, Capt. Chris 164
Bennett, Lt. Cornelius 259
Bennett, Sgt. John 229
Bickham, William D. 23, 56
Big Hill, Kentucky *see* Richmond, Battle of
Biggs, Lt. Col. Jonathan 205, 214
Bischard, Sgt. Daniel 224, 248
Blair, Maj. Gen. Frank 182, 226, 229–230
Bloodgood, Lt. Col. Edward 66
Blythe's Ferry 115–116, 126, 128
Bond, Maj. Frank S. 137, 140
Bourke, Pvt. John 55
Brackett, Maj. Alfred 111
Bradley, Lt. Col. William 197
Bradyville 86, 89–91, 280; skirmish 64, 280

Bragg, Gen. Braxton 11–12, 26, 29, 57, 59, 64, 69–70, 75, 77–78, 81, 165–166, 178–180, 182, 291; at Chattanooga before the Battle of Chickamauga 103–105, 112–113, 116, 118–120, 123–125, 127–142; at Chickamauga 142–144, 148–149, 155, 161–162; at Stones River 35–36, 38–39, 41–43, 51; Tullahoma Campaign 87–92, 97–102
Brandon, Pvt. John 245
Breckinridge, Maj. Gen. John C. 52, 138, 153
Brentwood, Tennessee 28, 86, 289; attacked 66
Brice's Crossroads, Battle of 243
Bridgeland, Col. John 17
Bridgeport 104–105, 111–113, 117, 123, 128, 133, 166, 215
Briggs, Maj. David 150, 167, 213
Bronson, Sgt. Eugene 50
Broomtown Valley 124–127, 132–133
Brown, Pvt. Mason 95
Brown, Pvt. Michael 194
Brownlow, Col. James P. 5, 70–***71***, 79, 84, 91, 111, 126, 135–136, 156, 165, 177, 181, 187, 195, 204, 213, 228, 240, 254, 256, 258–260, 279, 299
Brownlow, Col. John Bell 71
Brownlow, William "Parson" 71
Brown's Mill, battle at 256–260, 293
Buell, Maj. Gen. Don Carlos 9–13, 18, 23, 26–28, 30–31, 72, 74, 104, 206
Buford, Brig. Gen. Abraham 30, ***37***, 41, 43, 49, 51–52
bugle(s) 61
Bull Run, First Battle of 83, 97, 109, 177, 208
Burdsall, Lt. Col. Henry W. 21, 55
Burke, Lt. Col. Joe 52
Burns, Robert 144

335

Burnside, Maj. Gen. Ambrose 55, 105, 123; Knoxville campaign 180–182
Burnt Church skirmish 226–228
Burr, Sgt. Robert 99

Calfkiller Creek skirmish 113–114
Campbell, Col. Archibald 5, 70, 73, 79, 84–85, 95, 99, 111, 114–115, 118, 124, 126, 134–135, 138–139, 150–151, 160, 165, 182–188, 190, 192, 194–195, 209–210, 292, 299
Campbell, Henry 171
Campbell's Station 181
Campbellton 238–239, 279–280; skirmish 253–254
cannon(s) 21, 43, 47, 51, 74–75, 94–95, 147, 188, 195, 224, 234, 246, 262, 271
Caperton 114–115
Capron, Col. Horace 263
Carlisle Barracks 22, 28, 30
Carter, W.R. 82, 107, 123, 137, 186–187
Carter's Expedition 69
Cassville, Georgia 282; Battle of 222–224, 289, 291
Cavalry Bureau 119, 199
Centre College 69, 88
Chadwick, Mary Jane 108
Chalmers, Brig. Gen. James 63
Chapin, Sgt. John 154
Chase, Salmon 82, 175
Cheatham, Maj. Gen. Benjamin 42, 133, 138, 251
Cheeks, Maj. Christopher 129
Chehaw Station skirmish 247
Chicago Board of Trade Artillery (Stokes') 82, 91, 145–146, 153–155, 169, 171, 179, 205, 214, 224, 302; Battle of Atlanta 250–251; Garrard's Raid 262; Kilpatrick's Raid 268–275; Noonday Creek 231–234
"Christmas Raid" 29, 69–70
Cincinnati Commercial Newspaper see Bickham, William D.
Clanton, Brig. Gen. James H. 246
Clark, William 240, 263
Clason, Rufus 279
Cleburne, Brig. Gen. Patrick 29, 135, 228, 274, 278
Coburn, Col. John 64–66
Colt revolving rifle 15, 33, 119, 209, 288, 290
Condit, Lt. Timothy 45, 53
Confederate Units: 1st Cavalry 44, 198, 273; 8th Cavalry 62, 188, 216
Cook, Lt. Col. W.R. 165
Cooper, Col. Robert Wickliffe 68, 84–85, 111, 165, 204, 213
Cooper's Gap 139, 162; skirmish 157–160

Corinth, Battle of 9–11, 15, 22, 151, 162
Corinth, Siege of 11, 18–22, 70, 78, 83, 126, 164, 177
court-martial 61–62, 72, 107, 109, 129, 159, 171, 174, 197, 293, 297
Cowell, Lt. Joseph 158
Cox, Maj. Gen. Jacob 234
Cox, Col. John T. 44
Crane, Capt. William E. 154, 261, 268
Crawfish Springs 144, 149–151, 153–155, 157–158, 290
Crews, Col. Charles C. 186
Crittenden, Maj. Gen. Thomas 11–14, 36, 40, 42, 50, 89–92, 97, 101, 105, 113–117, 123, 125, 127–128, 133, 135–138, 140–142, 144–145, 157, 161, 175, 291
Crofts, Sgt. Thomas 20, 43, 229, 274
Crook, Brig. Gen. George 21, 103, **109**, 111, 114, 117, 120, 123, 127, 131–134, 136–141, 178–179, 190, 197–199, 210, 290–292, 295; Battle of Chickamauga 143–144, 150–151, 153–155, 157, 161; Wheeler's Raid 164–176
Croxton, Brig. Gen. John 149, 213, 238, 279, 291–292, 294; during McCook's Raid 253, 255–**258**, 259–260
Cruft, Brig. Gen. Charles 202–203
Culver, Capt. Elisha 67
Cupp, Lt. Col. Valentine 45, 111, 154–155, 167
Curry, Col. W.L. 24, 71, 86, 97, 124, 169, 237, 265, 270, 274

Dahlgren, Col. Ulric 208
Dallas, Battle of 226–228, 289
Dalton, Georgia 125, 127, 133, 136–137, 180, 199, 200, 225, 267, 278–279; advance on 211–212, 216–218, 220–221; reconnaissance 202–203
Dana, Charles A. 118–**119**, 199; rumors 176
Dandridge 186, 188, 192–193, 197, 289; skirmish 184
Davidson, Brig. Gen. Henry B. 148, 170–171
Davis, Maj. Charles 94
Davis, Brig. Gen. Jefferson C. 62, 125, 182, 202–203, 278
Davis, Maj. N.H. 30–32
Deweese, Lt. Col. John 165
Dibrell, Col. George 110, 113–114, 116, 118, 141, 160, 202, 216, 234, 255, 262, 280
Dickinson, Lt. Col. William H. 16, 34, 54
Dickinson College 64–65, 70

discipline 9, 16, 19–20, 31, 33, 72, 78, 105–107, 114, 129, 163, 182
disease(s) 67, 294, 297–298
Dodge, Col. Grenville 77, 250
Dornblaser, T.F. 99, 114, 273, 275
Dorr, Col. Joseph Bartlett 5, 205, 209–**210**, 211, 213, 216, 229, 288, 293–294; during McCook's Raid 256, 259–260
Dougherty's Gap 138, 140–141, 143–144, 149
Dover, Tennessee, skirmish 63–64
drums 61
Ducat, Col. Arthur 13–16
Dumont, Col. Ebenezer 24
Dunlap, Major 85
Dunn, L.K. 60
Dyer's Bridge 146, 148, 160

Edwards, Richard 207
Eggleston, Col. Beroth 84, 204, 214, 268, 272, 296
Elliott, Brig. Gen. Washington Lafayette 5–6, 193–194, 199–200, 204–205, 208–210, 212–213, 216, 219–221, 223–224, 228–229, 231, 235–237, 265, 267, 281, 284–285, 288, 290–291, 298; East Tennessee Campaign 175–**178**, 179, 181, 183–184, 188, 190–191
Ezra Church, Battle of 247, 253–254

Fair Garden 194–196, 289
Farmington, Battle at 170–174, 289
Faulkner, Col. John K. 69, 84–85, 165, 197, 213–214, 294–295
Ferguson, Brig. Gen. Samuel 228, 269, 272–273
Ferrier, Sgt. Daniel 217
Fidler, Maj. William 204, 213
Flat Rock skirmish 261–263, 289
Fleming, Capt. Eli 61
Fobes, George 31
Forrest, Lt. Gen. Nathan Bedford 2–3, 13–15, 18, 24–**25**, 26, 29–30, 35, 56, 63–64, 66, 76–77, 79, 81, 83, 85–86, 88, 95–96, 98, 101–103, 105, 109–110, 114, 116, 119, 123, 126–128, 130, 132–134, 141–142, 146–147, 149, 166, 170, 172, 176, 190, 197, 201, 203, 204, 220, 243–244, 280–281
Fort Deposit 115–116
Fort Donelson 21, 26, 63, 83, 210
Fort Heiman 83
Fort Henry 83
Foster, Col. John 194
Franklin, Tennessee: December 11, 1862, skirmish 28–29; December 26–27, 1862, skirmishes

38–40; April 10, 1863, skirmish 75–76
Fredericksburg, Battle of 35, 57, 199
Freeman, Capt. Samuel 76
Fremont, Maj. Gen. John C. 83
Fremont's Hussars 83
French, Lucy Virginia 77
Fulton, Col. John 146

Gaines Mill, Battle of 69
Galbraith, Lt. Col. Robert 61, 93, 114, 117, 166
Gallatin, Tennessee 13–15, 18–19, 29
Gano, Col. Richard 74
Garber, Hezekiah 21
Garesche, Col. Julius 29, 42–43, 80
Garfield, Brig. Gen. James A. 67, 71–72, 78, 80, 82, 101–102, 112–**113**, 121, 123–128, 130, 133, 136–137, 139–141, 144, 158–160, 165–166, 175, 291, 297
Garrard, Col. Israel 184–185, 192, 196, 267
Garrard, Brig. Gen. Kenner 201, 203, 204–205, 210–212, 222, 224, 226, 236–238, 243–244, 248–255, 265, 268, 272, 276–277, 281–282, 284–286, 288–289, 291; arrives at Resaca 214–220; biographical **199**; Noonday Creek 228–235; Roswell 239–241; Stoneman's Raid 261–263
Garrard's Raid: July 21–24, 1864, 249–251; July 27–30, 1864, 261–262; August 18–22, 1864, 267–268; *see also* Garrard, Kenner
Garrett, Sgt. George 62
Gay, Capt. Ebenezer 12
Georgia Units: 1st Cavalry 36, 186; 2nd Cavalry 186; 3rd Cavalry 17–18, 91, 99, 135, 186; 4th Cavalry 90, 99, 168, 216, 227; 6th Cavalry 186
Gerould, Sgt. Otis 33
Gettysburg, Battle of 104, 199, 208
Gibson, Col. William 44, 228
Gilbert, Maj. Gen. Charles 12, 65–66
Gilbert, Lt. James 52
Gillem, Brig. Gen. Alvan 204–**206**, 207, 210, 212, 279–280, 282–283, 286
Gist, Brig. Gen. States Rights 132
Glass Mill, Battle at 150–155, 157, 161–162, 166–167
Glick, Pvt. Solomon 195
Goddard, Lt. Col. C. 96
Godley, Maj. John 70, 84, 111, 165

Gooding, Othniel 190, 279
Goodrich, Charles 107, 109, 139, 155, 193, 217
Gordon('s) Mill *see* Lee and Gordon's Mill
Granger, Maj. Gen. Gordon 69–70, 73, 75–76, 85, **89**–93, 96, 100–101, 107, 114, 117, 137, 140, 144–145, 156, 175, 182, 200, 209
Grant, Maj. Gen. Ulysses 10–11, 29–30, 80–81, 87–88, 114, 118, 176–179, 182, 191–192, 198–199, 204, 212, 231–232, 242, 249, 281, 288, 295
Gratz, Maj. Louis 111
Gray, Maj. Horace 111, 165
Gregg, Brig. Gen. John 146
Grierson, Brig. Gen. Benjamin 281
Griest, Alva 223
Griffith, Col. J.C. 168
Guy's Gap 87, 91–93, 101

Haggard, Col. David R. 68
Hall, Col. Albert 66
Hall, Col. Bolling 200
Halleck, Maj. Gen. Henry 10–12, 15–16, 35, 55, 59, 63, 78, 81–82, 88, 104, 109, 100, 113–114, 127, 131, 164, 221, 230, 238, 244, 252, 262, 264–265, 283
Hamilton, Col. William 245, 247
Hanback, Lt. Lewis 76
Hardee, Lt. Gen. William 12, 36, 41–43, 57, 88, 92, 199, 202, 223, 250–251, 254, 277–278
Harker, Col. Charles 14, 136
Harlan, Col. John M. 29
Harnden, Capt. Henry 213, 227
Harrison, Col. Thomas (CSA) 153, 193
Harrison, Col. Thomas J. (U.S.) 78–79, 84, 136, 205, 208, 214–215, 252–254; McCook's Raid 256–261; Rousseau's Raid 245, 247
Hartstuff, George 21
Hartsville, battle of 17, 24–25, 28, 288
Hatch, Brig. Gen. Edward 281
Haynes, Lt. Col. William 112
Hazen, Col. William B. 67, 123, 228
Healy, George 120, 247, 260
Hempstead, Sgt. Henry Mortimer 90, 153, 155, 157, 196
Herb, Pvt. Felix 93
Hill, Maj. Gen. Daniel H. 135
Hill's Gap skirmish 168
Hindman, Maj. Gen. Thomas 133, 135, 138, 154
Hoblitzell, Lt. Col. William T. 68, 84, 111, 128–129, 158–160, 165, 178

Hodge, Col. George B. 170–173
Holly Springs raid 29, 35, 57
Hood, Lt. Gen. John Bell 7, 148, 180, 199, 221, 223–224, 226, 228, 236, 248–254, 256, 261, 265, 267, 276–278, 280–283, 289, 298
Hooker, Maj. Gen. Joseph 88, 175, 179, 212, 215, 221, 223, 226, 236, 252
Hoover's Gap 87, 89, 91, 96
horses 7, 9, 14, 16, 22, 24, 29, 33, 36, 45, 50–53, 58–60, 62, 67, 76, 78–79, 81, 85, 90–91, 93–94, 96–97, 99, 103, 108, 114–115, 117–118, 120, 127, 131, 137–138, 141, 149, 151, 154, 156, 164, 166, 169, 172, 175, 178–179, 182, 185, 187, 193, 195, 197, 200, 202–203, 207, 209–210, 213, 216–217, 220, 224–225, 229, 232, 241, 245–246, 248, 260–261, 265, 274, 290–291
hospitals 156–157, 162, 250
Howard, Maj. Gen. Oliver 164, 182–183, 211, 215, 217–218, 220–221, 223, 227–228, 239, 252–254, 262, 265, 277
Howe, Capt. Daniel Wait 225
Howland, Maj. Horace 204
Hughes, Col. John 181, 200, 202
Humes, Brig. Gen. William Y.C. 254, 257
Huntsville, Alabama 22, 25, 113, 115, 117, 172, 178, 197–198, 203, 279; expedition 108–109

Illinois Units: 27th Infantry 76; 92nd Mounted Infantry 198, 205, 215, 218, 250, 270, 273–274; 98th Mounted Infantry 62, 168, 179, 205, 214, 218; 123rd Mounted Infantry 62, 146, 168, 179, 205, 214; *see also* Chicago Board of Trade Artillery (Stokes')
Indiana Units: 2nd Cavalry 12, 15, 17, 25, 28, 34, 53, 55, 84, 111, 114, 127–128, 135, 150–151, 160, 165, 167, 173, 182, 192–196, 204, 209, 213, 216–217, 224, 253, 258–260; 3rd Cavalry 26–27, 35, 39–40, 46–47, 53, 55, 75, 80, 84, 93, 95–96, 100, 111, 113–114, 116–117, 123, 140, 144, 161, 165, 179, 205, 213, 270, 272; 4th Cavalry 67–69, 84, 100, 111, 115–116, 127, 139, 150–151, 160, 165, 193, 195–196, 204, 209, 213, 216–217, 227, 231, 253–259, 294; 8th Cavalry 6, 205, 208, 213, 215, 245–247, 253, 258, 260, 268, 272, 274; 17th Mounted Infantry 62, 168, 179–180, 198,

205, 213–214; 18th Indiana Artillery (Lilly's) 171, 185–186; 22nd Infantry 51; 39th Mounted infantry 6, 68, 78, 98, 136, 208; 72nd Mounted Infantry 62, 146, 164, 168, 179, 198, 201, 205, 213–214, 222, 240, 263, 296
Iowa Units: 5th Cavalry 63, 82–83, 90, 105, 117, 120, 166, 170, 172, 177–180, 245–247, 260, 270, 272; 8th Cavalry 210, 235, 248, 253–254, 256, 259–264, 288, 293–294; 12th Infantry 211
Ireland, Chaplin John 22–23
Iuka, Battle of 10–11, 22–23, 162
Iverson, Brig. Gen. Alfred 234, 255, 261, 283

Jackson, Brig. Gen. James 17, 21
Jackson, Brig. Gen. William Hicks 181, 228, 237, **254**–258, 263, 270, 273–274
James, Lt. Col. Thomas C. 70
Jenkins, Lt. William 100
Jennings, Maj. James H. 48–49, 214, 229, 272
Johnson, Andrew 70, 204, 206
Johnson, Brig. Gen. Bushrod 145–147, 180
Johnson, Brig. Gen. Richard Johnson 39, 43–44, 46, 201, 281, 286
Johnson, Col. Robert 70
Johnston, Pvt. Jarratt 232
Johnston, Gen. Joseph 7, 81, 88, 104, 110, 128, 132, 182, 280; Atlanta Campaign 200–202, 206, 210–213, 215–224, 226–236, 238–239, 243–244, 247, 249, 251
Jones, Lt. Andrew 197
Jonesborough/Jonesboro 244, 268, 270–271, 277–278, 282, 284, 287, 289
Jordan, Lt. Col. Henry 205
Jordan, Col. Thomas 64–**65**, 66, 70, 74, 84–85, 91, 173, 182–183, 188, 191–192, 194, 200, 205, 280

Kansas Units: 2nd Infantry 72, 143; 8th Infantry 73
Keim, Maj. Gen. William 64, 70
Kelly, Brig. Gen. John H. 228, 279
Kelly, Lt. Col. Robert 213, 257
Kennesaw Mountain, Battle of 230–232, 236–238, 289
Kennett, Col. John 12–17, 21, 34, 36, 43, 46–48, 53, 55, 73–74
Kentucky Units (CSA): 2nd Cavalry 26, 64, 179; 3rd Cavalry 41, 168; 5th Cavalry 41; 6th Cavalry 41
Kentucky Units (U.S.): 1st Cavalry 12; 2nd Cavalry 12, 67–68, 77, 84, 98, 100, 111, 118, 154–155, 161, 166, 169, 179, 205, 214–215, 245, 253, 258, 260, 268, 272; 3rd Kentucky 15, 17–18, 28, 34, 38, 42, 47–49, 53, 55, 58, 60, 62, 205, 215, 218, 270, 273–274; 4th Cavalry 64, 66, 68, 75–76, 84–85, 90, 99, 105, 111, 116–117, 126, 158–159, 161, 165, 194, 196, 204, 213; 4th Mounted Infantry 213, 238, 253, 255–257, 259; 5th Cavalry 12, 68, 99–100, 105, 111, 126, 128–129, 158–160, 178–179, 194, 198, 201, 205, 215, 270, 273–274; 6th Cavalry 66, 68–69, 84–85, 99, 105, 111, 116, 126, 135, 158–159, 161, 165, 196, 204, 213; 7th Cavalry 66, 68–69, 84–85, 105, 111, 120, 126, 128, 165, 193, 196–197, 204, 209, 213, 237, 295; 9th Cavalry 12; 11th Cavalry 28; 20th Kentucky Infantry 68
Kilpatrick, Brig. Gen. Hugh Judson 5, 204–205, **207**–208, 210–212, 214–219, 244, 252, 262, 264–265, 280–286, 289, 281, 295, 297; Kilpatrick's Raid 267–278
Kilpatrick's Raid 268–277
Kitchell, Lt. Col. Edward 205, 214
Klein, Lt. Col. Robert 27, 35, 39–**40**, 46–47, 55, 75, 84, 111, 165, 205, 214, 270, 272, 275
Knoxville, Siege of 180–183
Kolb's Farm 236
Kryder, George 107, 172, 191, 209, 228

LaFayette, Georgia 124, 133–142
La Grange, Col. Oscar 83–**84**, 111, 126, 128, 134–135, 150, 165, 182–184, 186, 188–190, 192–196, 204, 211, 213, 216–217, 219, 227, 292, 294
Lamson, Lt. Col. Horace 204, 213, 217, 227, 258, 294
L'Anguille Ferry 83
Larson, Sgt. James 235
Laughlin, Maj. James 34
Lee, Lt. Gen. Stephen Dill 277
Lee and Gordon's Mill 133, 135–136, 139, 142, 144–**145**, 148, 153, 155
Lesslie, Maj. Joseph 195
Lexington Rifles 26
Liberty Gap 87, 91, 96
Lilly's Artillery see Indiana Units, 18th Indiana Artillery
Lincoln, Abraham 59, 62, 72, 81–82, 97, 100, 109
Lochiel Cavalry see Pennsylvania Units, 9th Cavalry

Long, Brig. Gen. Eli 5, 53, 73–**74**, 77, 80, 84, 89, 91, 97, 100, 109, 111, 117–118, 124, 144, 149, 156–157, 161, 179, 182, 188–189, 202–203, 204, 213–214, 226, 228, 230–231, 262, 267, 277, 281, 284–285, 295; Battle at Glass Mill 151–155; Kilpatrick's Raid 268–276; Wheeler's Raid 166, 168, 170, 173
Long's Raid (Cleveland, TN) 179–180
Longstreet, Lt. Gen. James 153, 180–184, 186, 191–194, 196, 199, 201
Lookout Mountain 110, 124–126, 128, 131–133, 137, 151, 157–159, 182
Lost Mountain 230–231, **236**, 238
Love, Capt. James 73
Lovejoy's Station 244, 252–256, 269–261, 263–265, 267, 270, 272–273, 275
Lowe, Col. William Warren 5, **83**, 105, 111–112, 120, 162, 166, 170, 172, 178–179, 205, 214, 218, 226, 230–231, 282, 285, 291, 297
Lowe's Hell Hounds see Iowa Units, 5th Cavalry
Lynch, Pvt. John 118

Maple, Lt. Thomas 52
Marshall, Eugene 172
Martin, Pvt. Frank 53
Martin, Brig. Gen. William T. 88, 93, 95–96, 124, 126, 130, 134, 147, 153, 155, 158, 167–168, 170, 181, 184, 186–188, 190, 194–196, 200, 220, 231, 278–279, 287
Mathews, Maj. Peter 81
Matthies, Brig. Gen. Charles 202
McCahan, Capt. Thomas 138, 151, 155, 167, 181
McCann, Maj. Dick 77
McClellan, Maj. Gen. George 11
McCook, Maj. Gen. Alexander 11–14, 21, 36, 38–39, 41–44, 46–48, 50, 55, 68, 89–92, 96, 105, 111, 121, 123, 129–**130**, 132–133, 135–143, 149, 156–158, 175
McCook, Brig. Gen. Edward 5, 15, 17, 27–28, 58, 84–85, 100, 150, 151, 156–158, 160, 162, 165–168, 170, 174, 178, 183, 186–188, 190, 192–198, 200–201, 203–205, 207–209, 211, 213, 215–219, 221–231, 235–240, 244, 248, 270, 276, 278–284, 286, 289–293; advance on Chattanooga **110**–112, 114–117, 124, 126–127, 130–132, 134,

136–141, 143–144; Battle of Chickamauga 150, 151, 156–158, 160, 162; McCook's Raid 250–265
McCook's Raid 253–261; *see also* Brown's Mill
McCown's Escort Company 46
McCrillis, Col. Lafayette 201
McIntyre, Capt. James 61, 84, 111, 139, 165, 204, 214, 230, 272, 275
McLain, John 38, 77, 107, 156, 234
McLemore's Cove 135, 138, 142, 149–150
McMinnville expedition 76–77, 289; capture during Wheeler's raid 168, 171–173
McNair, Brig. Gen. Evander 146
McPherson, Maj. Gen. James 204, 206, 211–212, 215–**216**, 217–220, 222–224, 227–228, 230, 232, 235–238, 241, 248–252, 267, 282, 284
McTeer, Maj. Will 60, 67, 77
Medal of Honor 55, 94, 217, 221, 251, 260, 298
Meigs, M.C. 78–79
Mercer, Cpl. George W. 107
Meridian Campaign 197–198, 201–202
Merrill, Pvt. Robert 131
Metcalfe, Col. Leonidas 69
Michigan Units: 1st Light Artillery 51, 215, 245–246, 253; 2nd Cavalry 12, 18, 64–66, 68, 70, 73, 84–85, 90, 99, 108, 111, 114–115, 117–118, 120, 134, 138, 145, 150–151, 153–157, 162, 165, 185–186, 192, 194–196, 204, 209, 213, 221, 241, 253, 279, 293; 4th Cavalry 16–18, 28, 33–34, 38, 40, 42–43, 48–50, 52–55, 62, 64, 74–77, 84–85, 91, 93, 95, 97, 100, 107, 111, 113–114, 124, 144–145, 147–148, 156, 161, 165, 172, 179, 190, 204, 214, 222, 229, 232–234, 268, 270, 272, 274–275; 7th Infantry 15; Dee's Artillery 15
Middleton expedition 79–80, 289
Miller, Col. Abram O. 6, 164, 168, 170–171, 178, 198, 205, 214, 220, 223, 228, 233, 234, 262, 287, 291–292, 296
Miller, Col. John K. 205
Millikin, Col. Minor 16, 19–20, 34, 45–46, 53
Minnesota Units: 2nd Light Artillery 12; 2nd Infantry 113; 5th Infantry 22; Minnesota cavalry companies 83, 209
Minty, Col. Robert 5, 15–**17**, 18, 24, 27, 33–34, 36, 38, 41–43, 48–50, 52–55, 58, 62–64, 66, 70, 73–74, 76–77, 80, 84–85, 110–120, 123, 126–128, 130, 133–134, 136–137, 140–141, 151, 156–157, 160–161, 163, 168, 171, 173–174, 178, 204, 214, 220, 222, 224, 227, 232–234, 250, 262, 284–285, 291–292, 295–296; Battle of Reed's Bridge 144–149; Battle of Shelbyville 92–96; Kilpatrick's Raid 268, 270, 272–275, 277; Tullahoma Campaign 91–94, 96, 98, 100–102
Missouri Units: 4th Cavalry 62
Mitchell, Capt. Joseph A.S. 15, 17, 34
Mitchell, Brig. Gen. Robert B. 5–6, 71–**72**, 73–74, 767, 84–85, 88–93, 97–99, 101, 103, 105, 107, 109–111, 120–121, 123, 133, 136–137, 139–144, 149, 151, 153, 155–158, 160, 162, 165–166, 168, 170, 172–176, 290–291, 297–298
Mitchell, Lt. Thomas V. 53
Mix, Maj. Frank **54**, 84–85, 95, 214, 272
Moore, Col. Absalom B. 24, 28–29
Moore, Maj. David A.B. 44, 53
Morgan, Brig. Gen. John Hunt 2, 5, 13–15, 17–18, 24–**25**, 26, 29–30, 35, 55–56, 65–66, 69–70, 74–75, 81, 86, 103, 147
Morgan, Brig. Gen. John T. 186, 195
Mossy Creek: battle 186–188; skirmish 183–186
Mott, Col. Samuel 186, 188
Mower, Brig. Gen. Joseph 243
Mundy's Battalion 69
Murfreesboro *see* Stones River, Battle of
Murphy, Maj. John 61
Murray, Lt. Col. Douglas 16, 20, 34
Murray, Col. Eli 5, 15, 17–**18**, 34, 47–48, 55, 205, 214–215, 218, 222, 224, 270, 273–274, 279
mutiny: 15th Pennsylvania Cavalry 30–32

Nash Farm, Battle of 272–277
Nashville and Chattanooga Railroad 104
Naughton's Irish Dragoons 83
Negley, Brig. Gen. James 12, 14, 36, 135–138, 140, 142
New Hope Church, Battle of 226–228
New Madrid and Island No. 10, Siege of 11, 21–22, 70, 177
New Market 184–186, 190, 289
New York Units: 2nd Cavalry 208; 5th Infantry 208; 21st Cavalry 208; 146th Infantry 199
Newell, Lt. Nathaniel 16, 19, 21, 34, 38, 74–75, 84–85, 111, 136, 165
Newell's Section *see* Ohio Units, 1st Artillery
Nicholas, Col. Thomas P. 68, 84, 111, 166
Nolan's Systems for Training Cavalry Horses 232
Noonday Creek, Battle at 232–235, 289
Nourse, Pvt. Benjamin 224, 231, 251, 271

O'Higgins, Father 43
Ohio Units: 1st Artillery 16, 19, 21, 34, 38, 48, 53, 74, 84–85, 90, 93, 111, 165; 1st Cavalry 12, 16, 19–20, 24, 34, 39, 41, 43–47, 52–53, 60, 71, 84, 86, 97, 100, 107, 111, 118, 123, 126, 154–155, 161, 166–167, 179, 183, 189, 204, 209, 214, 228, 232, 237, 268, 270, 272, 274–275; 2nd Cavalry 70; 3rd Cavalry 12, 16, 19–20, 34, 38–39, 41, 43–44, 46–48, 51–53, 60, 64, 67, 75, 80, 84, 97, 99–100, 107, 111, 118, 126, 154, 161, 171–172, 179, 183, 190–191, 204, 209, 214, 228–229, 268, 272, 274–275; 4th Cavalry 12, 14, 16–17, 19–20, 34, 39, 41, 44, 51–55, 64, 74–75, 80–81, 84, 97, 100, 111, 118, 133, 154, 161, 166–169, 179, 203, 204, 214, 228, 268, 272, 275; 5th Cavalry 180; 9th Cavalry 245, 247, 253; 10th Cavalry 68, 70, 84, 105, 112, 117, 166, 179, 205, 224, 268, 270, 272, 274; 10th Infantry 43, 52; 40th Infantry 75; 41st Infantry 67; 118th Infantry 186–188; 121st Infantry 66; 125th Infantry 66
Opdycke, Col. Emerson 66
Orton, Colonel 85
Osage Rifles 83
Osborn, Capt. Thomas 74
Otis, Capt. Elmer 14, 16, 21, 33, 35, 46, 48, 55, 61

Paine, Maj. Nathan 213, 253–254, 260
Palmer, Maj. Gen. John 36, 38, 90, 149
Palmer, Col. William J. 28, 30–31, 62, 133, 138, 188, 205
Paramore, Col. James W. 46–47, 97
Parry, Dr. George 232
Patrick, Lt. Col. Mathewson T. 83–84, 166, 205, 214, 245

Patten, Dr. James C. 281
Patten, Lt. Col. Thomas J. 166–167, 214
Peach Tree Creek, Battle of 247
Pearre, Mary 62
Pegram, Brig. Gen. John 30, 36–**37**, 41, 43, 52, 126, 133–134, 144, 148, 160
Pennsylvania Coal Company 28
Pennsylvania Units: 7th Cavalry 12, 16–18, 28–29, 34, 38, 42–43, 48–50, 53, 55, 60, 62, 67, 74–75, 80–81, 84–85, 92–95, 99–100, 108, 111, 113–114, 144–145, 147, 161, 165, 179, 204, 209, 214, 222, 226, 229, 231–235, 242, 268, 272, 275–276; 9th Cavalry 12, 64–66, 68, 70, 79, 84–85, 90–91, 99–100, 111, 114–115, 138, 150–151, 155–156, 160, 165, 167, 173, 181, 185–189, 192, 194, 200, 204–205, 209, 273, 280; 15th Cavalry 6, 16, 26–32, 35, 39, 41, 43, 48–55, 61–62, 133–**134**, 137, 188, 219, 287
Perryville, Battle of 17–21, 24, 26–27, 45, 63, 68, 70, 73, 143
Peters, Dr. James B. 81
Pickens, Col. W.C. 165
Pickett's Mill, Battle of 226–227
Pike, Pvt. Benjamin 241
Pike, Cpl. James 133
Platter, Col. John A. 69–70, 84, 111
Poe's Tavern 115–116
Poinsett Tactics 60
Polk, Lt. Gen. Leonidas 12, 57, 88, 92, 136, 138, 160, 218, 223–224, 226
Pomeroy, Lt. Col. Henry 111
Pope, Maj. Gen. John 177
Post, Col. P. Sidney 156
Potter, Lt. Henry Albert 66, 76, 147, 172
Presdee, Maj. Joseph 111, 165
Prickitt, Sgt. Daniel 60, 67
Pugh, Maj. John 16, 21, 34, 54
Purdy, Maj. George H. 213, 258–259

Ranney, Dr. George 221
Ransom, Col. O.P. 19–20
"Rape of Athens" 71–72, 107
Ray, Col. Daniel 63, 75, 105, 115, 150–151, 155, 158
Rea, Capt. John 183, 189
Reed, Frances 95
Reed's Bridge, Battle at 144–**146**, 147–150
Resaca, Battle of 212, 215–221
Reynolds, Brig. Gen. Daniel Harris 270, 272–273
Reynolds, Brig. Gen. Joseph J. 63, 76, 96, 115, 140

Rhoads, Lt. Amos **94**, 100
Riggs, Maj. C.M. 60
Riggs, Capt. John B. 129
Rippetoe, Lt. William 205, 214
Robie, Lt. Col. Oliver 54–55, 75, 84, 111, 166, 204, 214, 272
Robinson, Lt. George I. 205, 214, 268, 272, 274–275
Roddey, Brig. Gen. Phillip D. 126, 166, 172, 175, 178–179, 198, 228–229, 244, 256–258
Rome Expedition 123–137
Roper, Lt. Col. William 165
Rosecrans, Maj. Gen. William S. 9–**12**, 13–17, 22–24, 26–27, 29–30, 61–63, 65, 67, 71–72, 75–82, 166–167, 172, 175–178, 180, 191, 198, 242, 262, 287–288, 290–291; advance on Chattanooga 108–110, 112–120, 123, 125–144; Battle of Chickamauga 148–149, 151, 155–157, 161–164; Stones River 33, 35–36, 38, 41–42, 47–52, 54–59; Tullahoma Campaign 86–92, 96–98, 100–105
Rosengarten, Maj. Adolph 27, 31, 35, 39, 41, 53, 55
Ross, Brig. Gen. Lawrence Sullivan "Sull" 228, 254, **257**, 259, 268, 270, 272–274
Roswell, Georgia (Union cavalry action) 239–241
Rousseau, Maj. Gen. Lovell 36, 38, 104, **245**, 247, 249, 251–252, 279, 283
Rousseau's Raid 207, 244–247, 289
Russell, Col. A.A. 108, 184
Russell, Lt. Col. Roswell 111, 138, 150, 155–156, 165

sabers 1, 6, 18, 22, 24–25, 34, 45, 50, 60, 62, 66, 71, 85, 87, 92–99, 124, 138, 156, 163, 167, 170, 172, 185, 187, 195, 209, 222, 224, 234, 254, 274, 280, 288
Sabre Brigade 18, 66
Sand Mountain 123–124, 264
Sanderson, Col. J.P. 104
Sanderson, Maj. Thomas 205, 214, 272
Savage, Maj. Edward 204
Schofield, Maj. Gen. John 211–212, 215–217, 219–220, 230, 236–238, 240, 265–267, 281, 298
Scott, Col. John 144, 146, 149, 156, 170
Scott, Capt. William H. 45, 53, 169
Scranton, Maj. Leonidas 65, **150**, 153–154, 195, 204, 213
Seibert, Maj. James 111, 165
Seidel, Lt. Col. Charles 84, 97, 111, 166, 214, 272, 275

Shackelford, Brig. Gen. James 181
Shelbyville, Battle of 92–96
Shelley, Pvt. Joseph 128
Sheridan, Maj. Gen. Philip 21, 70, 73, 79–80, 103, 105, 127, 156, 209, 288, 295
Sherman, Maj. Gen. William T. 3, 6–7, 35, 68, 80, 164, 179, 182–183, 191, 197–199, 201–202, 204, 206–**212**, 213, 215–226, 229–245, 247–253, 255, 261–268, 291, 294, 295, 297
Shiloh, Battle of 1, 18, 20–21, 23–24, 26, 28, 37, 68, 78, 126, 210
Sigmund, Lt. Jacob 147
Simonson, Capt. Peter 222
Simpson, Lt. John 148
Sinclair, Maj. William H. 15, 80, 127, 153
Sipes, Lt. Col. William B. 18, 84, 94–95, 204, 214
Slocum, Maj. Gen. Henry 21, 164, 277
Smith, Maj. Gen. A.J. 69, 243, 245, 277
Smith, Col. Baxter 28, 79
Smith, Col. Charles C. 70, 84, 166, 205, 214, 297
Smith, Brig. Gen. Green Clay 66, 68, 74
Smith, Lt. Col. R.W. 263
Smith, Brig. Gen. W.F. "Baldy" 179
Smith, Maj. Gen. William Sooy 179, 197–198, 201, 281, 286, 291
Snow Hill skirmish 70, 74–75, 86, 289
Snyder, Henry 95
Spalding, Lt. Col. George 205, 279
Sparta, Tennessee, skirmishes 110, 112–115, 118, 181–182, 200–202
Spears, Brig. Gen. James 160
Spencer, Lt. Col. William 31
Spencer rifles and carbines 209, 216, 222, 247, 275, 288, 290
Squire, Elbert 97, 124
Stanley, Maj. Gen. David S. 9–**10**, 11–29, 61, 63–64, 67, 69–76, 78–82, 84, 86–103, 154, 157, 161–164, 174–176, 178, 191, 220–221, 223, 275, 278, 281, 286–288, 290, 292, 298, 299; advance on Chattanooga 105–109, 111–112, 114, 117–121, 123–134, 136–137, 139–143; conversion to Catholicism 22–23; relieved of command 175–176; Stones River 31–36, 38–39, 41–45, 47–50, 52–59
Stanton, Edwin 11, 15, 33, 57–59, 76, 104, 118, 164, 177, 267
Star, Capt. Owen 77, 214, 260, 272

Steedman, Maj. Gen. James 75, 146, 148, 237, 278
Stephens Maj. Mashack 245–246
Stevens, Maj. Mashack *see* Stephens, Mashack
Stewart, Lt. Col. James W. 204, 213, 216–217, 226–227
Stokes, Capt. James H. 82, 84, 166, 171, 179
Stokes, Col. William B. 27, 35, 61, 84, 112, 175, 200–**201**, 202
Stoneman, Maj. Gen. George 119–120, 206, 211, 215–**218**, 219, 222–226, 228–232, 235–240, 243–244, 247–248, 250, 253–256, 261, 265–268, 276, 282–285, 291
Stoneman's Raid: July 10, 1864, 247–248; July 27, 1864, 251–252, 261–264
Stones River, Battle of 3, 5, 32–60, 62, 64, 68, 73–74, 80, 82, 112–113, 289
Stover, Lt. William 196
Streight, Col. Abel 77–78, 86, 101
Strickland, Sgt. Maj. H.A. 76
Stuart, Lt. J.E.B. 1, 22, 88
Sturgis, Brig. Gen. Samuel 179, **184**–188, 190, 194, 196–198, 200, 217, 220, 243, 281, 290–291
Summerville skirmish 133–134

Tennessee Units (CSA): 1st Cavalry 36; 1st and 19th Cavalry Battalion(s) 258; 2nd Cavalry 36; 4th Cavalry 28, 38, 79; 8th Cavalry 110; 17th Infantry 147; 25th Infantry 98; 26th Infantry 98; 44th Infantry 147; 48th Infantry 273; Freeman's Artillery 76; White's Artillery 43–44, 46
Tennessee Units (U.S.): 1st (1st East Tennessee) Cavalry 52–53, 58, 61, 67–68, 70–71, 79, 82, 84, 90–91, 99, 107, 111, 114–115, 118, 123, 127, 35, 151, 156, 160, 165, 181, 185–186, 187–188, 194–195, 204, 208–209, 213, 228, 231, 240, 253–254, 256, 258–259, 279; 2nd (2nd East Tennessee) Cavalry 26–27, 35, 41, 44, 46–47, 51–54, 60–**63**, 75, 84, 100, 105, 111, 118, 126, 156, 158, 160, 165, 198, 201, 205, 279, 287; 3rd Cavalry 52, 60, 62, 67, 77, 165, 205, 208, 279; 4th Cavalry 28, 67, 70, 205, 208–209, 216, 245–247, 258–260, 279; 5th (1st Middle Tennessee) Cavalry 26–29, 35, 43, 48–50, 53–54, 61, 64, 74–75, 84, 93, 100, 105, 112, 114, 117, 166, 200–202, 205, 207, 279–280; 8th Cavalry 205, 279;

9th Cavalry 71, 205, 279; 10th Cavalry 205, 208, 279; 10th Infantry 206; 12th Cavalry 205, 208, 279; 13th Cavalry 205, 208, 279
Texas Units: 1st Legion Cavalry 273; 3rd Cavalry 272–273; 6th Cavalry 172, 256, 268, 273; 8th Cavalry 44, 153, 193, 195, 217; 9th Cavalry 256, 273; 11th Cavalry 193, 195
Thatcher, Capt. Marshall 65, 73, 120, 128, 138, 163, 185–186
Thomas, Maj. Gen. George 11, 24, 29, 38, 98, 129, 135, 156–157, 160, 174–175, 177, 179, 191, 193, 198–202, 206, 211–212, 221, 232, 235, 248, 267, 276, 281, 290
Thomas, Julius 71, 107, 127
Thomas, William 66, 187
Thompson, Edgar 28
Thompson, Heber 145, 147, 226, 231, 235, 242
Thompson's Station, Battle of 64–66, 86
Thornburg, Lt. Col. Duff 205, 232
Thornburg, Lt. Col. Jacob 205, **207**
Torrey, Maj. William H. 204, 213, 253, 256–260
Trecy, Father Jeremiah 23, 148
Trenton expedition 117–118
Tullahoma Campaign 3, 5, 60, 86–102, 104–105
Tupelo, Battle of 243
Turchin, Brig. Gen. John 71–**72**, 73–74, 76, 79–80, 84–85, 88–89, 97–99, 101, 107–109, 143, 291
Tweedale, Pvt. John 55

U.S. Army Units: 1st Cavalry 74; 2nd Cavalry 20, 69, 83, 199; 3rd Cavalry 183; 4th Cavalry 12, 14, 16, 21, 27, 35, 46, 52–55, 61–62, 64, 73, 75–76, 79–80, 93, 95, 113–114, 136, 139–140, 144–145, 147–148, 165, 168, 180, 198, 201, 230, 232–235, 268, 270, 272, 275; 4th Light Artillery Battery 12; 5th Cavalry 69
Upton, Brig. Gen. Emory 281

Vale, Capt. Joseph 60, 66, 87, 92, 111, 114, 222, 276
Van Cleve, Brig. Gen. Horatio 36, 112–113, 115–117
Van Dorn, Maj. Gen. Earl 29, 35, 57, 64, 75–76, 79, 81, 86
Varnell's Station skirmish 216–217
Vaught's Hill 66
Vicksburg 81, 87–88, 104, 114, 118

Vimont, Lt. Col. Thomas 111, 128, 197
Vogel, Pvt. John 134–135

Wade, Col. William B. 188
Walker, Brig. Gen. William H.T. 138, 146, 148, 160
Walter, Edward 172
Ward, Maj. Frank B. 27, 31, 35, 39, 53, 55
Warner, Capt. Philip 111
Waters, Capt. Gilbert 100
Watkins, Col. Louis 5, 68–**69**, 84–85, 105, 111, 113, 115, 117, 120, 126, 128–129, 135–136, 141, 143–144, 151, 157–162, 165, 178, 194, 196, 204, 213, 237–238, 265, 285, 291, 294
Watts, Lt. Col. Elijah 98, 154–155, 205, 245
Western and Atlantic Railroad 124, 215, 223, 236, 243
Wharton, Brig. Gen. John 28–30, 36–**37**, 39, 41, 43–52, 81, 88, 91, 124, 126, 130–131, 134, 136, 138, 153, 155, 158–159, 167, 170, 181
Wheeler, Maj. Gen. Joseph 3, 5, 15, 24–**26**, 30, 36–39, 41–43, 49–52, 55–57, 59, 63–64, 81, 86, 88, 91–93, 95–96, 98, 100, 103, 105, 110–111, 116, 119–120, 124, 126–128, 130, 132–135, 139, 141–142, 149–151, 153–157, 165, 178–179, 181, 184, 190, 200–202, 206, 216, 218–219, 221–223, 226, 231, 234, 239, 250–251, 254–255, 257–264, 283, 287, 289, 297
Wheeler's Raid: October 1863, 1, 65–174; August–September 1864 264, 267, 278, 280, 282
Whitaker, Brig. Gen. Walter 146, 149
Wickliffe, Capt. John D. 77
Wilder, Col. John T. 6, 62–63, 77, 91, 96–98, 101–102, 113, 115, 118, 144, 143–146, 148–149, 151, 160–161, 164, 167, 178–179, 205, 213, 222, 231, 287, 296
Wilder's Brigade *see* Miller, Abram; Wilder, Col. John T.
Williams, Col. Edward C. 70
Williams, Brig. Gen. John 181, 234, 279
Willich, Brig. Gen. August 42, 44
Wilson, Sgt. James 93
Wilson, Maj. Gen. James H. 6–7, 191, 199, 280–281, 286, 291–298
Wilson's Creek, Battle and Campaign of 10, 22, 72, 143
Winchester, Battle of 177
Winslow, Col. Edward 281

Winston's (Gap) 124–127, 139–140, 144

Wisconsin Units: 1st Cavalry 82–84, 90, 100, 107, 109, 111, 115, 131, 139, 150–151, 155, 158, 160–161, 165, 167, 173, 193, 195–196, 202, 204, 209, 213, 216–217, 227, 253–254, 261, 279; 5th Artillery 48; 10th Artillery 216, 273; 22nd Infantry 64

Wolfley, Maj. Lewis 205
Wolford, Col. Frank 192, 196
Wood, Pvt. George 108
Wood, Brig. Gen. S.A.M. 39
Wood, Brig. Gen. Thomas 36, 73, 135, 145, 148
Wright, Brig. Gen. Marcus 180
Wulsin, Pvt. Lucien 272
Wyeth, John Allan 98
Wynkoop, Col. George 18

Wynkoop, Maj. John E. 16, 19, 34, 48, 55
Wynkoop, Nicholas 19

Young, Maj. Morris 180, 215, 272

Zahm, Col. Lewis 12, 14, 16, 19–*20*, 27, 33–34, 36, 38–44, 46–48, 50–55, 73

www.ingramcontent.com/pod-product-compliance
Lightning Source LLC
Chambersburg PA
CBHW081537300426
44116CB00015B/2658